Close-up and Macro Photography

Close-up and

Macro Photography

Its Art and Fieldcraft Techniques

ROBERT THOMPSON

Routledge
Taylor & Francis Group
NEW YORK AND LONDON

First published 2018
by Routledge
711 Third Avenue, New York, NY 10017

and by Routledge
2 Park Square, Milton Park, Abingdon, Oxon OX14 4RN

Routledge is an imprint of the Taylor & Francis Group, an informa business

Library of Congress Cataloging in Publication Data
A catalog record for this book has been requested

ISBN: 978-1-138-65846-2 (hbk)
ISBN: 978-1-138-65847-9 (pbk)
ISBN: 978-1-31562-080-0 (ebk)

Designed and typeset in Adobe Caslon Pro by Alex Lazarou

For Jonathan, Ethan, Olivia and Noah

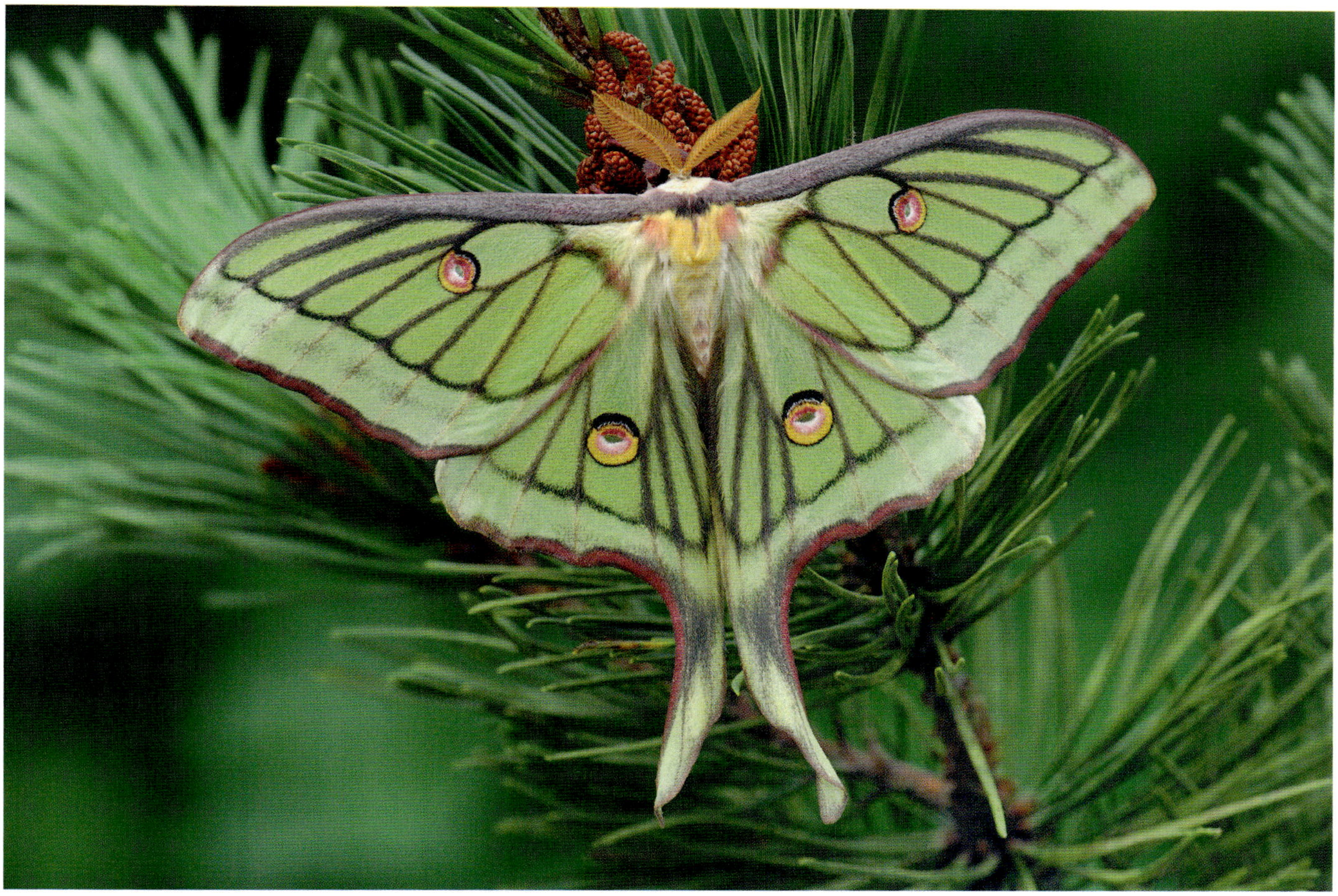

Contents

Part One
Digital Fundamentals

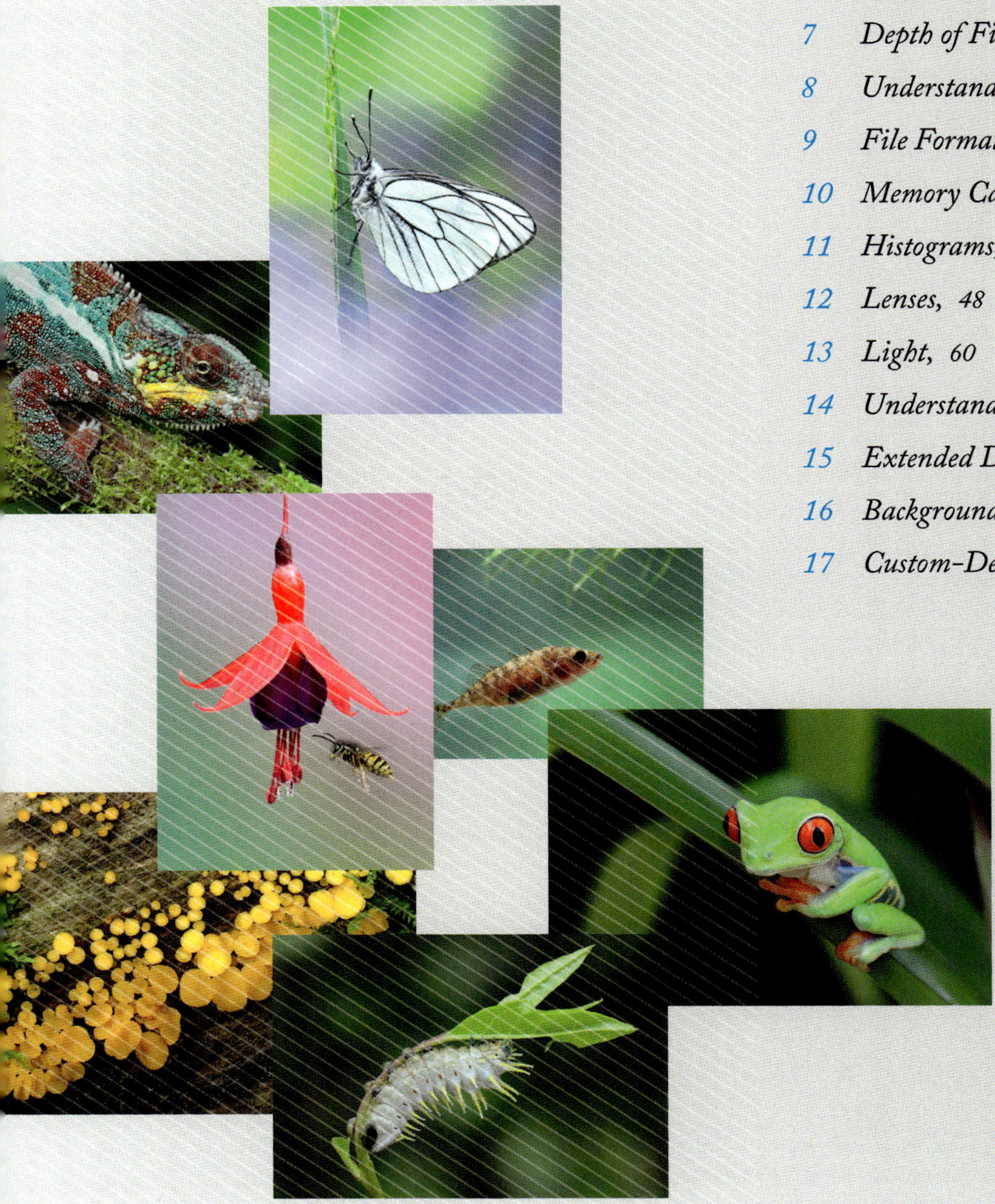

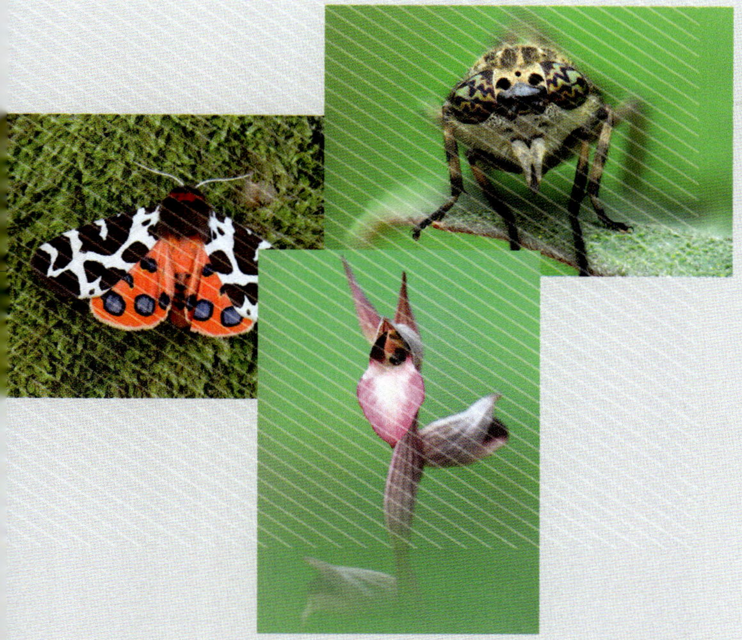

Part Two
Fieldcraft and Methodology

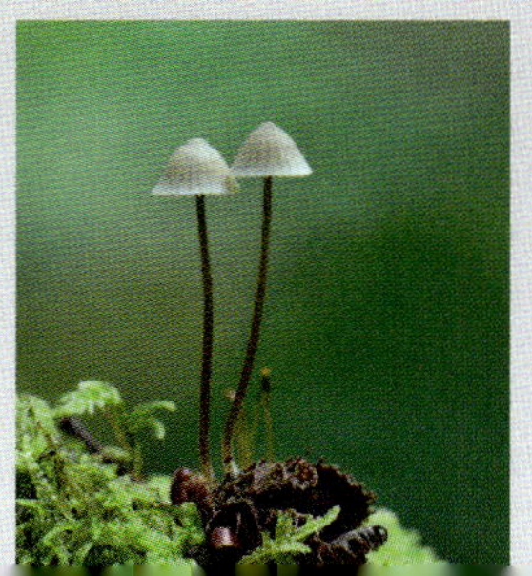

Part Three
Portfolio Case Studies

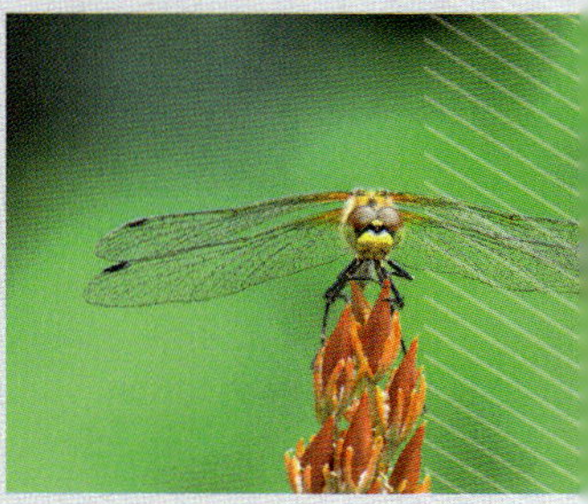

Part Four
Digital Workflow and Presentation

Acknowledgements

The success of any publication is not down to the work of a single individual but relies on the collaboration and goodwill of others who work assiduously in the background to ensure the final product meets with everyone's expectations.

I would therefore like to express my appreciation to the following people.

First of all, my profound thanks to my wife Catherine and children who are always supportive and cheerfully put up with my extended periods of absence both at home and further afield. Also my good friend and photography companion John Spencer, who has accompanied me on many of my field trips and workshops across Europe.

I would also like to express my sincere thanks to Routledge for supporting this project, in particular Judith Newlin, editor of Photography and Visual Arts, Elise Poston, Editorial Assistant and Abigail Stanley, Senior Production Editor for all of their help through the editorial and production stages of this publication. They have patiently endured my numerous questions, phone calls and been extremely supportive throughout the whole process. My thanks also to Kimberly Duncan Mooney, who initially commissioned the book; Paul Harcourt Davies for kindly reviewing the manuscript; John Douglas, Louise Borbely and Alexander Hyde, for their assistance with some of the more challenging identifications and to Alex Lazarou for designing and typesetting the book.

My grateful thanks to the following people: Rob MacNeice at Nikon UK for his help and assistance with additional equipment and also to Stewart Dunwell; Angus Bicker, manager at Calumet Photographic, Belfast; Adam Pensotti at Canon Europe for his help with equipment; Mehdia Mehtal at Canon UK; Paul Cockrill at UK Optics; Susan Sex, Orchid illustration and Chuck Pistole at Wimberley.

I have, over the years, met and corresponded with many fellow naturalists and photographers, too many to acknowledge individually. Some have become great friends and share my passion and enthusiasm for the natural world. My grateful thanks to them for freely sharing with me their knowledge, expertise and those special places close to their heart.

Finally, to my late parents Jane and Samuel Thompson, who encouraged my love of nature from an early age, supported me throughout all my endeavours and instilled in me the value and respect for the natural world in all its Biodiversity.

Introduction

Exploring the natural world in close-up has, for me, been a journey of enlightenment, knowledge, and discovery. I have spent most of my life engaging with nature, intrigued by its beauty, complexity and fragility. For the masses who go about the daily routine of life, most are oblivious to the smaller world and its significance in sustaining the ecological equilibrium in our own.

My fascination with nature stems back to my childhood days which were spent exploring an extensive parkland estate where I grew up. During the summer months, I often witnessed the profusion of bright blue damselflies that congregated among the bankside vegetation of the 105-acre lake adjacent to our home. My attraction to nature and insects had its beginnings then, and although my interest in natural history has extended to encompass other related fields I have always sustained my fascination with insects, particularly dragonflies, butterflies and moths. Many people see only the big picture, unaware of the microcosm of life around us, which is one of astonishing beauty and mystery. Through visual inquisitiveness and curiosity, we can discover the underlying harmony and connectedness of nature in minute detail, from the scales on a butterfly's wing to the dewdrops clinging precariously to a fine blade of grass; all of which can be captured in incredible detail and immortalised in print and screen.

Historically, macro photography was deemed to be a niche; a specialist branch of photography practised by those with a natural history interest primarily in entomology and botany. In fact, many of the early macro specialists had a zoological background and their transition to photography mainly came about through their own professional fields of interest. Macro photography today has evolved considerably since the 1980s. Advances in digital capture combined with the latest in post-processing software make it possible to photograph and depict subjects in a way that was simply impossible to achieve with film. Photography post digital is undergoing continual change; state of the art lenses, improved camera technology and innovative software mean the process of photography itself is never static. The digital revolution has been a significant factor in raising the profile of macro and its popularity among the masses. Virtually every camera and the majority of mobile phones now have the capability, albeit in a rudimentary form, to capture acceptable images in close-up.

I should also point out from the start that the word 'macro' is a term often incorrectly applied to close-up photography. It is frequently misused, especially by camera and lens manufacturers, to describe a 'close-up facility' on a lens or compact. The definition of macro photography ('photomacrography') in the real sense relates to magnifications from 1:1 (life-size) to around 20:1. Photographing subjects below life-size is referred to as close-up photography, which is the category that the majority of subjects fall into. However, for the purpose of this book and to reduce confusion, I have used the word 'macro' in the general context when discussing close-up photography as a whole.

In some of my previous macro photography publications, I have only been able to give a brief overview of some of the most commonly photographed subjects. This book is aimed at photographers who want to learn more about the techniques and methodology for successful macro photography. Also, those who have a working knowledge and understanding of the methods employed and naturalists who want to learn more about the equipment and techniques needed to obtain successful photographs in the field.

The book is divided into four sections. Part one deals with equipment and understanding the fundamentals of digital photography. The second part is operating in the field and familiarising oneself with some of the current techniques for capturing successful close-ups. Part three is the most comprehensive section, describing in detail through portfolio case studies the biology and ecology of the most popular subjects and how best to go about achieving great photographs in the field. There is also a reference section at the end of each topic to encourage further study. You should consider this to be a starting point, and I urge you to develop your own ideas and methods. There are many online forums on the web these days where you can seek additional information. I would encourage you to check these out. One in particular which stands out from the rest is www.learnmacro.com, which has a wealth of additional information on equipment and techniques. In part four I have given a brief, but simplified, overview of my own workflow and some thoughts as to how to present your work, also looking at the long-term preservation of your most valuable images.

Throughout this publication, I have, in the majority of cases, illustrated my own Nikon equipment. I am not suggesting for a moment that this imagery is only achievable with this brand; of course it's not. Any of the current photographic systems will deliver comparable results. Fieldcraft and an understanding of the subject, underpinned with technical competency, are the real secrets of consistently good imagery; I have never discovered any shortcuts.

One final, but important point is the ethical issues regarding the subjects you photograph. There have been many debates and articles published on this topic. As photographers, we have a duty of care to the creatures of the smaller world and the habitats they occupy. Be mindful of this and consider their welfare and environment at all times; their wellbeing should always take precedence over any photograph.

Robert Thompson FRPS FIPF

// FACING PAGE //

White Prominent *Leucodonta bicoloria*
The natural foodplant for this amazing species is Birch. It was thought to be extinct in the British Isles since it had not been seen for over seventy years. It was rediscovered in 2008 in southwest Ireland. When at rest, it blends naturally with the trunk and branches of the tree making it difficult to detect. I used flash to control the visibility of some distracting foliage in the background.

Nikon D810, 200mm micro Nikkor, 1/60sec at f16, flash, ISO 100.

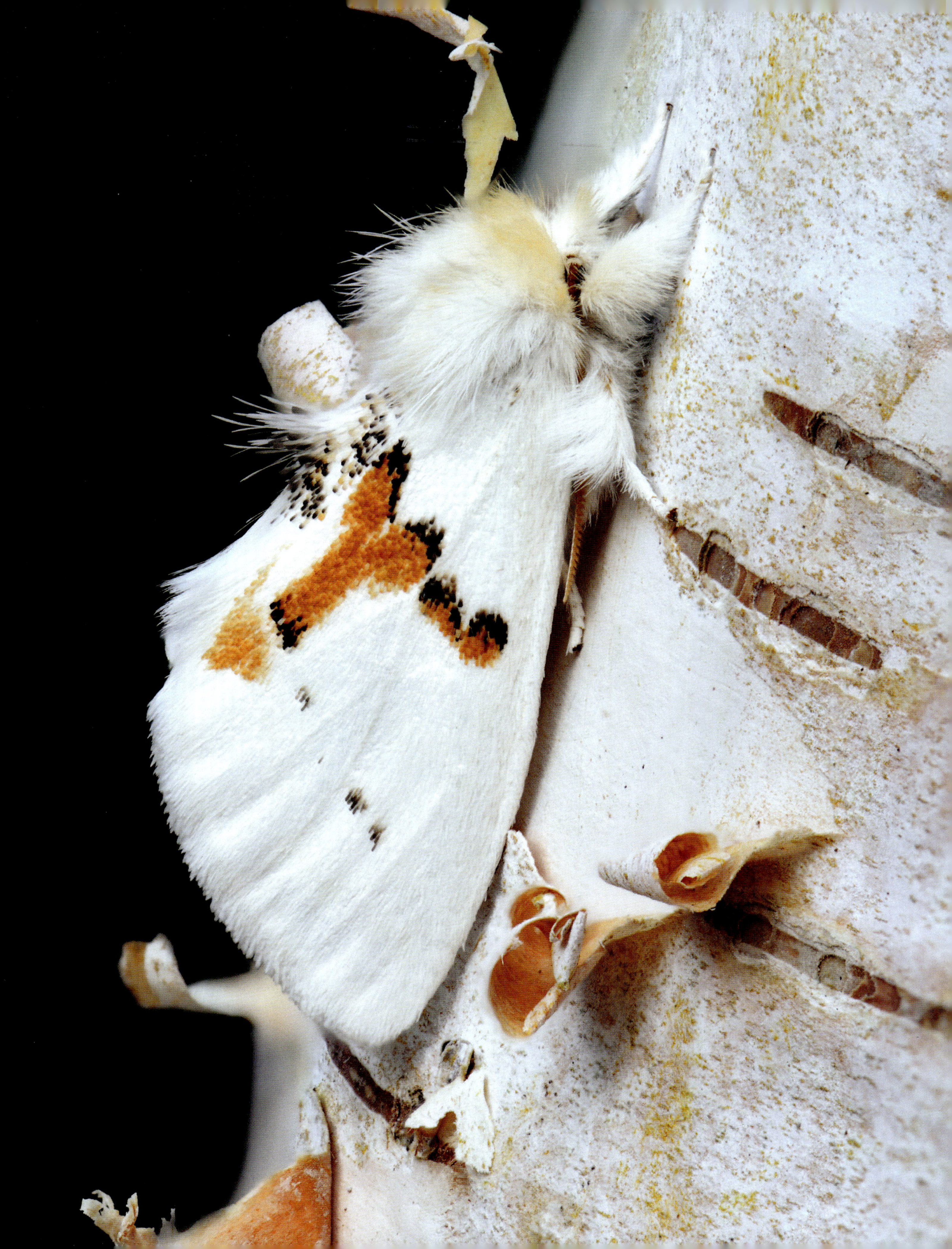

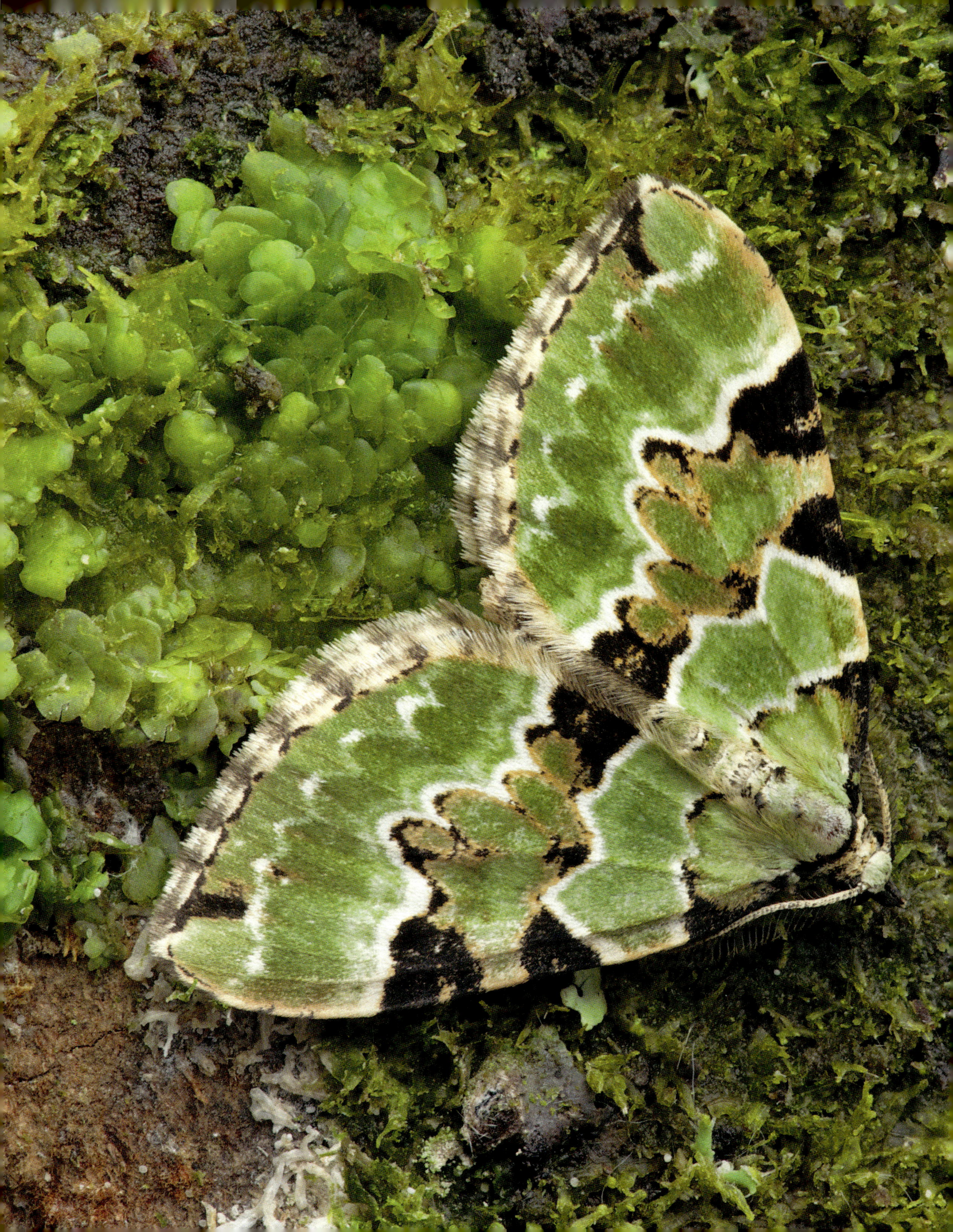

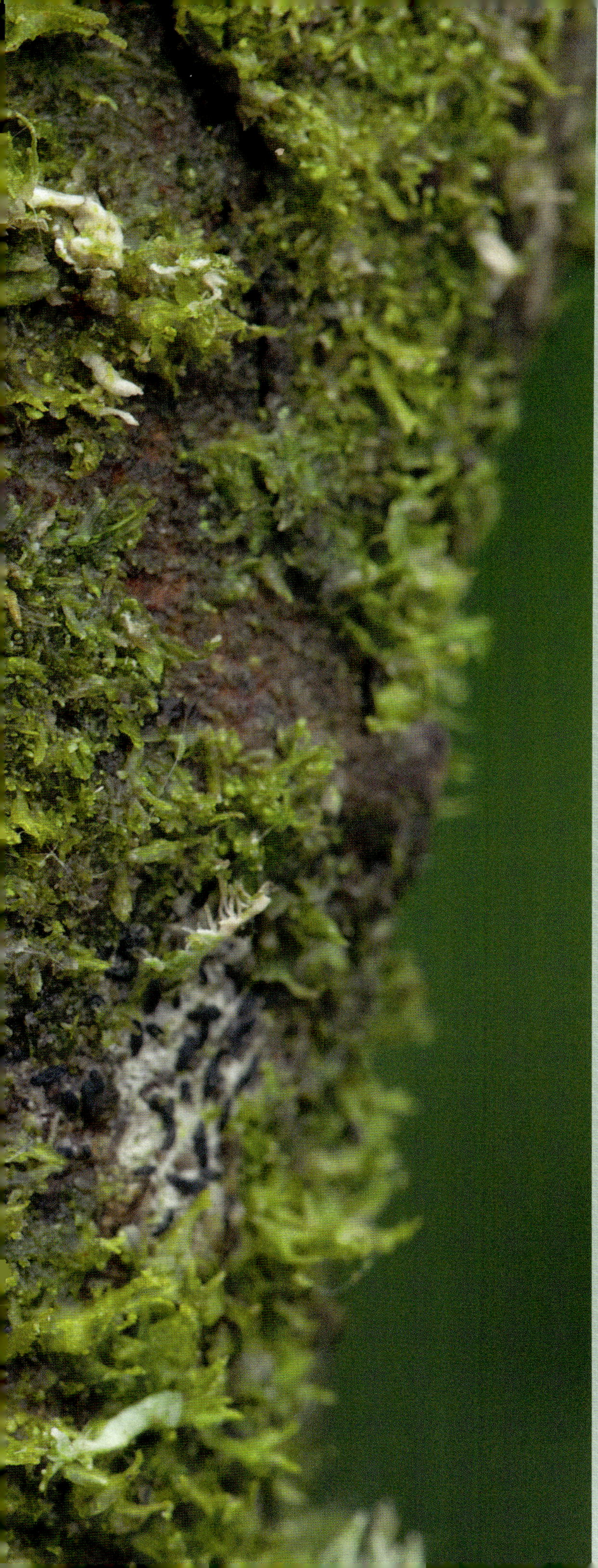

Part One

Digital Fundamentals

Green Carpet
Colostygia pectinataria

ONE

Having a Photographic Roadmap

PHOTOGRAPHY for most people starts with taking pictures of family and friends. Photographs are an excellent way to remind us of travel and significant events in our lives. Most people are happy to keep their photography casual and have no aspirations other than being able to take reasonable photographs when the need arises. For those who want to progress and take it to another level, it is the beginning of a journey that for many will develop into a lifelong passion, exploring and engaging with the natural world at every level.

The photographic world underwent its own metamorphoses during the digital revolution. It's a very different and competitive platform these days; one that requires considerable commitment, determination and persistence if you want to get noticed. Social media has an enormous influence on photography, with global websites like Facebook and Flickr providing a platform for people to share millions of photographs worldwide. The smartphone has redefined snapshot photography and has become the driving force in social imagery among the masses. Where this will eventually end, who knows.

The future of photography as a business is challenging, but also exciting. Branding has become a major factor, with many photographers taking advantage of the abundant resources that social media can deliver. It has also provided a global platform for photographers to showcase and market their work; something that would have been much harder to achieve in the past. Digital has without doubt redefined the photographic world in every sense of the word. It does not, however, define your skill or ability as a photographer, but being part of it is essential, in my opinion, if you want to get your work recognised. It's important from the start to identify where your photographic interest lies and what your long-term aims and objectives are. Twenty years ago, the aspiration of most photographers then was to get their images published in magazines, brochures and ultimately books; that desire hardly even warrants a conversation these days. Marketing and branding oneself is a vital part of today's photographic culture and, most importantly, the business of photography itself. Most professionals have a specialisation; one aspect that they have a particular interest in. My knowledge of insects, especially dragonflies, butterflies and moths was instrumental in developing my interest in macro. For me and many others, it was a natural progression from studying insects in the field to capturing what I observed on film and subsequently digitally. I have always been fascinated with the natural world and all of its intricacies from a very early age. I have never lost that passion or enthusiasm; it has matured and developed with me throughout my life.

// FACING PAGE //

1.1 ~ Owly Sulphur *Libelloides coccajus*
A rare insect found in some parts of Europe particularly France and Italy. I spotted this resting adult very early in the morning in a wonderful flowery meadow in the Gargano, Italy. It still had remnants of overnight dew which added to the overall ambience of the photo.

→ Nikon D3X, 200mm micro Nikkor, 1/8sec at f/8, ISO 200.

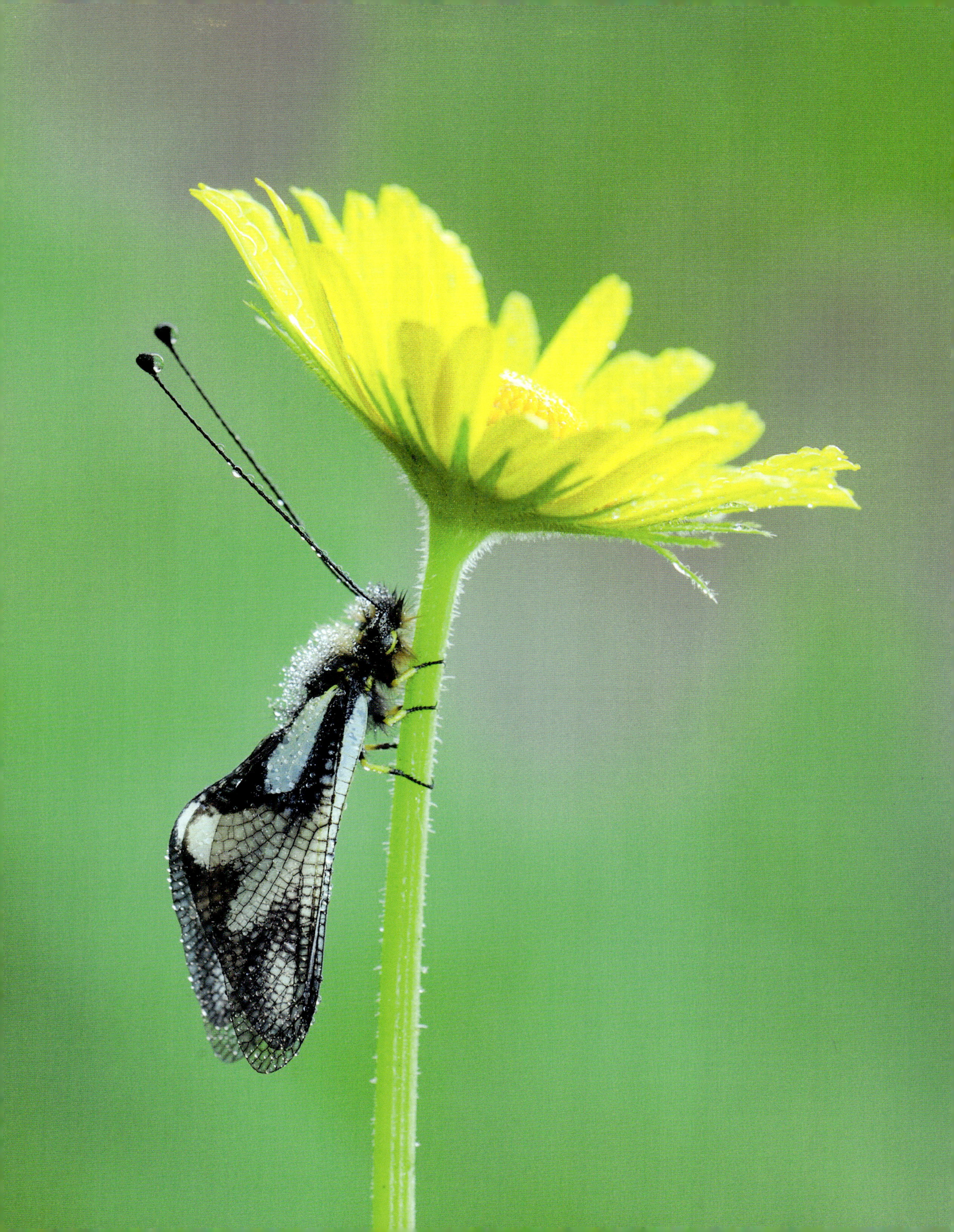

Achieving Consistency and Style

Developing a style or achieving a particular look to your work which is identifiably yours takes time. The process of creating visual consistency in your imagery irrespective of where your photographic interest lies is the result of practice, technical know-how, a creative mind and, above all, patience. Don't expect to get it right every time. Style is not instantaneous; it evolves over time. As your photography matures, so does your style; it develops with you. Training your mind to establish those subjects that meet your criteria comes with practice. It's important therefore to study your work regularly and methodically. Analyse those images that are successful and those that were not, asking yourself why they failed and can you correct or avoid that mistake in the future. It is often the simple things or changes in practice that become game changers.

It is also fair to say that modern digital cameras have, to a degree, removed much of the control and the learning process away from developing photographers. Many of today's younger photographers have never used or exposed a single roll of film. Working with transparency film in the past was a great master and totally unforgiving if you got the exposure wrong; there was no way back. Having an intimate knowledge of your camera and its exposure system was vital, as was the choice of processing laboratory; all three were inextricably linked! Today everyone sees Photoshop as the great redeemer of exposure transgressions; 'a digital hospital for sick images' as it's so often been called. Somehow exposure does not carry the same penalty as it did in the days of analogue capture.

Another aspect of the learning process is evaluating the work of other accomplished photographers in their fields. The mentors of macro during my early years were Stephen Dalton, Paul Harcourt Davies, Heather Angel and John Shaw; all highly successful photographers and authors in their own right. I got to know two of them particularly well over the years. Regardless of how experienced you think you are, we all seek knowledge and inspiration. It's an essential part of the development process regardless of where your level of expertise lies. The fact that we buy and subscribe to various publications endorses this fact. While it's important to look at and admire the work of others, you should aim to develop your own approach and not emulate what has already been done. No photographer, irrespective of their skill or expertise, would claim to produce visually eye-catching images with every push of the shutter. Light, composition, lens selection and an interesting subject form the core of a great photograph. Getting all of these elements to gel in a single image is a tall order even for the most accomplished photographers. Learning to recognise subjects that are pictorially or graphically strong comes with practice. For every good picture, many others have been condemned to the bin. If you want to progress as a nature photographer, you need to engage with your subjects and equipment frequently, evaluate your results critically and modify your techniques accordingly until you achieve your objective. Those photographers that can amalgamate artistic vision with technical competency are what separates them from the rest.

Maintaining Focus and Interest

One of the problems new photographers often experience is maintaining long-term interest. Initial enthusiasm often wains after a while, and the desire and drive begins to diminish. One of the reasons is the lack of direction and not having an overall purpose or plan. Receiving feedback on your work is one way of raising motivation, but having a long-term goal; something you can work towards that will help keep the motivation and passion alive is important. I have been fortunate throughout my career to have worked on several high-profile natural history projects for the government and the National Parks and Wildlife Service, documenting photographically nationally important species that were part of an on-going recording

// FACING PAGE //

1.2 ~ Cone-head *Empusa pennata*
The best images often happen by chance. While running a workshop in Sicily I spotted this immature mantis at rest on this orchid. I was careful not to spook it as its elegant posture would be lost. It was just a question of waiting until it turned its head towards me.

→ Nikon D3X, 200mm micro Nikkor, 1/8sec at f/8, ISO 200.

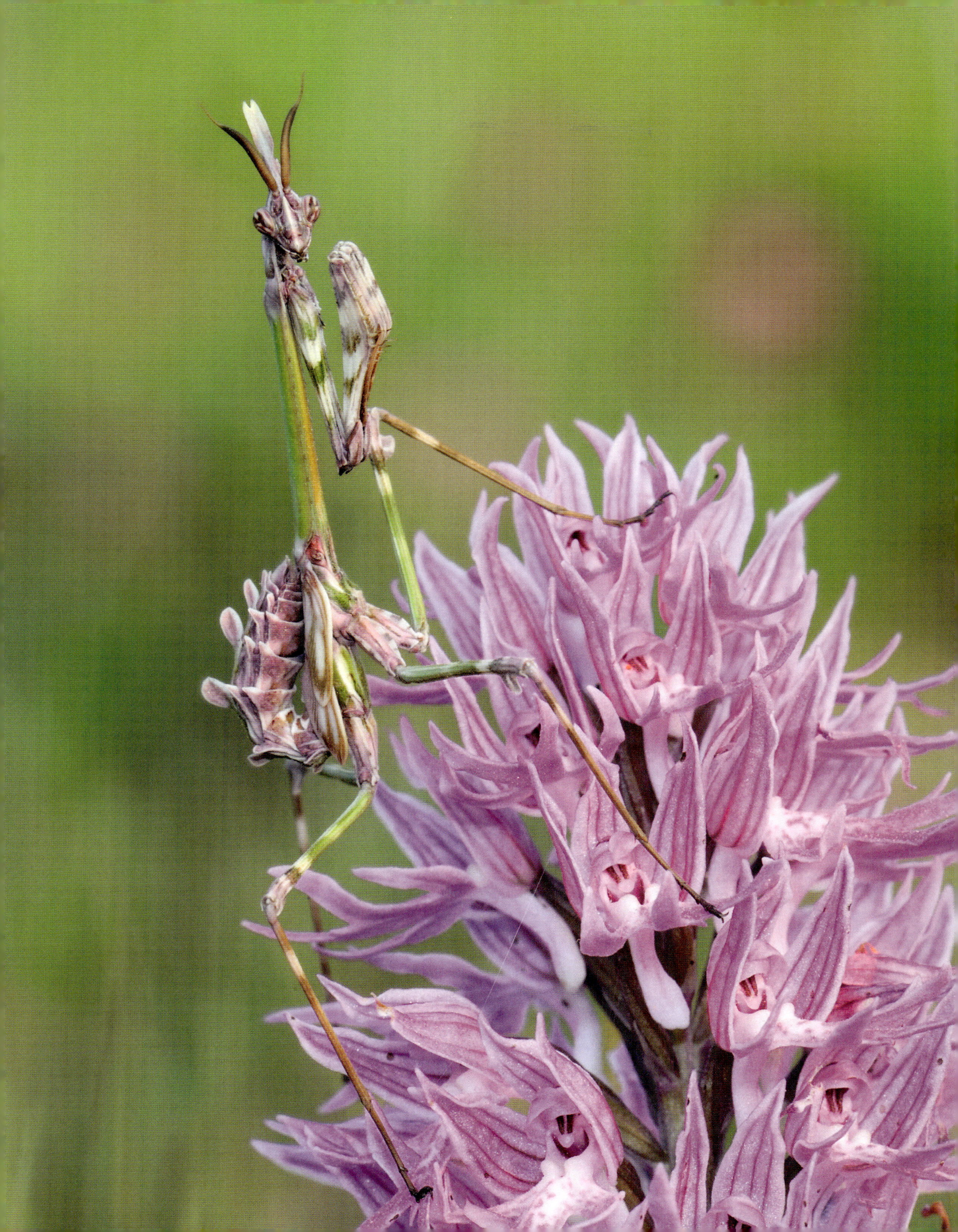

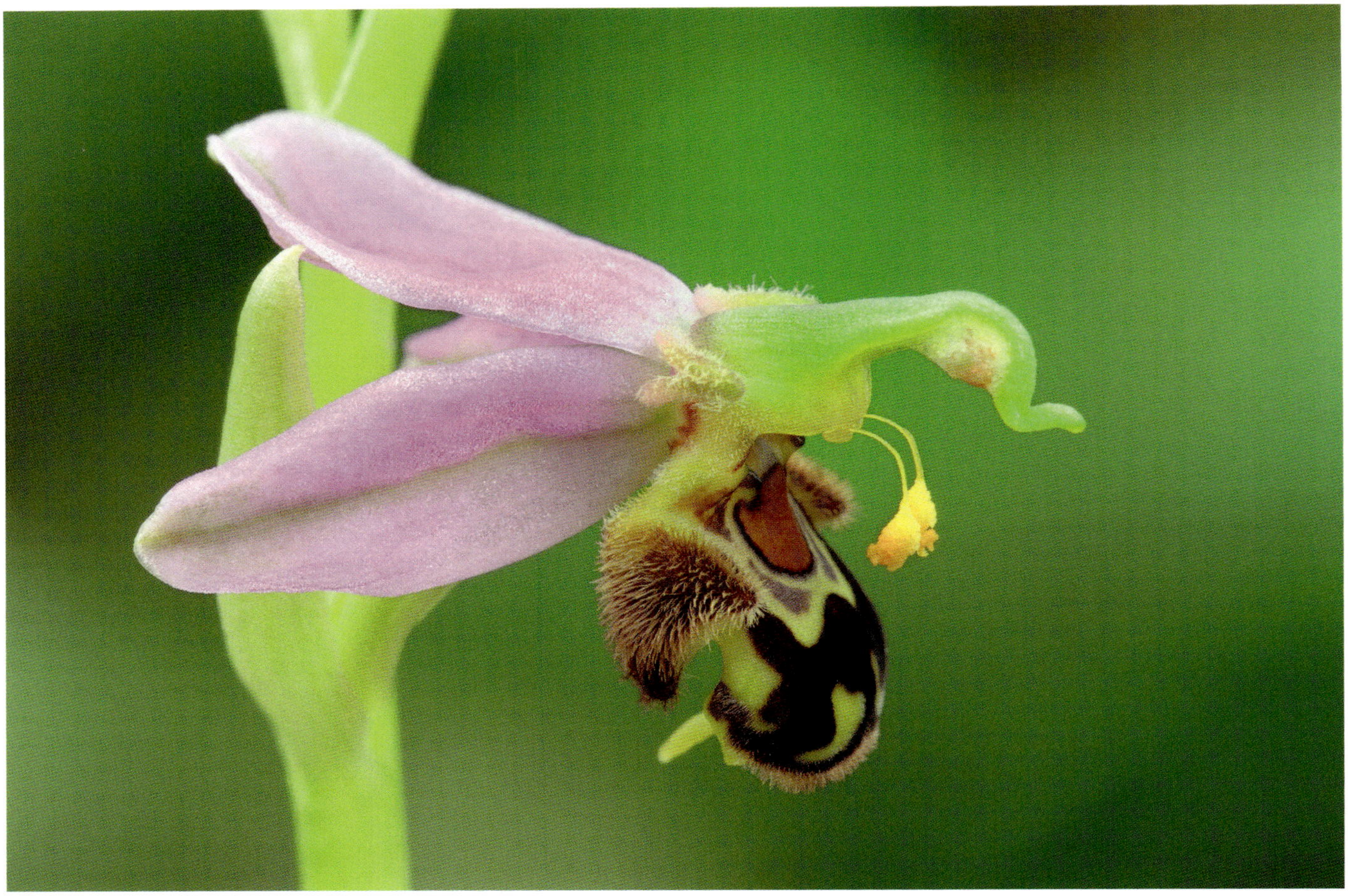

1.3 ~ **Bee Orchid** *Ophrys apifera*
A striking and familiar orchid found throughout Europe and the Mediterranean. A long lens in this case helped to isolate the plant from its background allowing the detail in the flower to stand out.

↳ Nikon D3X, 300mm Nikkor, + ext. tube, 1/15sec at f/8, ISO 200.

programme. While working alongside some of the top biologists in their respective fields, I found myself being attracted to subjects that I would not typically engage with at such a detailed level.

Lichens are one example where I was commissioned for eight years to work with several of the UK's top lichenologists on recording and documenting the country's lichen flora. My knowledge of lichens was rudimentary; although I had photographed for stock many of the common species that were easily identified, beyond that I had no real interest since many of them are extremely difficult to identify correctly. However, working with several lichenologists on the project I not only made new friends but also learned an incredible amount about this group of plants and became hooked myself. I now have accumulated an extensive collection of images of a wide range of species, many of which are defined as nationally scarce or endangered. The point I'm making here is the fact that if you have the motivation, you can initiate your own long-term project. If the images were to contain the appropriate location data, then it adds real value to the photographs, especially in the long term. Local projects help to build a picture of the flora and fauna that reside in your area. Photography can also play a critical role in documenting rare and threatened species, in addition to providing evidence of their existence in a particular habitat or location. Material such as this is a real valuable long-term asset.

As a professional freelance natural history photographer, I have covered many different commissions and projects over the years, from shooting aerial

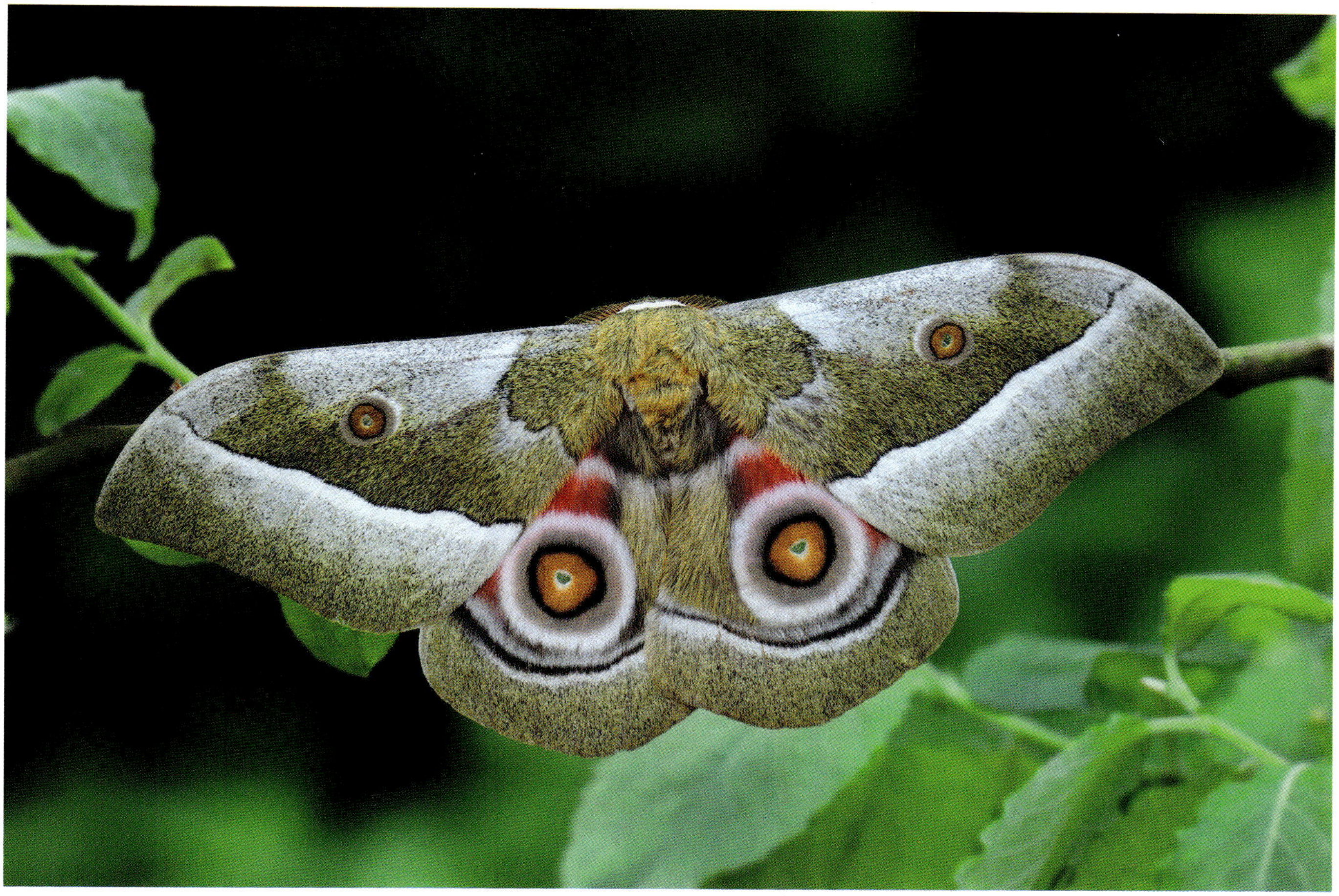

1.4 ~ **Zambezi Emperor Moth** *Gonimbrasia zambesina*
A large, colourful species, resident in Africa and found in eastern coastal lowlands and along the Zambezi river valley. Like many members of this family they have large eyespots on their hindwings which are concealed when at rest.

↳ Nikon D3X, 200mm micro Nikkor, 1/15sec at f/11, fill-in flash, ISO 200.

landscapes at 2000ft to photographing some of the largest underground cave systems in Europe; these are some of the more unusual commissions I have undertaken. However, I have my own long-term projects running in the background. The first of these is Europe's wild orchid population. My initial enthusiasm for these plants was sparked by a publication I purchased in the late 1980s written by Paul Harcourt Davies; one of macro's great veterans and a highly successful photographer and exponent of all things close-up. One of the many fascinating aspects of that book was the thumbnail account of each of the countries and Mediterranean islands that he visited. I have spent over twenty years (call it a busman's holiday) travelling around Europe in a similar way photographing its flora and fauna, with a particular emphasis on insects and orchids.

My other long-running project is on wild silkmoths of the world. I have always had a passion and scientific interest in these residents of the night, having written a book on the moths of my own country. Wild silkmoths are without a doubt one of the largest and most impressive groups of insects in the world. The majority of species are to be found in the tropics, but a small number occur in Europe. Over a twenty-year period, I have studied and photographed many species from around the world, some of which have rarely been photographed. Having long-term projects running in the background is a great way of keeping your motivation high. It also means that you have material which you can utilise in some form, perhaps at some point in the future.

Marketing Your Images

Breaking into a photographic market that is already heavily saturated with imagery from just about everywhere you can think of is far from easy, but not impossible. If your aspiration is to sell your work, then you need to consider your approach carefully from the start; you'll regret it later if you don't! Creating successful photographs routinely is a challenging business; technical competency is only one aspect, but this on its own is insufficient. Developing a discerning and artistic eye for stock images that sell comes with experience and hours of practice in the field. There are no shortcuts that I've discovered! Another point worth considering is the aesthetic or scientific approach. Both are ok, but the final result can be somewhat different. In my experience, I find much more demand for natural scientific imagery, especially those that have a pictorial quality about them, but are still, from an ecological point of view, correct. The photographic requirements of natural history publishing are often somewhat different than those of the photographic press, something I have always been mindful of over the years.

Finally, no matter what your long-term aims and objectives are the important thing is to get out and enjoy your photography and engage with the natural world whenever you can; you will not regret it!

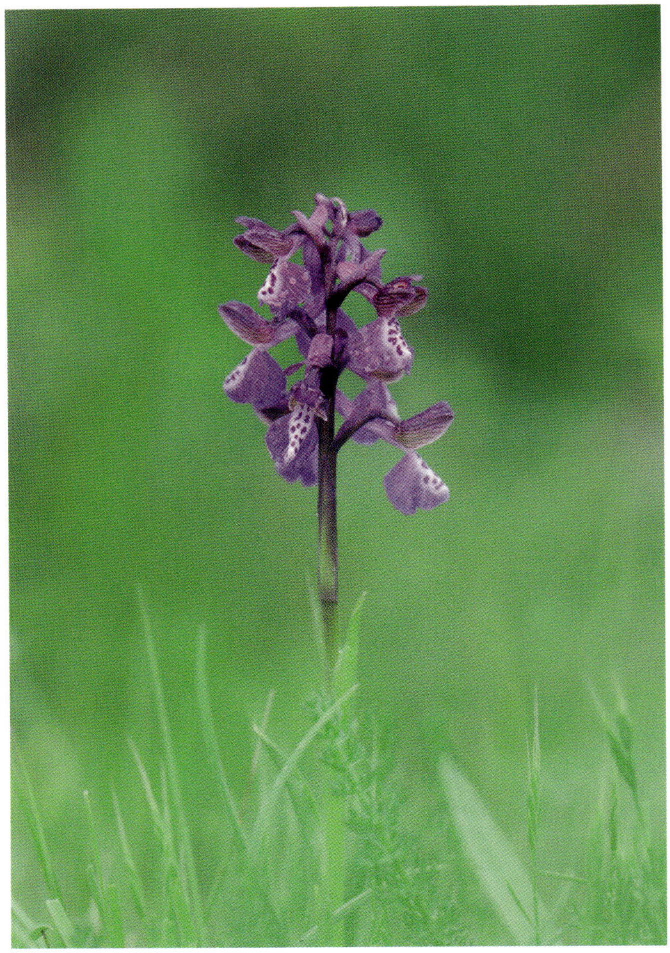

1.5 ~ **Green-winged Orchid** *Anacamptis morio*
When the opportunity presents itself I like to take advantage of the conditions at the time. A heavy rain shower left droplets on the flowers. I shot through the foreground vegetation which produced a more atmospheric result. It is always worth considering both the impressionistic and scientific approaches when in a position to do so.

↘ Nikon D3X, 300mm Nikkor, 1/60sec at f/5.6, ISO 200.

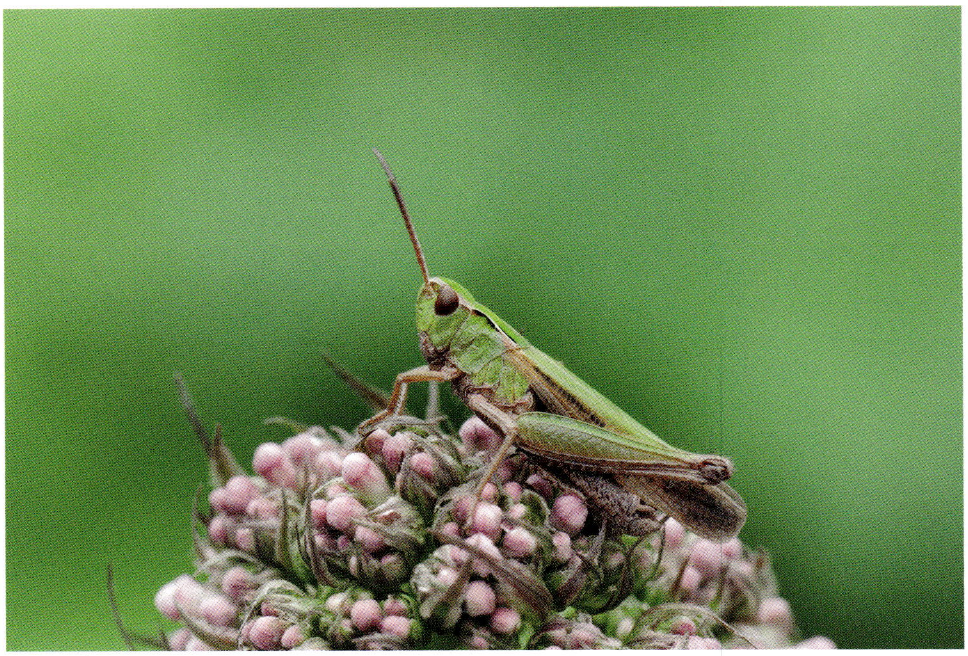

1.6 ~ **Common Green Grasshopper** *Omocestus viridulus*
I was walking around a meadow in the Alps in early evening when I came across this adult resting on the flower head. The plant was taller than the surrounding vegetation which meant I could select a smaller aperture while still keeping the background well diffused.

↘ Nikon D3X, 105mm micro Nikkor, 1/30sec at f/11, ISO 400.

TWO

Digital Cameras

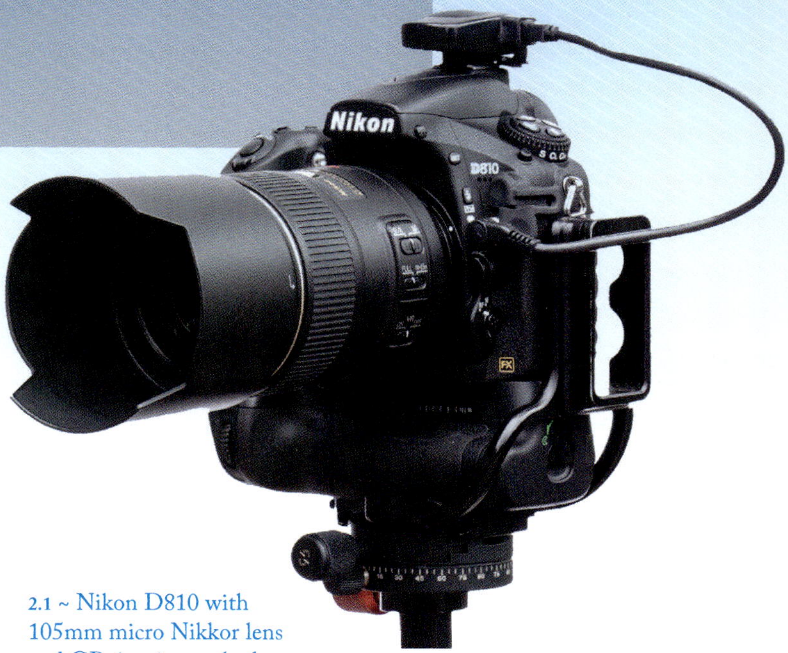

2.1 ~ Nikon D810 with 105mm micro Nikkor lens and GP-1 unit attached.

THE DIGITAL REVOLUTION has, without doubt, transformed the way we think about photography and how we make pictures today. The diversity and complexity of cameras makes selecting a system a daunting task for anyone wishing to photograph the world in close-up. Current advances in electronics and design have taken digital capture to extraordinary levels of performance and sophistication in a relatively short time; that trend is likely to continue for some time to come.

Virtually all the modern digital cameras today are capable of delivering excellent results if used correctly. The digital single-lens reflex (DSLR) camera, is the obvious choice for professionals and serious enthusiasts who require the ultimate in terms of image quality and resolution. However, there are some points worth considering before you purchase as, once committed, it is financially difficult for most people to change. Investing in any system is usually a long-term commitment and should not be undertaken lightly. It is worth spending a little time researching the pros and cons of different brands and the range of accessories (especially those relevant to macro) before you decide. Another important point is defining where your main interest lies and whether that system can accommodate all of your future needs should you decide to expand into other aspects of nature photography. For those who are serious about close-up photography, the DSLR camera provides the greatest versatility and range of accessories, which are capable of delivering outstanding image quality.

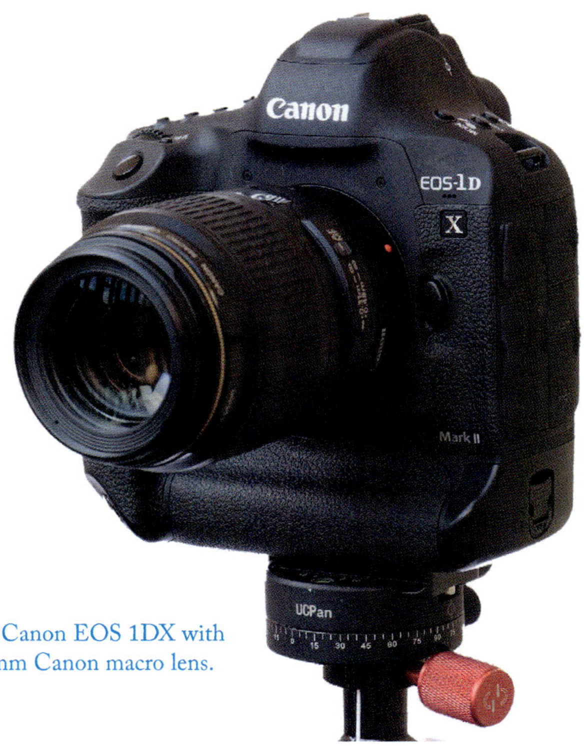

2.2 ~ Canon EOS 1DX with 100mm Canon macro lens.

Sensor Size and Crop Factor

Before the digital revolution, there were a number of different film formats. The most widely used in nature photography was 35mm. Medium Format was practically standard issue in the professional and commercial sector and the choice adopted by many landscape photographers. When digital cameras were first introduced, it seemed more practical, from a manufacturer's point of view, to design sensors that replicated traditional film formats for a number of reasons. First of all, photographers were familiar with established sizes and most already owned a range of lenses and accessories for their format. To reconfigure sizes at this point would have meant redesigning lenses and other equipment; this would have been a monumental task for the majority of camera manufacturers. It would also have been financially prohibitive for the vast majority of photographers to adopt that sort of radical change virtually overnight.

Sensor Types

Sensor sizes and megapixels continually attract a lot of attention and debate among photographers; much in the same way as the historical rivalry between camera brands has done for years. There are essentially two types of sensor used in digital cameras today: the Charged Coupled Device (CCD) and the Complementary Metal Oxide Semiconductor (CMOS). Both sensors function in a similar way and deliver comparable results. CCD sensors provide excellent image quality but are more expensive to manufacture and consume more power than other types. They are used in many compact cameras due to their smaller size, but also in some DSLRs in both 35mm and medium format.

There are three basic size groupings for sensors: The Four Thirds system, adopted by Olympus and Kodak, which use a sensor size of 13.5 x 18mm. APS-C, which is similar to the original APS film size where many DSLR cameras fall into. However, to confuse matters even more not all APS-C sensors are the same size. Nikon's DX-format uses a sensor size of 23.6 x 15.7mm, with a crop factor of 1.5x. Canon is slightly smaller at 22.3 x 14.9mm with a crop factor of 1.6x. What this effectively means is the difference in size between a 35mm film frame and the sensor in your camera. APS-C sensors also multiply the focal length of a 35mm lens and they also affect the angle of view. A 100mm lens attached to an APS-C camera with a crop factor of 1.5x results in an effective focal length of 150mm. If you multiply the focal length of the lens by the crop factor of the camera, you get the equivalent focal length of the lens needed to replicate the equivalent angle of view on a 35mm camera. The calculation is a simple one.

Focal length x crop factor = equivalent focal length.

100 x 1.5 = 150mm

It has also been stated that smaller sensors deliver greater depth of field than larger full frame sensors; this is not correct. Magnification and depth of field are inextricably linked! As magnification increases, depth of field decreases for the selected aperture. Therefore, on a smaller sensor, the depth of field may appear greater, but that's because the sensor area is less and the magnification of the subject is reduced if it's reproduced in its entirety within the frame. Depth of field is consistent for a given magnification irrespective of the sensor size. For example, if you have a 105mm macro lens on a full frame camera and your subject occupies all of the viewfinder. If you exchange the camera body with a micro 4/3 body fitted to the lens via an adapter you no longer see all of the subject only a section of it, that's because this camera has a sensor size which is only one quarter of the area of a full frame camera. Inexperienced photographers often assume incorrectly that the subject is magnified; that's because you are only reproducing part of it.

If you are making an A4 print, then the smaller sensor has to be enlarged twice as much as that from the full frame sensor. It may appear initially that you have used twice the magnification, but in reality the depth of field is the same from both sensors. If you increase the magnification on the full frame sensor to replicate what has been recorded on the smaller sensor, you would need to increase the magnification of the subject by a factor of 2. As a result of the increased magnification on the full frame sensor the depth of field would naturally decrease. This is where inexperienced photographers often assume that you get greater depth of field with smaller sensors, which is of course not true.

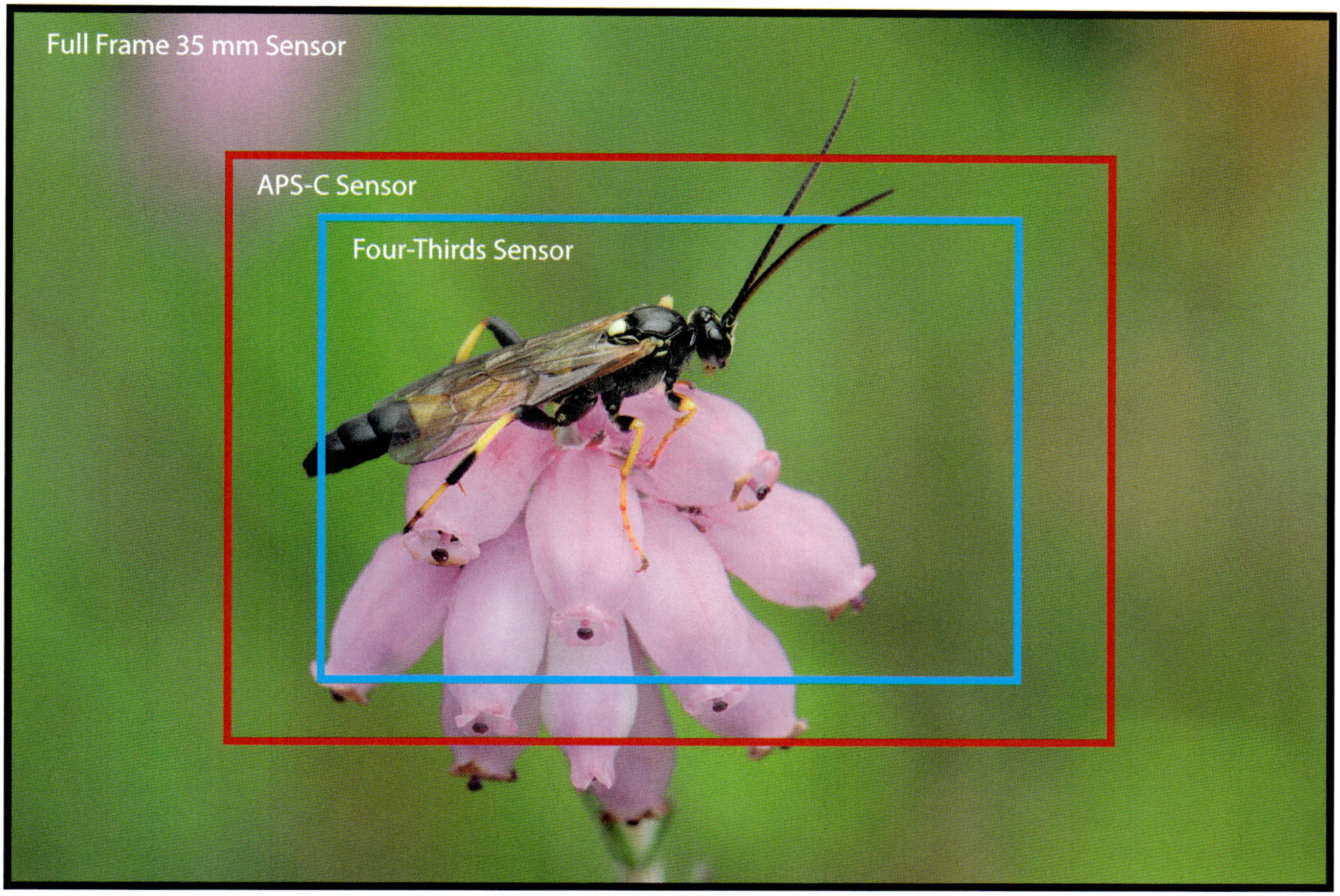

2.3 ~ **Parasitic Ichneumon Wasp** *Amblyteles armatorius*
The full frame sensor illustrating the 36mm x 24mm format. The coloured rectangles represent the APS-C (red) and Four Thirds (blue) formats showing the capture area in relation to the full frame sensor.

↳ Nikon D3X, 200mm micro Nikkor,1/15sec at f/16, fill-in flash, ISO 200.

The full frame sensor is based on the 35mm film format (36 x 24mm) that was used traditionally in film SLRs. Historically, almost all DSLRs used the smaller APS-C format. The main reason was sensor technology was still very much in its infancy. The production costs of full frame sensors are naturally higher because you are getting fewer chips from a silicone wafer when compared to an APS sized unit. However, having said that camera manufacturers now offer more full frame cameras in their line-up. The price has come down, and they are more affordable than in the past.

Full frame sensors have a number of advantages. They have a higher dynamic range and are therefore capable of capturing a greater range of tones within an image compared to a smaller sensor. ISO performance is also better, mainly because the individual pixels are larger, which generates a greater signal-to-noise ratio, delivering a much smoother result with less digital noise. Even if all things are equal, a full frame sensor will always appear cleaner at 100% since it requires less enlargement than a smaller format. Sensor size also has an influence on the background behind the subject. A full frame sensor can produce a more diffused appearance at a given aperture due to the larger size and the increase in magnification. For example, if a subject occupies the same area within the frame in both formats at the same aperture then the background appearance will be different. A 35mm sensor is also better at isolating the subject from its background, the reason being that in order to fill the frame you need to get closer to your subject than you would have to with a smaller format. However, the smaller format does have some advantages. For example, if both cameras were twelve megapixels and the subject occupies only the central

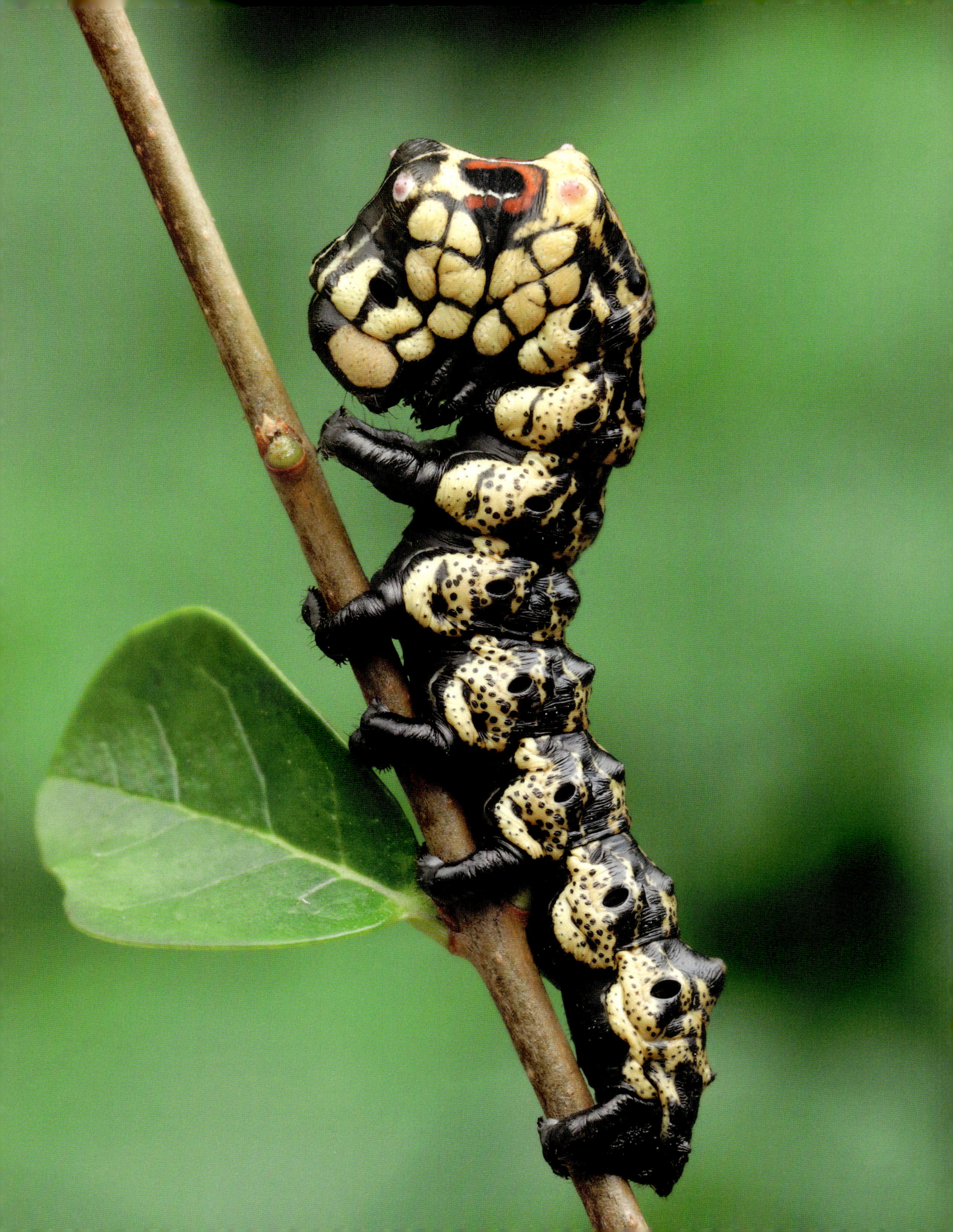

portion of the full frame sensor. If you crop the image, you have reduced the file size to perhaps six or seven megapixels. However, if the subject were photographed on the APS-C format, it would require no cropping, and you still have a twelve-megapixel image producing a larger file size for printing.

Diffraction is also very relevant in macro photography since smaller apertures have to be employed to provide reasonable sharpness throughout the image. Diffraction is a property of light waves where they spread when passing through an aperture. It manifests as a softening of the finer details within the subject especially as magnification increases and, most significantly, at smaller apertures.

With a larger sensor, diffraction is less of an issue because you do not have to enlarge the picture as much, therefore, allowing you to use smaller apertures. These points may not seem that significant, but in many aspects they are and it is important to understand these principles before you make any decisions regarding the choice of formats. Lenses and other accessories are more expensive for full frame, and the increased weight can be a problem for some people. However, 35mm is better catered for in lenses and accessories than most of the smaller formats.

Important Features

There are so many cameras currently on the market that it's impossible to discuss them in any significant detail. New models are continually being released or updated. Most of the relevant and important information can be found on the web. Below are some aspects you should pay particular attention to when choosing a camera for macro photography.

// FACING PAGE //

2.4 ~ **Owl Moth** *Brahmaea certhia* (larva)
A large impressive caterpillar that occurs throughout China and South Korea. Photographed with an APS-C sensor.

↘ Nikon D2X, 200mm micro Nikkor, 1/30sec at f/11, ISO 200.

Mirror Lock-up

Mirror lock-up, from a macro photographer's point of view, is an important feature in a camera. Using a tripod does not necessarily guarantee a sharp result. You are at a greater risk when using slower shutter speeds, especially between 1/8sec–1sec. Before an exposure can take place, the mirror is raised to allow the light to reach the sensor. The speed at which the mirror makes contact with the pentaprism before the shutter opens can induce a slight vibration, which can degrade the sharpness of finer detail in the image. Modern cameras have greatly improved damping, which has reduced the problem; however, vibration is not always immediately apparent when viewing the image at normal size. Raising the mirror before exposure prevents this from happening. Some high-end and pro-level cameras allow you to delay the exposure for a fraction of a second before the shutter opens. When this feature is engaged it reduces mirror bounce. Nikon refer to it as 'Exposure Delay Mode'. Many recent cameras have what is termed 'electronic front curtain shutter' which helps eliminate shutter vibration; it should be used in combination with a remote release and mirror-up.

Depth of Field Preview

Another essential feature is a depth of field preview button. When you look through the viewfinder, you are previewing the image with the diaphragm in the lens set to its widest aperture. However, this is not how the image will appear when exposure takes place unless you are shooting wide open. A depth of field preview button lets you see the image at the actual taking aperture; you can also check the zone of sharpness and identify any distracting highlights. These are often out of focus initially when composing: they only become apparent when the lens is stopped down to the taking aperture. Initially, when the preview button is activated the focusing screen darkens as the aperture closes. It can be difficult to see the image clearly but, with practice, you quickly get accustomed to this and identifying distracting foliage and highlights in the background. Depth of field has a profound effect on the appearance of the final image; being able to preview it before exposing the photo is important.

High-resolution LCD Screen

The LCD screen on the back of your camera allows you to preview the image and other relevant information pertaining to exposure etc. It also provides a visual record of the histogram, which allows you to see if the image is over, or underexposed and whether the shadows or highlights have detail present. Some of the high-end cameras have high-resolution LCD screens, which are capable of allowing you to zoom in on individual aspects within the photograph, and check for sharpness. I find this extremely useful for performing initial edits. It also means I'm not transferring unwanted images to my computer taking up valuable hard drive space.

High-resolution screens also allow the photographer to take advantage of the 'Live View' function. The camera's LCD monitor now operates as an external viewfinder permitting the photographer to see the scene in real time. It achieves this by allowing the image to be continuously projected onto the sensor, which is then transferred to the LCD screen. Your camera needs to be on a tripod to use this function correctly.

Live View has a number of advantages in close-up photography. First of all, it allows you to compose and preview your photograph before exposure and identify any distracting elements, in the background or around the edge of the frame. Photographing subjects at ground level, or in awkward positions can make it difficult to compose and focus accurately. Using Live View makes the process much easier since you have a visual display of the subject, and you can make the appropriate adjustments if necessary; this is especially useful when working at higher magnifications where precise focus is paramount. You can, in some models, use Live View in combination with your depth of field preview to ascertain the degree of sharpness in your image. It is also useful in low light and when photographing in heavily shaded woodland. Having said that, I don't use this feature as routinely as some photographers do. I still prefer the viewfinder, but there are situations where it has a distinct advantage over the conventional optical viewfinder.

Resolution

Since the production of the first digital SLR, the megapixel race has been a major selling point for camera manufacturers. Resolution relates to the density of pixels contained within the sensor and the ability to distinguish fine detail within the subject. Many of the current DSLRs have a pixel resolution that exceeds twenty megapixels; this equates to twenty million pixels; one megapixel being equal to one million pixels. The higher the number of pixels means an increase in the overall file size of each image. Cameras with higher resolution sensors are also capable of capturing more information and resolving finer detail, which in theory should produce a sharper photograph. However, the quality of the sensor and the optics of the lens are equally important if you are to get the best from your camera's sensor. There are some advantages in using higher resolution cameras, but not necessarily in every aspect. If you do not intend to produce prints larger than A3 then an eight-megapixel camera would be perfectly adequate and will produce a high-quality A3 print, which is the equivalent of a two-page spread in an A4 book or magazine. However, cameras with a resolution of twenty plus are the average these days, which gives you reasonable latitude for cropping an image if necessary. You can also upsize your photos through interpolation in various software programs such as Photoshop or ON1 Resize, with excellent results and no real perceptible loss in quality.

Below are the typical sizes for prints which can be obtained from different cameras ranging from 12–36 million pixels.

MEGAPIXEL SIZE	PIXEL RESOLUTION OF THE SENSOR	PRINT SIZE AT 300DPI (INCHES)
12	4256 x 2832	14 x 9
24	6048 x 4032	20 x 13.4
36	7360 x 4912	24.5 x 16.4

There are occasions when the higher resolution sensor has a distinct advantage. Getting close to a subject is not always possible for a number of reasons. It may be timid and easily spooked, or the difficulty of the

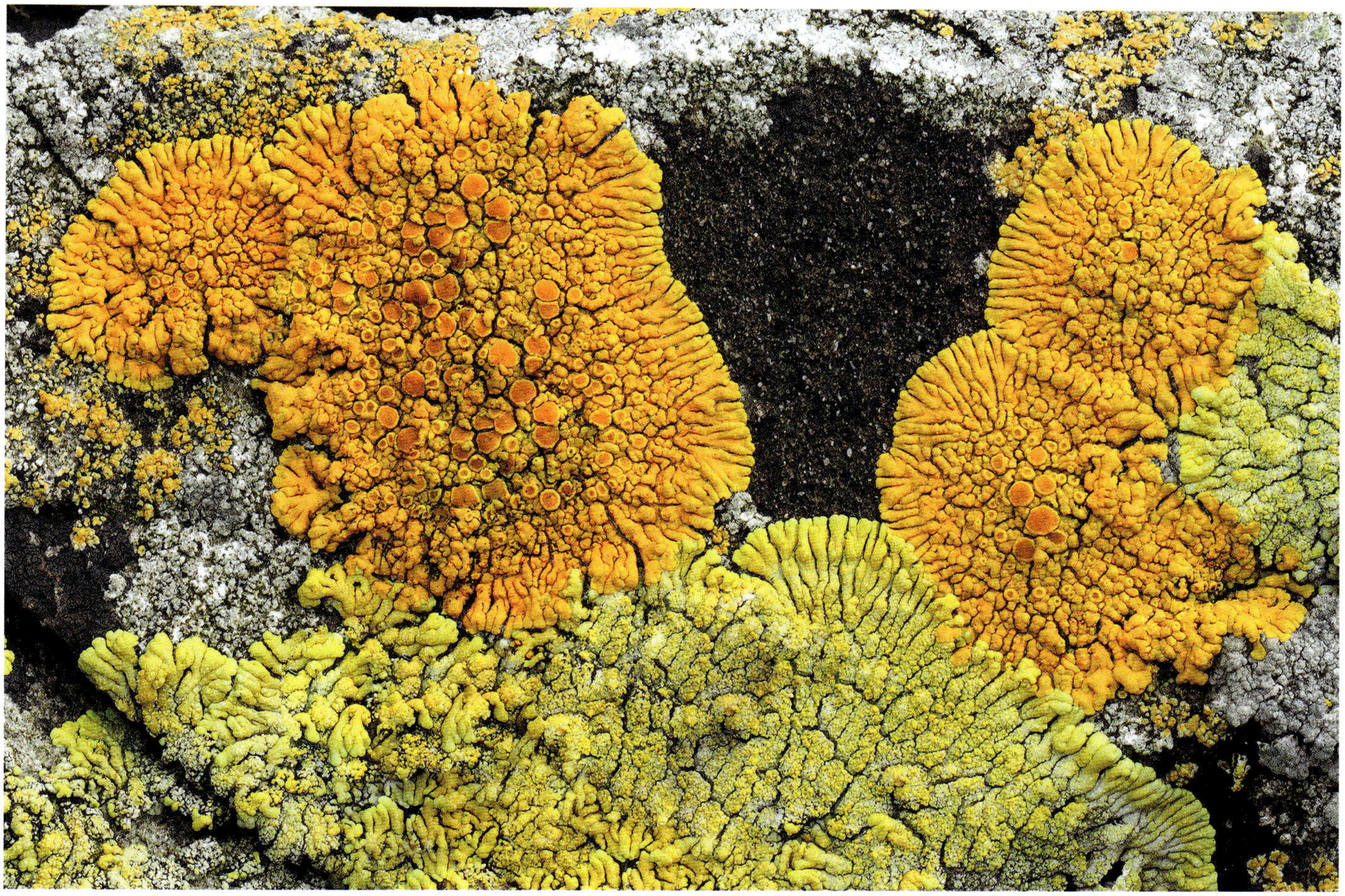

2.5 ~ **Lichens** *Caloplaca thallincola*, *Caloplaca verruculifera* and associated species.
If used correctly, most DSLRs these days are capable of delivering superb detail and image quality, which is clearly evident in these coastal lichens.

↘ Nikon D3X, 200mm micro Nikkor, 1/60sec at F/16, ISO 200.

terrain may prevent you from getting in closer. Whatever the reason, shooting with a high megapixel DSLR provides a large enough file size which you can crop when necessary and still retain a reasonably high-quality photograph.

Higher megapixel cameras are less forgiving when it comes to vibration and focusing errors; this is especially relevant in macro photography. For example, if you were photographing with a twelve-megapixel camera and you had an exceptional one-off image that was perhaps just a fraction soft it may still be usable. However, in a thirty-six-megapixel camera, you would have three times the number of pixels that were soft and when enlarged the softness would be considerably more apparent, and the image is more than likely not useable. With each new release of camera bodies comes increased pixel numbers and improved ISO performance among other minor enhancements. We are probably reaching the peak in terms of resolution, with some full frame cameras now at fifty megapixels. Further developments are likely to concentrate on reducing digital noise and increasing dynamic range, which has been improving, but at a slower rate. Bear also in mind that higher megapixel cameras do not necessarily produce superior image quality. Packing more pixels into a relatively small sensor brings its own problems in terms of ISO performance and increased file sizes. Lower megapixel DSLRs often produce much cleaner images due to their larger pixel dimensions.

THREE

Tripods & Camera Support Devices

Tripod Selection

THE VAST MAJORITY of photographers would agree that the most tedious piece of equipment they lug about on a daily basis is a tripod. They are, by nature, cumbersome; the legs seem to snag on every passing branch, and most can be slow to set up correctly. In the time taken to erect one, attach your camera and remote release, the moment has usually passed; the light has gone, or the insect is now in the next meadow! We have all been there, myself included!

However, despite the criticisms, there are lots of reasons why you should use a tripod. They provide stability, sharpness, precision framing, focusing and the means to continue working in low light situations. All of these advantages are extremely important in close-up photography. There are of course those that claim they can obtain sharp images by handholding, if you don't print and post only on the web then it may not be an issue, but printing does highlight any shortcomings. I rarely handhold a camera and shoot every image I can from a tripod, only resorting to a monopod when the subject or the terrain dictates otherwise. The benefits gained far outweigh the inconvenience in my opinion.

Tripods come in a variety of designs and sizes. Most adhere to the same fundamental design principle; extendable legs, central column and supporting plate for your camera. Avoid cheap, flimsy models with a compact design. A tripod suitable for close-up photography needs to have the capability of shooting at ground level. Many of your subjects will be from ground level to around a meter high. It's import that your tripod can operate comfortably and efficiently within this range. My own preferred choice is Benbo and Uni-loc; both are virtually identical in design with only minor differences. I have several models in various sizes and have used them throughout my career. I have never had any reason to switch to other brands or designs. They can be placed in virtually any position from ground level upwards and locked with a single action, by tightening the lever. These tripods are ideally suited to close-up and general nature photography. They are, I admit, a little tricky to navigate at the start, but with a little practice, you quickly become accustomed to the way they operate. You do however, need to exercise care when unlocking the lever and must always support the central column holding your camera; otherwise, it will collapse to the ground. Other manufacturers who have suitable designs include Gitzo's Systematic and Manfrotto's X ranges, which are ideally suited to low-level photography. Investing in a good tripod can be expensive, but consider the number of years of service it will give you. It is an important part of your photographic kit so don't cut financial corners. Carbon fibre designs, while lighter and more expensive, are also worth considering; many are just as sturdy as their aluminium counterparts.

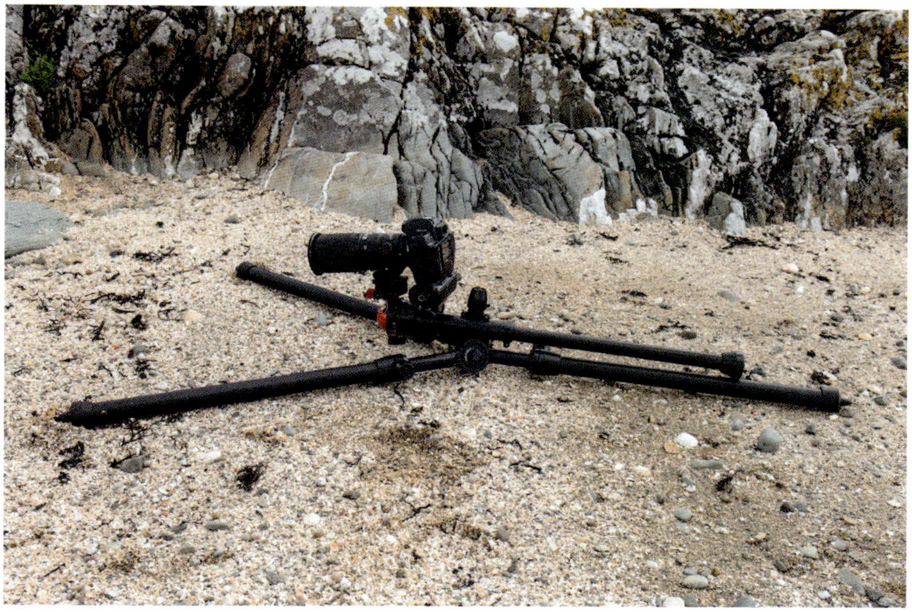

3.1 ~ Make sure your tripod is capable of working at ground level and is sturdy enough. Many of your subjects will be found relatively low down. I have always used Benbo and Uni-loc which are excellent tripods for field photography.

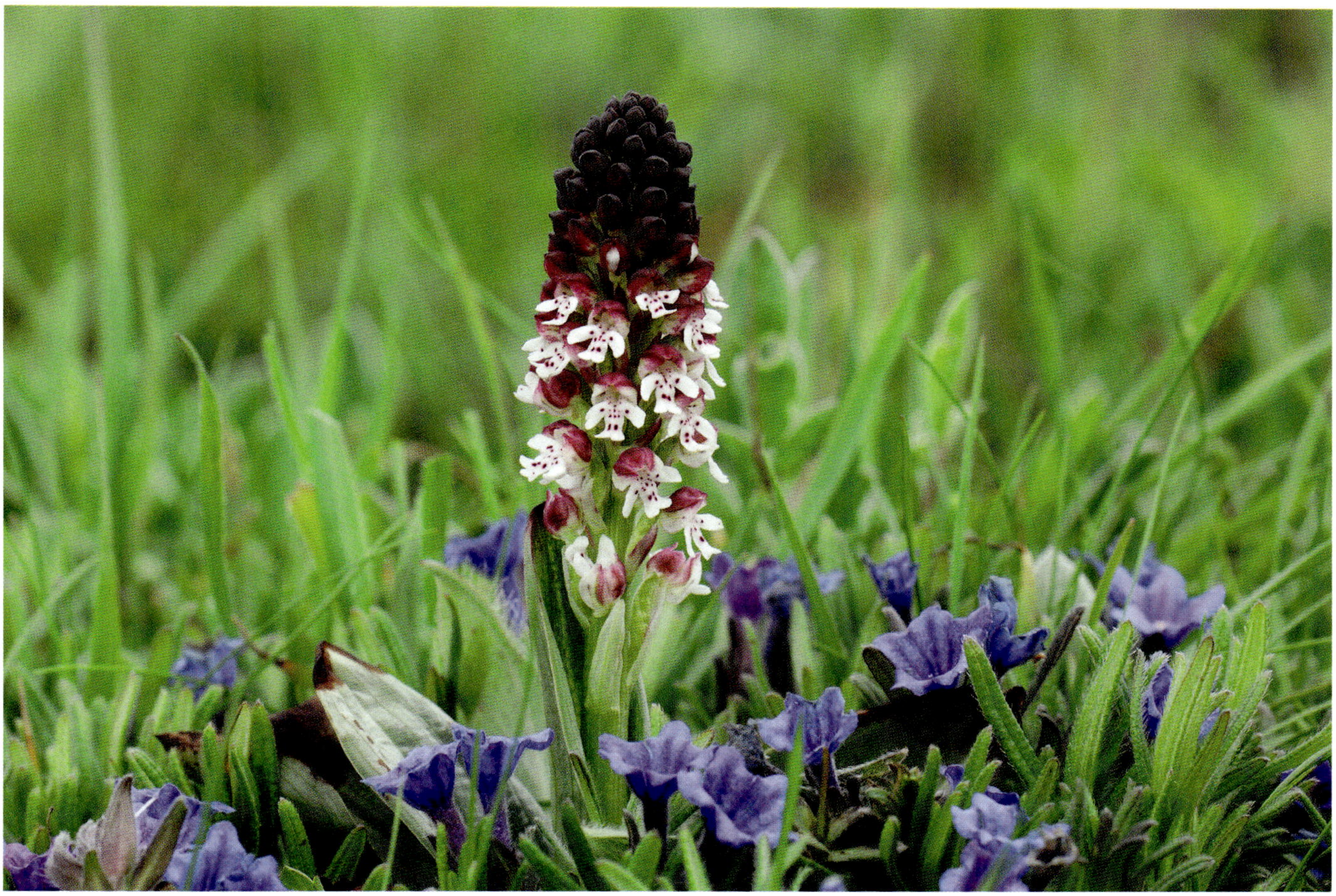

3.2 ~ **Burnt-tip Orchid** *Neotinea ustulata*
Photographing in exposed mountainous areas such as the Picos de Europa means you often have to deal with a persistent breeze. This orchid was stunted and only a few inches high. In these situations, you need to switch to shutter priority to maintain a high enough speed to deal with subject movement.

↘ Nikon D2X, 105mm micro Nikkor, 1/250sec at f/8, ISO 400.

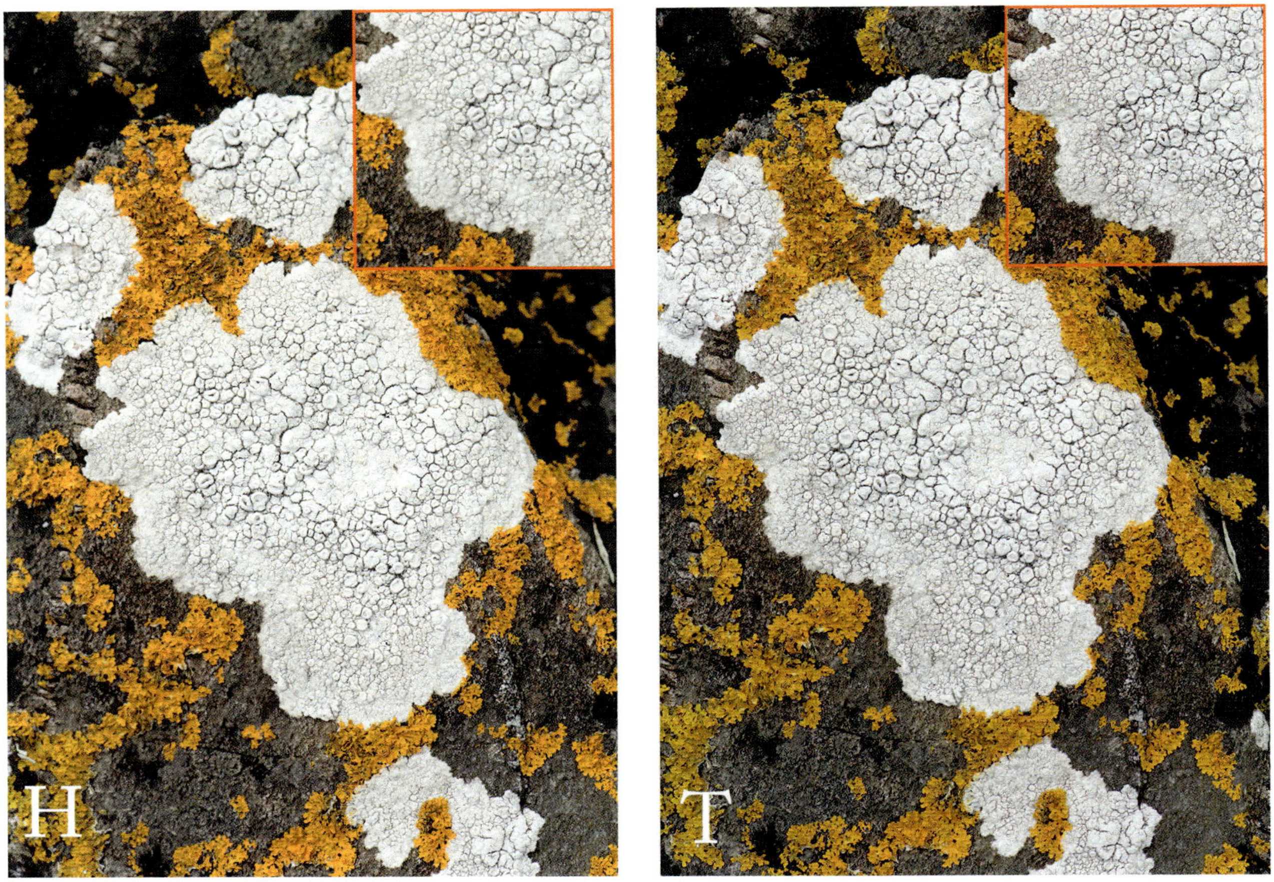

3.3 ~ *Ochrolechia parella*
I photographed this lichen on a tripod (top right) and selected the best of several handheld shots at the same shutter speed, aperture and magnification (top left). You can clearly see in the 100% enlargement insert (top right in both images) that the tripod image is much sharper.

↳ Nikon D810, 105mm micro Nikkor, 1/250sec at f/11, ISO 400.

Tripod and Handheld Shooting

The digital revolution has, in many ways, changed the way we work; high-resolution sensors and improved performance at higher ISO values have seen a shift towards more handheld photography in some photographic sectors. It is often stated that a tripod kills spontaneity, which is perhaps true in some photographic disciplines such as sport for example where the situation often demands an immediate response. It's also true that many great photographers have captured outstanding images of decisive moments shooting freehand. In close-up photography a camera mounted on a tripod will produce a sharper image than the corresponding handheld shot; this is especially evident in the reproduction of subtle detail. However, what a tripod may lack in speed it more than makes up for in terms of discipline and evaluation, giving you time to analyse everything within the frame before you push the shutter. When you view your images initially on screen, or at a relatively small size, the difference between a handheld and a tripod shot may not be that obvious. However, when viewed at 100% the softness in the fine detail from the handheld shot is clearly visible. You have no control when handholding over the point of focus and you cannot replicate it precisely in successive shots as you can when using a tripod. If your images are intended purely for web-based projects, then it may be acceptable if you are not enlarging up too much. However, if you plan on printing or exhibiting your work, any minor defects or shortcomings when enlarged will be clearly visible. With large megapixel cameras very much in vogue these days, it is even more important that you have a sound technique and a stable platform to shoot from.

The Pros and Cons

Here are some of the advantages a tripod can bring to your photography.

- It supports the camera and allows you to place it exactly where you want it, making it easy to compose your images accurately.
- You can also make minor adjustments to the composition and compare the difference.
- When working in a cramped, or an uncomfortable position, a heavy lens and camera can be difficult to frame and hold for any length of time.
- A tripod is a precision device which allows you to shoot photographs in succession, producing accuracy in your framing, focus and sharpness; this is especially critical when taking multiple images at slightly different focusing points to extend the depth of field. The technique is commonly referred to as 'Focus Stacking', or 'Extended Depth of Field'.
- When shooting in close-up, you are often working in poor light and are forced into using slower shutter speeds. Without a tripod, this would not be possible unless you increased the ISO setting.
- Working from a tripod allows you to use any shutter speed and aperture combination to achieve a particular result while working at the camera's optimum ISO.
- It is essential for higher magnifications, life-size and above.
- You have the freedom to concentrate on the subject without having to keep your eye fixed to the viewfinder.

The disadvantages of not using one limits your options in some aspects. For example:

- You would be restricted to photographing in high contrast light; a situation that is not ideal in close-up photography.
- You will be forced to work at lower magnifications with a limited range of shutter speeds and be constrained to wider apertures and higher ISO settings.
- Attaining consistency in terms of sharpness, accuracy of framing, focus and composition would not be possible.
- Extended depth of field (Focus Stacking) is harder to achieve when handholding a camera.

Tripod Heads

Maintaining total stability at the moment of exposure is critical in obtaining sharpness in an image. It is extremely important in macro photography, where any shortcomings in your technique or equipment are clearly magnified in the result. Many of the common problems seen in photographs frequently relate to the tripod (which is often inadequate) and the head, which is not suitable for the camera setup placed upon it. Even the slightest vibration will compromise the sharpness. One of the benefits of buying a tripod separately is the fact that you can choose which style of head suits you best. A good tripod head should be able to hold your camera assembly firmly in all positions, without creeping. Cheaper heads often suffer from this, even when tightly secured. As magnification increases, this becomes more of a problem, and you often have to frame slightly off-centre to counteract for the movement of the camera.

There are many different types of tripod head available; all are modelled on two principal designs, the ball-and-socket and the conventional pan-and-tilt. It's hard to advise any photographer on what suits his or her style best. The ball-and-socket is a popular choice for many nature photographers. They are quick to adjust and allow continuous rotational movement around a sphere that can be locked in any position. The negative aspect is not being able to make precise adjustments in vertical and horizontal planes, although I have not found this to be a drawback, certainly in close-up photography.

Pan-and-tilt designs are a popular choice among landscape photographers, where precise adjustments are often necessary. The head allows movements in three directions, a forward and backwards tilt, a left and right tilt and also horizontal panning. Each movement has a separate locking lever. They can be a little fiddly to get used to at the beginning, but for static close-ups they work extremely well. If possible, I recommend trying both designs with your setup before you purchase. Another option is geared heads, which are used by many photographers. Although more expensive, they are the ultimate in precision and use a tooth and cog mechanism to allow precise control over framing. They don't require locking or unlocking between adjustments, unlike standard pan-and-tilt heads.

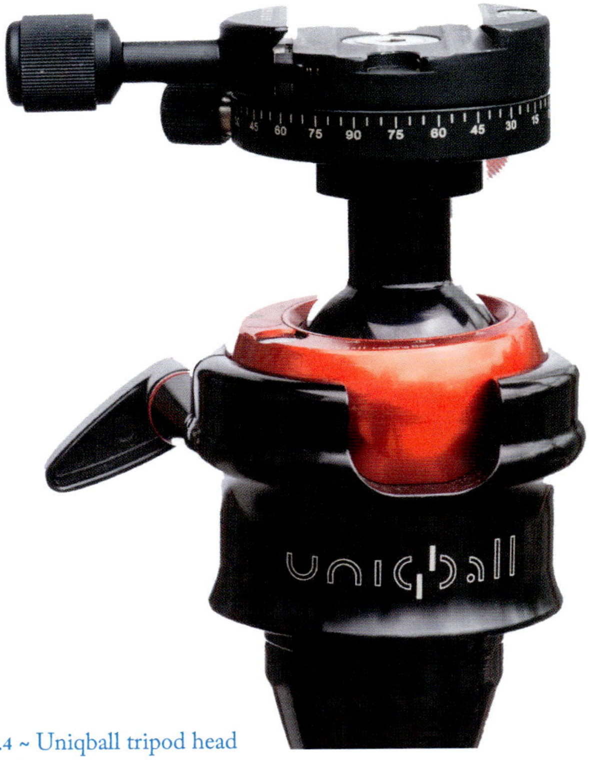

3.4 ~ Uniqball tripod head with panoramic base.

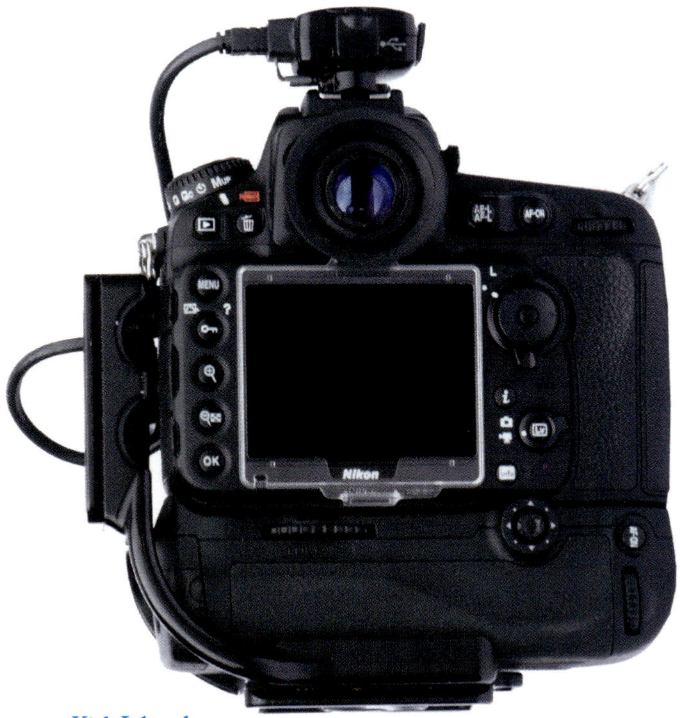

3.5 ~ **Kirk L bracket**
These can be purchased for your individual camera.

The best tripod heads are expensive but think of it as a long-term investment. Kirk Enterprise Solutions, Really Right Stuff and the Uniqball have an excellent reputation for high-quality equipment and are worth exploring. I now use the Uniqball most of the time. It is an excellent product designed by photographers themselves. A quick search on the web will give you access to reviews from photographers who may already be using these models. After all, you would hate to have some of your best opportunities and images compromised due to an inadequate tripod or head!

Quick Release Brackets

Another useful camera accessory is a quick release L-bracket. These are universally custom-made brackets that are attached to your camera's body to allow you to connect and remove your camera quickly from your tripod head. You can also switch between portrait and landscape positions without having to reset the shooting position. It also keeps the camera's centre of gravity directly on the tripod head where it can provide maximum stability and support. There are some companies, for example, Really Right Stuff, Kirk Enterprise and Manfrotto, that manufacture units which are specifically designed for popular camera bodies. Most of the companies who produce L-brackets are now adopting the 'Arca-Swiss quick release system', which is widely recognised as being one of the best in terms of connectivity and stability. Many of the L-brackets have this mount as standard.

Monopod

A monopod has limited use in close-up photography, but it is extremely useful in situations where the terrain makes it difficult to use a tripod without disturbing the surrounding vegetation. I have found it helpful when stalking insects, in particular butterflies and dragonflies that are perched on prominent pieces of vegetation. It is more useful at lower magnifications, or when stalking larger insects. I frequently increase the ISO so I can work at a higher shutter speed. A monopod is not a substitute for a tripod, but it will help to improve your stability and the sharpness in your images.

Most monopods can be a little long for working close to the ground. I normally reduce the length and attach a spike to the end so I can force it into the ground when I'm the right distance from the subject; my body adds additional support as well. You also need to add a small ball and socket head so you can make adjustments to the camera angle, otherwise you will only be able to work at right angles to the ground.

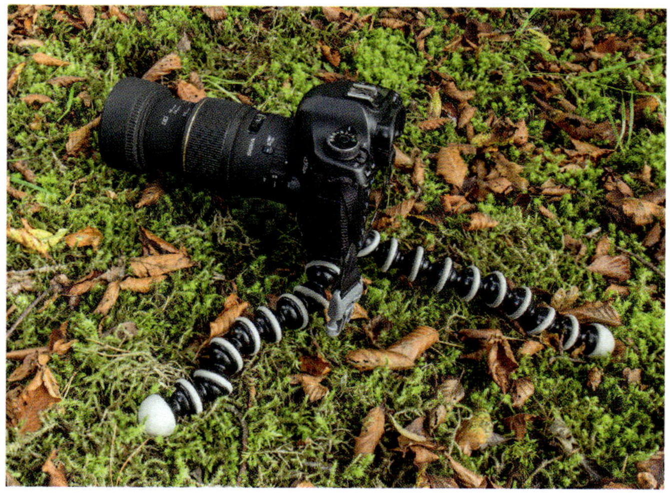

3.6 ~ **Gorillapod**
There are some situations where this support might be useful, particularly at ground level using a small lightweight setup. It has, in my opinion, limited use.

Beanbag

When you need to get your camera as close to the ground as possible, a beanbag is a useful way of achieving this. It provides a stable platform for low-level photography. Tripods that are capable of resting flat on the ground still have the height of the tripod head and therefore sit higher even at their lowest position. I find a beanbag extremely useful when using my 200mm macro at ground level. The bag can be shaped to fit the contour of the camera and lens; it also provides good support and helps dampen the vibrations. There are several different designs, but the single bag is more suited to close-up photography. They are ideal for when you want to shoot through the foreground vegetation to create a soft-focus foreground.

Most beanbags come empty, you select the filling of your choice. Rice, beans, corn, buckwheat, or polystyrene balls (which are considerably lighter) can be used as the filling. When selecting a bag, make sure the platform is wide enough to support your lens and sufficiently deep enough to balance the lens and body. The heavier the fill, the more stable it will be, but also bear in mind that you have to carry it about.

Gorillapod

Joby's flexible Gorillapod (GP8) is another camera support that has some merit in situations where the ground vegetation may prove problematic. The legs are extremely flexible and can be bent around suitable supports, for example, branches or fence posts. I do, however, feel it has limited use, since most of the time an adequate support is never in the ideal position. If you were using it primarily for ground work, then it might have more merit. When I need to position my camera on the ground, I tend to prefer a custom-designed ground spike, or a large beanbag, simply for speed and simplicity. However, if you are doing a lot of low-level photography using a smaller focal length macro and don't want to carry a tripod then perhaps it might serve a purpose.

Ground Pods and Frames

Another device that is popular with some photographers is a 'Ground Pod'. The Kirk Low Pod is perhaps the most well-known. It is a rectangular structure with raised rubber feet, which help to grip and keep the frame stable, especially on rocks and uneven surfaces. The tripod head is connected to a central metal base. Once the camera is attached, the whole assembly is still quite high off the ground and not much lower than a typical tripod designed for low-level use. If weight was an issue and you were working low-level subjects in relatively even terrain, then it might have some value in terms of speed and use. I much prefer a beanbag, which is less hassle and lower to the ground.

FOUR

Exposure & Metering Modes

VIRTUALLY ALL DSLRS have a range of exposure modes. The most common are, Programmed Auto, Shutter Priority, Aperture Priority and Manual. In close-up photography, the most frequently used settings are Aperture Priority and, to a lesser degree, Manual.

Programmed Auto Mode (P)

In this mode, the camera selects both the f/number and shutter speed. You set the ISO value, and the camera will choose the appropriate shutter speed and aperture combination, based on the available light present. The downside is you have little control over the depth of field, or how much of the subject will be in sharp focus. Also, the whole exposure process is now controlled by the camera. Programmed Auto Mode, in my opinion, is not the ideal for shooting close-ups and is best suited to general candid photography, or situations that require a quick response, for example, changing lighting conditions.

Aperture Priority

When depth of field is the principal factor, then Aperture Priority is the obvious choice. You select the desired f/number relevant to the depth of field you require and the camera automatically chooses the appropriate shutter speed to produce the correct exposure. Changing the f/number will result in the camera making an alteration to the shutter speed to maintain the proper exposure. What do we mean by correct exposure? Put simply, one that achieves the desired result. Like other program modes, Aperture Priority renders your subject as mid-toned. Subjects that have a lighter or darker tone value frequently require an adjustment to the exposure.

Aperture Priority in combination with Evaluative (matrix) metering is my preferred choice for routine close-ups of static subjects and general landscape photography. I can choose the appropriate f/number to maintain sufficient sharpness throughout the subject, or select a larger one to control distracting background highlights. Adjustments can be easily made using the exposure compensation dial to modify the histogram if necessary based on the tonality of the subject. Any changes in the ambient light will be evaluated by the camera and the shutter speed altered accordingly to maintain the correct exposure. In certain situations, where the tonality of a subject is continually changing between shots, then I prefer switching to manual mode where I have total control over all the exposure settings.

// FACING PAGE //

4.1 ~ **Seed Bug** *Lygaeus equestris*
For routine close-ups, Aperture Priority is my preferred setting.

→ Nikon D810, 200mm micro Nikkor, 1/30sec at f/16, ISO 400.

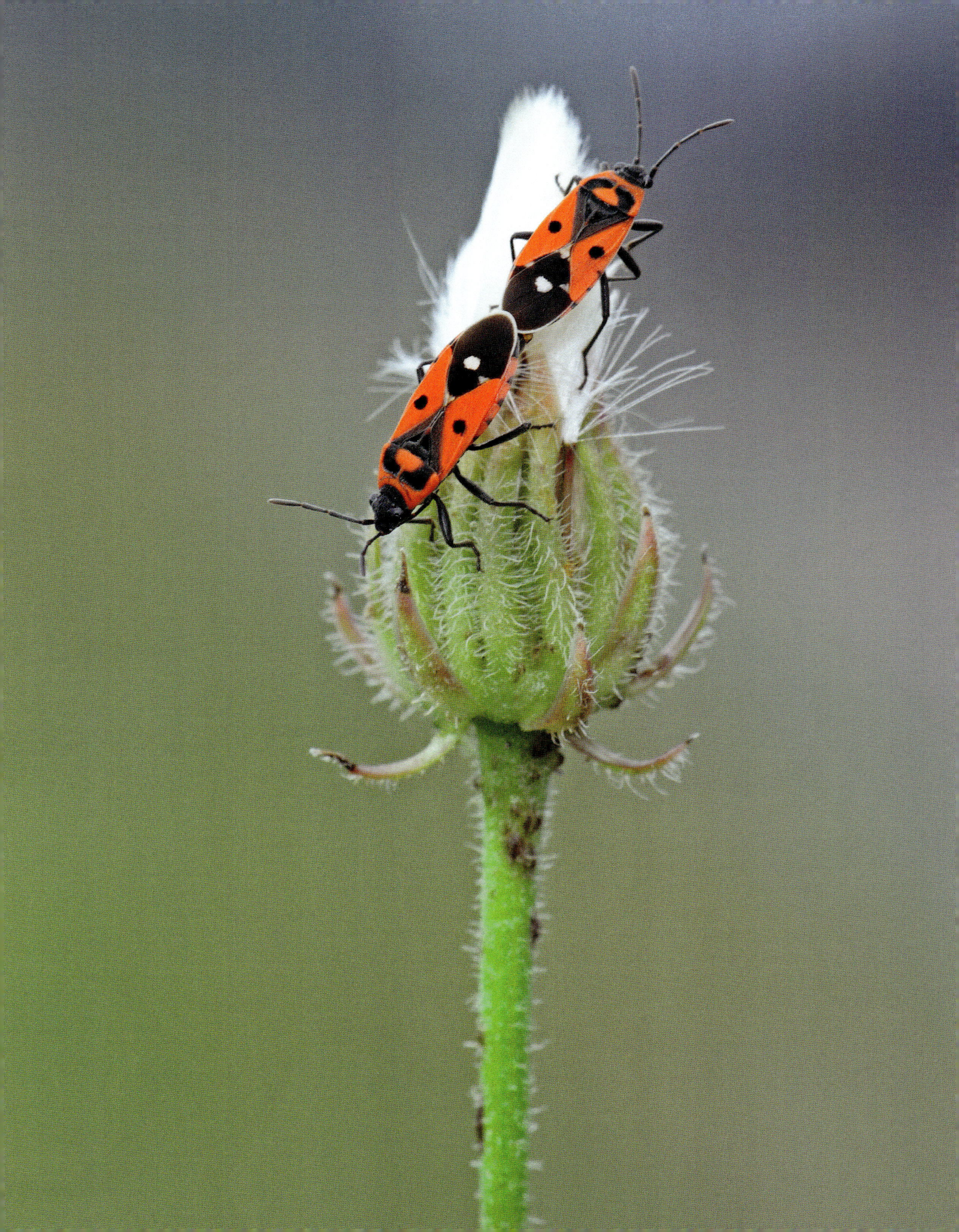

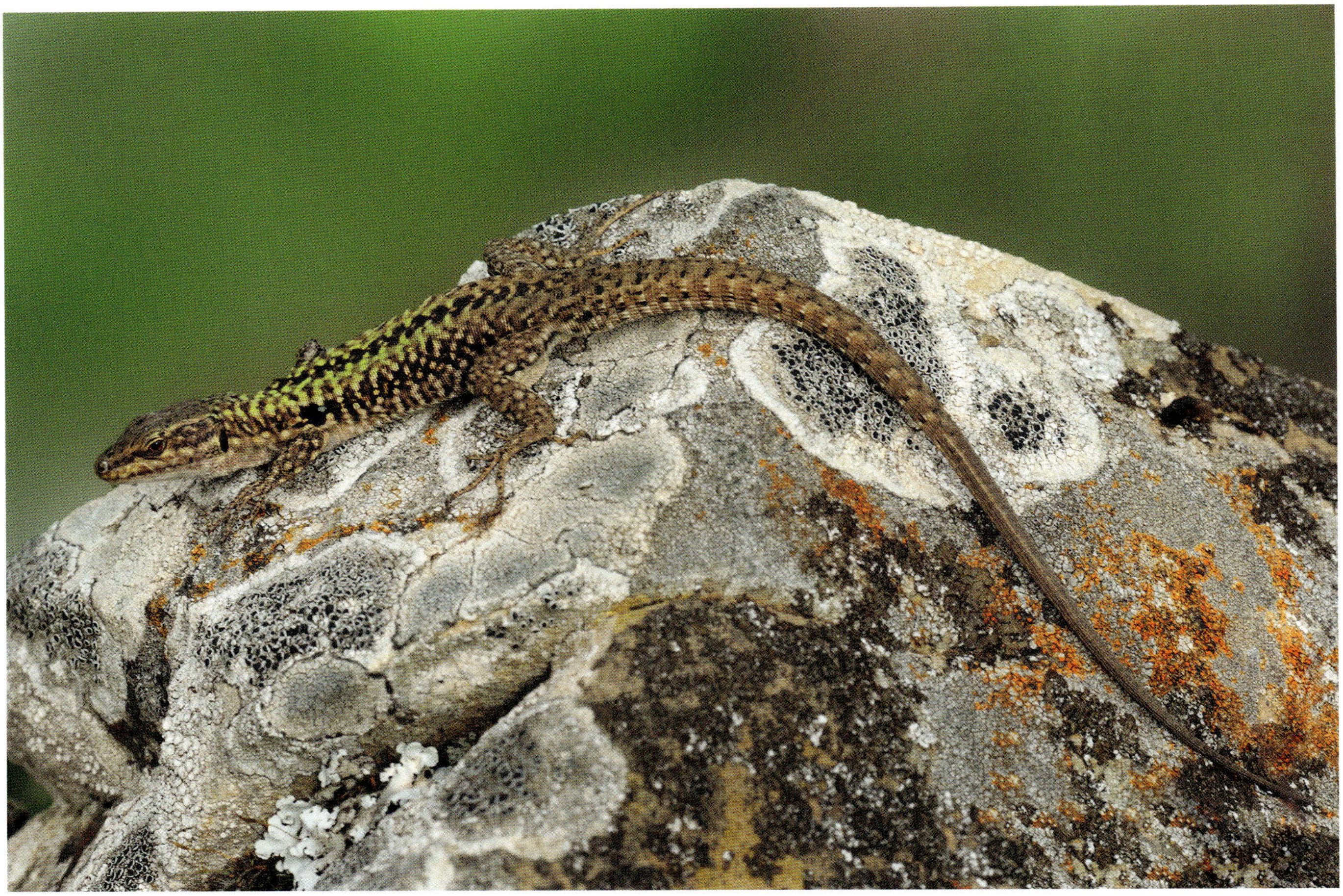

4.2 ~ **Italian Wall Lizard** *Podarcis sicula*
I prefer Shutter Priority in some situations when a creature is unpredictable.

→ Nikon D3, 200mm micro Nikkor, 1/125sec at f/8, ISO 200.

Shutter Priority

The primary advantage of Shutter Priority is when you need a fast shutter speed to freeze movement or eliminate camera shake during exposure. Once the shutter speed has been set, the camera automatically selects the appropriate f/number. I occasionally use this setting when stalking active insects, or when the terrain makes it difficult to use a tripod. One of the disadvantages of selecting a faster shutter speed is that the camera reciprocates by choosing a wider aperture which often means compromising on the depth of field. However, the ISO is so good these days that one can quickly select a higher setting to avail of smaller apertures without any significant loss in image quality.

Exposure Compensation

Modern through-the-lens (TTL) metering systems deliver excellent results in the vast majority of situations. They work on the principle that every subject is mid-tone. However, they are not infallible, especially in high contrast situations, where the subject is perhaps backlit, or exceptionally light or dark; these circumstances can

// FACING PAGE //

4.3 ~ **Four-spotted Chaser** *Libellula quadrimaculata* (female)
The large expanse of water behind the subject affected the camera's meter reading, rendering the image underexposed. Switching to manual is a sensible solution in this case, where you have complete control of the exposure.

→ Nikon D800, 200mm micro Nikkor, 1/60sec at f/11, ISO 200.

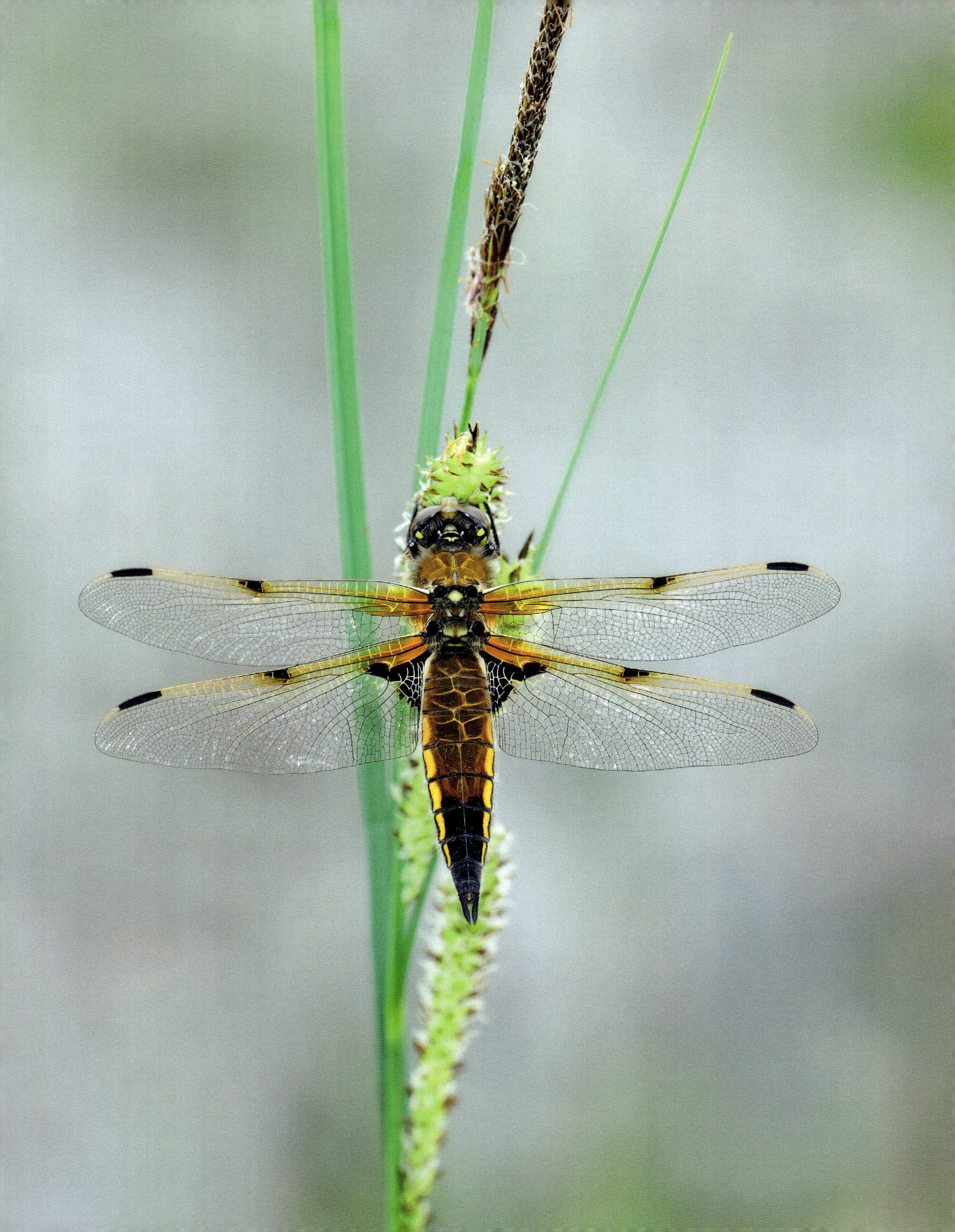

easily deceive even the best metering systems. If shooting in Aperture or Shutter Priority, you may need to make adjustments from the camera's suggested reading via the exposure compensating dial or button which is usually located on the top of your camera. The +/- dial increases or decreases the exposure in incremental stages depending on how your camera is programmed. Settings of 1/3, 1/2, and up to full stop increments are usually possible on most DSLRs. Changing the base exposure via the exposure compensation dial will be displayed automatically in the viewfinder and the LCD displays on your camera. For example, when in Aperture Priority if you increase the exposure compensation button by ½ stop the camera is extending the shutter speed by ½ stop from the selected one. When in Shutter Priority, the camera is opening the aperture by ½ stop from the selected f/stop. It is important that you understand how exposure compensation works in either of the automated settings. Most cameras allow compensation up to about five stops in either direction. Be mindful that any adjustments you make via the exposure compensation dial remain in place until you restore it to its default position. It is always wise to reset the dial when finished as you can easily forget. Remember, any subsequent images you take will have that setting applied to them during exposure.

Manual

Working entirely in manual when shooting close-ups is no longer that popular among photographers. However, there are situations when I like to have complete control of both the aperture and shutter speed, especially when making adjustments for subjects that are not mid-tone. If the subject occupies a small area within the frame, your camera's meter can be easily influenced by the surrounding area and produce a result that is over or underexposed.

Manual mode gives you complete control over the whole exposure process. Initially, it may seem to be a slower way to work, but is my preferred choice when faced with challenging lighting conditions. Once you have established the correct f/number and shutter speed the camera will retain these settings until you change them irrespective of the changing light. I always switch to manual when shooting for Extended Depth of Field (see page 77) to ensure there is no deviation in the exposure between shots. Another practical situation is when you can't for reasons of space, or position, have your eye in contact with the viewfinder; any stray light entering will have no effect on the exposure when your camera is in manual mode.

Metering Modes

The metering systems on today's modern DSLRs are complicated and sophisticated. However, despite their complexity, they are not foolproof. Most cameras have four metering modes, Evaluative (Nikon call it Matrix), Centre-weighted, Spot and Manual. I don't, as a rule, when shooting close-ups frequently switch between metering modes. I find in the vast majority of the cases, matrix metering is perfectly adequate and quicker to implement than spot metering. If I have to make a change to the suggested exposure, I can do this quickly using the Exposure Compensating dial. Despite all of the current innovative technology, a camera's metering system is not intuitive and, therefore, cannot predict the type of result you are trying to achieve. As a photographer, you need to have a comprehensive understanding of exposure and how to apply the necessary skills to correct errors and attain the desired outcome. If you are a Nikon user and find the exposure compensating button awkward to use Nikon allows you to reassign it to the main command dial, therefore making it easier and less fiddly to make the adjustments. Some photographers make use of this function, it's down to personal choice.

FIVE

Understanding ISO

DESCRIBED AS ONE of the three photographic triangles or pillars, ISO is the acronym for International Standards Organisation; a non-government body responsible for setting industrial and commercial standards in a wide variety of subjects. ISO along with shutter speed and aperture determine the exposure of a photograph. Your camera's image sensor is responsible for collecting the light passing through the lens and converting it into a visible picture. Put simply, ISO is the measurement of the sensitivity of your camera's sensor to available light. The abbreviation itself originates from the days of analogue capture when the ISO number on the film cassette referred to its speed. The ISO setting on your digital camera still functions in the same way as it did with film, except that it is now analysing how sensitive the sensor in your camera is to light.

All DSLR cameras have a native, or an optimum default ISO setting, which is the lowest ISO number that the camera can produce the highest image quality with little or no discernible noise visible. Most DSLRs have a native ISO between 100–200; a few higher specification models are capable of slower speeds of 50. The ISO scale on your camera works in geometric progression, for example, 100, 200, 400, 800, 1600, 3200, 6400. Advancing the ISO value from 200 to 400 is the equivalent of a one-stop increase, continuing to 800 represents a two-stop increase and so on. It is easier to think of the numerical progression in terms of stops; doubling or halving the number is the equivalent of one stop. Many of the current cameras allow you to make smaller incremental changes to the ISO value in 1/3-, or 1/2-stops. I don't see any significant advantage to be gained in making an adjustment of 1/3-stop, but certainly a 1/2- to 1-stop adjustments do have merit.

The lower the ISO setting, the less responsive the camera's sensor is to light and, therefore, requires a longer exposure time to obtain a correctly exposed image. The higher the ISO value, the more sensitive your camera's image sensor is to light. However, the downside is that increasing the ISO value adds digital noise to your pictures in a similar way that faster film speeds produced increased grain. The dynamic range is also reduced, and this becomes more apparent at much higher ISO settings, especially in shadow areas where it becomes grainy in appearance. Any increase in digital noise will affect image quality, especially the fine detail where it is most obvious. Nevertheless, the current DSLRs have excellent high ISO performance that has real benefits when you require faster shutter speeds or need to arrest moment and camera vibration. However, you should always select the lowest ISO that the situation requires. If high ISO settings are something that you are going to use on a frequent basis, then it would be prudent to research your camera's sensor performance in this area. With so many DSLRs on the market supporting different sensors, some will undoubtedly perform better at higher ISO settings than others.

In close-up photography, ISO selection is particularly relevant. There are situations when you have to resort to hand holding the camera. Increasing the ISO allows faster shutter speeds, which reduces the

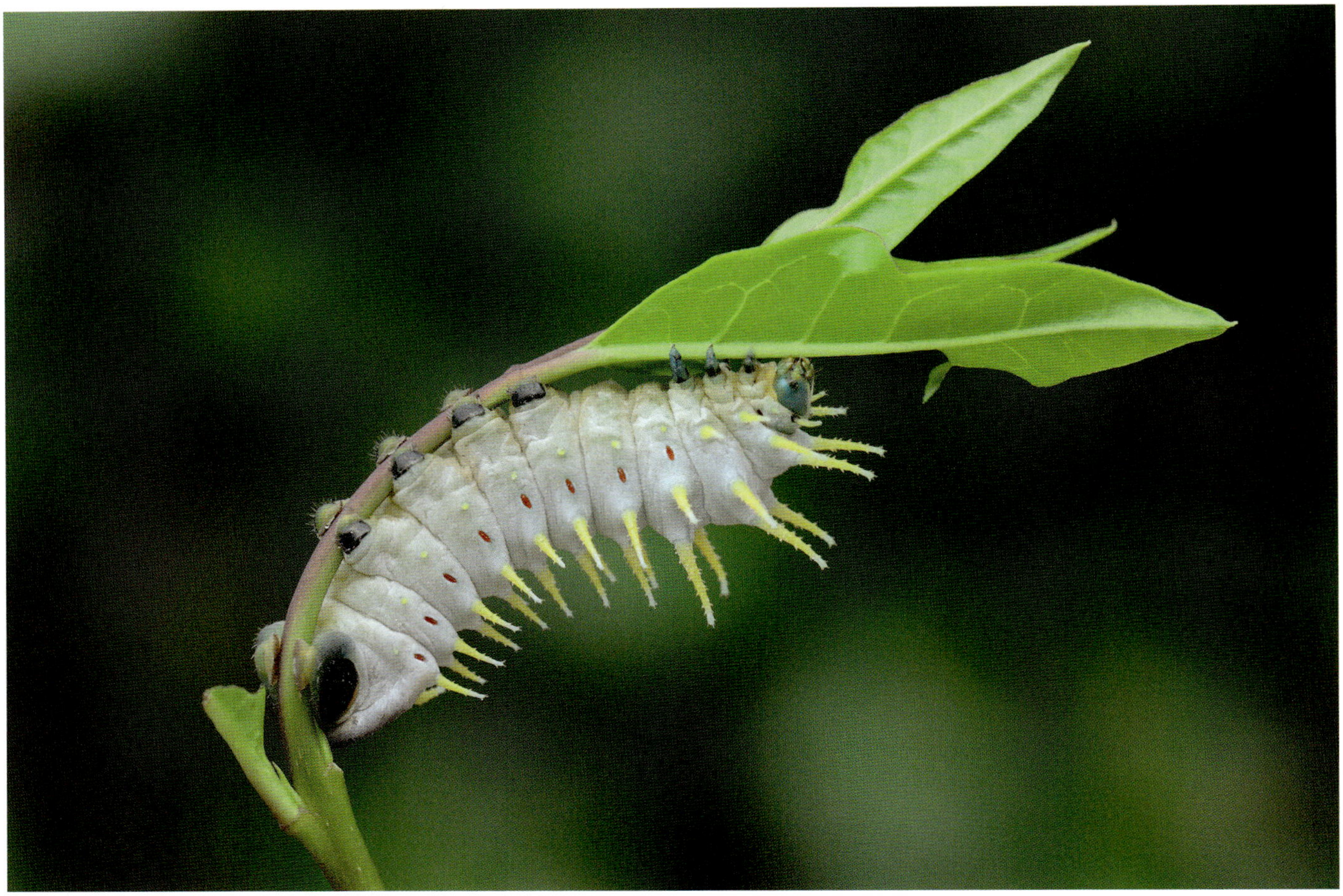

5.1 ~ **Hercules Moth** *Coscinocera hercules*
Operating at the camera's native ISO setting produces images with no discernible noise visible if exposed correctly.

↳ Nikon D800, 200mm micro Nikkor, 1/30sec at f/11, ISO 100.

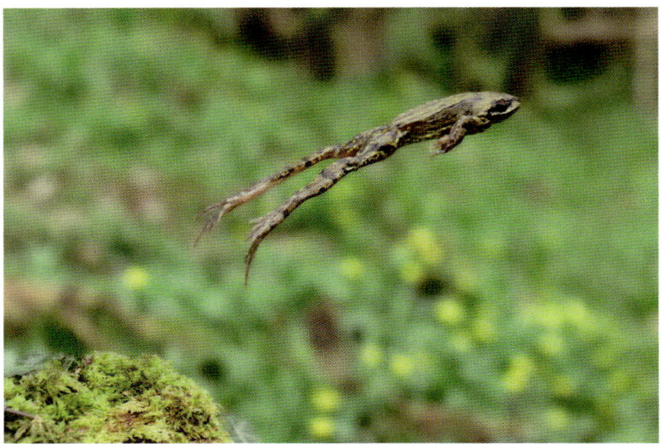

5.2 ~ **European Common Frog** *Rana temporaria*
Modern DSLRs even when pushed to the limit can still produce acceptable results.

↳ Nikon D810, 24–70mm, 1/2000sec at f/8, ISO 6400

risk of movement due to camera shake and increases your likelihood of obtaining sharper images. At higher magnifications depth of field is so shallow that it is sometimes necessary to advance the ISO to allow the use of smaller apertures combined with higher shutter speeds; this increases the depth of field while maintaining a fast enough shutter speed to arrest movement. Having said that, recent developments in sensor technology mean that the image quality even at ISO speeds of 800–1600 deliver excellent results with little visible sign of increased noise.

SIX

Aperture

THE WORD APERTURE derives from the Latin word *apertura*. Along with shutter speed and ISO, they form the three major components in photography often referred to as the 'Exposure Triangle'. The aperture controls the amount of light entering the camera and is the primary factor that determines the overall appearance of the photograph. Selecting a small aperture increases the depth of field, or the degree of sharpness in the image, while shooting wide open creates very shallow depth of field, isolating the subject from the background. Understanding how aperture, shutter speed and ISO work together is fundamental to creating great photographs.

The aperture in a lens operates in a similar way to the iris in your eye, which expands and contracts to regulate the amount of light passing through the pupil to the retina, which is the equivalent to the camera's sensor. A dilated pupil is comparable to a large aperture on a lens which lets more light through. The iris or diaphragm in a lens controls the size of the aperture which regulates the light passing through to the camera's sensor. In photography the size of the aperture is described in 'f-stops' or focal ratio, which relates to the diameter of the lens aperture. The f-stop number is determined by the focal length of the lens, divided by the diameter of the aperture. The focal length refers to the lenses' field of view, or the angle of view (as it's sometimes called) and is always expressed in millimetres and defines the area that the lens can capture.

The f-stops are expressed as a series of alphanumeric symbols on the lens. The smaller the number, the larger the aperture; this is often confusing to the beginner since we are used to having larger numbers representing greater values; the opposite is true in this case. The number of f-stops on a lens can vary depending on its focal length and speed. Typically, the average lens has an aperture range as follows:

f/2.8 f/4 f/5.6 f/8 f/11 f/16 f/22

Each of the numbers represents either a halving or doubling of the amount of light (depending on which way you go) from its adjacent neighbour. For example, moving your aperture from f/4 to f/5.6 represents halving the amount of light reaching the sensor, while opening the aperture from f/4 to f/2.8 accounts for a doubling of the amount of light reaching the sensor. Some expensive lenses have faster apertures of f/2 or even f/1.4. However, these lenses have no real advantage in close-up photography since you are unlikely in most situations, to be shooting with the lens wide open.

The iris or diaphragm of the lens consists of a number of thin metal blades that move inwards or outwards as the diaphragm ring is rotated; this creates a hole of variable size which the light can pass through. In photography terms, we are referring to the diameter or size of the opening itself which expands or contracts depending on the aperture selected. The greater the number of blades the smoother the transition between out of focus objects in the background will be. Nikon's 200mm f/4 micro-Nikkor lens has a nine-blade aperture unit which produces a more rounded and

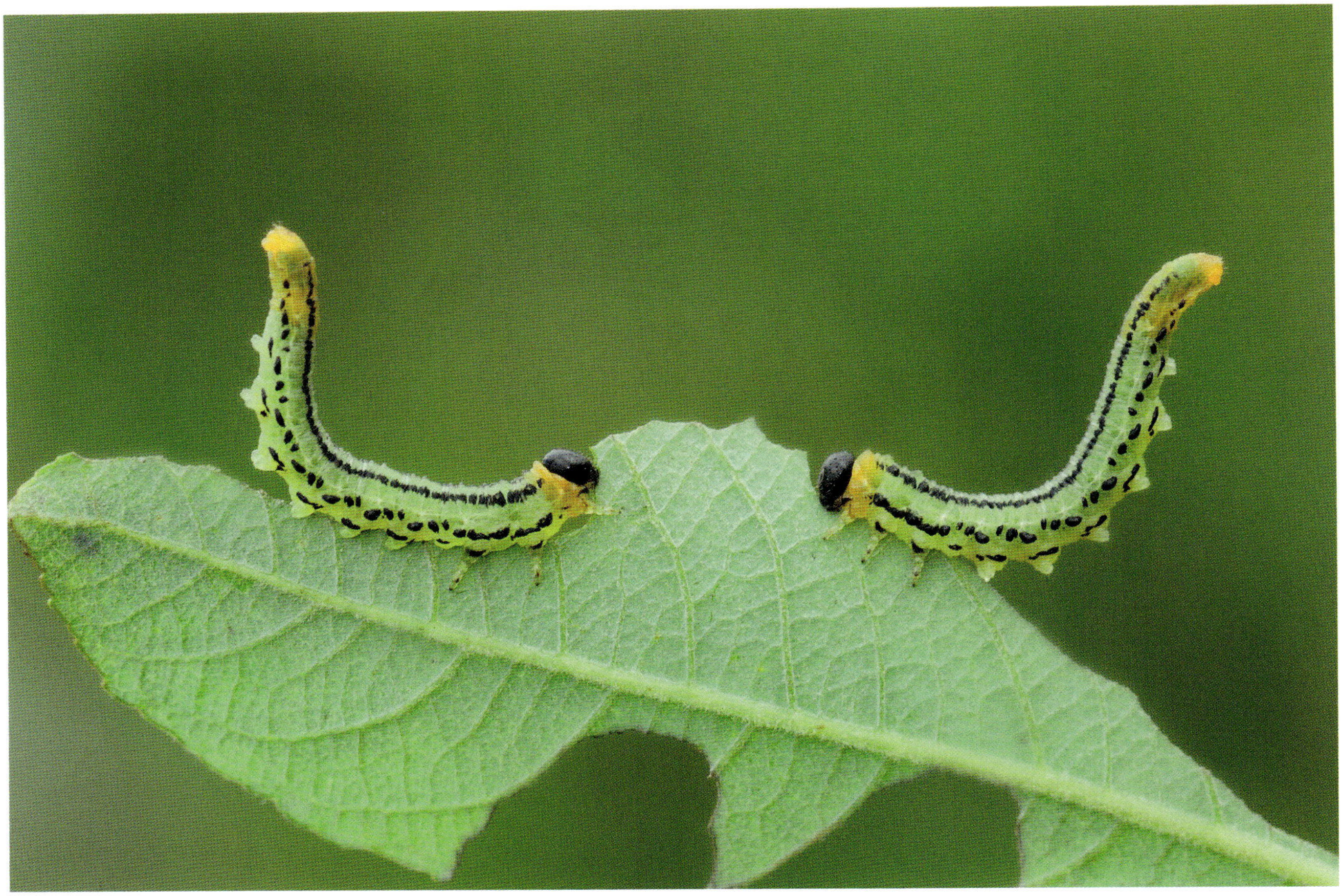

6.1 ~ Sawfly Larvae *Nematus pavidus*
Modern lenses have diaphragms with greater numbers of metal blades, which produce a smoother diffusion in the out of focus points in the background as can be seen in both these examples.

→ Nikon D3X, 200mm micro Nikkor, 1/30sec at f/11, ISO 200.

smoother transition between out of focus points in the background. All modern cameras have what is termed automatic aperture control, which allows you to view the subject at the lens's maximum aperture for composing and focusing. During exposure, it is automatically stopped down to the taking aperture. There is no correct aperture for every picture. The subject, focal length of the lens, its position and the overall look you desire are all important factors to be considered. It is not always desirable to have the whole subject in focus. Some of the most pictorial images are often those with shallow depth of field.

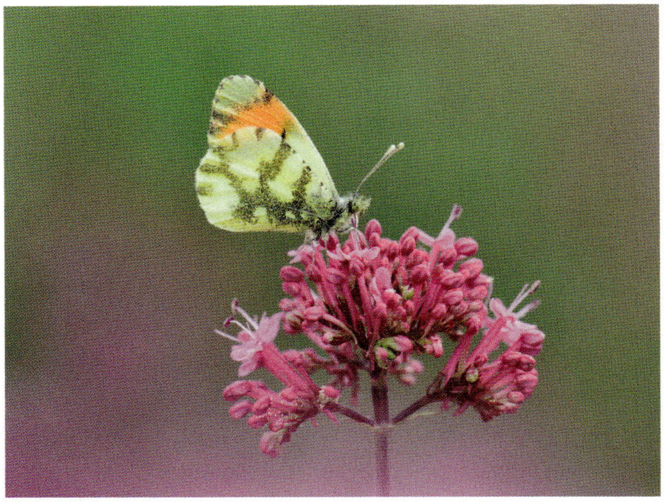

6.2 ~ Provence Orange-tip *Anthocharis euphenoides*
An attractive species similar to the Orange-tip *A. cardamines*, but males have a pale yellow upperside. Its distribution is mainly the Iberian peninsular and the south of France with a preference for woodland rides and meadows.

SEVEN

Depth of Field

UNDERSTANDING depth of field is one of the most important parts of the photographic process. Becoming familiar with how the aperture, magnification and the focal length of a lens all interact with each other is essential in photography as a whole; not just in close-up. In general, photography depth of field is normally defined as approximately one-third in front of the plane of focus and two-thirds beyond it. However, in macro the zone of sharpness is more evenly matched. In theory, true focus is only achievable on a single plane; at the point on which the lens is focused. The area either side of the point of focus is still relatively sharp. This range, or zone is defined as the depth of field.

The selected aperture along with magnification are the controlling factors that determine depth of field; both are inextricably linked. As magnification increases, depth of field decreases. Smaller apertures provide greater depth of field while larger apertures reduce it. Magnification or reproduction ratio has a bearing on how much of a subject you can keep in acceptable focus. Depth of field also has an impact on both the aesthetic and technical quality of a photograph. Photographing a subject at f/5.6 and at f/16 will produce a very different appearance in both photographs. At f/5.6 the degree of sharpness, both in the subject and the background will be considerably less, but the overall effect can be quite pleasing to the eye. At f/16, the subject will have a greater degree of sharpness throughout, but the background will look different and may have unwanted vegetation appearing that was diffused or less obtrusive when shooting at a wider aperture.

It has often been stated that long focal length lenses have less depth of field and wide angle lenses have more. This is not necessarily the case, as the degree of acceptable sharpness is controlled by a number of different factors: the aperture selected, the focal length of the lens, magnification and camera-to-subject distance. If the magnification and aperture remain constant, then all lenses will deliver the same depth of field irrespective of their focal length. If you photograph a subject at 1:1 with a 50mm macro lens and again using a 200mm macro lens at the same magnification and aperture you will achieve the same depth of field in both cases. However, the lens to subject distance, the angle of view and the background will all be different; this will be evident in both images.

In general photography, depth of field can be measured in metres, since most of the time the subject is a reasonable distance away. For example, a subject photographed five metres away at f/16 will have substantial depth of field. Any slight focusing error at this distance will have less effect on the final image since a small aperture would be sufficient to retain the subject in focus. In close-up photography, the situation is rather different. If we photograph a subject at 30 centimetres away at f/16, the lens-to-subject distance is now significantly reduced – the depth of field can be measured in millimetres. Any slight focusing error or movement in the camera becomes a serious issue. The only way you can increase depth of field is to use smaller apertures, decrease the magnification of the subject or use a focus stacking technique if possible. Having said that,

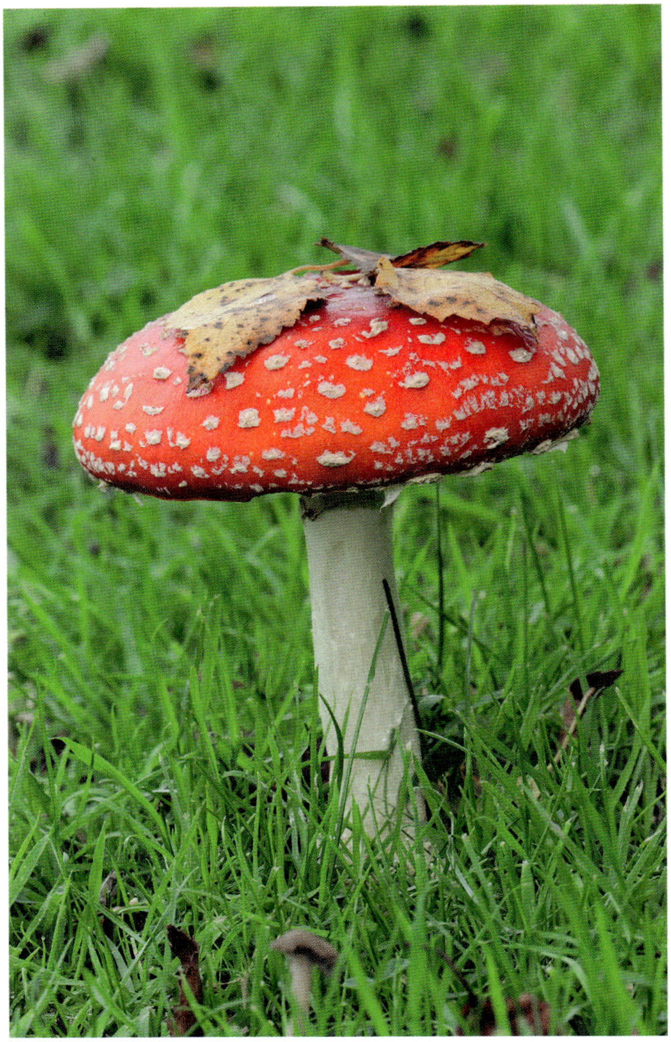

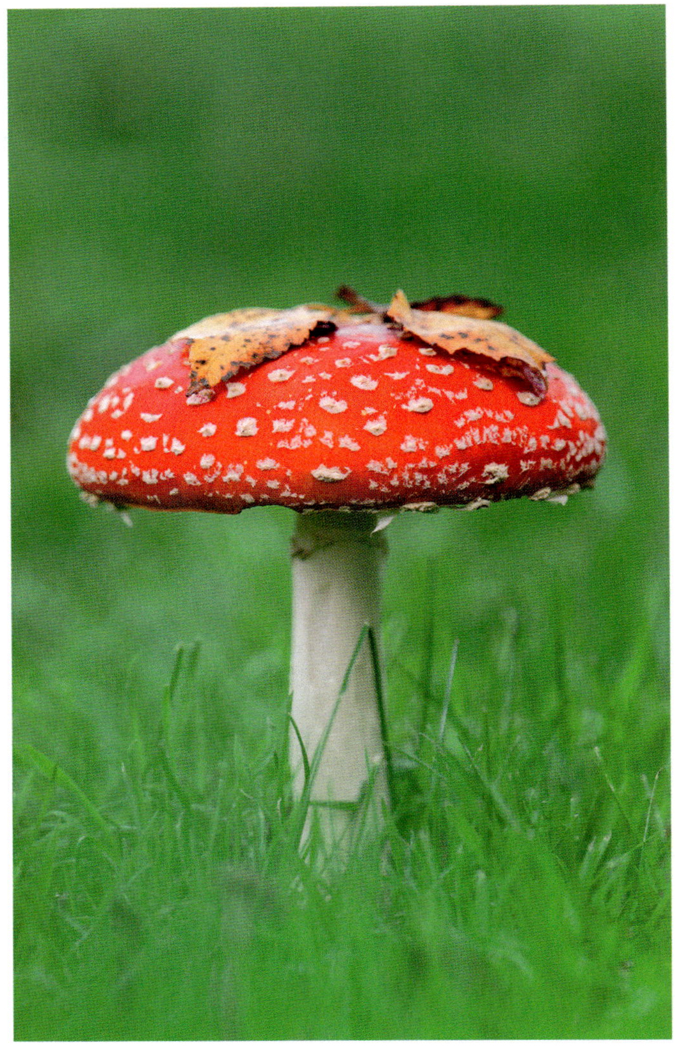

7.1 ~ **Fly Agaric** *Amanita muscaria*
Both these images are taken from a similar viewpoint. It can be clearly seen how the choice of aperture has an important bearing on the aesthetics of both photographs.

↘ Nikon D3X, 200mm micro Nikkor.
Left image f/16, ISO 100, right image f/5.6, ISO 100.

adopting the principle of selecting a smaller f-number for all of your images may seem the most logical approach. However, for reasons already stated this is not best practice. When you use apertures beyond the lens's sweet spot you encounter diffraction, which becomes more obvious at smaller apertures. The image can appear soft, there is also a lack of sharpness and overall contrast. It also forces you into slower shutter speeds and the final image may not be to your liking anyway. There is no ideal aperture, or 'one solution fits all'. You must choose your aperture according to the type of result you desire. In some cases, you may not want the entire subject in focus, or it may not be possible to obtain complete sharpness throughout.

// FACING PAGE //

7.2 ~ **Narrow-leaved Helleborine** *Cephalanthera longifolia*
I wanted to control the background in this image and selected an aperture that gave me enough depth of field to maintain focus on the plant.

↘ Nikon D3X, 200mm micro Nikkor, 1/ 125sec at f/8, ISO 100.

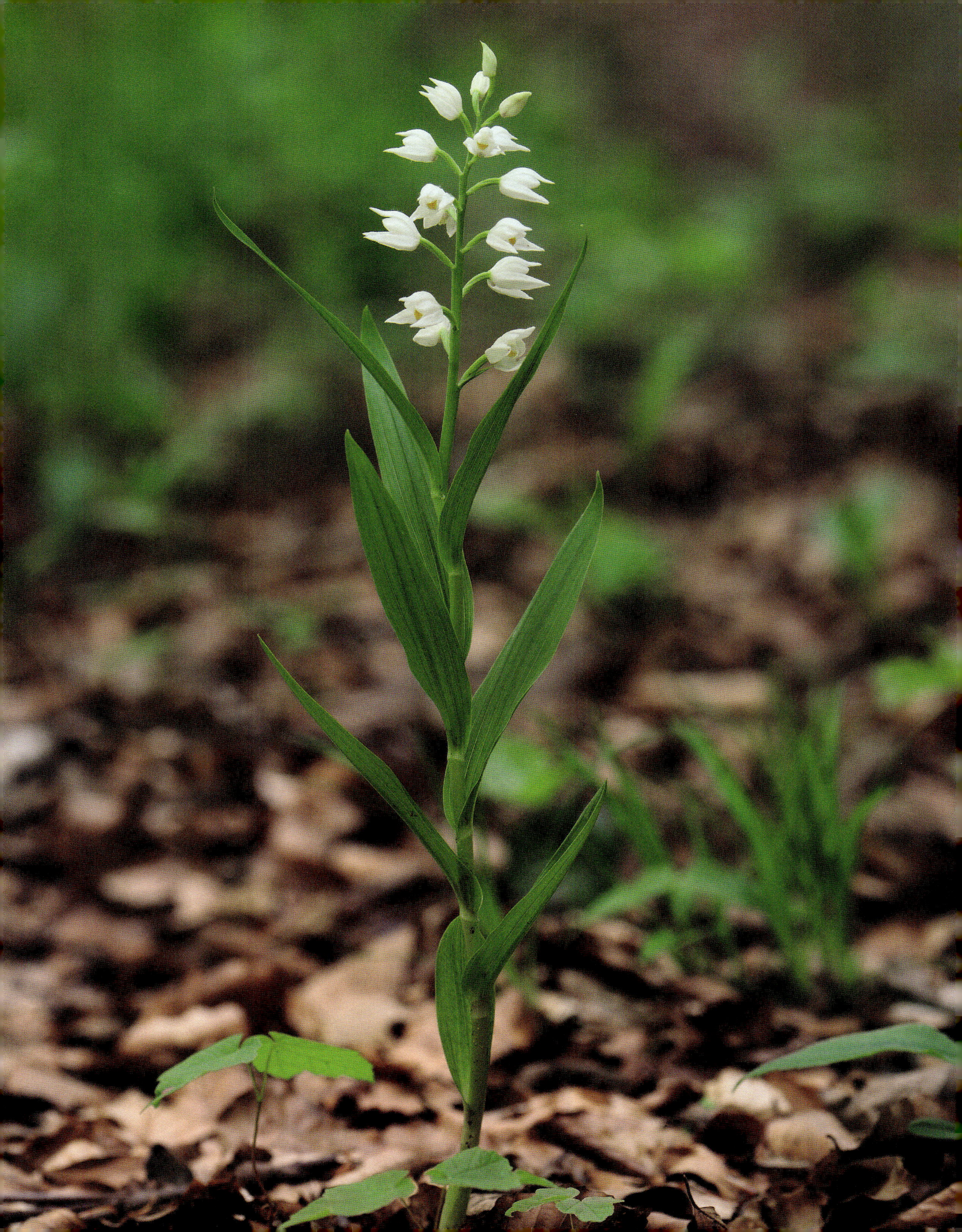

EIGHT

Understanding White Balance

WHITE BALANCE, is one aspect that beginners new to photography often have difficulty understanding. Colour is an important part of our lives, it enriches our visual experience of the world; without it we would be deprived of so much beauty. From the moment we wake up we encounter light in many different colours and forms. Most of the time we are oblivious to its nuances since our visual system automatically adjusts to the many variations in colour temperature. Unlike our eyes, the image sensor in a camera sees it differently and requires our input to ensure it records as faithfully as possible what we see.

There are two most important aspects of light as photographers; we need to comprehend the quality of light and the colour of light; both are different. Light is a form of electromagnetic energy that travels in waves ... when spread out according to wavelength a spectrum is created ...visible light forms only a very narrow part of that spectrum. Not all of these energy waves are visible to the human eye. The part that we can see is called the visible light spectrum, which is divided into thirds. The predominant colours are red, green and blue which we understand as (RGB). At the high end of the spectrum are the short wavelengths we recognise as being blue, while at the low end the long wavelengths we identify as being red. All of the intermediate colours in the visible spectrum lie between these two extremes. At the blue end of the spectrum and beyond our vision are the short wavelengths of ultraviolet and X-ray. Infrared radiation and radio waves lie beyond the long wavelengths at the red end of the spectrum.

The quality of light is measured through its 'colour temperature' which is constantly changing throughout the day and is measured in units of Kelvin (K). Sunrise and sunset contain a greater percentage of red wavelengths, which makes the light warmer and more pleasing to the eye. A higher colour temperature contains more blue wavelengths which give a much cooler look to photographs. Sunlight around mid-day is considered to be neutral and has a colour temperature of around 5,500K. All other light sources are equated to it.

The chart below shows the various types of light and their approximate Kelvin measurements.

LIGHT SOURCE	COLOUR TEMPERATURE IN KELVIN (K)
Candlelight	1,000–1800K
Sunrise/Sunset	2,500–3,000K
Tungsten	2,900–3,200K
Electronic flash	5,000–5,500K
Mid-day summer sunlight clear sky	5.500–6,500K
Overcast sky	6,000–7,500K
Outdoor shade	7,000–8,000K

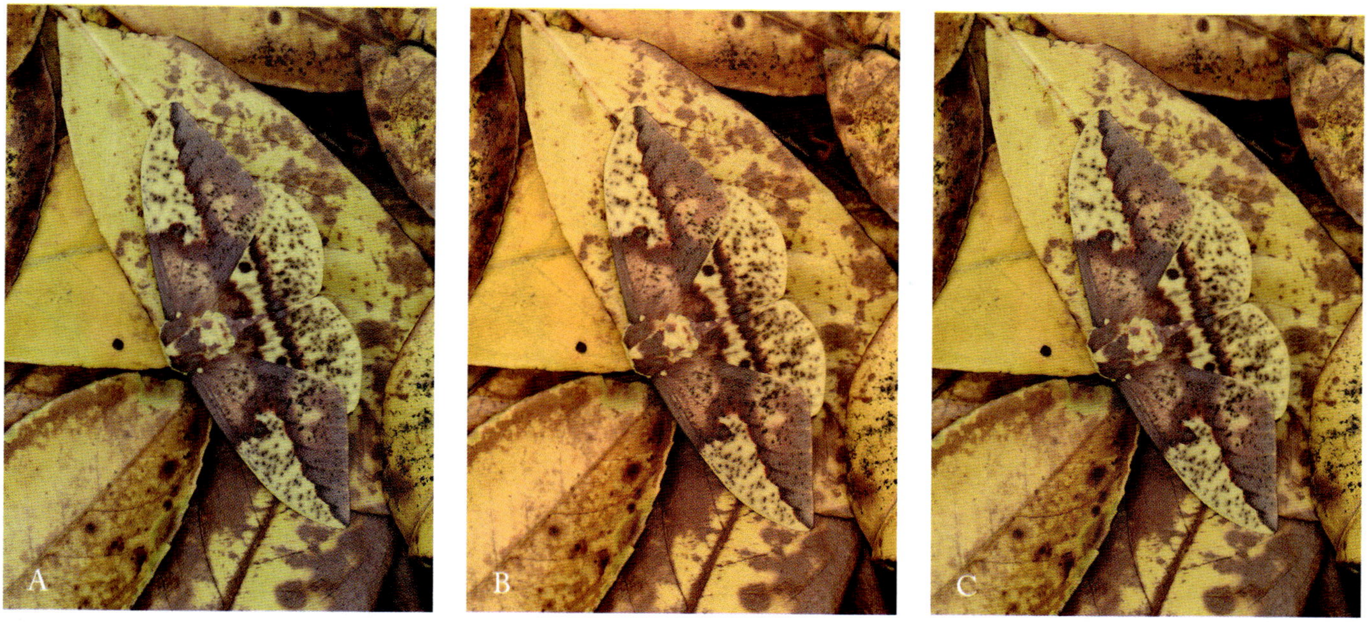

8.1 ~ **Oslar's Eacles** *Eacles oslari*
This series of images shows how the colour temperature varies depending on what preset you have selected. A is the recorded value by the camera. B is set to shade. C is cloudy.

↳ Nikon D810, 105mm micro Nikkor, 1/15sec at f/11, ISO 200.

DSLRs come with a built-in series of White Balance presets for the most common lighting conditions. These will give reasonable results in average situations, but it can be difficult to match the presets to more challenging shooting conditions. There is also an 'Auto White Balance Mode' (AWB), which some photographers use routinely, although reliable in most situations it is not foolproof. One of the disadvantages in relying entirely on the AWB setting is the fact that the light can change subtlety when shooting a sequence, and some images may have a slightly different colour cast. Many DSLRs have a custom White Balance setting where you can tweak the colour temperature to achieve a more accurate match. There are some products on the market, such as Lastolite EzBalance, ExpoDisc and even a simple grey card, that are specifically designed to help you attain the correct White Balance. These can be positioned and photographed in the same light as the subject for an accurate assessment of the colour temperature.

In close-up photography, you are likely to be photographing subjects in locations that are more challenging in terms of light and shade. Fungi in woodland are a good example where the light illuminating the subject may be heavily influenced by the green cast from the canopy. Shooting in the shade under a clear blue sky in the early morning is another situation that often produces a cool result. If you are shooting JPEGs as opposed to RAW, then you will need to be more careful when setting your White Balance in-camera as it is not so easy to correct in post-production.

I rarely use the AWB setting for a number of reasons. Using your camera's custom White Balance presets gives you much greater flexibility over the colour temperature. I have created several custom presets for various lighting conditions in the field, which I can quickly access to give me the type of result I like. Another important reason is all of the images I shoot will have a fixed colour temperature, which makes it easier to apply a global change in post-processing if necessary without having variations between individual images. This is important when shooting multiple photographs for extended depth of field.

If you are shooting in RAW then setting a specific White Balance is not as important since the data at this stage is still in its unprocessed state. You can even leave the camera on Auto and change it in the conversion software, which has a lot more options in terms of colour temperature. A RAW file will only have a specific White Balance setting applied to it when converted into a readable graphics format such as JPEG or TIFF.

// OVERLEAF //

8.2 ~ **Amethyst Deceiver** *Laccaria amethystina*
I prefer to use the custom White Balance setting of my own. I have several for difficult lighting situations.

↳ Nikon D3X, 300mm Nikkor, + ext. tubes, 1/6sec at f11, ISO 200.

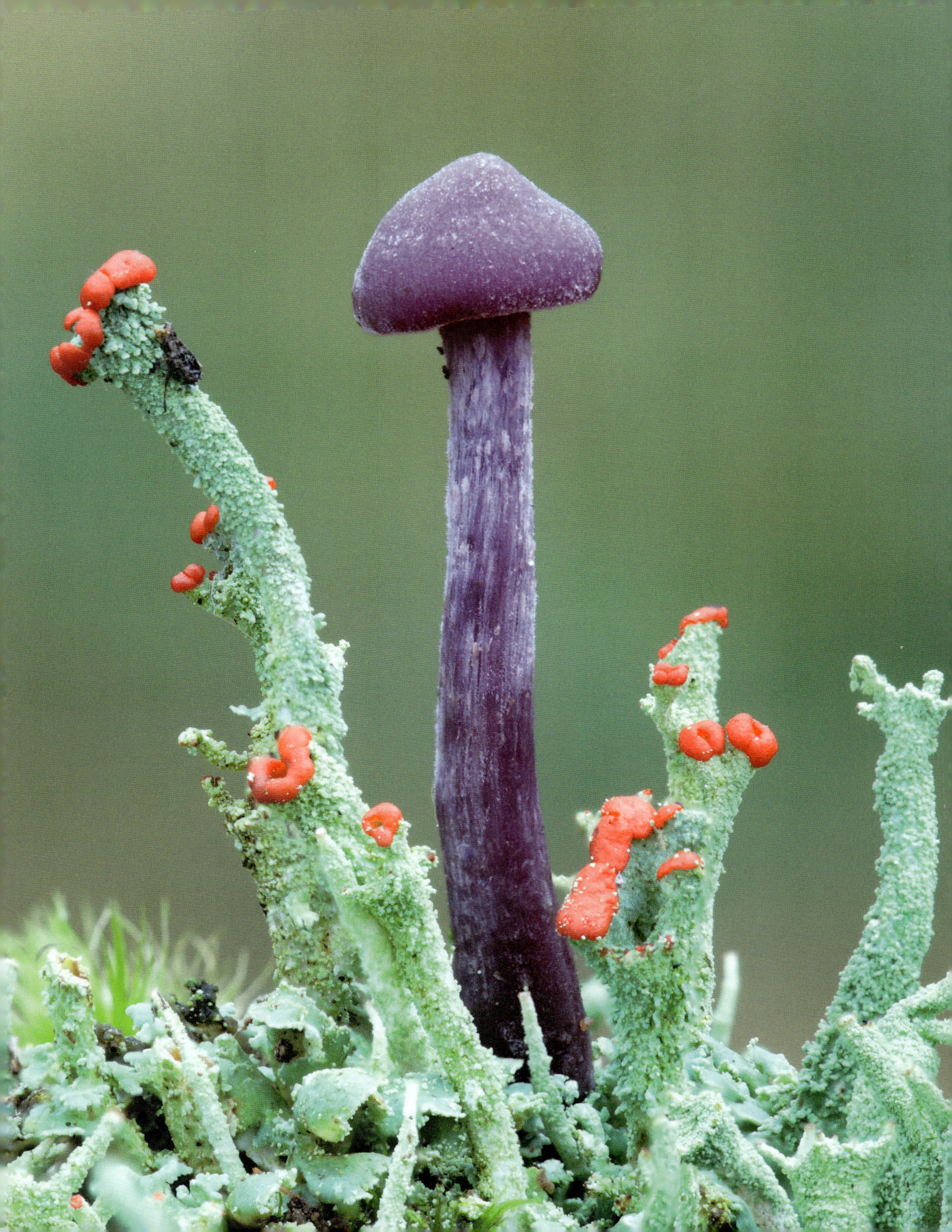

NINE

File Formats

WHETHER TO SHOOT RAW or JPEG is a question that crosses the mind of most photographers at some point. The three most commonly used in-camera file formats are JPEG (Joint Photographic Experts Group), TIFF (Tagged Image Format) and RAW, which is an in-camera lossless format. RAW files are often called digital negatives since they equate to film which, although it contains the information required to produce a viewable image, is not visible in its original state. There are many different types of digital image formats around, but making the right choice is important if you want to get the best in terms of quality and reproduction from your images. There are many opinions on the pros and cons of shooting RAW and just as many on the merits of the JPEG format. Some photographers claim you can get similar results to RAW from a JPEG if set up properly in-camera and exposed correctly. While this may be true to a point, there is considerably less latitude with a JPEG file in terms of corrections in post-processing compared to a RAW file. It is important from the start to decide what file format you are going to use. They all have merit and if used correctly in the appropriate context deliver excellent results. Your decision primarily lies with the type of photography you do and what your long-term aims are regarding your images.

Shooting RAW

Virtually every publication these days expounds the virtues of shooting RAW. Regardless of your camera brand, virtually all DSLRs have the capability to record unprocessed data captured by the camera's sensor. Each camera manufacturer has its own RAW file format. With Nikon the file extension is NEF (Nikon Electronic Format), Canon has two formats CRW (Canon RAW Format) and CR2 (Canon RAW 2nd edition), but in principle, they all work in the same way. One of the advantages of shooting RAW is that it gives you the maximum amount of information possible and

FORMAT	BIT VALUE	TONES PER CHANNEL	COMBINED TONES
JPEG	8	256	16.78 million
RAW	12	4,095	68.68 billion
	14	16,383	4.39 trillion

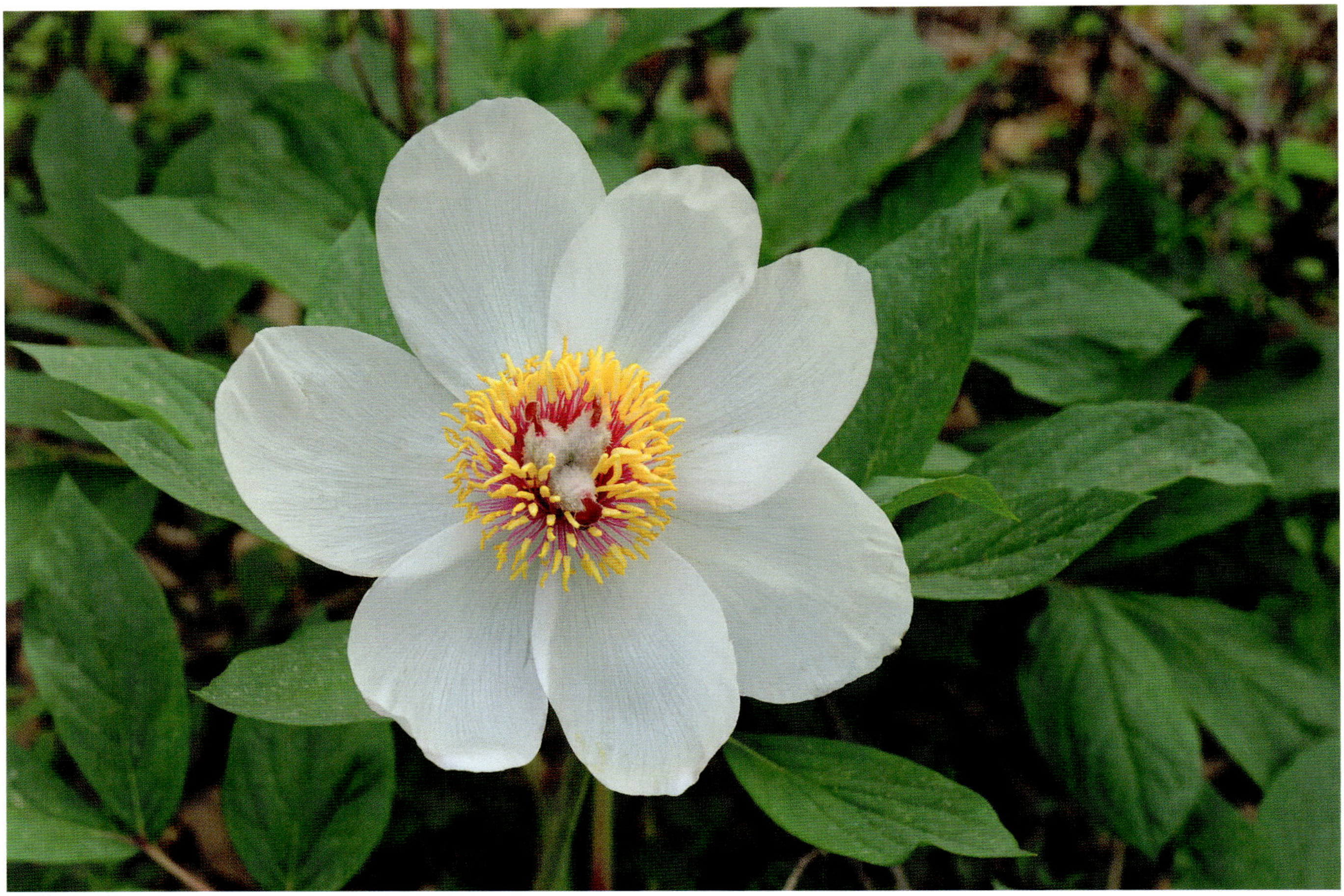

9.1 ~ **Peonie** *Peonie russii*
If you want to extract the maximum information from your sensor, then shoot RAW.
↘ Nikon D3, 24–70mm Nikkor, 1/8sec at f11, ISO 200.

in an unprocessed state; this allows you to make individual changes to various aspects within the file, such as exposure, White Balance, contrast, saturation and much more in a non-destructive way. RAW also allows you to record a much wider range of brightness levels compared to a JPEG file. What is meant by this is the amount of tonal range from the darkest shadows to the brightest highlights within an image. The range of tonal value that a file is capable of displaying is termed its bit depth level.

The RAW file's greater tonal range equates into more colours and smoother gradation between them; this is one of the reasons why most professional photographers prefer this format. The advantages are often seen in areas of smooth continuous tone, for example, blurred backgrounds or blue skies. RAW also allows you to make a wider range of corrections in exposure errors, brightness levels and contrast before you begin to see deterioration in the image quality. However, the downside is all RAW files have to be processed in your computer using the camera manufacturers own conversion software, or third party developers such as Adobe Camera Raw. Once the files have been processed, they can be converted into a universal format recognised by all devices.

Reasons to Shoot RAW

There are significant advantages for shooting RAW which include:

- Non-destructive editing, which allows you to make adjustments and corrections without affecting the original file.
- A wider range of brightness levels and greater dynamic range.
- Better correction software for under/over exposed images.

- Greater detail and information from the original file.
- Different colour spaces to suit your particular needs and workflow.
- White Balance, which can be altered, or be assigned a precise colour temperature.
- Files are much better quality since you have a greater degree of latitude in terms of processing.

Some Negative Points

- Needs additional computer time for processing and conversion into a readable file format for display on various devices.
- Requires more hard drive space for storage than a JPEG file. A typical RAW file may be around 30MB compared to a large JPEG file, which is about 8MB.
- RAW files will fill your camera's buffer more quickly than JPEG files.
- Some camera manufacturers don't disclose all of the information to third party developers in terms of decoding the processes within the file.
- Long-term security. There is a risk that in the future, as technology improves, these files may not be supported by the camera companies or third party developers; this is one of the biggest concerns among photographers. Conversion to Adobe's DNG format assures support in the long-term should this be the case.

Shooting JPEGs

One of the reasons often stated for adopting the JPEG format is instant access to files that can be shared and uploaded to any device straight from the camera and read by any image program. While this may seem a logical approach, there are disadvantages. First of all, JPEG is a 'lossy' file format, in other words, the information is compressed, and some of it is discarded. Every time you open a JPEG file and make adjustments to it, you potentially degrade the image quality if you don't save it as a separate file. You need to create a duplicate file to work on; otherwise, the quality in your original will deteriorate. There are also pre-shooting constraints, which you have little control over; White Balance, colour saturation, contrast and colour space. JPEGs also have a lower dynamic range; the information is taken directly from the sensor and processed using sophisticated algorithms in-camera. Colour and resolution are also slightly compromised; this becomes more apparent if the compression applied to the file is high. Once the information is discarded, it is gone and not retrievable. It is much harder to apply changes, or correct technical issues in post-production, such as blown highlights or deep shadows, without drastically affecting the image quality. JPEGs have much fewer brightness levels (see chart page 37) compared to RAW; therefore, greater care is required during exposure, since there is less latitude for retrieving blown highlights or correcting the White Balance. Many of the options available to you in RAW are not accessible when shooting in the JPEG format. Posterisation or banding is often much more visible in JPEG files especially in images that have continuous tone or where the background is well diffused. However, having said that, the image quality of modern JPEGs is excellent considering how much data is discarded. If the type of photography you do lends itself to shooting JPEGs, then make sure you set the in-camera options carefully to get the best from the files. You need to pay particular attention to image size, which should be set on large and optimal quality. Also, consider the White Balance and sharpness settings.

Shooting TIFF

Of the three most commonly supported in-camera file formats in DSLRs, TIFF is the least useful in terms of shooting. I see no advantage whatsoever in using this format in-camera. Firstly, files are limited to 8 bits per pixel compared to 12 or 14 bits in RAW. Also, their tonal gradation is considerably less. File size is also an issue; a typical 12-million-pixel camera would produce an uncompressed TIFF file of around 36MB per image. Certain camera functions like burst rate would be compromised due to the file's size, and memory capacity on cards would fill quickly. I doubt very much if there are any photographers that shoot with this format on a regular basis if at all.

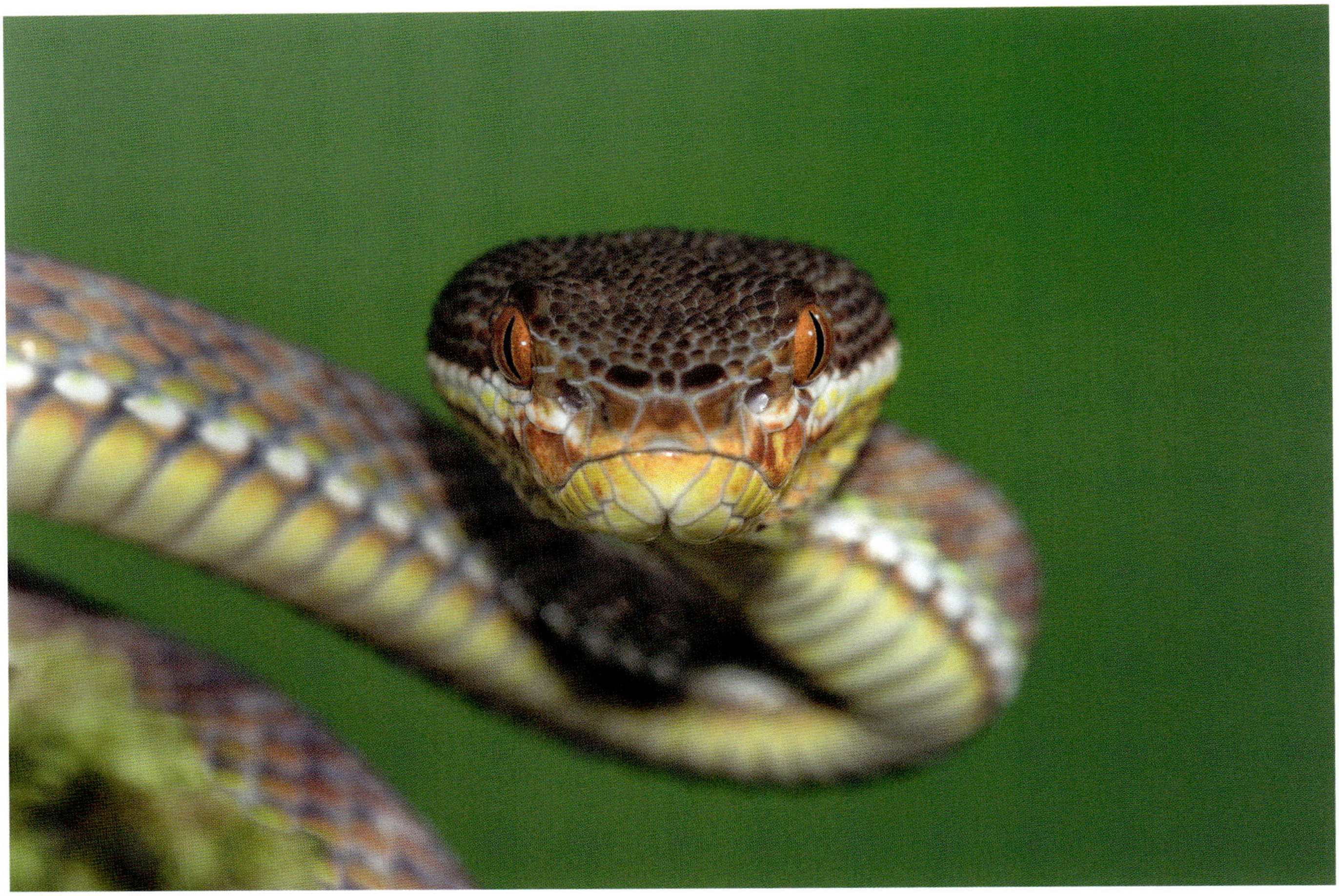

9.2 ~ **Mangrove Pit Viper** *Trimeresurus purpureomaculatus*

↳ Nikon D810, 200mm micro Nikkor, 1/ 60sec at f/11, flash, ISO 200.

My Own Approach

I shoot RAW all of the time for the simple reason that I have the maximum amount of information from the image available to me. I have the option to downsize, or convert into another format of my choosing. I prefer to generate any JPEG files I require for the web from the corrected RAW files, which have been processed, tweaked and cleaned, that way I get the completed file from the master image with my preferred changes. Once my images are downloaded and after processing and cleaning, I automatically convert some of my RAW files into TIFFs, which are stored on my hard drives. They can be edited and manipulated without any loss of information. TIFF is also recognised as one of the printing industries standard file formats and is the usual choice for many professionals for image storage. I provide my stock images to all of my agencies as TIFFs.

Some photographers shoot RAW + JPEG in their cameras. I don't have any use for this approach. The JPEGs will look different to your RAW images when processed and tweaked. Another disadvantage is the extra space taken up on your memory card or additional card slot since you are now duplicating the same image in two formats. It is a very simple procedure to convert the finished master file into a JPEG. For multiple conversions, you can set up an action in Photoshop, which will automate the conversion process for you.

TEN

Memory Cards

THERE ARE MANY different memory cards available these days offering a range of different speeds and specifications. It can be a bit perplexing for those who are not familiar with some of the technical jargon. First of all, the quality of an image is not affected by your choice of card. Although Lexar and SanDisk are leading names, your images won't look any better on these cards than they would on a cheaper lesser-known brand. However, having said that inexpensive cards might not give you a reasonable read and write speed, therefore, slowing down the performance of your camera. They might also have less support if you are in the unfortunate situation where you need to avail of data recovery.

There are two important points to consider when purchasing a memory card. The first is its read and write speed and the second is the capacity. The read speed defines how fast the information or data can be extricated from the card. The faster the card's read speed, the quicker your images will be transferred to your computer. The write speed indicates how quickly your images can be saved to the card. For example, if you were a bird photographer with a particular interest in flight photography, the write speed of your card would be of significant importance, since a camera capable of delivering a high burst rate would be at the mercy of how fast the images could be written to the card.

In macro photography, you are not as a rule shooting a high burst rate; therefore, you do not require very expensive cards with significantly high read and write speeds. However, this may well change in the not too distant future as some manufactures such as Panasonic are using 4K video to extend depth of field in an image. The Panasonic GH4 has what is termed a '4K Post Focus Mode'. When a short burst of video at 4K is made at 30 fps and the point of focus shifted throughout the sequence; this generates a stack of images which can then be combined to produce extended depth of field. If you are shooting RAW, many of the files from current cameras are quite large and would naturally benefit from a relatively fast read and write speed. But this does not mean you have to purchase the state of the art card just for its transfer rate.

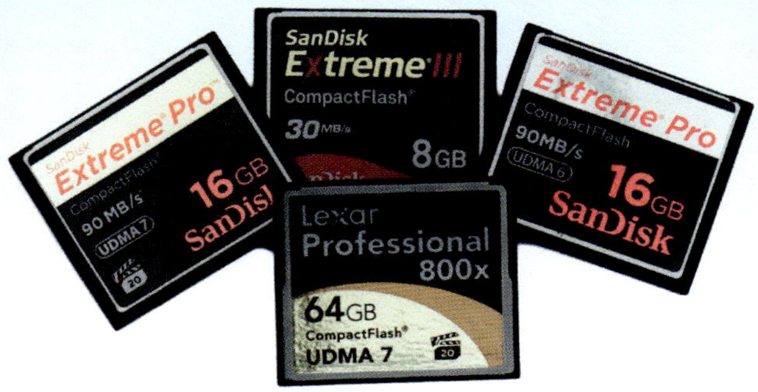

10.1 ~ Assortment of memory cards.

The second point is the card's capacity, which is important especially if you are using a high megapixel camera. Memory cards around 32GB are perfectly adequate for most DSLRs. I have always been cautious about using large capacity cards. I had a bad experience some years ago with a card and despite all my efforts I could not retrieve the data from it. Cards are more reliable these days, especially those from the top brands. Until recently I have tended to stick with cards around

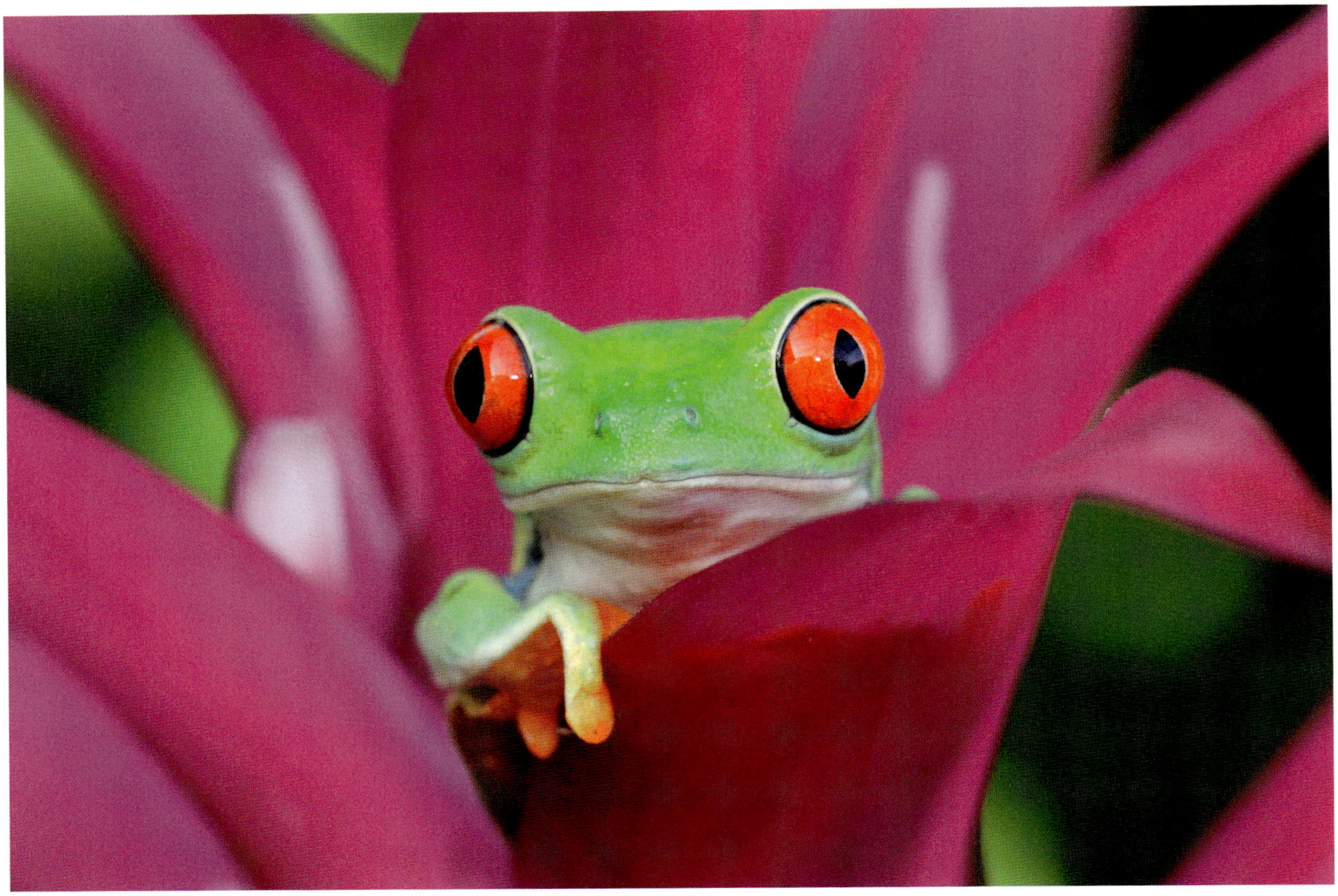

10.2 ~ Red-eyed Tree Frog *Agalychnis callidryas*

↬ Nikon D3, 200mm micro Nikkor, 1/60sec at f/11, flash, ISO 100.

32GB with the D810. Most of them were SanDisk Extreme Pro. However, on recent workshops in Europe, I have started to use 64 GB 800x Lexar Professional cards for general macro and have found them ok. The fast high-performance cards are naturally going to be more expensive. It would be wise to check what your camera's capable of delivering first.

Card Types

Compact Flash or CF cards

These cards have a long history dating back to the mid-1990s. They are widely used on high-end DSLRs and have a high storage capacity and are pretty robust in their construction.

SD (Secure Digital) Cards

The most commonly used memory card in traditional DSLRs. They are small, thin and not as robust as CF cards. Some high-end professional cameras have slots for both CF and SD cards.

SDHC (Secure Digital High Capacity) Cards

These are the same as SD cards, but with a much higher capacity. If you have an older DSLR, which predates SDHC, then it may not recognise it.

SDXC (Secure Digital Xtra Capacity) Cards

Released in 2009 these are essentially SD cards, but with a maximum capacity of 2TB and high-speed transfer rates. These cards utilise the exFat file system and are not backwards compatible with older DSLRs.

XQD

Designed to be the successor of CompactFlash, this card is capable of very fast read and write speeds; well beyond what's currently available. It is targeted at high-end stills and video cameras. They are ideally suited to photography that requires very fast action, for example, wildlife and sports photography.

Getting the Best from Your Card

These are just a few tips on how to get the best from your card and hopefully prevent problems arising.

- SD cards are less robust than their CF equivalents. Treat them gingerly when removing them from a card reader or camera.
- Most professional cards such as Lexar and SanDisk come with an image recovery program if you have deleted images accidentally.
- It's a good idea to have several cards with different storage capacities rather than one single large capacity card. Memory cards can occasionally fail; it's better to lose part of your shoot than all of it.
- When you have downloaded your card, format it in-camera not on the computer. Reformatting in-camera will clear all of the images and remove any remaining information that might still be present on the card, which could lead to card failure. It has been stated that reformatting on a computer can cause problems.
- Deleting images on the card rather than reformatting increases your chances of developing a fault. Reformatting reorganises the folder structure and reduces the chance of database errors.
- If you are going on a photo tour or holiday, consider splitting your images between more than one card as a safety precaution.

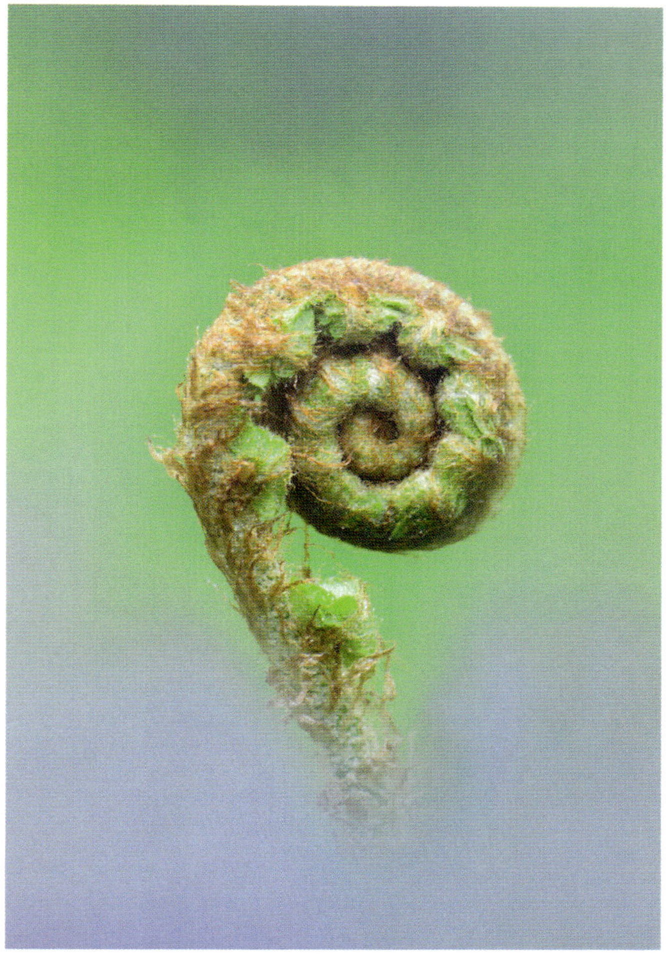

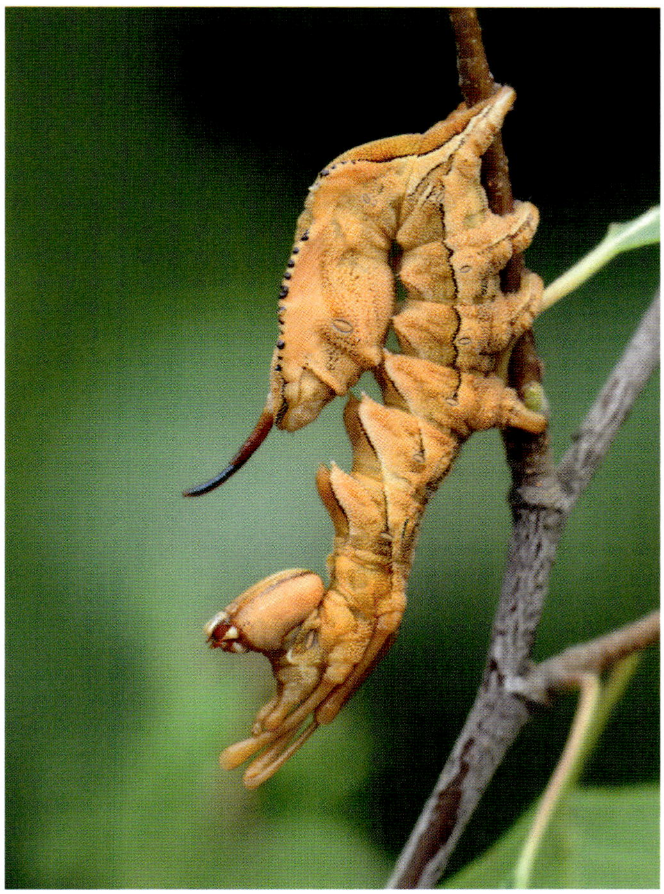

// THIS PAGE ~ TOP //

10.3 ~ Common Male Fern *Dryopteris filix-mas*
I used the bluebells in front to blur the foreground to focus attention on the unfolding frons.

Nikon D810, 200mm micro Nikkor, 1/125sec at f/5.6, ISO 100.

// THIS PAGE ~ BOTTOM //

10.4 ~ Lobster Moth *Stauropus fagi* (larva)
A rather bizarre looking larva with spindly legs and a lobster-like tail.

Nikon D810, 200mm micro Nikkor, 1/30sec at f/11, fill-in flash, ISO 200.

ELEVEN

Histograms

BEFORE the digital revolution, when I was shooting 120 roll transparency film, you were never entirely sure of how your images might look until you got the roll back from the lab. You did, of course, calibrate your camera's meter to ensure that your exposures were consistent, but during processing, there could be so many variables that it was always a relief when you set them on the light box and saw that all was well. The digital revolution has brought many advantages to photography and being able to preview your images in advance is the biggest benefit of all for any photographer.

Today the celluloid roll has been replaced with the digital sensor and a two-dimensional graph called a histogram. Understanding histograms is one of the most important aspects of digital photography, but it is also one of the least understood parts of the exposure process. All too often photographers evaluate their exposures from the image portrayed on the LCD screen rather than analysing the information contained in the histogram. It's ok for a quick visual of the composition, but you should be looking at the histogram. Virtually all digital cameras now can display a histogram in some form to show how the image has been exposed and where the tonal values lie within the picture. There is no perfect shape to a histogram; every photograph you take will produce a different graph. Understanding how to interpret a histogram is the key to creating correctly exposed pictures and provides the photographer with a graphic illustration of the complete tonal range within the photograph. In digital photography, there is no perfect exposure. What you have is a series of tonal values falling within the sensors dynamic range. The histogram is a graphical representation of the pixels exposed in the photograph. The horizontal axis ranges from pure black (0) on the left side, which represents the shadow areas, to pure white (255) on the extreme right, which indicate the bright, or highlight areas within the image. The central section comprises the mid-tones (18% grey). The vertical axis and the height of the peaks in the histogram represent the number of pixels within that particular tone.

Understanding the Histogram

When we make an exposure with our camera, the histogram appears on the back LCD screen if that particular function is activated within your camera's menu system. There are some things we can check just by looking at the graph. First of all, we can access whether the image is well exposed, in other words, are the tones evenly distributed within the graph from edge to edge? In an ideal histogram, they should just tail-off or touch the end of the baseline without spiking up the sides and have a symmetrical arch in the central region. If you have gaps on either side of the graph, this indicates that you are missing some information. You can retake the photograph after shifting your exposure a little to increase tonal range and rectify the gap. If your graph

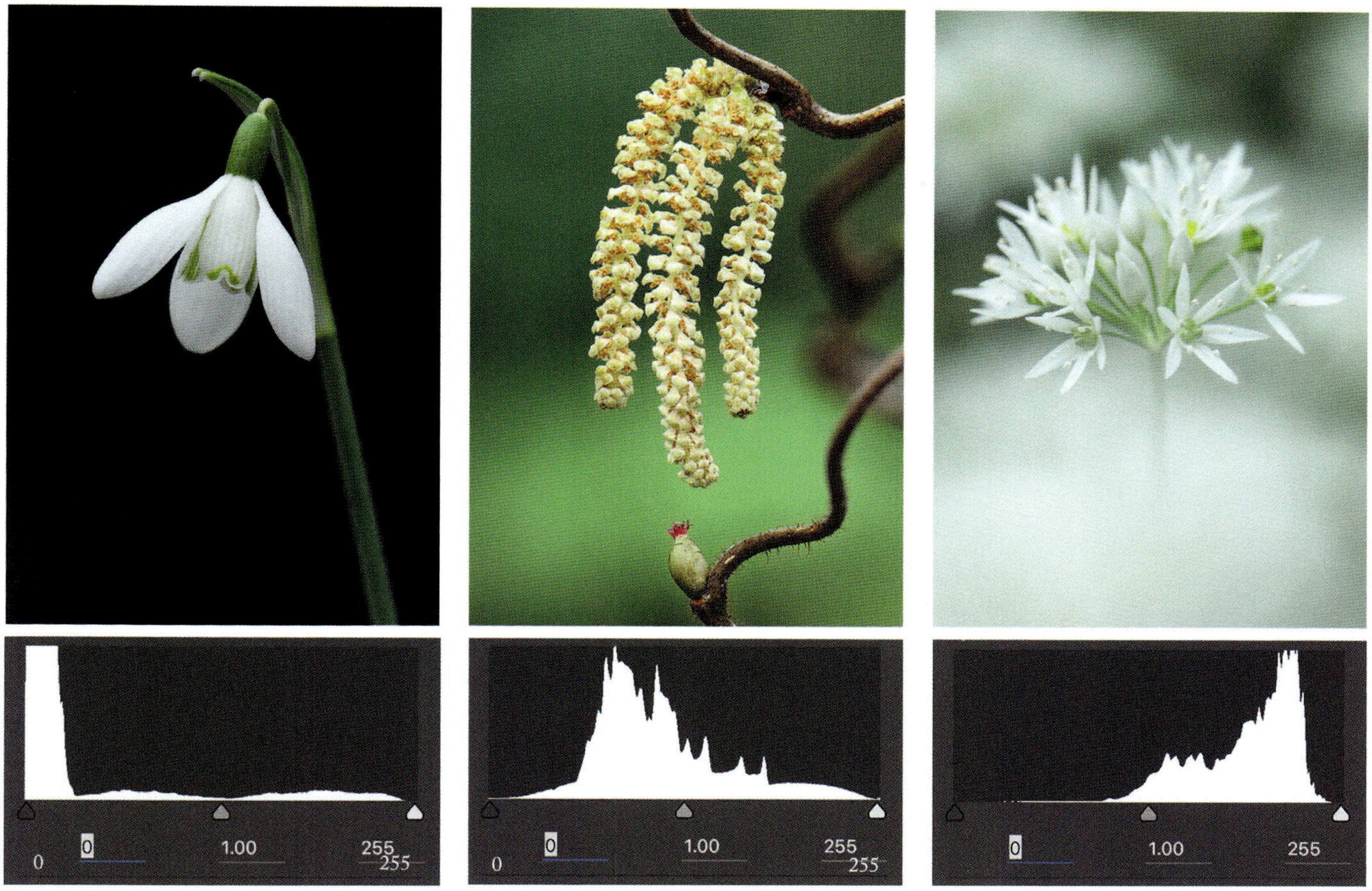

11.1 ~ Histograms vary significantly depending on the subject, the background and the desired result. The three examples show the difference in the graphs and how they differ depending on the composition and tonal information contained in each image. (A) The background is virtually black hence the histogram is heavily weighted to the shadow area. (B) A typical balanced histogram with no spiking. (C) The virtually white background means there is very little shadow detail present.

indicates sharp vertical spikes running up the edge, then you have what is termed 'clipping' of those tones. You really can't recover information from areas within the histogram that has been clipped, particularly on the highlight side of the graph. It is possible to recover some information from the shadows, but pushing it too far will increase any digital noise present. There are techniques and software available to blend different exposures together to overcome the limitations of dynamic range; this is standard practice in landscape photography, but less so in close-ups, as it can be difficult to implement the technique with active subjects such as insects.

Sometimes the tonal range within a scene is beyond the capabilities of the sensor. High contrast situations, for example, a perching butterfly or damselfly against the sun, or tones that produce deep shadows. In these circumstances, you are likely to clip the blacks, or whites or perhaps both. In these situations, you have to make decisions; you may want to preserve the highlights at the expense of clipping the shadow detail. If you are unsure, take both exposures and decide later. Most cameras today have a setting called 'highlight warning'. It is a quick method of checking your image for overexposed highlights. If it's not already active on your LCD screen, you may need to access your menu and turn it on. Once you have taken your shot, any highlights that are beyond the tonal range will flash. You can then make an adjustment to the image to correct this.

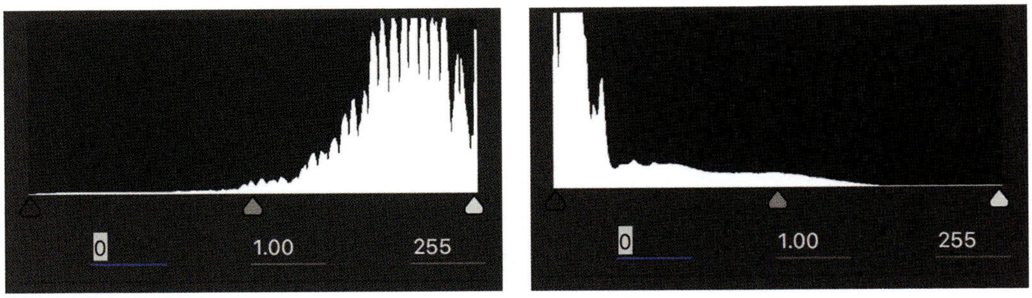

11.2 ~ Example showing over and underexposure. The highlights are obviously clipped on the left illustration resulting in information being lost. The right example clearly shows underexposure. It is possible to retrieve some information from the shadows but at a price of increased noise.

Exposing to the Right

One of the most commonly talked about techniques in digital photography is called exposing to the right or ETTR. If you want to obtain the highest quality from your digital images, then you need to shoot in RAW. Exposing to the right is a technique aimed at getting the maximum amount of information and performance from the camera's digital sensor when set to its base ISO. When used correctly, your images will have greater signal-to-noise ratio, improved tonal range in the shadow areas and greater latitude when post-processing. Executed carelessly and the danger is that you completely blow the highlights in your image rendering them totally white, making it impossible to recover any information at all. Images, when ETTR is employed, have the appearance of being overexposed on the LCD screen, but this can be corrected in post-processing. You should also be mindful of clipping the highlights at the edges of the histogram. The amount of adjustment possible in an image depends on the dynamic range or contrast ratio of the scene. If you find it difficult to evaluate the histogram, then use the highlight warning indicator (or 'blinkies'), which flash when there are white areas within your exposure that contain no data. Some photographers find this method easier to operate rather than analysing the histogram. The highlight warning indicator is not as accurate, but it's better than doing nothing at all.

Another point worth mentioning is that the histogram displayed on your camera's LCD screen is not an exact representation of the actual tonal value of your RAW file. It is generated from the processed JPEG image that is embedded in your RAW file. Although the histogram may indicate blown highlights, there may still be some recoverable data during post-processing in the RAW file itself. Exposing to the right when in Aperture Priority means using your exposure compensation dial to make any exposure adjustments; this produces slightly longer exposure times, which might be an issue if hand-holding your camera. However, increasing the ISO is a better option than trying to correct an underexposed image which is likely to generate more noise.

A Final Thought

ETTR requires time to implement and when shooting close-ups of active subjects can be difficult in many situations to apply. The real benefits gained from ETTR are perhaps not as significant as one might think. In situations where speed is essential, working with the meter's suggested reading is best practice. The difference between the two is not that significant, and many current sensors have a much better dynamic range, so it begs the question is it worth it in terms of close-up photography? Perhaps yes if you are photographing a static subject why not implement it, but when speed is a priority then I would prefer to play it safe and know that I have not blown any highlights, I can always correct in post-production. If you are shooting JPEGs, then there is no real benefit for implementing ETTR. The file already has significantly reduced data when compared to a RAW file, and this may lead to colour shifts among other things. As photographers,

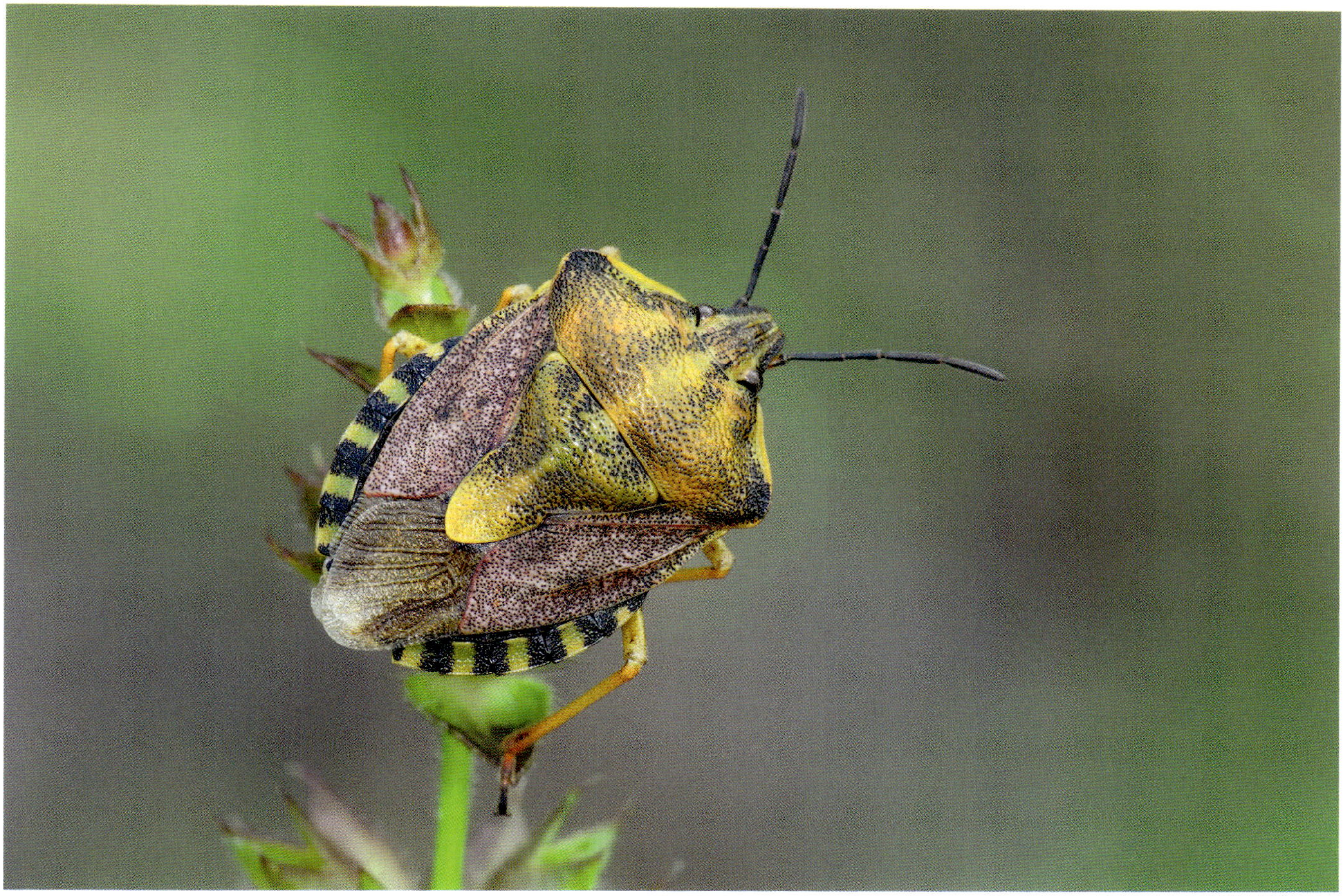

11.3 ~ **Shieldbug** *Carpocoris purpureipennis*
I would prefer to have a slightly underexposed histogram than one which I have lost valuable detail in the highlights. You can always retrieve information from the shadows but not from areas that contain no detail.

↘ Nikon D800, 200mm micro Nikkor,1/30sec at f/11, ISO 200.

we naturally want to squeeze that last bit of tonal data out of our images. Landscape photographers have more time to implement this technique. To get the best from it then other components within the photograph such as the camera's base ISO, composition, lighting and focus are equally critical factors. Histograms also vary considerably depending on the subject, its background and the result you desire.

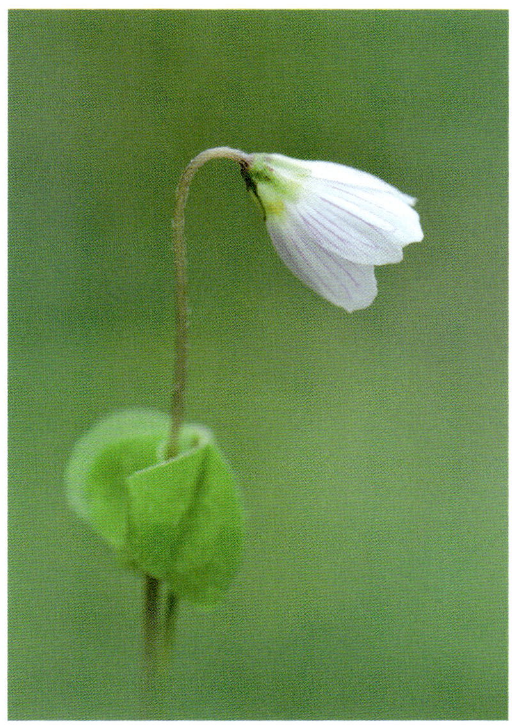

11.4 ~ **Wood Sorrel** *Oxalis acetosella*
You need to exercise due care when employing ETTR with very pale subjects. It is very easy to blow the palest of highlights especially with moving subjects.

↘ Nikon D810, 200mm micro Nikkor, 1/15sec at f/11, ISO 100.

TWELVE

Lenses

Lens Overview

THERE ARE A broad range of lenses available today for most DSLRs. Many of these can be used in close-up photography. Some have, what is termed, a 'macro mode', or close focus capability. However, the reproduction ratio is usually low; around 1:4 life-size at the most. The overall sharpness and performance are not comparable with a true macro lens, which is designed to deliver its optimum performance when used in close-up. However, if you are on a budget and photograph close-ups, occasionally you can still take some great images with modest-priced accessories such as close-up lenses and extension tubes which allow the lens to focus closer than normal.

Since the digital revolution, all of the modern lenses manufactured are now optimised for digital sensors. Some lenses perform much better in close-up than others. It is worth spending a little time testing your own lenses and evaluating their results. Different focal length lenses affect the working distance between lens and subject. Also, the angle of view changes as the focal length of the lens increases. These factors all have a bearing on how much of the background will appear in the final image. It is also important that you don't confine yourself to working with a single lens, be it a macro or even a medium telephoto, as the focal length and the angle of view significantly influence the overall appearance of the final photograph.

For example, if your primary interest is insects or venomous reptiles, then the working distance between the lens and subject is an important factor. You ideally want a long focal length macro or a medium telephoto to reduce the risk of disturbing your quarry. Doubling the focal length of a lens with a 2X converter doubles the working distance between the lens and subject. Therefore, a 100mm macro lens in combination with a 2X converter will give you twice the working distance in addition to doubling the magnification. If you are planning on shooting a lot of close-ups and budget is not a restriction, then purchasing a dedicated macro is the sensible approach. If your passion is flower photography, then you would want to have at least one wide-angle lens to show plants in relationship to their natural environment. Also working distance is not as important since the subject is static.

Lenses Suitable for Close-up Photography

There are a number of lenses of different focal lengths, which provide different perspectives and opportunities to capture images from environment portraits to extreme close-ups.

// FACING PAGE //

12.1 ~ Beautiful Pit Viper *Trimeresurus venustus*
A highly venomous species, which is best photographed with a longer macro.

→ Nikon D810, 200mm micro Nikkor, 1/30sec at f/8, ISO 200.

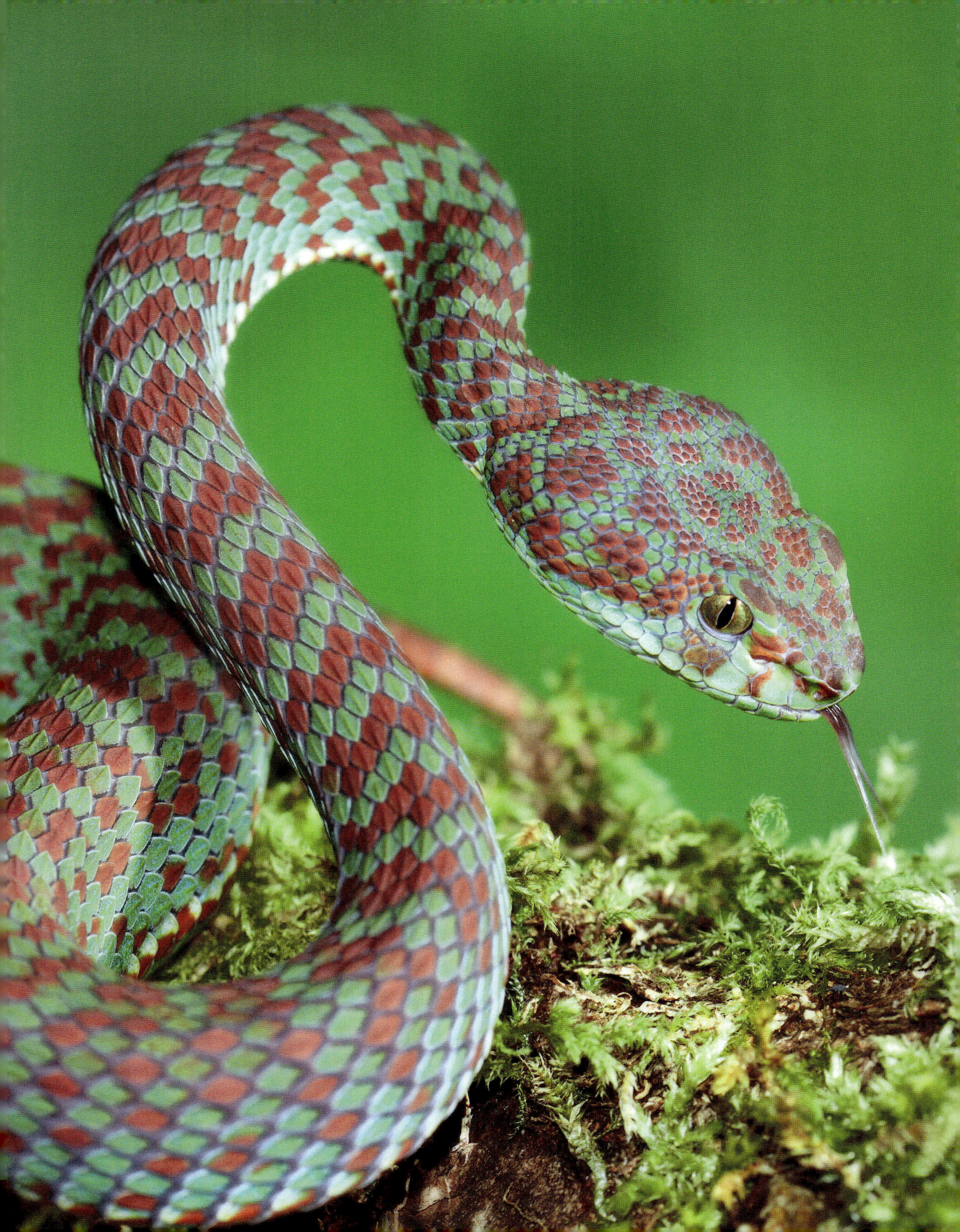

Standard Lens

A standard lens has a focal length of 50mm and was the universal lens sold with analogue SLRs for many years. Modern DSLRs tend to come now either as body only or with standard zooms usually in the region of 24mm–70mm on a full frame DSLR. The standard lens is often understated and not as popular with close-up enthusiasts. However, its lightness is a distinct advantage when handholding a close-up assembly. Unlike some other lenses, it also has minimal distortion and usually has a fast maximum aperture, around f/2. It is ideally suited to close-up attachments for example; extension tubes and close-up lenses and can produce excellent results. They also make excellent lenses for reversing on bellows, or extension tubes. They do have some limitations particularly if you are interested in photographing insects. Its short focal length means you need to get relatively close to your subject, which is not always obliging.

Wide-Angle Lenses

These lenses are not usually associated with close-up photography, but used in the right situation can produce images with real impact. They are an essential part of the landscape photographer's repertoire of equipment but are frequently overlooked in terms of their close-up value. Lenses with a focal length of 35mm and below are termed as wide-angle. They also have a very close minimum focusing distance and are ideally suited to showing your subject in relation to its environment. Wide angles also have a broader field of view than normal human vision and therefore an exaggerated perspective. The wider the focal length, the more exaggerated the perspective is. One of the most important factors is the minimum focusing distance from the subject to the front element of the lens. You can easily find out from the information supplied with the lens, or by doing some field tests.

Fixed focal length wide angles tend to perform better than zooms and normally have a very close-focusing distance, usually only several centimeters from the subject. For maximum impact, you will be positioning the camera at ground level, commonly referred to as the 'bug's eye view'. Insects, flowers and fungi take on a whole new perspective from the conventional macro view. There is normally a distinctive mark; usually, a circle bisected with a horizontal line on the top of your camera, which relates to the sensor's position.

Getting the best from wide angles in close-up invariably means having a point of interest in the frame. Positioning your subject up close in the foreground, off centre will lead the viewer's eye into the frame. These lenses work best with larger subjects, for example, flowers and insects such as dragonflies, butterflies and moths. The major drawback is you have to get extremely close to your subject to take advantage of the wide field of view.

Prime Telephoto Lenses

A telephoto lens is usually defined as having a focal length greater than 50mm. They have a narrow field of view compared to normal human vision, which is approximately 140° by 80°. These lenses magnify distant subjects and are therefore more susceptible to camera shake since minor hand movements are more likely to produce blur. The difference between a telephoto and a non-telephoto lens is down to focal length. Telephotos can be grouped into three categories short, medium and super according to their focal length. See table below.

SHORT TELEPHOTO	MEDIUM TELEPHOTO
85mm–100mm	200mm–300mm

All telephotos produce images with a flattened, or compressed perspective. It is often stated that the focal length of a lens determines the perspective. However, perspective only changes when your position relative to your subject is altered. Perspective is an extremely important compositional tool in photography and when used correctly has a significant bearing on the appearance of an image. Short to medium telephotos focus reasonably close without the need for additional accessories, but most are used in combination with supplementary close-up lenses, or extension tubes to allow them to focus closer than their minimum focusing distance. Telephotos are useful lenses when you want to isolate a subject from its background. Their narrow-angle of view helps to create a well-defused background.

One of the negative aspects of larger telephotos is their weight. They are usually heavier, frequently difficult to handhold and are best supported on a tripod, or a beanbag when working at ground level. Telephotos also have reasonably good working distances between lens

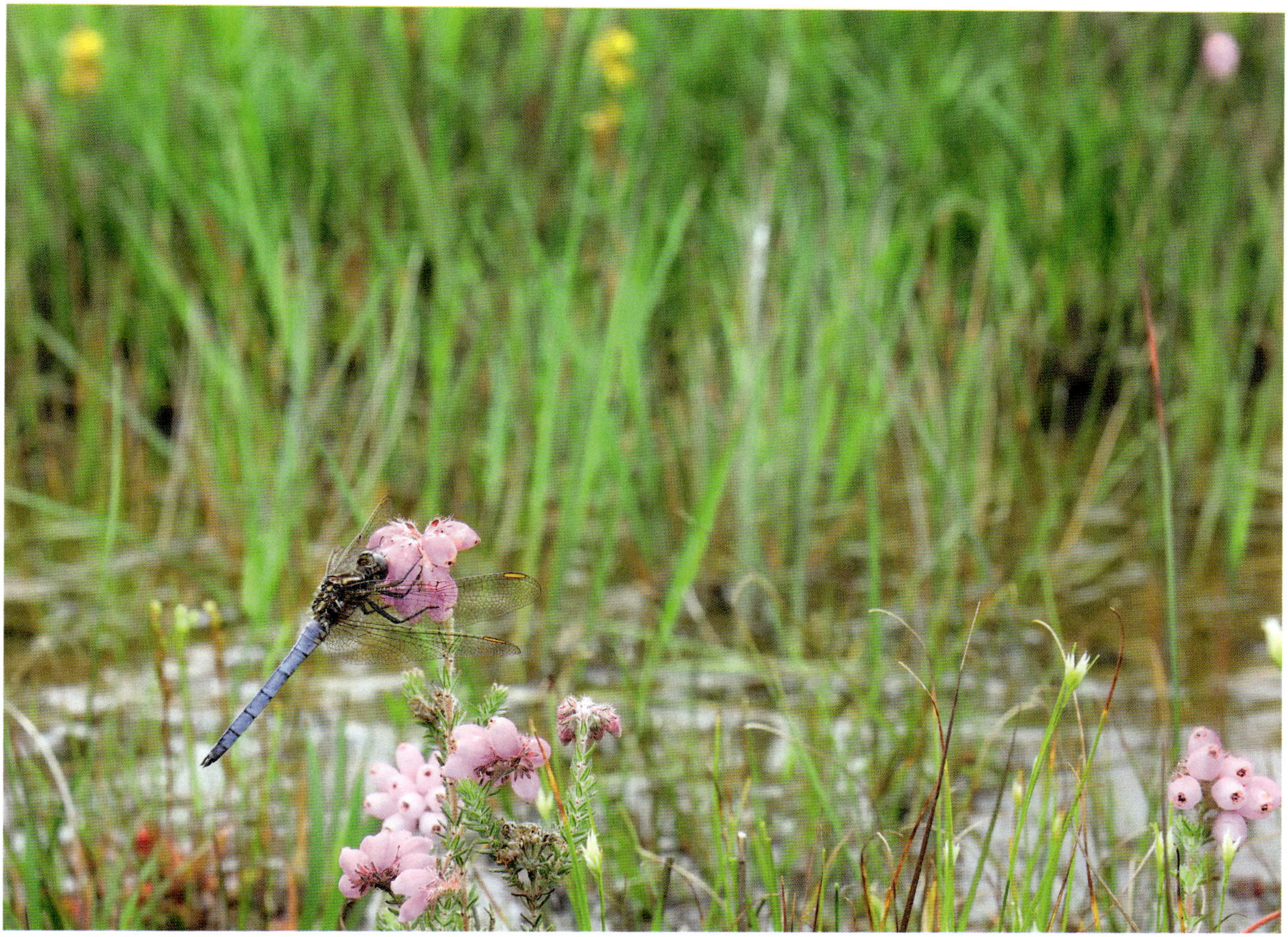

12.2 ~ **Keeled Skimmer** *Orthetrum coerulescens* (male)
↪ Nikon D3X, 24–70mm Nikkor, 1/30sec at f/8, ISO 200.

and subject and are excellent lenses for photographing active and timid subjects. Lenses with a focal length of 200mm or higher are frequently used by photographers who have an interest in insects. They provide a good working distance between lens and subject. Plant photographers also use them to isolate flowers from their often-cluttered backgrounds to make them stand out.

Short, fixed focal length telephotos are a good alternative when used in combination with extension tubes. They are cheaper than buying a long telephoto macro and can ease the frustrations when photographing larger active insects. Their greater lens to subject distance reduces the risk of hitting the vegetation with your tripod legs and spooking your quarry. Minor adjustments to framing or tripod position are more easily accomplished.

Zoom Lenses

The optical quality of zooms, or variable focal-length lenses have come a long way since the days of film. They are a popular choice now across virtually all the photographic disciplines and are usually referred to by their focal length range, or zoom ratio. For example, a 70–210mm would be a 3x optical zoom. The calculation is a simple one; you divide the longest focal length by the shortest,

200/70 = 3

The most popular focal lengths in a full frame sensor are in the range of, 24–70mm, 70–210mm and 200–400mm. In an APS-C sensor, 18–55mm, 55–200mm and 55–300mm are typical of the range.

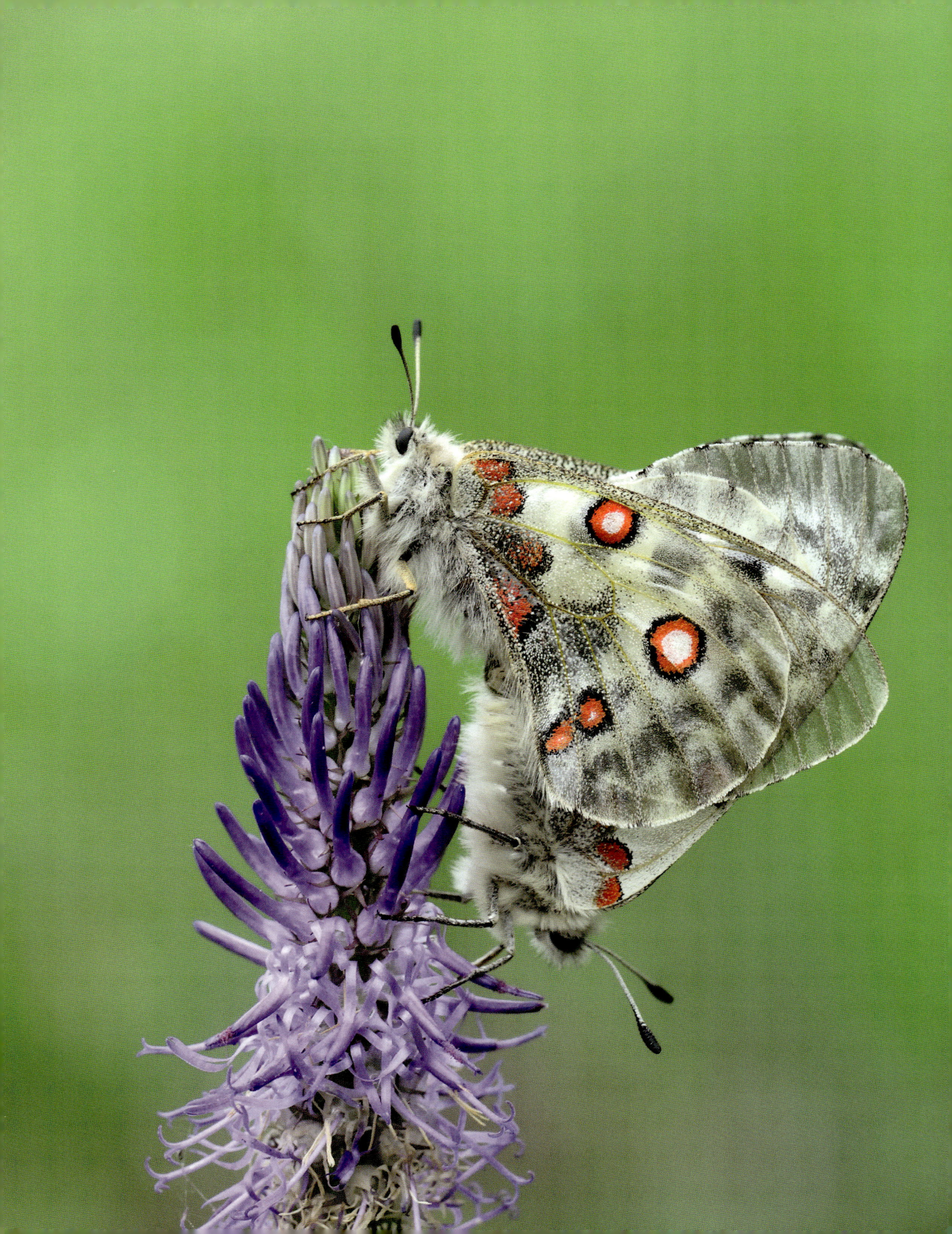

Many photographers already own at least one zoom lens among their lens collection. If used in conjunction with a high-quality two-element supplementary lens, or extension tube it allows you to alter the composition of your subject by zooming through a range of focal lengths. You can also increase or decrease the magnification with supplementary lenses depending on the focal length setting on the lens. If you are using extension tubes the shorter the focal length the larger the magnification, but the trade off is a much closer working distance. Working at a focal length of around 200mm provides greater flexibility, but at a lower magnification. You can achieve very acceptable results with these lenses providing you exercise good photographic technique. Some zooms have a built-in macro setting, but this is often fixed at a particular focal length.

Legacy Lenses

Most photographers have older lenses and systems from the analogue era that are now redundant. Don't however abandon them entirely. Micro 4/3 and other camera systems can be used with special adapters which allow you to use lenses you may have lying about from other systems. They can also be used with mirrorless cameras with the appropriate adapters. One disadvantage with legacy lenses is the lack of electronic coupling to the camera body; you have to manually stop down the lens to obtain the correct exposure. One advantage with mirrorless cameras is they incorporate an image intensifier in the viewfinder or for the LCD screen which provides a brighter screen even when the lens is stopped down to the appropriate aperture.

Some adapters are now available for Canon lenses that permit electronic coupling with a mirrorless body for exposure metering and autofocus. Unfortunately, due to patent restrictions adapters are not currently available for Nikon users. Being able to utilise lenses from various systems opens up a whole new world for those who love to dabble and experiment. There is insufficient room in this publication to elaborate in great detail but visiting the online resource 'Learn Macro' given in the Introduction covers this and many other macro topics in much greater depth.

// FACING PAGE //

12.3 ~ **Apollo** *Parnassius apollo*
One of Europe's iconic butterflies. A 300mm combined with ext. tubes is an excellent choice when you need to keep your distance and want a well-diffused background.

↳ Nikon D800, 300mm Nikkor, + ext. 1/60sec at f/8, ISO 200.

Macro Lenses

Virtually all of the leading camera and lens manufacturers make at least one macro lens. Nikon, Canon and Sigma offer different focal lengths. Although they are designed to deliver their optimum performance in close-up, they can also be used for general photography as well. Macros are highly corrected lenses, especially for flatness of field. This has particular relevance when photographing two-dimensional subjects, for example, illustrations, or documents where you need the lens to be sharp across the entire frame. When applied to three-dimensional subjects such as insects or flowers, it is not as critical. The slight softness due to the curvature of the glass in a normal lens is of no real significance since in most cases the subject does not occupy the entire frame to the extreme edges. One of the main advantages of these lenses when working in the field, is being able to compose and photograph from infinity to life-size without having to add and remove extension tubes.

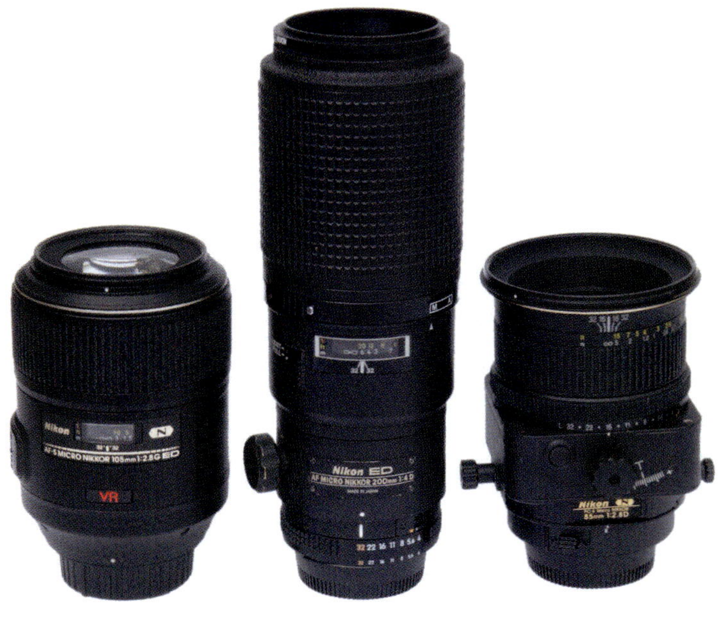

12.4 ~ Nikon's 105mm, 200mm micro Nikkors and the 85mm tilt and shift macro lenses.

Virtually all modern macros can focus from infinity to life-size without the need for any additional extension. Contemporary computerised lens designs have floating element arrangements, which change their position inside the lens barrel as the lens is focused. This reduces the need for additional extension. The majority of older, pre-digital macros had an expanding tube that increased in size as the focusing ring was rotated. The majority were restricted to half life-size and required an additional tube to achieve life-size. A point worth bearing in mind if buying second hand. The majority of macro lenses fall into three categories.

SHORT FOCAL LENGTH MACROS	MEDIUM TELEPHOTO MACROS	LONG TELEPHOTO MACROS
55mm–60mm	90mm–105	180mm–200mm

Short Focal Length Macros

These lenses, which are in the range of 55mm–60mm, are often referred to as short focal length macros since they are similar to a standard lens on a full frame DSLR. They are an excellent general purpose macro and more suited to tabletop photography, also copy work and in situations where you are tight for space. The downside is the close working distance between lens and subject and while light in weight have limited use in field photography. Static subjects such as flowers and fungi are fine since working distance is not such a critical factor. However, for active creatures, it would be considerably more challenging. Their wider field of view means they encompass much more of the background behind the subject, which can be problematic in some cases. Another factor to consider is working off a tripod with a short focal macro can be very frustrating as you are much more likely to disturb the surrounding vegetation with the tripod legs and spook your quarry.

Medium Focal Length Macros

These lenses are by far the most popular and the best compromise in terms of weight and working distance. Nikon's 105mm and Canon's 100mm are among the most popular focal lengths. Sigma also produces a 105mm, which is an alternative. A typical 100mm macro will give you twice the working distance of a 50mm macro; this makes it an excellent choice when stalking active creatures, or supporting the various macro flash systems currently available from different camera manufacturers. Image stabilising systems such as Nikon's VR and Sigma's OS systems are standard in macros around this focal length. They give you greater flexibility when handholding at normal focusing distances, but caution is need when utilising VR and autofocus in close-up. Reproduction ratios under 1:2 with VR engaged seem to work ok, but at higher magnifications, it may be more of a hindrance when used in combination with autofocus. It is best to switch to manual. However, having said that I do use autofocus at magnifications beyond 1:2 with excellent results but I always use a monopod for additional stability, and this may make a difference. I know some photographers have indicated that at higher magnifications it can have a negative effect producing softer images as a result of vibration. I think in these circumstances it is wise for inexperienced users to resort to manual. Macros in this focal range give you greater all-around versatility and also make good medium range telephotos for general photography.

Long Focal Length Macros

Macro lenses with a focal length of 150mm–200mm are more specialised and often used by photographers who have a particular interest in insects, especially dragonflies, butterflies and other timid creatures. Many professionals also find them useful in flower photography, since their narrow-angle of view and flattened perspective creates a more diffused appearance to the background making the subject stand out more clearly. These lenses are essentially tripod lenses and considerably more expensive than other macros and therefore not as popular in the amateur sector. Nikon, Canon and Sigma all offer lenses in this focal range. If you plan on doing a lot of insect photography, then it is worth considering a longer focal length macro. Despite their cost and weight, there are some advantages with these lenses. First of all, the working distance between lens and subject is greater. Second, all of the lenses have a built-in tripod collar, which allows rapid change from horizontal and vertical framing without having to turn the whole camera assembly on its side, which can lead to a very unstable setup. Working off a tripod is much

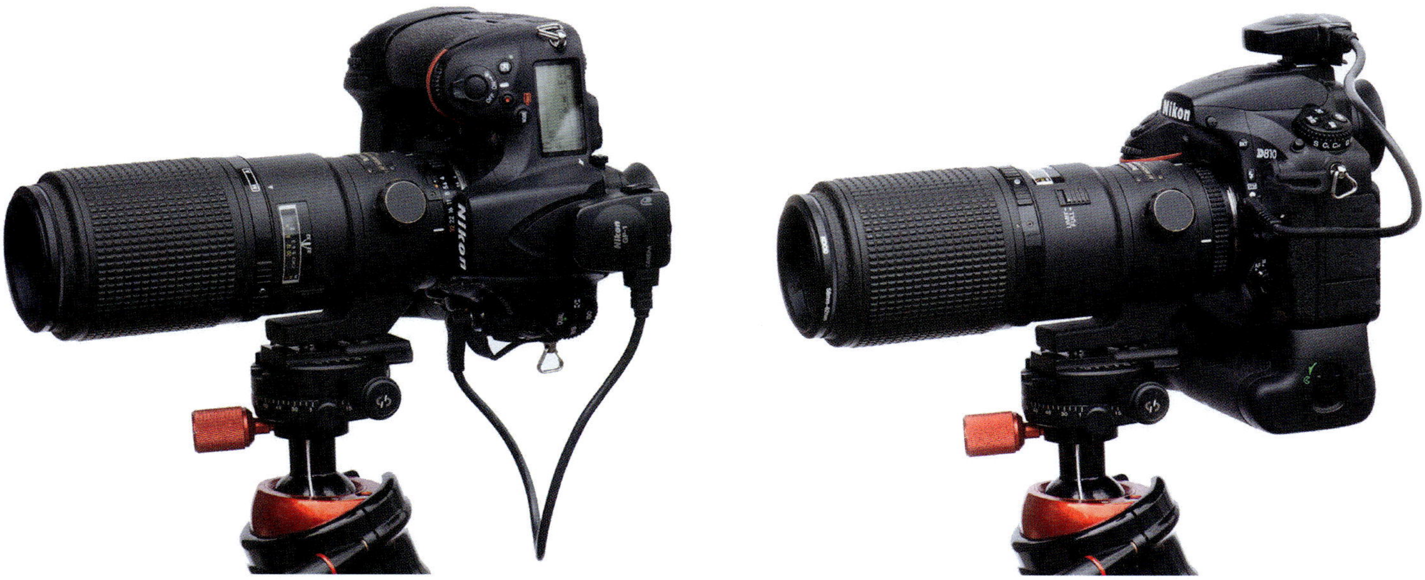

12.5 ~ Having a tripod collar on a long focal length macro allows you to rotate the camera into a vertical format without having to refocus or recompose the image. It also keeps the centre of gravity directly on the tripod head.

easier and with the increased working distance you are less likely to knock the surrounding vegetation (spooking your quarry), or getting your tripod legs snarled up among the ground foliage. I use Nikon's 200mm micro Nikkor for the majority of my close-up work and only resort to the 105mm when stalking active insects, or where space is an issue.

Special Purpose Macros

Tilt and shift, or perspective control lenses as they are often called, were mainly designed with architecture in mind to assist photographers in managing perspective. Both Nikon and Canon offer lenses in the range of 85mm and 90mm respectively. These lenses have a range of movements similar to those found on large format cameras, which were often used by landscape and studio photographers to correct vertical and horizontal distortions and to extend the depth of field without the need to stop the lens down to smaller apertures. While they don't have the same versatility as a proper large format lens and camera, they allow reasonable movements, which will correct many common problems, but in most situations, you still need to stop the lens down. They do have some merit, but in close-up, it's more limited. I frequently use my Nikon 85mm PC-E (E standing for electronic version) when working with relatively flat subjects such as lichens, or bryophytes growing on stones. This is a sharp lens and employs Nikon's CRC system (Close Range Correction), which delivers outstanding results if used in the appropriate setting. Commercial photographers and those engaged in product or food photography tend to have more use for this type of lens.

Nikon PC-E 85mm Macro

Nikon's PC-E Nikkor 85mm has macro capability up to 1:2 (half life-size), which is very useful. The lens has automatic aperture control and manual override using the aperture ring. The lens does not have autofocus capability which is not a significant disadvantage since the vast majority of close-up and macro photography is carried out in manual mode. The PC-E does not fully integrate with all Nikon bodies and it's important to check the compatibility before buying this lens. It can be used as a straight, conventional macro lens without having to employ any of its tilt and shift capabilities.

LENS MANUFACTURER	FOCAL LENGTH OF LENS	MAXIMUM REPRODUCTION POSSIBLE	CLOSEST FOCUSING DISTANCE CM
NIKON			
AF-S (DX) Micro-Nikkor	40mm	1:1	16.2
Micro-Nikkor (FX)	55mm	1:2	27.4
Micro-Nikkor (FX)	105mm	1:2	40.8
AF- (FX) Micro-Nikkor	60mm	1:1	22.2
AF-S (FX) Micro-Nikkor	60mm	1:1	18.2
AF-S (DX) Micro-Nikkor	85mm	1:1	27.4
AF-S VR (FX) Micro-Nikkor	105mm	1:1	30.4
AF (FX) Micro-Nikkor	200mm	1:1	49.2
PC-E (FX) Micro-Nikkor	45mm	1:2	25.2
PC-E (FX) Micro-Nikkor	85mm	1:2	39.6
CANON			
(APS) EF-S	60mm	1:1	20.0
EF IS USM	100mm	1:1	30.0
EF L	180mm	1:1	48.0
MP-E	65mm	5:1	24.0
SIGMA			
EX DG	70mm	1:1	25.7
EX DG OS HSM	105mm	1:1	31.2
APO EX DG OS HSM	150mm	1:1	38.0
APO EX DG OS HSM	180mm	1:1	47.0

A selection of the main macro lenses currently offered by Nikon, Canon and Sigma and their maximum magnification and minimum focusing distances. Some are older lenses, which are no longer in production, but can be bought second-hand.

Extension Tubes

These are black hollow tubes manufactured in different lengths and usually sold in a set of three. The tubes fit between the lens and camera body. Most camera manufacturers offer a set of extension tubes, but many independent companies also make them to suit some popular camera mounts. They are usually cheaper than the camera manufacturers own brand. Although relatively inexpensive, they are a very useful accessory. All modern extension tubes retain the automatic functions of the lens. When you purchase a set, it's a good idea to check with independent makes that when combined there is no vignetting at the corners of the frame and

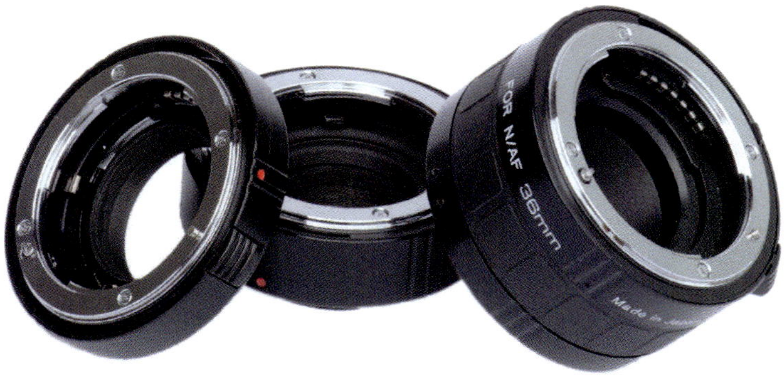

12.6 ~ **Automatic extension tubes**
These retain all of the automatic functions of the lens.

that you have full integration between lens, tube and camera body. When extension tubes are used in combination with any lens especially short and medium telephotos they allow the lens to focus closer than its minimum focusing distance. If your interest in macro is only casual, then extension tubes combined with telephotos work equally as well. You will see no real perceptual difference between them except at the extremity of the frame. There are many situations where a longer telephoto with extension tubes can produce a more pleasing result.

What Extension Tubes Do

Two things happen when an extension tube is added to your lens. First, the lens can now focus closer than its minimum focusing distance, producing an increase in magnification, but it will not now focus at infinity. Secondly, there will be a fall-off in light reaching the sensor. The amount of light fall-off will vary depending on the focal length of the lens. For example, adding a 25mm extension tube to a 200mm lens will produce a magnification of around one-eighth life-size. If you add the same extension tube to a 50mm lens, you now have a magnification of half life-size, but with greater light loss. The greater the extension, the higher the magnification but also the light has to travel further to reach the camera's sensor.

Extension and Magnification

The amount of extension that you require to achieve a particular magnification depends on the focal length of the lens. For example, if you want to achieve 1:1 (life-size) with a 50mm lens you would require 50mm of extension. If you doubled the focal length of the lens to 100mm then 50mm of extension would equate to a maximum magnification of 1:2 half life-size. At 200mm it is a quarter life-size. Therefore, the amount of extension increases proportionally with the focal length of the lens. Working at magnifications greater than half life-size in the field with extension tubes on longer lenses becomes difficult due to weight and the ineptness of the whole setup. You can easily work out the magnification rate by applying this simple formula.

Magnification = extension ÷ focal length of lens used

Teleconverters

Teleconverters or multipliers as they are sometimes called are hollow tubes which contain optical elements that magnify the image in front of it by a precise amount. They are frequently used with long focal length telephotos to increase the focal range of a prime lens. Advances in optical design have greatly improved the quality of current converters. When working with a lens stopped down you effectively use light rays passing through the centre of the teleconverter where it is very highly corrected – which is why image quality is often extremely good when they are used for macro work. Using them in combination with a macro is the easiest way to obtaining magnifications beyond life-size. They deliver excellent results providing you apply the same meticulous approach to your work. The majority of leading lens manufacturers produce converters that are optically colour-matched to their own range of lenses. Although this makes them more expensive, it is always advisable (if possible), to purchase these units, that way you will get the best in terms of optical quality and matching overall colour balance and contrast.

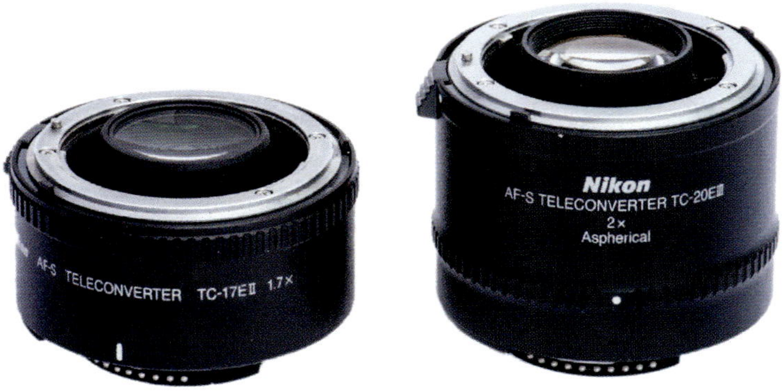

12.7 ~ **Nikon's TC-1.7E II AF and AF-S TC-20E II teleconverters**
The 1.7x combined with the 105mm micro Nikkor is my favourite combination in the field.

Image Quality

All converters will have a slight effect on image quality. They will also magnify any minor errors on your part such as focusing and also aberrations present in a lens. All converters reduce the light intensity reaching the sensor by a given factor. For example, a 1.4x when added to a 200mm f/4 lens now becomes a 280mm f/5.6, reducing the exposure by one stop. If you add a 2x converter to a 100mm macro, which is focused at 1:1 (life-size), it doubles the magnification, but not the focal length. You now have the capability to photograph subjects up to 2:1 (twice life-size) but at the expense of losing two stops of light. At this magnification, you really need to be working off a tripod where possible. Since the depth of field is so shallow, any minor focusing discrepancy becomes a major issue. Adding a 2x converter when the lens is focused at infinity doubles the focal length and reduces the angle of view, but it still retains its minimum focusing distance.

Extension Tubes and Converters

If you require magnifications beyond 2:1 (twice life-size), there are different ways you can achieve this. However, there are pros and cons with each procedure. A simple way to increase magnification is to add an extension tube to your setup. Where you place it has a direct bearing on the magnification possible. If magnification is your primary objective, then you need to put the tube next to the lens followed by the converter; this arrangement produces the highest magnification since the converter magnifies everything in front of it. If lens-to-subject distance is your primary aim then you

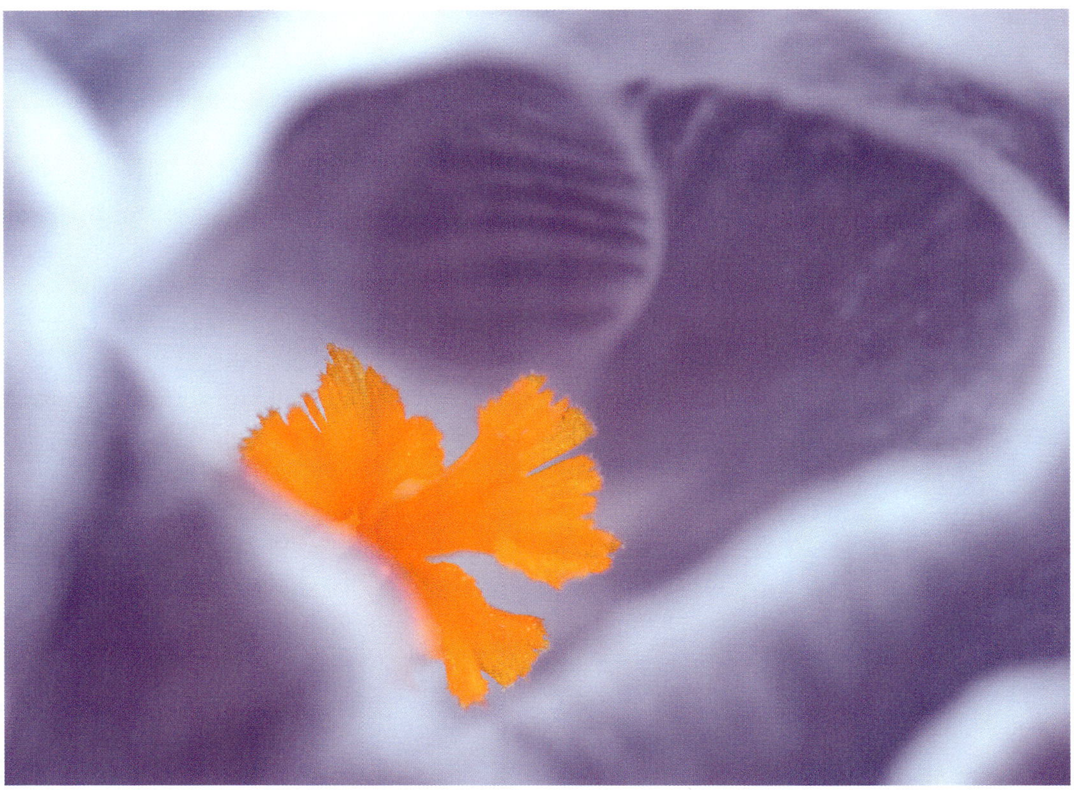

12.8 ~ **Crocus species**
The image quality of teleconverters is so good now that there is less need for other elaborate setups when photographing beyond life-size.

↝ Nikon D810, 105mm micro Nikkor, + 2x converter. 1/8sec at f/16, ISO 400.

should place the extension tube behind the converter; this results in a lower magnification but increases the lens-to-subject distance. Other methods of achieving magnifications greater than 1:1 will be discussed in the section entitled, 'Beyond Life-size' (page 124).

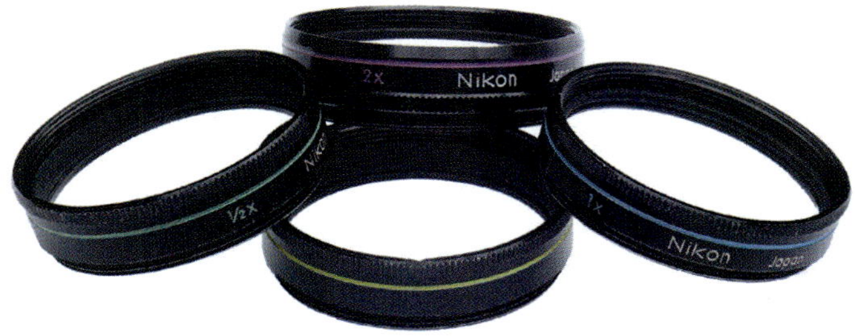

12.9 ~ **Some of Nikon's close-up lenses**
Magnifications up to twice life-size are possible with these two-element lenses.

Close-up or Supplementary Lenses

There are occasions when you will want your lenses to focus closer than their minimum focusing distance. If your interest in close-up photography is casual, then you might want to consider a cheaper alternative method of achieving this. One of the least expensive ways is to use supplementary or close-up lenses. These are positive lenses that screw into the filter threads on the front of your lens.

Close-up lenses come in two types, cheap, single-element units (which you want to avoid) and two-element colour-corrected lenses, which, although more expensive, produce much better results. Their small size makes them an ideal accessory for travel photographers where weight may be a significant factor. Some of the major manufacturers design them to work in combination with specific lenses and offer a range of magnifications (usually expressed as diopters). Lenses in the region of 150mm to 200mm work best with close-up lenses. They produce greater magnifications and better working distances between the lens and subject. They can be used on shorter focal length lenses however; the working distance is much closer making it difficult to work with active creatures. Canon, Hoya and Sigma make a range of close-up lenses in different strengths. Unfortunately, Nikon no longer do, but you can still pick them up second-hand.

Auto Focus and Live View

Virtually all cameras and lenses have auto focus capability nowadays. It has transformed many aspects of mainstream photography. Therefore, it would be easy to assume that attaining correct focus on a subject would be a relatively straightforward process, given the sophistication of these modern focusing systems. However, in terms of macro photography, its use is somewhat limited. It can be more of an annoyance than an advantage, especially when your subject is positioned off-centre. It often struggles to lock onto smaller subjects, especially in low light, or in situations where the contrast is poor. Manual focus is by far the best option in the vast majority of situations. It also allows you to choose your point of focus with greater accuracy.

For those whose eyesight is perhaps not as sharp as it once was there are various focusing aids which are now standard in some cameras. The most recent of these is 'focus peaking' which is designed to assist you when focusing manually. It highlights the edges of in focus elements within the frame allowing for very precise focusing. Focus peaking is likely to become standard in most high-end cameras and eventually other models as well.

Another alternative is Live View, which is becoming more popular with photographers. You can preview the image at 100% without any clipping and use it as an additional focusing aid to access sharpness and also make minor focusing adjustments. Some cameras also let you preview the final image at its taking aperture when the depth of field preview is engaged. You can analyse the zone of sharpness and view the final image as it will appear. This technique works best with static subjects and when working from a tripod. It can also highlight any unwanted elements within your frame which you may not have picked up when focusing through the viewfinder. I rarely use auto focus except when stalking active subjects with a monopod (see 'Macro on the Move', page 111). I shoot virtually all of my images with manual focus, that way I can control precisely where I want the point of focus to be in the frame.

THIRTEEN

Light

A SUCCESSFUL photograph is defined by the amalgamation of a number of key components, but at the forefront of these is light. The word photography itself means 'painting with light'. Even when all of the other elements are in place, without light it amounts to little. Light is the very essence of photography and the accomplishment of any photographer, professional or amateur, is based on his or her understanding of how light works. As a photographer, you have to learn how to make the best of it in any given situation and turn it to your advantage.

Light is constantly changing and not just in intensity but also in colour and quality throughout the day. The red and orange hues of early morning are replaced by the cool blues during the middle part of the day. As late afternoon approaches, the light becomes more directional again, and the blues are replaced by warmer reds and yellows of late evening. It is the light that creates the emotional impact and ambience in the final photograph.

In macro photography, it is important to understand light in all of its forms, both natural and artificial. No single lighting condition is perfect for all aspects of close-up photography. The strong, directional light favoured by landscape photographers, would be challenging for plant photography. Dull, overcast skies may not be the most inspiring for shooting the landscape vistas, but they are often the best option for the majority of subjects in close-up. It is much easier to render detail and the finer subtleties within an image in overcast conditions. However, the soft and warm directional light at dawn and dusk is still the best time to capture atmospheric photographs.

Natural Light

Natural light is unique, it has a richness and quality that cannot be emulated with any artificial light source. In its softer form, it adds mood and atmosphere, while in contrast, its harsh, directional rays can obliterate the texture and finer details in a photograph. Our eyes are naturally more efficient than any digital sensor and as photographers we are subject to the constraints of the dynamic range of our camera's sensor, which is less sensitive to the nuances of one's natural eyesight. Directional light is often divided into three distinct categories, frontlight, sidelight and backlight.

Frontlight

As its name implies, frontlight is the most popular lighting position in general photography. It is, however, the least dramatic, since the light source normally emanates from behind the camera and photographer. The shadows cast fall behind the subject and are either out of the camera's viewpoint, or quite subdued. The aim of frontlight is to highlight features and details of the subject. It is the easiest to deal with in terms of exposure, since all of the subject in the frame is evenly lit, which gives a more predictable result. It can, however, produce a more flattened, two-dimensional appearance, which is not always desirable in conventional photography. Working in close-up with a short focal length lens often means that it can be difficult in some situations to prevent your own shadow from placing the subject in shade; this is something you need to be mindful of especially when stalking insects. Despite some of its shortcomings, frontlight is still the most popular lighting position and it works well for the vast majority of subjects.

Sidelight

If you want to emphasise texture and shape, then lighting your subject from the side is the preferred approach. Images take on greater depth and character, often with a three-dimensional look.

Sidelight defines the subject more clearly than frontlight, separating it from its background. Shadow detail is usually more pronounced, which emphasises sharpness. In macro photography, sidelight requires more careful control of exposure, as there is a danger of blocking up shadow detail, giving your image an under-exposed look. The time of day and the changing seasons also affect the direction and angle of the light. In winter the sun is low in the sky throughout the whole day, which presents less of an issue than high summer at mid-day, where the light is often harsh and casting strong shadows. Sidelighting works best in the early morning, or late afternoon when the light has lost some of its intensity. It is softer with less contrast and more visually pleasing in a photograph.

Backlight

Shooting into the light when the sun is directly in front of you is technically more challenging, but it is a useful technique when you want to accentuate shape, texture and form. It is advisable to switch your camera to manual mode and spot metering where you have greater control over the exposure. Metering a backlit subject generally requires overexposing from the camera's suggested meter reading. The degree of compensation is

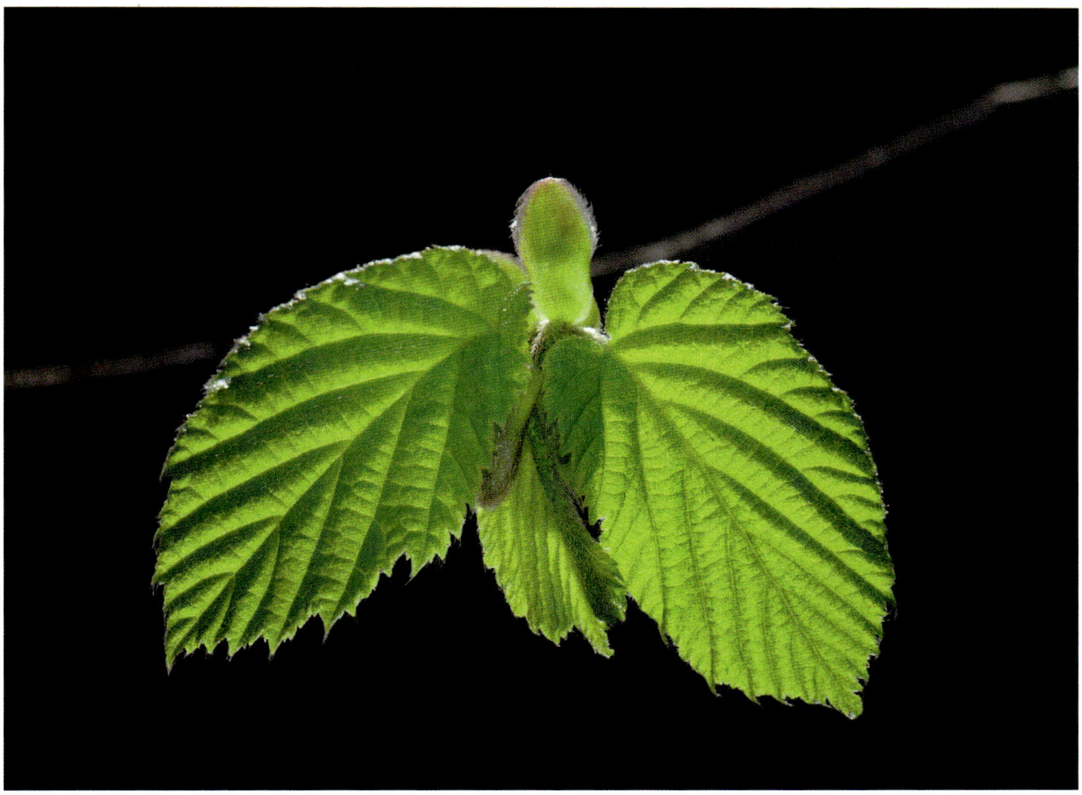

13.1 ~ Backlit hazel leaves

↘ Nikon D800, 200mm micro Nikkor, 1/60sec at f/8, ISO 100.

largely dependent on how you want the final image to appear. In most situations, making little or no adjustments to the camera's metering system will usually render the subject as a silhouette, lacking colour and detail, but strongly emphasising its outline against a lighter background. Backlight creates mood and atmosphere in a picture, often producing a rim of light around the subject, highlighting its finer intricacies; the fine hairs on the stem of a plant, the translucent veining in leaves and winged insects are good examples of where backlighting works extremely well. Early morning and late afternoon, when the sun is low in the sky, are the ideal times for backlit pictures. Be mindful when pointing your lens directly towards the sun as it can induce flare, which will degrade the image quality. Use a lens hood and if necessary shield extraneous light with your hand above the lens and out of the frame.

Photographing in Full Sunlight

We have no influence over the weather and therefore frequently find ourselves faced with conditions in the field, which are not always conducive for good macro photography. It's hard to quantify in real terms what the ideal weather is, since various conditions produce different results. Most photographers would agree that the bright, harsh light that you get from a cloudless mid-day sun is perhaps the most difficult to deal with. The strong, directional light at this time of the day creates harsh shadows among the vegetation, which is challenging even for the best of sensors to deal with. To be honest, I tend to avoid photography at this time of the day except when the sky is overcast. Also, the light has a cooler appearance which is reflected in the photograph. In the days of film, it was common practice to use a warming filter to correct some of the blue in the image. Now we can simply correct it in our chosen software. We can't restrict our photography to ideal conditions – that's just not practical, but we can make use of other accessories and techniques to help overcome some of the problems.

Over the last twenty years, I have travelled widely in Europe, documenting its wide diversity of flora and fauna. One of the biggest challenges is the weather. In the Mediterranean, you can expect plenty of sun, and it is always wise to plan ahead and have the appropriate equipment to help overcome some of the lighting difficulties. I always carry at least one large diffusion screen, complete with light aluminium rods, which I can push into the ground. I can erect this quickly beside a plant and it will diffuse the light, therefore, reducing the shadows and contrast. It is often the difference between getting something that is very acceptable, or failing miserably. When you have invested time and money in travel, you want to be sure that you can achieve an acceptable result irrespective of the conditions. If you have to photograph in bright sunlight, then it is worth taking a little time to look for subjects that are isolated and well separated from their backgrounds. They are less likely to have dark shadows and are more evenly lit. With a little foresight, you can still produce some very acceptable results even in the toughest of lighting conditions.

Diffused Overhead Light

Diffused lighting is preferred for general macro photography, since the overhead clouds act as a giant diffuser, reducing the sun's intensity. The strength of the diffusion is regulated by the density of the clouds. Photographing in overcast light accentuates any fine detail in the subject and also produces rich, saturated colours with virtually no shadows. You have complete freedom to shoot the subject from any angle without having to compromise on your composition and framing. Photographs taken in overcast light often have a slightly flattened appearance with little relief. You can add a touch of fill-in flash to boost the contrast and vibrancy if you feel it is needed. Subjects with delicate colouring, for example, flowers and some fungi, are best photographed in overcast conditions. Achieving the correct

// FACING PAGE //

13.2 ~ Tongue Orchid *Serapias lingua*
I often use long lenses and shoot through foliage to create a soft appearance to the image and background. I also used a diffuser to soften the light, producing a balanced look to the photo.

↘ Nikon D3, 300mm Nikkor, 1/125sec at f/8, ISO 200.

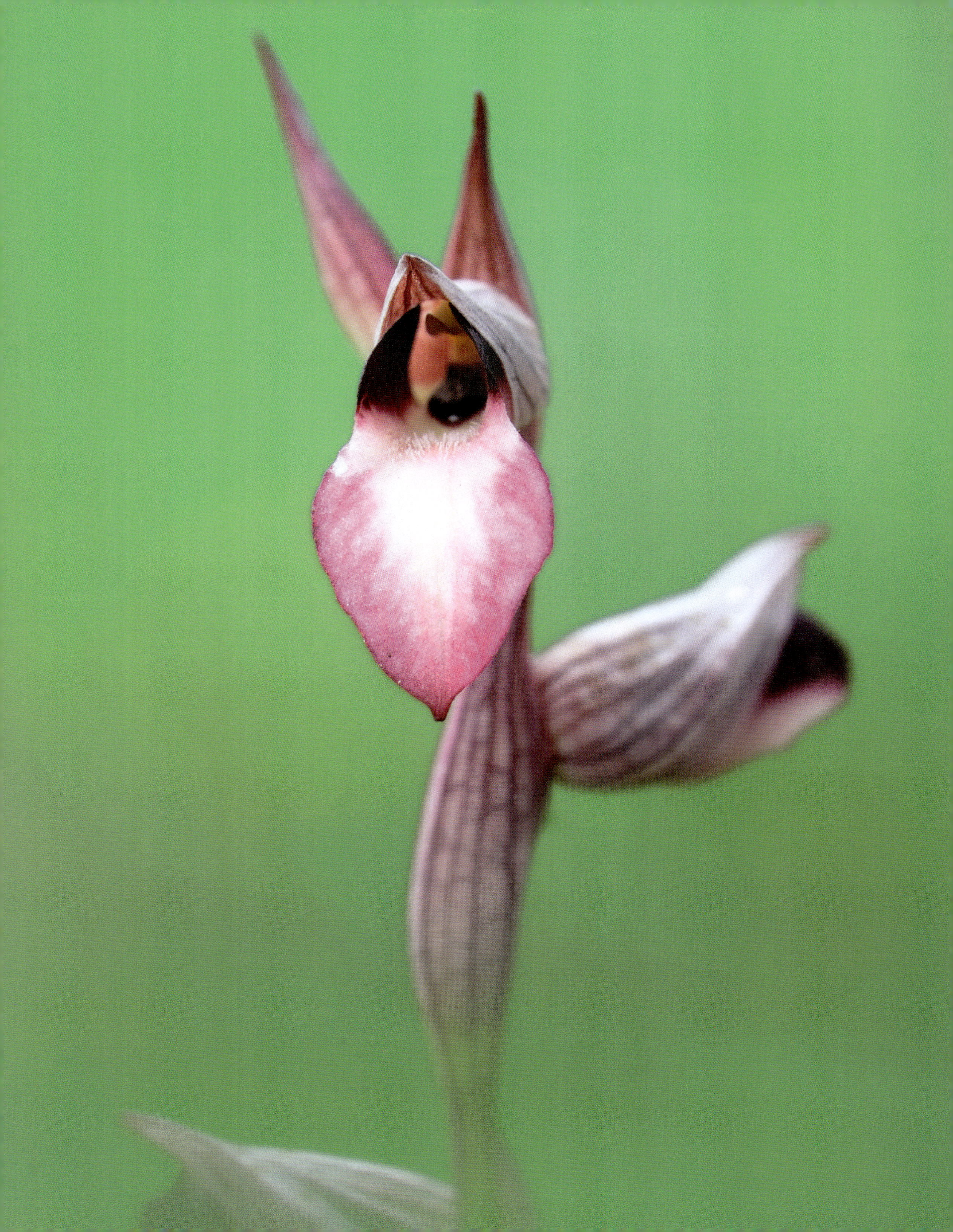

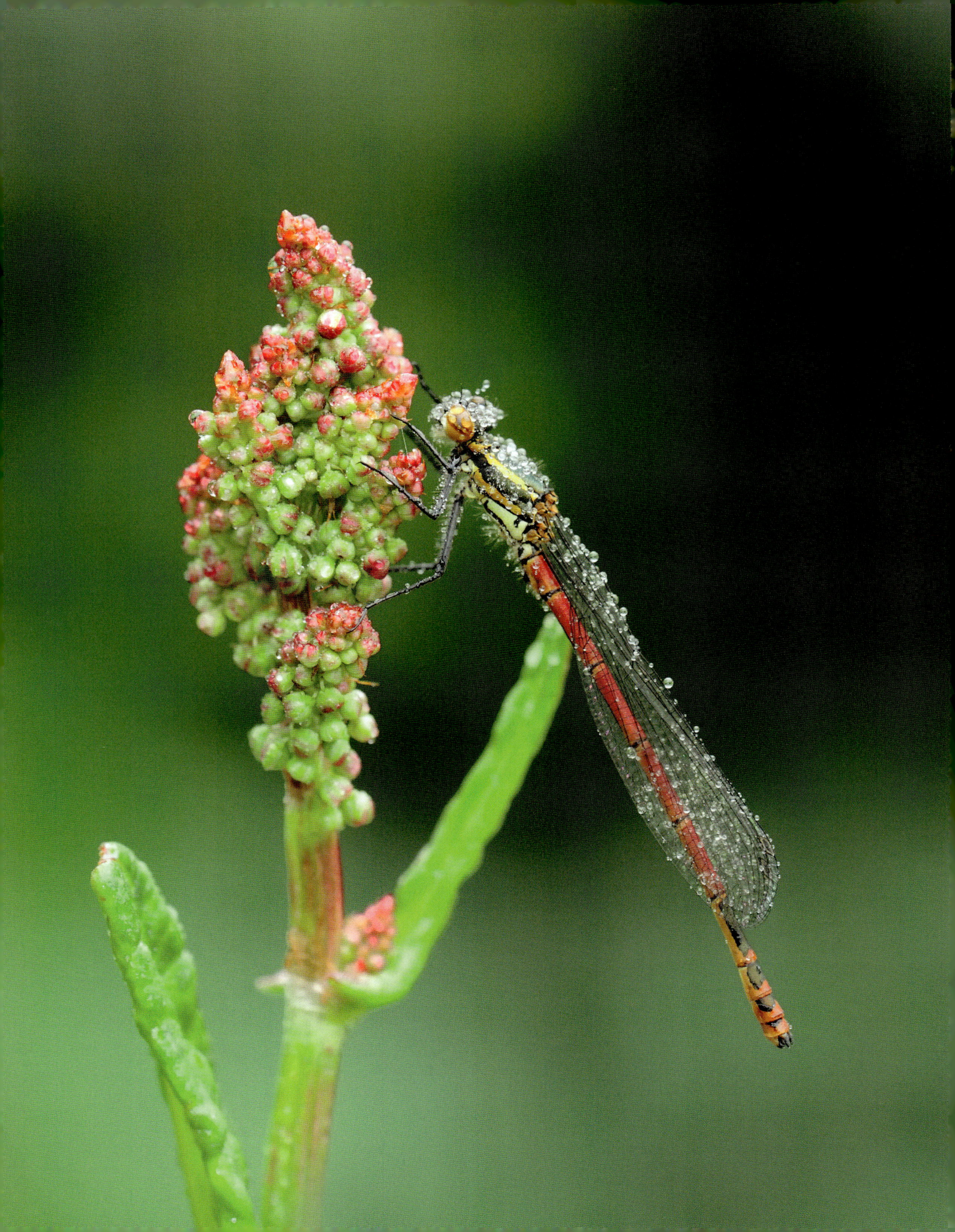

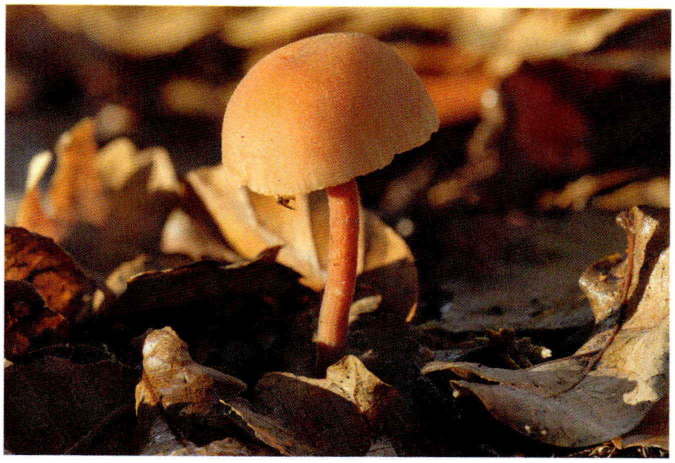

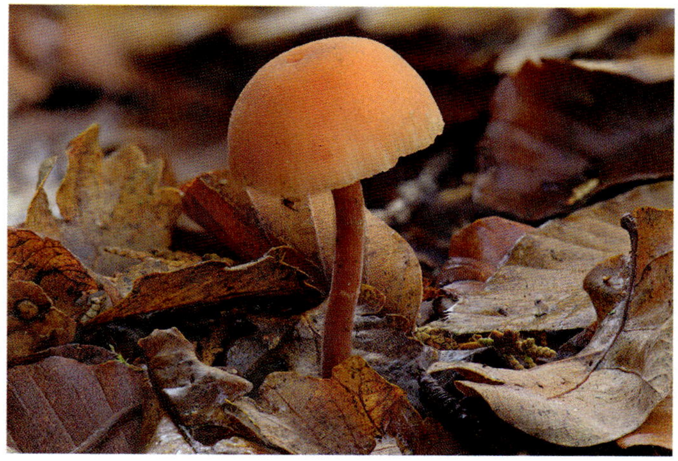

13.4 ~ **The Deceiver** *Laccaria laccata*
Left image without diffusion. Right with diffusion.

↳ Nikon D810, 200mm micro Nikkor, f/11, ISO 200.

// FACING PAGE //

13.3 ~ **Large Red Damselfly** *Pyrrhosoma nymphula* (male)
Light rain has the potential to produce some fine atmospheric images.

↳ Nikon D3X, 200mm micro Nikkor, 1/2sec at f/8, ISO 200.

exposure is relatively straightforward since the light remains consistent. Given the choice, I prefer to photograph the majority of my close-ups in overcast light; despite being often underrated, its simplicity provides the potential to create some great pictures.

Photographing in the Rain

Most photographers naturally prefer to be out in the field when it is dry. However, on days when there is light rain, it is worth making the effort to go out and explore. Flowers and fallen leaves will have an array of water droplets on their petals. Insects will not be capable of flight and therefore forced to rest low down among the foliage. Fine rain in the form of light mizzle is the most interesting, as it produces a series of fine water droplets on foliage, spider's webs and torpid insects. Don't be put off by a little inclement weather. There are often excellent opportunities for great atmospheric shots to be had. However, prolonged, heavy rain is neither comfortable to be in, nor to photograph. Foliage becomes totally saturated with water with little in the way of atmospheric shots to be had.

Diffusers

Although modern digital sensors have a much greater dynamic range than film ever had, no sensor can emulate the tonal values of the human eye. These shortcomings are clearly evident on a bright sunny day when the contrast levels are high even for the best sensors to cope with. We could, of course, choose to photograph only on overcast days, but that's not a practical solution, and chances are, the sun will make an appearance just when you don't want it to. We can't control the weather, but we have accessories at our disposal that will help us overcome some of the problems that mother nature throws at us. High levels of contrast are especially detrimental for close-up photography; the intense light causes dark shadows within the image. We want at all cost to avoid these situations. One way to overcome the problem is to use diffusers.

A diffuser is a device that is placed between the light source (usually the sun when working in natural light) and the subject. It softens the light and reduces the contrast. A diffuser is an important accessory in close-up photography. I regularly carry two different sizes with me. What photographers often forget is that you need to diffuse not only the subject but the background behind it as well. I have often had photographers on my workshops who have purchased a small collapsible diffuser. When I have asked, 'Why so small?', the common reply has been, 'Because it is light and easily transportable in the field.' You need to carry a

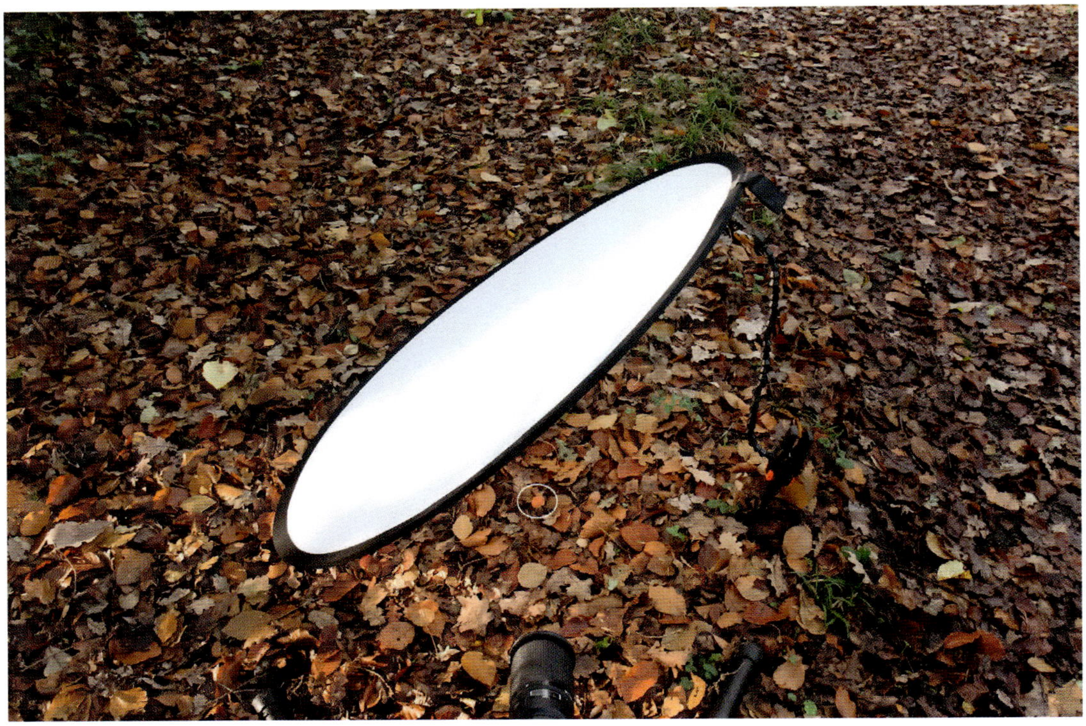

13.5 ~ The diffusion screen in place.

relatively large unit; one that is capable of diffusing the light, both on the subject and the background behind it, otherwise you can end up with a split exposure. Diffused light on the foreground and subject and a line running across the background where the light is still illuminating it. This may not be that noticeable in the viewfinder initially, since you are viewing the subject wide open, but it will be apparent at the taking aperture. You need to check your depth of field to ensure your diffuser is clearly covering the required area. In some situations, you may need to elevate your taking position or switch to a longer focal length lens to reduce the background coverage. Simply place the diffuser as close as possible to the subject without it intruding into the frame. It can be supported with a flexible gooseneck on a spike if strong enough.

Some commercial companies, for example, Lasolite and Photoflex make a professional range of diffusers. The circular units are best suited for macro and easily carried. Professional units are entirely neutral and do not usually have any colour cast associated with them. Many photographers make their own diffusers, but you need to run a test with a grey card to ascertain if the material used produces a colour cast.

Reflectors

The primary purpose of a reflector is to redirect light into the shadow areas of a subject brightening them up and reducing the overall contrast. Reflectors come in all shapes and sizes. They can be easily fabricated from a range of different materials. One of the simplest reflectors is stiff, bright, white card. It produces an overall soft effect that is not that strong. Crumpled kitchen foil spread out over thick card is another excellent reflector and easily carried in your bag. It is a more efficient reflector than a white card. The foil is more reflective on one side than the other. It's down to personal preference which side you prefer. Crumpling the foil before attaching it to your board produces a softer effect than just leaving it smooth. Some commercial companies provide a range of reflectors in various sizes that fold up into relatively small circular pouches, which are fairly light and easily carried.

FOURTEEN

Understanding Flash

NATURAL LIGHT is usually the first choice for conventional macro photography, but it has limitations, especially when working at higher magnifications. Flash is an indispensable tool and the most efficient way to address camera blur and motion. It provides an independent light source, which allows you to operate in challenging situations and achieve results that would be difficult, or perhaps impossible to accomplish with natural light. Other benefits include the use of smaller apertures in situations where you need greater depth of field while using the camera's optimum ISO. This is especially important when you photograph at magnifications greater than life-size, since the zone of sharpness is so shallow. Flash, if used as the primary light source, enhances contrast, giving your images a little more vibrancy especially in poor light. It also gives you (when necessary) the freedom to operate independently of a tripod.

Today's modern units, although more sophisticated, have greater integration and accuracy when it comes to TTL ('through the lens') flash exposure. As a result, those coming fresh to digital photography have benefited greatly from the latest smart flash technology, missing out on all of the formulas and mathematical calculations that were synonymous with exposure and film in the past. This hit or miss approach was a constant source of frustration for many photographers. However, today's modern DSLR cameras have taken much of the difficulty out of calculating flash exposure with the minimum of effort on the part of the photographer.

Notwithstanding the importance of flash in macro photography, it does, however, have some negative aspects. It can produce harsh looking shadows and dark backgrounds due to flash fall-off, also unwanted highlights, but if used skilfully and with the appropriate diffusion the results are excellent. Some units have a relatively slow flash duration of around 1/500, which may not be quick enough to freeze the movement in faster-moving subjects. If you plan on doing a lot of flash photography, then it may be worth checking out the unit's minimum and maximum flash duration speed before you purchase. Flash can also be used in different ways with daylight, but its presence in an image should be subtle and as natural as possible.

TTL Flash

All modern DSLRs support TTL flash metering. Virtually all of your flash photography in the field will be carried out using the TTL mode on your flash unit. Your camera has a separate flash meter (not to be confused with your camera's built-in ambient meter) that regulates the light output from the flash unit at the moment of exposure via a sensor in the camera body. It terminates the light when the correct amount has been given for the chosen aperture. As long as the flash is within range to illuminate the subject, the correct exposure will be attained. The closer the flash is placed to the subject the shorter the duration of the flash. It

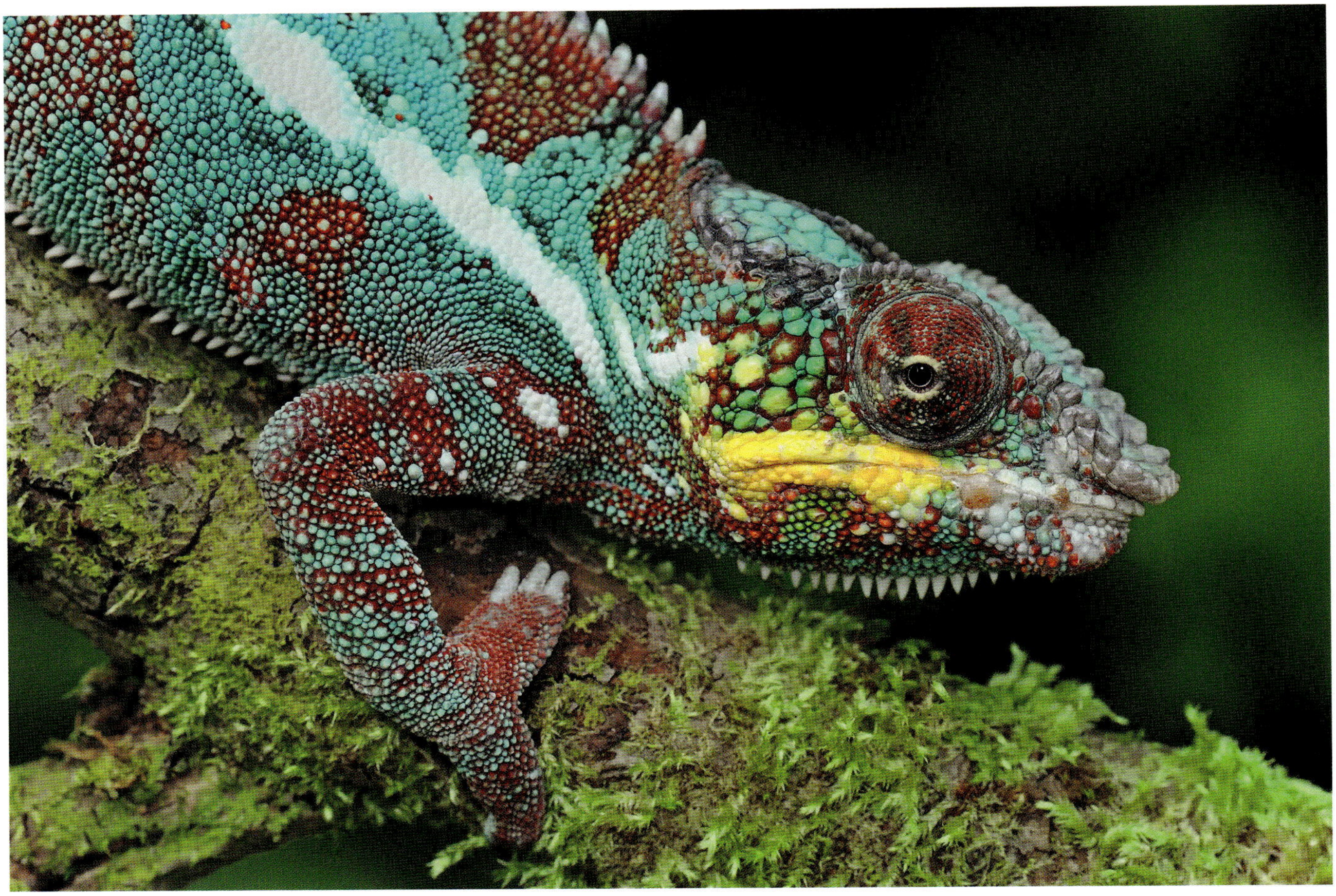

14.1 ~ **Panther Chameleon** *Furcifer paradalis*
Flash is an important tool in macro photography and the best way to eliminate motion and blur.

↘ Nikon D3, 200mm micro Nikkor, 1/60sec at f/11, flash, ISO 200.

seems like an answer to all of the flash exposure problems; no more incorrect exposures, but in reality, like any other metering system, it is not foolproof. You will have to make some exposure adjustments for subjects, which are lighter or darker than a typical mid-tone value. One other point worth mentioning is when you work in Aperture Priority you cannot alter the flash exposure by changing the aperture. Any compensation has to be made through the autoexposure compensating dial on the camera, or on the flash unit itself. You need to be aware that positioning your subject off-centre, or if it only occupies a small part of the frame, then your meter may be influenced by the larger background area and may render the subject over or underexposed. If possible, purchase your camera's own flash units. First of all, they will have complete intergradation with your camera, and you will get all of the benefits of a fully compatible system. Independent manufacturers often state that their flash units have total integration, but that's not always the case.

Manual Flash

Prior to TTL flash, determining the correct exposure was done manually, which involved numerous calculations. Running a test film initially to establish the correct exposure values for a given aperture based on the guide number (GN), provided by the manufacturer was common practice. The formula for this was:

GN = aperture x flash-to-subject distance

// FACING PAGE //

14.2 ~ **Bruising Webcap** *Cortinarius purpurascens*
Using manual flash is an excellent way to control the amount of ambient light in the picture. In this case, I wanted the background to appear darker to eliminate some distracting foliage in the distant background.

↘ Nikon D3X, 200mm micro Nikkor, 1/30sec at f/11, flash, ISO 100.

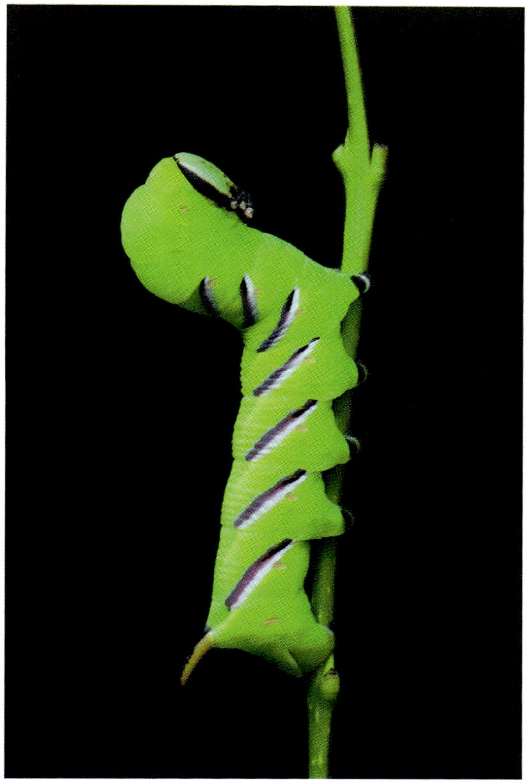
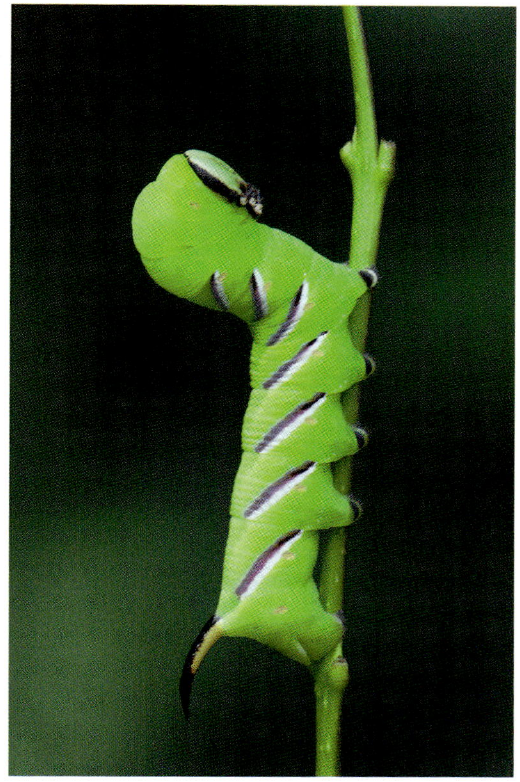

14.3 ~ **Privet Hawk-moth**
Sphinx ligustri
Full flash and fill-in flash. The caterpillar on the left was photographed using full flash. The background is virtually black due to flash fall-off. The image on the right was photographed balancing the flash with ambient light, which produced a more pleasing appearance and allows the detail in the background to register.

↳ Nikon D810, 200mm micro Nikkor, 1/60 sec at f/11, flash ISO 100 (left),
1/8 sec at f/11, fill-in flash, ISO 100 (right).

produce black backgrounds due to flash fall-off and harsh shadows when used with small apertures. If used in combination with lower magnifications and wider apertures on a bright day, the sun acts as a second light source and reduces the effect of flash fall-off on the background.

Mixing Flash with Daylight

When you photograph a subject using ambient light (daylight) as the primary light source and you add flash, you are using fill-in flash. The flash itself is not the major light source but adds supplementary lighting to the darker shadow areas of the image in a similar manner to a reflector.

The important factor here is to consider the lighting ratio; in other words, the amount of flash you need to add to the image. Gauging the balance between flash and daylight is often confusing to inexperienced photographers. To understand this concept, you need to think of flash in terms of stops, like the apertures on a lens. When applied correctly, it can be a useful aid in controlling contrast. I use fill-flash a lot in my routine macro work, especially when working in shaded woodland where the light is often poor. Unlike full flash, fill-in flash works in harmony with daylight.

Many of the smart flash units have what is termed automatic fill-in, where the flash works in conjunction with your camera body. It decides the amount of flash to output. You can alter the intensity of the light by adjusting the compensation dial to fine-tune the balance. Alternatively, you can change the output directly on the flash unit in incremental values of one-third of a stop. You need to carry out some tests with your camera and flash setup changing the values incrementally to establish the correct ratio. The amount of reduction required depends on the tonal value of the subject, the lens to subject distance and the overall effect you are seeking. For example, when I'm using my Nikon D810 with the 105mm micro Nikkor I normally reduce the flash output value by −1 to −1.5 stops. The flash is delivering one and a half stops less light compared to the ambient reading. This produces a more natural result in an average mid-tone subject, adding some light to the shadow areas of the photograph. You will have to make some exposure adjustments with subjects that are darker or lighter to prevent over or underexposure. Fill-flash, if applied correctly should be subtle, integrating naturally with the ambient exposure, showing little evidence of its presence.

Fill-in flash is of limited use when photographing active creatures. It will only work if the subject remains perfectly still, which is unlikely in the heat of the day. Any movement will be apparent in the photo producing a second image commonly referred to as ghosting. In these situations you need to resort to full flash.

Flashgun Size and Diffusion

The ideal choice of flashguns for macro are the small, lightweight units, which are easily positioned near the front of the lens and as close to the subject as possible. The size of the flash reflector lens is large in comparison to the subject, which in theory produces a softer, diffused light. However, the light emitted can still be too harsh, causing hot spots especially on the wing cases of various insects. Many macro photographers (myself included) are do-it-yourself enthusiasts and are always making, or modifying some piece of equipment. There are different diffusers available commercially that will fit most flash guns. However, many photographers make their own. The diffuser should be large enough to spread the light and soften the shadows. It should also be thick enough to reduce hot spots, but not too dense as to reduce the intensity of the flash too much.

I prefer to use a single flash in most cases rather than a dual setup. You don't want to produce an image totally flat and devoid of some relief. A single diffuser, in my opinion, if big enough is usually adequate in most cases. Diffusers are best used in conjunction with a dedicated macro flash system, or flash bracket. Macro lenses in the region of 100mm are ideal for handheld close-ups. They are lighter and better suited to macro on the move. Also, the diffuser is closer to the subject. Where you position the flash unit is important. In most cases, high axial lighting provides the best overall result with the shadows falling directly behind the subject. Placing the flash on the hot shoe can cause problems. The close working distance between the lens and subject can partially block the light from illuminating evenly. Bear in mind that shadows are more apparent when the subject is resting on leaves and other flat foliage, or when the light is coming from the side.

High-speed Flash

In literally a blink of an eye, it is possible these days to capture an insect in flight with today's modern DSLRs thanks to advances in camera electronics and photoelectric triggering devices.

Digital image capture has made the process of taking photographs of natural history subjects and many others less arduous. Nevertheless, it still requires a considerable amount of knowledge and patience to achieve even a handful of great images. I have always had an interest in this technology but don't get to use my own high-speed flash setup as much as I did in the past.

During the 1970s, Stephen Dalton pioneered high-speed flash photography of insects and other natural history subjects using custom-designed flash units capable of very high flash durations in the region of 1/30,000 sec. I joined his agency in my mid-twenties twenty-seven years ago, and I got to know him. We both shared a passion for insects, among other things. He wrote the Foreword for my first photography book on insects. Many of his photographs from that period are still as good today and have not been bettered.

Many of the current smart flash units can deliver very acceptable results of fast moving subjects. Switching your flash gun to manual and reducing the power setting down manually to say, 1/16 power or less, and upping your ISO gives a much faster burst of light, but the actual light output is naturally reduced. One way to overcome this problem is to place your flash units much closer to the subject where the light has less distance to travel. With some models you may require cables to use them off camera; however, many modern flash guns, for example, most of Nikon's SB Speedlights, are wireless and can be positioned off-camera and fired from the

// FACING PAGE //

14.4 ~ Common Wasp *Vespula vulgaris*
I personally prefer a little movement in the wings to indicate motion.
↳ Nikon D810, 200mm micro Nikkor, f/11 flash, ISO 200.

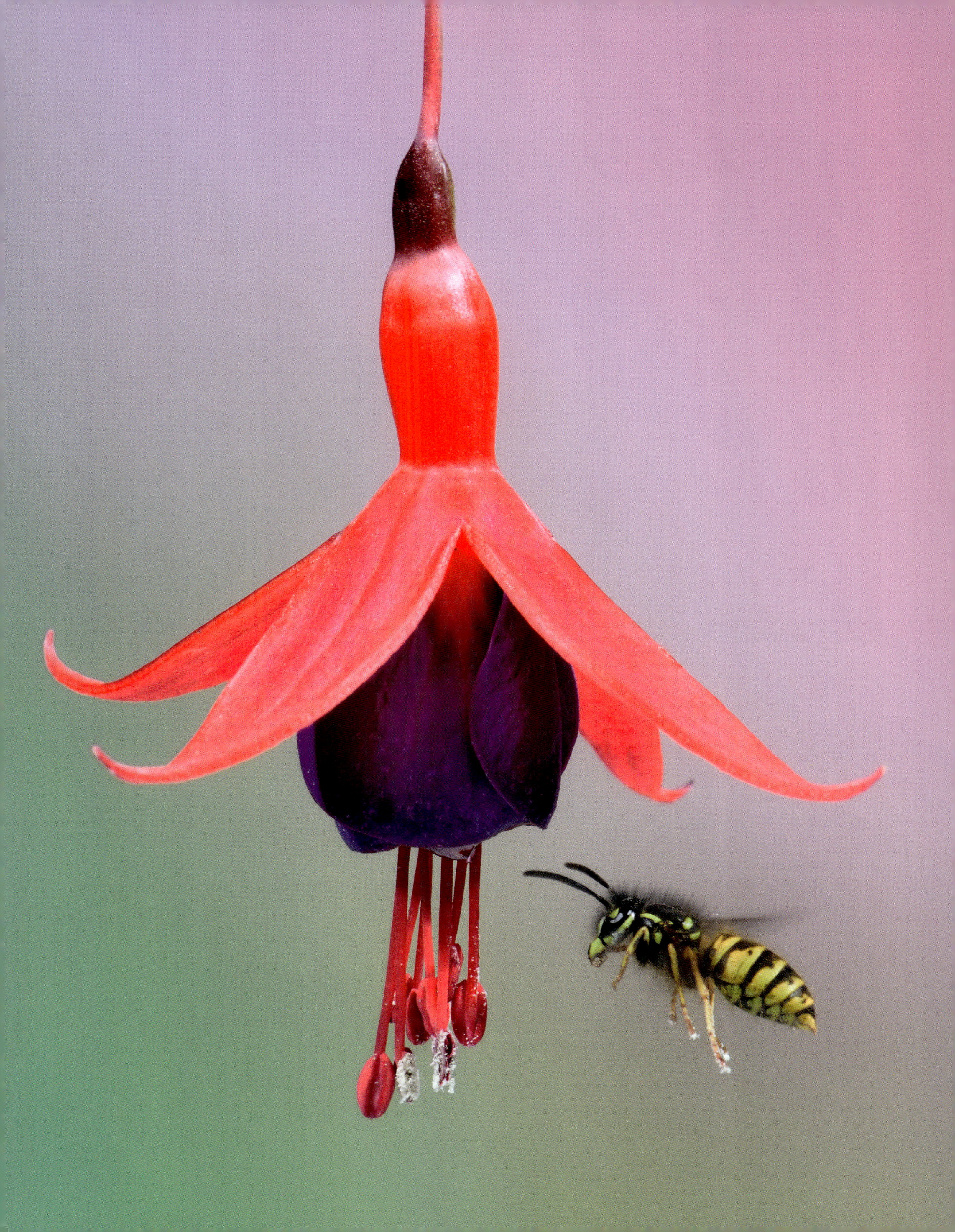

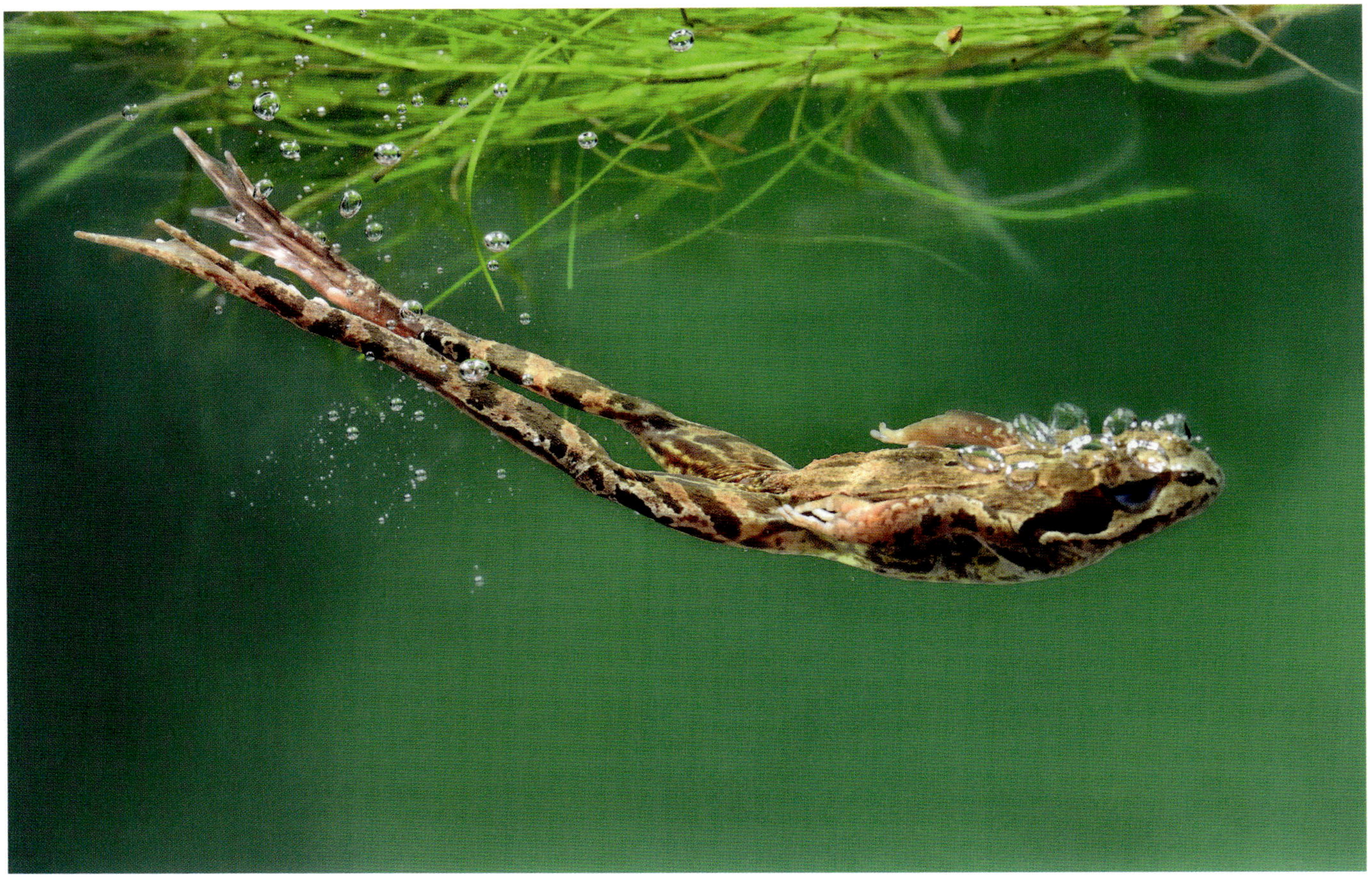

14.5 ~ **European Common Frog** *Rana temporaria*

↘ Nikon D810, 200mm micro Nikkor, f/11, flash, ISO 200.

commander unit on the camera's hotshoe. There are some photoelectric devices on the market from companies like Photo Trap and Cognisys, which manufacture a range of specialised equipment for high-speed flash photography. You can achieve reasonable results in the field by adopting a 'wait and see' approach, where you set up your equipment prefocus on a flower and wait and see what appears. The methodology and practice of high-speed flash photography is a highly specialised technique and beyond the scope of this publication.

Commercial Macro Flash Systems

There are a number of commercial macro flash systems on the market. Most have a hefty price tag, but you are essentially paying for convenience and ease of use. It can be a significant investment for some photographers who may find it difficult to justify the expense if they are not using it on a regular basis. A macro flash system should be easy to assemble and not too fiddly to use. The last thing you want is for your set up to let you down at the crucial moment. Some of the designs have the flash units fixed, which restricts their use. This becomes more of an issue when you use a longer focal length macro, which has a greater lens to subject distance. The flash units are much further back and may lack the power to light the subject adequately when using smaller apertures.

Nikon's R1C1 Macro Flash, which replaced the SB29s, is one of the most versatile systems on the market at present. It's entirely wireless; the flash units connect to a circular housing attached via a ring secured in the filter threads of the lens. The flash guns can also be detached and placed at the subject if required even though the camera and lens are much further back. Additional units can be added to the ring and their light output can be adjusted individually if required. The flashes can be triggered and their light output adjusted directly via a commander unit which fits on the hot shoe, or from the built-in flash on some of the more recent camera bodies.

Canon also manufactures both a ring light and a macro twin light, as do independent companies such as Sigma, which can be used with many of the major camera brands. The Sigma unit offers dual flash, which can be fired simultaneously or independently. It also has a range of adapter rings which allows the unit to be used on a variety of different lenses.

Ring Flash and Twin Flash Units

Conventional ring flashes are more commonly used in the field of medicine and dentistry, where you require shadowless lighting. This is especially important in dentistry since you are photographing the oral cavity, which can be hard to light evenly, especially in the buccal corridors (between the cheeks and teeth) and the distal extremities of the mouth. When used in close-up photography, the lighting tends to be rather flat. Modern ring flashes are primarily now twin flash setups, which are mounted on each side of a large circular ring. The flash units can be rotated via the ring, but cannot be removed individually. The control unit is usually mounted on the camera's hotshoe. This device can be attached to a number of lenses via an adapter ring which screws into the lens. Unlike a conventional ring flash, you can adjust the light output individually for creative flash control, which produces a more natural result with shadow relief. The disadvantage is they are fixed and cannot be removed. Also, the flash guide number is relatively low, and flash fall-off is often more evident with these particular units. They are much better suited to shorter focal length macros and when photographing at higher magnifications where the flash units are much closer to the subject.

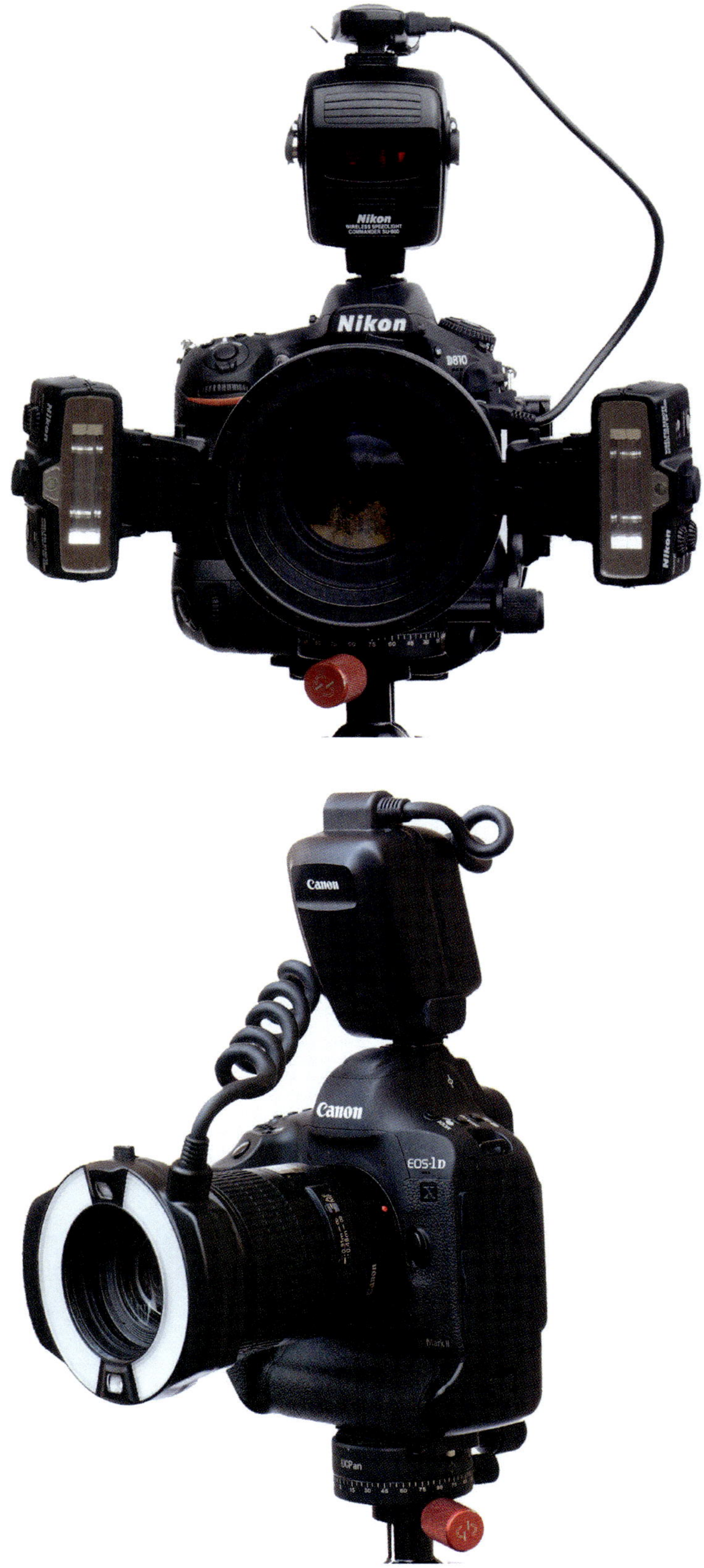

14.6 ~ Nikon R1C1 Macro Flash System and Canon MR-14EX II Speedlite
Whichever system you use they all deliver excellent results. You will always have to modify your exposures when dealing with challenging lighting conditions or high contrast situations.

Custom-designed Flash Brackets

Although convenient, commercially made flash systems are not ideal in every situation. Many photographers, myself included, have, over the years, designed

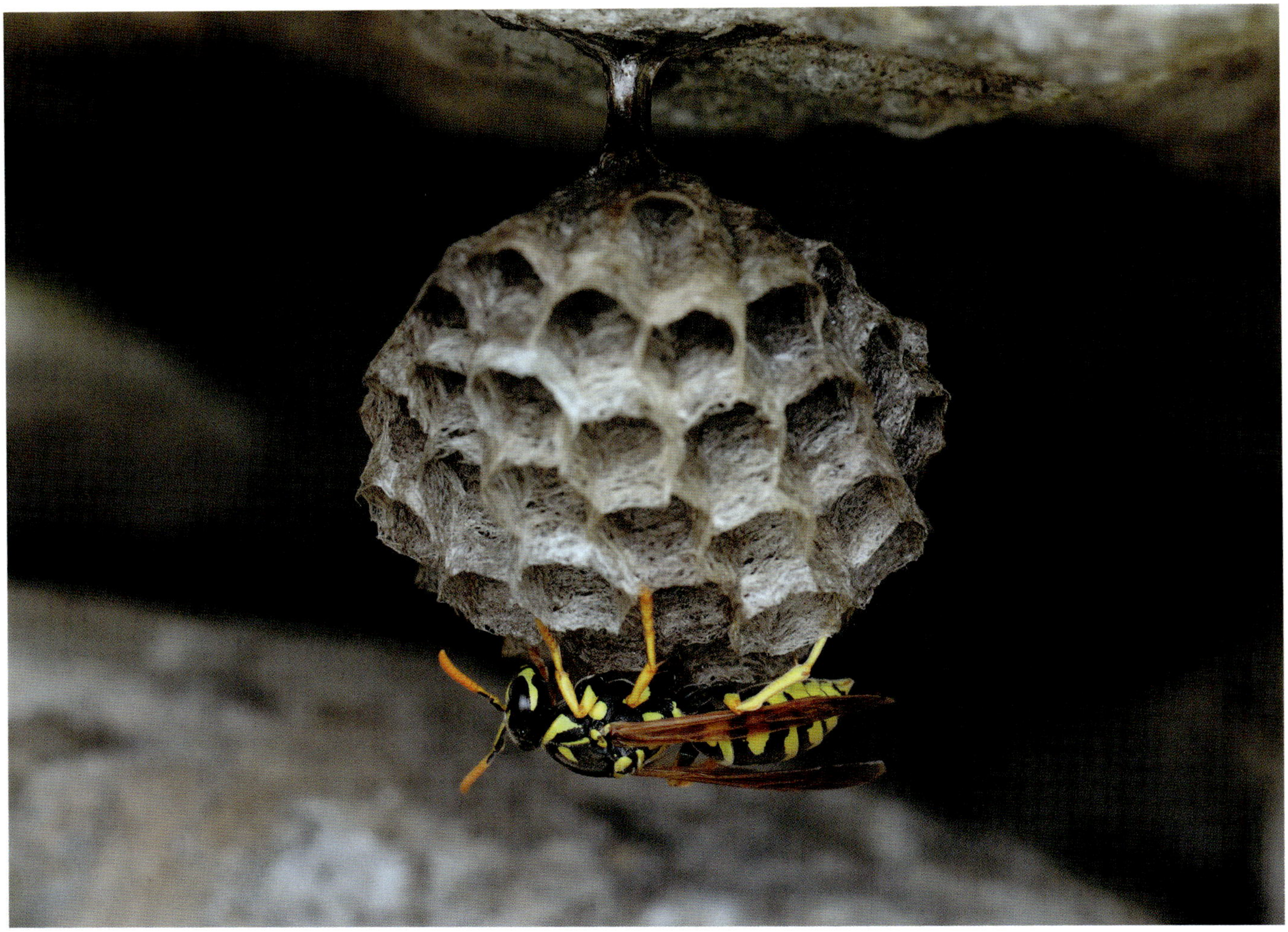

14.7 ~ **Paper Wasp** *Polistes gallicus*
Full flash on the custom bracket works well in situations such as this where this wasp is moving continuously.

↳ Nikon D3X, 200mm micro Nikkor, 1/125sec at f/16, flash, ISO 200.

and constructed custom flash brackets. I have illustrated some of these in my previous photography books. Commercial macro flash systems are an alternative to homemade designs, but their price is often prohibitive for many photographers. With so many accessories available in DIY stores and on the internet, it is relatively easy to acquire the appropriate material to fabricate your own bracket. I often use my custom-made flash bracket when photographing in TTL mode at higher magnifications with a single flash positioned above the lens. This design has worked well and seems adequate in most situations. Some insects, for example beetles, are prone to hot spots, in particular with a twin setup. I use a home-made diffuser on the flash unit when stalking insects. It is quite simple to make; check out the internet, there are many examples there. Some commercially manufactured brackets are available from Kirk, Really Right Stuff and Novoflex.

Any commercially made flash system is always going to be expensive. It you are a keen do-it-yourself aficionado, for a very modest outlay you can easily construct a flash bracket that will produce very similar results. On page 90 is an example of one of my custom-made units. The components are easily obtained.

FIFTEEN

Extended Depth of Field

COMBINING several images together to make a composite photograph is not a new concept, it's been used in the photographic world for a long time. Thanks to recent advances in software development it can be applied to close-up and macro photography to extend the depth of field in a photograph.

'Extended Depth of Field', or 'Focus Stacking' has been used in a rudimentary form by museums and in the world of microscopy for quite a long time. In mainstream photography, it really took off with the introduction of software developed by Combine ZM and Helicon Focus in the early 2000s. Since then, Adobe Photoshop and other programs like Zerene Stacker have also become popular alternatives. The basic idea of extended depth of field is taking a series of photographs, each one shot at a slightly different focusing point and blending them into a single composite image.

Understanding the Problems

The age-old problem in macro photography is, of course, depth of field. The f/16 culture as I call it was so evident in the 1990s, it was expounded from the photographic pulpit of virtually every magazine. Creative macro photography is not necessarily about shooting everything at f/16, other important factors, such as the photographer's style and interpretation, are also significant issues; overall sharpness in a subject is not always essential and in some cases it may be counterproductive. However, when complete sharpness is paramount then techniques like focus stacking can help to a point overcome the problem.

In conventional macro photography we are often forced to compose and photograph from a particular position to maximise the depth of field. Being restricted to certain positions constrains creativity, especially if you want to illustrate the subject from a more oblique angle. Using smaller apertures is not necessarily the solution as it means slower shutter speeds and an increased risk of diffraction.

As magnification increases, depth of field decreases, with less of the subject appearing in focus. Where it becomes evident is at magnifications approaching life-size and above. The zone of sharpness is significantly reduced, even at smaller apertures. While the laws of physics and optics cannot be ignored, Focus Stacking, or Extended Depth of Field, can certainly overcome some of these restrictions that conventional photography places upon us.

Applying the Technique

Focus Stacking is an amalgamation of two tasks; the first is capturing a series of images, each taken at different focusing points to achieve complete sharpness throughout the subject, or to a point of your choosing. The second is combining them in an appropriate

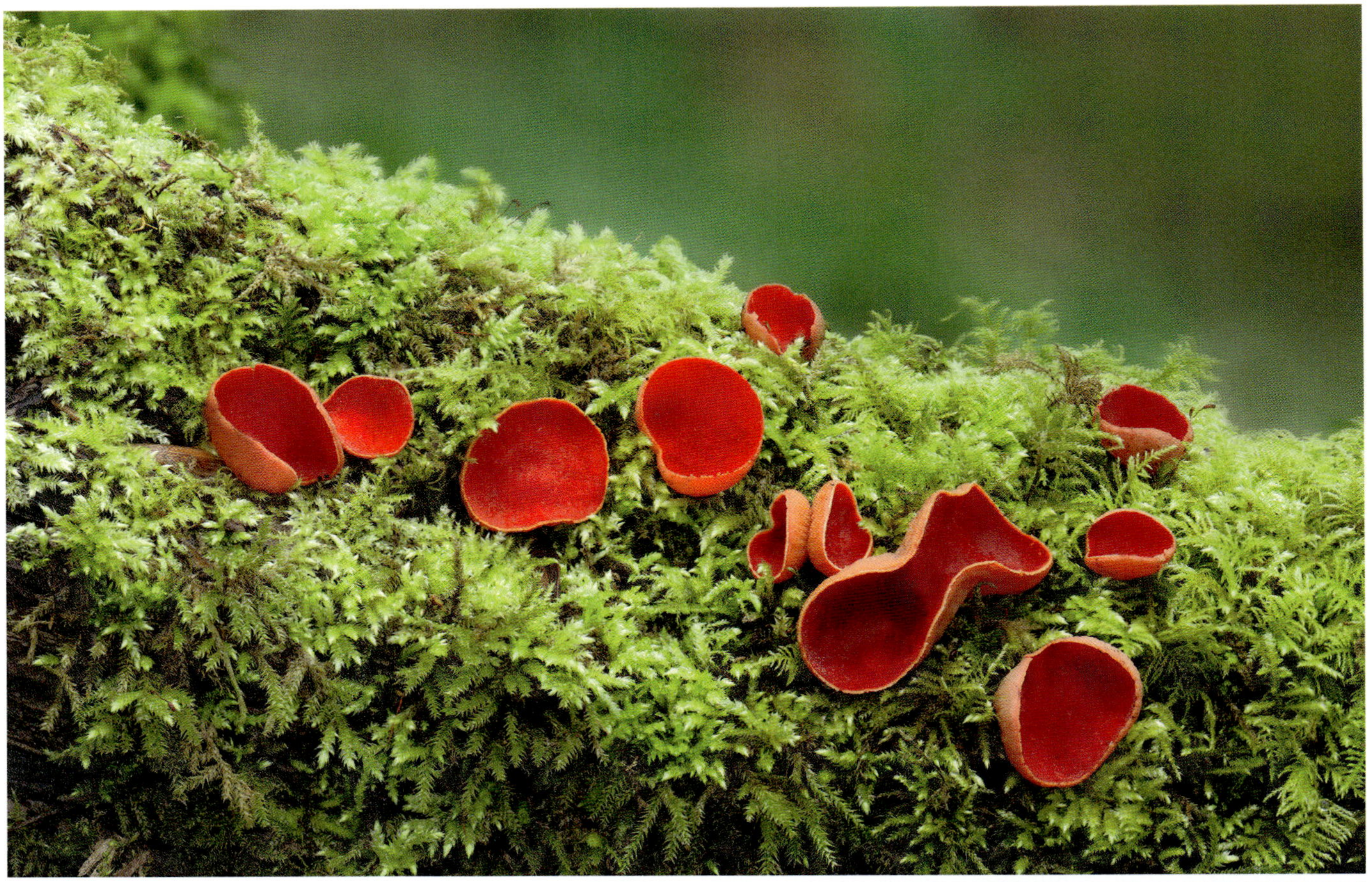

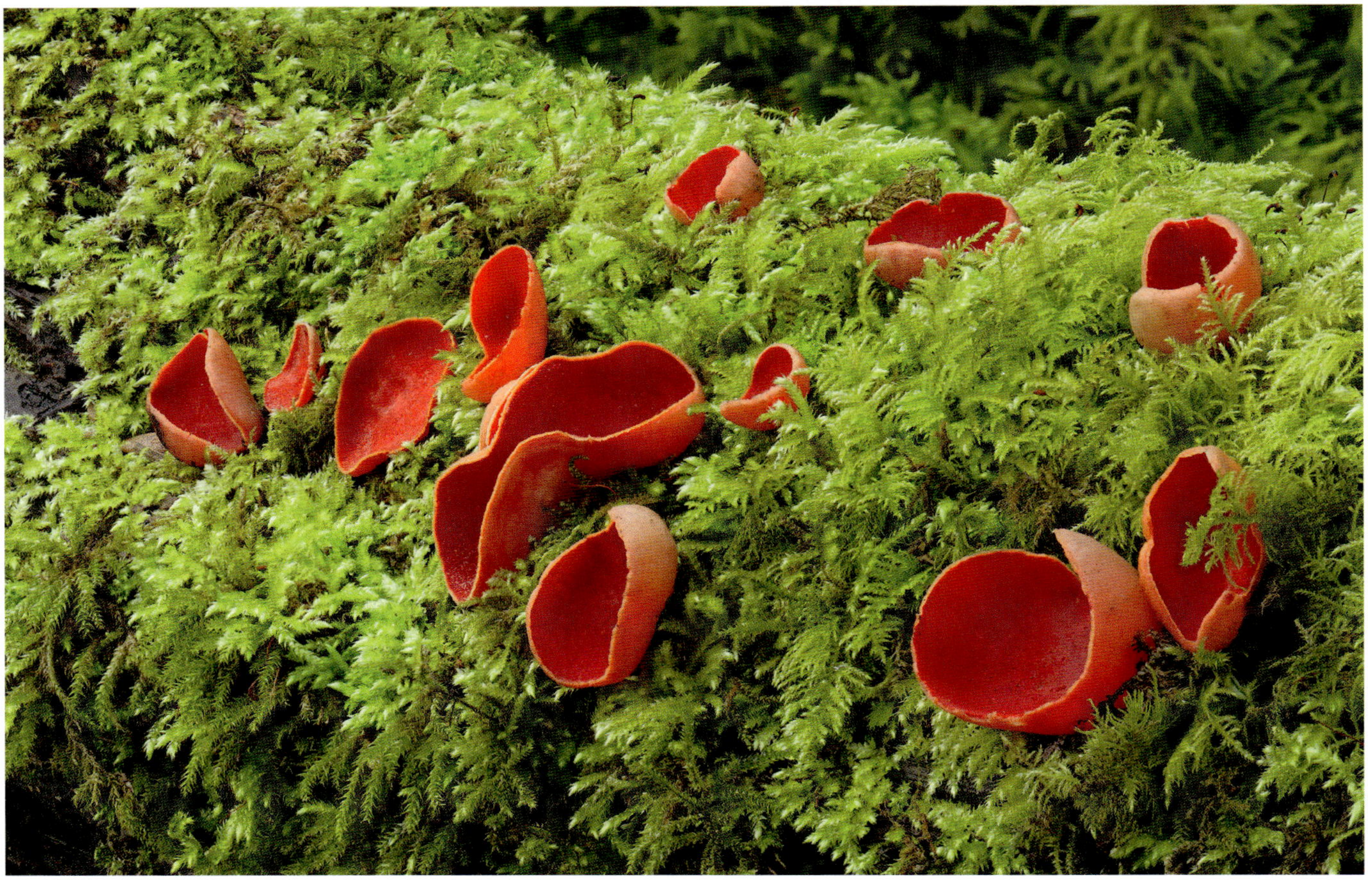

piece of software into a single composite photograph. Although it may seem a relatively straightforward process, there are pitfalls and issues throughout the process, examples being, digital artifacts and movement of the subject. Many photographers have their own preferences and methods of how they apply the technique. I don't use it exclusively, or on a regular basis, but apply it in situations where the subject would benefit from its application.

There are basically two methods of approach. The first, and probably the most widely practised of the two, is changing the point of focus by rotating the focusing ring on the lens in small, incremental stops. This method works relatively well up to around life-size, but is less reliable for higher magnifications, which can lead to various artifacts during the blending procedure. Rotating the focusing ring is actually changing the magnification slightly within each frame, although the software takes this into consideration during the process. At higher magnifications, rotating the focusing ring has virtually no effect, as depth of field is so shallow.

The second, which is less popular, is mounting the camera assembly onto a focusing rail. In this case, you are changing the point of focus by moving the entire camera assembly in small, precise movements, which seems to produce better results at higher magnifications. One of the downsides is lack of real stability as the whole assembly can be cumbersome to position and operate. Most of the high magnification photography is carried out in a studio setting. Many of the table-top setups use the focusing columns from old microscopes with adapted tripod and camera mounting plates; these deliver greater precision and stability when fine-focusing.

Both approaches have their pros and cons. To get the best from this technique you need to do the following:

- work from a tripod to ensure stability and continuity in each image in terms of framing and focus;
- switch your camera to manual so there is no variation during each exposure;
- change the White Balance from auto to manual and set a specific colour temperature. This is to ensure continuity throughout the exposures otherwise any change in the light could affect the colour balance of each image;
- decide where you want the image to appear sharp from and where it should end;
- carefully advance the focusing ring of the lens in very small, even incremental movements during each exposure until you reach the end of the area you want in focus;
- overlap the depth of field in each consecutive frame to ensure a smooth blending free from artifacts;
- a successful image stack often contains up to thirty images and at higher magnifications frequently more.

It is a good idea to experiment with a static subject first until you familiarise yourself with the technique. With practice, you become familiar with just how much to adjust the focusing ring on the lens. Personally, I don't record every single part of the image in focus – I prefer to let focus gradually fade out a little, this produces a more natural result in my opinion. At the end of the sequence, I shoot a blank to mark the end of the stack. If I'm repeating the process again I now have a reference point of where the new sequence commences and the previous one ends.

Focus stacking is a widely practised technique; good as it is in many aspects, it is not the ultimate solution in every case, but when used correctly and in the appropriate situation, it can deliver excellent results. You can also work with larger apertures to control cluttered backgrounds. It will work well in most situations where the subject for example remains perfectly still. It is much more challenging when applying the technique

// FACING PAGE ~ TOP //

15.1 ~ Scarlet Elf Cup *Sarcoscypha coccinea*
We are often restricted in our choice of viewpoint in order to maximise the depth of field for the selected aperture.

↳ Nikon D800, 200mm micro Nikkor, 1/8sec at f/16, ISO 100.

// FACING PAGE ~ BOTTOM //

15.2 ~ Scarlet Elf Cup *Sarcoscypha coccinea* (composite)
Extended depth of field allows us to take advantage of more oblique viewpoints creating a feeling of depth to the photograph.

↳ Nikon D800, 200mm micro Nikkor, 1/8sec at f/16, ISO 100.

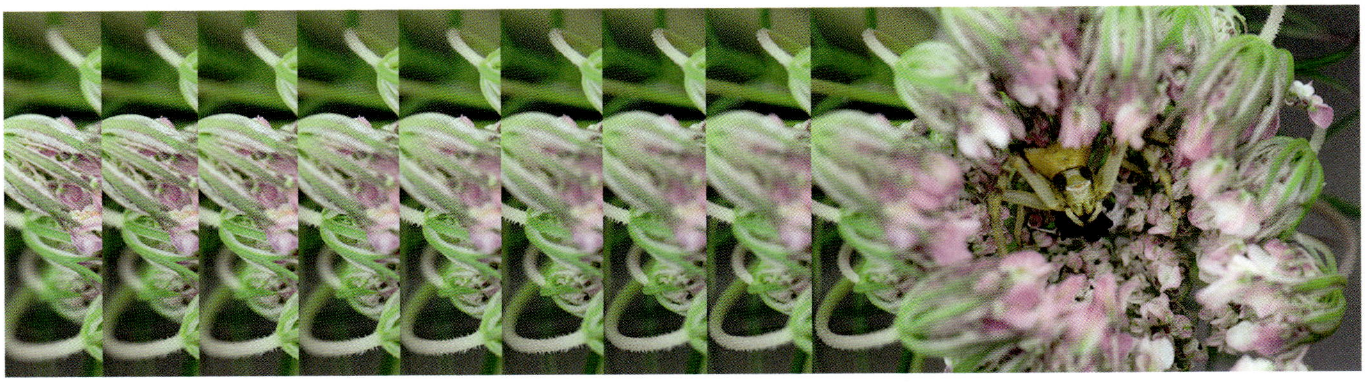

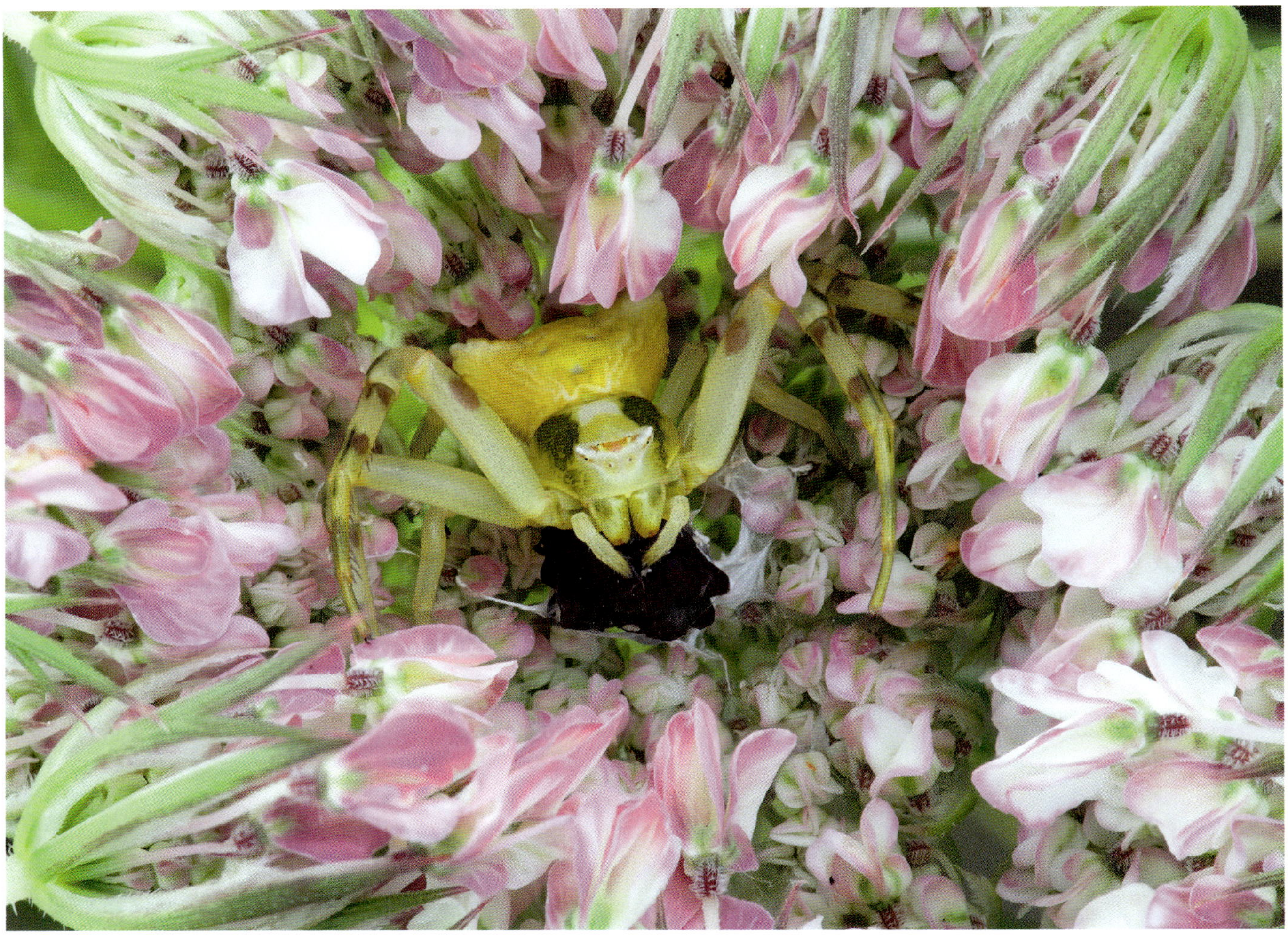

// TOP //

15.3 ~ **Crab Spider** *Thomisus onustus*
Image stack showing point of focus in each photo.

// BOTTOM //

15.4 ~ **Crab Spider** *Thomisus onustus*
Finished, composite image. It would not have been possible to retain sharpness from the top of the flowers to the spider without using extended depth of field.

→ Nikon D810, 200mm micro Nikkor, 1/15sec at f/11, ISO 200.

to active subjects such as insects. The movement of any part of the subject will create artifacts in the final composite; for example, moving legs or antennae, and these will require a considerable amount of time to remove.

Image stacking is fast becoming an accepted method for dealing with depth of field issues. Recent technical advances have meant that an image stack can be created in camera very quickly by changing focus automatically. The images are combined using the camera's internal software. Olympus offers this facility in some compact cameras as do the top of the range DSLRs. It certainly begins to make focus stacking in the field less challenging for mobile subjects.

Extended Depth of Field Using 4K Video

Panasonic cameras offer a 4K video approach, creating an image stack in a slightly different way utilising the 4K 'post focus mode'. Essentially, the camera allows a short burst of video at 30 fps whilst shifting the focus from the nearest point of focus on the subject to the background. The individual frames from the video burst are combined to produce the stacked image. The video clip can be reviewed initially in QuickTime or a similar program and edited to remove unwanted images. You can also use a wide aperture such as f/5.6 to keep the background well diffused. I have seen the results from this technique and they are excellent. Although this technology is relatively recent it is likely to become standard in the camera bodies of most manufacturers that offer 4K video and eventually 6K video. The next Panasonic professional camera the GH5 will allow 4K post focus at 60fps (meaning you can use it for higher magnification work with smaller steps between frames and also 6K post-focus. For further information on this technique visit the online resource Learn Macro already mentioned in the Introduction pages.

Extended depth of field is an alternative in some situations. It does not replace conventional macro photography in any sense of the word, but should be used when there is a distinct advantage to be gained. There are many well-illustrated references to focus stacking on the web. A large percentage of these are studio-based setups; some of the high magnification examples of insects on a wide variety of sites and forums have undoubtedly been sacrificed in order to facilitate the photographer's vanity. Some are obviously the result of unethical procedures, with most of the specimens being either dead, or severely compromised. It's hard to envisage any active insect remaining perfectly still while a photographer rattles off fifteen or twenty images only a matter of millimeters away.

Software Selection

Once you have obtained your sequence of shots you need suitable software to blend the images together. I have already mentioned a number of popular software programs, which are specifically designed for this task. My own preference is for Helicon Focus, but there are others equally as good. Not all of the programs allow you to combine images in their RAW format; some require conversion to TIFF or JPEG. I have a directory in which I send my stacks for conversion, once this has been completed, I delete the stack from my drive, but I still have the RAW files should I ever need to repeat the process again. It's important to adopt some sort of routine as to how you deal with the accumulation of multiple shots otherwise your drive after a period of time will be overrun with files, which you are unlikely to use again. Importing the files is a straightforward process in Helicon Focus and a simple click of the render button and the rest is relatively automatic. The default settings work pretty well for the vast majority of cases. As you become more familiar with the program you can alter some of the other settings, which will improve the final result in more challenging composites. You can plot the development of the composite as it works its way though the images. I usually make two copies by saving it twice; one is filed in my RAW file directory, and the other will be stored in my TIFF library to be used when necessary; that way, I always have an untouched backup copy.

Not every subject lends itself to this technique. The most successful composites are of static subjects; lichens, fungi and most plants are all possible, but working in the field brings its own challenges. Wind and subject movement are perhaps the biggest problems to overcome when stacking. Obtaining successful

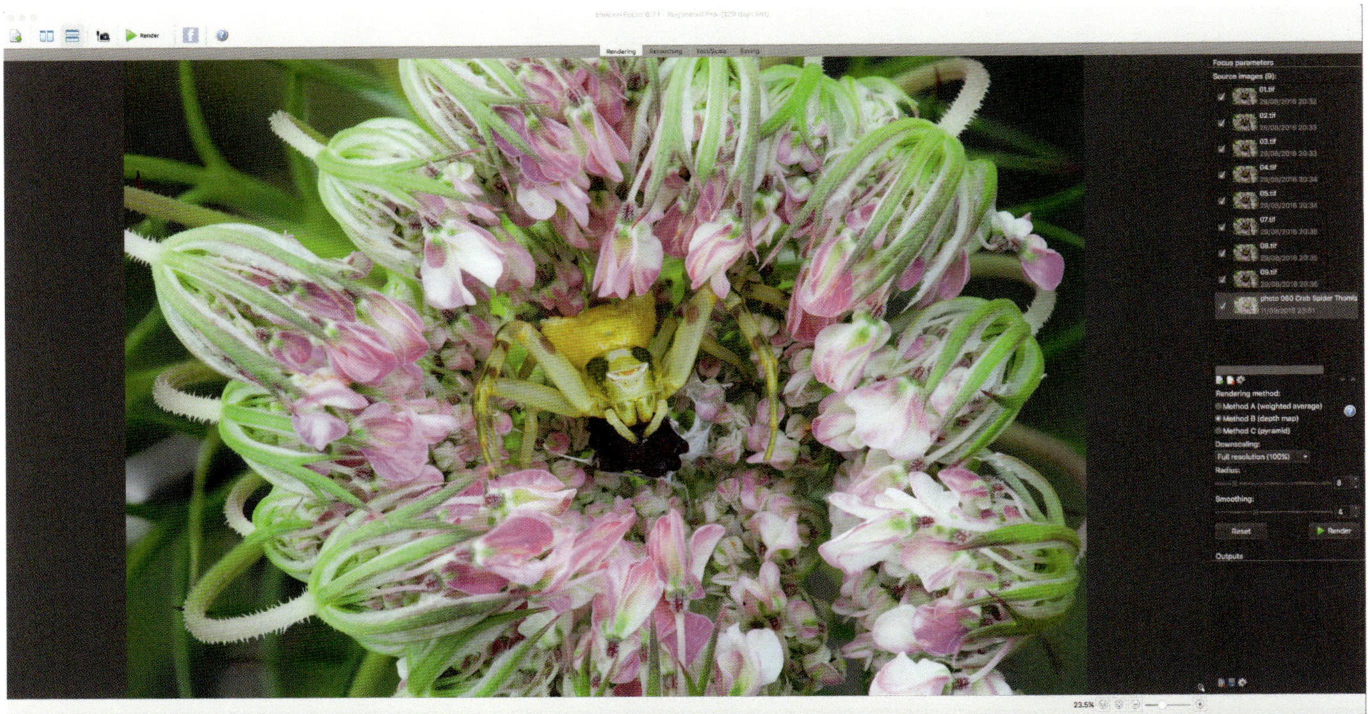

15.5 ~ Screen shot showing Helicon Focus with the finished composite.

composites of insects can also be a very frustrating experience. Obviously, you have to be able to record your sequence with the subject remaining perfectly still. This can be more challenging than it seems. There are few insects that will tolerate a large lens thrust in their face in the middle of the day. Choosing the right day and time is as important as mastering the technique itself. Dragging yourself out of a warm bed in the early hours when insects are torpid on the vegetation from the night before is one of the most productive times. The secret is, work quickly, but methodically and use a long focal length macro. Any movement of the subject during the process will produce artifacts during the blending process. Twitching antenna and legs seem to be the most common issues, which is why I don't apply the technique on a regular basis with insects. Digital artifacts are one of the side effects of composites; many are relatively straightforward and are easily dealt with; others are not and can be extremely time-consuming to correct. Sometimes one stack will have artifacts present and the following stack shot a few seconds later is trouble free, I don't really have any answer as to why this should be, having repeated the process in exactly the same way. Another problem is the volume of individual images that are necessary to complete each composite, which can be well into double figures, especially if you are working at much higher magnifications. Any corrections in the RAW stage have to be applied to all the images in the stack. Working with high megapixel cameras such as the D810 produces extremely large file sizes, so storage and processing are more time consuming. You can also fill cards pretty quickly if you are applying this technique to every image you shoot.

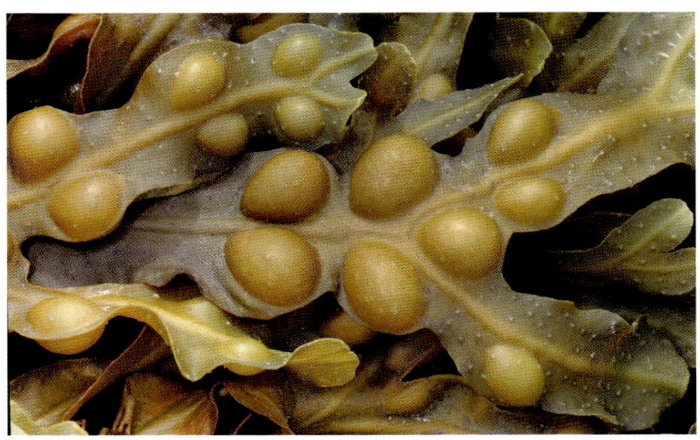

15.6 ~ **Bladder Wrack** *Fuscus vesiculosus* (composite)

→ Nikon D810, 200mm micro Nikkor, 1/15sec at f/11, ISO 200.

SIXTEEN

Backgrounds

MANY PHOTOGRAPHERS new to macro photography often underestimate the significance of the background behind the subject and how it contributes to the overall aesthetics of the photograph; this usually becomes apparent when the photographs are analysed on screen. Blades of grass and other intruding bits of vegetation that were not apparent in the viewfinder suddenly appear from nowhere. It is important to check the background as it will appear in the photograph by engaging the depth of field preview button before you take the shot. There is also an assumption that any lens can take close-ups if the appropriate accessories are added and of course that is true to a point, but the focal length of a lens will determine how the image will look. Lens selection in close-up photography is important; it defines the overall appearance of the photograph. If you want to show the subject within the context of its environment, then you need to select a short focal length lens. It will incorporate a much wider field of view behind the subject. If you want to isolate your subject from the background, then you need to select a longer focal lens. Photographers often reach for the same lens out of habit when they want to shoot close-ups. I use a variety of lenses. My decision on which lens to use is based on how I want to illustrate the subject.

It is fair to say that the vast majority of close-ups are taken with medium to long focal length macros, but don't overlook other lenses particularly in the region of 300mm. These lenses are often extremely useful at dealing with difficult backgrounds.

Background Control

One of the major factors that has an influence on the background is the angle of view of the lens. It determines the amount of background visible within the frame. No matter how good the subject is, the background can make or break the photograph. With longer lenses, you can be a bit more selective in where you place the camera; often a slight shift in position is enough to change the background appearance quite dramatically. It is always a good idea to take a few minutes and look carefully at the subject and what's behind it. Look for areas in the background that have a more uniform colour and try to incorporate these within the frame; they will produce a more diffused appearance. The aperture also plays a part in background control. Shooting at f/5.6 is going to look quite different than f/16. The latter will obviously give you greater depth of field, but make a lot more of the background, or distracting elements within it visible. Check carefully at the taking aperture to see how it will look when the exposure is made. You can usually pick up any distracting highlights at this point and carefully remove them. One of the worst scenarios is to be in what I call, the 'half-way house' position, where the background clutter is only partially in focus, but still sharp enough to be a distraction. Try to avoid this situation, either by switching lenses to a shorter focal length to bring it into focus or, using a much longer lens at a wider aperture, even if it means losing a little depth of field towards the end of the subject.

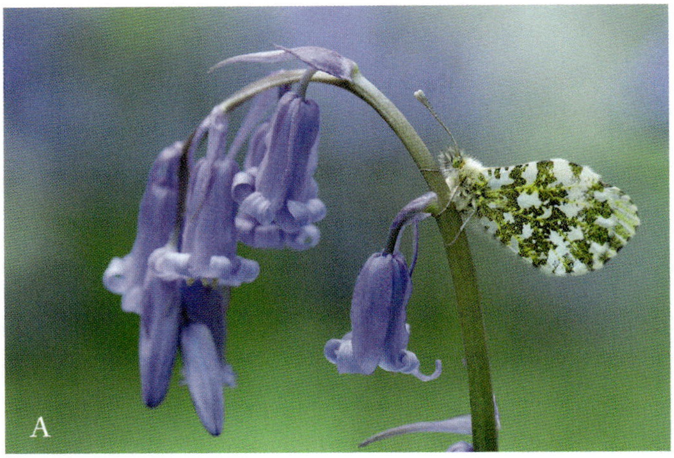

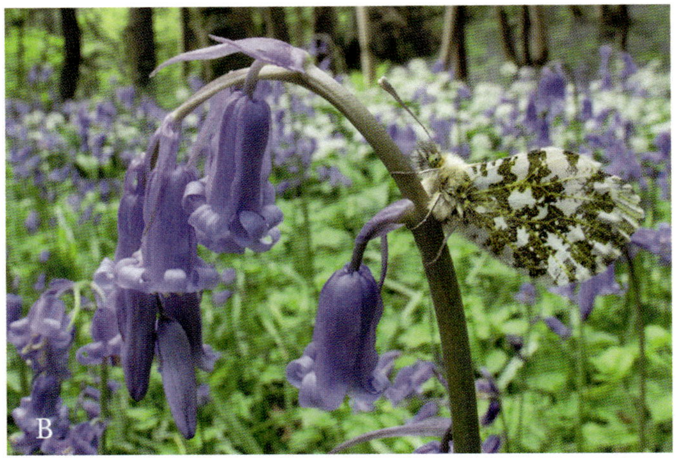

16.1 ~ **Orange-tip** *Anthocharis cardamines* (female)
Example showing how different focal length lenses at a similar magnification and aperture affect the final image and the background behind the subject.

↳ (A) Nikon D810, 200mm micro Nikkor, 1/15 sec at f/11, ISO 200 (left).
(B) Nikon D810, Laowa 15mm macro 1/30 sec at f/11, ISO 200.

Artificial Backgrounds

I prefer to photograph subjects in the field against their own natural backgrounds, where the light falling on the subject and the background are usually the same. Some photographers choose to create their own, both for the studio and outdoors. This is accomplished either by spraying different coloured paints onto a stiff card to replicate out-of-focus foliage or photographing vegetation by deliberately blurring it and then printing the result out on an inkjet printer. You can often tell the difference since the light often appears dissimilar on the artificial background when compared to natural foliage. Vegetation varies considerably in colour and shade; there are differences in the absorption of light. On a bright day, you can also get shadows appearing on the background, which detracts from the picture. There can be reflectance issues depending on how they are situated. It was also common practice in the studio in the past to photograph subjects against plain backgrounds, but this approach is very outdated now, and I don't recommend it. There is a greater emphasis now on photographing subjects behaving naturally in their own environments.

Bokeh

The word Bokeh is of Japanese origin and is a term used to describe the soft out-of-focus parts or blur of a photograph and how the lens renders the transitions between different parts of the image. It is especially evident in photographs that contain highlights in the background. Long telephotos and macro lenses are well suited for creating a soft diffused look to an image, and the technique is popular among photographers.

The aesthetic quality of the bokeh is largely down to the design and construction of the lens diaphragm. The greater the number of blades used in the construction the more rounded the aperture is; this produces a much smoother result. Many of the current macro lenses contain around nine blades, which produces a visually pleasing transition between components in the background. Other lenses, particularly those of earlier design, had less and were more angulated and not as

// FACING PAGE //

16.2 ~ **Sawfly Orchid** *Ophrys tenthredinifera*
Highlights in the background can make or break an image. It's important to check your depth of field preview to see how the final photograph will look? The bokeh in the background of this orchid has a nice smooth transition which is much more pleasing to the eye.

↳ Nikon D3X, 200mm micro Nikkor, 1/60sec at f8, ISO 100.

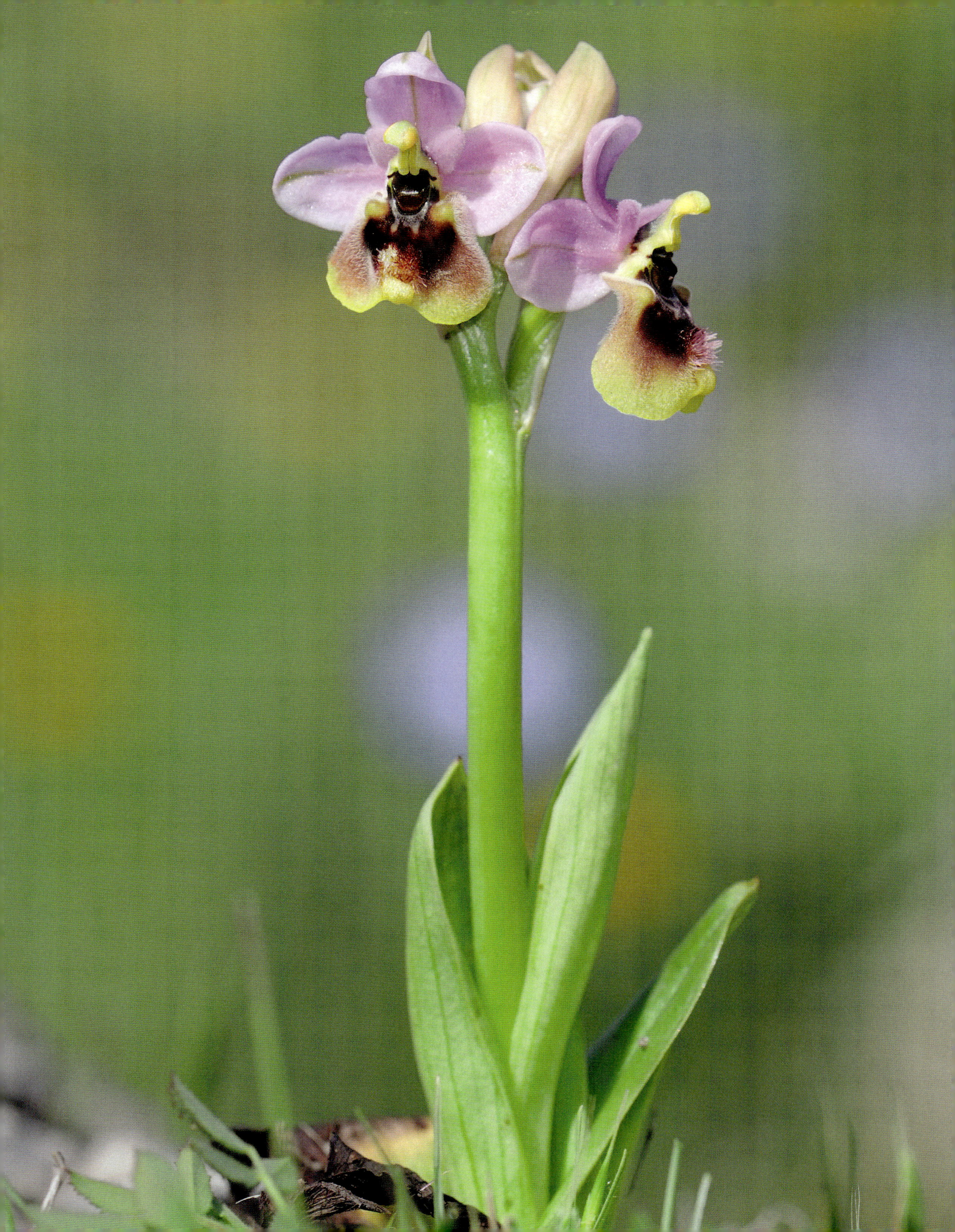

pleasing to the eye. Bokeh is most evident in those parts of the image that lie just beyond the depth of field. The light diffracts and produces a series of disc-like patterns that assume the shape of the selected aperture.

The technique for achieving good bokeh in close-ups is relatively straightforward. Ideally, you want to shoot at a relatively wide aperture of around f/5.6 or f/8. Use Aperture Priority mode, which will adjust the shutter speed but not the aperture. Try to have as much distance between your subject and the background. The shallower the depth of field, the more visible bokeh will be. One of the most popular subjects for illustrating bokeh in close-ups is flowers, especially when backlit by the sun. Using bokeh often adds softness and mood to an image, especially in situations where the background is not that photogenic.

Perspective

What determines perspective is the position from where you take the photograph. The perspective does not change when you switch to a different focal length lens; what alters is the composition, or framing within the viewfinder of the subject.

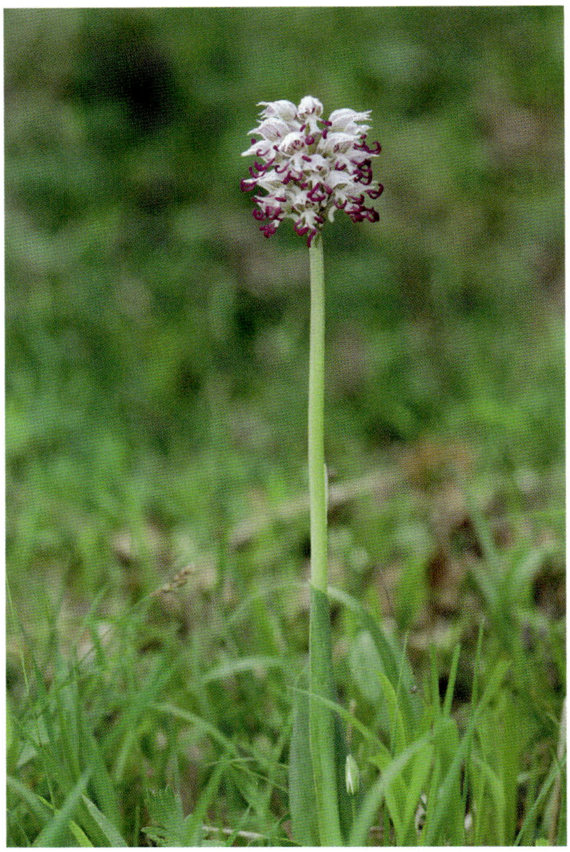

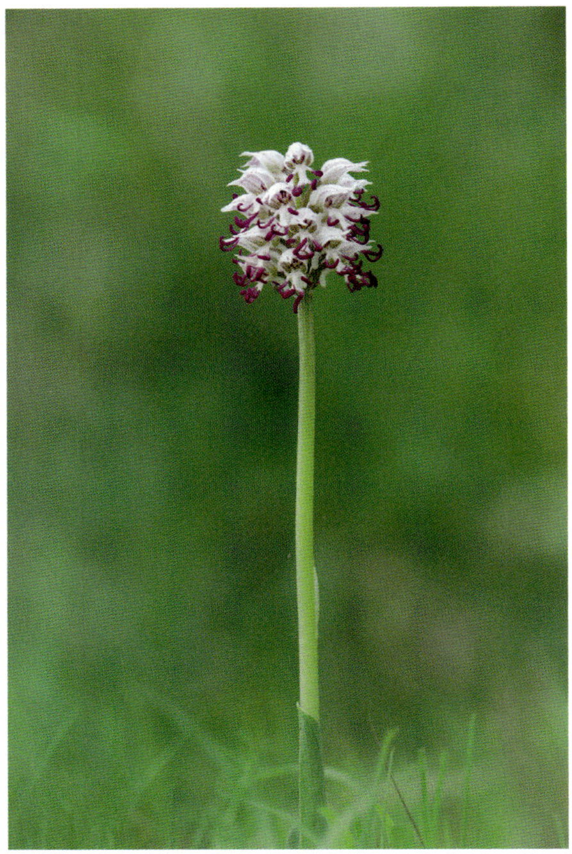

16.3 ~ **Monkey Orchid** *Orchis simia*
These two images illustrate the subject taken from the same viewpoint but the appearance of the background is different. The image on the left is shot with a shorter focal length lens at a smaller aperture, but the background is obtrusive. In the image on the right, I chose a longer lens, which gave me a greater working distance. I selected a wider aperture and allowed some of the taller vegetation in the foreground to blur creating a better balance between subject and background.

↪ (left) Nikon D810, 105mm micro Nikkor, 1/8sec at f/16, ISO 100.
(right) Nikon D810, 200mm micro Nikkor, 1/30sec at f/8, ISO 100.

SEVENTEEN

Custom-Designed Equipment

Macro photography has perhaps more do-it-yourself equipment enthusiasts than any other photographic discipline. Most of the accessories currently offered by camera and independent manufacturers are often too generalised. A few companies such as Nikon and Olympus had a more comprehensive range of macro equipment in the pre-digital era but many of these accessories were never updated. Most macro aficionados (myself included) found it necessary to modify, or fabricate something that was more specific to our needs.

Over the years, I have designed and modified all manner of equipment to make the process of capturing images less troublesome in the field. Some of my devices work very well, while others often require tweaking. Most of the equipment outlined below is particularly relevant to me and the way I work in the field. It may not be of use to everyone, but consider it a starting point towards making your own devices. I have omitted some that are specific to high magnification macro, which is entirely studio based.

All of the equipment outlined below is constructed from relatively simple components, most of which are easily bought from any good DIY store, or online. The equipment illustrated here is light, easily carried and quick to assemble in the field; this is important as you don't want to be battling with components that are going to take a while to erect and take down. I normally construct a prototype and test it for a while identifying where its good and weak points are then try to improve on the original device.

Flexible Stem Stabilizer

The wind is the bane of the macro photographer and one of the most difficult problems to contend with in the field. You can, with experience, get around most other issues, but a plant blowing about in the breeze is challenging to say the least. The Flexible Plant Stabiliser is one of my most important accessories; I never leave home without it. I've been using one for over twenty years; long before the Wimberley Plamp was around. The unit is quite easy to construct and especially versatile. The components consist of a long thin gooseneck; the ideal ones are about one centimetre in diameter and about 50 centimetres in length. Some come with a protective black plastic coating, which is ideal. An alternative is to spray the metal gooseneck black, which also works fine. The spike is a preformed hard plastic ground peg used to secure the ropes of a tent. They come in various sizes; select one that has a slightly larger diameter than the base of the gooseneck. It can be easily attached to the base with a strong resin glue.

The crocodile clip is attached to a small straight piece of wire; the round end of the clip is clamped around the top of the wire. The wire from an old coat hanger, or something similar, cut to about four centimetres in length is ideal. Fill the top of the gooseneck with resin or similar and put Vaseline on the wire, which is now attached to the clip. Embed it in the top and before it sets completely, rotate it slightly; this means that you can twist it round in the gooseneck to accommodate the position that it is bent in.

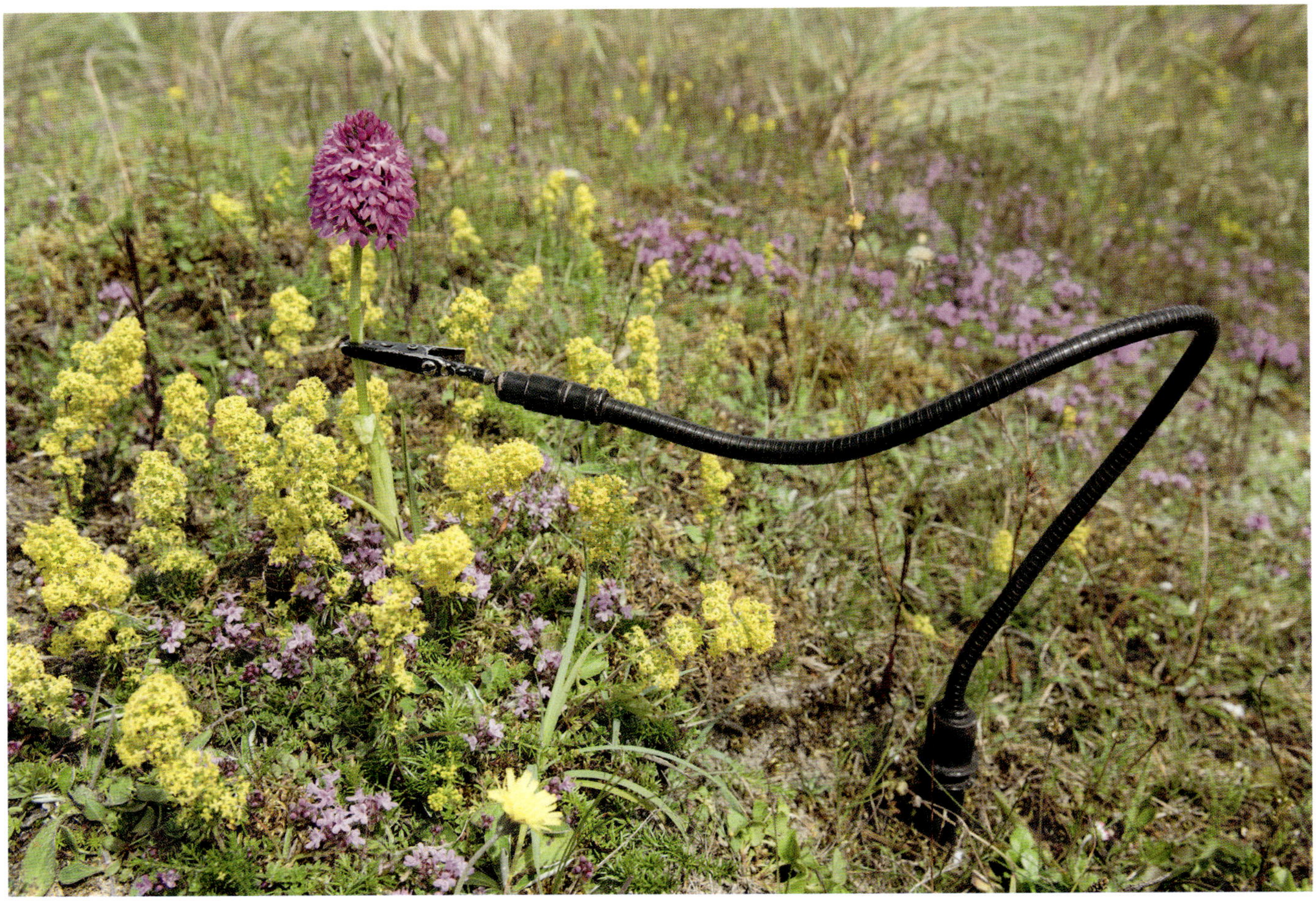

17.1 ~ **Pyramidal Orchid** *Anacamptis pyramidalis*
The stem stabiliser securing the stem of the Pyramidal Orchid.

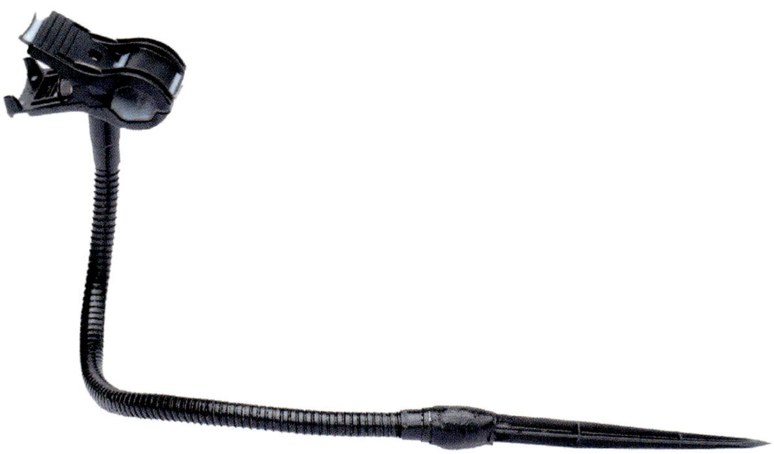

17.2 ~ Portable Flash Ground Spike. Useful in woodland situations when you need to position flash units close to the subject.

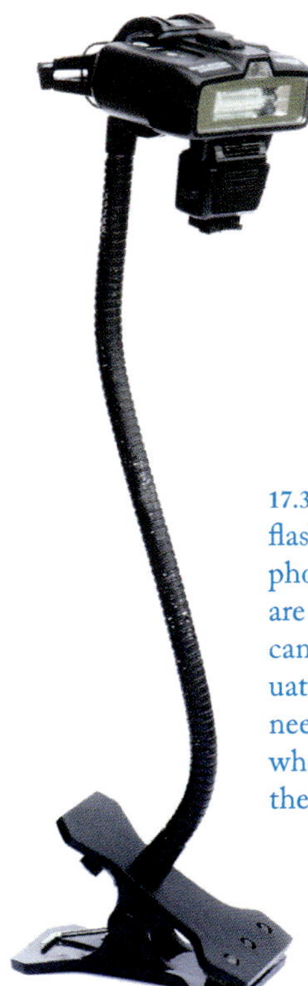

17.3 ~ Portable flexible flash clamp for rock pool photography. These units are extremely versatile and can be used in other situations where you might need flash. See page 262 where they are attached to the tripod legs.

The clip itself needs a little modification to ensure it does not damage the plant stems. The first thing you need to do is file the teeth flat and squeeze both sides together carefully with pliers to ensure they have an even contact. Next, you need to deactivate the tension in the spring; this will allow you to position the clip over the stem of the plant without decapitating it. Once this is done, you can then close the clip safely on the stem. You simply push the spike into the ground beside the plant and bend into contact. Adopting this approach means you have complete freedom to manoeuvre and position your tripod independently without the fear of snapping the flower stem. I have larger crocodile clips in various sizes to deal with the stems of fallen branches that contain different species of lichens and mosses. They are all interchangeable with the top of the gooseneck.

Having a stabiliser attached via a clamp to your tripod leg is not a good idea, in my opinion. If it's blowing a gale, then stay at home and pick another day. No device is going to make a difference in these conditions.

Portable Flash Ground Spikes

There are some situations, especially when working in woodland where you might need to position your flash guns much closer to the subject, or perhaps when you need to add additional light to the background. The difficulty is supporting them in the correct position. These portable flash spikes are a modification to the flexible plant stabiliser, where I have attached two Nikon flash holders supplied with the SB-R 200 macro flash units. These flexible arms allow me to place the flash units in any position I choose and their light output controlled via the commander unit supplied with the macro flash kit, or directly from the camera itself. They are really useful especially when you need a third hand.

Flexible Flash Clamps for Rock Pool Photography

One of the most challenging environments to work and photograph in is the seashore. You not only have the elements to deal with but the tide and frequently the difficulty of the terrain. Your equipment is exposed to a higher risk of potential damage from sand and the salty environment. It frequently involves very early and late afternoon sessions since you are at the mercy of the tides. Most of the photography at rock pools requires flash. Positioning them is often difficult and there is always a risk that they can fall into the water, which will destroy the units.

The flash holders are made from a pair of LED angle-poise lights purchased from a local DIY store. The light unit was cut off, and the wire stripped out. The bases have a spring loaded clamp which will clip onto your tripod legs. I secured a pair of Nikon clamps for the SB-R 200 series on top of the goosenecks. These would then hold the flash guns firmly in place. I can then connect the flexible flash clamps to the tripod legs (see page 262 (figure 38.13)). You can manoeuvre them into the correct position with the security of mind that they will not fall off. This approach allows for quick assembly and positioning when needed. The same units can also be used when working low down on rocks, for example when photographing lichens or other low-growing plants. You can practically use them in any situation where you require flash.

Portable Dark-field Unit

Dark-field illumination is very much a technique of microscopy, but the same light setup can be easily replicated in the field. The base unit is a laboratory clamp and stand with a black acrylic table. A square hole one centimetre smaller all round is cut out of the black acrylic top. Below this is a black acrylic base plate with the flash guns placed either side and angled upwards. The four sides of the mini tank are constructed out of five-millimetre-thick, transparent Perspex. The shallow tank is seventeen centimetres square by eight centimetres deep; this is adequate to cover most aquatic subjects. The two-millimetre glass is secured to the base with silicon. You can vary the depth of the water depending on the subject. The same setup can also be used for conventional photography of marine and freshwater subjects.

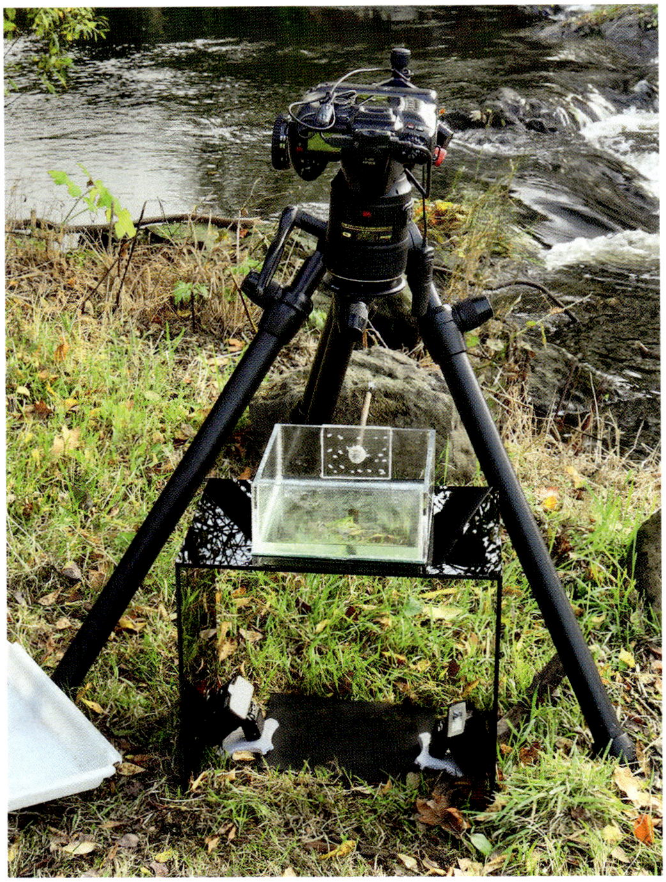

17.4 ~ Portable dark-field setup for freshwater and marine photography. The small square tank is deep enough to accommodate various sizes of aquatic creatures. See page 250 for example of damselfly larva.

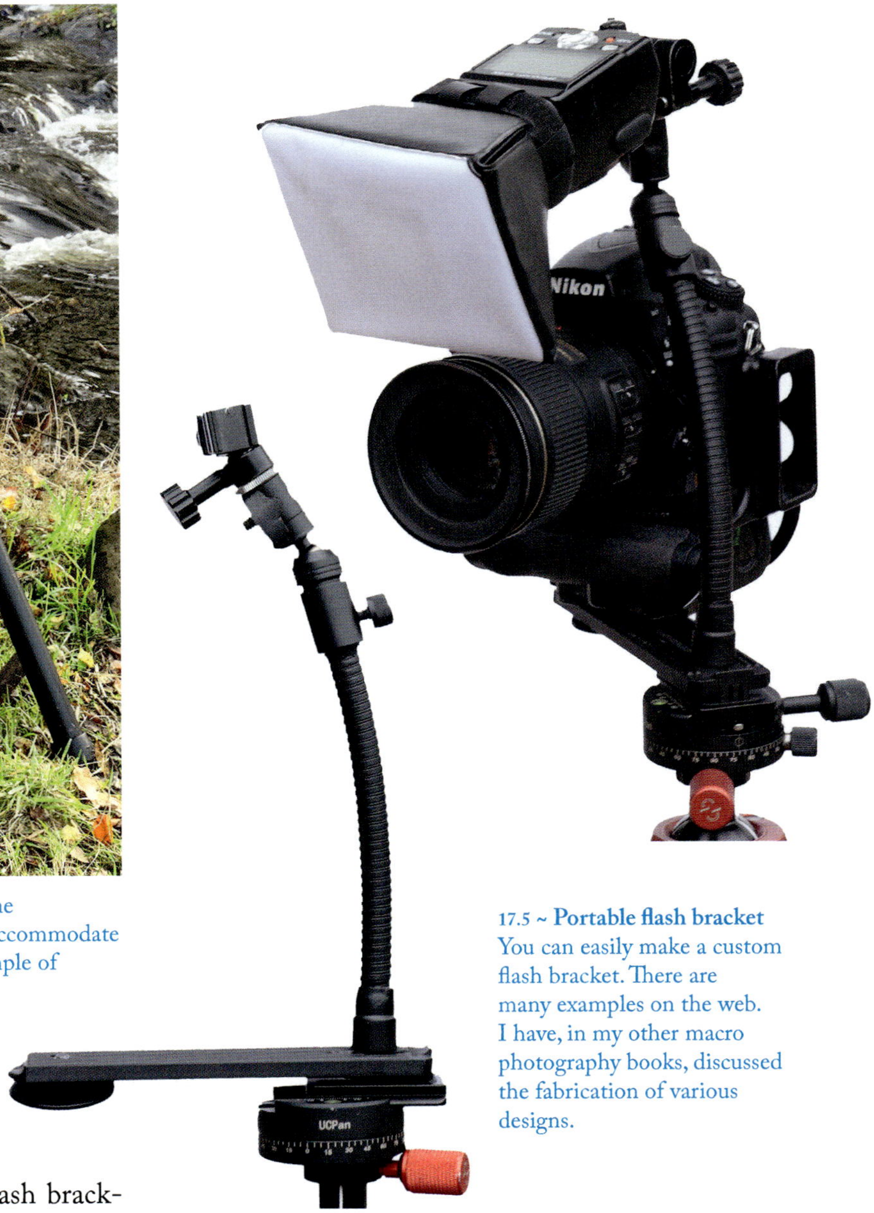

17.5 ~ Portable flash bracket
You can easily make a custom flash bracket. There are many examples on the web. I have, in my other macro photography books, discussed the fabrication of various designs.

Portable Flash Bracket

There are endless examples of commercial flash brackets available on the market. Most do not allow the flash unit to be positioned near the end of the lens, where the subject can be evenly illuminated. When I want to stalk insects using full flash, I currently use this simple home-made design. I find it very effective and when used in combination with a diffuser produces very acceptable results.

The base of the flash bracket is cannibalised from an old hammerhead flash unit. The gooseneck is the flash supporting arm and is approximately eighteen centimetres long and is secured to the base with a large, flat screw. A large universal hotshoe accessory is secured on the top of the gooseneck and tightened with a small threaded screw. You can pick up similar units online. Once the bracket is attached to the base of the camera body, it can be secured and tightened. The flash with diffuser is held horizontally at the edge of the lens.

// FACING PAGE ~ TOP //

17.6 ~ Black Leg Poison Arrow Frog *Phyllobates bicolor*
Photographed with the portable flash bracket.

↳ Nikon D3, 105mm micro Nikkor, 1/60sec at f/11, Flash, ISO 200.

// FACING PAGE ~ BOTTOM //

17.7 ~ Longhorn Beetle *Morimus funereus*
While running a workshop in Croatia, I came across this large longhorn beetle crawling over the bark of a log. The easiest way to deal with active subjects is to employ flash. It provides sufficient light and freezes movement. I used the flash bracket with diffusion.

↳ Nikon D3X, 105mm micro Nikkor, 1/60sec at f/11, Flash, ISO 200.

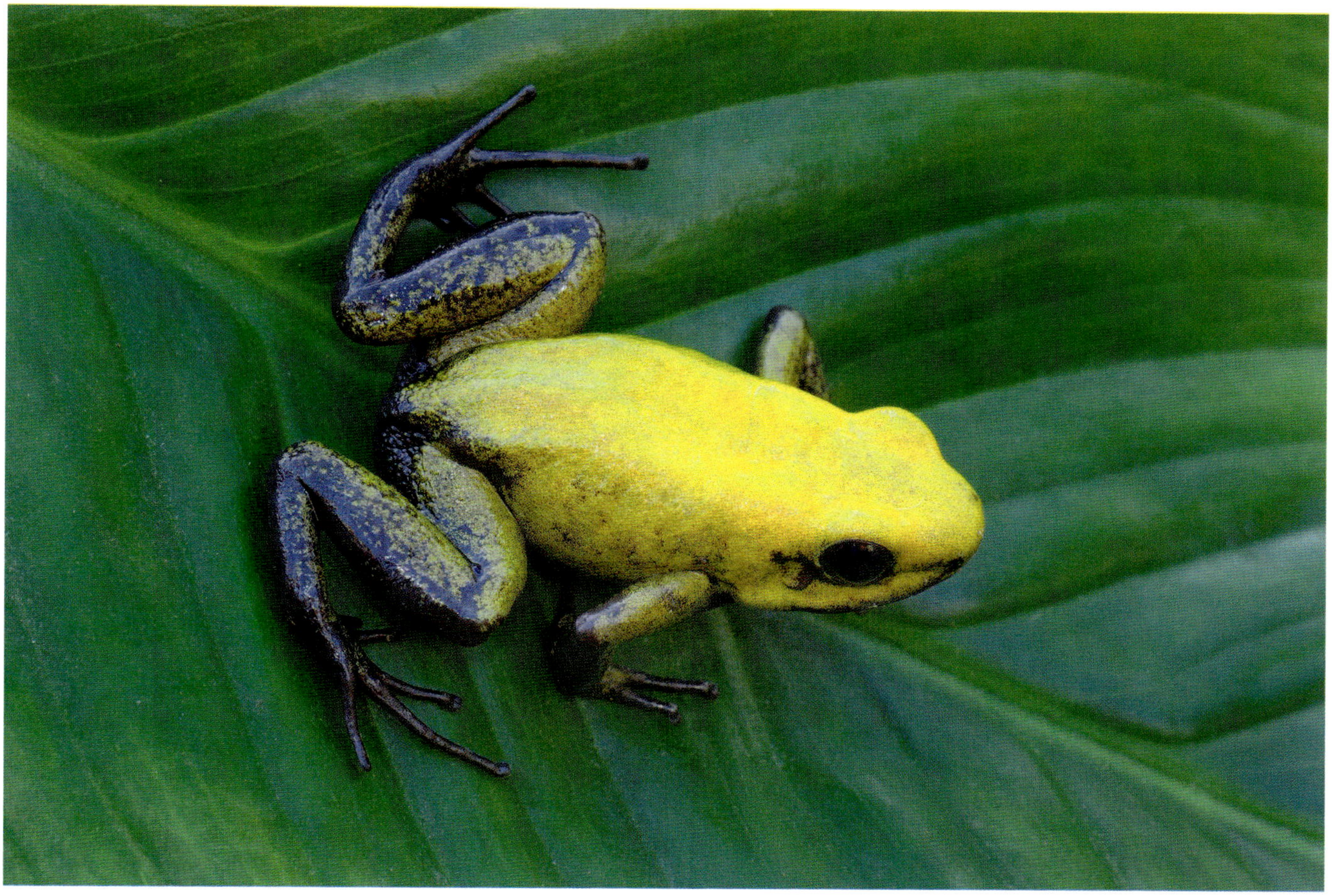

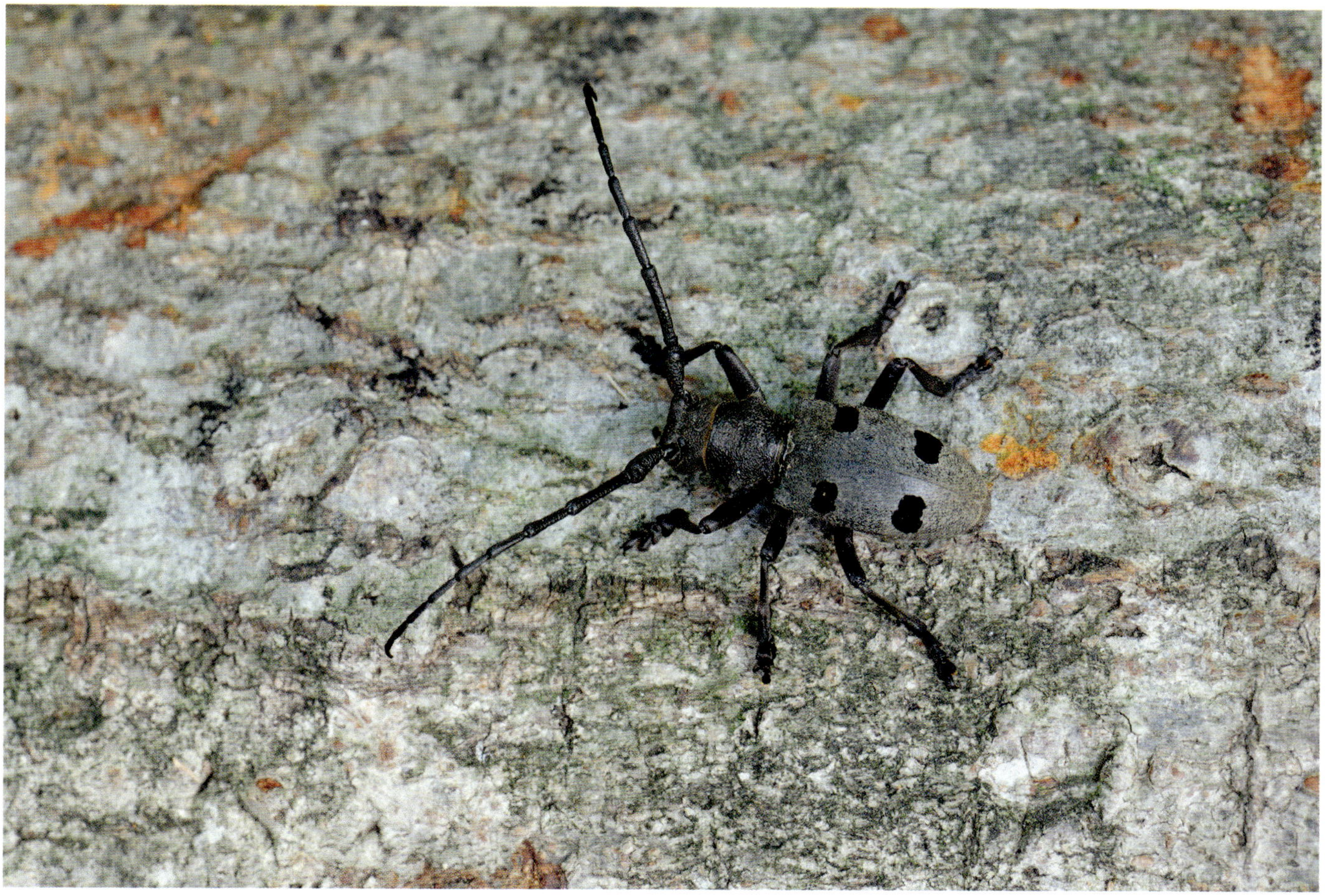

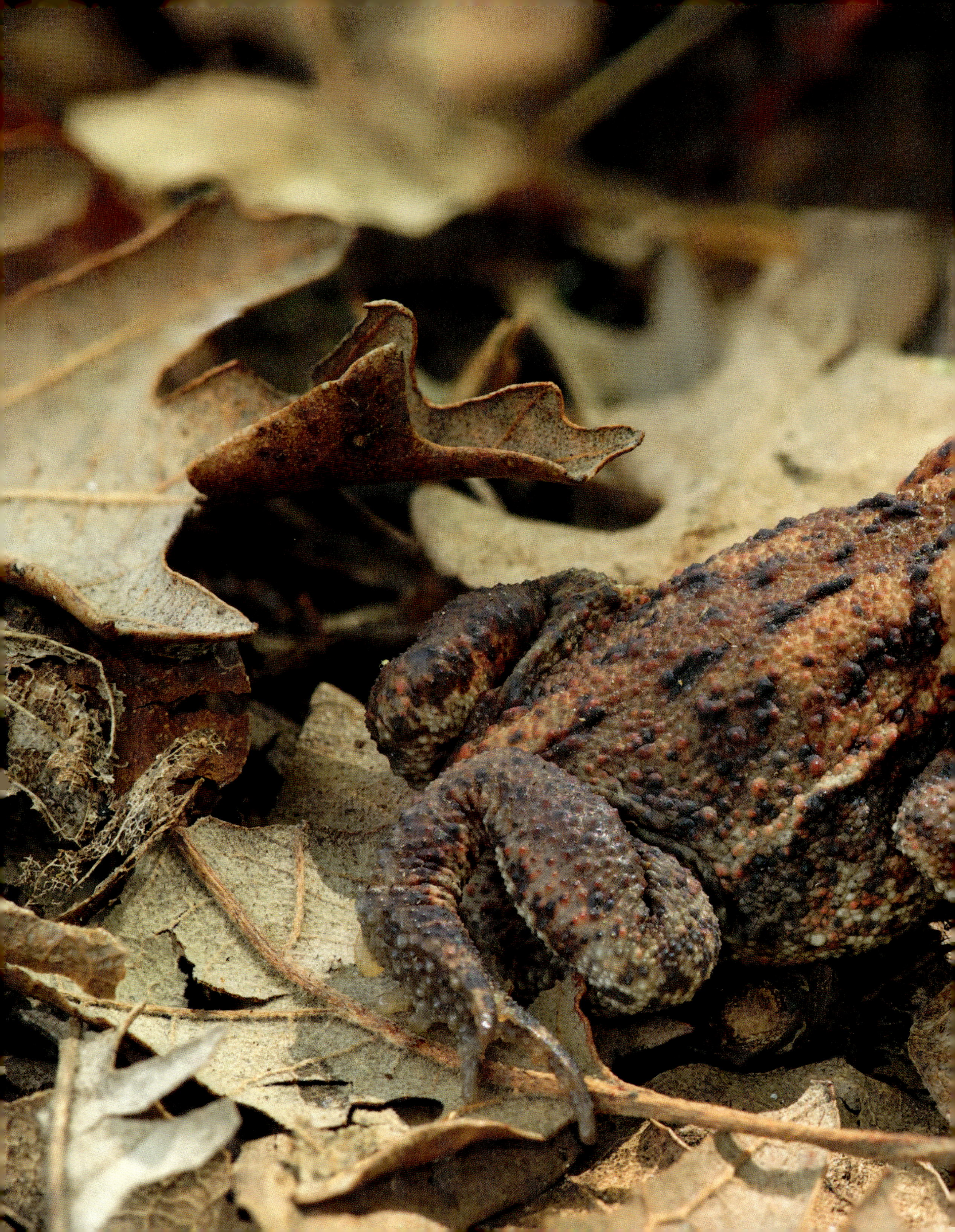

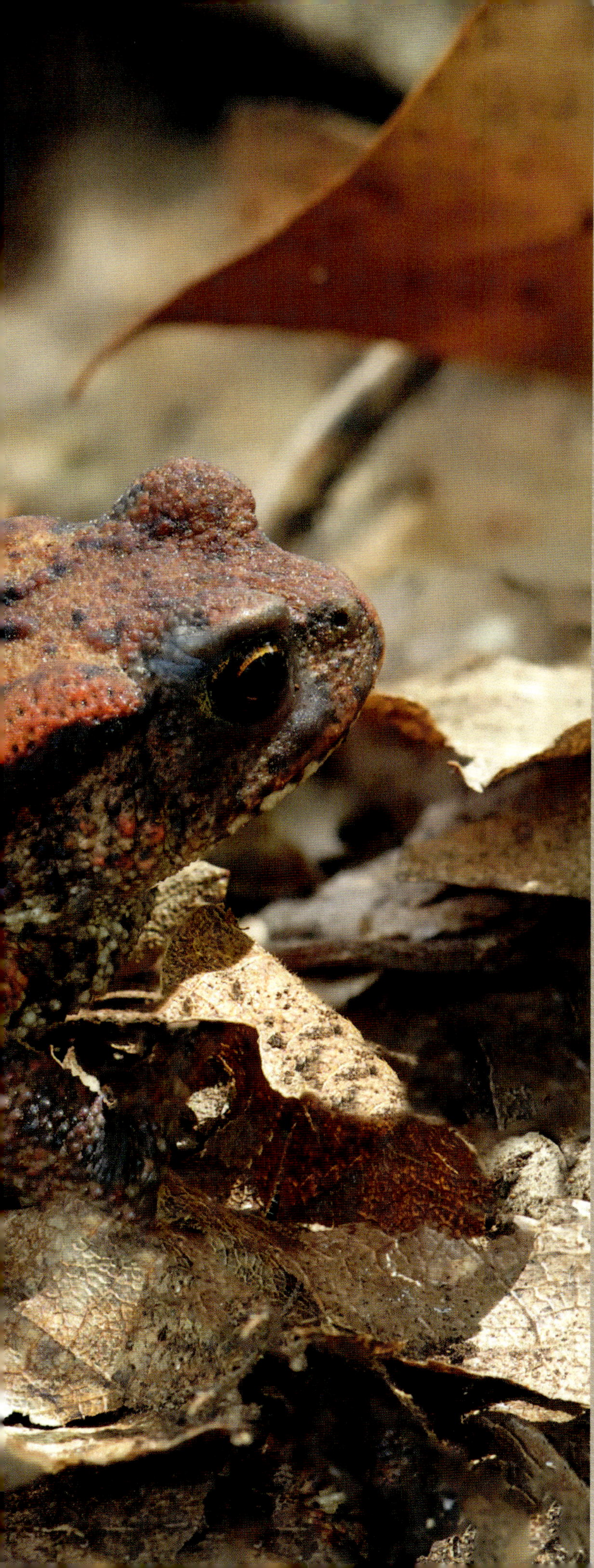

Part Two

Fieldcraft & Methodology

Common Toad
Bufo bufo

EIGHTEEN

Setting Up Your Camera for Macro

CAMERAS have become so sophisticated these days that many inexperienced photographers are often perplexed at the array of menus, functions and settings that appear before them on the LCD screen. To be perfectly honest, many of the settings are unlikely to be of use certainly in shooting close-ups. The terminology used to describe certain features may differ slightly between camera brands. Since I shoot with Nikon, I have outlined some of the features and settings that I consider are important. There are many others which are not essential.

Metering Modes

I use Aperture Priority for most of my macro photography, since depth of field is the important factor which I want to control. I switch to Shutter Priority when subject movement is an issue. Manual is my preferred choice when I'm engaging extended depth of field or where it's important to have continuity in the exposure of images.

Image Quality

One of the first decisions you need to make is the choice of format you are going to work in. The advantages and disadvantages of different formats have already been discussed. I only shoot RAW since it gives me the greatest flexibility when it comes to image manipulation and final appearance. I also select 14-bit lossless compression. If your camera has this option, then use it, if not then 12-bit. I don't see the need to record both RAW and JPEG formats. I prefer to convert my processed RAW files into JPEGs if required. The advantage here is that they include any modifications that were carried out in post production. Remember, unlike RAW files which are processed on your computer, JPEG files are processed in-camera based on the settings you have chosen. There is much less latitude with this format in terms of adjustment. If you do want to shoot JPEGs make sure you have selected the appropriate settings to provide the highest image size and quality.

White Balance

Since I only shoot RAW, setting a precise White Balance in-camera is not that critical as I can change the colour temperature in post-processing software. I rarely use any of the auto presets: I prefer to use a custom White Balance setting where I can set a particular colour temperature; this is usually around 5000K.

// FACING PAGE //

18.1 ~ Giant Waxy Monkey Frog *Phyllomedusa bicolor*

↳ Nikon D3, 300mm Nikkor, + ext. 1/60sec at f11, flash ISO 100.

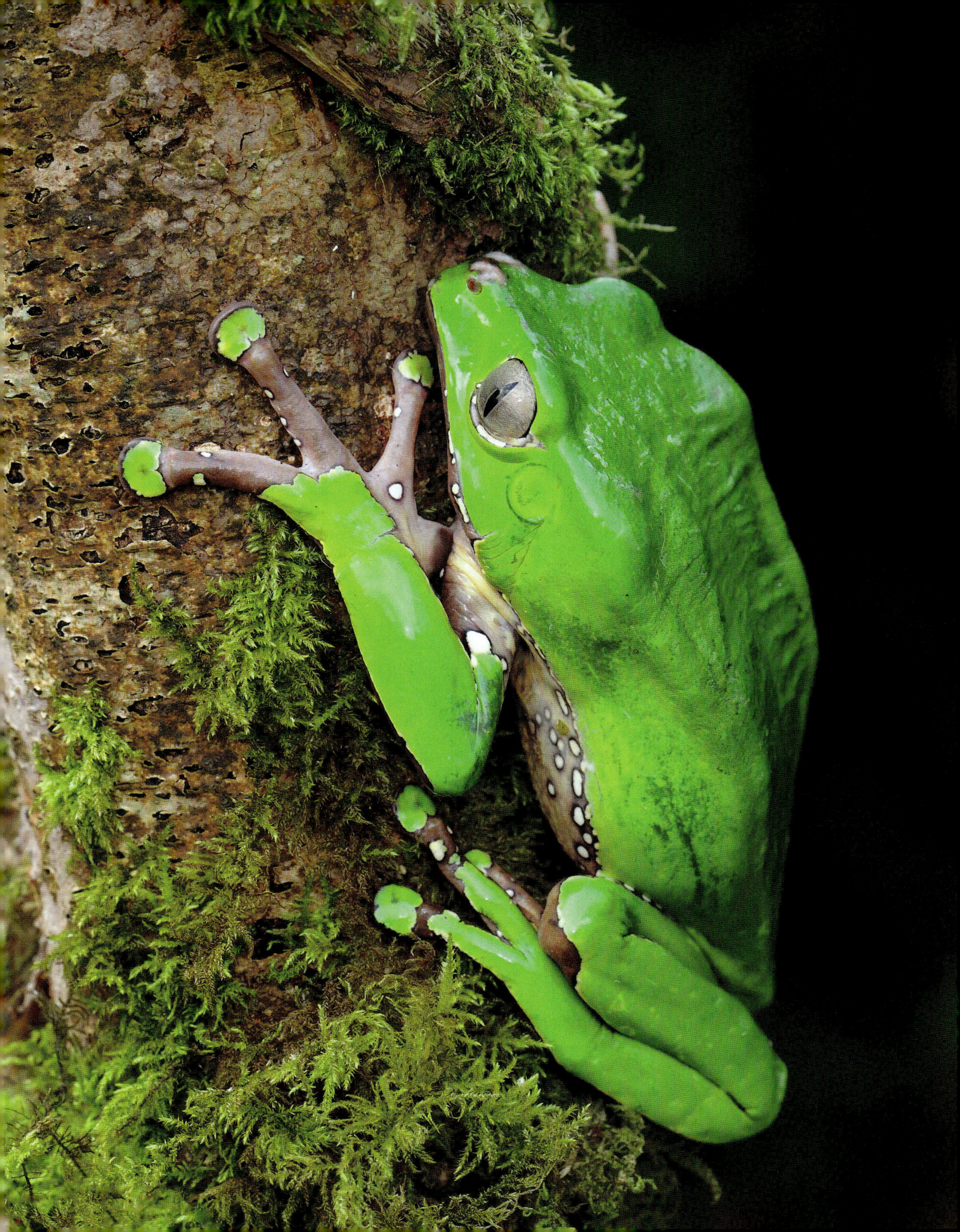

I have a few other custom settings programmed in for specific conditions, for example, photographing in heavily shaded woodland. One of the advantages of a custom White Balance setting is that you can make a modification to the colour balance and apply it globally to all of your images knowing that they will have the same colour value. On a preprogrammed setting this is not always the case since the colour temperature can vary between shots.

Colour Space

The options here are SRGB or Adobe RGB. Since I'm shooting RAW, I can always change the setting, but I have it set to Adobe RGB. If you're shooting JPEG, then SRGB is probably a better option, especially if you are displaying the majority of your images on the web.

Image Review

Make sure you selected this option so you can see your image immediately after shooting and access the histogram. Don't evaluate the exposure of your photograph based on the brightness of your LCD screen. It has nothing to do with the exposure, use it merely to evaluate the composition.

Playback Menu

There are a number of options here to choose from. Ensure that you have selected shooting data which will display all the various settings including shutter speed aperture, lens, White Balance etc. that have been used to take the picture. The highlight or blinkies option should also be checked, which will identify any areas within the image that are overexposed. The RGB histogram should also be checked.

Picture Control

I generally have this set on Vivid with some modification to the saturation levels. I can change this to standard or neutral if I choose depending on the subject.

Rotate Tall

Leave this option unchecked since it rotates the vertical images so you can view them with the camera in a horizontal position, which reduces their size.

Focus Point Wrap

I find this feature useful on some occasions when I'm composing a subject in the far left or right of the frame. If my focus point is in the extreme right of the frame and I need it to be on the far left rather than navigate my way back through each focus point you can simply advance it further to the right which brings it back to the left again.

Flash Sync Speed

Your maximum sync for flash is limited to the specification of your shutter, in most cases it is generally 1/250 sec and all speeds below this. Nikon has a setting called Auto FP or high-speed sync which you can leave on. The flash is discharged is a series of pulses but it does reduce the power of the flash. It has no bearing on the normal sync speed.

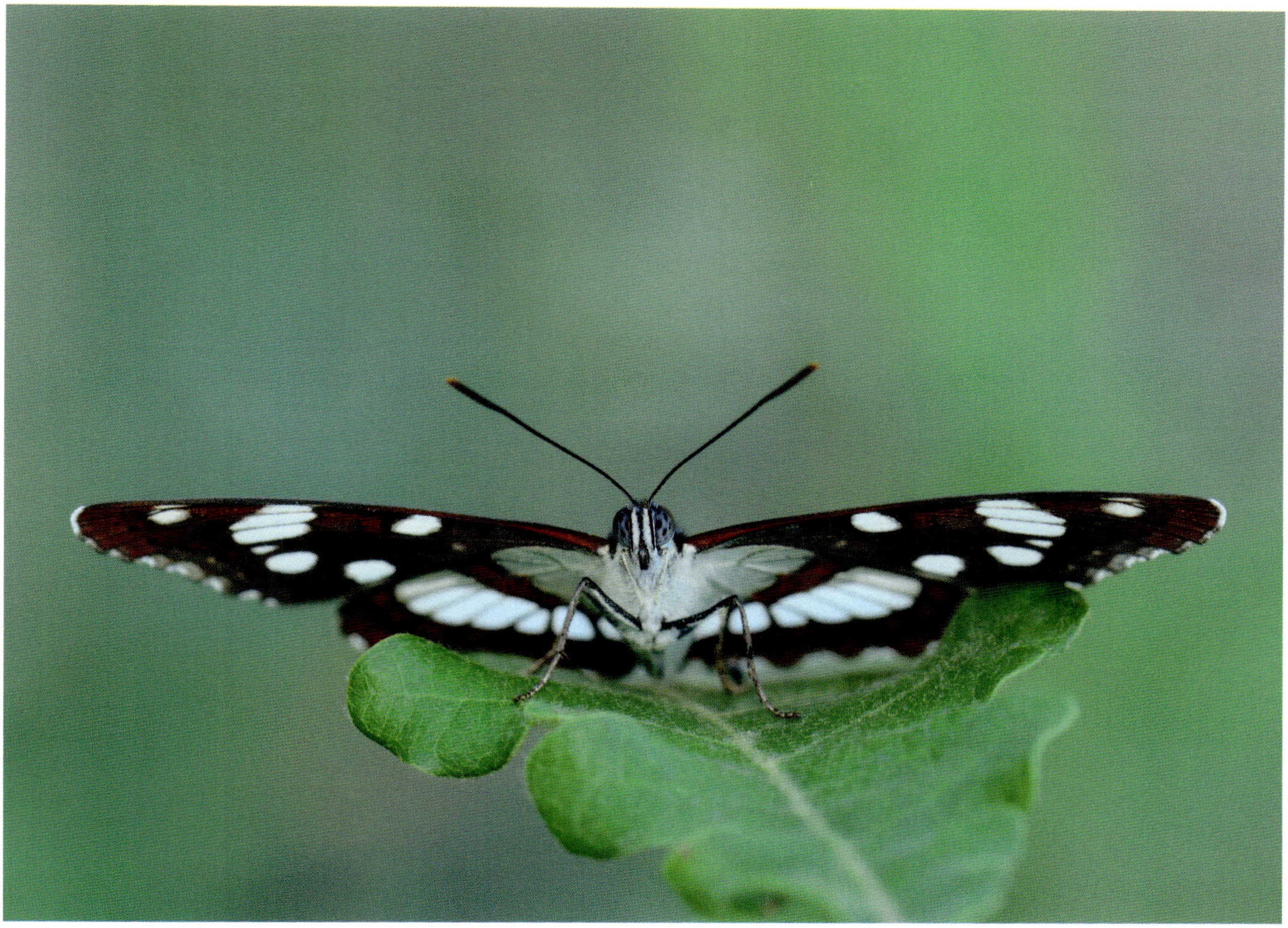

18.2 ~ **Southern White Admiral** *Limenitis reducta*
Don't be afraid to explore your subject from different viewpoints. I try where possible when working at slower shutter speeds to use mirror lockup whenever I can. Used in combination with electronic front-curtain shutter or equivalent in other camera brands reduces your risk of blur as a result of shutter vibrations.

↪ Nikon D3X, 200mm micro Nikkor, 1/15sec at f/8, ISO 200.

File Naming

If you are operating with more then one camera body you might want to differentiate between both. Nikon allow you to insert three characters that precede the file name so you can distinguish between both cameras. My D810 has my initials RST followed by the number, which separates it from the other bodies which have different characters.

File Number Sequence

I prefer to have this function set to on since the file number will continue from the last image taken in the card or when a new card is inserted.

Long Exposure Noise Reduction

I don't have this feature turned on as a rule. If I'm working in a heavily shaded wood and my shutter speed is greater that twenty seconds, I occasionally turn the feature on. It uses what is termed black frame subtraction where the camera records a second exposure of equal length, examines the noise and subtracts it from the first exposure. The problem is if your exposure time is doubled, which is ok if the subject is static but not so good if it's mobile.

Electronic Front-curtain Shutter

Working in close-up increases the risk of blur due to mirror or shutter vibrations as I have already stated. A focal-plane shutter consists of two curtains; the front curtain opens to start the exposure, and the rear curtain closes to end it. The risk of vibration increases at higher magnifications and slower shutter speeds. Many of the most recent cameras have what is termed, 'Electronic Front-Curtain Shutter'. When engaged in close-up work, it's a good idea to engage this feature along with mirror up. Bear in mind also that on Nikon cameras 'Exposure Delay Mode' helps to reduce blur caused by mirror bounce, but has nothing to do with blur caused by the camera's shutter.

Personal Menu

Most cameras have a custom menu which allows you to save a list of particular settings that you want to use or change on a regular basis. Rather than scrolling down through endless lists of functions you can save them to a custom menu which you can access in a few seconds. These are some of my frequently used settings:

- Virtual horizon
- Exposure delay
- Multiple exposure
- Long exposure noise reduction
- Lock mirror up for cleaning
- Clean Image sensor

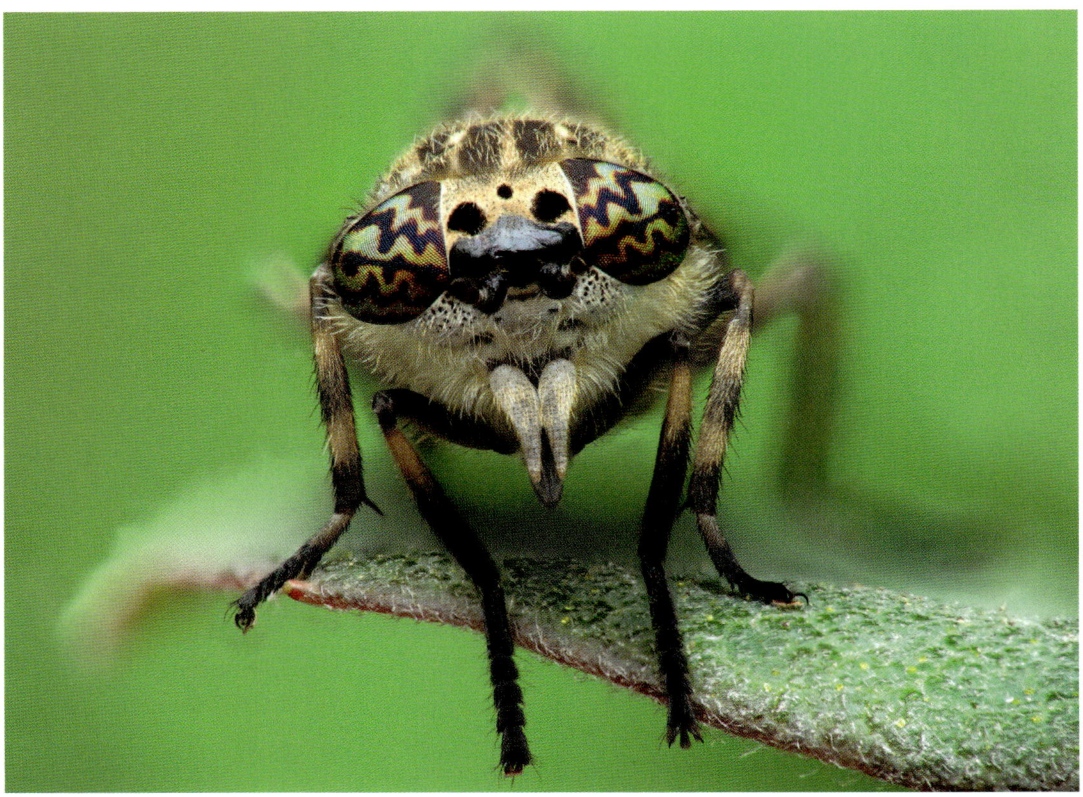

18.2 ~ Clegg Fly
Haematopa pulvialis
The risk of vibration and blur is always there, especially at higher magnifications. The electronic front-curtain shutter helps to reduce it.

↘ Nikon D810, 105mm micro Nikkor, + 1.7x converter. 1/60sec at f16, flash, ISO 400.

NINETEEN

Composition & Orientation

We all view the world from a horizontal perspective. It, therefore, seems rational that we routinely compose our photographs in a similar way perhaps more so out of habit than choice. Many subjects appear to lend themselves to this approach which probably accounts for its dominance, particularly in landscape photography. Horizontal compositions create a feeling of space and balance while vertical arrangements emphasise height and depth. We naturally view photographs from left to right, but we subconsciously analyse vertical arrangements usually from top to bottom. Those coming new to photography often find it more challenging to visualise and compose in a vertical format.

Exploring the world in close-up is somewhat different from what we perceive in everyday life. However, having said that, composition is equally important in the macro world as it is in other photographic disciplines. The formation of any photograph begins with evaluation; being able to recognise subjects that may have potential and to visualise those possibilities and how they might materialise into something tangible. Composition is more than merely arranging the principal elements within the frame. It is often complicated and frequently subjective. Explore subjects with strong lines and sweeping curves, especially those that run through the central portion of the frame. If we consider the relevance and importance of each component, its size and position within the overall configuration, we can significantly increase its impact on the viewer. In close-up photography, the subject is naturally the dominant component within the frame, but its impact can be diluted by peripheral elements which can be a distraction. It is, therefore, important to identify what is essential and eliminate the rest.

There are many philosophies regarding compositional etiquette. The 'Rule of Thirds' is perhaps the oldest and the most widely known in photographic circles; its origins can be traced as far back to the Ancient Greeks who employed the Golden Ratio, which is a close approximation to the 'Rule of Thirds'. It was also widely practised during the Renaissance period. The philosophy still holds true today and can be a useful guide in many situations. The concept focuses on subject placement within the compositional frame to create an aesthetically pleasing result. The basic principle behind the rule is the division of the image frame by two horizontal and two vertical lines producing nine equal parts. Where the lines intersect creates four key points. Placing the main subject, or part of it at one of these intersections is said to create a stronger composition with additional depth and impact visually. However, not every subject lends itself to this approach. It is there merely as a guide, but not to be slavishly implemented at every push of the shutter. The morphology and structure of the subject often dictate the choice of format. For example, long, slender-bodied insects such as antlions or damselflies and many plants are often better suited to a vertical composition or a slightly oblique arrangement. The vertical format may not be the most popular method, but it does dominate the publishing world. Just look at the many magazines and other printed media, and you can

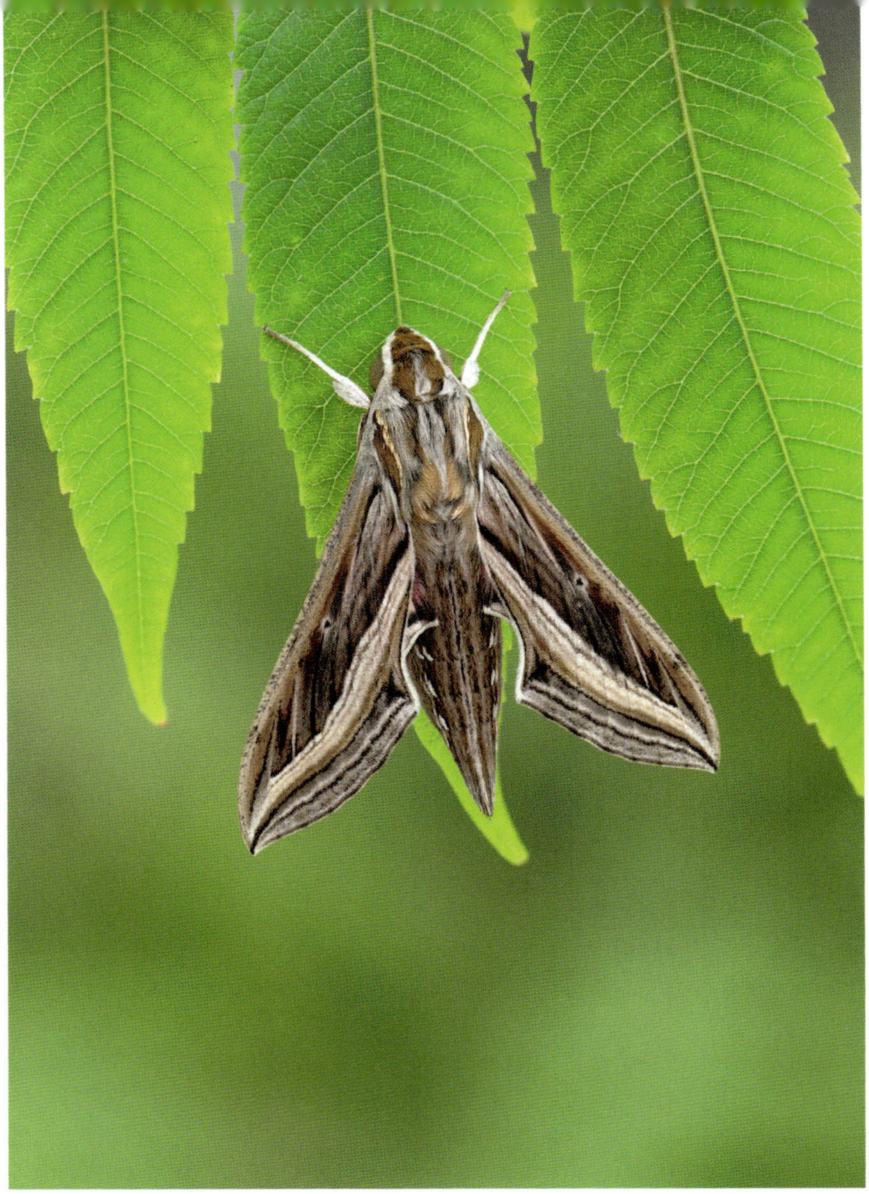

// THIS PAGE ~ TOP //

19.1a ~ Silver-striped Hawk-moth
Hippotion celerio
When you are unsure of what format works best explore both, even intermediate positions and decide later what suites the subject best.

↳ Nikon D800, 200mm micro Nikkor, 1/30sec at f/11, fill-in flash, ISO 200.

// THIS PAGE ~ BOTTOM //

19.1b ~ Silver-striped Hawk-moth
Hippotion celerio
Of the two compositional formats, I prefer, in this case, the horizontal version. Achieving a similar outcome vertically would mean a reduction in the size of the moth.

↳ Nikon D800, 200mm micro Nikkor, 1/30sec at f/11, fill-in flash, ISO 200.

// FACING PAGE //

19.2 ~ Double-striped Pug
Gymnoscelis rufifasciata
Placing the subject off-centre often produces a more visually pleasing result. The subtle colouring of reds and browns helps this species to blend naturally with its background.

↳ Nikon D3X, 105mm micro Nikkor, 1/15sec at f16, fill-in flash, ISO 200.

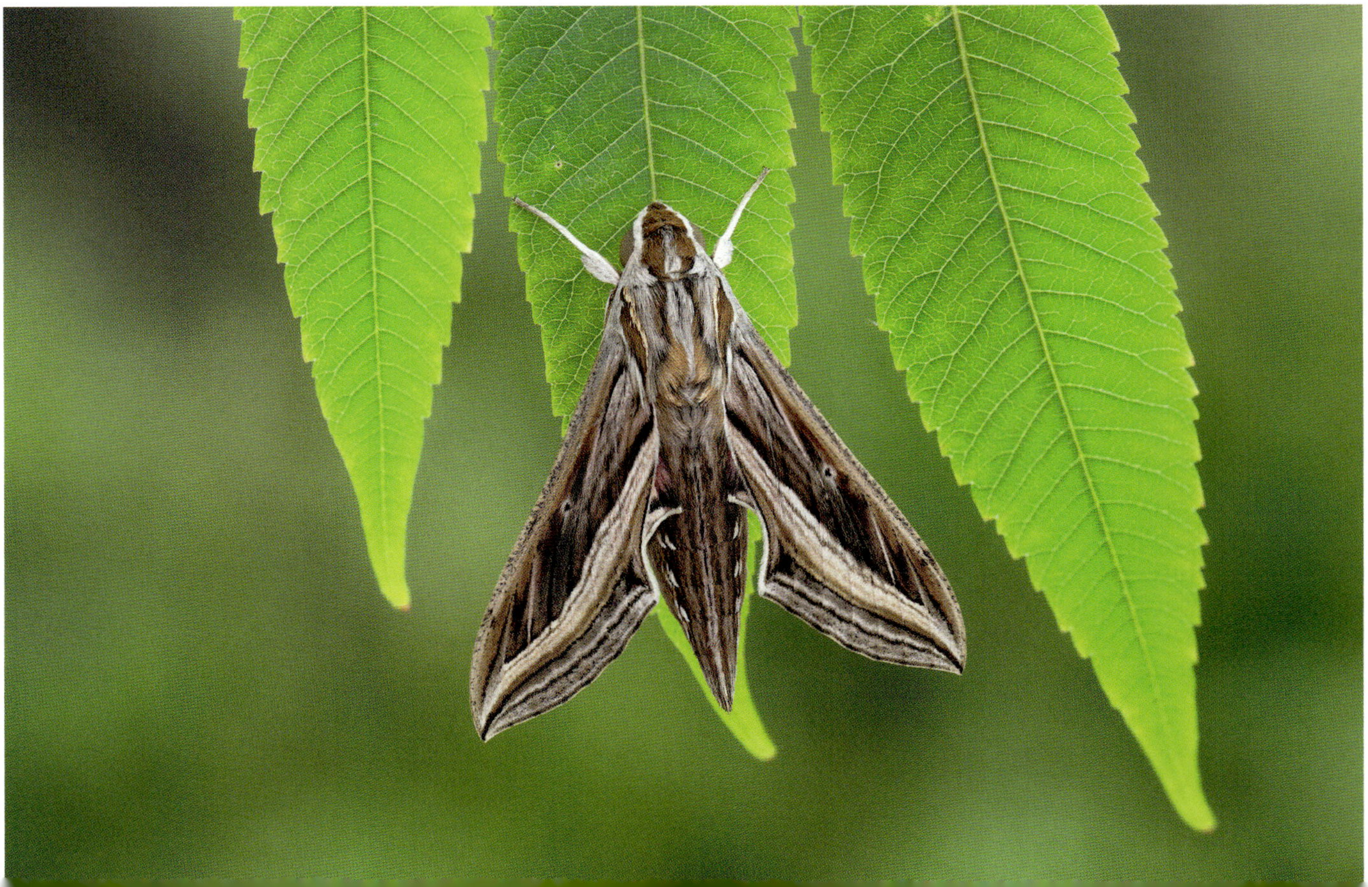

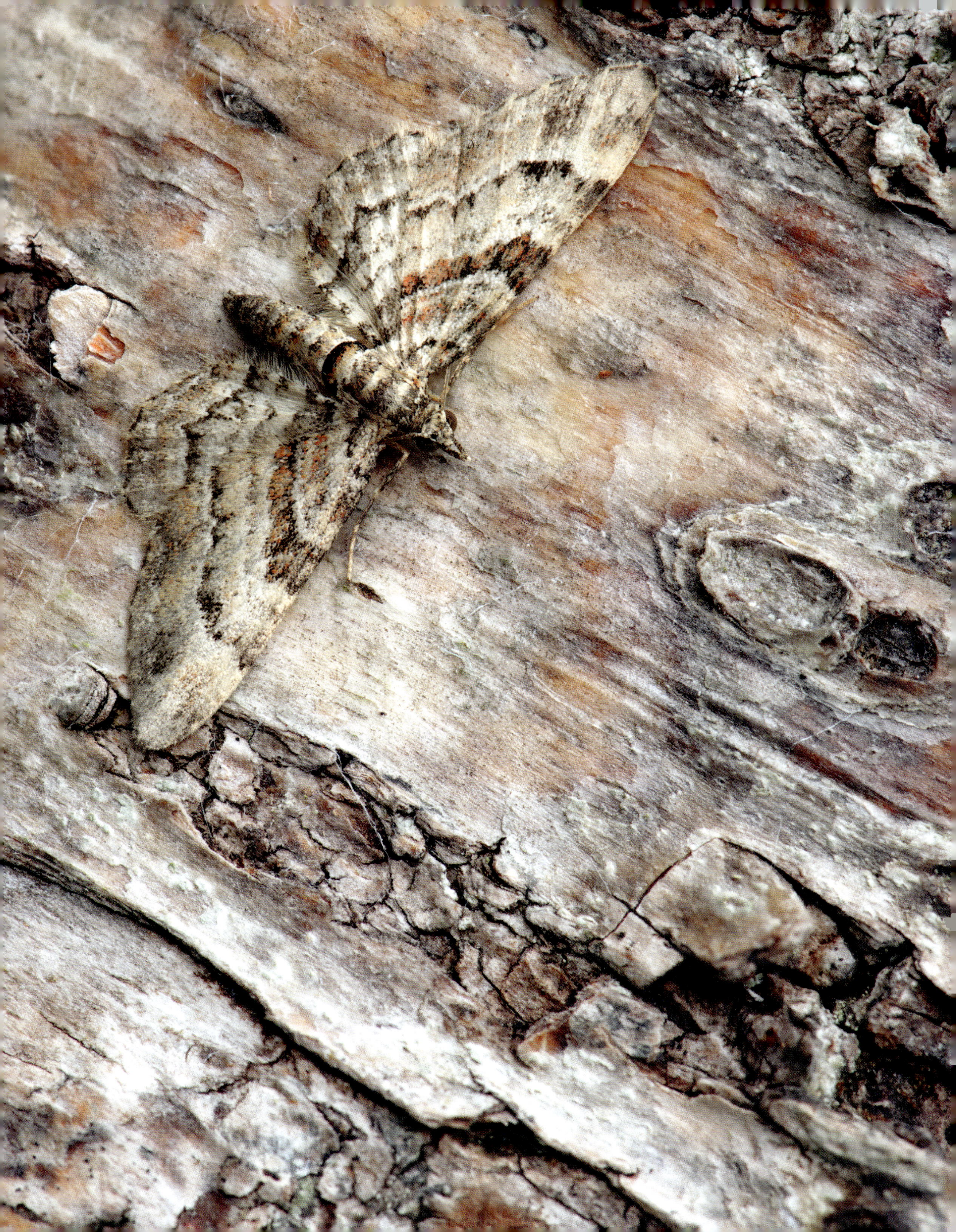

see why. Professional photographers providing stock imagery are well aware of this and do evaluate subjects in both formats. Normally, where a subject's length is longer than its overall width, it is usually a good indication as to the choice of format. Don't get too hung up on theories, with experience comes instinct; trust your own judgement; the anatomy and position of the subject are your best indication as to how you should frame it. However, don't feel that you must shoot every image in both formats, there are many intermediate positions. I frequently compose between the two, depending on how the subject is resting. A wide range of DSLRs have a grid system which you can access in the menu bank. Some photographers find it a useful aid when composing and leave it on all of the time.

Understanding Positive and Negative Space

Positive and negative space is another concept that has been associated with the art world for hundreds of years. It's also a frequently used term in the photographic world and if applied correctly, can improve the impact of your photographs. Positive space is the subject itself; negative space is the remaining area within the frame either side of the subject. Negative space is that part of the compositional structure that frequently receives less attention, but its importance in the overall balance of a photograph is often underrated. If used correctly, negative space can significantly strengthen and enhance an image; it also defines and accentuates the main subject while at the same time controlling the attention of the viewer. Although there are no clear distinctions about the association between positive and negative space, or how much of the compositional frame each should occupy, both need to be considered when composing an image for it to be effective. Placing the subject in the centre of the frame is not the most creative approach since it splits the negative space diluting its effectiveness. Lateral or asymmetric placement in most cases offers greater potential and generates more visually pleasing photographs with greater impact. The origins of many strong graphic images stem from this approach.

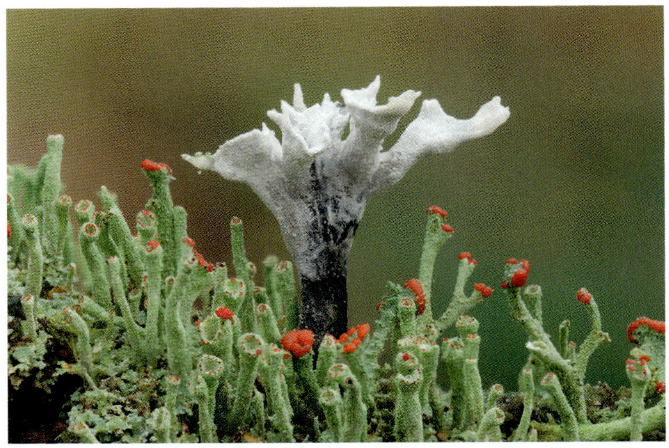

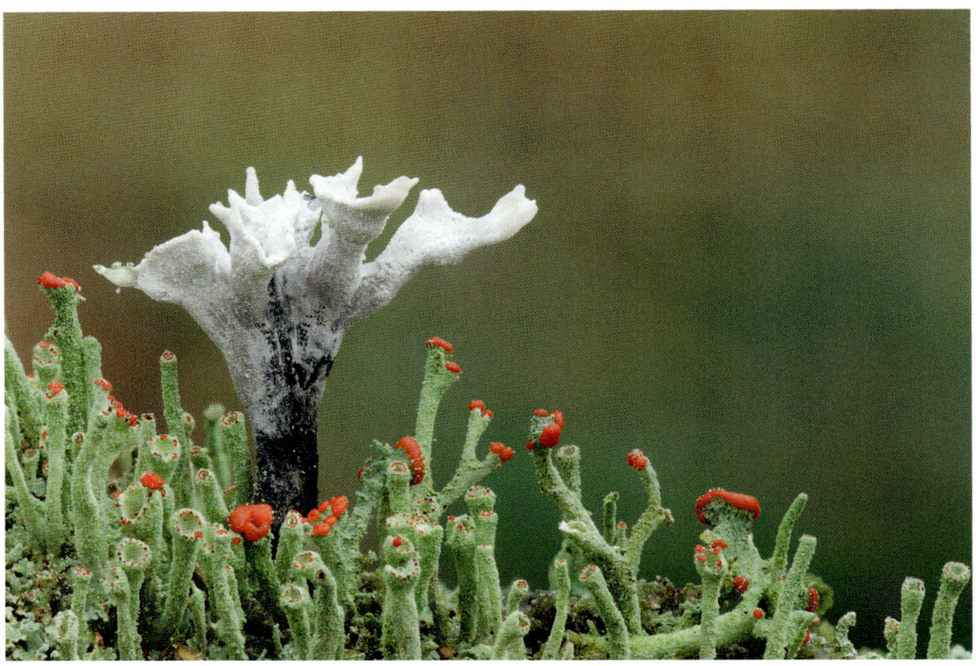

19.3 ~ **Candlesnuff Fungus**
Xylaria hypoxylon & Cladonia coccifera
Where you position the subject within the frame has an important bearing on the balance and impact of an image. Placing the subject in the centre does not necessarily produce a well balanced picture in every case. Asymmetric placement often produces images which work in harmony with the surrounding negative space giving a more pleasing result. I personally prefer the image where the subject is placed off centre.

↘ Nikon D810, 200mm micro Nikkor, 1/8sec at f/16, ISO 200.

TWENTY

In the Field

PHOTOGRAPHING in the field brings its own challenges. In addition to mastering your camera and techniques, you have to contend with other factors that can affect the end result, such as light, weather and the unpredictability of the organisms themselves. It can be a bit overwhelming at the start for those photographers coming fresh to macro. Initial enthusiasm can often override any methodical approach. There is a lot to take in, and it's better to focus your attention on one aspect initially until you become proficient with your techniques; this will increase your confidence and hopefully lead to better photographs. It's a good idea to have an objective in mind and focus on it rather than trying to cover everything that moves.

Despite the challenges, seeing and photographing your quarry in its natural environment is still the best option for many reasons. First of all, they are in their biological habitat and are likely to behave in a more natural way. Photographing creatures in artificially contrived settings is often more challenging for the photographer as well as the subject and when stressed they are less likely to behave in a natural manner.

Working a Subject

Most photographers are familiar with this term, but how many actually take the time to explore a subject methodically. In the majority of cases shooting close-ups of active creatures means you have little time to evaluate the situation or take multiple images from various locations. The majority of photographers are usually happy if they manage to get in close, maintain focus and get one good representation of the subject, even if it is from the standard position. However, having said that, there are many occasions where you will have time to evaluate your subject from different positions and with other lenses. I have often seen photographers shoot a series of images from one location without even looking at another, making the assumption that they have covered the species. I have on many occasions proved to myself that exploring other options and positions often produces a better result. Sometimes the difference is marginal, but there are times when it is not, and I was glad I kept my options open. You can't, of course, apply it to every situation, but there are many situations where you can, and you should get into the habit of doing so. A good example might be, instead of reaching for the same lens, to use a wide angle or a longer telephoto. Try exploring the subject head-on or from the side. Slow down, take the time to examine the subject, look at its position and the background and most importantly the direction of the light. Also check its condition. Photography has a habitat of highlighting any damage or wear sustained by specimens or flowers. I would usually avoid species, for example, that had damaged wings or blemishes on the flower heads unless it happened to be rare.

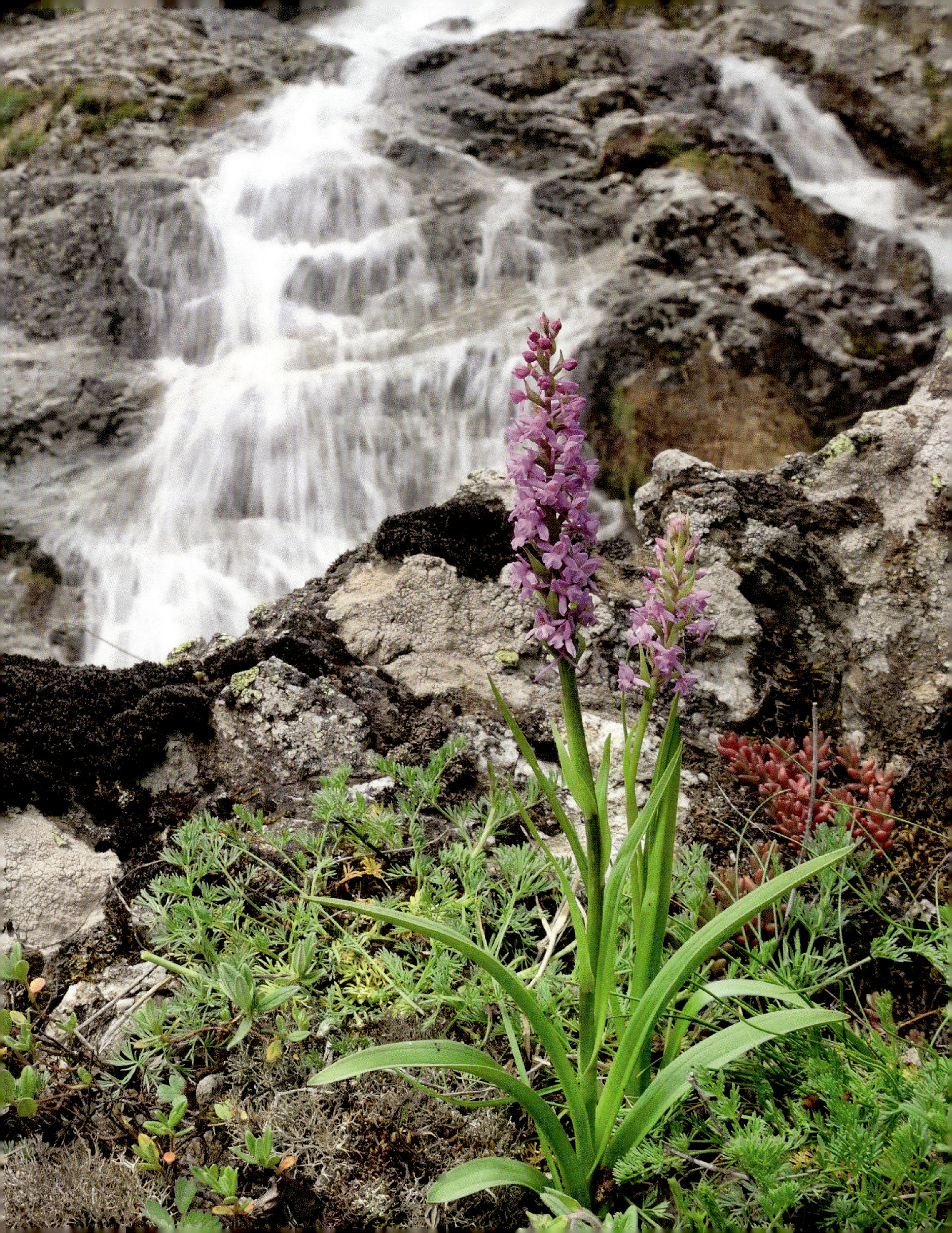

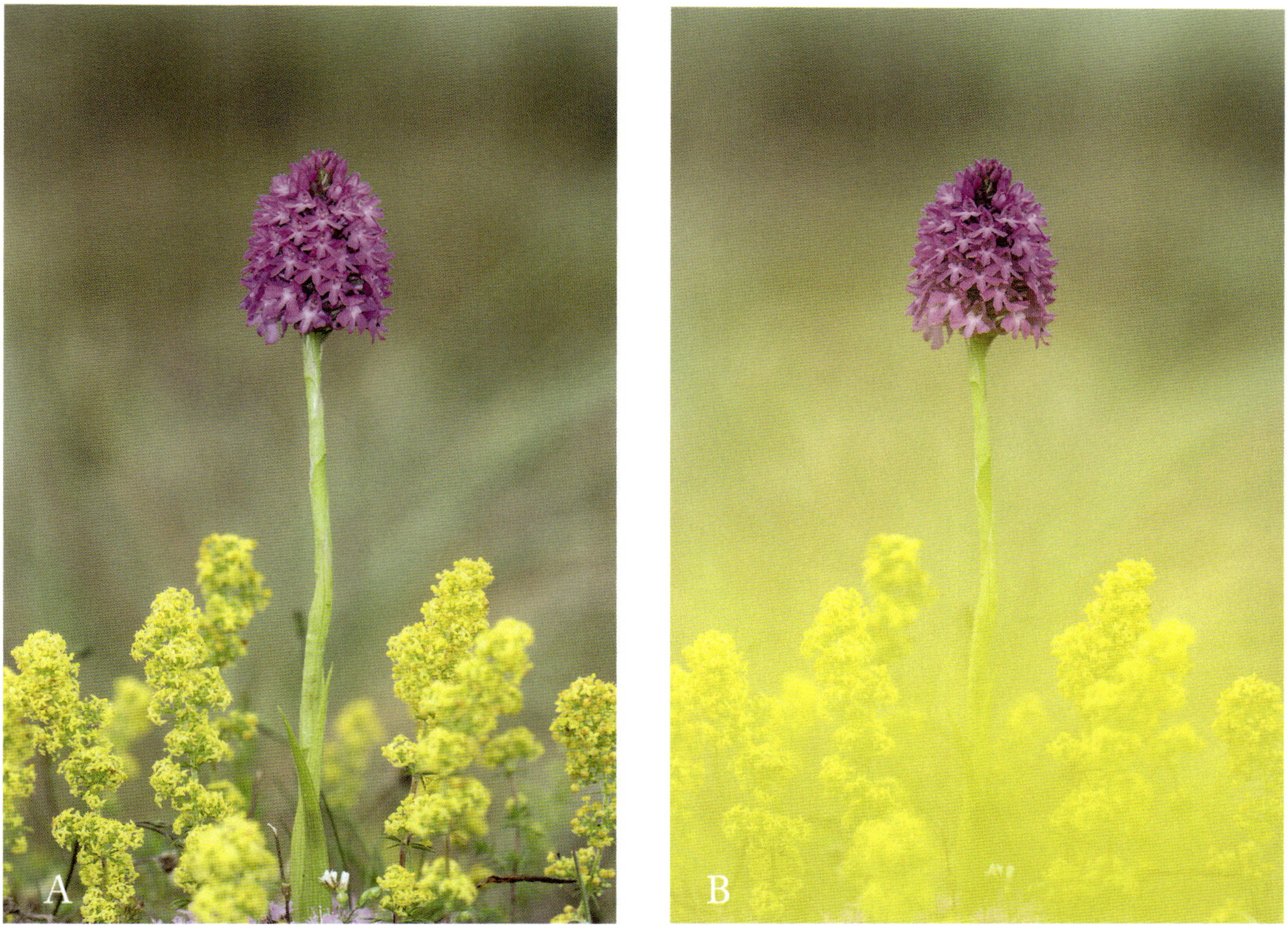

20.2 ~ **Pyramidal Orchid** *Anacamptis pyramidalis*
(A) Conventional approach.
It is easy to fall into the trap of analysing and photographing every subject in the same manner.
(B) Impressionistic approach.
Using a little imagination and shooting at a wider aperture through the bedstraw flowers in the foreground produced a different result.

↘ (A) Nikon D810, 200mm micro Nikkor, 1/30sec at f11, ISO 200.
(B) Nikon D810, 200mm micro Nikkor, 1/125 sec at f5.6 ISO 200.

// FACING PAGE //

20.1 ~ **Fragrant Orchid** *Gymnadenia conopsea*
Don't restrict yourself to a couple of lenses. Explore the subject with other lenses such as a wideangle especially if the backdrop is interesting as in this case.

↘ Nikon D800, 24mm PC-E Nikkor, 1/30sec at f16, ISO 200.

Scientific and Artistic Approaches to Image Capture

There are many different methods and approaches to photography. One topic that frequently comes up in conversation is the scientific and artistic approaches to macro. Both have equal merit, and it's up to the photographer as to how he/she would like to illustrate the subject. The scientific approach is frequently used in natural history publications and field guides. Photographs tend to show the whole or the salient parts of the subject in sharp focus and frequently in the context of their environment. The artistic or impressionistic approach is centred around pictorialism, which focuses on aesthetics and the emotional impact of the image which takes precedence. Creative lighting and shallow depth of field is often the trademark of this approach. It has in recent times become extremely popular among photographers. Flower photography is perhaps the best example in the macro world where pictorialism is best illustrated. I like to shoot both styles and have a need for accurate representation of the subject as well as an impressionistic approach.

TWENTY ONE

Wide-angle Macro

SINCE the digital revolution, macro photography has increased in popularity not only among nature photographers but also those people who want to explore the close-up world, be it in their garden or further afield. Digital technology has made it relatively easy these days to get acceptable images even with modestly equipped compacts. Wide-angle or Environmental Macro as it's sometimes called is a less known genre of conventional macro photography, but one that is gaining popularity among photographers. The concept is to show the subject in close-up and in context with its natural habitat, unlike traditional macro photography where the focus in on the subject and not its environment. This is a brief overview of the technique; there is not the space to cover it in-depth. There are many interesting articles on the web describing wide-angle macro in detail. There is also an excellent e-book on the subject written by two well-acknowledged and experienced exponents of this technique. See 'Additional Resources' at the back of this publication for more information.

Which Lenses Work Best

Wide-angle lenses are not commonly associated with close-up photography in the traditional sense, but they can be used to great effect showing the subject in relation to its environment. I have used them for many years in my work employing their increased field of view to set the subject within the context of its habitat. There are a broad range of lenses from fixed focal lengths to zooms which can be used for this technique. Some are better suited to wide-angle macro than others, but to get the best from them, you need to be aware of the characteristics of your lenses, such as the minimum focusing distance, maximum reproduction ratio and the working distance. In practice, your working distance between the lens and subject is going to be extremely tight and in some cases will be difficult to light the subject adequately.

There are a good selection of lenses currently available from well-known brand names and independent companies. Most photographers usually own at least one wide-angle zoom, which are often expressed in terms of their power; therefore, a 24–70mm is defined as a 3X zoom or a 12–24mm as a 2X zoom. Wide-angle zooms vary greatly when it comes to minimum focus capability, and this is the important aspect that you need to consider. Those in the short focal range such as the 10–20mm, 12–24mm or 14–24mm tend to have the best overall close-focus performance.

// FACING PAGE //

21.1 ~ *Orchis mascula* **var.** *tenera*
Much information can be gleaned about the habitat of a species if shot with a wideangle lens. It sets the species in context with its environment.

↝ Nikon D2X, 24–70mm Nikkor, 1/15sec at f11, ISO 100.

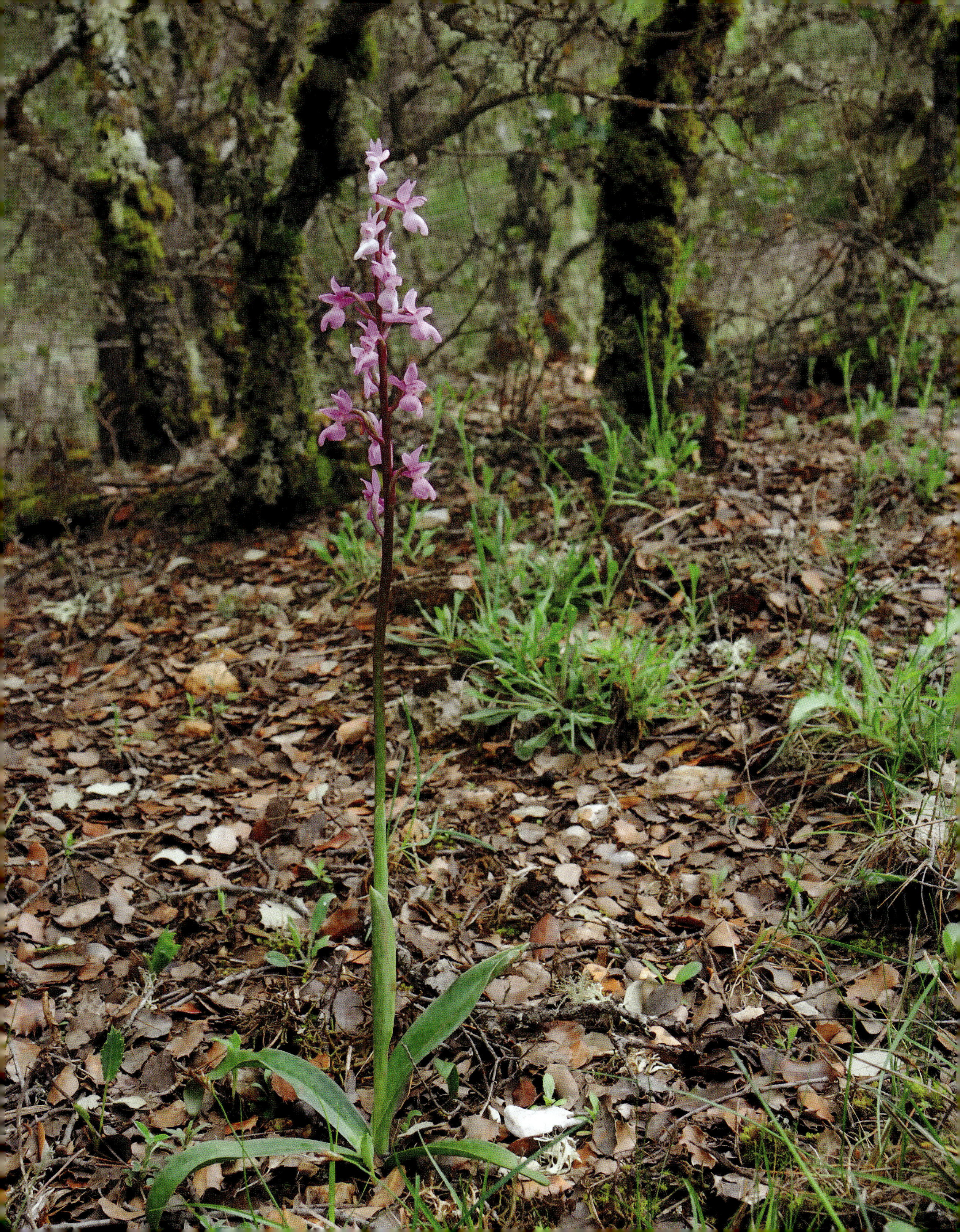

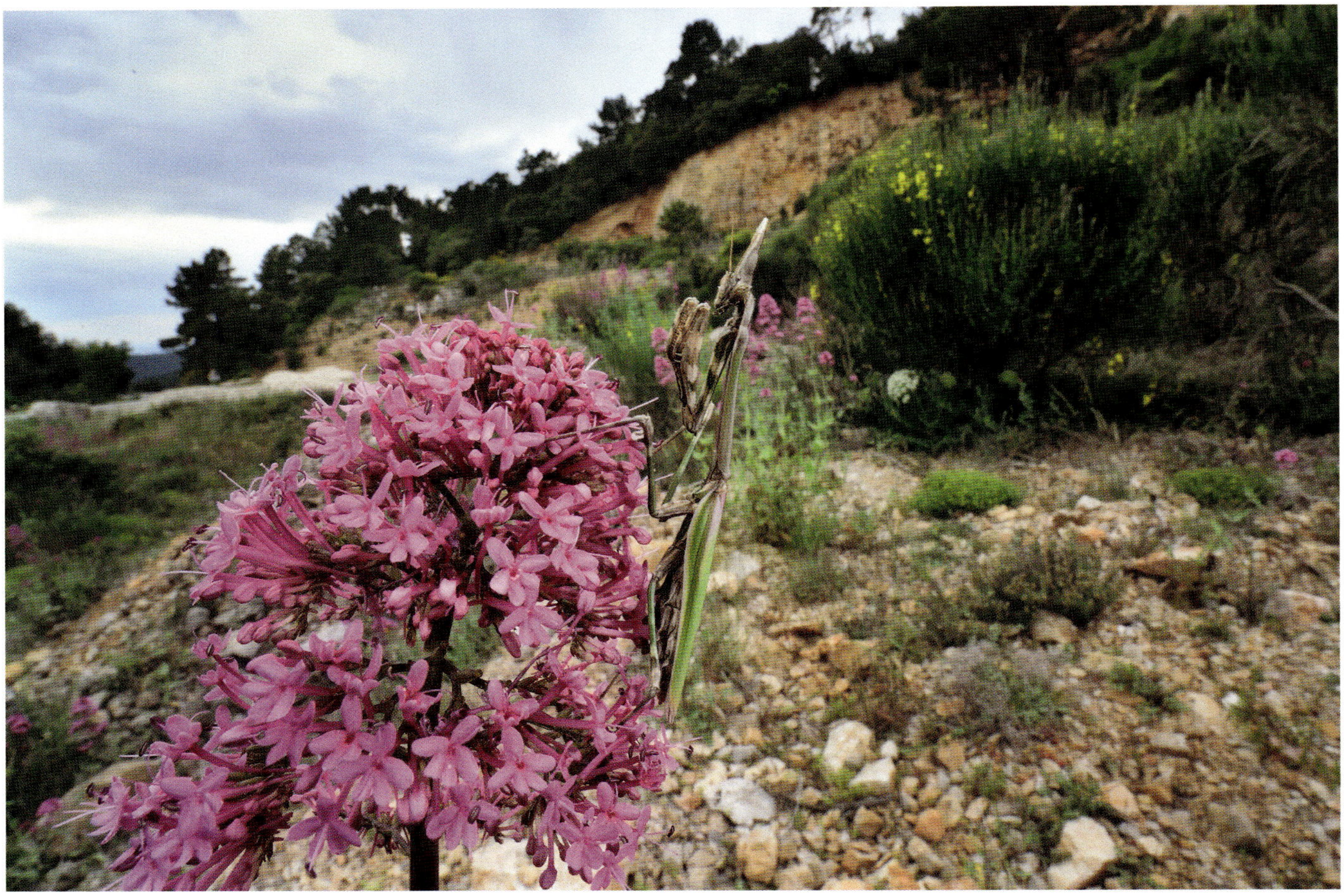

21.2 ~ **Cone-head Mantis** *Empusa pennata*
An excellent lens for setting the subject in context with its environment.
→ Nikon D810, 15mm Laowa macro, 1/8sec at f16, ISO 200.

Nikon's 14–24 mm is an excellent ultra-wide-angle lens and delivers very sharp results, its overall minimum focusing distance is 0.28m from the camera's sensor. It has a maximum magnification 0.15X which is adequate for larger plants, but when shooting smaller subjects, such as insects, you have to zoom in to increase the magnification at the expense of decreasing on the wider view in the process. The greatest magnification is naturally at the lens's longest focal length. This is one of the challenges associated with this type of photography. Canon also produces similar lenses in the same focal length with comparable specifications. Independent lens manufacturers such as Sigma are also worth considering the 10–20mm EX DC HSM for the APS format has a minimum focusing distance of around 24cm from the sensor and a maximum magnification of 0.15X, which makes it ideally suited to this technique. Fixed focus wide-angles, particularly older, manual lenses are also worth considering. They deliver a better performance on minimum focusing distance and magnification compared to most of the current autofocus lenses.

Special Purpose Wide-angle Macro

As far as I'm aware, and at the time of writing, the Venus Laowa 15mm f/4 wide-angle macro is the only true wide-angle macro which has the capability of achieving 1:1. The lens is manual focusing with stop down metering; a method that was a familiar routine for many of us mature macro photographers before the luxury of electronic pairing, which is standard on virtually all modern lenses. This lens also has a small built-in shift facility of six millimetres up and down which is useful in some

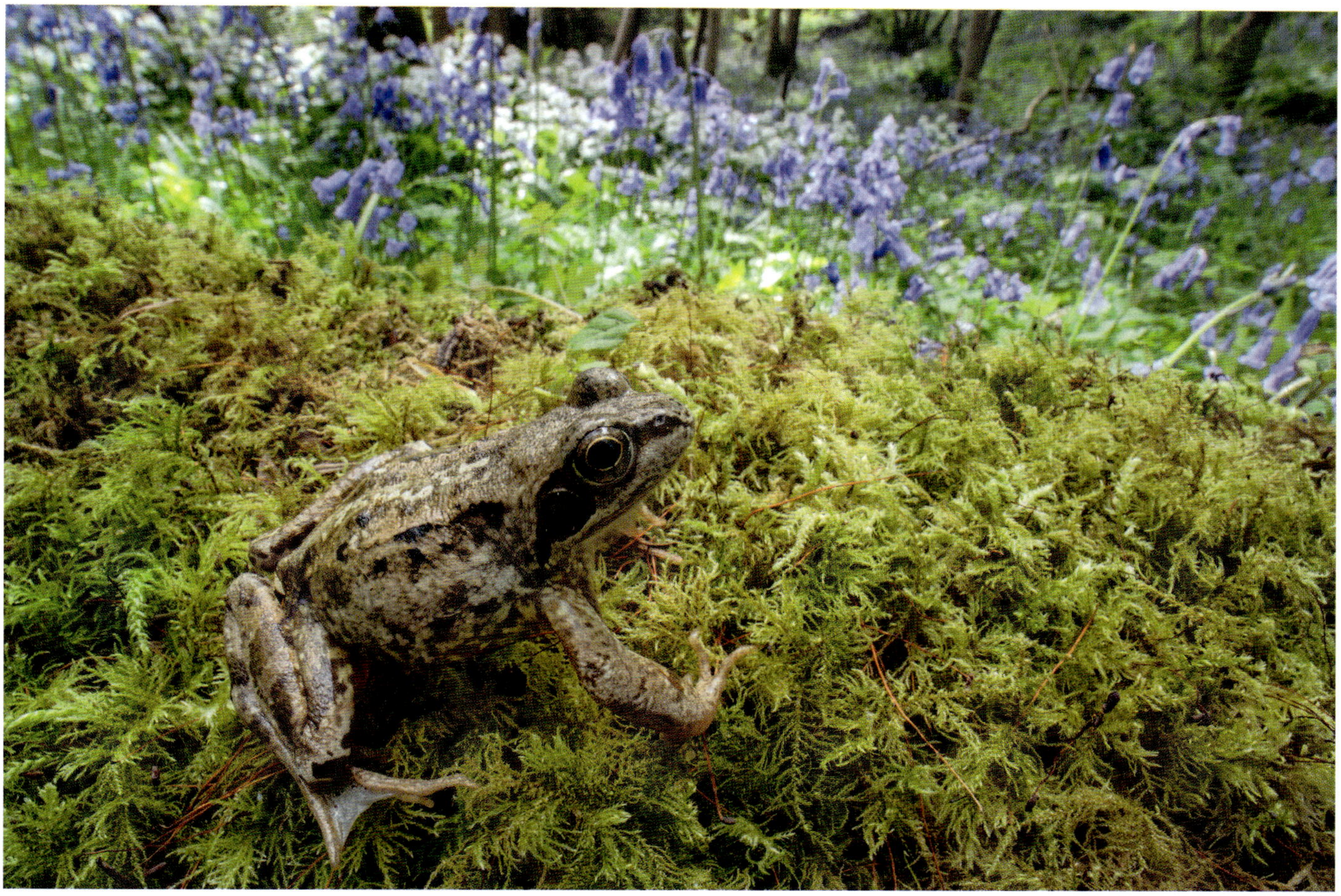

21.3 ~ **European Common Frog** *Rana temporaria*

↳ Nikon D810, 15mm Laowa macro, 1/15sec at f11, ISO 200.

situations. Focus is best achieved by selecting your reproduction ratio and moving the camera and lens assembly in and out. The results from this lens are visually impressive and anyone who wants to pursue this technique will find a lens like this extremely useful. Whether it is possible in the field to photograph an active insect at life-size is debatable, since the lens to subject distance is down to a matter of millimetres. Resting adults are certainly possible at slightly smaller magnifications. Nevertheless, the optics are extremely sharp, and it does produce some amazing results.

Rectangular (or Diagonal) Fisheyes have an extremely good close focus capability and are also ideal for wide-angle macro – the 15mm f/2.8 is a case in point. This is a full frame lens and when used with APS-C or smaller format, the central image portion of the lens is used and the distortion within this is not excessive – in fact, it can be of use creatively.

Which Subjects Work Best?

It is possible to apply this technique to a range of subjects, but flowers are ideally suited to wide angle macro. Most are of a reasonable size and in many cases close to the ground. Those plants that inhabit mountainous landscapes are often stunted to reduce the impact of the pounding winds and the inhospitable environment in which they exist. Some grow in quite scenic localities with attractive backdrops which create impact and show this technique at its best.

Photographing insects at such close quarters poses more of a problem. Larger species, for example butterflies, can be approached when confined to the vegetation. Larger dragonflies, mantids, beetles and cicadas are also achievable since they are mostly inactive when at rest. Smaller insects are much more challenging, since they require higher magnifications usually beyond half life-size which is not feasible in many cases without a complicated setup. Additional extension would also be required, which is likely to bring the lens virtually into contact with the subject. I have experimented with some smaller species, but it can be very hit and miss.

Amphibians and certain reptiles work well with this technique. However, like so many creatures you need to be mindful of their needs and welfare. Amphibians, in general, do not handle very well, their highly sensitive skin is easily damaged if continually fingered by dry hands. Most amphibians can be approached pretty closely if you refrain from sudden movements.

Lighting Options

Lighting subjects which are close to the rim of the lens can be difficult since you have so little room for manoeuvring flash units. Photographing in natural light on an overcast day is less of an issue; however, when the sun is shining behind you the shadows will fall directly on the lens and subject. Employing flash is one alternative but trying to position it close to the subject is difficult when you are virtually a centimetre from it in some cases. Fill-in flash where the light output is reduced and balanced with the ambient light is one solution that does work, but at very close working distances it can still be awkward to position it. Some devoted photographers of this technique have designed elaborate lighting setups to overcome the problem, and from what I have seen, the results are excellent.

When adopting the wide-angle approach, like conventional macro you still need to pay attention to the background. Depending on your magnification and focal length it can still be a distraction rather than complementing the subject. This is particularly true at higher magnifications where it can appear obtrusive rather than balanced.

Wide-angle macro is a fascinating technique and one which every macro photographer should explore at some point. It requires an intuitive eye to get the best from it but this comes with practice and identifying those opportunities that work. It offers an alternative to producing photographs in the conventional way, with the emphasis clearly on the subject's environment; an aspect that is often overlooked.

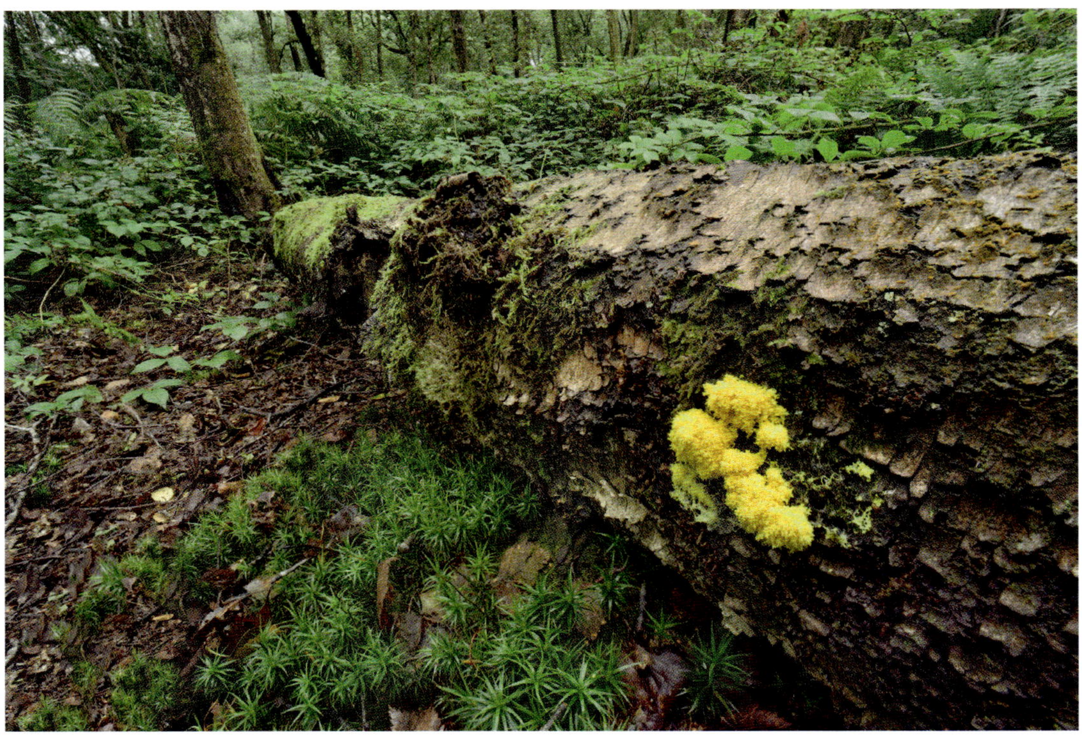

21.3 ~ **Slime Mould**
Fugio septica
Environmental close-ups have a role in conventional close-up photography. So much additional information can be gleaned about the habit they occupy.

→ Nikon D810, 15mm Laowa macro, 1sec at f11, ISO 200.

TWENTY TWO

Macro on the Move

HAVING preached the virtues of using a tripod earlier in this book, I now find myself defending valid reasons as to when it becomes a hindrance rather than an advantage. Don't misunderstand me, I still shoot every image I can with one, but there are situations when it becomes challenging to photograph active insects for a number of reasons. Rough, overgrown terrain makes it difficult to manoeuvre a tripod without disturbing the surrounding vegetation, forcing your quarry and anything else to make a hasty exit.

During the pre-digital era, pursuing insects on the move with a camera (in my case medium format) was a much more challenging ordeal. There was no fast, responsive autofocus, or image stabilisation and only one chance to get it right. You often had a two-week wait for the return of your films to see if you achieved your goal. By then you were either back home, or somewhere else with no chance of a repeat if things went wrong. You also had less choice when it came to faster films; we were all devoted Velvia converts and resorting to higher ISO films was always the last option; this is especially true in my case; I would often go to great lengths especially with flash to avoid using a higher ISO film. Photographing insects in the middle of the day was far from easy, especially when they were on the move and resting only briefly between spells of activity. Where possible I would avoid the warmest part of the day, but when working abroad or visiting a site only briefly, you don't have the luxury of cherry picking your ideal times.

Photographing creatures in hotter climates like the Mediterranean means you are going to face much warmer temperatures most of the time, even in early morning and late evening. The abundance of insects often means that you will want to photograph at more challenging times of the day. The digital revolution has made this more achievable. Now when photographing abroad, I can have instant feedback on any aspect, from my LCD screen and the opportunity to evaluate my results and reshoot were necessary all without leaving the field. I still prefer the additional support, especially when using a high-resolution camera and as a rule, I rarely shoot freehand. I prefer to use a monopod for extra stability. No matter how proficient you are, having additional support is an advantage, especially when working at higher magnifications. You have much better control, and you can also drop your speed a little if the situation demands it.

My preferred setup for mobile macro is a Benbo monopod, but any reasonable make will suffice. I use a small light ball and socket head, which gives me flexibility when it comes to framing and orientation. The monopod also has a homemade spike on the end so I can apply pressure to force it into the ground when in position. I prefer to use a medium focal length macro, for example, the 105mm micro Nikkor with single flash unit. It is reasonably light, and it also has vibration reduction which I can engage at lower magnifications to facilitate working at slower speeds when I don't want to compromise on the ISO. I can also engage smaller apertures, but most importantly it's the lightness of the whole assembly and its quick response that works for me.

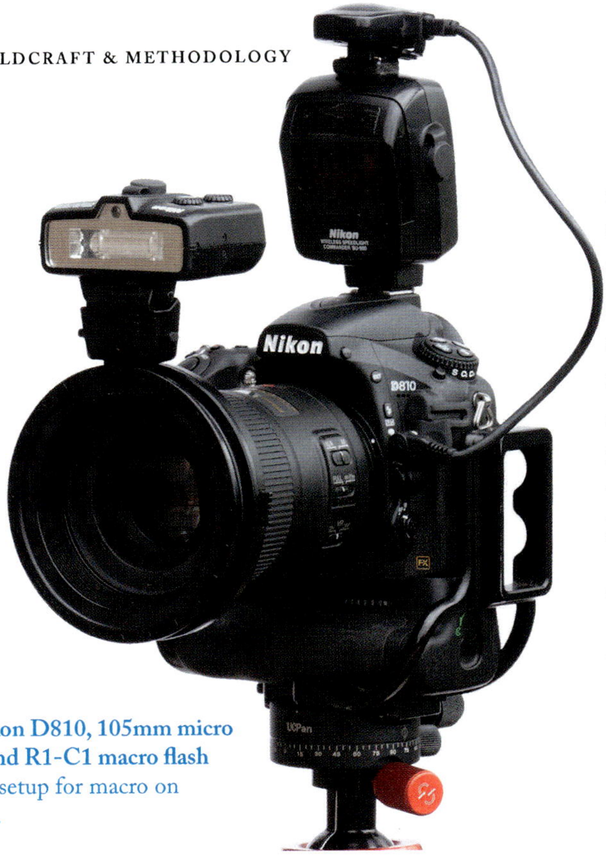

22.1 ~ Nikon D810, 105mm micro Nikkor and R1-C1 macro flash
My ideal setup for macro on the move.

Actively stalking insects is one of the few occasions when I prefer to use autofocus mainly for speed and to keep my hand movements to a minimum. For example, when in a meadow I tend to target a species and watch to see if it settles for a reasonable amount of time before moving on to the next flower or is it merely a fleeting stop? Those insects that are in a hurry are not worth pursuing since you are unlikely to get in close enough before they move on again. It's better to observe and focus on those that seem to settle for longer periods; you will have a much better chance of success. Try and select subjects with a relatively clean background behind them, although this is not always possible, a quick check before moving in will give you an idea. It's also important to keep your shadow off the subject and keep yourself below the skyline, otherwise it will highlight your movements even more. Another useful accessory when you are on the move is knee pads; they are invaluable and save your knees when you have to kneel down on rough terrain. Don't expect to nail every species you target, but with a little patience, an understanding of the scene and a careful approach you can get some great images.

22.2 ~ Sharp-tailed Grasshopper *Euchorthippus declivus*
→ Nikon D800, 105mm micro Nikkor,1/125sec. at f/11 fill-in flash, ISO 400.

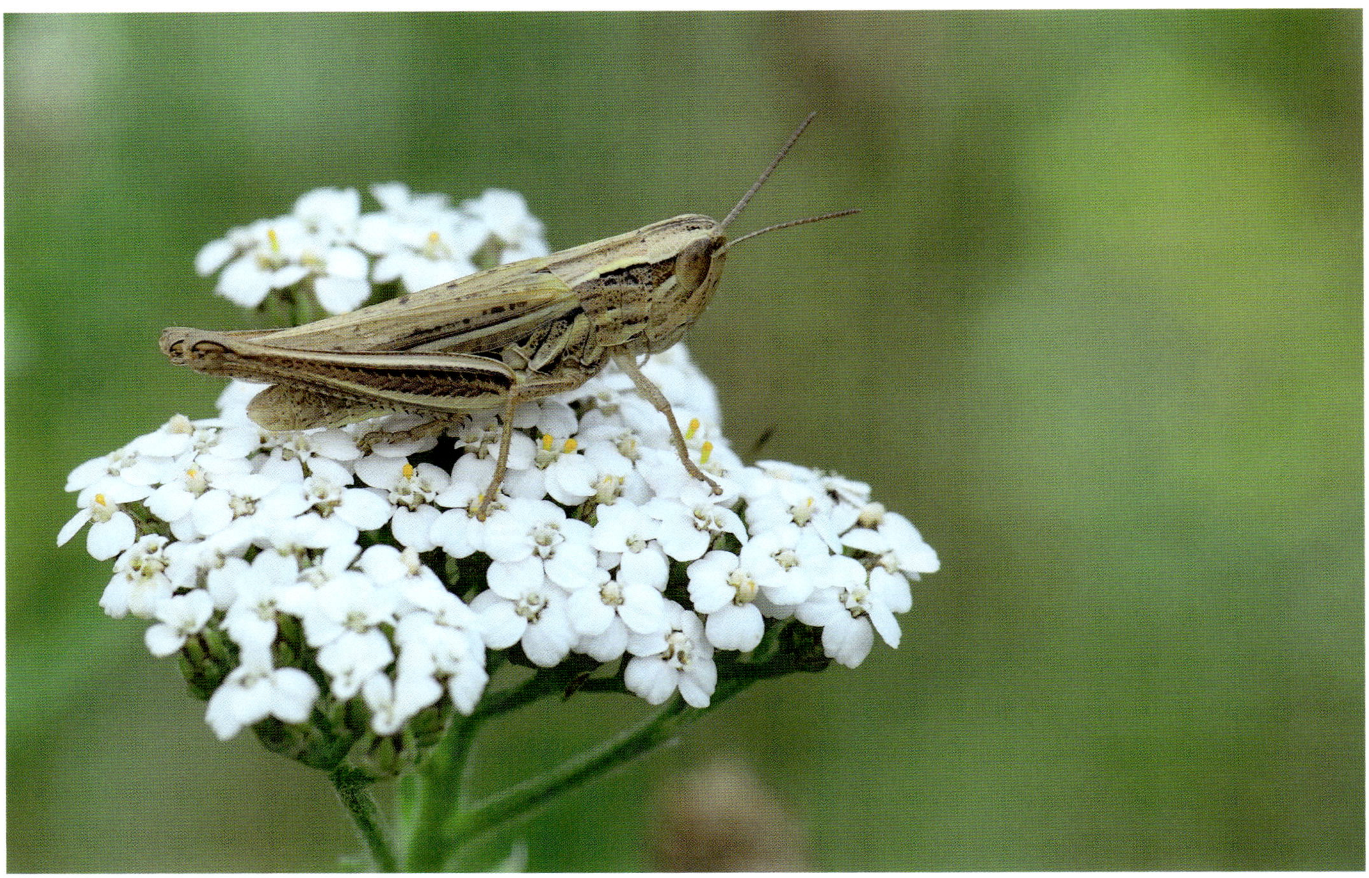

TWENTY THREE

The Outdoor Field Studio

I FIRST became aware of this technique about 2010 when a friend of mine Niall Benvie along with Clay Bolt developed a clever initiative in 2009 entitled 'Meet Your Neighbours', whereby people could reconnect with nature and wildlife in a unique and more intimate way. The concept centres around photographing the subject as a high key colour image where the background is entirely white, giving your subject a distinctive but identifiable look. The reasoning behind this approach is total engagement and appreciation of the subject without the distraction of a background, context or anything else. Over the years, the initiative has grown into a worldwide project with many photographers from different countries contributing to it following its rather unique photographic template. The technique outlined below is a brief overview; I suggest that you consult the excellent e-book by Niall Benvie (see 'Additional Resources') which describes the equipment and the various techniques in much greater detail. The method is particularly useful in book publishing and graphic design. Images can be directly imported onto the page without having to resort to cut-outs which from experience are frequently challenging and time-consuming to do. Composites are produced with ease and can be used to illustrate a wide diversity of subjects.

Getting Started

The equipment needed to create the high key photographic style of the field studio is not that expensive or complicated. You can achieve the result with a very modest setup. The background is opaque white acrylic or Perspex, which is relatively easy to acquire. You can purchase it online or from sign manufacturers who will cut it to your preferred dimensions. A piece around 3–5mm in thickness and approximately A3+ in size is adequate for the majority of close-ups of plants. The background is placed directly behind the subject and can be held in place with lightweight rods, clamps and clips which will be outside the field of view. Two flash units are required,

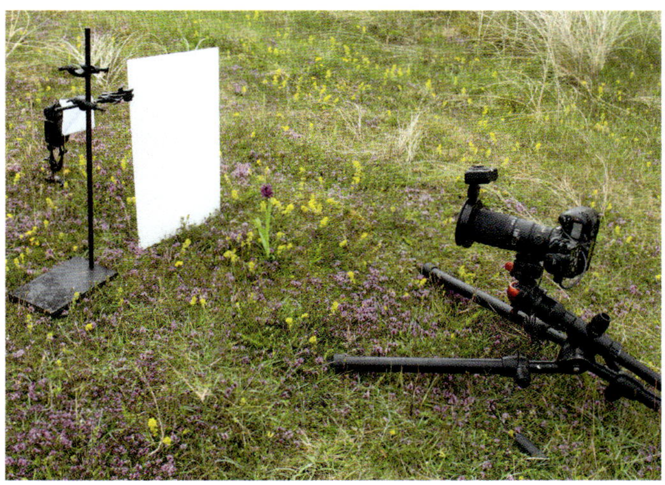

23.1 ~ Outdoor field studio setup
Note background flash. The front flash is normally diffused with an opaque envelope stiffener which is held in front of the flash unit.

one to be positioned behind the Perspex to create the backlight and the other (the master) placed in front. Excellent results can be achieved with any pair of flashguns; they don't have to be state of the art, old manual units work just fine as long as you have the appropriate sync leads. Front diffusion is provided by a flyweight envelope stiffener or another diffuser something similar which should be placed closer to the subject than the flash.

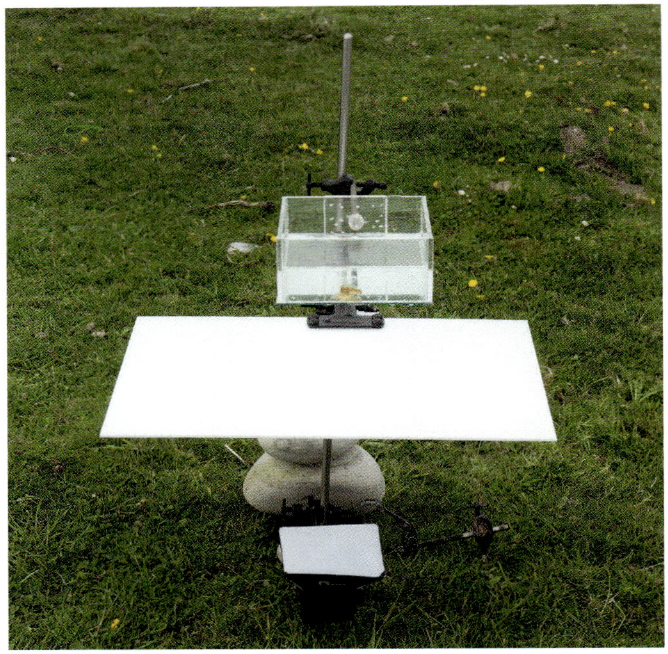

23.2 ~ Seashore field studio setup

Establishing the Correct Exposure

If you are using Speedlights, it's important to determine the correct position relative to the subject. You want the background to be white, but not entirely overexposed; half a stop is adequate since a certain amount of light travels through the Perspex to the subject making it appear to glow. The closer the background is, the greater the radiance. With experience, you become more familiar with the distance and how far it needs to be to achieve the correct exposure. Once in position, make a series of test exposures with the background flash only and make the necessary adjustments to the flash output or via the ISO or aperture. The correct value is obtained when the highlight warning in your camera shows the background flashing but not the subject. The histogram reading will naturally show a bias to the middle and right side of the screen with virtually no values registered on the left side. With pale subjects, you need to keep the background further back to achieve the desired result otherwise finely featured or translucent parts of your subject may become overexposed and blend with the background. With darker subjects, it's the opposite, the background needs to be closer. When you are satisfied that the background exposure is correct, you can perform a similar procedure with the front flash. Better results are obtained if you use diffusion; this can be accomplished by using a softbox attached to your flash unit or a large opaque envelope stiffener which produces a similar result. You want to place the diffuser relatively close to the subject and vary the position of the flashgun until the correct exposure is attained. You need to run some test exposures to make sure the subject is not overexposed.

Photographing Invertebrates

Invertebrate and aquatic photography require a different approach. Most photographers have their own methods, but mostly they all produce the same recognisable look. For aquatic photography, I have a tank which is constructed from white acrylic with a clear back and front panel. I can make adjustments to the white back panel to achieve the correct exposure. It works perfectly fine for the majority of subjects. Photographing active insects is a bit more challenging. Ideally, it is better to create distance between the background and the subject rather than placing it on a white piece of Perspex. For speed of use in the field I use a large laboratory clamp with a clear transparent box which can be secured and positioned above the white Perspex; this can be altered where necessary to create distance from the background. The flash is positioned below the Perspex sheet, which can also be adjusted up or down to establish the correct background exposure. The front flash is diffused with a softbox; this quick assembly unit is handy when working at rockpools and the coast.

The high-key images produced by the outdoor field studio provide a fresh alternative to conventional photographs of subjects in their natural surrounding. The focus can be on local species without the need to travel far. Unlike traditional macro, it can be practised in the field, even when the conditions aren't ideal for routine close-up photography.

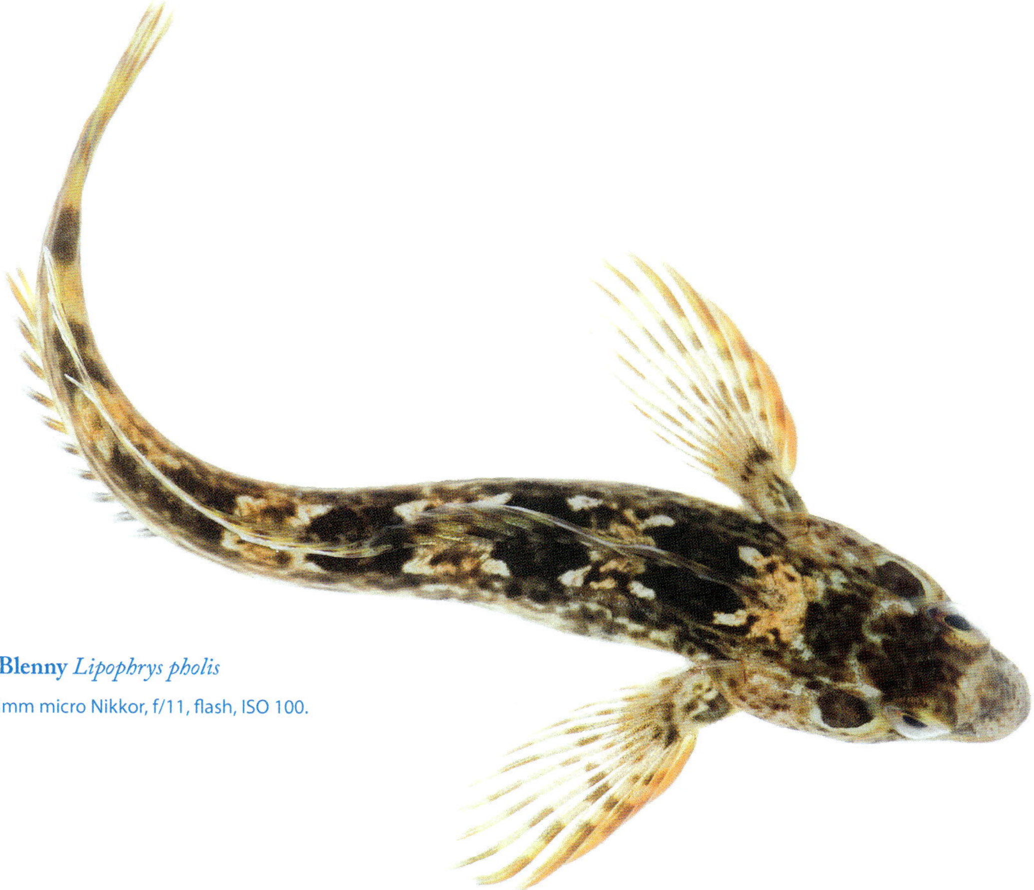

23.3 ~ **Common Blenny** *Lipophrys pholis*

↘ Nikon D810, 105mm micro Nikkor, f/11, flash, ISO 100.

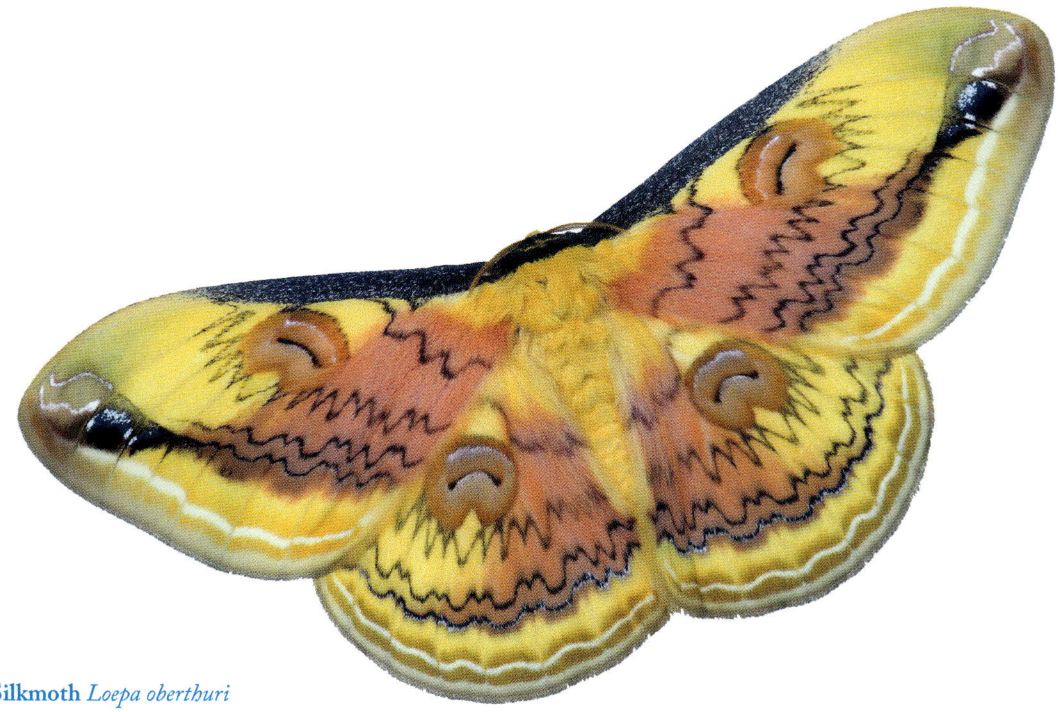

23.4 ~ **Giant Silkmoth** *Loepa oberthuri*

↘ Nikon D810, 105mm micro Nikkor, f/11, flash, ISO 100.

TWENTY FOUR

Photographing Further Afield

TRAVELLING around the world has never been easier or more affordable than at present. Naturally, most photographers given the opportunity want to see and expand their interest to cover other subjects in foreign destinations. Photographic workshops are the most popular way of doing this. There is an abundance of companies and photographers offering this service and will take you to see and photograph high profile species and iconic locations for a price. However, before you sign up for such a trip, it is worth thinking about what your aims and objectives are. Why do you want to visit that particular place and what do you hope to get from it? Many workshops are expensive and sometimes photographers' expectations are greater than the reality of what it is or the conditions were less than favourable at the time. Nature does not negotiate with photographers.

One of the advantages of workshops or any photographic tour is the fact that everything is planned for you, right down to your meals in most cases. Some photographers prefer it this way and are happy to pay for others to lead them by the hand. I run a number of workshops myself, which are ideally suited to those with a passion for the close-up world. There is no doubt that a new location with different subject material set amidst stunning scenery can go a long way to revitalising and developing newfound enthusiasm.

Successful photography abroad requires planning, research and selecting the most appropriate time that will coincide with your intended targets. Visiting any foreign destination without having aims and objectives is not an ideal approach. You can waste your time not to mention your hard-earned cash on a trip that falls short of your expectations. When planning my trips to Europe, be it for a workshop or for shooting stock, I obtain all of the relevant information well in advance, the flowering times of plants, the emergence of butterflies and other insect groups which I want to target. I always try to find accommodation close to the locations I plan on visiting. What you want to avoid is spending more time travelling than photographing. I normally have a target list, and I will check the emergence times of everything before my visit. I tend to plan many of my scheduled trips almost a year in advance and usually during the winter months when there is more time to research locations accurately. When working abroad, it is essential to have an itinerary and to know where you are going and what you are targeting. You don't want to be wandering about aimlessly hoping that you can turn species up by chance. In my experience, it rarely ever happens.

Having a connection with societies, organisations and local photographers in the respective countries that you plan on visiting is indispensable. There is a network of naturalists who belong to various local natural history groups, which are willing to share information in return for something back. I have been a member of a number of organisations both in the UK and Europe for many years. Most produce reports and journals that have accounts of members' trips to various locations at home and further afield. These are often a minefield of information. I have built up a network of friends through

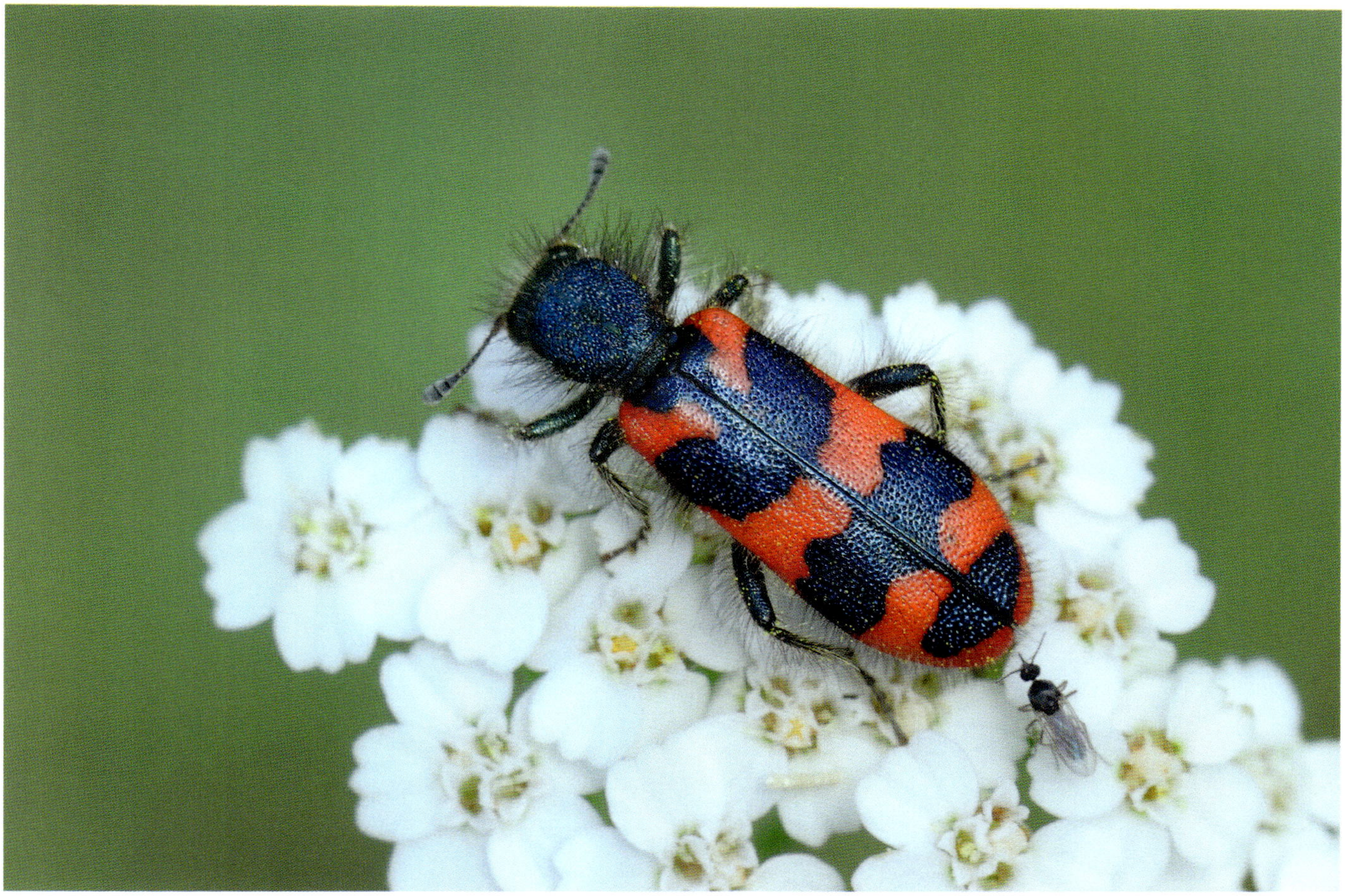

24.1 ~ **Bee-eating Beetle** *Trichodes alvearius*

↘ Nikon D810, 200mm micro Nikkor, 1/60 sec f/11, flash, ISO 200.

correspondence and meetings with many knowledgeable botanists and entomologists who have experience in different fields of natural history. Most have travelled widely in Europe and the Mediterranean. These contacts are important since they can provide information on sites from particular regions and the flowering and flight times of different species. This kind of information is invaluable.

Writing articles and passing on information to others is one way of ensuring reciprocation. Various natural history journals are often a good source of material; many publish accounts of trips made by members. These can be extremely helpful when planning trips. There is usually contact information, and I have found over the years, most people are genuinely helpful. I can also reciprocate with information on locations that I have been to and the trust develops. There are also many resources online where you can obtain information.

Airline Travel

With travel so widely available these days, even to relatively remote destinations, you would think from a photographer's perspective that's a good thing. However, there are caveats to that freedom and independence and it comes in the way of security, scrutiny and restrictions. There is no doubt that safety is an important issue and at present they are paranoid about it in many airports. Gone are the days when you could get through to the departure lounge with only the mildest of checks. Airport security is the bane of the photographer's life. We all stretch the rules just a little taking that extra lens or piece of equipment which we might use but never do. I am of course guilty myself of pushing the boundaries.

On some flights my photographic bag gets pulled and after careful packing at home, everything hits the table for inspection. Equipment is scrutinised, and I

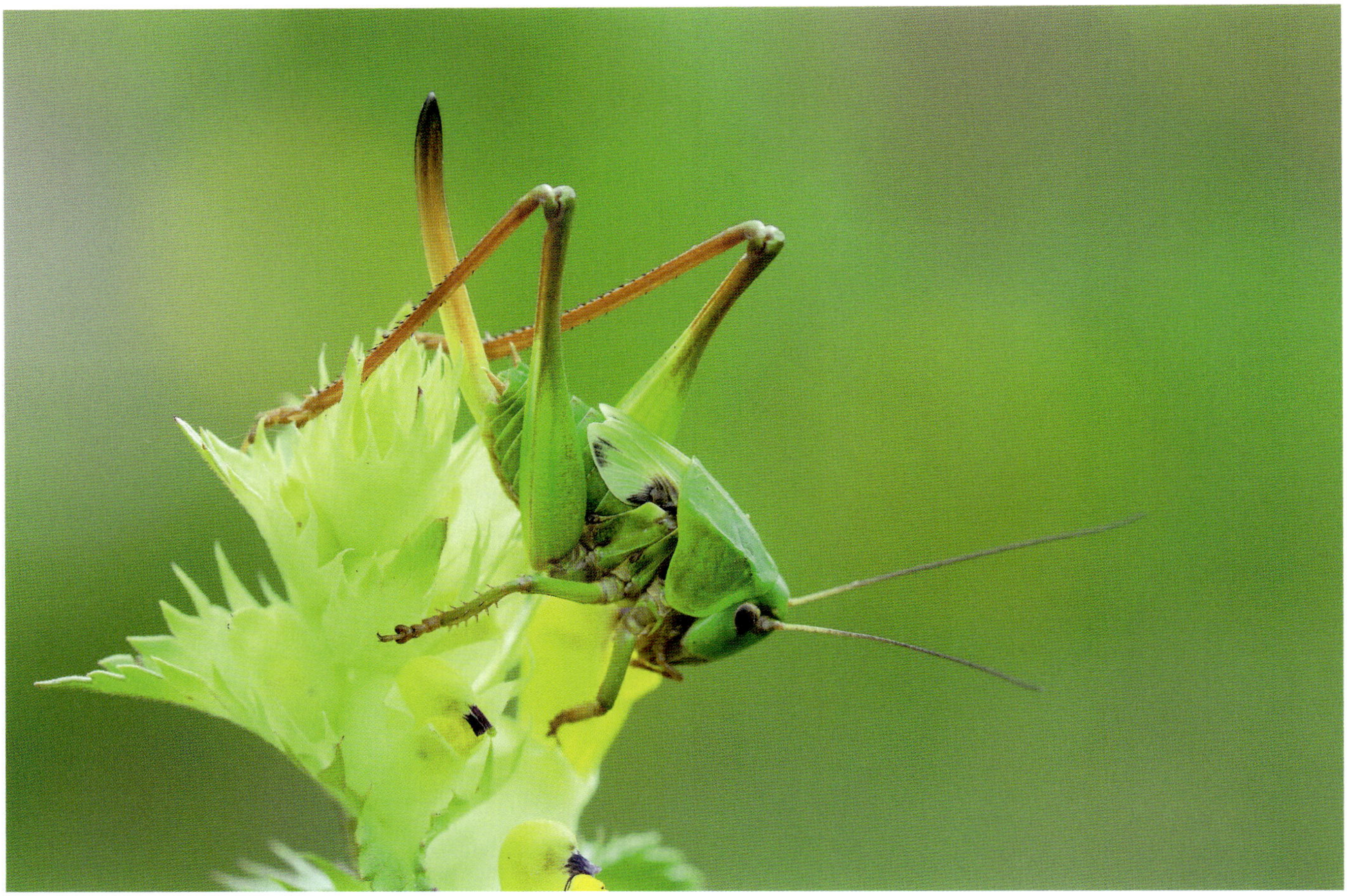

24.2 ~ **Wart-biter** *Decticus verrucivorus*

↘ Nikon D800, 200mm micro Nikkor, 1/80sec at f/11, flash, ISO 200.

have on some occasions been asked to push the shutter button on my camera bodies. There are, however, some airlines and airports which are a bit more lenient. Weight restrictions on hand luggage is the biggest problem. Some airlines don't have a policy on hand luggage but many now do. There are some airlines I simply won't fly with and I try where possible to stick to the few that are more forgiving with weight, even if it means driving for longer to my destination. Hand luggage is becoming a major problem for airlines since many people are carrying more onboard to avoid being overweight with their hold luggage. On flights that are full it's becoming common practice for staff to select some hand luggage and put it in the hold since there's no room for it in the overhead lockers. So, the moral here is don't be last on the plane. Like it or not it's a fact that when photographing abroad, you have to prioritise and take only what you realistically are likely to use. My diffusers and additional accessories, which are not as vital, go into my main hold bag. My photographic kit comes on board with me always. It usually contains a MacBook Pro, two camera bodies, a 200mm macro, 105mm macro, 24–70mm zoom and 14–24mm zoom and also four camera batteries. I also take the alkaline insert for the battery grip should I need to change for some reason, this way I can keep shooting if my main bag gets delayed with the charger in it. Included also is my macro flash system, my compact flash cards, filters, electronic release (plus a back-up) and a phone charger, which get dispersed around my person. I consider these also to be essential items. I can just about fit this all into a regulation size bag.

Virtually all carriers allow one piece of hand luggage usually around 56 x 45 x 25cm. I do adhere to these dimensions and resist over packing side pockets as they may push it beyond the regulation size or attract a pair of scanning eyes behind the check-in desk. Carry all of your necessary equipment on board; if parted from your main luggage bag as a result of theft or misplacement by the carriers, you have the means to function at least in some capacity. Arriving at your destination only to find that your gear has disappeared for one reason or another is every photographer's nightmare. Just because you have slipped through the radar of the check-in desk doesn't mean you're out of the woods. Be prepared, you can still get pulled at the boarding gate; I have had this happen to me on more than one occasion.

Since I'm a frequent traveller, I have a template which is a list of equipment I need to take with me. I just check each item off the list. There are many good photographic bags on the market which meet the regulation size. Think Tank is one example, who produce bags that comply with the guidelines and are worth a look. Personally, I avoid bags with metal handles and wheels. I have found that these are the first ones targeted by airline staff when they are forced to consign hand luggage to the hold due to excess baggage on board. I also purchase priority boarding so I am among the first to board the aircraft. I can place my photographic bag in the overhead locker directly above me for peace of mind before the masses are allowed on. It's also sensible to have camera equipment insured separately as the majority of insurance companies linked with airlines have minimal cover. As a back-up, if travelling beyond the European Union, you should photocopy your passport, licence and insurance and email to yourself; that way should you lose your documents you have some proof of identity. I also have a photograph of my backpack with my photo gear in place; should anything happen, it can be useful for insurance purposes.

When photographing away from home, it's a good idea to make notes of species that you have found, their flight or flowering times and locations. I use the Nikon GPS unit which is attached to my camera. It provides in addition to GPS reference, altitude, capture date and the default metadata. Information like this is very useful should you want to return again at some other time. I also carry a few extra tools and bits such as black insulation tape and a small screwdriver set in case I have to do a makeshift repair on something.

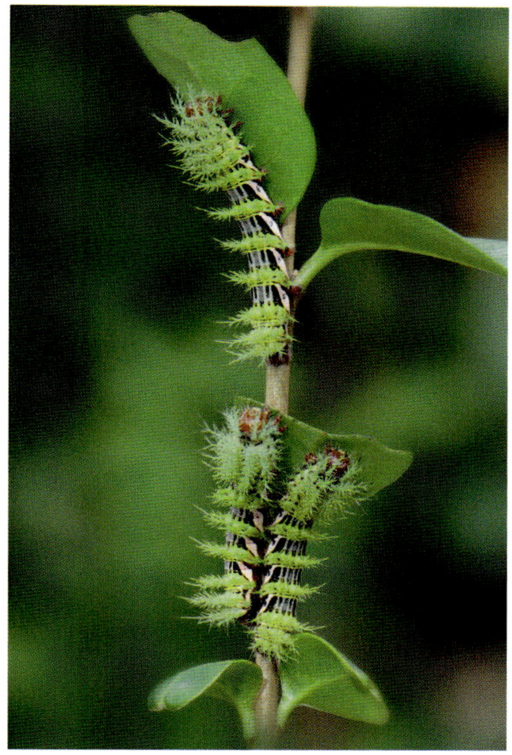

24.3 ~ *Automeris naranja* (early instar larvae)

↘ Nikon D2X, 200mm micro Nikkor, 1/15sec at f/11, fill-in flash, ISO 200.

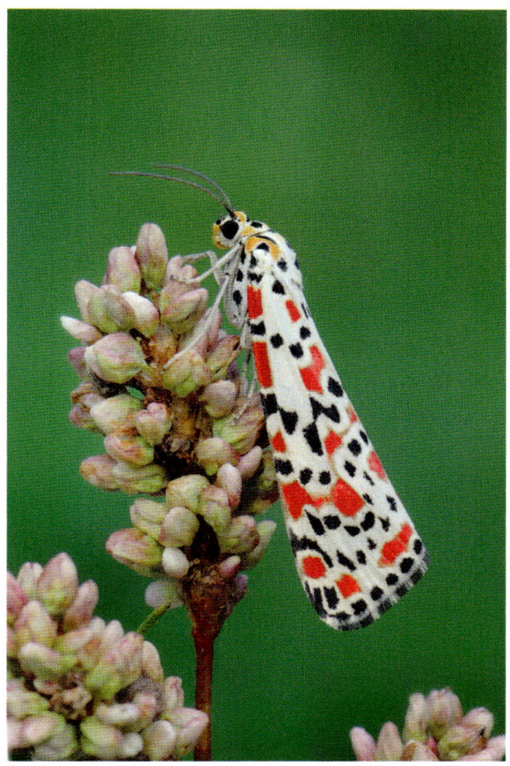

24.4 ~ **Crimson Speckled Footman** *Utethesia pulchella*

↘ Nikon D2X, 200mm micro Nikkor, 1/30sec at f/11, ISO 200.

TWENTY FIVE

Photographing in Challenging Conditions

THE WIND more than any other of nature's elements is the bane of every close-up photographer. The majority of other problems can, in most situations be overcome, but a persistent breeze is extremely annoying. Finding a sheltered spot away from exposed areas is usually the best option. You will often find that insects are of the same opinion and seek calmer well-sheltered areas where the temperature is a degree or two warmer. Early morning or late evening is a good time for photography; any breeze always seems to be that bit calmer earlier or later in the day. Erecting a wind break for plant photography gives some protection, but if the breeze is relentless without intermittent relief, it becomes virtually impossible to work. I have often been photographing abroad in the Mediterranean and the south of France when the Mistral, a cold northwesterly wind, blows. Clear conditions often accompany it which is even more annoying since you are dealing with bright conditions as well; not the ideal combination for good close-ups. Coastal habitats are more exposed than inland sites, and you should consider locations that will offer some protection from the wind if you are going out on windy days.

Raising the ISO on your camera and using shutter priority is a sensible approach. Also switching your camera to continuous shooting mode increases your likelihood of capturing one or two decent images. There is no easy solution when the elements are against you other than to try another day. Early morning starts do have a slight advantage in that resting insects are still torpid from the cooler overnight temperatures.

Photographing in light rain often produces interesting atmospheric images providing it is not raining relentlessly. I often like to visit wetland areas in these conditions. Insects are grounded and forced to rest among the vegetation until the temperature rises. Light water droplets add an extra dimension to flowers, other vegetation and enhance the general ambience of the photograph. Calm conditions with little to no wind often accompany these weather patterns. Also, the light is often heavily diffused making it ideal to capture all of the finer subtleties of the subject. You can also use a tripod which allows you to work at the camera's optimum ISO and control the point of focus. Light rain devoid of wind is one of my favourite times to explore with a camera.

Try to avoid shooting in clear blue skies. The shadows are at their heaviest particularly among rank vegetation which produces very unflattering backgrounds. If you are shooting in bright conditions look for subjects that are isolated from nearby foliage, they will produce much better photographs with cleaner backgrounds.

// FACING PAGE ~ TOP //

25.1 ~ Wild rose thorns
→ Nikon D810, 200mm micro Nikkor, 1/15 sec at f/11, flash, ISO 100.

// FACING PAGE ~ BOTTOM //

25.2 ~ Ground Crab Spider *Xysticus Species*
This predatory spider was well clear of surrounding vegetation. The light was intense, I used fill-in flash to help lighten the shadows a little.

→ Nikon D810, 200mm micro Nikkor, 1/60sec at f/16, fill-in flash, ISO 100.

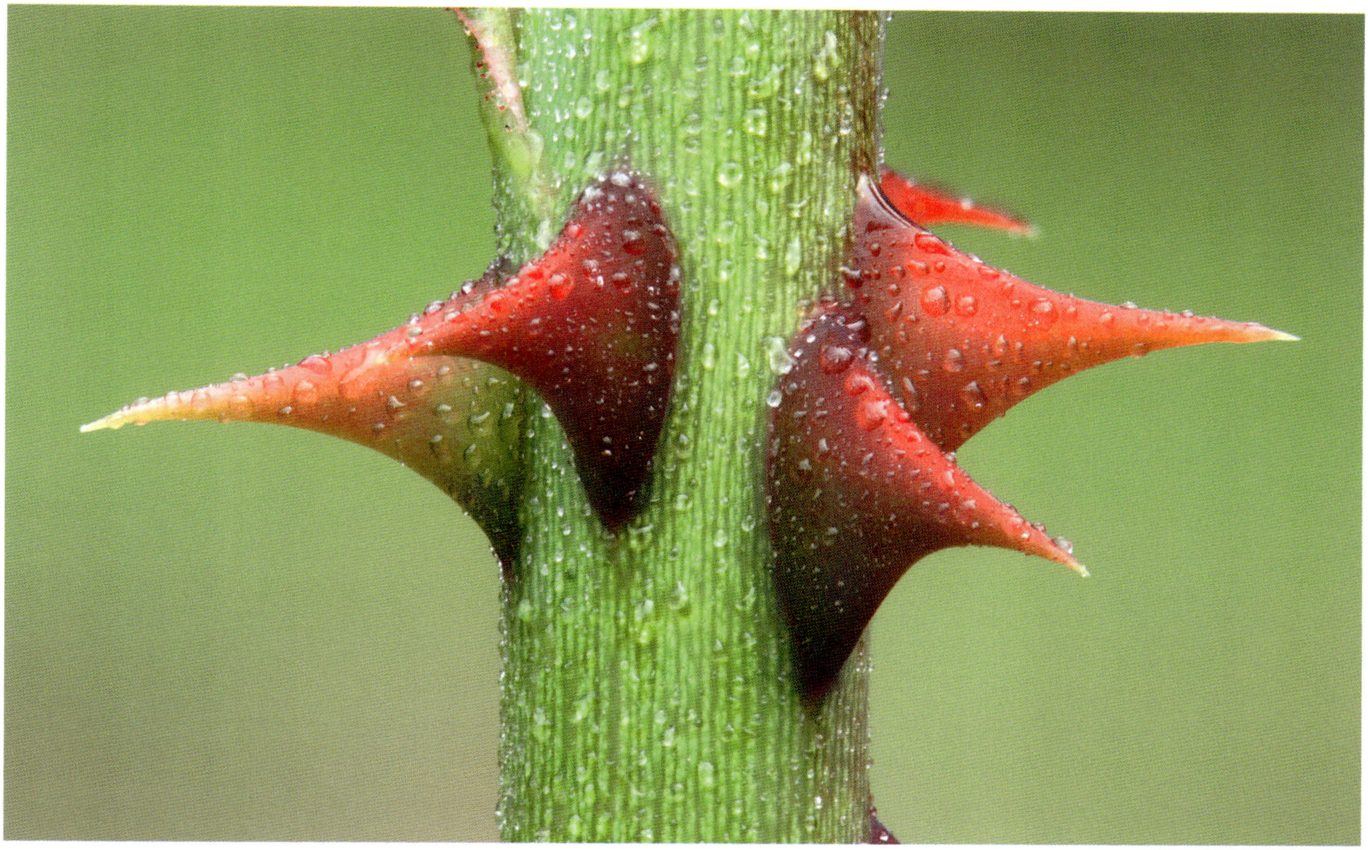

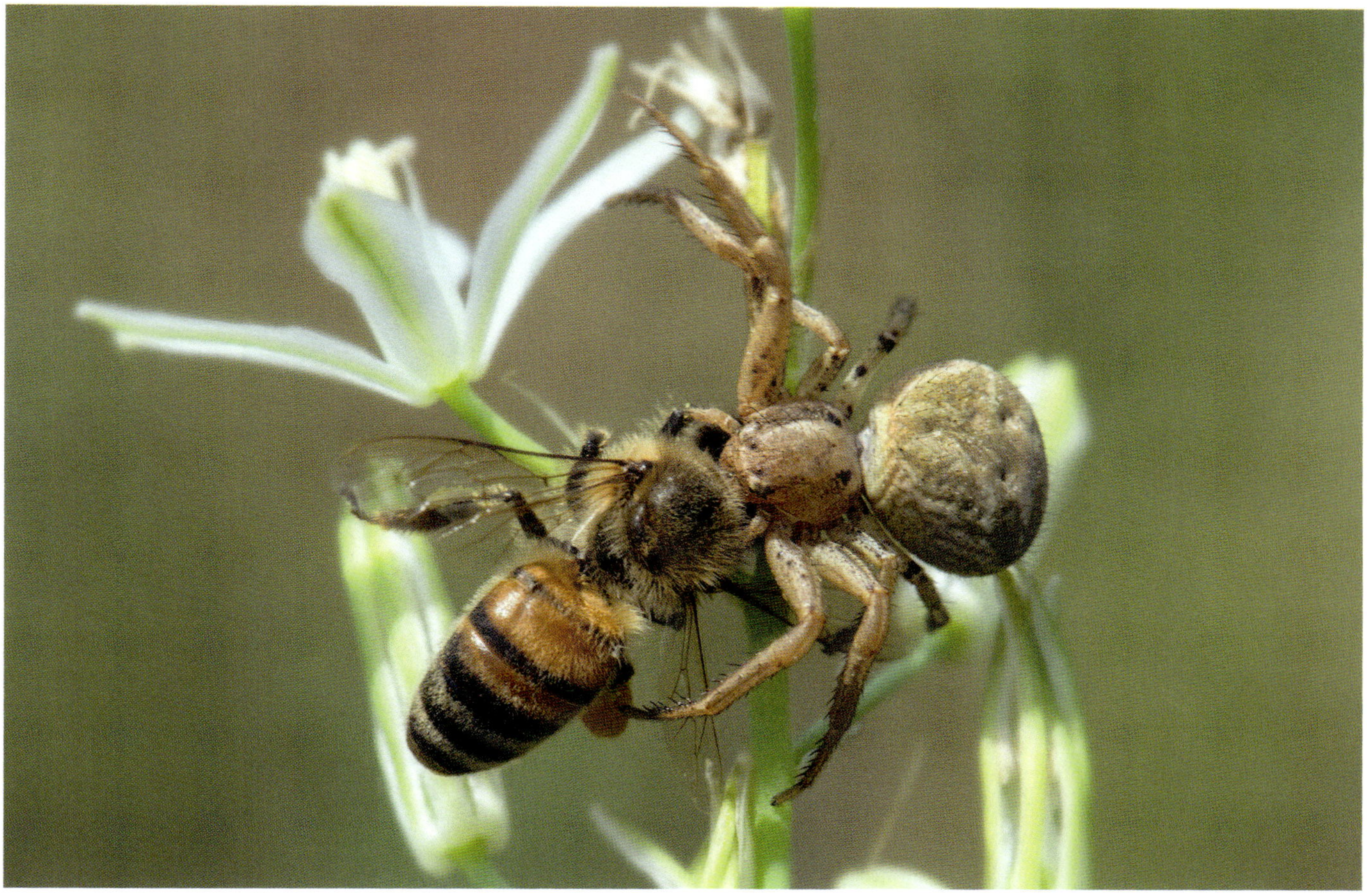

TWENTY SIX

Macro Through the Seasons

THERE is no doubt that spring and summer are the busiest and most productive seasons in the macro calendar. The flora and fauna are at their peak and most colourful. Insects and flowers attract the largest group of photographers; however, it's imperative to keep up your photography through the least productive months. It's easy to slip into seasonal dormancy when autumn comes to an end. Many photographers reduce their field activity in exchange for the warmth and comfort of the fire, and to catch up with the backlog of unprocessed images accumulated through the spring and summer months.

Winter is the least productive of the four seasons for macro photography, but having said that it's not entirely devoid of subject material. Grey, overcast skies and lingering cold can dampen the enthusiasm for all but the diehards. The winter months may not have the salubrious feeling that spring brings, but it has its own character and charm. If you can put up with the cold, and the rain doesn't dampen your fervour, you may be surprised to know that there are many other seasonal subjects worth exploring. By December insect life has all but gone, or those that overwinter have entered hibernation. There are some moths which are active during this time, but not many. Larger autumn fungi are also over, although brackets and smaller species can persist throughout this period.

Winter is also a good time for mosses and lichens; most are generally at their best photographically. A visit to a mature woodland or bog will provide a broad diversity of species, many of which are colourful and worthy of attention. Exploring heathlands will produce various sphagnum mosses with their vibrant green and red colouring. The bark of different species of tree is also worth investigating for abstracts. December and January are the months of frost and ice. Frozen streams and pools provide a range of designs and an assortment of leaves entombed in ice. A crisp frosted coating can transform relatively normal subjects into something worth photographing. Frost is generally at its best very early in the morning, and pre-dawn light can give a subject a soft, cool, pastel look. The glistening dew, frosted spider's webs and leaves, all provide a broad range of possibilities. The last remnants of overlooked berries can still be found attached to the branches of trees and hedges. Various grasses and an assortment of seed heads of numerous flowers take on a whole new perspective when cloaked in an icy coating. As sunlight beckons and the temperature rises (even a degree or two), the moment is literally melting away. During mornings such as these, I often find myself on my way home again by ten, having had the best of the day.

// FACING PAGE ~ TOP //

26.1 ~ Frosted hawthorn berries
Crataegus monogyna
It is not uncommon to find small numbers of these berries peppered across bare hedgerows during the winter. What makes them interesting is when they are engulfed with small ice crystals.

↝ Nikon D810, 200mm micro Nikkor, 1/15sec at f/11, ISO 100.

// FACING PAGE ~ BOTTOM //

26.2 ~ Frosted gorse flowers
Ulex europaeus
Winters seem to have got milder and its not uncommon to see a few early flowers on this shrub in most years. Ordinary subjects take on a new look when tiny crystals of ice form on them.

↝ Nikon D810, 200mm micro Nikkor, 1/8sec at f/16, ISO 100.

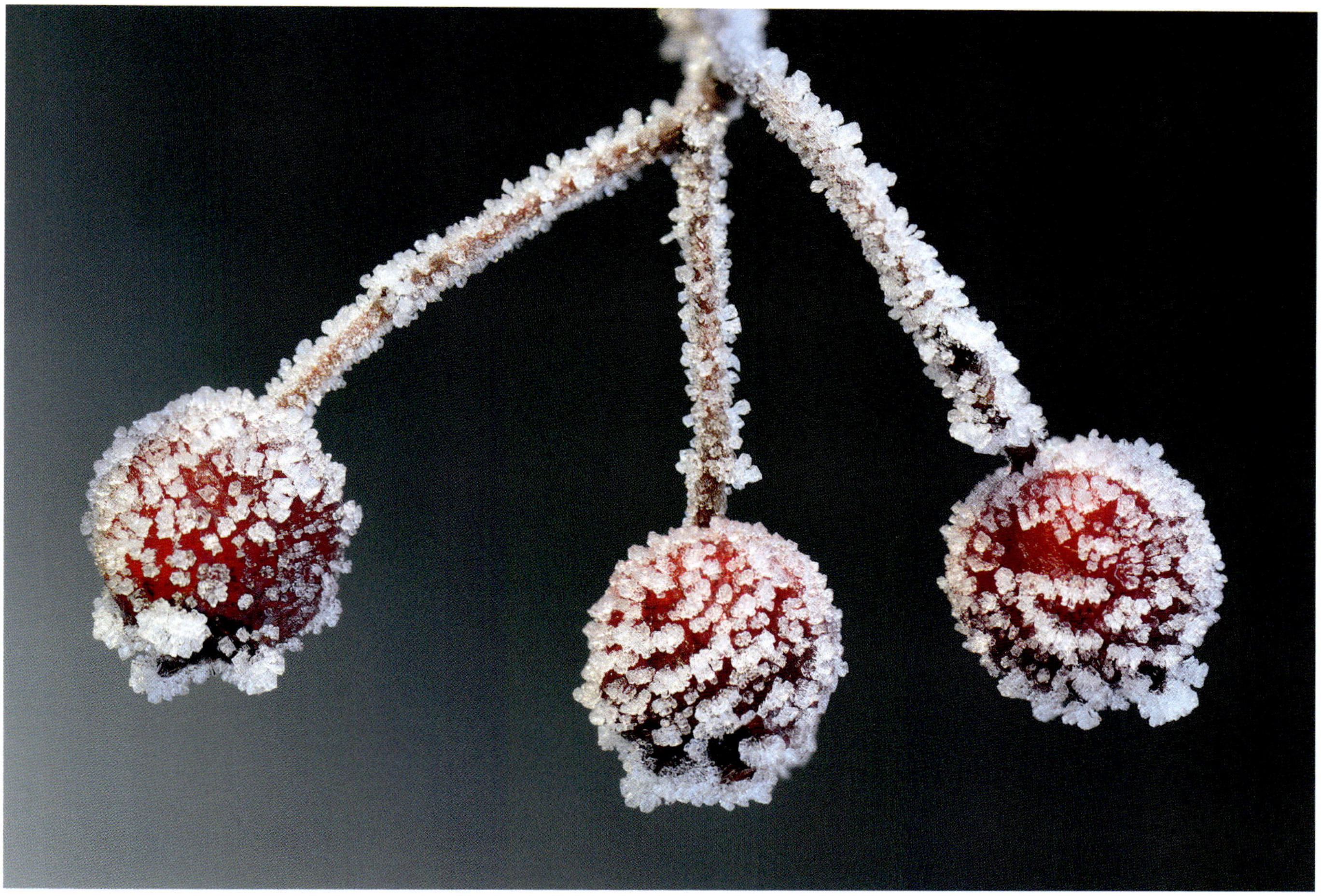

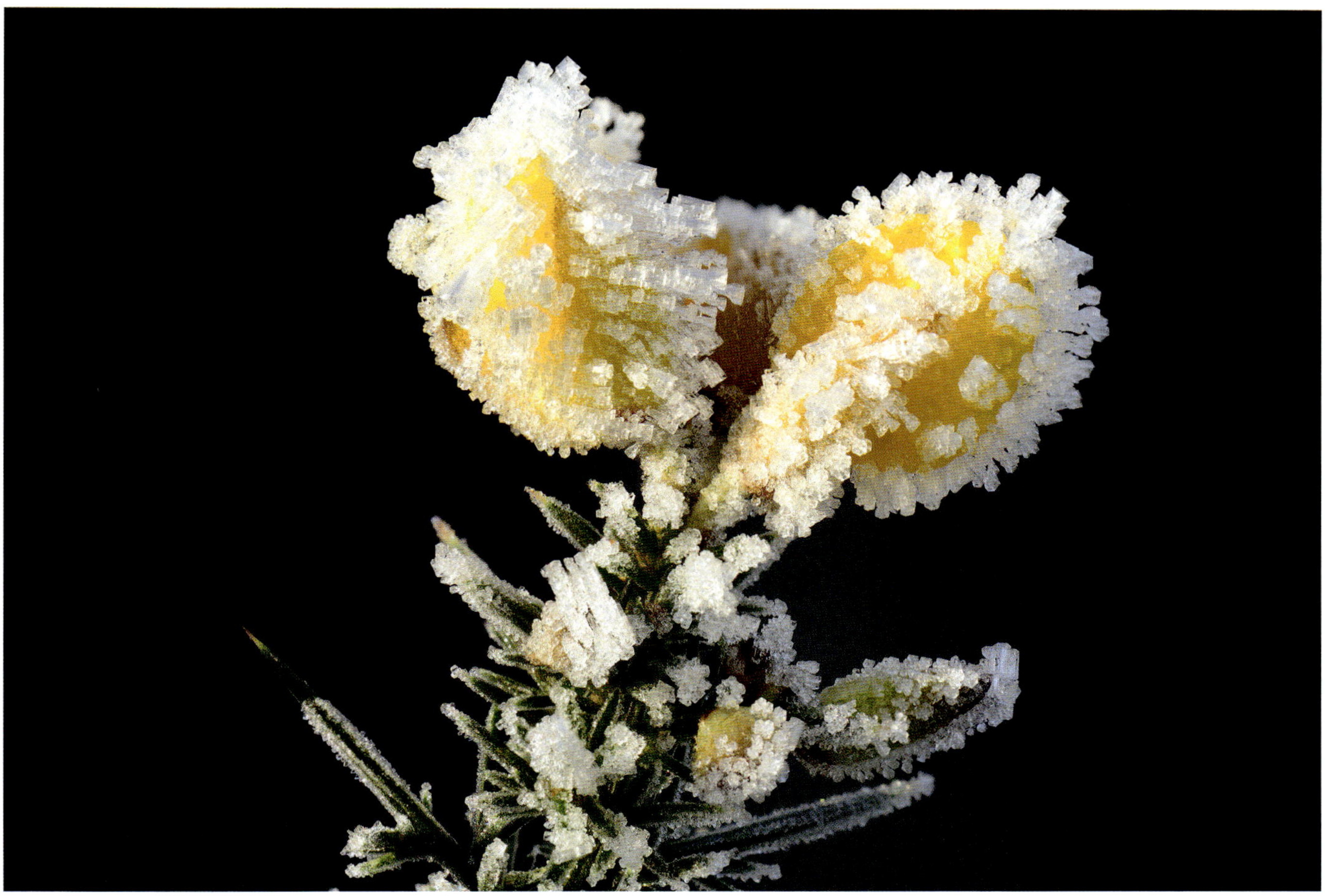

TWENTY SEVEN

Beyond Life-Size

IT IS FAIR to say that the majority of macro photographers operate within the realms of 1:1. Photographing beyond life-size requires a more methodical approach, combined with a good sound technique if you are to produce consistently good results. The disappointments are much higher at this level, but you are entering the realms of true macro photography or photomacrography, to be more precise. Working at higher magnifications can reveal many aspects of a subject that are beyond the normal field of vision.

Understanding the Terminology

As mentioned briefly at the beginning of the book, the term 'macro' is often incorrectly applied to close-up photography. It is also misrepresented by many, including camera and lens manufacturers to describe a 'close-up facility' on a lens or compact camera. The definition of macro photography in the real sense relates to magnifications from 1:1 (life-size) to around 20:1.

Magnification and reproduction ratio are also terms that many photographers new to close-up

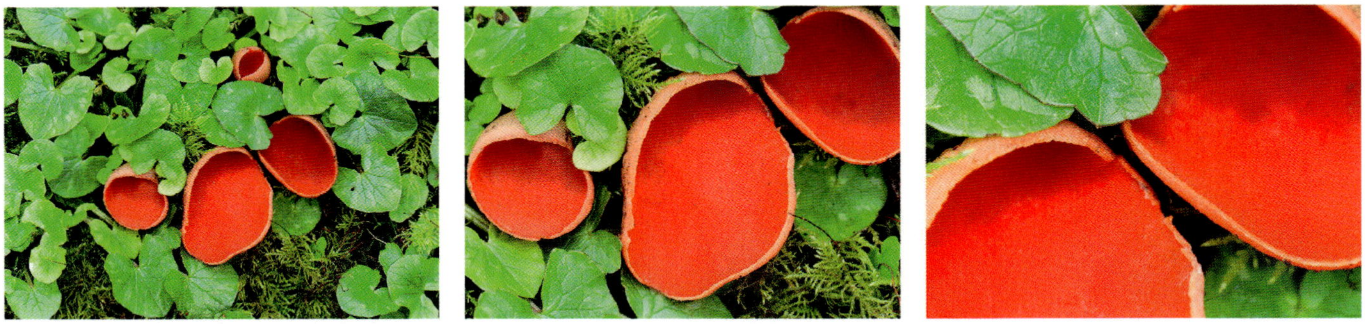

27.1 ~ **Scarlet Elf Cup** *Sarcoscypha coccinea*
Example of different reproduction ratios.

→ Nikon D810, 105mm micro Nikkor, ISO 100.

// FACING PAGE ~ TOP //

27.2 ~ **Black Darter** *Sympetrum danae* (male)
The bi-coloured compound eyes can contain up to 30,000 individual hexagonal rods and cones, giving them the most acute vision in the insect world.

→ Nikon D810, 105mm micro Nikkor, + 2X converter, 1/60sec at f/16, flash, ISO 200.

// FACING PAGE~ BOTTOM //

27.3 ~ **Variable Damselfly**
Coenagrion pulchellum (male)
Extreme close-up of the male's eyes and head.

→ Nikon D810, 105mm micro Nikkor, + 2X converter, 1/60sec at f/16, flash, ISO 200.

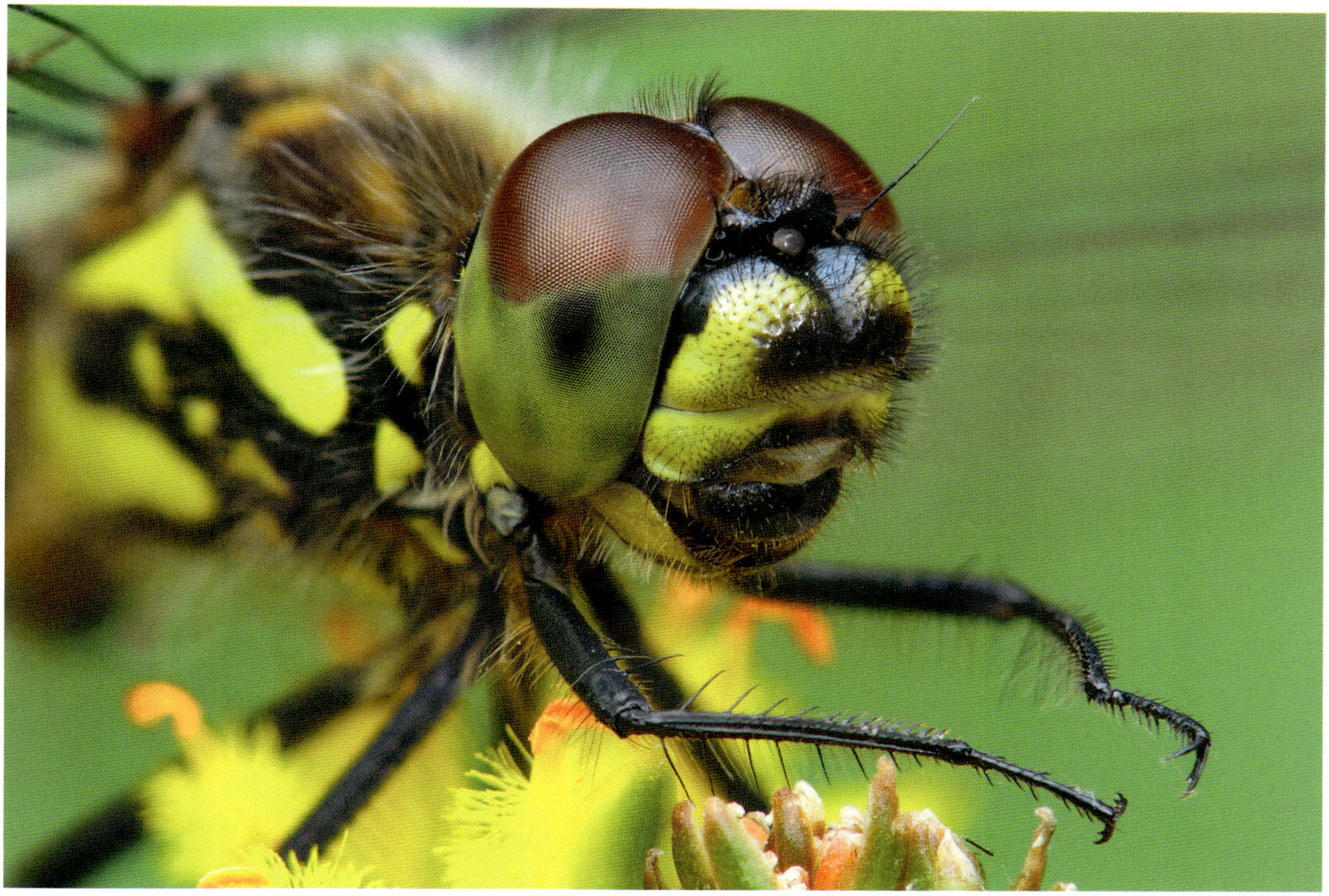

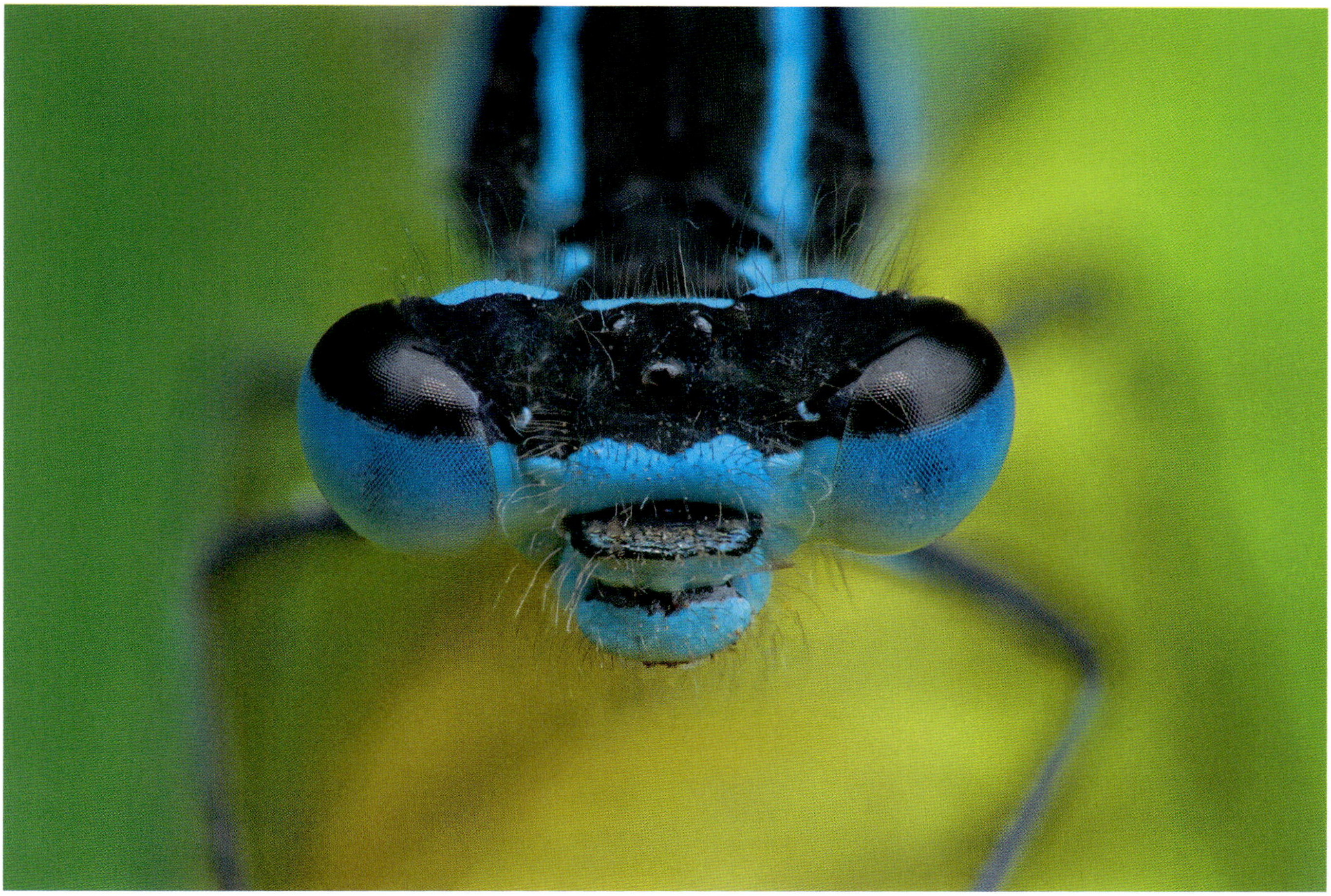

photography find confusing. Magnification is the relationship between the actual size of the subject being photographed and its image size or reproduction ratio on the camera's sensor. The term reproduction ratio is defined as the relationship between the two and is expressed as ¼, ½, ¾ and 'life-size', or 1:1. Photographing any subject below life-size means that it will appear on the sensor smaller than its real size; conversely, shooting a bumble bee at 2:1 would mean it appears at twice its normal size on the imaging sensor.

Getting Beyond Life-size

Most modern macro lenses deliver their best optical performance at their minimum focusing distance which is 1:1. However, to attain magnifications beyond life-size requires additional pieces of equipment and a more intelligent approach regarding technique. There are several ways in which we can obtain higher magnifications. Extension tubes are the most obvious choice for many photographers. Inserting them between your macro lens and the sensor is one way of increasing the magnification above life-size. One of the advantages of extension tubes is there is no loss of image quality since there are no additional lens elements within the hollow tubes, and they are a relatively cheap way of going beyond the 1:1 barrier. The downside is, of course, the increased weight and fall off in light as we have already discussed. For example, if you owned a 100mm macro, then you would need 100mm of extension to take you up to 2:1 or twice life-size; not that practical for field photography, in my opinion.

Reversing Rings

Reversing rings are one of the cheapest close-up attachments which allow you to mount a lens in reverse on the camera. The accessory has a rear lens mount on one side and a male filter thread on the opposite end. The female filter thread of the lens attaches to the male thread on the adapter which then connects to the body. It is possible to attain a high level of magnification depending on what focal length of lens you reverse. But the downside is the lens to subject distance which will be significantly reduced. Wide angle lenses will produce a greater magnification when reversed, but the working distance will be much closer. It is also better to use a prime lens rather than a zoom. The disadvantage of reversing a lens is you loose all of the automation including open aperture viewing. Focusing has to be carried out manually with the diaphragm wide open and then closed to the appropriate aperture. This approach is feasible if you are dealing with static subjects, but considerably more challenging with active creatures. The quality of the images from a reversed lens is excellent. It is possible to obtain automatic reversing rings, but they seem to be limited to a couple of major brands. Novoflex makes an automatic reversing ring adapter for Canon as do Vello. Unfortunately, there is no equivalent for the Nikon system which is a real pity.

Bellows

One of the traditional methods of attaining higher magnifications was attaching lenses onto bellows. They were widely in vogue pre-digital and popular among the macro fraternity. Most of the major camera companies at that time had a set of automatic bellows as part of their macro line up. The image quality is maintained since there are no glass elements within the unit. Many of the earlier bellows retained automatic function which made the process much easier. Unlike extension tubes bellows gave you variable magnification with greater accuracy. Most of the expensive units were mounted on a double rail system; one to expand and contract the bellows and the other to move the assembly in and out to focus. Their popularity post-digital has declined, and major manufacturers no longer make them. Leading German manufacturer Novoflex produces bellows for a couple of major brands, but they have a limited appeal these days and are simply too time-consuming for serious field photography. They are better suited to a studio setup where you have greater control over lighting and background arrangements. I have used all of these methods in the past myself and designed and modified many pieces of equipment to make the process easier, but I no longer feel it is necessary to use bellows, although some photographers still do. Digital

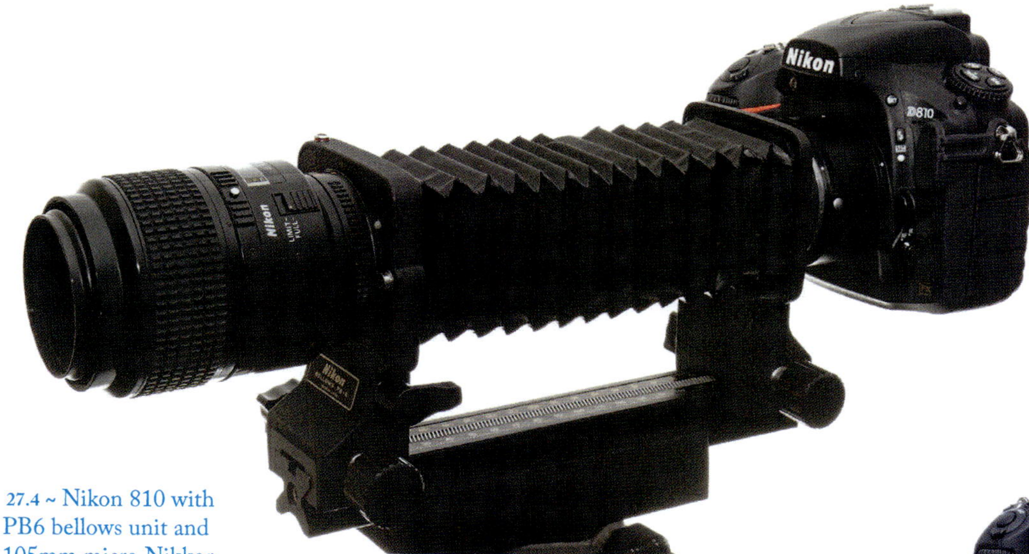

27.4 ~ Nikon 810 with PB6 bellows unit and 105mm micro Nikkor

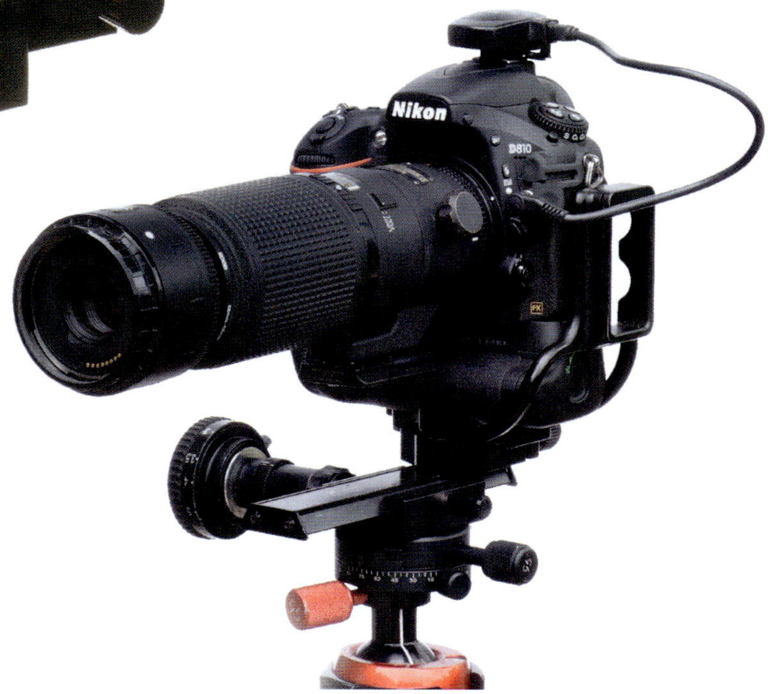

27.5 ~ Nikon 810 with 200mm micro Nikkor lens and stacked 80mm Mamiya lens reversed. Also quick release bracket and GPS unit

technology and advancements in optics have opened up many alternative approaches. The results today are certainly superior to those achieved with film in the past.

Stacking Lenses

When I need magnifications greater than 2:1 my preferred approach is combining two lenses together to achieve this. Depending on the combination I can obtain magnifications in the region of 5:1. Stacking two different lenses together was a popular practice among photographers in the 1990s. The technique had some merit at that time. However, the big disadvantage was the vignetting in the corners which were nearly always present to some degree irrespective of the lens combination used. Transparencies had to be masked to overcome the problem or duplicated. The ideal prime lens for stacking is a 200mm macro or any other similar focal length macro will work equally as well. A standard, short focal length lens can be reversed and attached to the front element of the prime lens using an adapter ring. I discovered that if you use a medium format lens such as Mamiya's 80mm or similar the vignetting disappears, and you can use the whole of the sensor area with no pixel wastage. Both lenses are connected via an adapter or coupling ring which can be made from a filter or step-up rings. These are then glued together. As a temporary measure, you can tape the lenses with black electrical tape if you want to get an idea of how it works. The aperture is controlled from the prime lens in the usual way. The attached lens plays no part in the exposure process. I also modified an extra lens bayonet cover to serve as a small lens hood by removing the central section, which then locks on the base of the stacked lens giving some protection to the delicate contacts. Magnifications up to 5:1 are possible utilising this setup. There is also no light loss or exposure issues, as it does not affect the electronic communication between the primary lens and camera. I have produced some very good results using this approach.

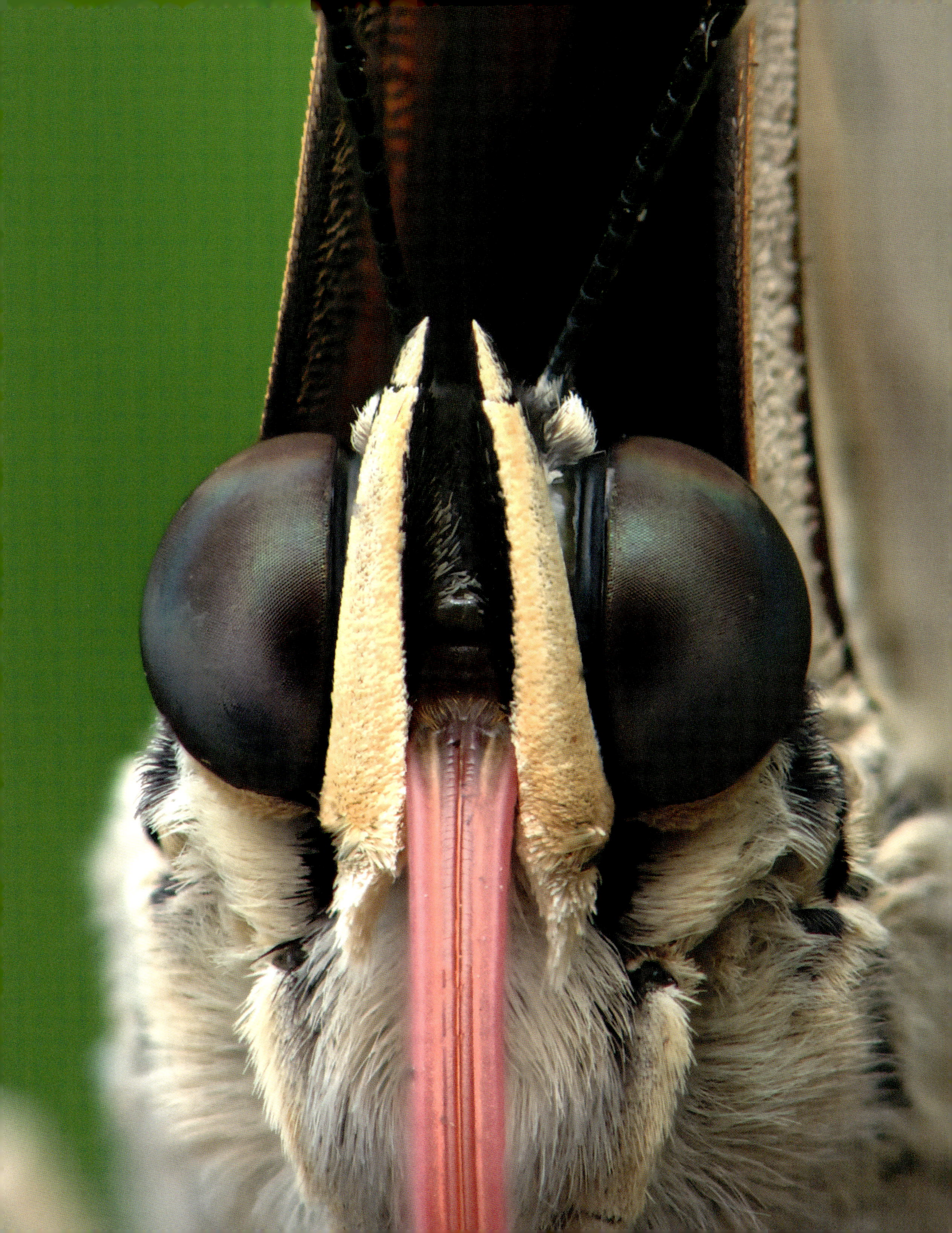

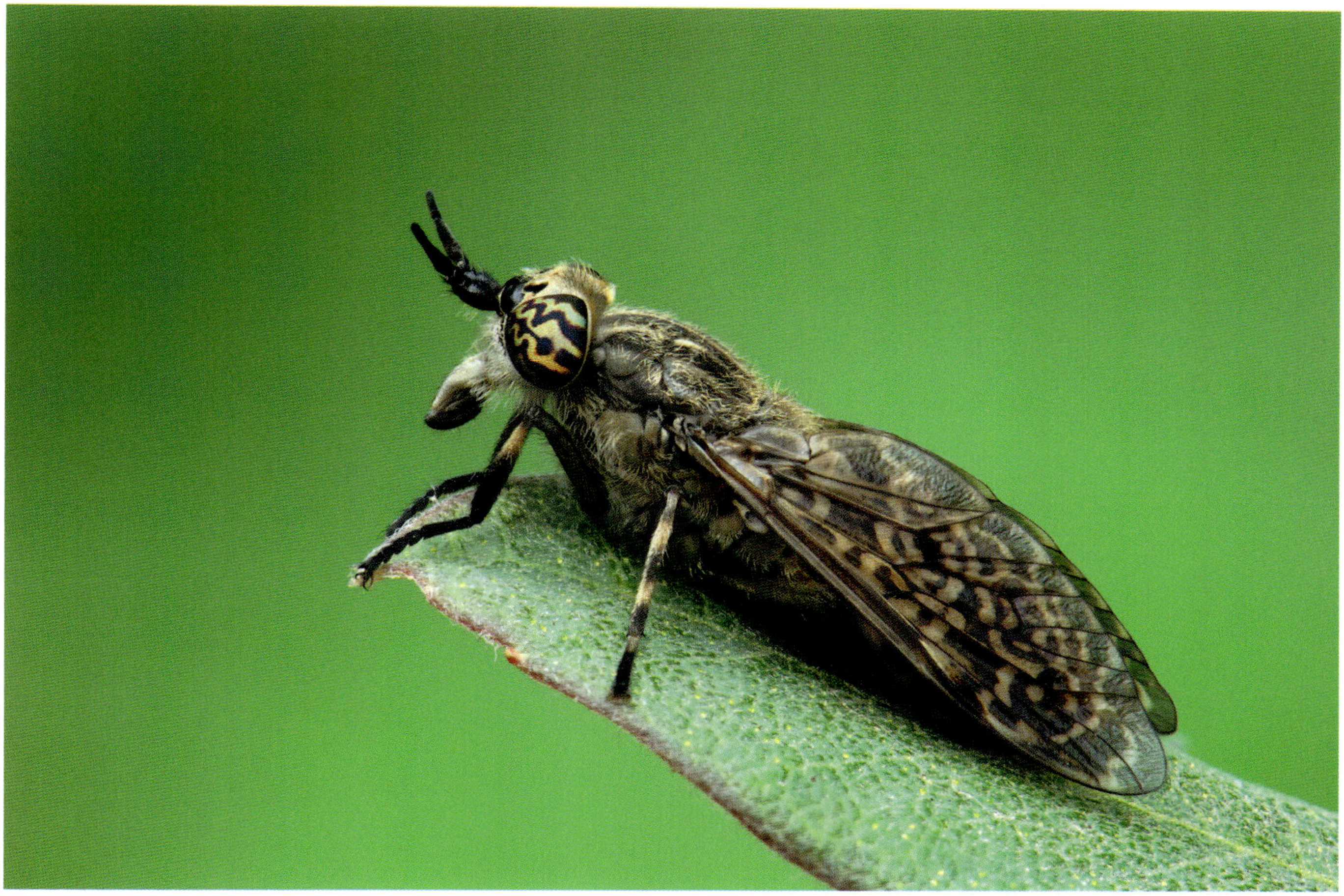

27.7 ~ **Clegg Fly** *Haematopa pulvialis*
A perfectly calm evening made it possible to capture this image at 1.5 times life-size. The mirror was raised first to eliminate any vibration.

↳ Nikon D810, 105mm micro Nikkor + 1.7x converter, 1/15sec at f/22, flash, ISO 200.

// FACING PAGE //

27.6 ~ **Shoemaker Butterfly** *Prepona omphale*

↳ Nikon D3X, 200mm micro Nikkor, with Mamiya 80mmm reversed via a coupling ring. 1/30sec at f16, ISO 200.

My Own Approach

Every photographer has their ideas and techniques for shooting at higher magnification in the field. My approach is a 105mm micro Nikkor in combination with a 1.7x or 2x teleconverter, which delivers pretty impressive results with only a reduction of one stop in terms of light loss when used in combination with the 1.7x converter. I can engage autofocus and VR and attach an extension tube if I want to push the magnification that bit further. Using a high megapixel camera such as the D810, means that I can crop the image down a little and still have a pretty usable file size. The big advantage of this combination is its lightness and portability; I can also handhold it with a macro flash assembly supported on a monopod when necessary, although I prefer to use a tripod with a focusing rail whenever possible. This makes the whole process much easier to manage. I find photographing up to around 2:1 in the field is more than adequate for the vast majority of subjects. If I need to obtain magnifications beyond that, I usually resort to the studio where I have much better control, although it requires a lot more preparation and effort to achieve an acceptable result.

Working at higher magnifications is a lot more challenging. Rotating the focusing ring achieves very little beyond life-size. It is much better to move the camera and lens assembly in and out on a focusing rail

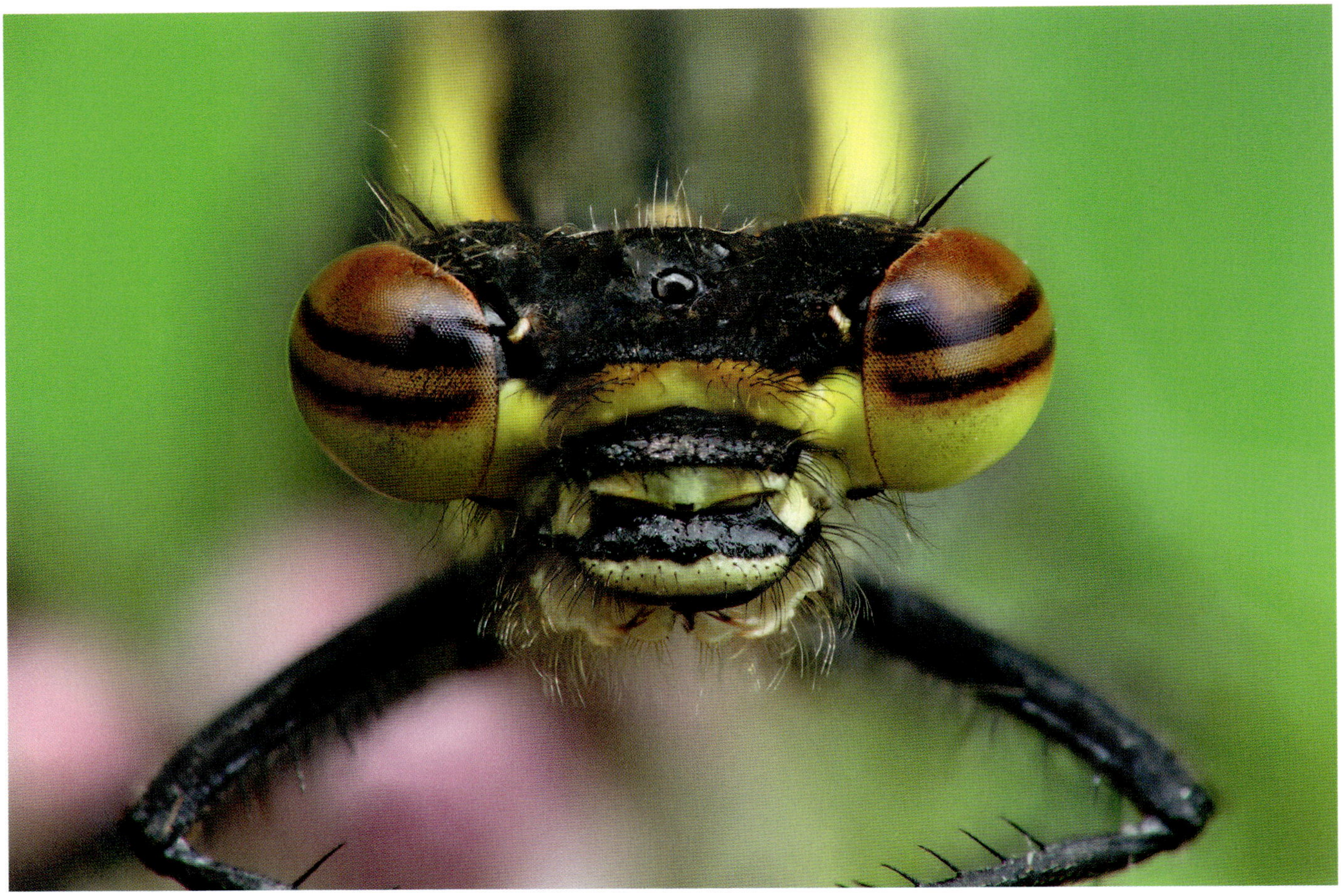

27.8 ~ **Large Red Damselfly** *Pyrrhosoma nymphula*

↘ Nikon D3X, 105mm micro Nikkor, + 1.7x converter, 1/15sec at f16, flash, ISO 200.

until the correct focus is achieved. As magnification increases, depth of field is extremely shallow beyond life-size. Working at higher magnifications usually means using flash as the primary light source, although in the right conditions, it is possible to use a combination of natural light and flash. There are many good macro flash systems about; although expensive they are worth the investment if you plan on doing a lot of this type of photography. A cheaper alternative is to make your own flash brackets as many photographers have. Information on how to do this is contained in the section on equipment in one of my previous macro photography books. There is also plenty of information on flash bracket design on the internet.

There is no doubt that photographing beyond life-size brings its own challenges. You are privy to the world that most people are oblivious to. When things go well, it does put you on a high, but it requires observation and patience along with an abiding enthusiasm for the subject. Chances are, most of your images will hit the trash can, but don't be put off, being selective in your choice of subject and choosing the appropriate weather conditions can tip the balance in your favour!

Special Purpose Macros

Canon MP-E 65mm Macro

This is a highly specialised macro lens, unique in many ways, offering a magnification range from 1:1 (life-size) up to 5:1 (5 times life-size). The MP-E 65 is a dedicated macro lens, designed specifically for high-magnification work and cannot be used for conventional photography since it can't focus at infinity. It's an all-manual focus lens with manual exposure. The lens-to-subject distance is naturally reduced from just over 10cm to less than 4cm at 5:1. Unfortunately, Nikon does not make an

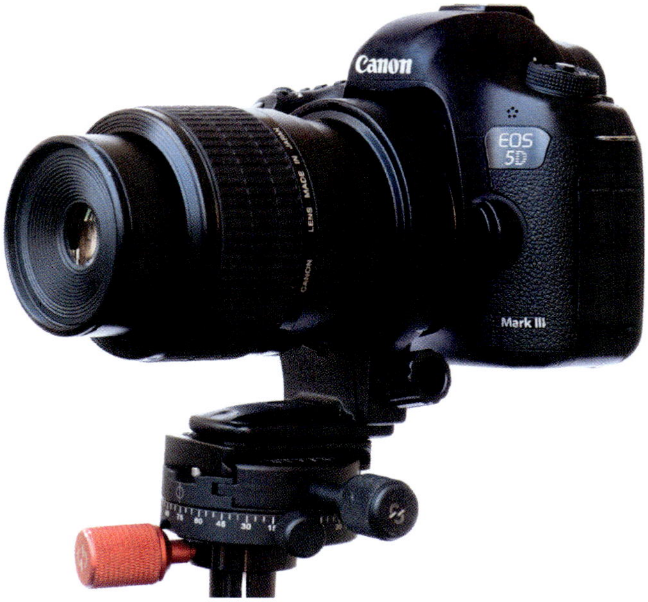

27.9 ~ Canon MP-E 65mm macro lens
An excellent lens delivering very sharp results. The lens is manual and capable of magnifications up to 5:1.

equivalent. It is very much a studio lens in some aspects, especially if you are going to take advantage of the higher magnifications. However, having a true macro lens delivering magnifications beyond the standard 1:1 without the need for additional accessories is a real advantage. As a Nikon user, I am rather envious of my peers who shoot with Canon having access to such an interesting lens. The MP-E65 has a mounting ring on the front which allows you to connect Canon's macro flash units. The short working distance can be a bit frustrating, especially when engaged at higher magnifications. It is certainly not a lens designed for a beginner, but once you familiarise yourself with the workings of it, the results can be quite impressive.

Laowa 60mm f/2.8 2:1 Ultra-macro

When a new macro lens is launched there is always an expectation that it will do something that the others can't do. The 60mm Laowa f/2.8 2:1 is the first macro lens capable of focusing from infinity (on an APS-C sensor) up to 2:1. It is a fully manual lens, so there are

27.10 ~ Black and Red Froghopper *Cercopis vulnerata*
↘ Nikon D810, 105mm micro Nikkor + 1.7x converter, 1/15sec at f/22 ISO 400.

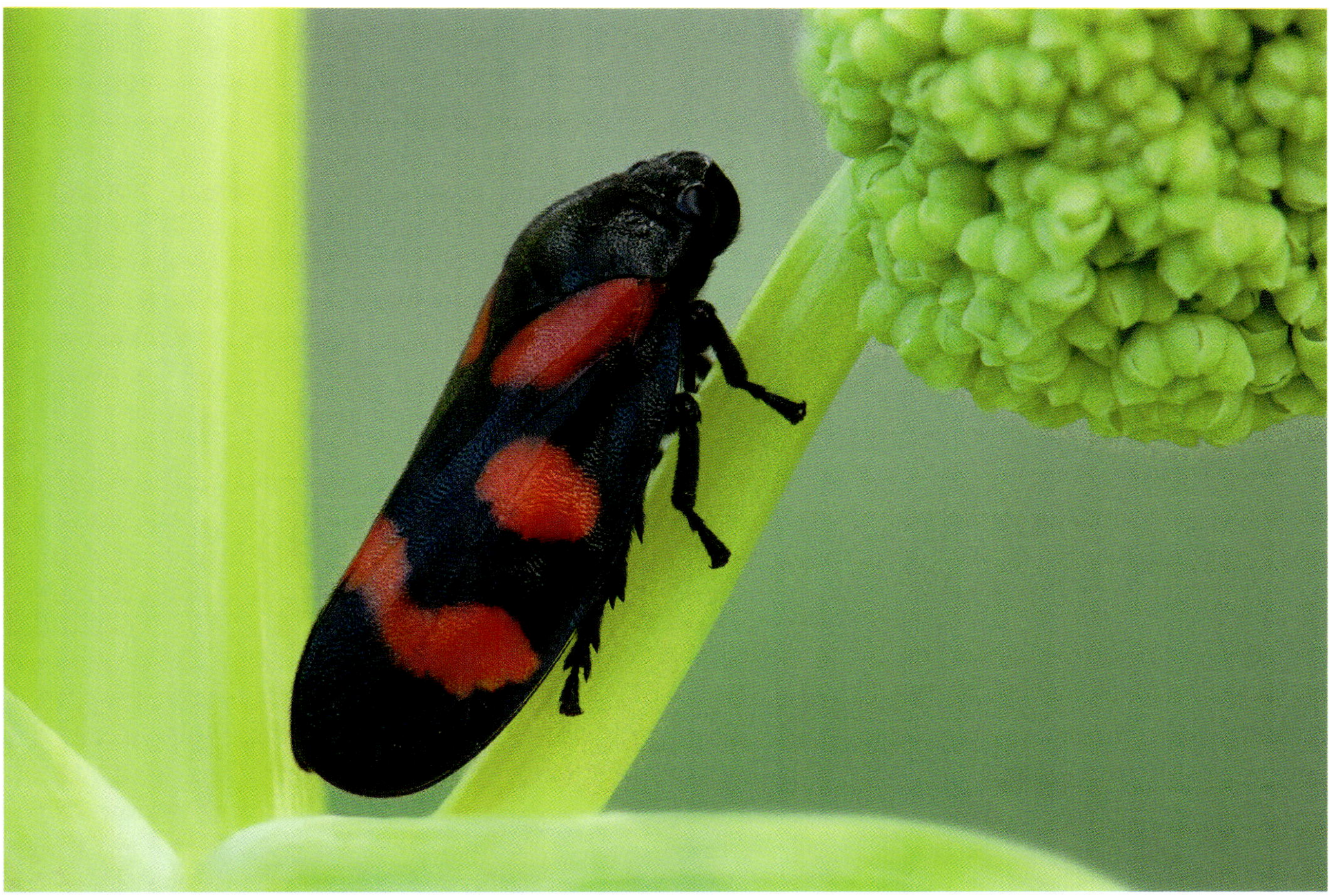

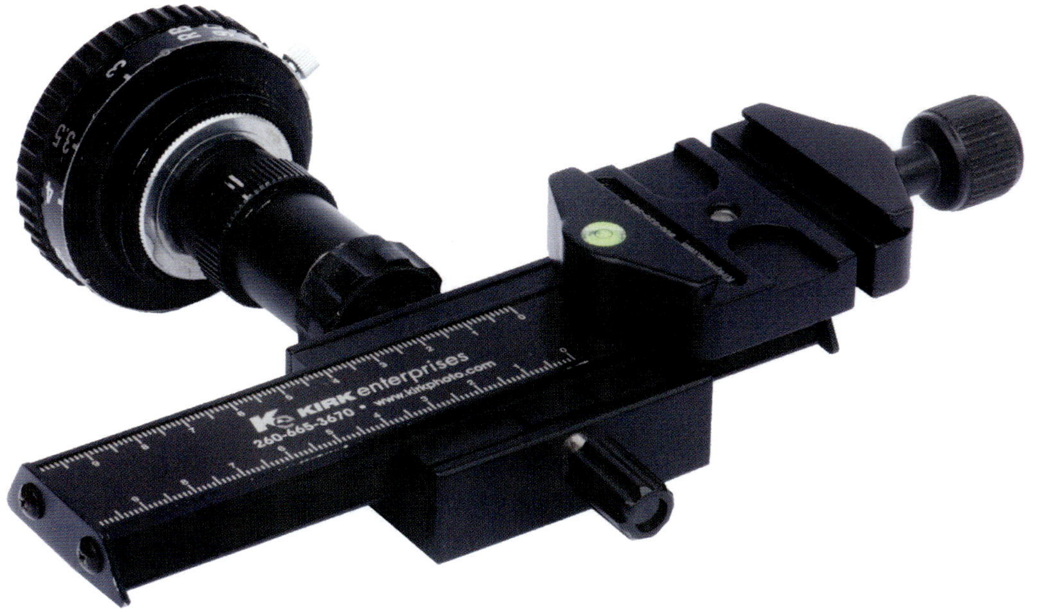

27.11 ~ **Kirk focusing rail**
I attached a larger focusing knob, which makes it easier to make fine adjustments.

no electronic connections between it and camera body. The lens consists of nine elements in seven groups and has an aperture range from f/2.8 to f/22 and a fourteen blade diaphragm which delivers very nice bokeh. Metering is carried out using the stop-down metering technique perhaps more familiar to those photographers that used film. The lens has a built-in extension tube which allows it to reach 2:1. At its maximum magnification, the lens to subject distance is around 5cm. Be also aware that when connected to the camera the aperture will naturally default to 00 since it assumes that there is no lens attached.

If you use this lens with a micro 4/3 body (via an adapter) and, with the crop factor of 2 you get a frame filled with what you would see at 4:1 magnification with a full frame camera, and with greater depth of field because of the lower magnification on the sensor.

It is very useful in the field because you have a continuous magnification range taking you from infinity and is supremely sharp with a very positive manual focus. Used with Live View with its inbuilt image intensifier it provides clear images even when stopped down. It has to be used with some sort of support, a focusing rail or a beanbag at least.

Focusing Rail

When photographing below life-size, you make adjustments to the focus by rotating the lens-focusing mount. What you are doing here is altering the position of the elements within the lens which is changing the magnification and composition of the image. It is easier to make changes at lower magnifications since it has little effect on the overall composition, however, at larger magnifications rotating the focusing ring has a considerable effect on the composition and magnification. Trying to make any adjustments by moving the tripod usually results in throwing the entire image out of focus. A focusing rail is the best approach when working beyond 1:1; it becomes an essential item in my opinion if you want to achieve precise focus. It is also useful when focus stacking at higher magnifications since rotating the focusing ring serves little purpose.

A focusing rail needs to be of a sturdy design capable of supporting a substantial setup while still being able to glide smoothly without being lumpy when weight is placed upon it. Kirk, Really Right Stuff and Monfrotto all produce excellent units. Most rails are of a rack and pinion design and fit between the tripod head camera assembly. The rail allows you to make fine focus adjustments by moving the whole assembly

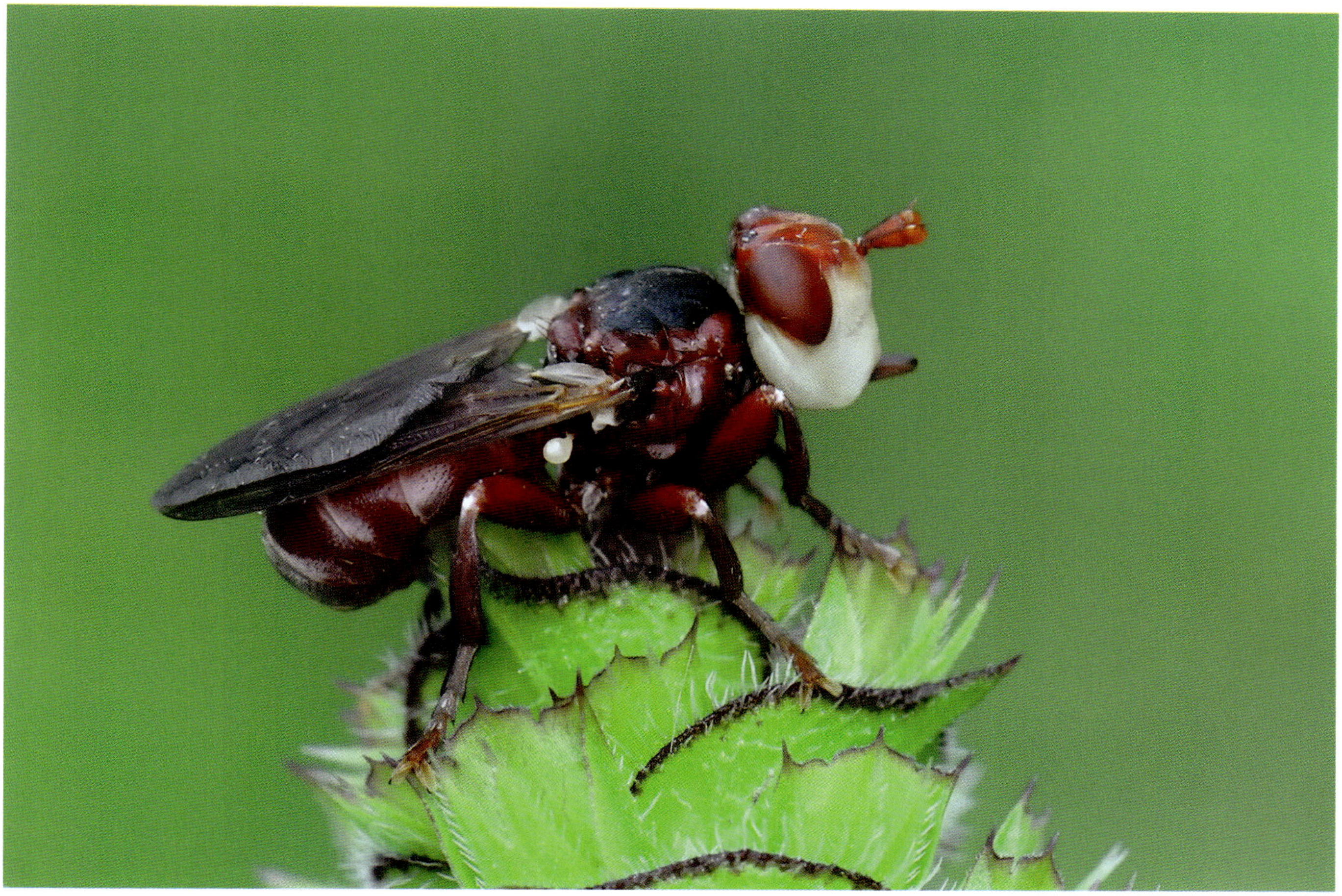

27.12 ~ **Conopid Fly** *Myopa buccata*
A focusing rail makes it much easier to work at higher magnifications in the field. You can make fine adjustments to focus without having to try and adjust the tripod. The Conopid is approximately 1.5 times life-size.

↘ Nikon D810, 105mm micro Nikkor + 1.7x converter, 1/15 sec at f/22 ISO 400.

forwards and backwards. While it is possible to work in the field above 1:1 without a rail, I find it more beneficial to work with it in place. It does give you greater control over the focus point and increased stability. Photographing subjects which are a metre off the ground is less of an issue. Working at ground level is more challenging as the height of the assembly makes it a lot harder to work at very low level. Vibration is another issue so it's important to have stability in your whole setup.

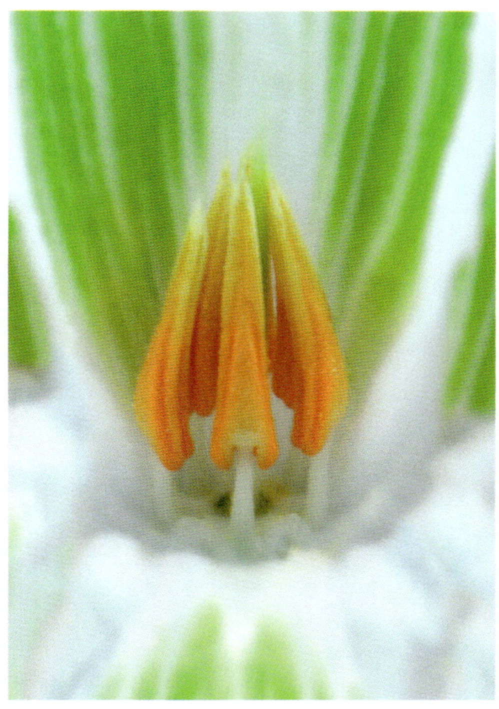

27.13 ~ **Snowdrop** ***Galanthus*** **species**
Magnification is approximately 3.5 times life-size. Focus-stacked using a focusing rail.

↘ Nikon D810, 200mm micro Nikkor, with Mamiya 80mmm reversed via a coupling ring. 1/60sec at f16, ISO 400.

TWENTY EIGHT

Accessories for Macro

Remote Device

PHOTOGRAPHING any subject, especially when using slower shutter speeds requires meticulous attention to technique even if the camera is mounted on a tripod. Depressing the shutter button carefully with your finger will impart a certain amount of movement and therefore affect sharpness and degrade the quality of the image. When shooting close-ups and working at higher magnifications, it is even more critical since any movement, even if minimal, will be magnified and clearly evident when your photograph is enlarged. I use a remote device for virtually all of my macro work except when I'm photographing on the move with a monopod. I can't emphasise strongly enough how important this is. All camera manufacturers make at least one. I have a few different units from Nikon, which I alternate between depending on what I'm doing. Most remote devices are relatively simple to use and consist of wire with a connection at the end which is inserted into the camera's terminal. Some models are fairly basic; other more expensive units offer more features, such as interval timer and a backlit control panel etc. They are also extremely useful when the mirror lock-up feature is employed.

Right Angle Finder

Pre-digital, I did use one of these devices on a regular basis and would have considered it an essential accessory for anyone shooting close-ups particularly when working at ground level. However, since the introduction of Live View they have become less popular. As its name suggests, it's an L-shaped right-angle finder which attaches to the camera's viewfinder. It's ideally suited for viewing and composing images when working at low-level and saves you having to lie flat on your

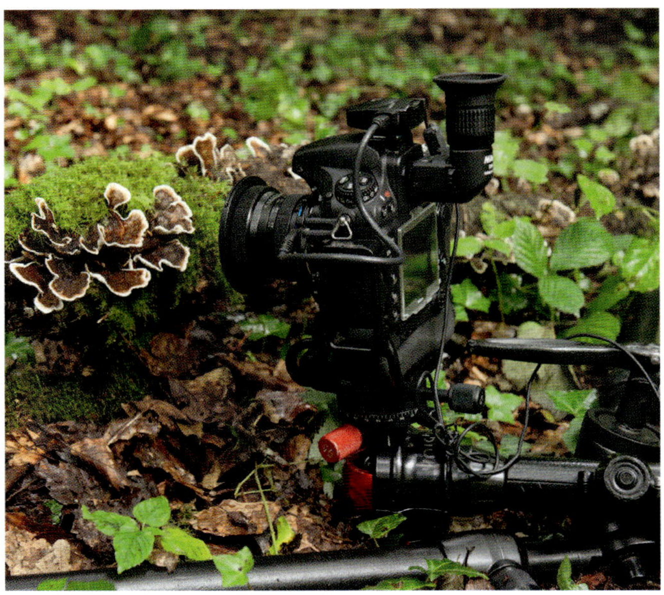

28.1 ~ Right angle finder
I still find this device handy when working at ground level.

chest, bending your neck at right angles while trying to peer through the viewfinder. I am not a regular user of Live View, but that's just down to personal approach. I still prefer to use the viewfinder for most of my macro photography, but there is still merit in having one in your bag.

GPS

I'm a big fan of 'GPS' and used a handheld unit for many years in the field. For speed and convenience, I now use Nikon's GP-1 unit. A large proportion of my work is archived at the National Museum from a number of high-profile projects that I've been involved with in Ireland. It's an essential part of my work to have location data and other relevant information attached to the image. This is particularly important when photographing rare and endangered plants and in cases where long-term monitoring of an area or habitat is taking place. Also, if you're providing images to photographic agencies, they require you to identify the subject and provide the relevant data with it. Getting into the routine of adding meaningful information to your images makes them a valuable asset and an important source of reference in the future.

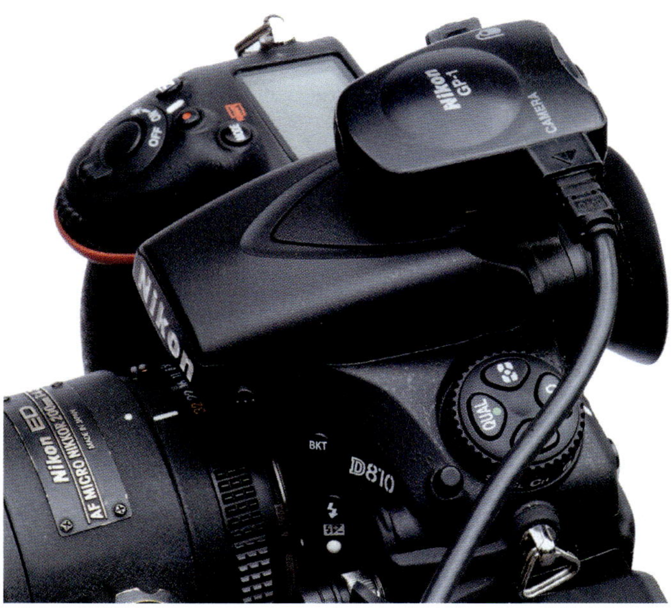

28.2 ~ **Nikon GP-1 unit**

Field Accessories

Knee Pads

Apart from the usual equipment in my backpack, I carry several other useful accessories which I think are important to have with you in the field. The first of these is a pair of knee pads which I use routinely when I'm photographing. It's surprising how much of your time is spent on your knees and how painful it can be, particularly amongst the ground vegetation which has all sorts of sharp bits of vegetation including brambles and thorns. Uneven surfaces with stones are also painful on the knees. I find it much more comfortable to use lightweight knee pads which allow me to move freely on the ground without the annoyance of thorns or stones perforating my skin.

Kneeling Mats

When working in wetland habitats, I also carry a lightweight kneeling mat similar to those used for gardening strapped to my backpack. It takes up little room and is useful for keeping the knees of your trousers dry. I also have a ground sheet for when I need to lie flat on the ground. These suggestions may sound like stating the obvious, but it's surprising just how many photographers carry nothing like this at all. You need to be comfortable when photographing at ground level, and if you are not it will be a constant source of distraction.

The Wimberley Plamp

One of the most popular macro accessories for stabilising moving subjects in the wind is the Wimberley Plamp. The original version, in my opinion, was stiff, and the clasp clamp which attached to your tripod leg meant that if you wanted to make minor adjustments to the position of the tripod you had to be extremely careful not to snap the stem of the plant it was supporting. I also found it difficult to make smooth, minor adjustments to the position since the individual segments were somewhat stiff.

The latest version of the Plamp has been redesigned with a few modifications and now supports additional accessories. The current design has a spike which is essentially a screwdriver that fits into a moulded tube; this can be reversed when not in use. It also has an improved head clamp with foam inserts.

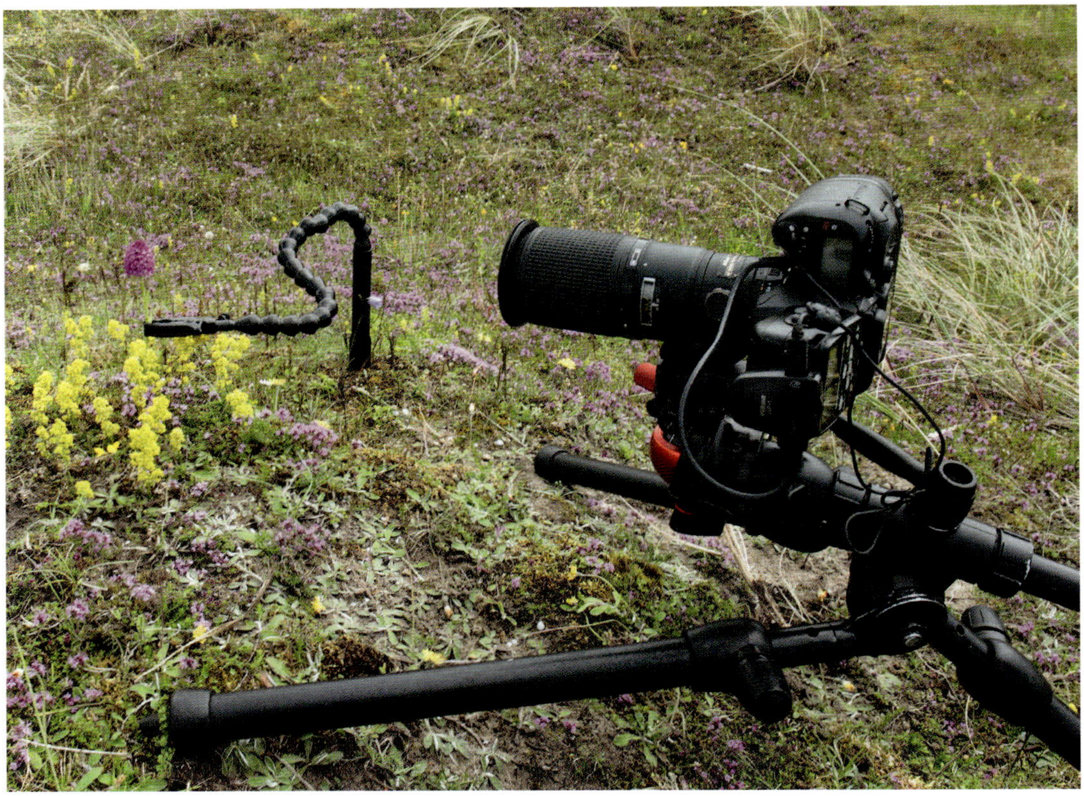

28.3 ~ The Wimberley Plamp
The latest version is a good improvement over the previous model.

There is also a notch for a diffuser, but I feel it's better to have a diffuser as a standalone unit. Most are too heavy in my opinion to connect to the device. I also found in the earlier model that the bolt that attaches the Loc-line tubing to the clamp becomes loose after a while. The connection on the latest version is a definite improvement. I had used my own design of stabilising device before the Plamp became available, but I carry both now as they each have their uses.

Other Bits and Pieces

I also carry a few other bits and pieces in my bag including clothes pegs small crocodile clips and string for holding back thin branches from the field of view. A small pair of scissors is useful when you need to remove an obtrusive piece of foliage. I also carry a small paint-brush for removing hairs, dirt and other small bits of debris off the leaves and flowers of plants. Inexperienced photographers frequently overlook these in the field, but they can often diminish the aesthetics of the image. If you don't have a stem stabiliser or a Plamp you can use two V-shaped twigs. The stem rests in-between the V-shaped branches which are pushed into the ground; the other branch rests slightly above, which supports the stem. It may seem crude, but it does work if you're stuck.

When the weather is changeable I don't want to keep taking down my equipment, so I use a clear plastic bag with a zip; the sort that a blanket comes in. It is light but thick enough to do the job. I can place this over my camera and zip it up.

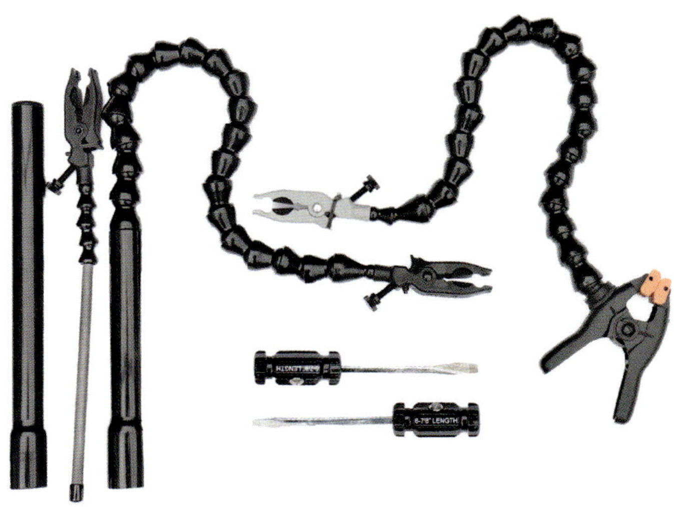

28.4 ~ Latest version of Wimberley Plamp and accessories.

TWENTY NINE

My Field Equipment

I AM frequently asked about what equipment I take out with me on a regular basis. It's a meaningless question in a way, since it all depends on what I'm going to photograph. I do however have a regular field kit for macro which covers most of the situations I'm likely to encounter. I don't carry everything listed here but switch between equipment depending on what I'm doing. I keep a second bag in my vehicle if I'm going to be working on a particular project, for example, creatures in freshwater or rockpools. I need to carry tanks and other accessories to be able to work *in situ*. I am not a committed photo junkie, but I do like to invest in equipment that I think will make my task easier. Unfortunately, I have found over the years that when it comes to macro you end up making bits and pieces yourself since some of the standard accessories offered by camera companies are often too universal and not of any real use.

Since the digital revolution, I have used Nikon equipment. I have found it to be excellent, and it works for me. Others prefer another brand such as Canon or Sony. To be honest, any camera these days is more than capable of delivering high-quality imagery. The important thing is to choose carefully; investing in a system is a long-term commitment and financially expensive. It is not that easy to switch when you have invested a considerable sum in lenses and accessories. I don't change equipment (particularly camera bodies) just as quickly now as I did a few years ago. I have owned every professional DSLR body that Nikon has produced to date, but I feel that the D800 and D810 are excellent cameras. There would certainly need to be something more than a mere increase in pixels for me to consider another jump at present.

Pre-digital I used Medium Format; in particular Mamiya's 645 and 6 x 7 formats. I had a long association with them but used their cameras because it suited my style of photography and for no other reason. I also had a Bronica SQAi system as well, which I did use on some occasions. It's easy to make a statement that expensive equipment accounts for good imagery which is, of course, untrue. Good equipment helps in the sense that it can withstand the elements and the pounding of everyday use and is generally reliable. Cameras don't make photographs, photographers do. Any system in the hands of an inexperienced operator no matter what the cost is capable of delivering poor results if used incorrectly.

Current Camera Bodies

At present, I use a Nikon D810 and D800, both with battery grips. I also have a D3X, which I used as my main camera body until I purchased the D800 and subsequently the D810. All of these cameras are capable of producing high quality imagery. When working abroad I prefer to take the D800 as my backup; the battery grip and all of the other accessories are transferable between both bodies which means I can cut down on duplication.

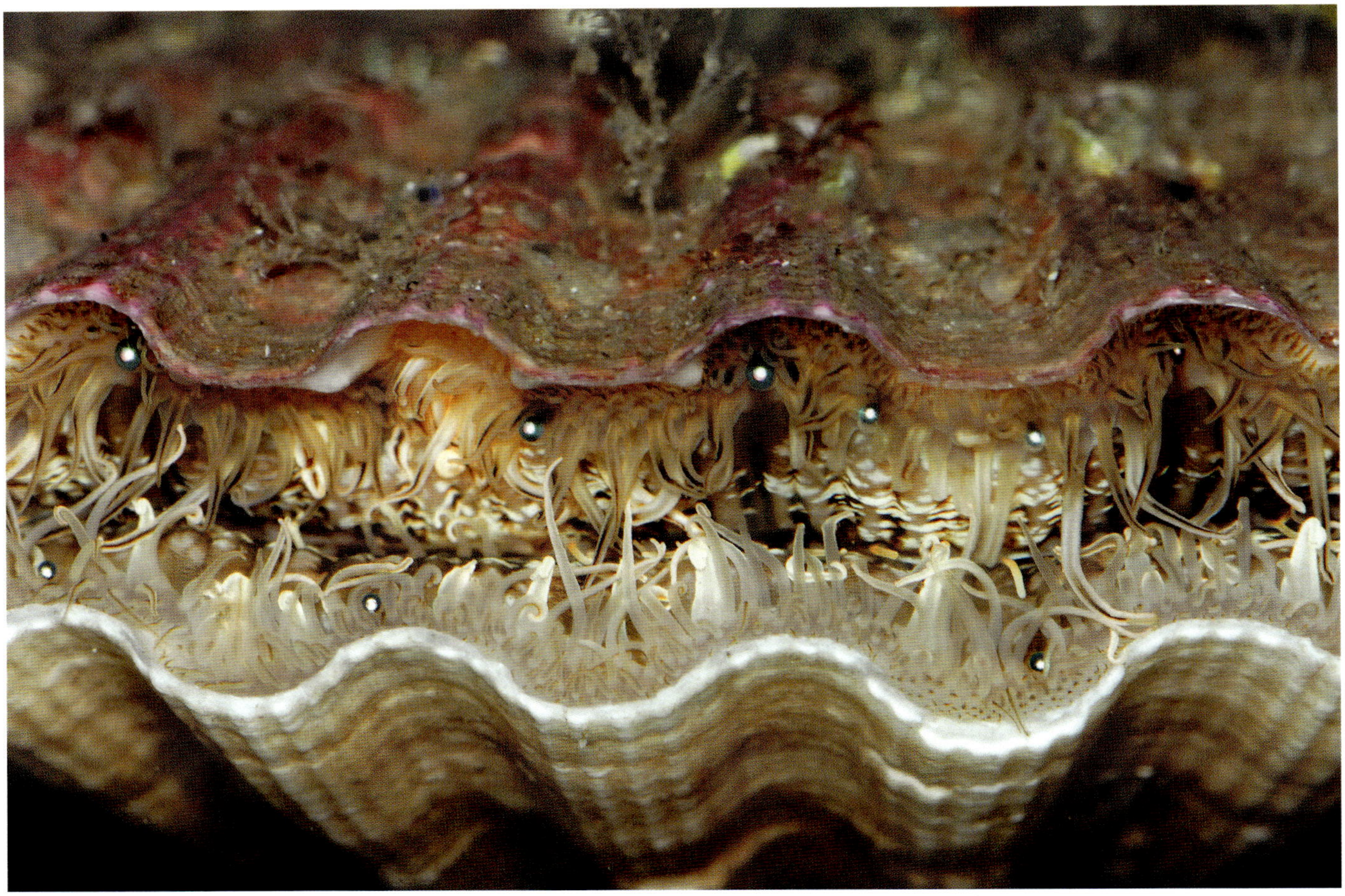

29.1 ~ **King Scallop** *Pecten maximus*
Close-up of the shell and mantle showing the array tentacles and small eyes.
Nikon D810, 200mm micro Nikkor, 1/6sec at f11, flash, ISO 200.

Nikon Lenses

- **14–24mm f/2.8 AF-S.** This is a great lens and excellent for showing plants in relation to their environment. One negative point is the fact that it does not accept conventional filters. The front element of the lens is large and dome-like making it difficult to attach a normal filter. There is also no screw thread on the lip of the lens. You can obtain filters for it from Lee, but these are very expensive.
- **24–70mm f/2.8 G AF-S ED.** One of my favourite all-around lenses and one I often use for habitat and *in situ* shots.
- **105mm micro Nikkor AF-S 2.8 G ED.** I use this lens mainly for macro on the move (see page 111) and in combination with a 1.7x teleconverter to get beyond 1:1 life-size in the field. Also, occasionally, when I'm in a confined area with limited space.
- **200mm micro Nikkor f/4 D IF-ED.** My most frequently used lens for close-ups. It delivers exceptionally sharp results and has a great working distance and a narrow-angle of view which is useful for background control. It is a heavy lens and is best used on a tripod.
- **300mm f/2.8 G ED VRII AF-S.** I like this lens a lot for portraits of plants, in particular, orchids and dragonflies. It does an excellent job of isolating the subject from its background creating a soft diffused look. It's quite a heavy lens so I don't take it with me routinely, only when I am after a particular look.

Other Lenses I Sometimes Use Include:

- 24mm f/3.5 PC-E tilt/shift
- 85mm f/2.8 PC-E micro Nikkor

Flash

- SB-800 x 2
- R1C1 Wireless macro flash system with commander unit x 2
- SB-29s macro Speedlight
- Series of diffusers and reflectors
- Range of CF cards up to 64GB
- Lowepro Pro Trekker 600 AW; favourite back-pack with bags of space
- Two other smaller Lowepro bags for travel.
- Kneeling mat and knee pads

Additional Accessories

- Nikon 1.7x teleconverter
- Kenko extension tubes
- Nikon GP-1 GPS unit
- Various remote release cables
- Portable storage and back-up
- MacBook Pro when away from home
- My own Stem Stabiliser

Tripods and Heads

- Uni-loc and Benbo, three different sizes
- Kirk quick release L brackets for camera bodies with Arca Swiss fitting.
- Kirk BH1 tripod head
- Kirk focusing rail
- UniqBall with a panoramic head. I use it virtually all of the time now

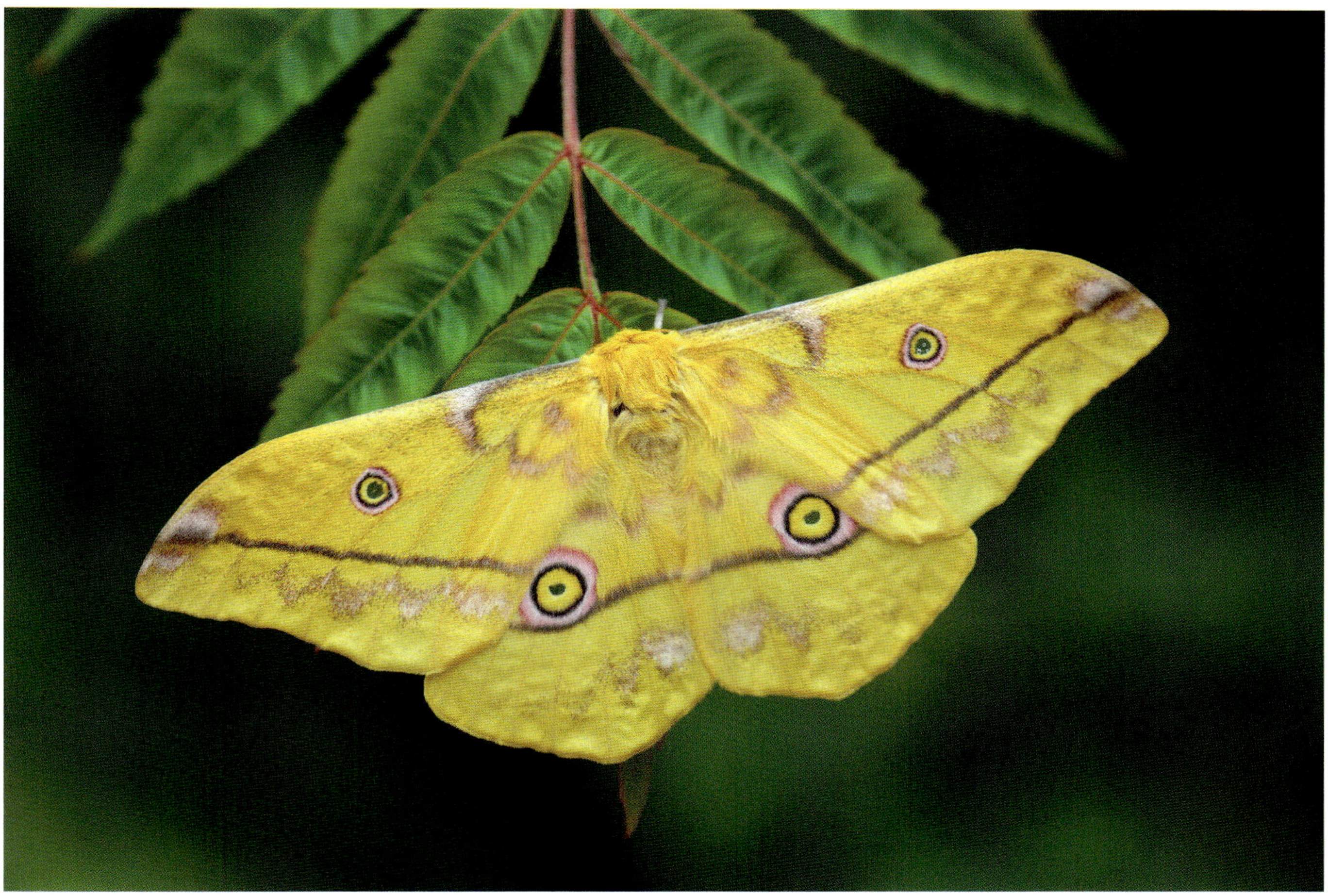

29.2 ~ *Nudaurelia dione* (female)

Nikon D810, 200mm micro Nikkor, 1/30sec at f8, flash, ISO 100.

THIRTY

Filters

DURING the pre-digital era, filters were an important part of the photographer's repertoire of accessories. So many can be replicated in image processing software, that it is no longer necessary to carry a large selection. I don't use filters very often in close-up photography now I have converted to digital. I prefer to reproduce what I see in nature as close as possible. However, having said that, I do carry a polarising filter and a couple of graduated neutral density filters.

Polarising Filter

Polarising filters are widely used in landscape photography for saturating clear blue skies and removing reflections of various objects. In close-up photography they are particularly useful for removing surface reflections from plants, foliage, water and rocks, especially after rain. They also add vibrancy and impact to your subjects in the right situations. I don't usually apply it to subjects photographed in early morning light as I like to convey the cool ambience of that time of day.

There are two types of polariser, linear and circular. A linear polariser is essentially composed of two elements that when rotated alter the direction of the light waves passing through the filter. Rotating the filter in one direction will allow horizontal waves to pass through while turning the filter through 90 degrees permits only vertical light waves. Linear polarisers are useful when you need to suppress light striking a reflective surface from a particular direction.

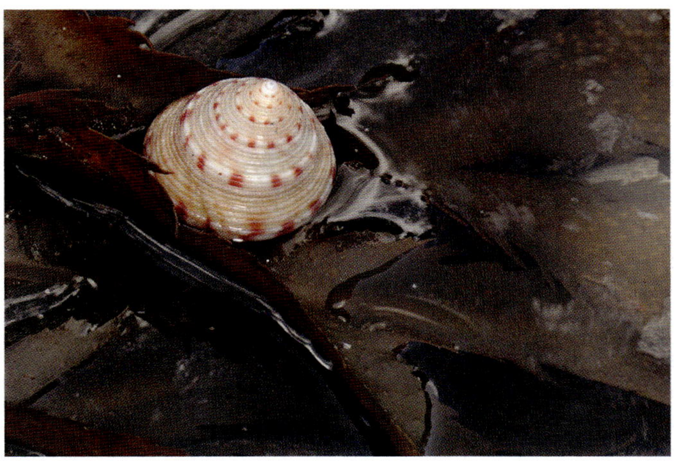

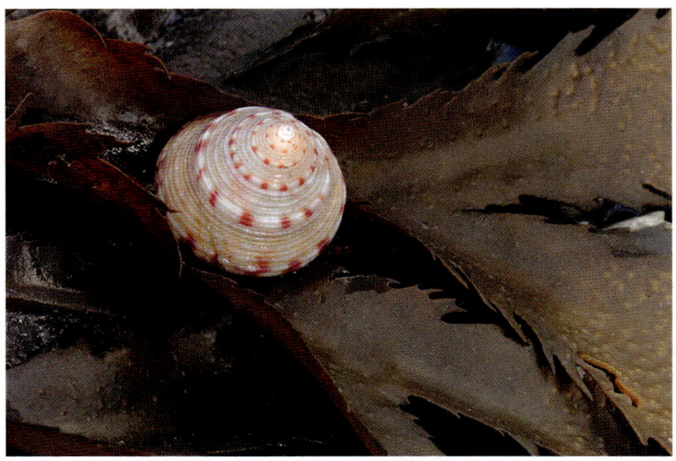

30.1 ~ Polarising filter
A polarizer is handy in situations such as this where you need to remove the surface reflection.

Circular polarisers are sensitive to both linear and circular polarisation. It incorporates a linear polariser combined with a quarter wave plate which is attached to the rear of the linear polariser, resulting in the light emitted being circularly polarised. Modern DSLRs have partially reflecting mirrors and this can lead to metering errors when a linear polariser is used. Circular polarising filters eliminate the problem, but tend to be more expensive. Polarising filters can reduce your exposure by up to two stops. You need to be aware of this, especially when photographing in shaded spots or when shutter speed is a priority.

30.2 ~ Dog Welk *Nucella lapillus*
The surface of this rock was slightly wet creating distracting highlights in the image. Attaching a polarising filter removed the surface reflections and increased the saturation slightly producing a more pleasing result.

↪ Nikon D810, 105mm micro Nikkor, 1/8sec at f/11, ISO 100.

Graduated Neutral Density Filters

These are rectangular resin filters that fit into a particular holder which is attached to the front of your lens. They are useful when shooting subjects in the context of their habitat. The holder can be rotated to darken areas within the frame which are lighter than the rest to balance the exposure. I don't use them as much now since I can in most situations bracket exposures and combine and blend in Photoshop when I need to. However, there are still some occasions, particularly where there is movement, that using a filter is an easier option. Graduated filters come in different strengths, for example 0.3, 0.6, 0.9. Each value represents an exposure increase of one stop. They also come in hard and soft versions. I prefer the soft version which is a more gradual transition between the full density of the filter to clear. Hard neutral density filters are better suited to situations such as seascapes where you have a cleaner uninterrupted horizon line.

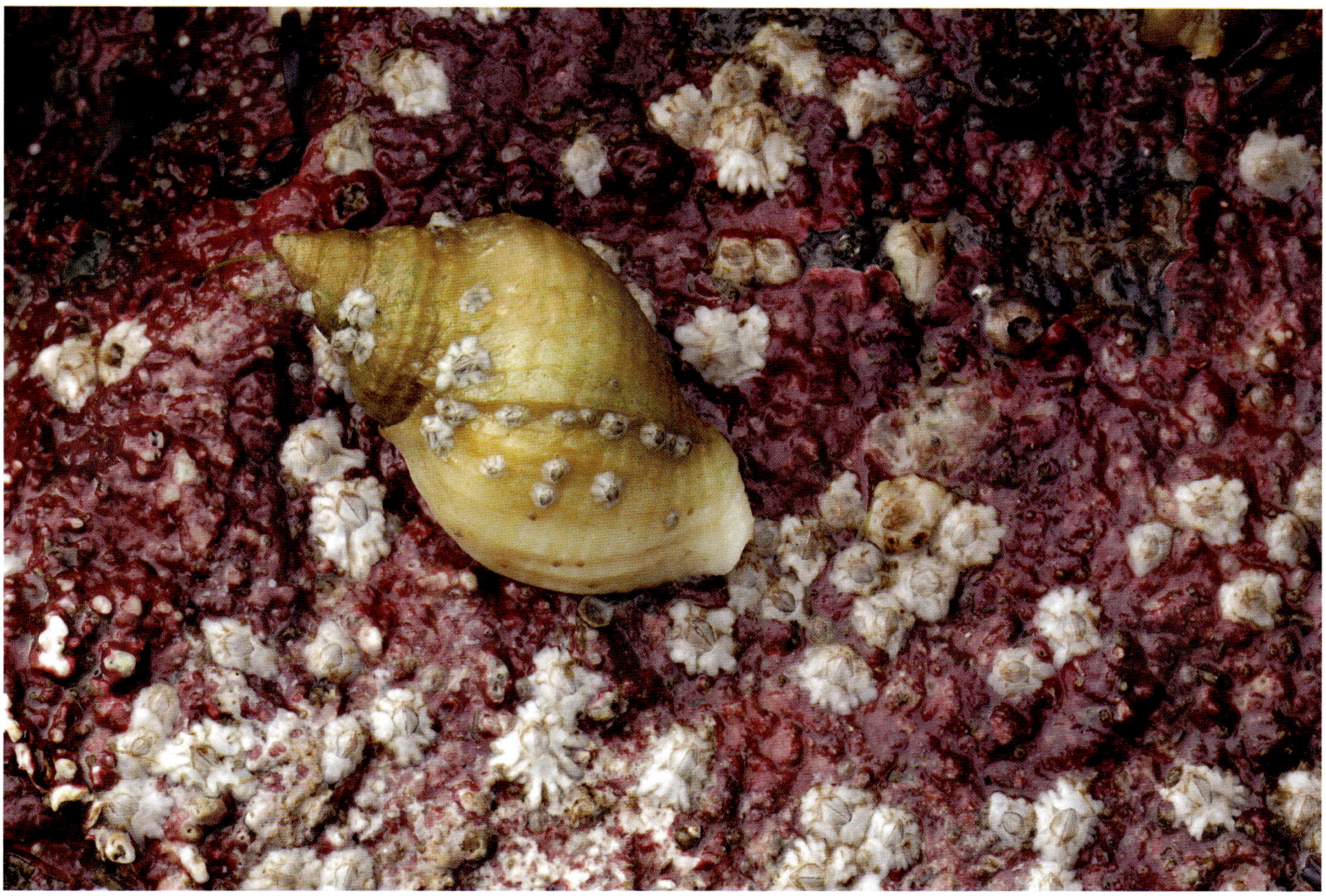

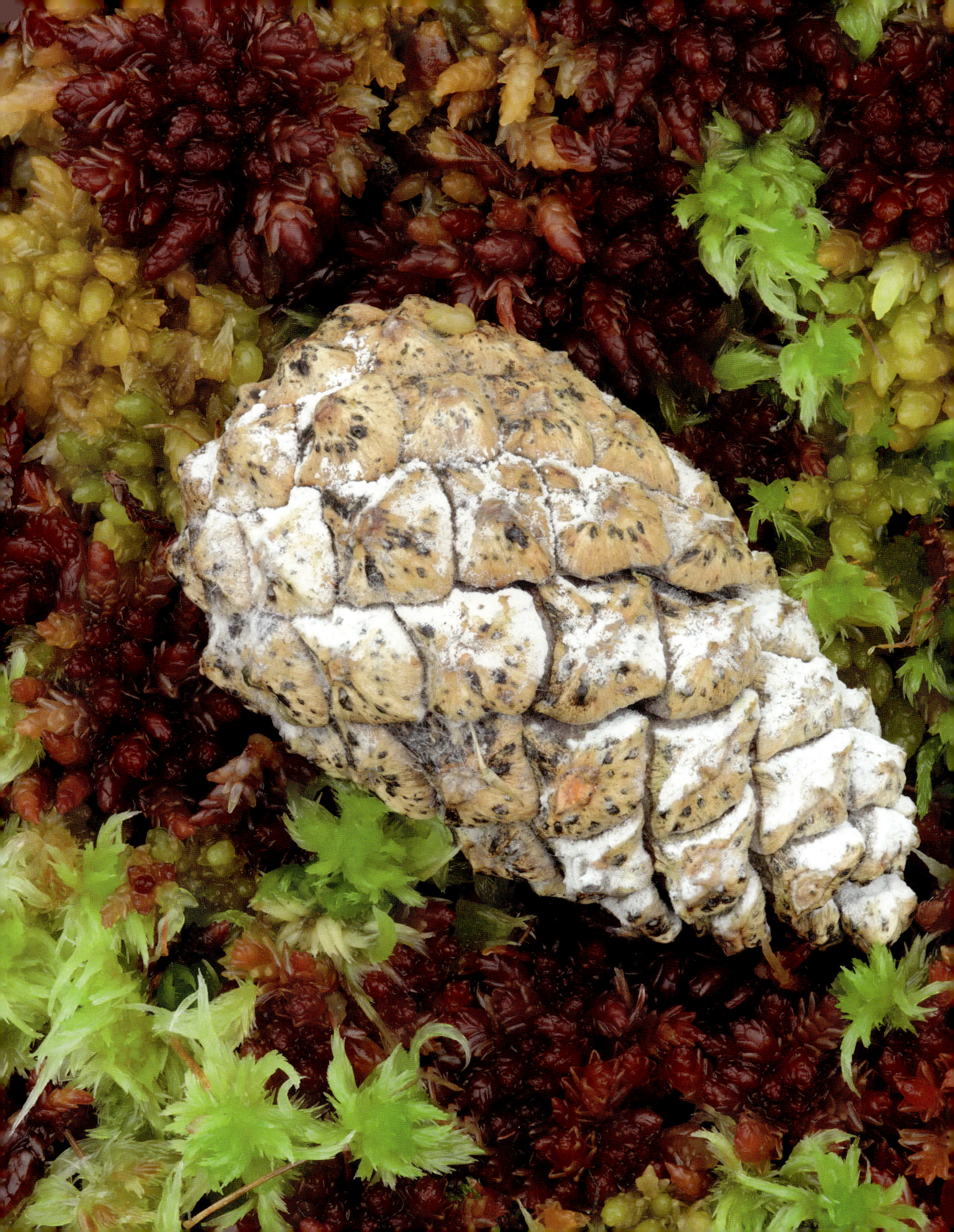

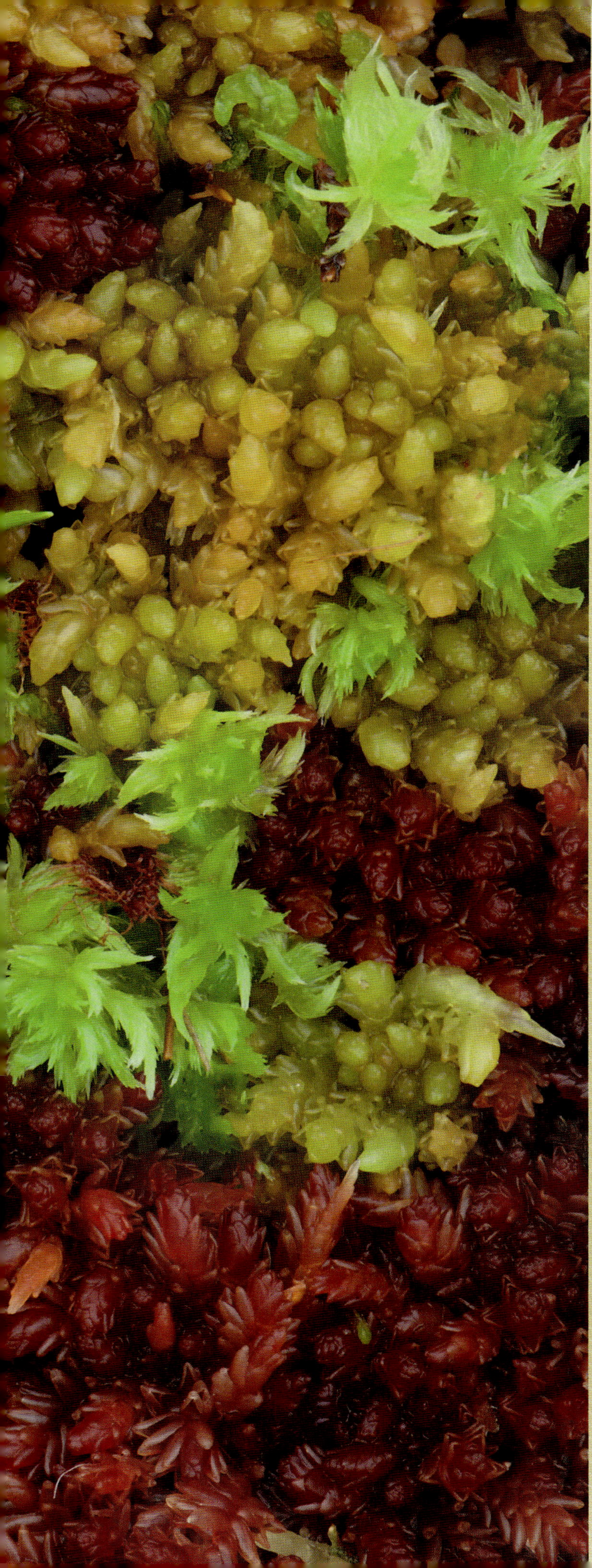

Part Three

Portfolio Case Studies

Fallen Pine Cone

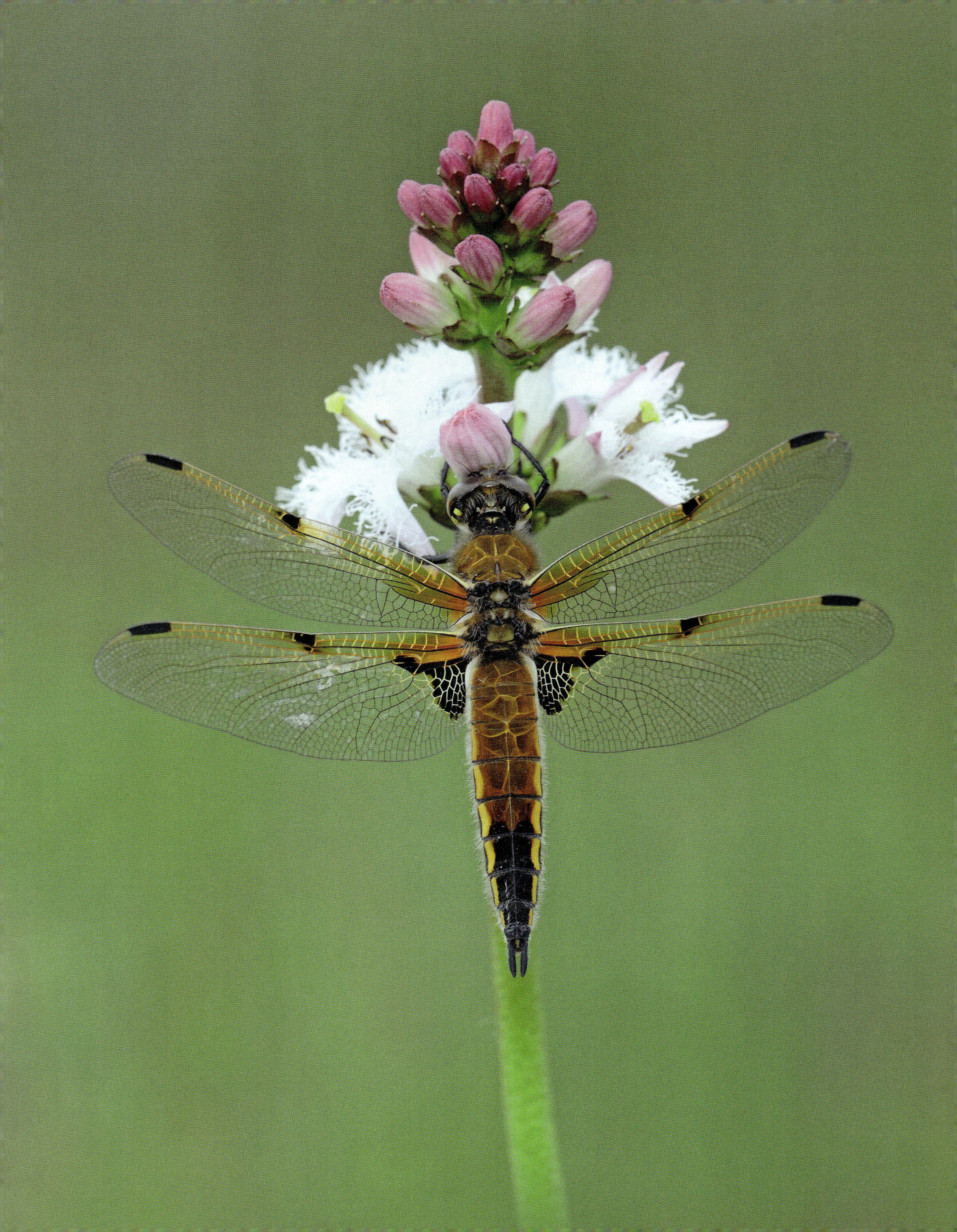

THIRTY ONE

Jewels of the Insect World

Dragonflies & Damselflies

Introduction

Dragonflies are an ancient and fascinating group of insects, whose origins date back over three hundred million years ago. Their ancestors flew in the vast prehistoric forests before the dinosaurs roamed the earth. They are one of the oldest insect orders in the world and still retain most of their primitive morphological structure, which has undergone little change since then. They are, without doubt, one of the largest and most colourful group of insects alive today, recognised as being benign, charismatic and appreciated for their beauty and vibrant colours. No other insect can match their speed or agility in the air; they are highly efficient predators with superb visual acuity, possessing 360° vision and an aerodynamic structure that is beautifully adapted for hunting and feeding on the wing. The modern names such as hawkers, emeralds, skimmers, darters and chasers reflect their true nature and character.

// FACING PAGE //

31.1 ~ Four-spotted Chaser *Libellula quadrimaculata* (female)
This is a very approachable insect. I chose a wider aperture to keep the background well diffused and carefully eased a neighbouring flower just out of the frame to keep the composition simple.

↘ Nikon D800, 200mm micro Nikkor, 1/30sec at f/8, ISO 200.

Like most insects, dragonflies are extremely popular among photographers, attracted by their size and bright, vibrant colours. Walking along the bank of a slow-flowing river, or sitting quietly at the edge of a small lake or pond with a camera will reveal many fascinating aspects about their habits and behaviour.

Biology and Life History

These enigmatic creatures are one of the most challenging groups of insects to photograph. Achieving captivating photos of their life history is an amalgamation of fieldcraft, observation and an understanding of their biology and habits.

Dragonflies are subdivided into two groups, the Anisoptera (true dragonflies) and Zygoptera (damselflies). The former are mostly large, robust insects, brightly coloured and fast fliers. True dragonflies rest with their wings held horizontal, or depressed forwards when active and at flight temperature.

Large dragonflies are referred to as hawkers; other smaller species are known as 'chasers', 'darters' and 'skimmers'. Many species are territorial, preferring to perch on prominent reeds or stems from which they conduct aerial sorties, waging battle with rival males

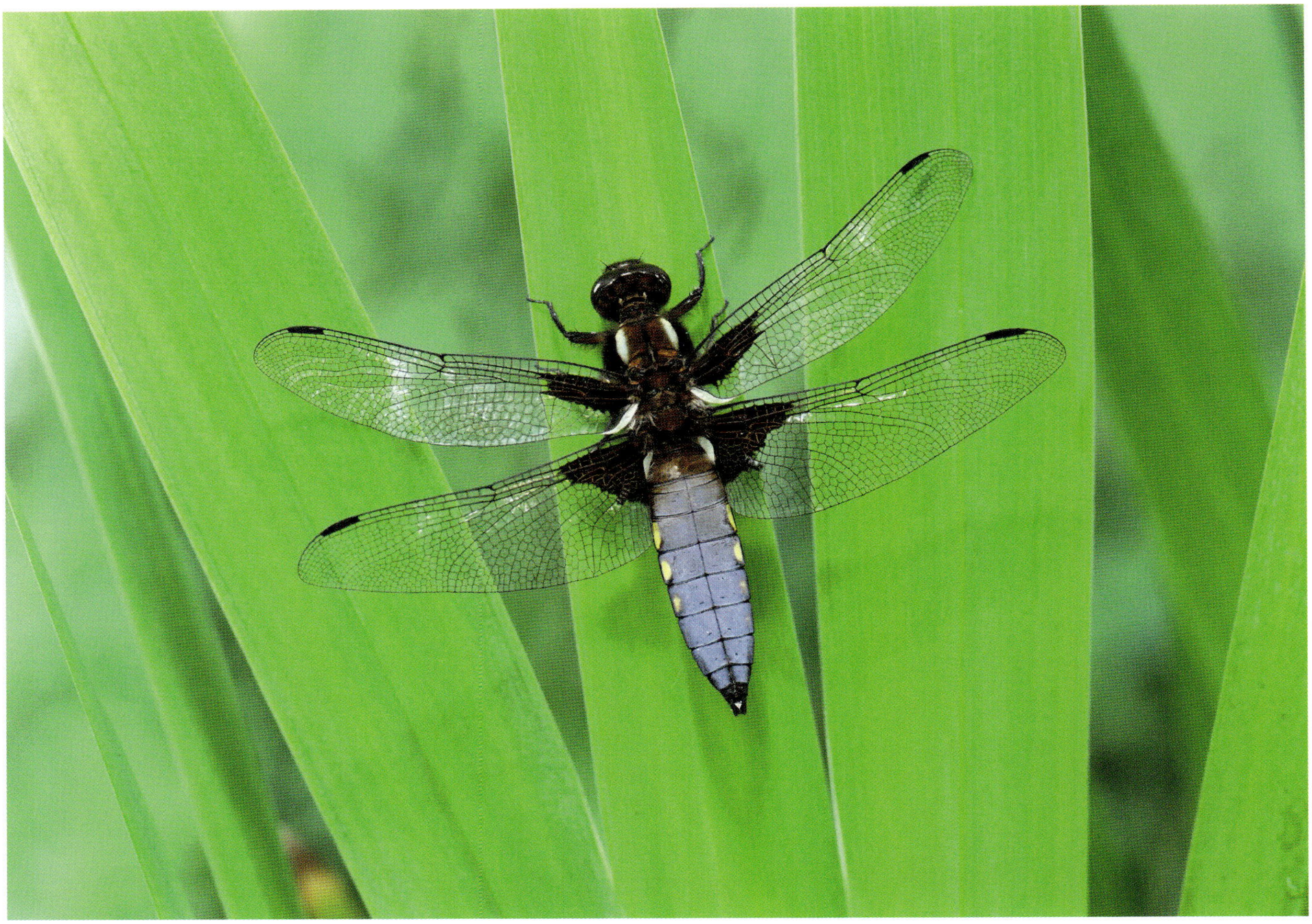

31.2 ~ **Broad-bodied Chaser** *Libellula depressa* (male)
The males of this species are quite territorial and can be difficult to approach closely.

↘ Mamiya 645 Pro TL, with 210mm lens, ext tube, Velvia, tripod.

and other species that invade their airspace. These smaller dragonflies are more commonly encountered and reasonably tolerant of approaching photographers. They tend to congregate around breeding pools, especially during mid-morning.

All dragonflies and damselflies are, by nature, aquatic insects and spend on average between one and three years (depending on species) below the water as a predatory larva. When mature, they need to leave the water to complete the transformation into a winged adult. They congregate in the shallow areas of lakes, ponds and streams where they select a suitable stem or piece of vegetation in which they can crawl up to complete the change. This often takes place under the cover of darkness, or early in the morning. Their adult phase as a winged insect is relatively short compared to their

// FACING PAGE ~ TOP //

31.3 ~ **Migrant Hawker** *Aeshna mixta* (larva)
The larval phase of dragonflies varies between one and three years; occasionally longer with some species especially at higher altitudes. Most dragonflies can easily be photographed in a small tank on location without having to bring them back to the studio.

↘ Nikon D2X, 105mm micro Nikkor, 1/60sec at f11, flash, ISO 100.

// FACING PAGE ~ BOTTOM //

31.4 ~ **Variable Damselfly** *Coenagrion pulchellum* (larva)
Damselfly larvae have slender abdomens and prominent feather-like appendages at the end of their abdomen. This makes them easier to distinguish from their larger dragonfly cousins.

↘ Nikon D2X, 105mm micro Nikkor, 1/6sec at f11, flash, ISO 100.

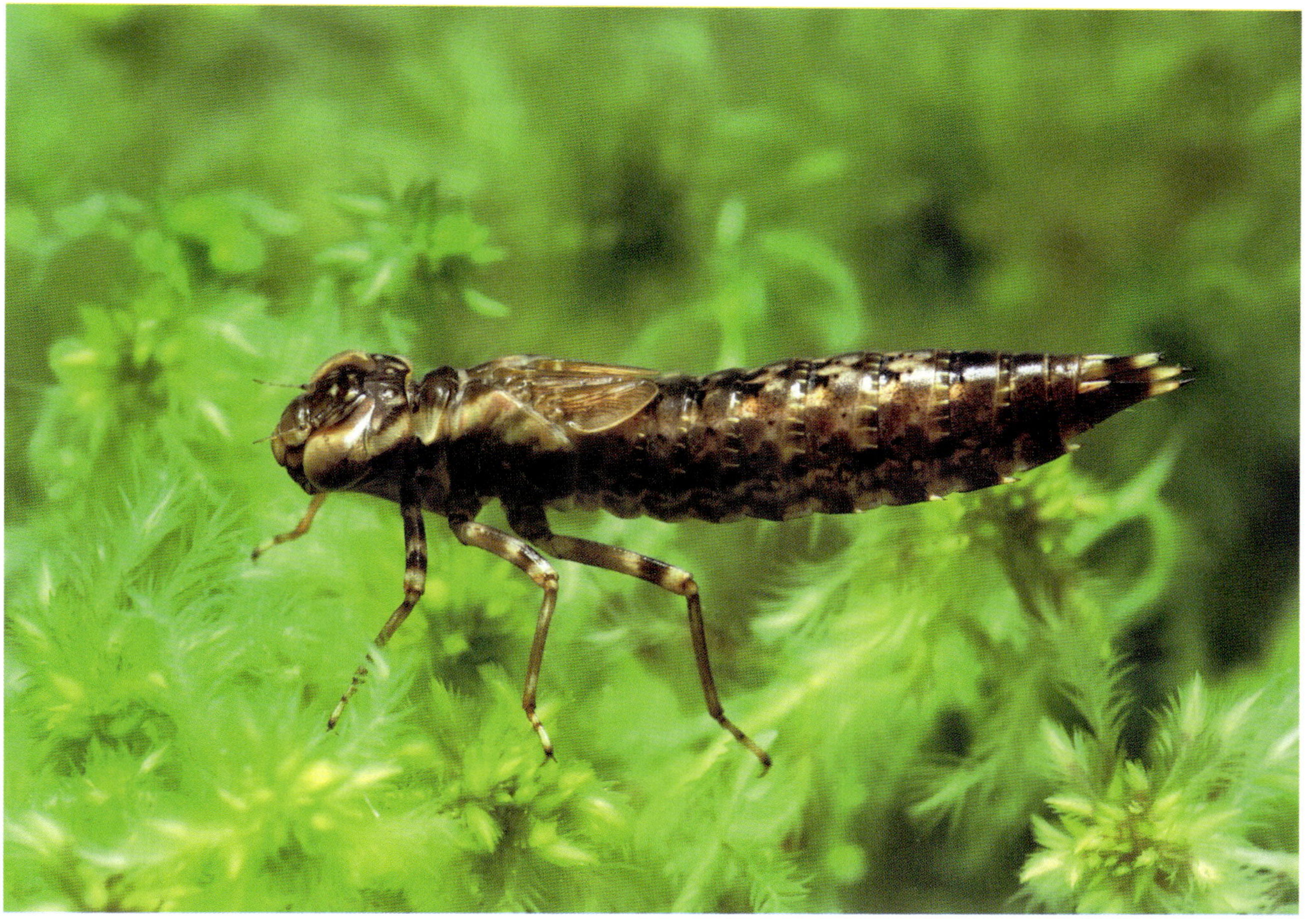

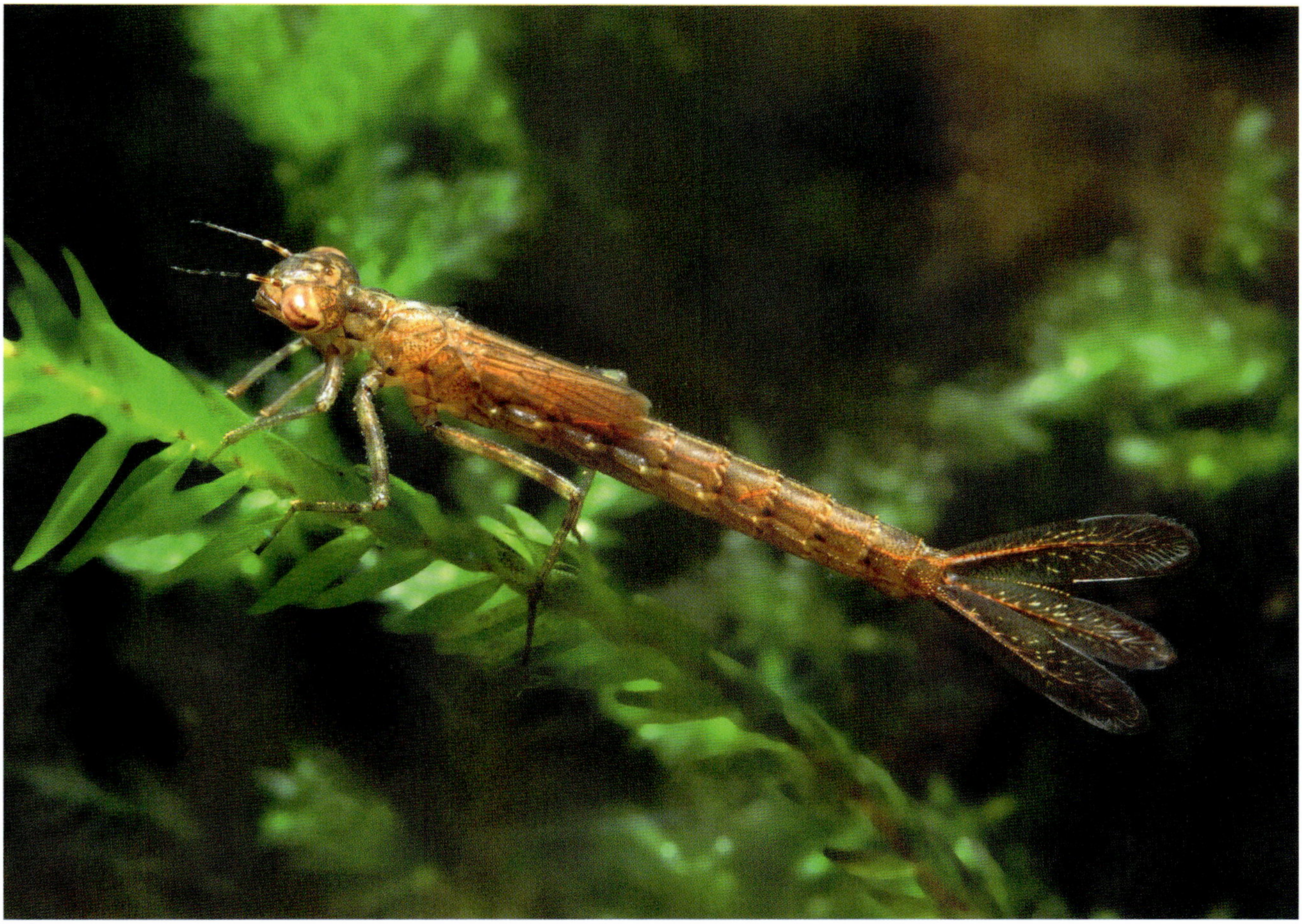

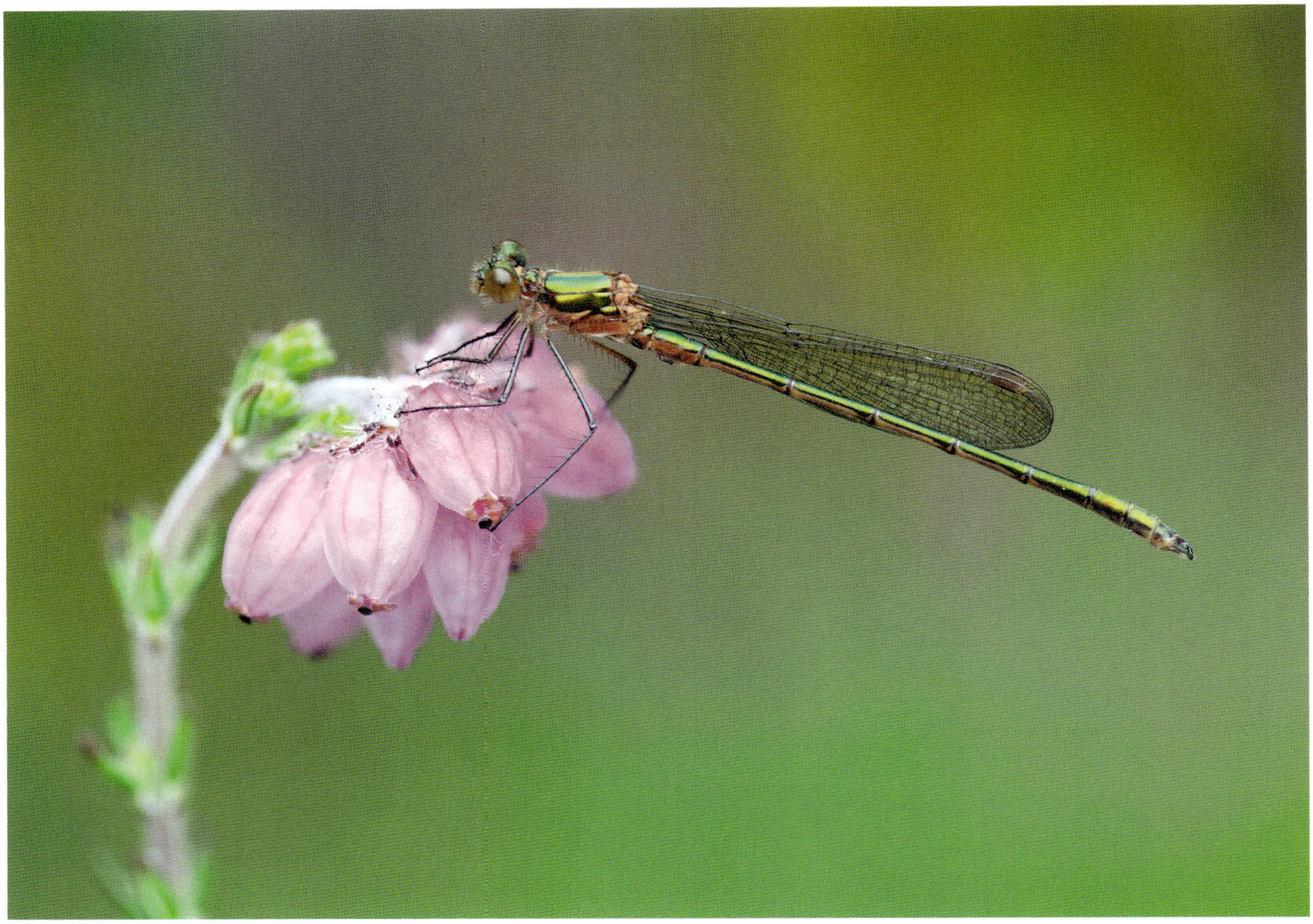

31.5 ~ **Emerald Damselfly** *Lestes sponsa* (immature male)
Keeping your camera parallel with the body of the damselfly means you will need less depth of field which will help to keep the background well diffused.

→ Nikon D800, 200mm Nikkor, 1/15sec at f/8, ISO 100.

overall aquatic lifespan; on average no more than a few weeks for most smaller dragonflies, but a little longer for larger species.

Damselflies, on the other hand, are much smaller insects with widely separated eyes that do not make contact, unlike dragonflies, which are large and occupy virtually all of their head. Damselflies have long, narrow, delicate bodies, which are rather fragile and easily damaged. They are much less agile in the air than dragonflies but are easier to find in sheltered spots near the water's edge among the lush vegetation. They are frequently targeted by photographers wanting to experiment with their setup since they are easier to approach than their larger relatives.

Fieldcraft

Where to Find Dragonflies

Dragonflies occur from late spring onwards, but the peak flight period is during the summer months. One of the first tasks is locating potential breeding sites in your area. It is important to explore the entire site,

// FACING PAGE //

31.6 ~ **Variable Damselfly** *Coenagrion pulchellum* (male)
Damselflies are generally much easier to locate and can be found in greater numbers than dragonflies. Manoeuvring a tripod through tall vegetation can be difficult. Using a monopod gives you more freedom to move around and react to evolving possibilities.

→ Nikon D3X, 105mm micro Nikkor, 1/30sec at f/8, ISO 200.

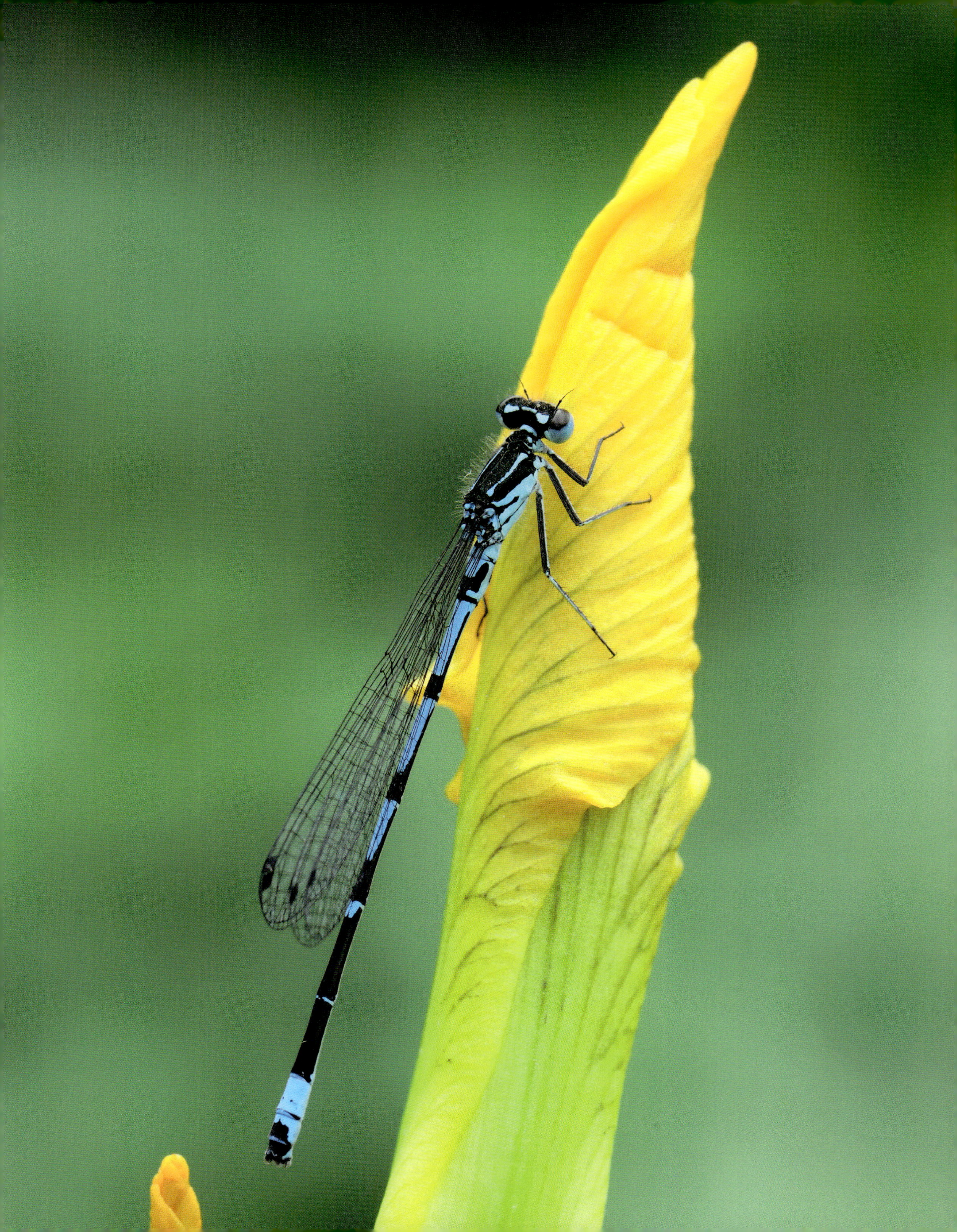

including any adjacent woodland and also to check how accessible the breeding pools are for photography. Most dragonflies tend to have a routine; mid to late morning is an especially important time for them. Males congregate at breeding pools and set up territories awaiting the arrival of females. Some species are extremely territorial, patrolling the same stretch of water frequently perching on a prominent piece of vegetation where they can survey their territory and spot a rival male or an approaching female. Identifying which perches are repeatedly used, means you can position yourself in advance, prefocus and wait. You can also encourage some species to rest in better locations by inserting a large stick or similar into the ground. Some interesting pictures can be obtained using this technique, but you need to be patient and remain relatively still.

By early afternoon interest at breeding sites tails off and adults usually disperse into sheltered rides and clearings in nearby woodland to hunt, rest and feed. These hot spots should be explored as adults often rest low among the vegetation where the temperature can be a few degrees warmer. Visiting a site early in the morning when the air temperature is well below that needed for flight can be a very productive time photographically. It is always wise to set your camera bag down and explore the area first, walking slowly and carefully checking the vegetation for emerging and roosting adults. The sheltered sides of lakes, ponds, and marshes tend to be the most productive; especially those spots that receive direct sunlight early in the morning. When you find a suitable adult, place a stick or something similar nearby as a visual reference so you can easily locate it quickly. The advantage of this approach means you can choose the most appropriate adults for photography and not waste valuable time on subjects which are not in ideal positions. It is always wise to assemble your camera and equipment away from the target area so as not to alarm the insect.

Photographing in the Field

Depending on the species and climate, most dragonflies become active and begin to fly at temperatures around 15°C (59° F). Some species from cooler, temperate climates fly at slightly lower temperatures. Early morning and late evening are the best times photographically to explore wetland locations; dragonflies are less active and generally clinging to vegetation, or perched on overhanging foliage. Morning photography is usually more productive because cooler, overnight temperatures mean dragonflies need a longer warming up period. In the late evening, the opposite occurs, adults are cooling down and will perch for more extended periods, but the air temperature is still warm so they are not as torpid, and most are still capable of flight if disturbed. The main advantage with evening photography is the softer directional light and the gradual drop in temperature.

Many of the larger hawker dragonflies frequently settle overnight among the vegetation close to breeding territories where they can be approached with care and photographed using a tripod. Unlike smaller species they are not capable of instant flight so rely on their colouration to break up their outline in the vegetation, Smaller dragonflies and damselflies, when disturbed usually drop into the deeper parts of the vegetation making them harder to photograph. On overcast days, if the temperature is low, adults remain inactive and rest in the vegetation until the temperature rises sufficiently for flight. However, don't be put off by inclement weather, some great photographic opportunities for atmospheric images are possible in light rain, or early morning when dew can form on the wings and abdomens of insects brought on by cool overnight temperatures and clear skies. However, this phenomenon is less common in the UK than the number of images in photographic magazines would have you believe. Days with intermittent sunshine and partial cloud can be productive photographically; adults settle into the vegetation more frequently, especially when the sun

// FACING PAGE ~ TOP //

31.7 ~ **Black Darter** *Sympetrum danae* (female)
Darters often perch on prominent bits of vegetation, which makes backgrounds easier to manage.

↪ Nikon D800, 200mm Nikkor, 1/15sec at f/8, ISO 100.

// FACING PAGE ~ BOTTOM //

31.8 ~ **Hairy Dragonfly** *Brachytron pratense* (male)
Hawkers are generally more difficult to get close to, especially when active. A longer lens with a tube is often a better approach.

↪ Nikon D800, 300mm Nikkor, + ext tube, 1/15sec at f/11, ISO 100.

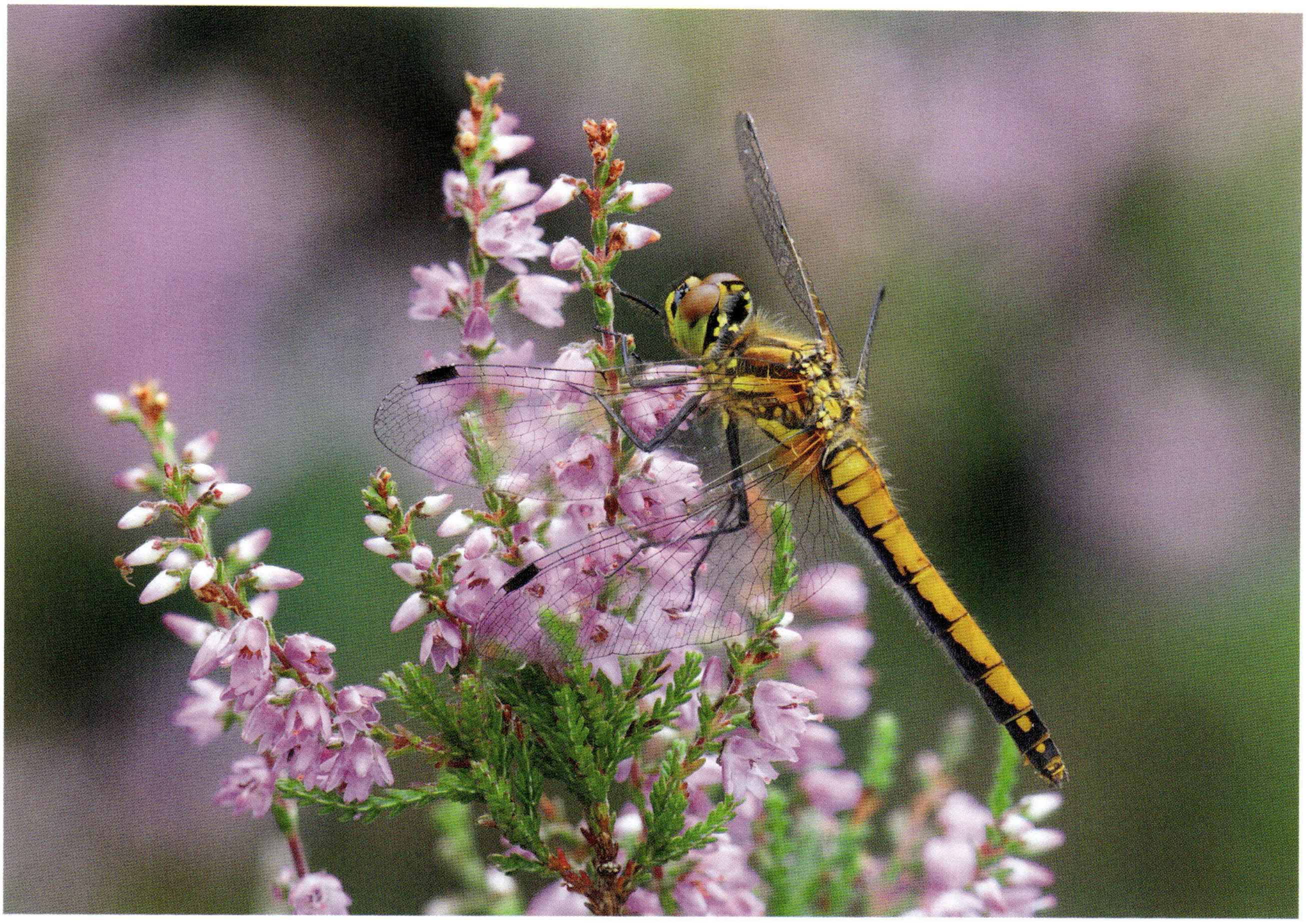

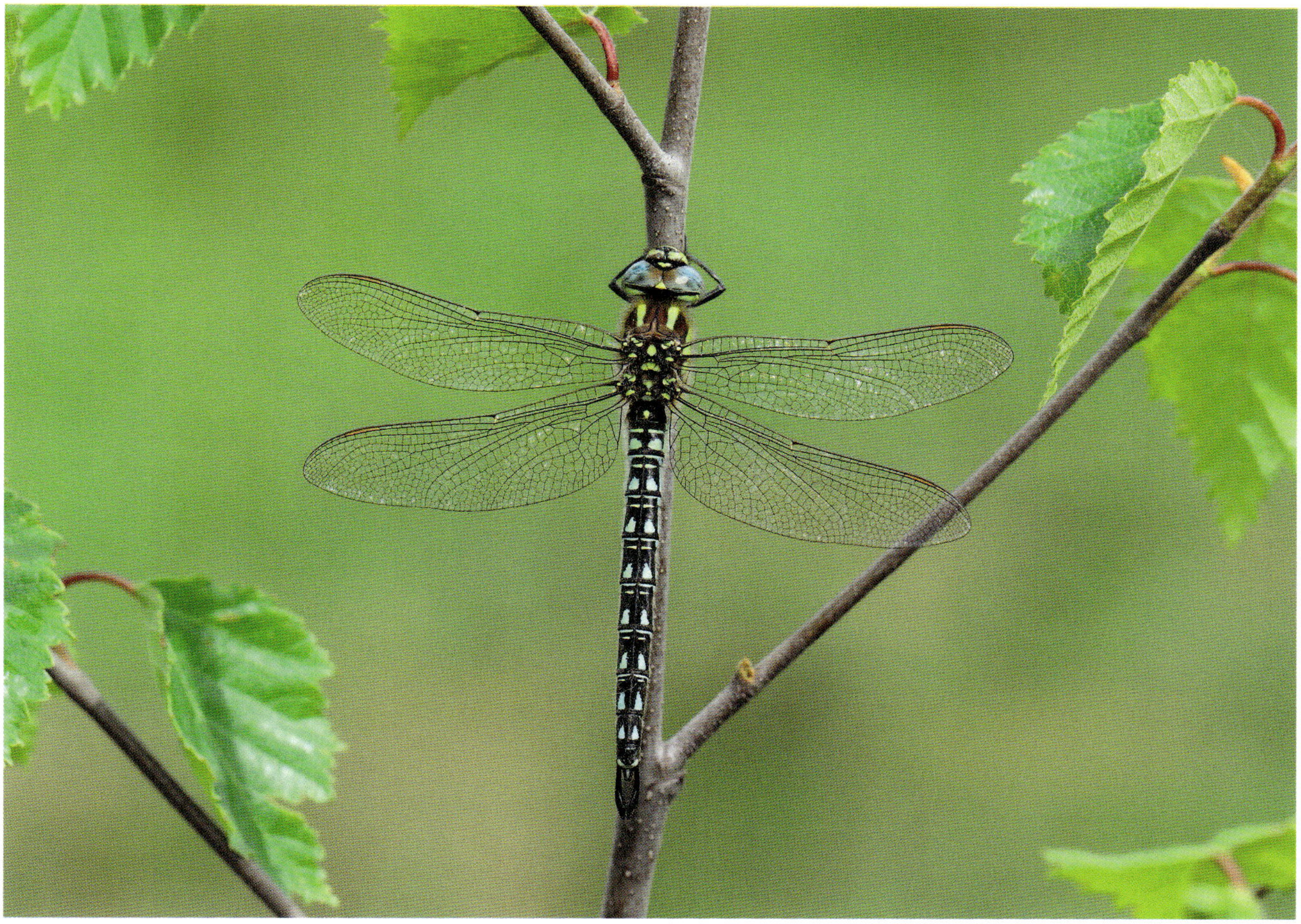

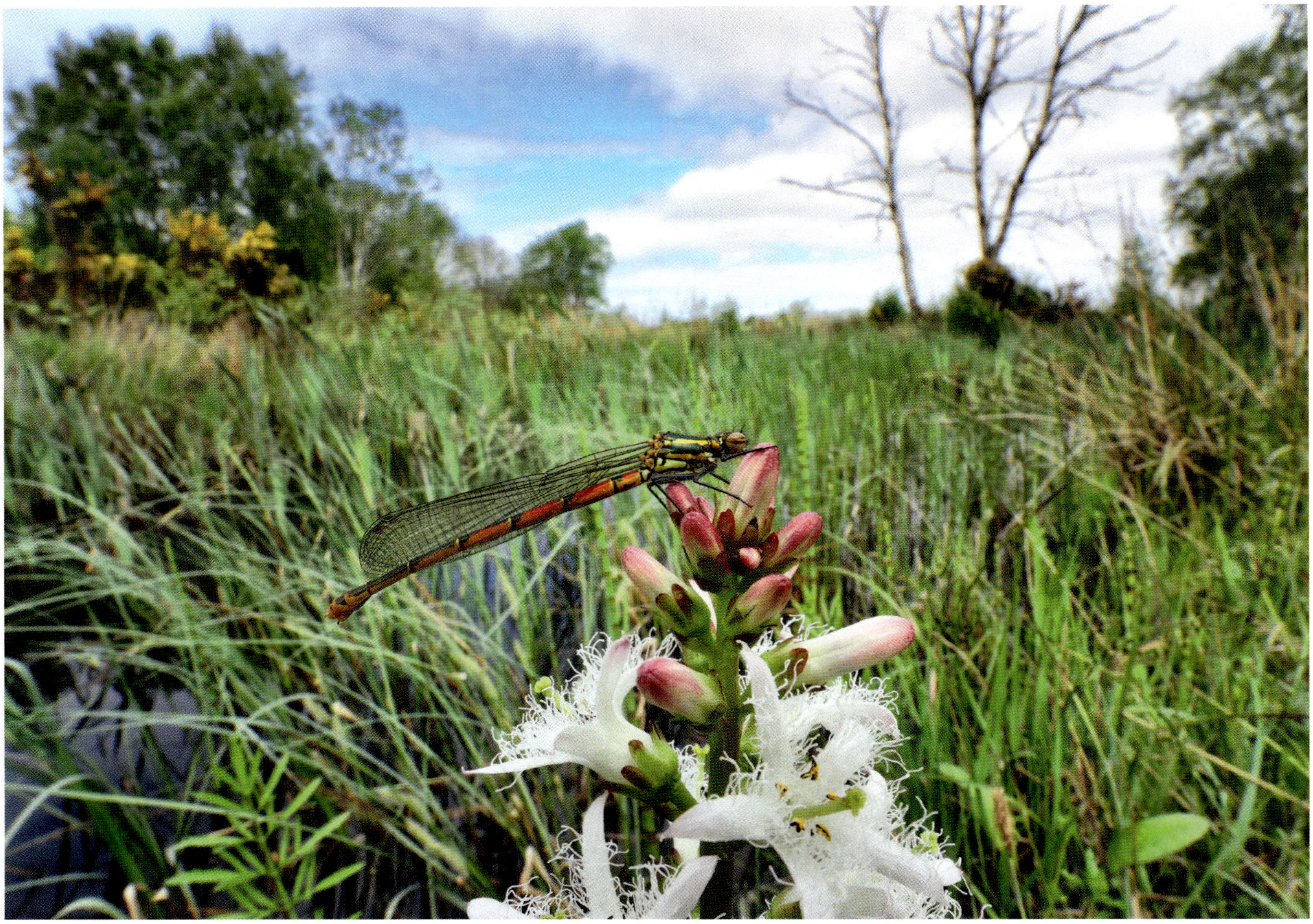

31.9 ~ **Large Red Damselfly** *Pyrrhosoma nymphula* (female)
Using ultra wide angle lenses allows you to set the insect in context with its environment.

→ Nikon D810, 15mm Laowa macro, 1/15sec at f11, ISO 200.

disappears behind the clouds. Avoid the temptation to rush in too quickly, some species are easily spooked and will fly immediately if they sense movement or danger. Take a visual marker as close as possible to where the insect has settled and wait for several minutes until their body temperature has dropped a little before advancing; they are more likely to remain concealed in the vegetation rather than take flight. In breezy conditions, dragonflies are more liable to be found where the temperature is a little warmer, and there is protection from the wind.

I prefer natural light for the vast majority of my dragonfly photography. However, having said that there are situations where flash is indispensable, especially when having to shoot into the light, or when you need to arrest movement. You should also consider using it as a fill-in on overcast days to boost the contrast and add vibrancy to the image.

'Manual focus' and 'Aperture Priority' are my preferred settings when working with dragonflies, but I do on occasions switch to 'shutter priority' when speed is the critical factor. Bear in mind that not every dragonfly you encounter is necessarily a competition winner. It takes time and practice to identify those that are worth pursuing. Some will be resting low down among the foliage making them difficult to isolate. Look for adults resting against a clean, uncluttered background; this will isolate the subject from its surroundings and emphasise the intricate veining in the wings.

Cooler, overcast conditions also allow you to work with a tripod; you have greater control over the point of focus, aperture and aesthetics of the final photograph.

However, it is not always possible to use one in every habitat. There are situations where the undergrowth makes it difficult to manoeuvre a heavy tripod without disturbing the surrounding vegetation. Switching to a monopod provides greater flexibility and additional support. It also takes the weight off your arms and provides some stability, which is better than operating free hand.

Dragonflies are by nature timid insects and highly perceptible to movement. Every creature has a circle of fear. If you operate outside that zone, they may be wary, but will continue about their business. Once that circle is breached, they become agitated and are likely to take flight. When pursuing your quarry, it is always good practice to nail a few shots from a greater distance in case you spook it; having bagged something you can then work your way into a more favourable position.

The ideal combination for dragonfly photography is a long focal length macro in the region of 180mm–200mm. You could use a shorter focal length of around 100mm, but your working distance at any given magnification would be closer. A telephoto with a focal length of around 200mm or 300mm in combination with extension tubes is an excellent alternative. This approach works quite well; the only downside is having to add and remove tubes depending on your subject distance. You can also place a converter behind an extension tube to gain extra magnification if required. Their narrow-angle of view also helps to control chaotic backgrounds. There are, however, situations when you need speed and flexibility. My preferred approach in these situations is a short focal length macro such as Nikon's 105mm set to autofocus (group function), VR in the on position and attached to a monopod. This allows me to adapt quickly to spur-of-the-moment opportunities or changes in an insect's position.

Wide-angle lenses with a focal length of around 24mm are also useful for illustrating an adult within in the context of its environment. This style of photography is very much in demand these days, but more challenging to achieve with this group of insects, but not impossible. Early morning and late evening, or overcast days are perhaps the best times to achieve these sorts of images. With modern, fast lenses and improved autofocus, flight shots have become hugely popular.

Despite being challenging insects to photograph, dragonflies are fascinating creatures to watch and much can be learned from observation. There is no substitute for time spent in the field; it provides, you with opportunities to practise and refine your photographic technique and improve your fieldcraft skills. Obtaining consistently good images is time-consuming; no single solution or method can be applied to every situation. Background knowledge, persistence and above all the ability to see and act on creative opportunities are the best strategies; there are no second chances with these insects.

Project Planning

The winter months are always a good time to plan for the coming season. There are many aspects of dragonfly behaviour and life cycle which are worth documenting photographically. Below are some ideas for projects, which are worth pursuing.

Collecting Larvae for Photographic Study

The larvae of dragonflies and damselflies spend most of their lives living among the weeds and detritus on the bottom of ponds, lakes and streams etc. The shape and structure of larvae vary considerably; a site may contain several different species, but they will all occupy various parts of the environment they inhabit. For example, most hawker dragonflies are weed dwellers, while many of the chasers live among the detritus at the bottom of the pond or lake. Others live in gravel or silt. It is important to research your target species beforehand. Many are habitat specific and won't occur anywhere else, others are more widespread and easier to find.

Early spring is the best time to visit sites to collect the larvae for photography. Most species begin to move in from deeper water to the shallow margins in preparation for emergence during the coming months. A bucket and a strong, heavy-duty pond net, along with a white tray to examine the contents are all that is required. Small glass tanks for larval photography are easy to construct and can be set up in the field or in the boot of your vehicle rather than transporting specimens back to the studio. If preferred, a few larvae can be taken back to the studio and photographed in an aquarium tank setup where you have precise control over the lighting. When the session is complete, it is important to return them to the same location.

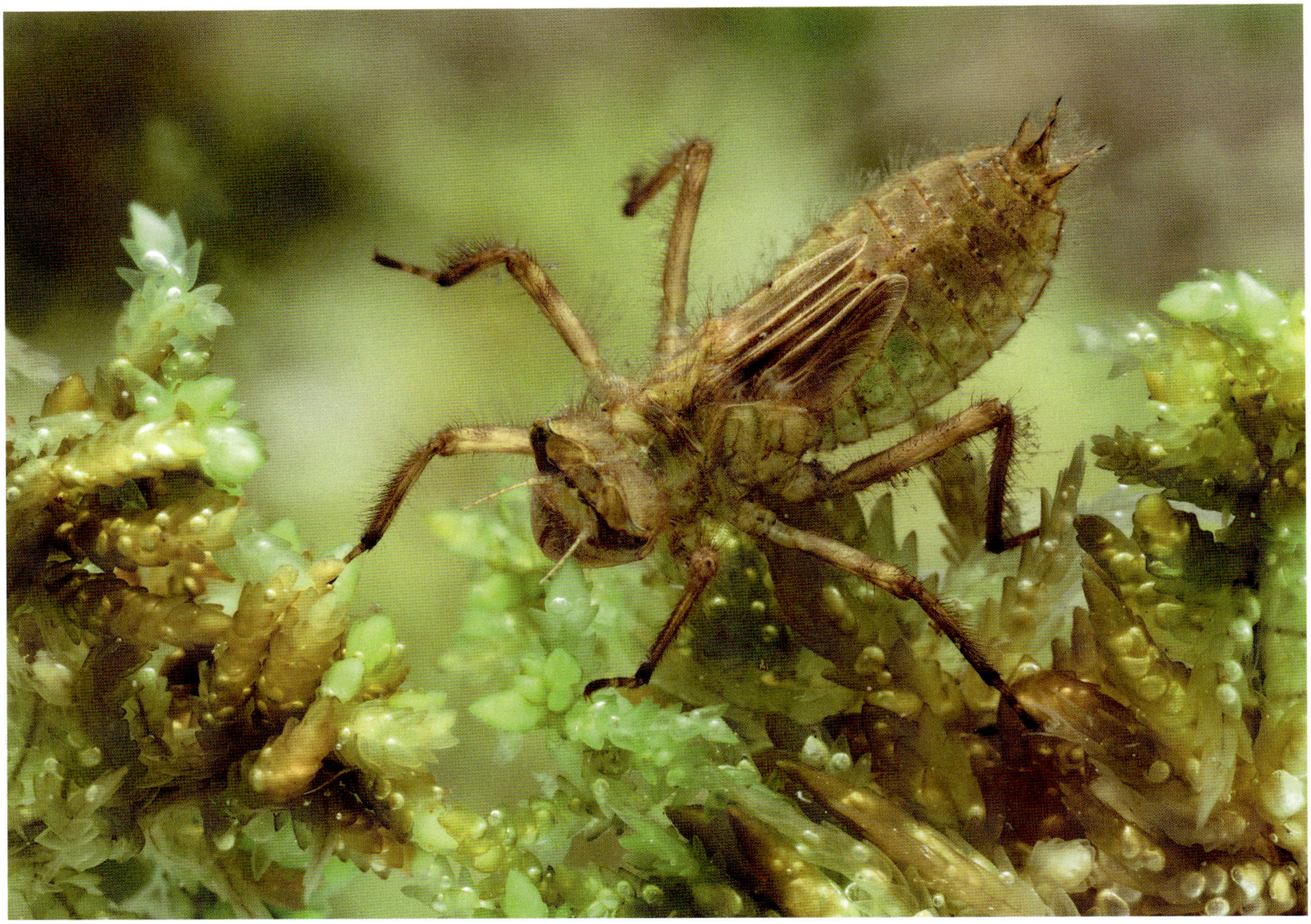

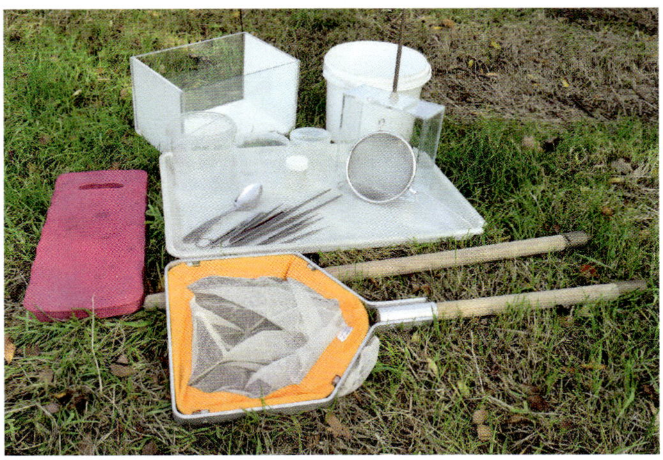

31.10 ~ Aquatic equipment for collecting specimens

// THIS PAGE ~ TOP //

31.11 ~ Four-spotted Chaser *Libellula quadrimaculata* (larva)
Most species in this family live among the weed, moss and detritus at the bottom of the pool or pond. Specimen photographed in the back of my jeep.

→ Nikon D3X, 105mm micro Nikkor, 1/60sec at f/11, flash, ISO 200.

// FACING PAGE //

31.12 ~ Four-spotted Chaser *Libellula quadrimaculata* (female)
Capturing the emergence and transformation of a dragonfly from larva to adult means being on site very early in the morning.

→ Nikon D3X, 200mm micro Nikkor, 1/30sec at f/11, ISO 200.

// OVERLEAF ~ LEFT //

31.13 ~ Large Red Damselfly *Pyrrhosoma nymphula* (female)
Damselflies are often at their most vulnerable just after emergence. Note the wings have a slight tint; this disappears as the adult matures.

→ Nikon D800, 200mm micro Nikkor, 1/15sec at f/11, ISO 200.

// OVERLEAF ~ RIGHT //

31.14 ~ Common Hawker *Aeshna juncea* (female)
Dragonflies and damselflies attain their mature colouring over time. It is worth photographing the different colour phases.

→ Nikon D800, 200mm micro Nikkor, 1/15 sec at f/8, ISO 200.

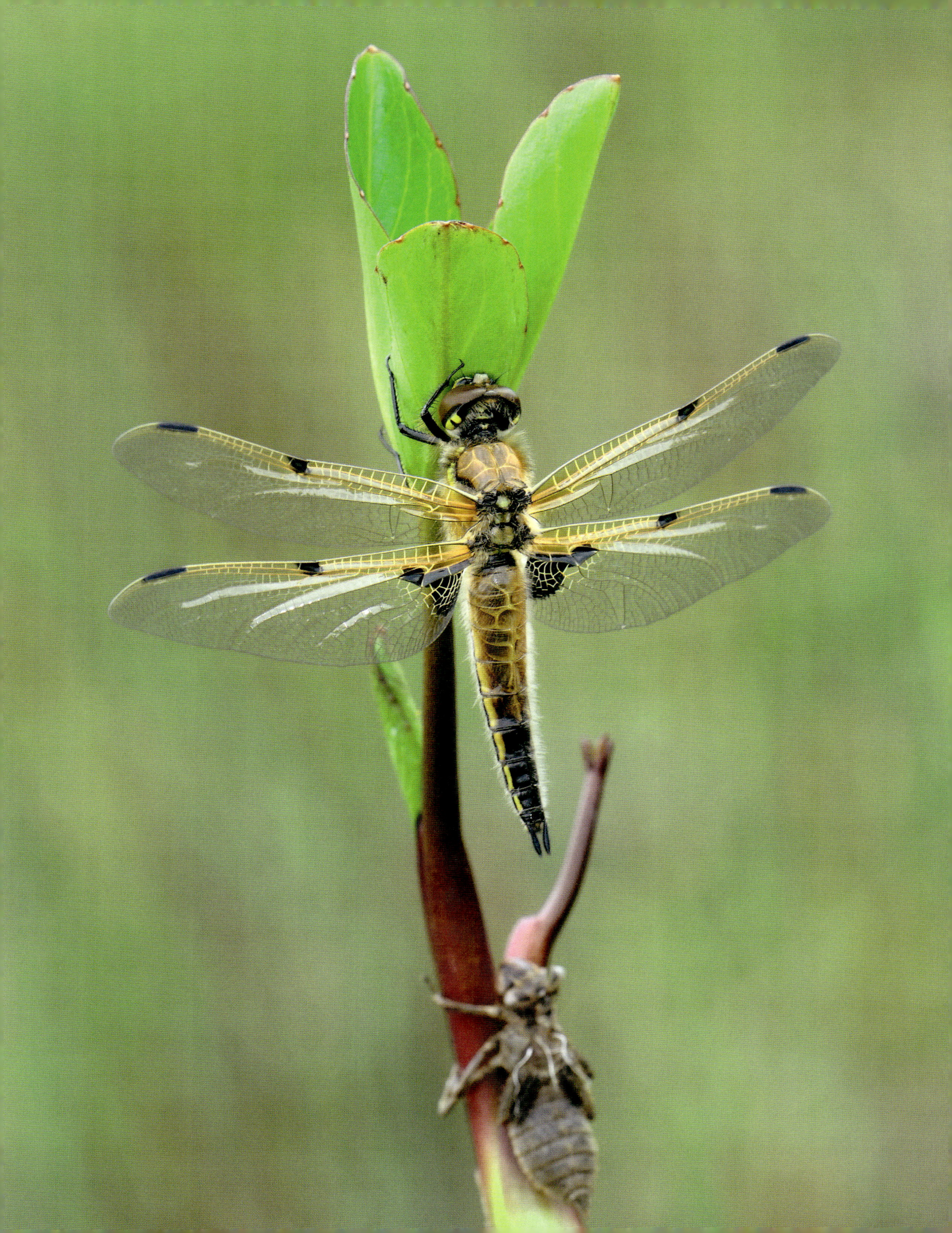

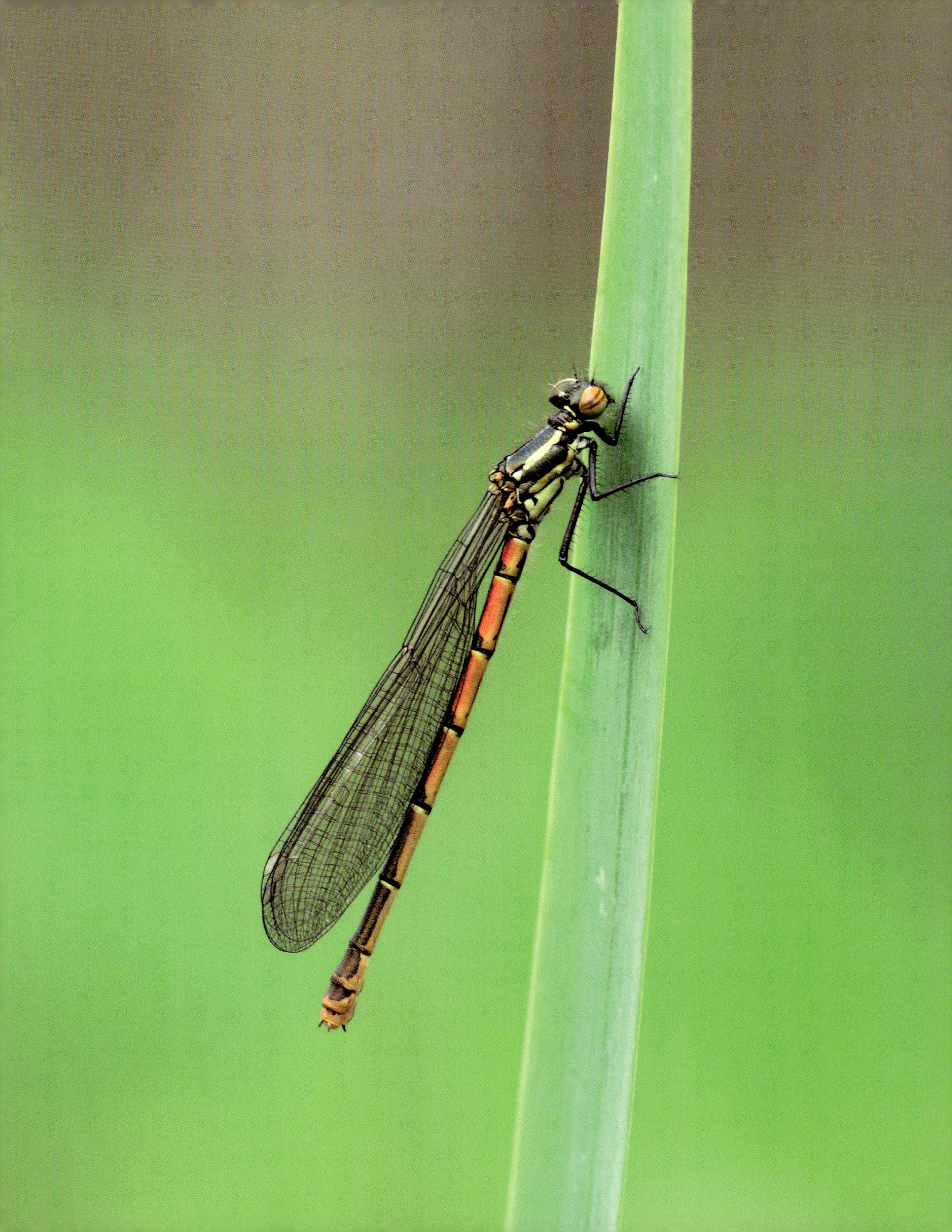

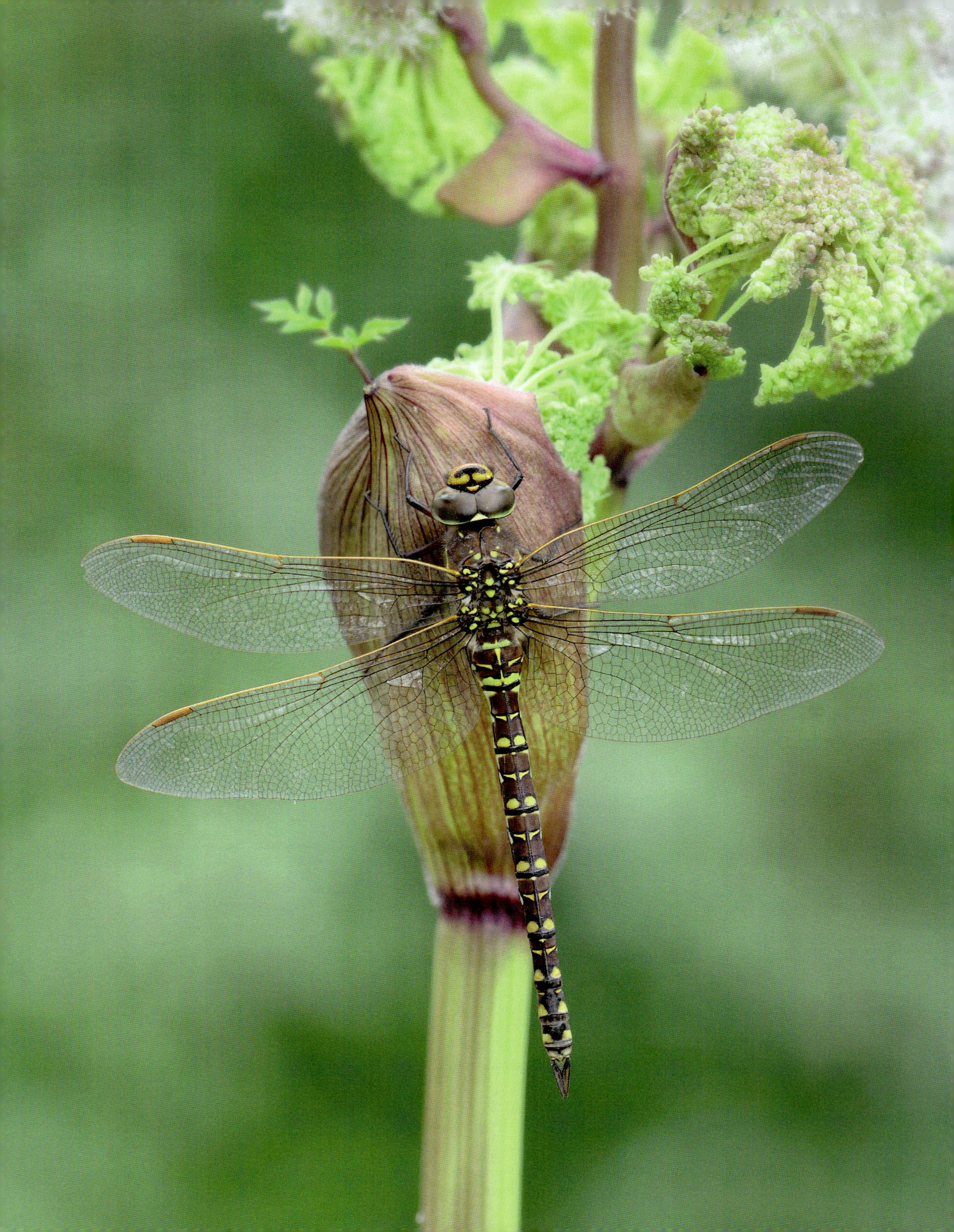

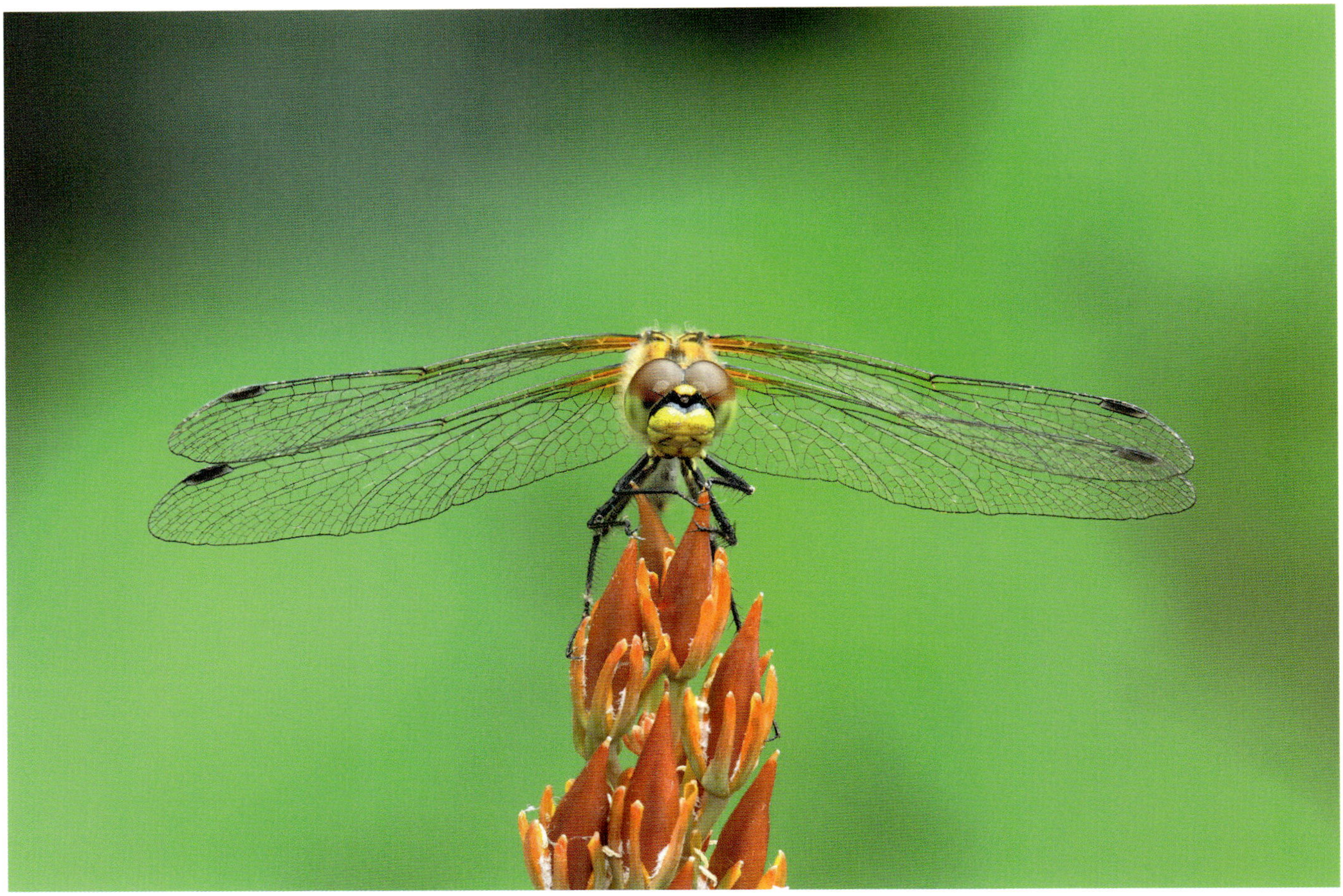

31.15 ~ Black Darter *Sympetrum danae* (male)
This is an attractive species commonly associated with bogs and wetland sites. Don't be afraid to vary your shooting position. You don't want to fall into the habit of photographing every species from the same angle.

↘ Nikon D3, 200mm micro Nikkor, 1/30sec at f/8, ISO 200.

Emergence Sequences

One of the fascinating aspects of a dragonfly's life cycle is the transformation from a larva to an adult. Many species begin to emerge after sunrise to complete the transformation to a terrestrial winged adult. Capturing this sequence is challenging; it requires arriving at a breeding site very early in the morning and systematically searching the marginal vegetation for adults. The second option is keeping some larvae in a tank at home, or a studio and monitoring their activity over a few nights when emergence is close. Many larger species emerge during the night for protection, so you may find yourself getting up at hourly intervals to check for activity. Virtually all of the damselflies prefer early morning; a systematic scan of the vegetation at the water's edge will often produce some individuals at different stages of emergence. They can be easily photographed *in situ*.

Immature Phase

Capturing the various colour phases is an interesting aspect of the development process. Their colouration after emergence is often weak; the abdomen is delicate and takes a while to mature and harden. The wings are not transparent and, usually, have a slight tint. This phase is often referred to as the 'Teneral Phase'. Only when the insect has attained its full colouration and is sexually mature will it return to the water and the breeding site. Other aspects worth photographing are feeding, mating and the cast off larval skins (exuviae) left on the vegetation after emergence.

When adults attain their rich, vibrant colours they are, for a short while in their prime and damage-free. This is the best time to photograph them before the colour fades; wings become marked and tatty as the result of territorial fights with rival males, or predation by birds.

PHOTOGRAPHIC TIPS

Below is some advice and suggestions, which you may find helpful.

- Be mindful of your silhouette against the sky; this highlights your movements even more.
- Don't position yourself between the insect and sunlight; it will either reorientate itself or fly off.
- If you are photographing in bright sunshine, target individuals which are perched on prominent pieces of vegetation rather than those resting among the cluttered foliage. This will reduce the shadows among the vegetation, which can often be a distraction. It's a good idea to use a fill-flash to help control shadow areas and produce a more balanced result.
- Select small pools for photography and observation; this makes it easier to get closer to your subject.
- Some dragonflies defend their territory from a prominent perch. You can often encourage a species (particularly chasers and darters) to a place of your choosing by pushing a small branch into the ground, to which you can pre-focus your lens; this technique works well on small pools with not too much vegetation.
- Don't confine yourself to a single lens. If you own longer telephotos use them with extension tubes; these combinations increase the lens to subject distance and are excellent for controlling background distraction and dealing with timorous species.
- Perfect your setup and fine-tune your technique on damselflies first, which are a lot more approachable.
- Purchase a good guidebook and read up on the biology and distribution of species in your area. Many regional guides on dragonflies have been published.

RESOURCES

Below is a list of current publications, which provide more in-depth knowledge on dragonflies and damselflies from different parts of the world. There is also a list of major societies and their websites devoted to the identification, study and photography of dragonflies.

FURTHER READING

Brooks, S., Cham, S. *Field Guide to the Dragonflies and Damselflies of Britain and Ireland.* British Wildlife Publishing.

Dijkstra, K., B. *Field Guide to the Dragonflies of Britain and Europe.* British Wildlife Publishing.

Needham, J. G., Minter, J. Westfall, Jr. & May, M. L. *The Dragonflies of North America.* IORI: Gainsville, Florida.

Nelson, B., Thompson, R. *The Natural History of Ireland's Dragonflies.* National Museums of Northern Ireland.

Silsby, J. & Parr, M.J. *Dragonflies of the World.* Smithsonian Books.

Thompson, R., Nelson, B. *Guide to the Dragonflies and Damselflies of Ireland.* National Museums of Northern Ireland.

WEBSITES

British Dragonfly Society: www.british-dragonflies.org.uk
Dragonfly Ireland: www.habitas.org.uk/dragonflyireland
Dragonfly Society of the Americas: www.odonatacentral.org
World Wide Dragonfly Society: www.worlddragonfly.org

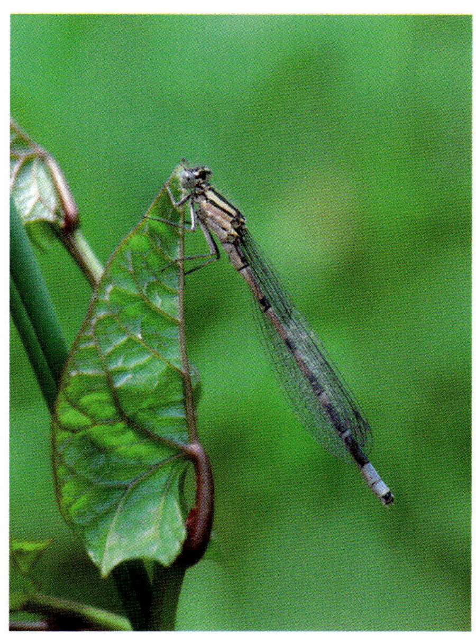

31.16 ~ Common Blue Damselfly *Enallagma cyathigerum* (immature male)
When freshly emerged, many damselflies have immature colouring, which is often quite different to the fully mature adult. As they hunt and feed their colour develops. The males of this species are bright blue when they reach sexual maturity.

Nikon D2X, 105mm micro Nikkor, 1/15sec at f/11, ISO 200.

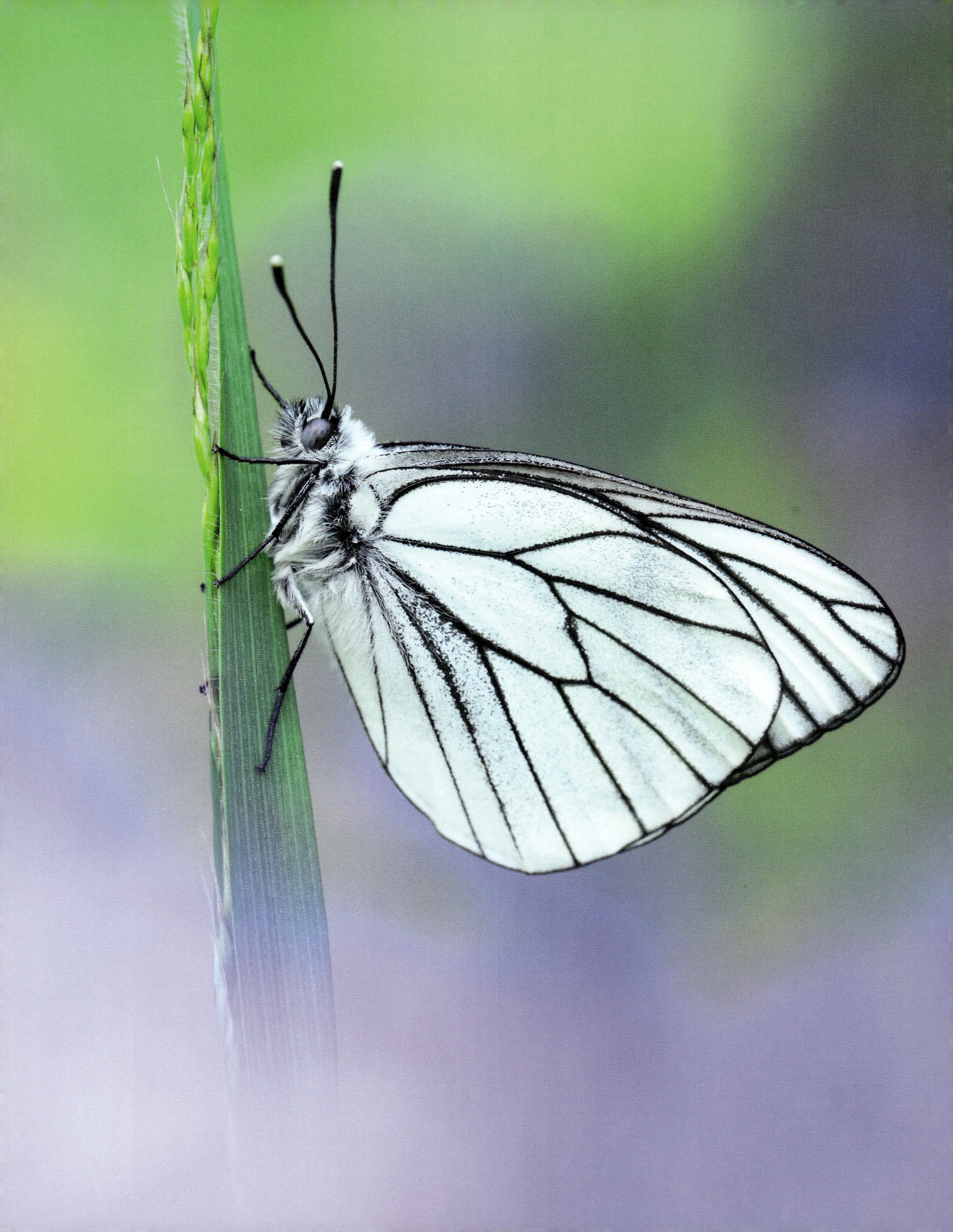

THIRTY TWO

Meadow Dancers

Butterflies

Introduction

Butterflies are without doubt the most popular and best-loved group of insects in the world. They occupy a special place in the affections of people and are admired for their beauty and elegance on the wing. Their bright, vibrant colours and graceful flight add an extra dimension to the countryside and bring colour and interest to parks and gardens throughout the spring and summer months. Like many insects, butterflies have a close association with plants as a food source both in the larval stage and as adults extracting nectar from a wide variety of flowers. This relationship, along with the temperature and climate, are the main factors that control their distribution as a species across the continents.

Despite their popularity among naturalists and photographers, many butterflies are in decline with some becoming scarce or even close to extinction. Their abundance in country lanes and meadows that were commonplace in previous generations is now sadly a thing of the past in many places. Changes in agricultural practice and the large-scale destruction of pristine habitats are the primary cause of their diminution.

Today the nets and collecting jars have mostly given way to cameras, with photographers pursuing them with the same degree of eagerness, but their trophies now are an amalgamation of pixels instead of dried specimens in a glass cabinet. Unlike preserved museum specimens, naturalists, through photography, are better able to capture the beauty and behaviour of butterflies, which has added significantly to our knowledge and understanding of the biology and ecology of these captivating insects.

Fieldcraft

Where to Find Butterflies

Butterflies in temperate climates begin to appear from the middle of spring and right through the summer until early autumn when the temperature starts to fall. Species that hibernate during the winter months can still be seen sipping the last of the nectar on mild sunny days in early autumn.

People's first encounter with butterflies is often in their gardens; they are important places for them to rest and feed. Gardens act as corridors between nature

// FACING PAGE //

32.1 ~ Black-veined White *Aporia crataegi*

↳ Nikon D800, 300mm Nikkor, + ext tube, 1/15sec at f/8, ISO 200.

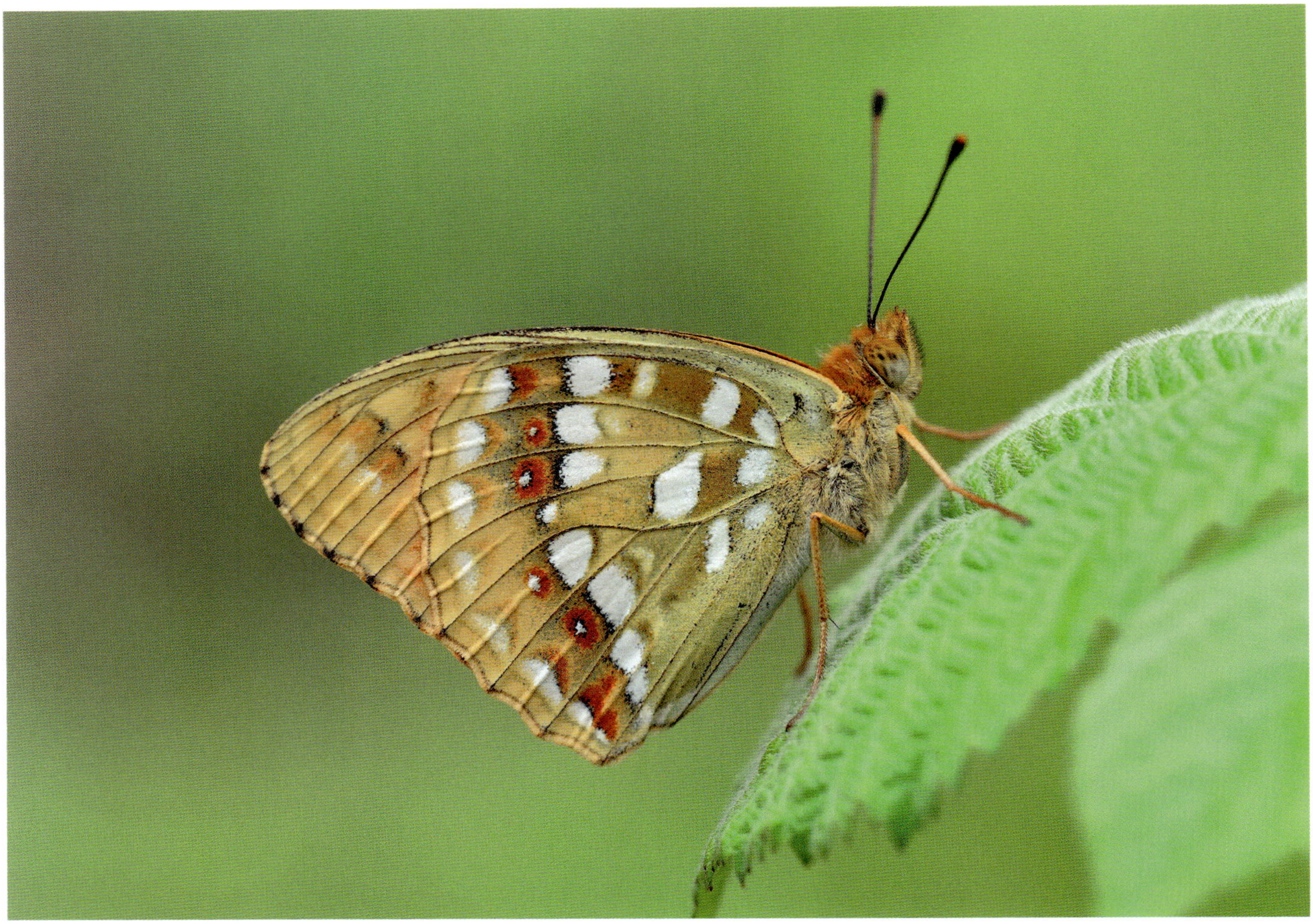

32.2 ~ High Brown Fritillary *Fabriciana adippe*
The overcast light and cooler evening temperature meant I could approach this insect more closely using a tripod. Fritillaries close their wings when roosting revealing the intricate patterns of spots on the underside of the hindwings. The arrangement is an important diagnostic feature which aids identification.

→ Nikon D800, 200mm micro Nikkor, 1/15sec at f/8, ISO 200.

reserves and natural habitats. Planting the right type of shrubs and flowers in your garden will attract those early species if you manage it carefully. A well thought out garden can attract others and provide you with an excellent range of subject material. Some of the best garden plants for butterflies include buddleia, lavender, ice plant, michaelmas daisies, teasel and red valerian. Spring flowers such as dandelion, bluebell and lady's smock are also a rich source of nectar and important for early butterflies and those emerging from hibernation. On warm spring days, they can be seen basking in the early morning on stones and walls to raise their temperature for flight.

Photographing other less common species will involve travelling to different habitats. Butterflies like many other insects are restricted by the distribution and availability of their food plants. You won't find species that are specific to coastal habitats in woodland locations. Visiting natural habitats in your local area such as old country lanes, roadside verges and meadows, where the vegetation has been left uncut will produce a range of species. Woodland rides, clearings, disused quarries, grassy hillsides and embankments where there is floral richness and diversity are also excellent locations for hairstreaks, whites, coppers and brimstones, etc. Coastal habitats are among the optimum sites and those with a rich botanical ground flora will produce the greatest range of butterflies. Some of the most colourful species that inhabit these locations include fritillaries, blues and skippers. Studying the flight times and foodplants of butterflies is the real key to finding other species. Other areas of importance include mountainous habitats;

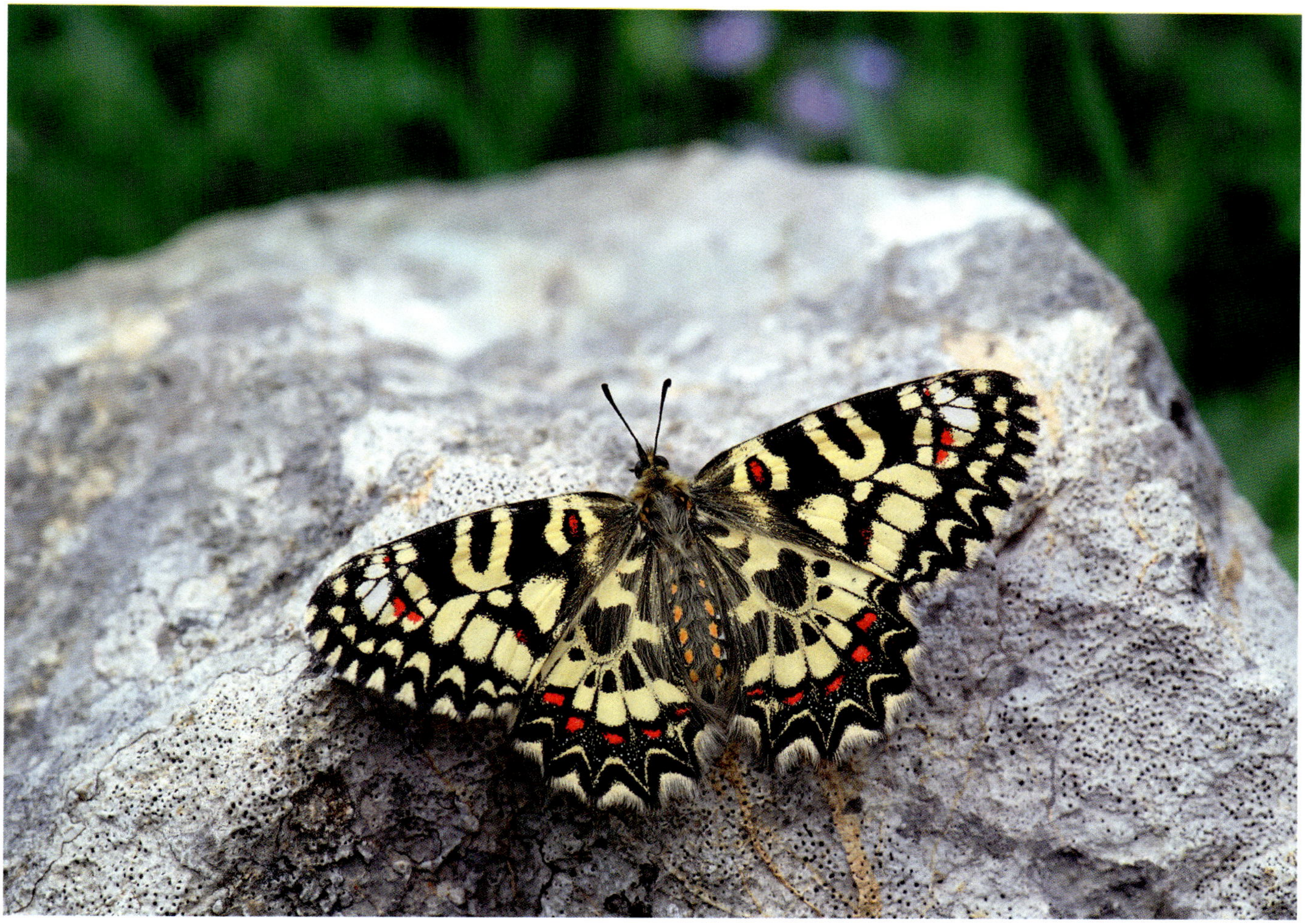

32.3 ~ Spanish Festoon *Zerynthia rumina*
Butterflies like to take advantage of early morning sunlight and are often seen basking on dark-coloured rocks, gravel paths and other reflective surfaces that catch the heat in the sun's rays. This helps them to warm up with their wings acting like solar panels.

↳ Nikon D2X, 200mm micro Nikkor, 1/15sec at f/8-11, ISO 200.

particularly those in Europe, such as the Alps, Pyrenees and the Apennines Mountain Ranges. These are among the richest regions for species diversity and numbers in Europe. Many of the habitats are set among chocolate-box backdrops with stunning vistas offering the butterfly photographer a wealth of subject material to choose from.

In the Field

The temperature at which butterflies become active varies between species and the climate they inhabit. An average temperature for spring species is around 14°C (57° F); but this only an approximate guide. Warmer regions such as the Mediterranean would have a higher temperature threshold for flight. Butterflies frequently select south-facing roosting sites, which give them shelter, but also these hot spots provide heat if the sun is shining early in the morning. They also like to bask on the ground, or on rocks and walls to expedite warming up. From a photographic perspective, they are often much more approachable and less inclined to fly at this time of day. Some roost overnight in and among flower heads to break up their outline. You need to scan the vegetation and flowers carefully for roosting adults. Others settle low among the vegetation where the ground temperature can often be a little warmer. I enjoy this time in the morning for butterfly photography. I can, for most of the time, use a tripod and exercise greater control on focusing, depth of field and general composition of the subject. The advantage with morning sessions is that butterflies are warming up from being torpid overnight.

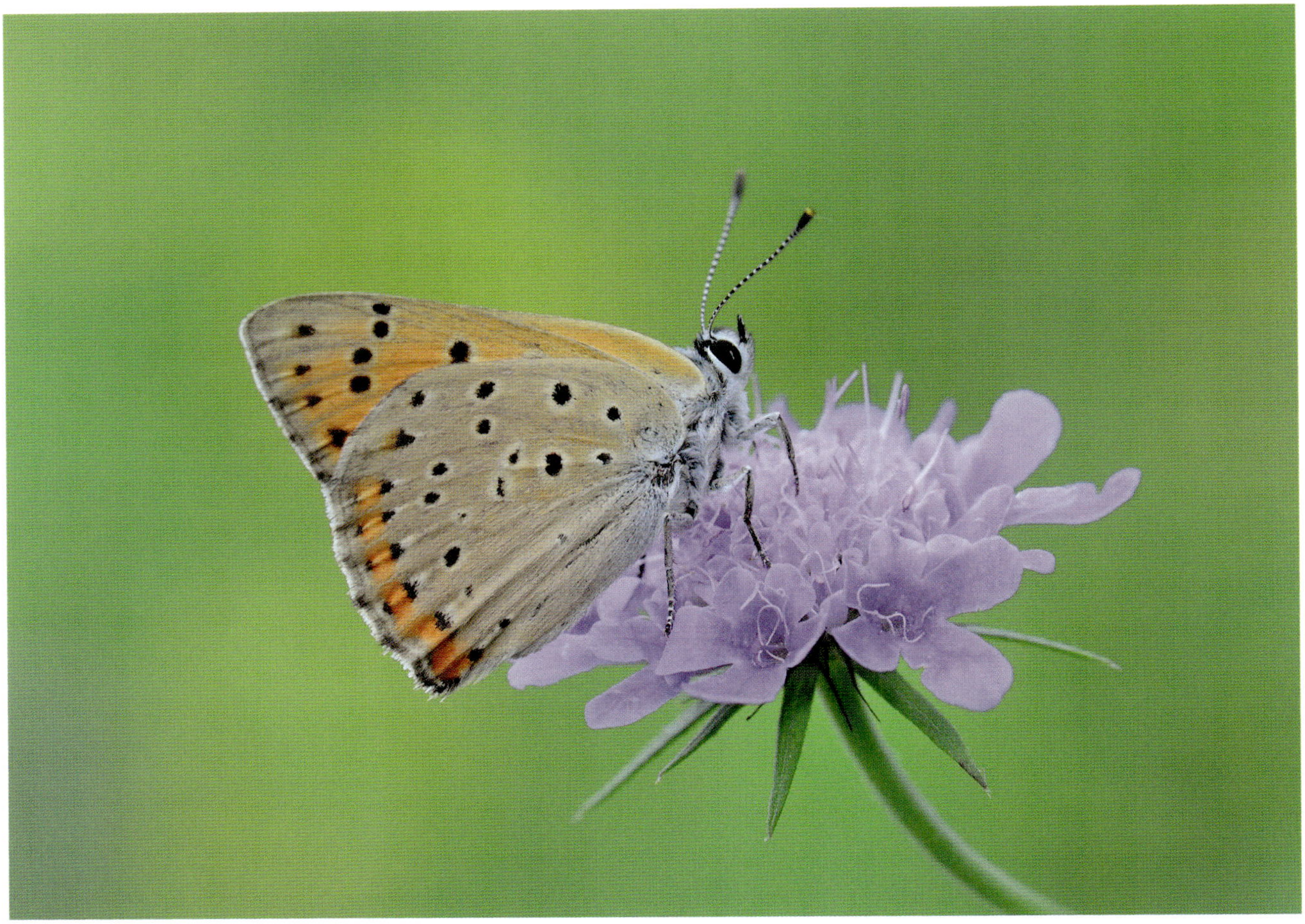

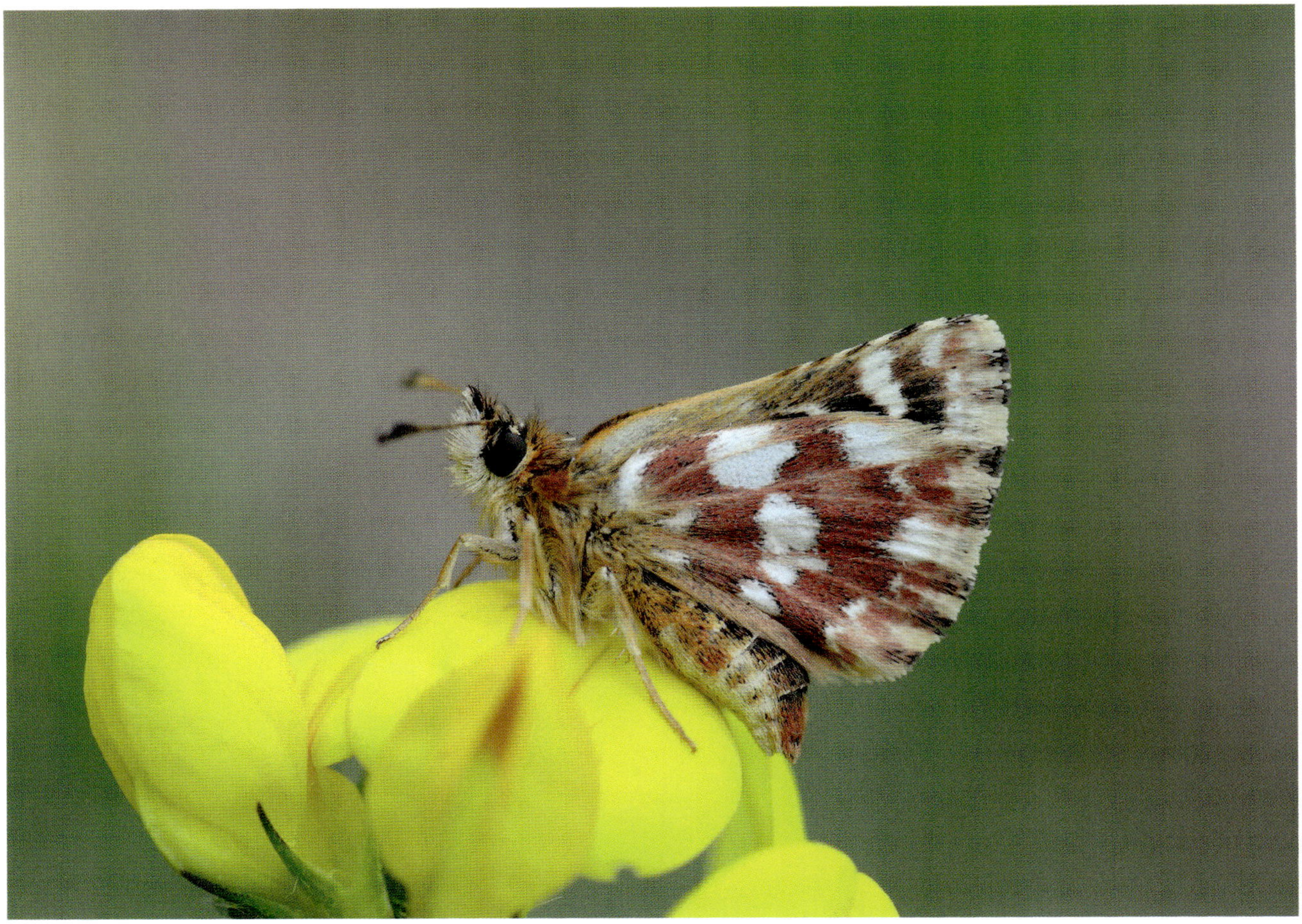

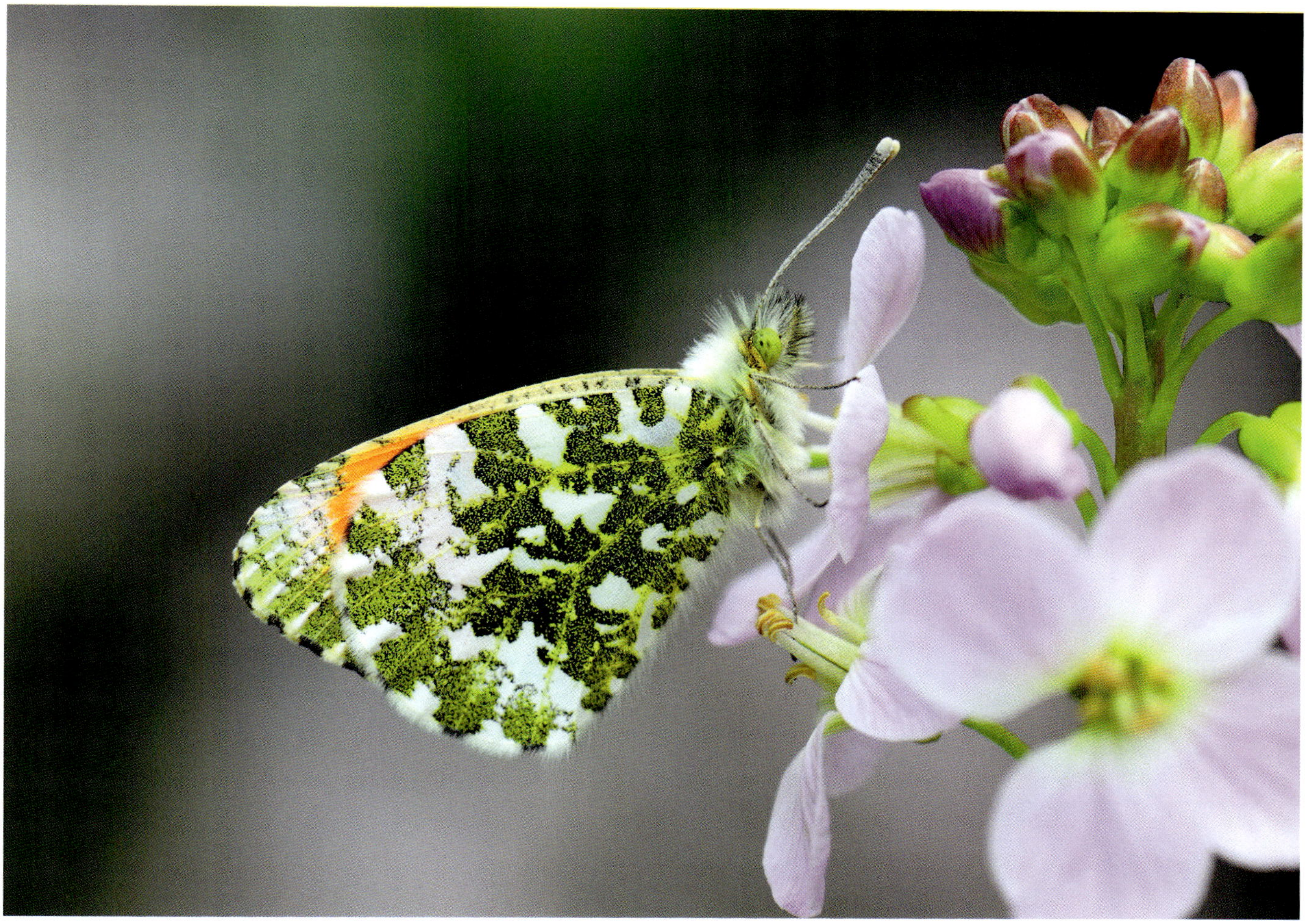

32.6 ~ **Orange-tip** *Anthocharis cardamines* (male)
Visiting a meadow early in the morning before the temperature rises can be very productive for photography. Adults can often be found resting on flower heads, or among the vegetation.

↳ Nikon D3X, 200mm micro Nikkor, 1/8sec at f/11, ISO 200.

// FACING PAGE ~ TOP //

32.4 ~ **Purple Shot Copper** *Lycaena alciphron*
The Alpine regions in Europe have a rich diversity of butterfly species. Exploring flower-rich meadows in France in early evening can produce a good variety of species. Many butterflies retire to the vegetation when the temperature drops and the sun disappears from view. I kept the camera back parallel to the underside of the wings of this copper and selected a smaller aperture to ensure the flower was also in focus.

↳ Nikon D800, 200mm micro Nikkor, 1/8sec at f/11, ISO 200.

// FACING PAGE ~ BOTTOM //

32.5 ~ **Red-underwing Skipper** *Spialia sertorius*

A small attractive butterfly that flies fast and close to the ground. I found this resting adult in late evening and was able to approach it carefully with a tripod. It was resting close to the ground so I engaged Live View to help with composing and focusing.

↳ Nikon D800, 200mm micro Nikkor, 1/15sec at f/8, ISO 200.

Much of the early part of the morning for butterflies is spent feeding and looking for a mate. This can be a more challenging time photographically, especially if it's warm and sunny. Adults are more restless and may settle on flowers only briefly, to sip nectar before moving on. You need to work quickly, but methodically and target individuals that look a bit more settled. If you watch a butterfly's behaviour, it will become apparent quickly if it's possible to get in close. Those that stop only briefly to visit flowers are unlikely to settle for more than a moment, so stalking is perhaps the best approach in these circumstances. Avoid the middle of the day when the temperature is at its hottest. Early evening is often a good time to photograph. The light is warm and directional; also, butterflies are not as preoccupied with

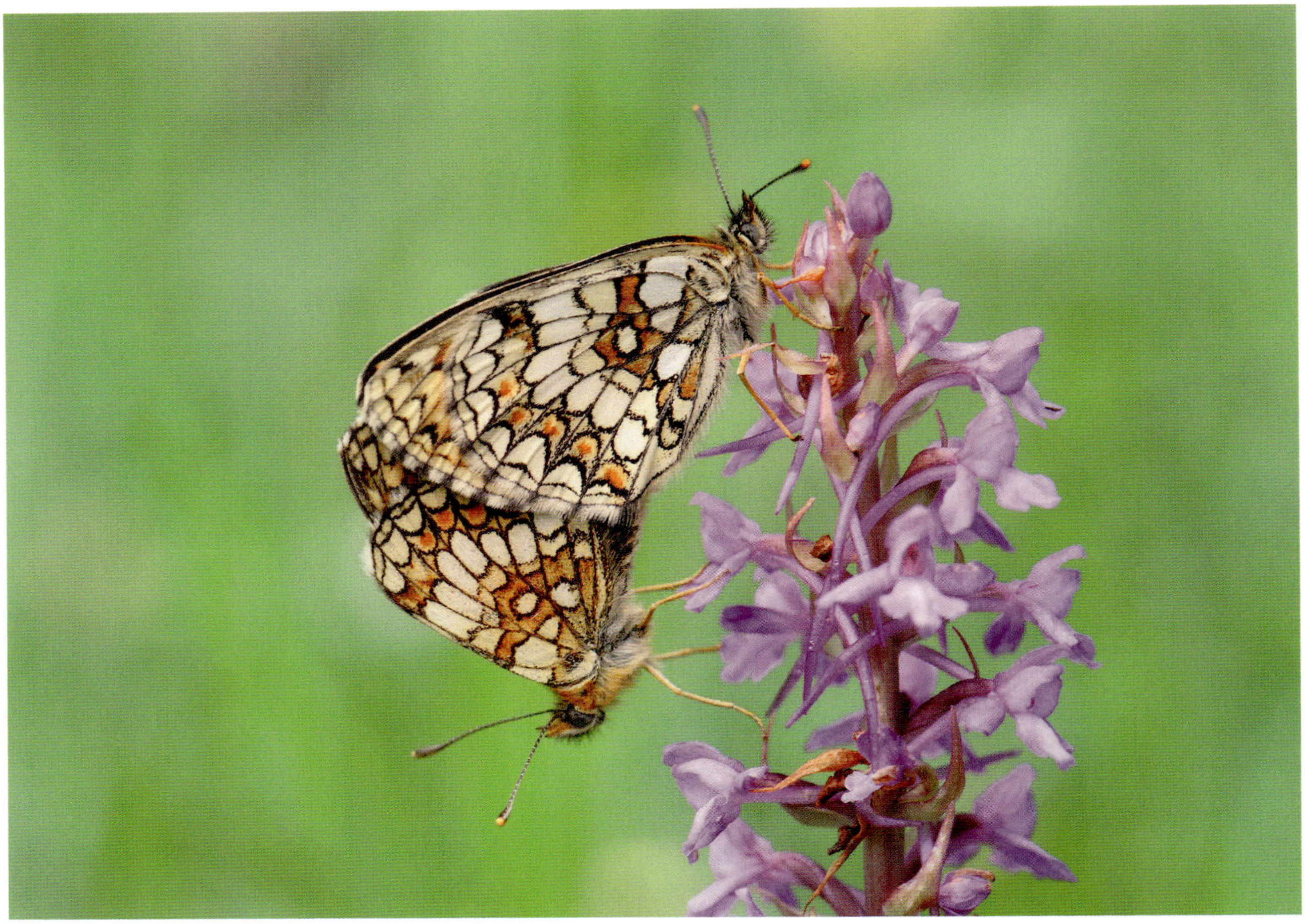

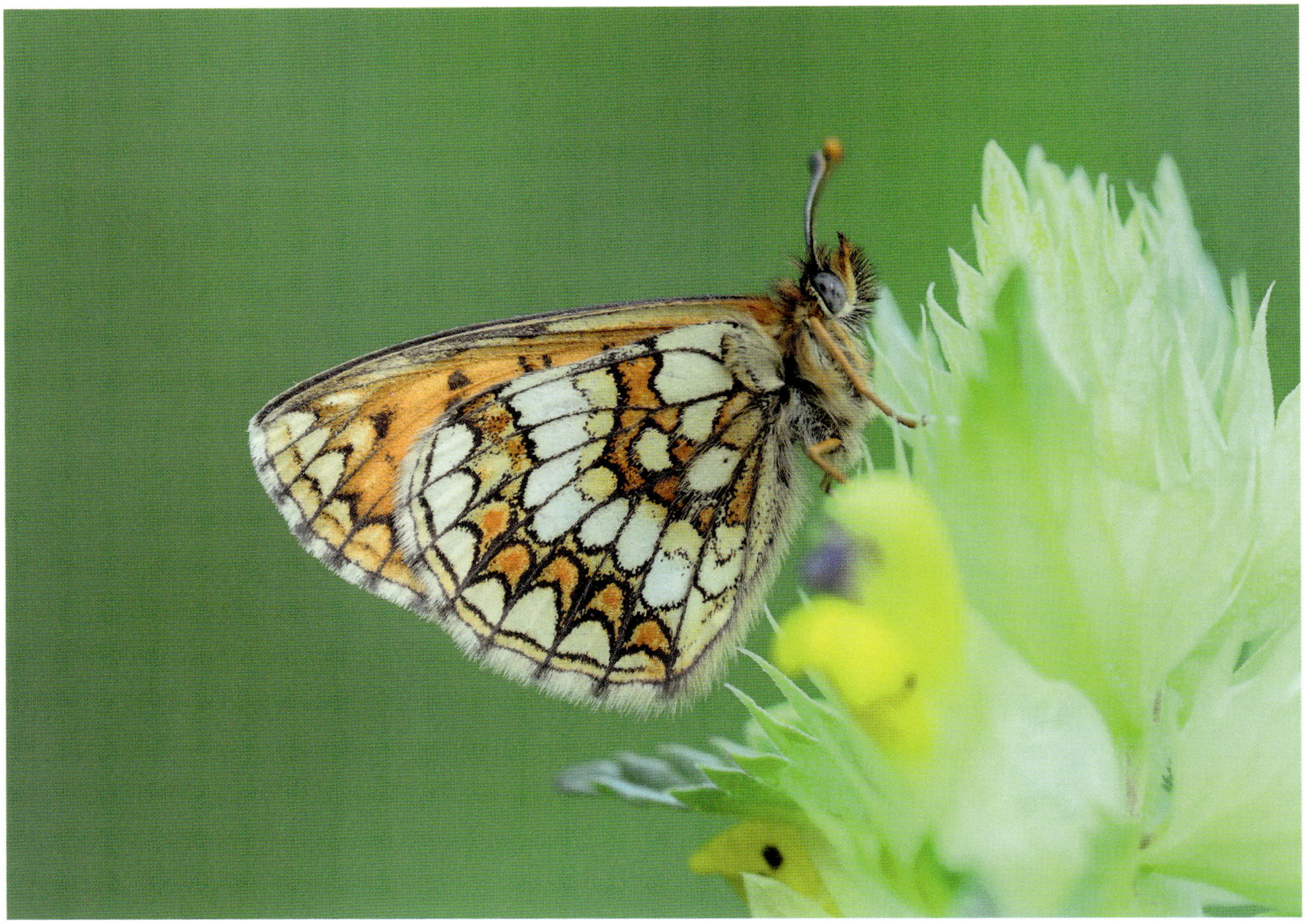

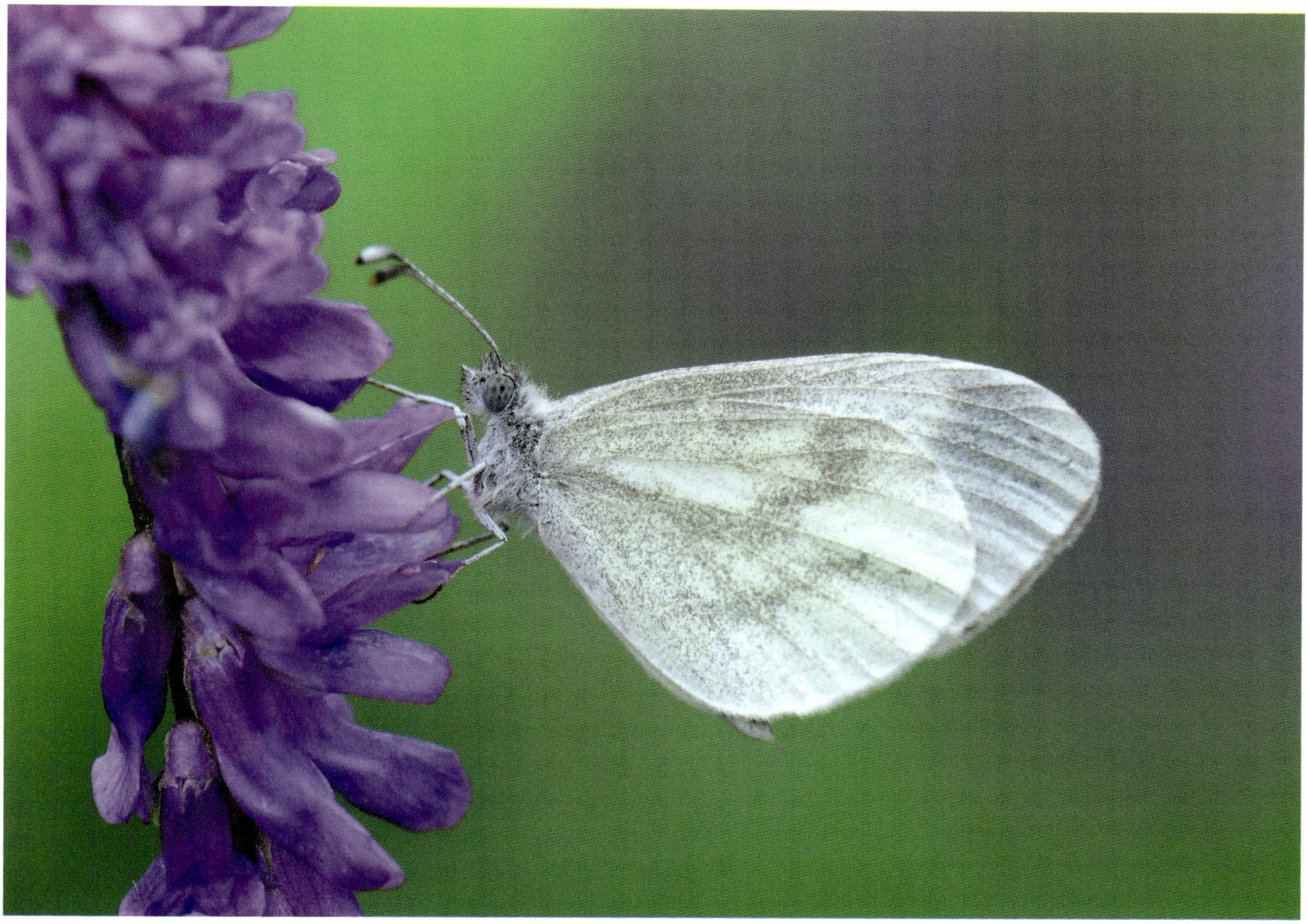

32.9 ~ Wood White *Leptidea sinapis*
A long lens has a narrower angle of view and can produce a well diffused background in the right circumstances.

↳ Nikon D800, 300mm Nikkor, + ext tube, 1/30sec at f/8, ISO 200.

// FACING PAGE ~ TOP //

32.7 ~ False Heath Fritillary *Melitaea athalia*
Butterflies are often more approachable when they are preoccupied with other matters. I was able to use the tripod and remove a distracting bit of foliage from the front of the orchid.

↳ Nikon D800, 200mm micro Nikkor, 1/30sec at f/8, ISO 200.

// FACING PAGE ~ BOTTOM //

32.8 ~ False Heath Fritillary *Melitaea athalia*
Fritillaries by nature are wary insects and can often be problematic for beginners to identify, especially when viewing the upper side of their wings. The undersides have distinct patterns, shapes and spots which make identification much easier.

↳ Nikon D800, 200mm micro Nikkor, 1/8sec at f/11, ISO 200.

feeding and finding a mate. They often settle for much longer periods of time in the vegetation; the light is also dropping along with the temperature, making them less agitated. Many blues for example roost early, and are usually very approachable, especially those that rest on grass stalks. Others break their outline up by settling in the middle of flower heads, among the ground vegetation, or on the overhanging foliage of shrubs.

Photographic Approach

Many of the principles outlined in the dragonfly case study apply equally with butterflies. Photographing early in the morning, or late in the day is the ideal time. Aperture Priority is my preferred setting with butterflies since they are not as wary as dragonflies. Some species close their wings when at rest, therefore, reducing the need for small apertures. I usually target adults on higher bits of vegetation which makes it easier to keep

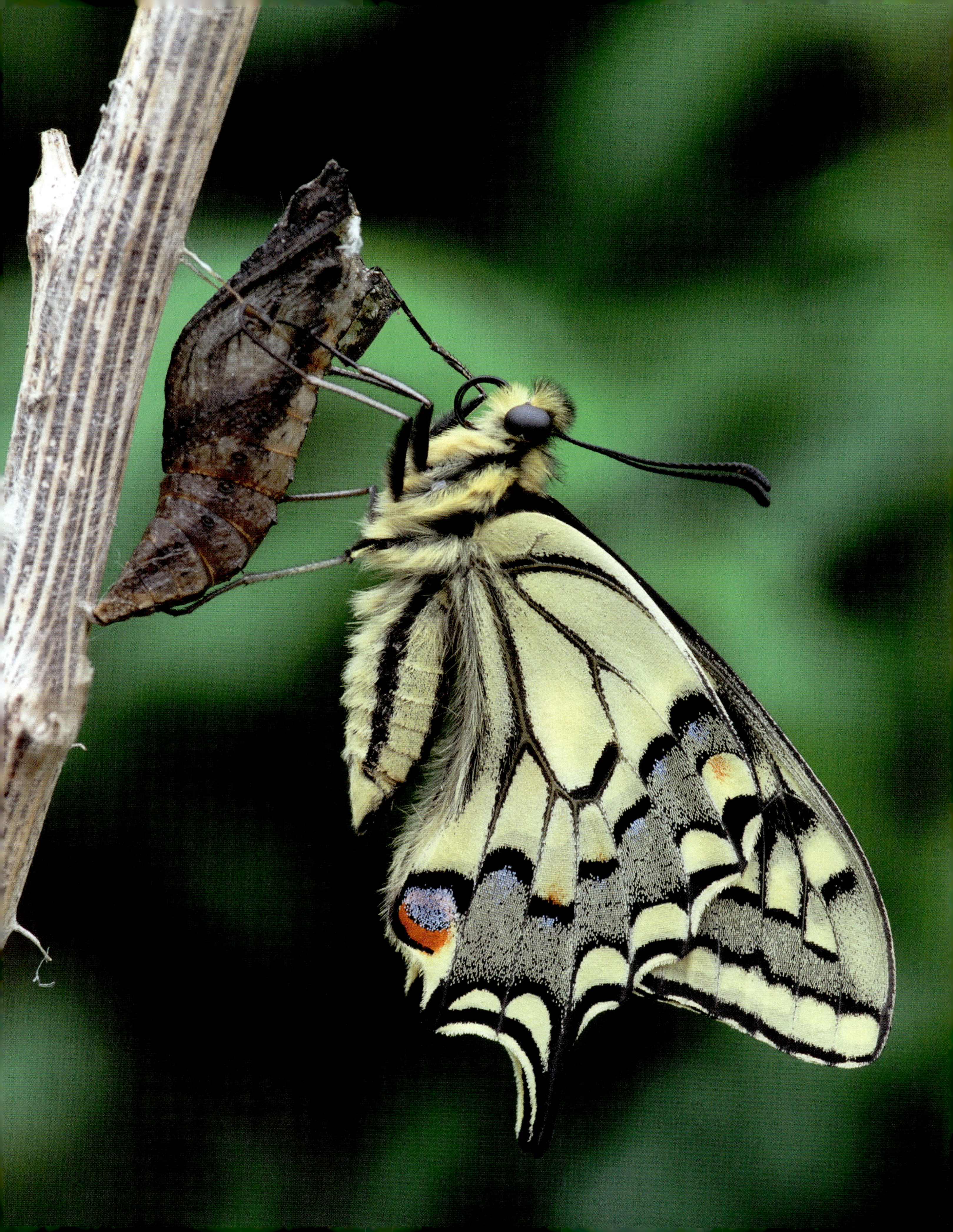

your camera parallel to the plane of the insect's wings. It will also help to keep the surrounding background more diffused if the flower stem is above the vegetation line. Some species settle on the flower heads themselves rather than seeking cover in the vegetation. For example, Orange Tips have a habit of resting among the seed heads of dandelions; the mottled appearance of the underside of their hindwings blends beautifully, making them difficult to spot. I do favour a 200mm macro for butterfly photography as they often tolerate a much closer approach. Lens selection is, therefore, not as critical. You can also obtain excellent results with a macro around 100mm–105mm, or a telephoto with extension tubes. These combinations are also better suited to macro on the move where you are constantly stalking active adults. On days of inactivity, I often shoot with a 300mm in combination with extension tubes. It allows me to shoot from a greater distance, which gives me time to evaluate the subject, the background and its position. In very overcast conditions, I like to supplement natural light with a hint of flash; this is easily accomplished using a single light unit from Nikon's R1C1 macro flash system positioned on top at the edge of the lens. You can rig up something similar with other makes; this provides just enough light to boost the contrast and add a little vibrancy to the photograph.

Butterflies lend themselves well to environmental portraits shot within the context of their habitat. Species photographed against a nice flowery meadow backdrop convey much about their habitat preferences and the environment they live in. A wide-angle lens around 17mm–24mm is ideal for *in situ* photos. This type of shot is difficult to achieve on a tripod unless taken on a cool, overcast day. My preferred approach is to handhold the camera, engage autofocus and VR, or equivalent if the feature is present, set the focus point to the far right to avoid placing the subject directly in the centre of the frame, that way you have an uninterrupted view of the background habitat.

// FACING PAGE //

32.10 ~ **Swallowtail** *Papilio machaon gorganus*
This newly emerged swallowtail will remain on its pupal shell until its wings are fully expanded and hardened.

↳ Kodak Pro SLR/n, 105mm micro Nikkor, 1/15sec at f/11, ISO 160.

Project Planning

Butterflies like most insects are seasonal, the spring being the start of the emergence period for many species in temperate regions of the world. The small number that hibernate throughout the winter months are the first species to make an appearance when the weather conditions are favourable.

Collecting Eggs, Larvae and Pupae for Photographic Study

Finding eggs, larvae and even pupae of butterflies in the wild can be challenging. Their existence depends on their ability to remain concealed from potential predators; the exception being those species which have other defence mechanisms that provide some form of protection from birds and small mammals. It is wise to start with a species that is fairly easy to find. The eggs of the orange tip, for example, are laid on the stalks and the underside of the flowers of lady's smock or garlic mustard. You will nearly always find a single orange egg on nearly every plant. When the larva has emerged, it can be reared on the foodplant and photographed at various stages in its development.

Some butterflies are considered pests. The larvae of the cabbage white butterfly feed on the leaves of brassica crops, cabbages, cauliflower and nasturtiums etc. As the larvae develop, they eat large holes in the leaves boring their way into the centre, which destroys the plant. The larvae are usually easy to spot among the leaves and can be reared to obtain photographs of the other parts of their life cycle. The larvae of Small Tortoiseshell and Red Admiral butterflies feed on stinging nettle plants. They can be easily found just by looking for areas where the foliage has been stripped.

The larvae of butterflies pupate in different ways according to which family they belong to. Most, (with the exception of a small number) pupate above ground; some species suspend themselves from the undersides of foliage, or branches and even under windowsills. The *Papilionadae* (Swallowtails) spin a tiny silken pad on the stem or leaf and then secure itself to it by a special appendage called a cremaster, which has tiny hooks that embed themselves in the silk pad to support the pupa. It also spins a silken girdle around its waist for support and additional security. Other butterfly larvae pupate in a silken tent, cocoon, or on the ground. With

// THIS PAGE ~ TOP //

32.11 ~ **Apollo** *Parnassius apollo*
On cool, overcast days, you can get up close to butterflies. Selecting a wide angle will allow you to show the species within the context of its environment.

→ Nikon D810, 24–70mm Nikkor, 1/30sec at f/11, ISO 200.

// THIS PAGE ~ BOTTOM //

32.12 ~ **Southern White Admiral** *Limenitis reducta*
A common species in southern Europe often seen in light woodland and gliding along shrubby tracks. Adults have an attractive blue metallic-like sheen to the upperside of the forewings. I was able to approach this resting adult in early evening. The light was overcast and I used a monopod for additional support.

→ Nikon D800, 200mm micro Nikkor, 1/8sec at f/11, ISO 200.

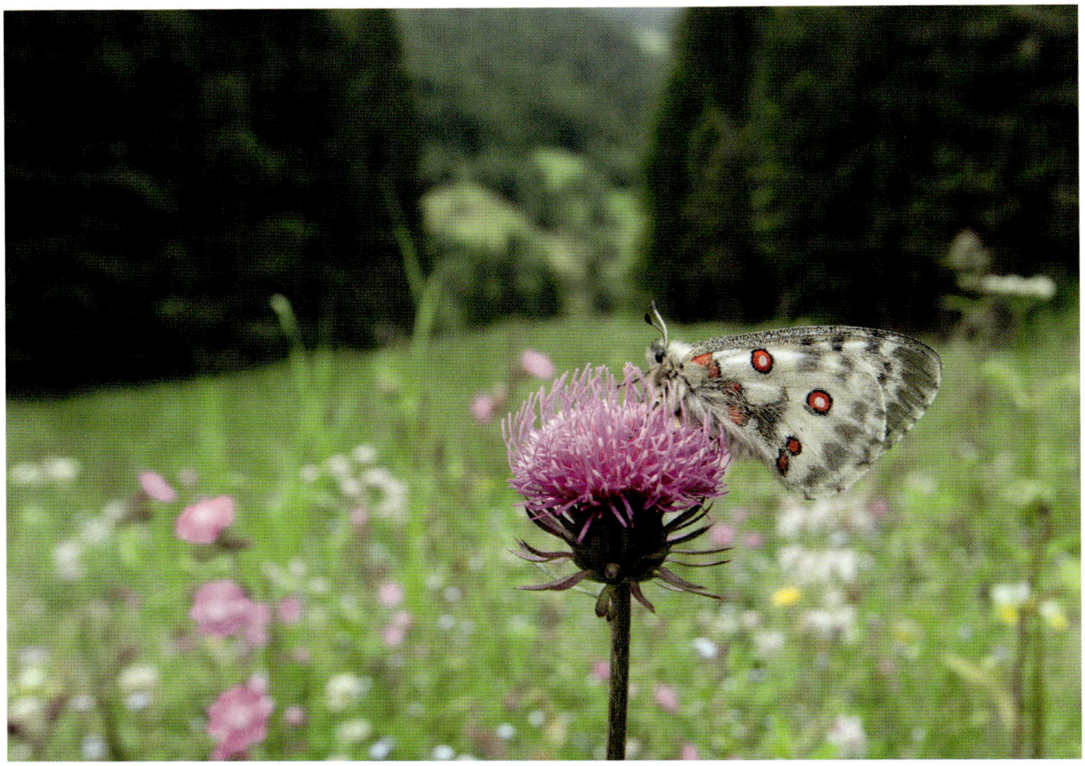

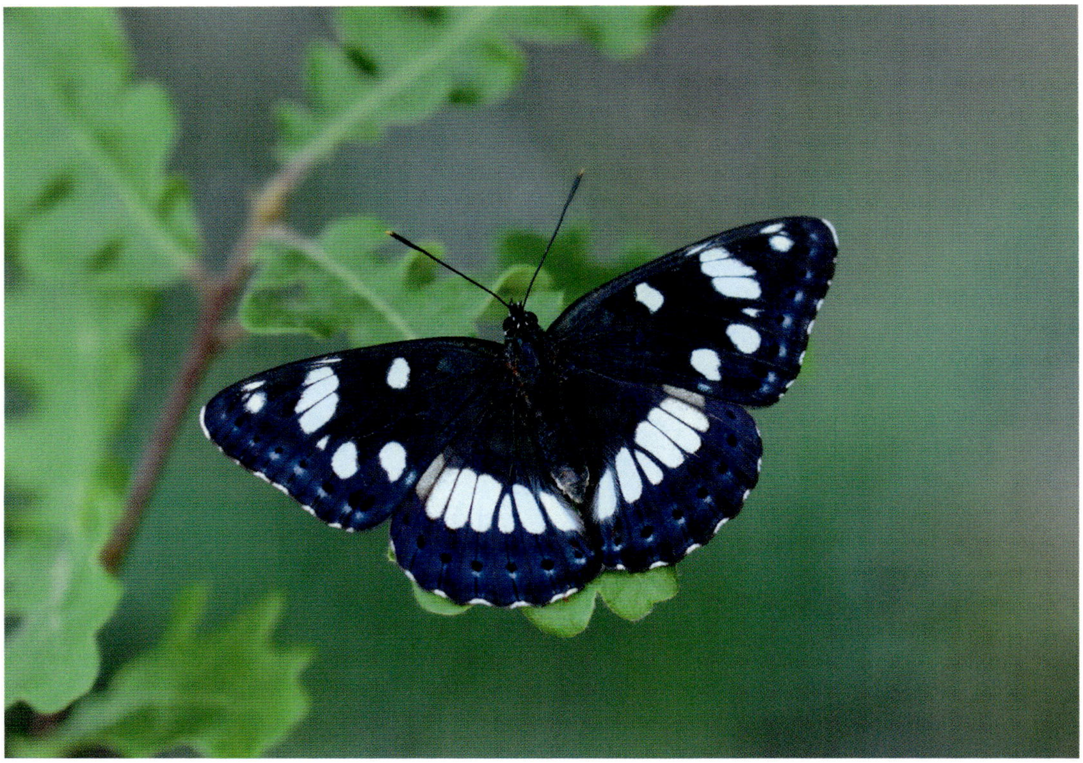

// FACING PAGE //

32.13 ~ Composite panel showing the many variations in butterfly pupae.

// OVERLEAF ~ LEFT //

32.14 ~ Image showing the wings of the adult butterfly which are clearly visible through the transparent pupal shell. The adult is very close to emerging.

→ Nikon D3X, 200mm micro Nikkor, 1/8sec at f/11, ISO 200.

// OVERLEAF ~ RIGHT //

32.15 ~ **Postman** *Heliconius melpomone*
Adults tend to rest on their pupal shell until their wings are fully hardened.

→ Nikon D3X, 200mm micro Nikkor, 1/30 sec at f/11, ISO 200.

BUTTERFLY PUPAE

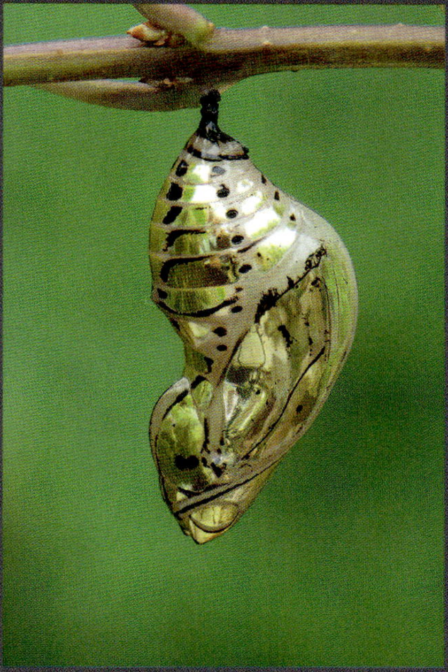
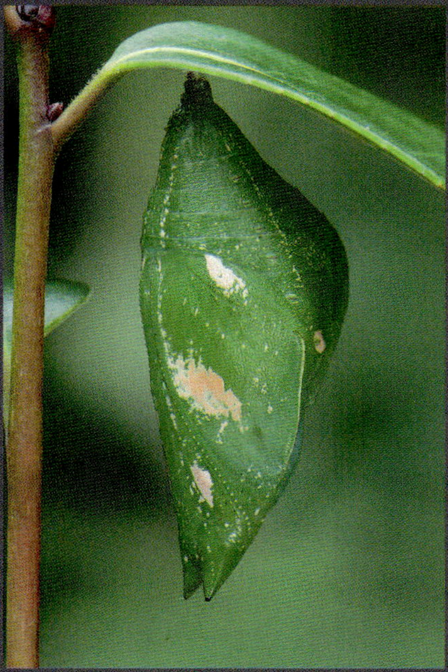
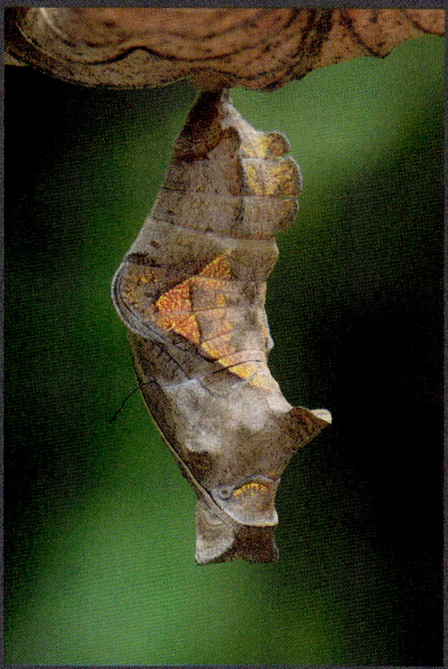
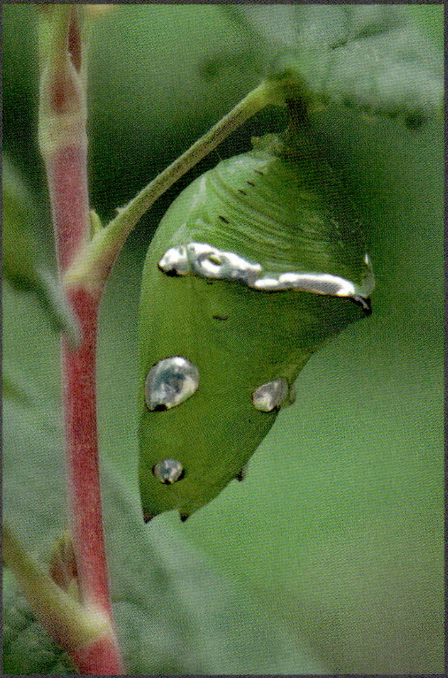
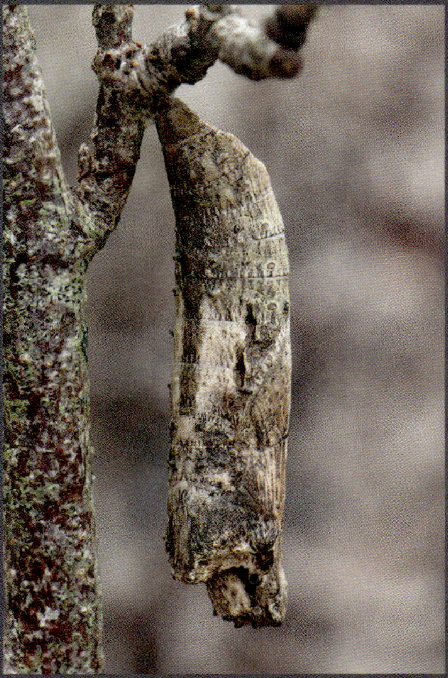
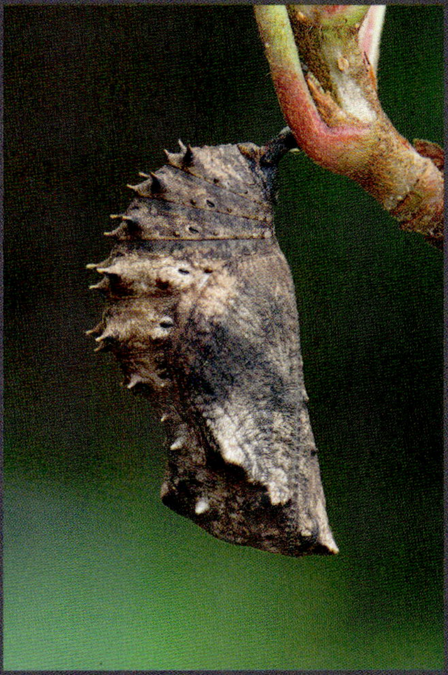

www.robertthompsonphotography.com

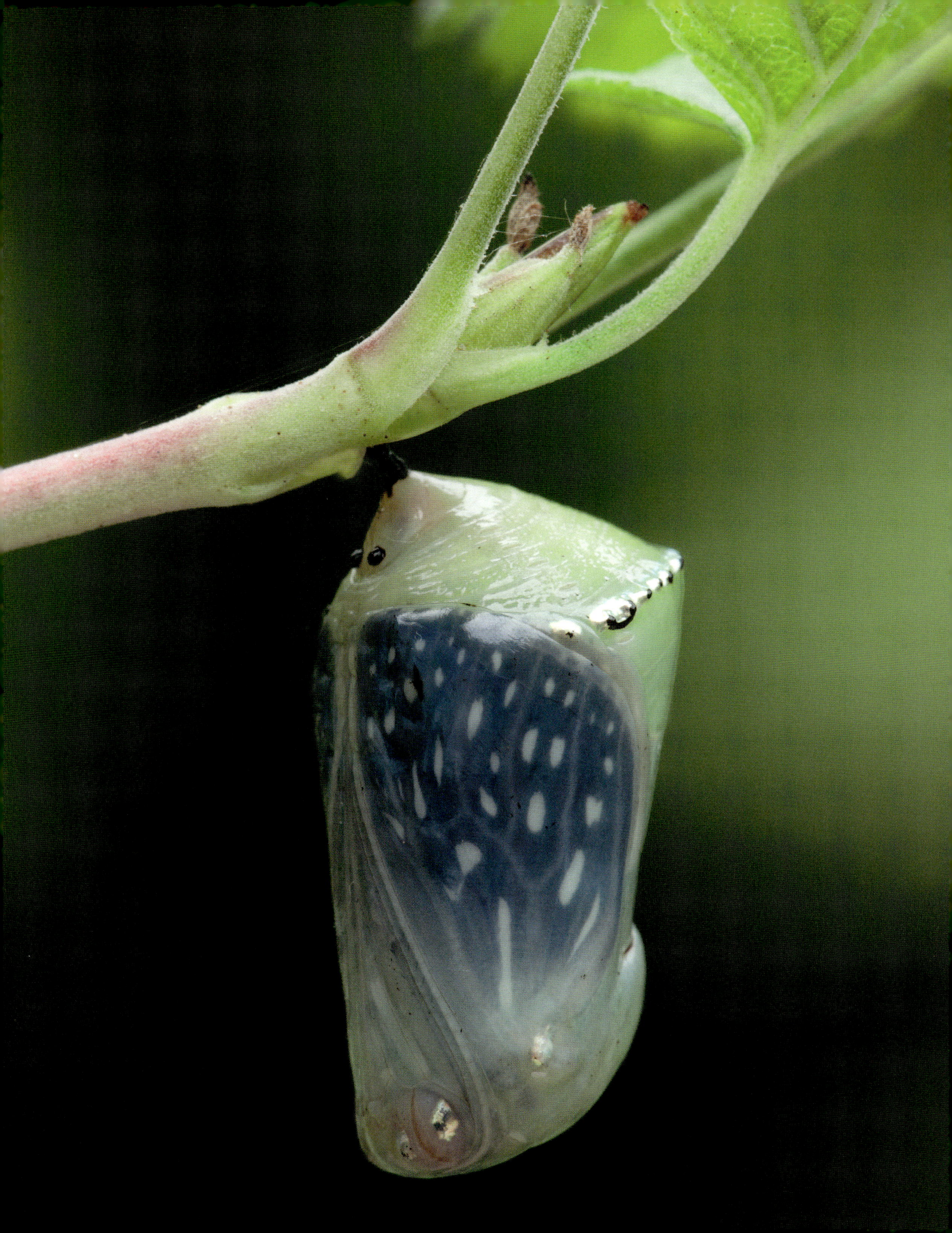

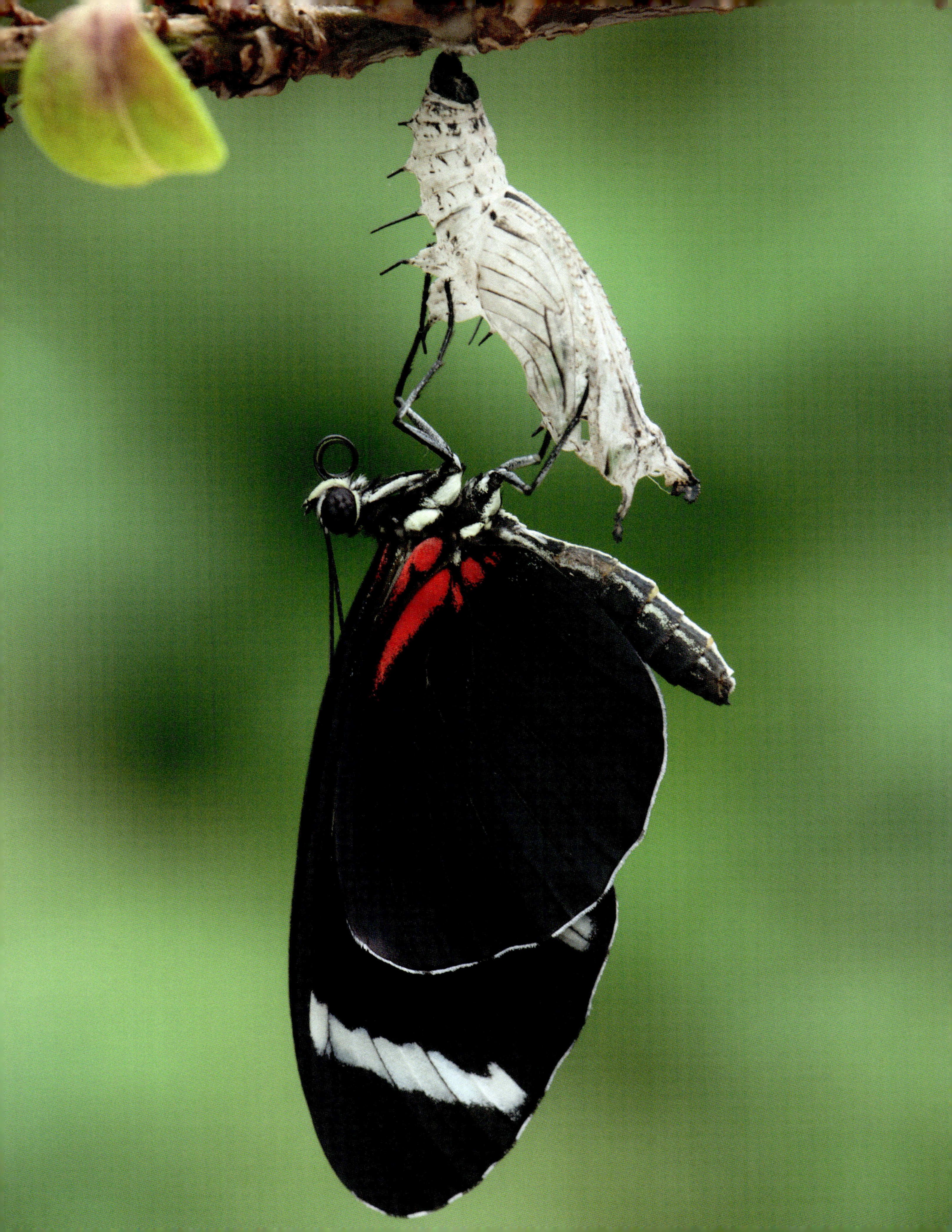

the exception of a few common species, the pupal stage of many butterflies can be quite difficult to find in the wild. The larvae are very choosy where they pupate since their very survival depends on not being discovered by potential predators.

Emergence Sequences

The pupae of butterflies are incredibly diverse and come in all shapes and sizes (see page 171). They make fascinating subjects for photography as do the emergence of the adults. To photograph an emergence sequence you need to plan in advance and keep a close eye on the transformations that are taking place inside the pupa. When the time is close, the colour and wing pattern of the butterfly start to appear through the darkening pupal case. Over the next few days, these changes intensify until the pupa darkens. The wings of the adult are now visible through the transparent shell. At this point, emergence is close. You need to have your camera and tripod in place to photograph the sequence, which takes place rather quickly. Most butterflies emerge in the early part of the morning. You should take a few test shots to establish lighting and background issues. The event takes place quickly so it's important that you have everything in place; there won't be time to experiment with camera positions or exposure settings. When emergence begins, it's a real fascinating experience to witness and one you won't forget.

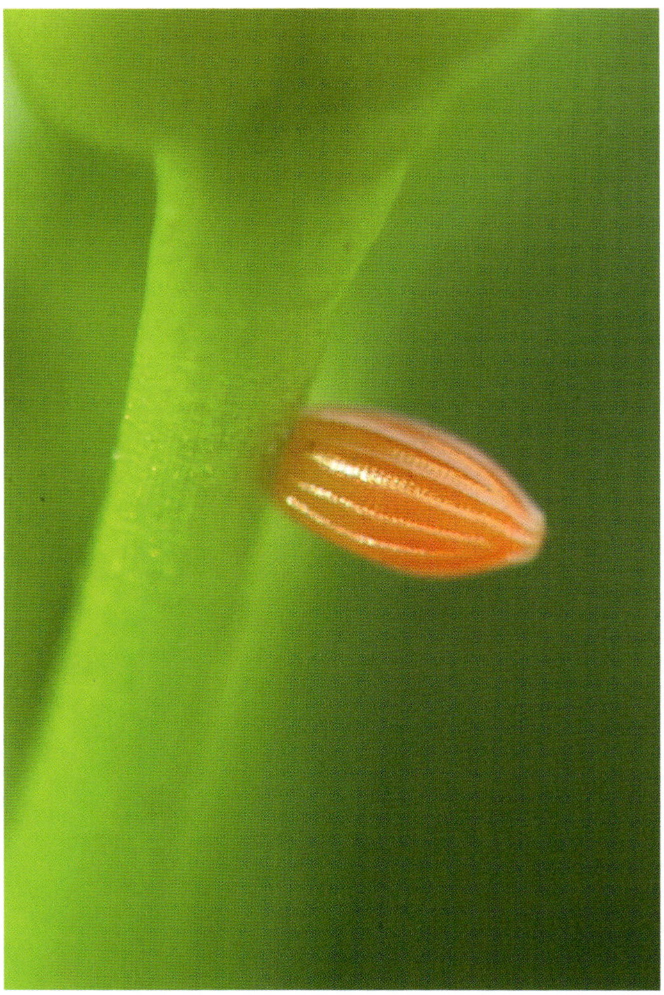

32.16 ~ **Orange-tip** *Anthocharis cardamines* (egg)
These are one of the easiest eggs to find. Almost every Lady's Smock flower will have one.

↳ Kodak Pro SLR/n, 200mm micro Nikkor, + ext tube, 1/8sec at f/16, ISO 160.

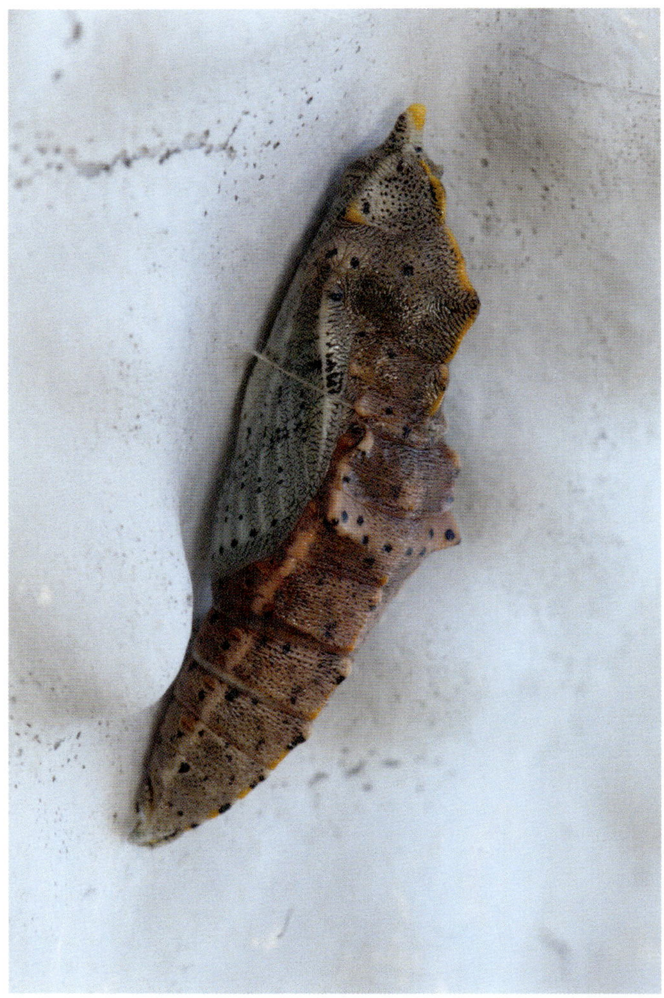

32.17 ~ **Large White Pupa** *Pieris brassicae*
The larvae of butterflies can select some unusual places in which to pupate. I found the pupa of this species in a sheltered spot on the wall underneath a large window sill.

↳ Nikon D2x, 200mm micro Nikkor, 1/8sec at F11, ISO 400.

PHOTOGRAPHIC TIPS

- Encourage butterflies into your garden by planting flowers and shrubs which they find attractive. They will also provide colourful props for photography.
- Explore suitable areas near your home first, such as roadside verges, woodland rides and clearings, and also coastal habitats rich in flowers. These habitats will contain a wide diversity of species.
- Don't confine your photography to ideal days. Go out in overcast and rainy conditions, butterflies are more approachable when restricted to the vegetation.
- Always check open or bare patches on tracks, also sunny spots on stone walls; butterflies often bask on them early in the morning.
- Look for south-facing areas with some shelter and flowers.
- Photograph all aspects of butterfly behaviour including feeding, mating and emergence.
- Try and capture complete life cycles. Start with common species, which are regarded by gardeners as pests. The eggs and larvae should be easier to find.
- Avoid species resting on cluttered vegetation on sunny days, as the shadows from surrounding foliage, can be distracting. Target those resting higher up in the vegetation where you can throw it out of focus.
- Make enquiries about local natural history societies in your area; they can provide you with information on species in your area.

Resources

There is a wide range of information on butterfly biology, life cycles and photography on the web. Below are some well-known publications and websites, which provide more in-depth knowledge of butterflies from around the world.

FURTHER READING

Glassberg, J. *Butterflies of North America.* Sterling.

Scott, J. *The Butterflies of North America: A Natural History and Field Guide.* Stanford University Press.

Thomas, J. & Lewington, R. *The Butterflies of Britain & Ireland.* British Wildlife Publishing.

Thompson, R. & Nelson, B. *The Butterflies & Moths of Northern Ireland.* National Museums Northern Ireland.

Tolman, T. & Lewington, R. *Butterflies of Britain & Europe.* HarperCollins.

WEBSITES

Butterflies & Moths of Northern Ireland: www.habitas.org.uk/moths

Butterflies and Moths of North America: www.butterfliesandmoths.org

Butterfly Conservation Europe: www.bc-europe.eu

Butterfly Conservation UK: www.butterfly-conservation.org

Moths and Butterflies of Europe and North Africa: www.leps.it

North American Butterfly Association: www.naba.org

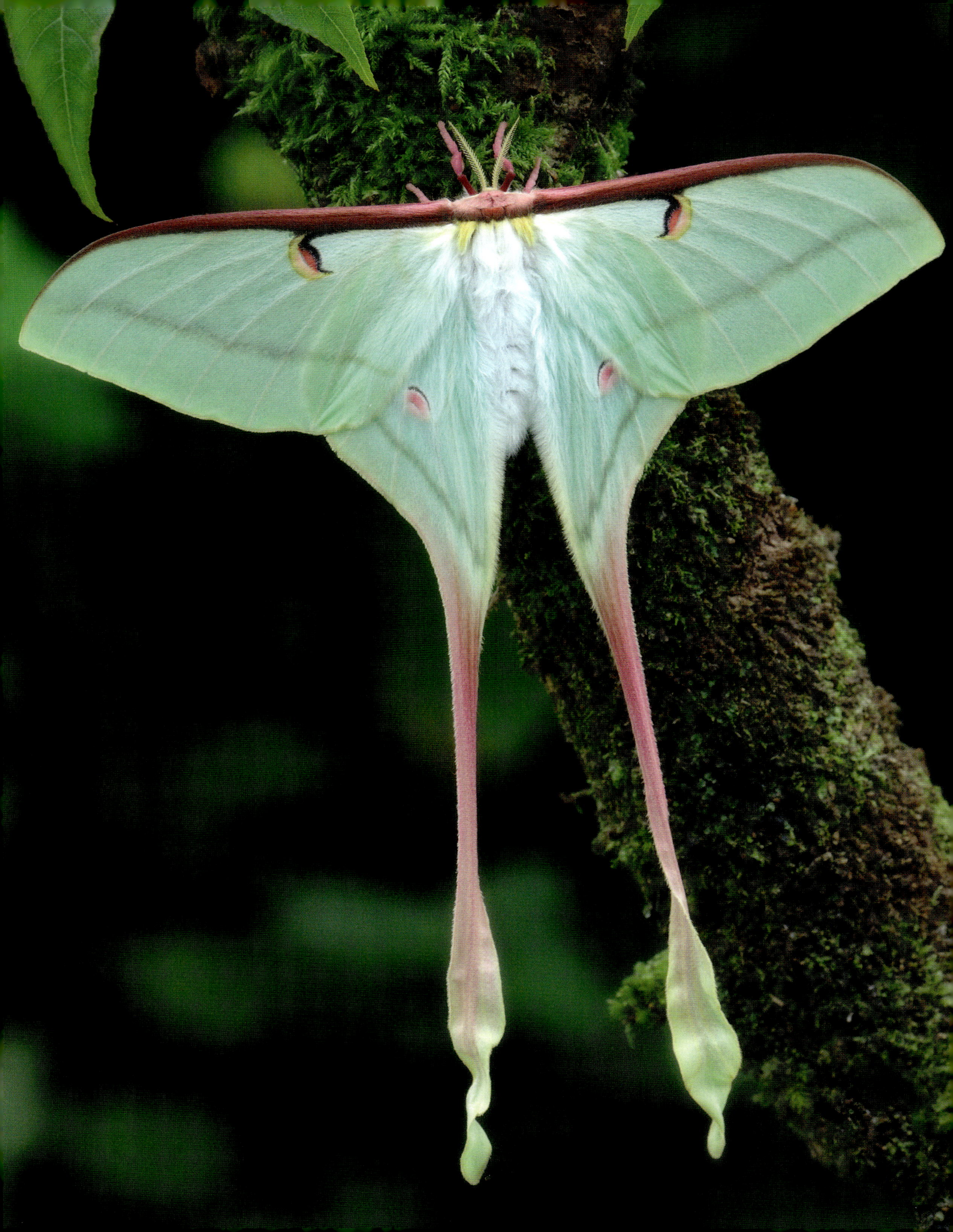

THIRTY THREE

Nature's Nocturnal Butterflies

Moths

Introduction

Moths have always been seen as the poor relatives of butterflies. It is fair to say that these inhabitants of the night receive much less attention than their flamboyant cousins. People's perception of moths is often one of indifference; however, they are much more unassuming creatures and secretive, yet their beauty, colour and diversity surpass many butterflies. Their reputation as devourers of clothes and carpets is grossly overstated; in fact, only a few species actually consume natural fabrics and textiles; the few that do are members of the microlepidoptera. The larvae of some moths are also regarded as serious pests in some parts of the world, but in general, the vast majority of species do not fall into this category.

Moths, like butterflies, are mainly plant-feeding insects; only a few species deviate from this habit. The majority of adults (but not all) feed on energy-rich nectar from flowers. Some are physiologically incapable of feeding as they lack the functional mouthparts; they store sufficient energy during the larval stage to see them through adulthood.

There is also a general misconception that moths fly only at night, which is not the case. There are as many moths that fly in the daytime, as there are species of butterfly in the British Isles. Over 2,400 species of Lepidoptera have been recorded throughout these islands; about 96% are moths. In the United States, it's around 11,000 species. When you look at moths in close-up, you will see that many have exquisitely beautiful patterns and delicate colouring. Most notable among these are the 'carpet moths', so-called because of their resemblance to oriental carpets. Other striking families include the brightly coloured tiger moths and the Saturniidae, or giant Silkmoths.

Scientifically, there is no difference between butterflies and moths, it's an artificially created division we have given to a group of Lepidoptera which have similar characteristics and fly during the daytime. We have given the name moths to the more primitive families into which the Lepidoptera are divided and also to the latter ones, which are considered to be more advanced. Inserted between these two groups are a small number of families, which we collectively call butterflies.

// FACING PAGE //

33.1 ~ **Dubernardi's Silkmoth** *Actias dubernardi* (female)
Silkmoths are the largest family of moths in the world. Many are highly colourful and make wonderful subjects for photography.

↪ Nikon D2X, 200mm micro Nikkor, 1/60sec at f/11, flash, ISO 200

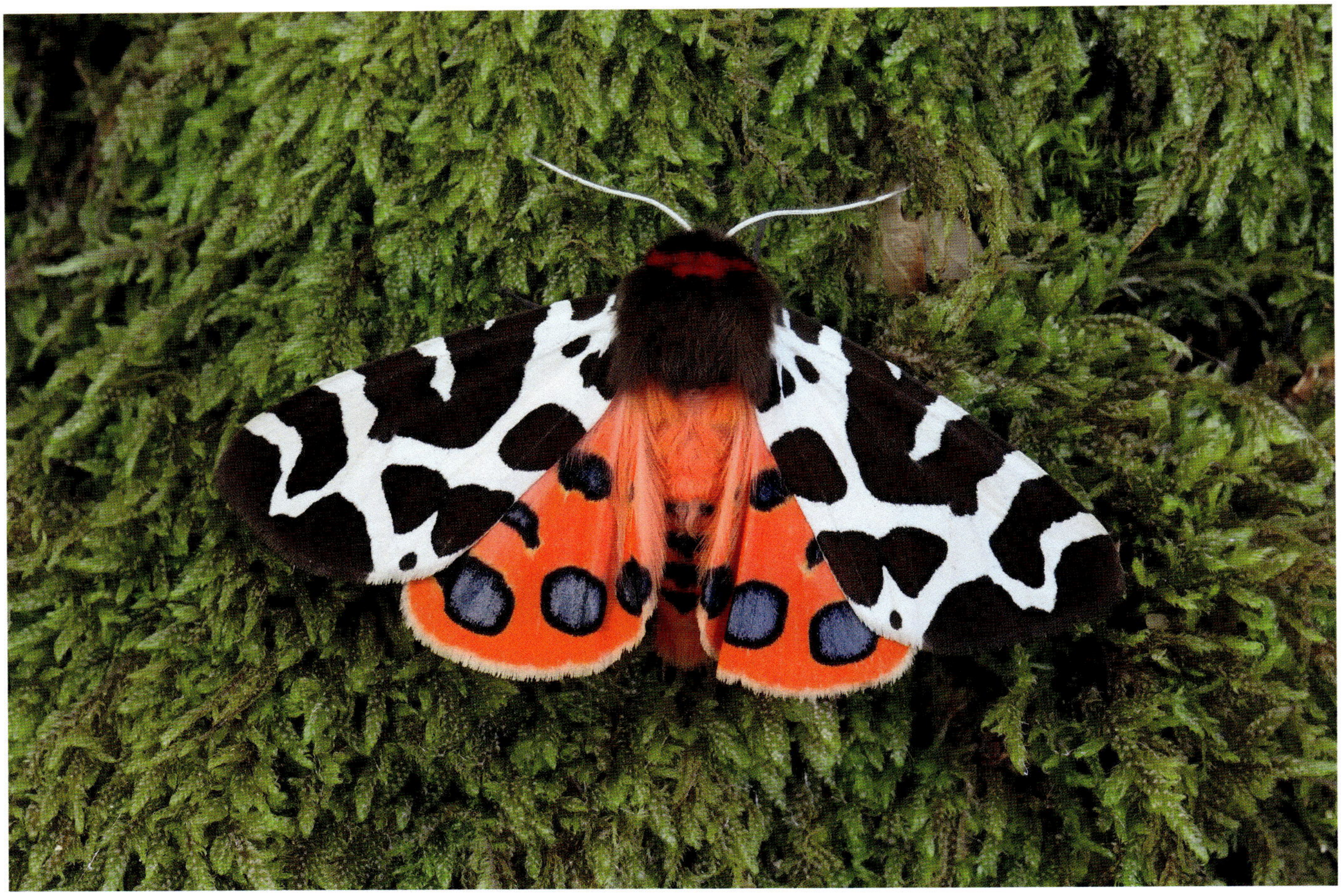

33.2 ~ **Garden Tiger** *Arctia caja*
A striking moth with chocolate brown and white patterned forewings. The bright scarlet hindwings contain a series of black dots and remain hidden when at rest. When threatened, the hindwings are reveled in an attempt to startle a would-be predator, buying the moth time to make its escape.

↳ Nikon D2X, 105mm micro Nikkor, 1/30sec at f/11, fill-in flash, ISO 100.

Moths are divided into two groups, the microlepidoptera and macrolepidoptera. All of the families of moths that precede the butterflies are known as microlepidoptera or 'micros' for short. All of the moth families that follow them are termed, the macrolepidoptera or 'macros'.

Biology and Life History

There are considerably more moths in the world than butterflies. Approximately 160,000 species have been scientifically described, with no doubt many more awaiting discovery. Their life cycle is the same as that for

// FACING PAGE ~ TOP //

33.3 ~ **Micro Moth** *Dioryctria abietella*
Modern converters are capable of delivering excellent quality when used with current macro lenses.

↳ Nikon D2X, 105mm micro Nikkor, + 2x converter 1/8sec at f/16, ISO 100.

// FACING PAGE ~ BOTTOM //

33.4 ~ **Early Thorn** *Selenia dentaria*
A very attractive species found commonly in a wide variety of habitats including gardens. The rich brown colouring helps to conceal the moth among leaves and ground vegetation.

↳ Nikon D3, 200mm micro Nikkor, 1/8sec at f/11, ISO 200.

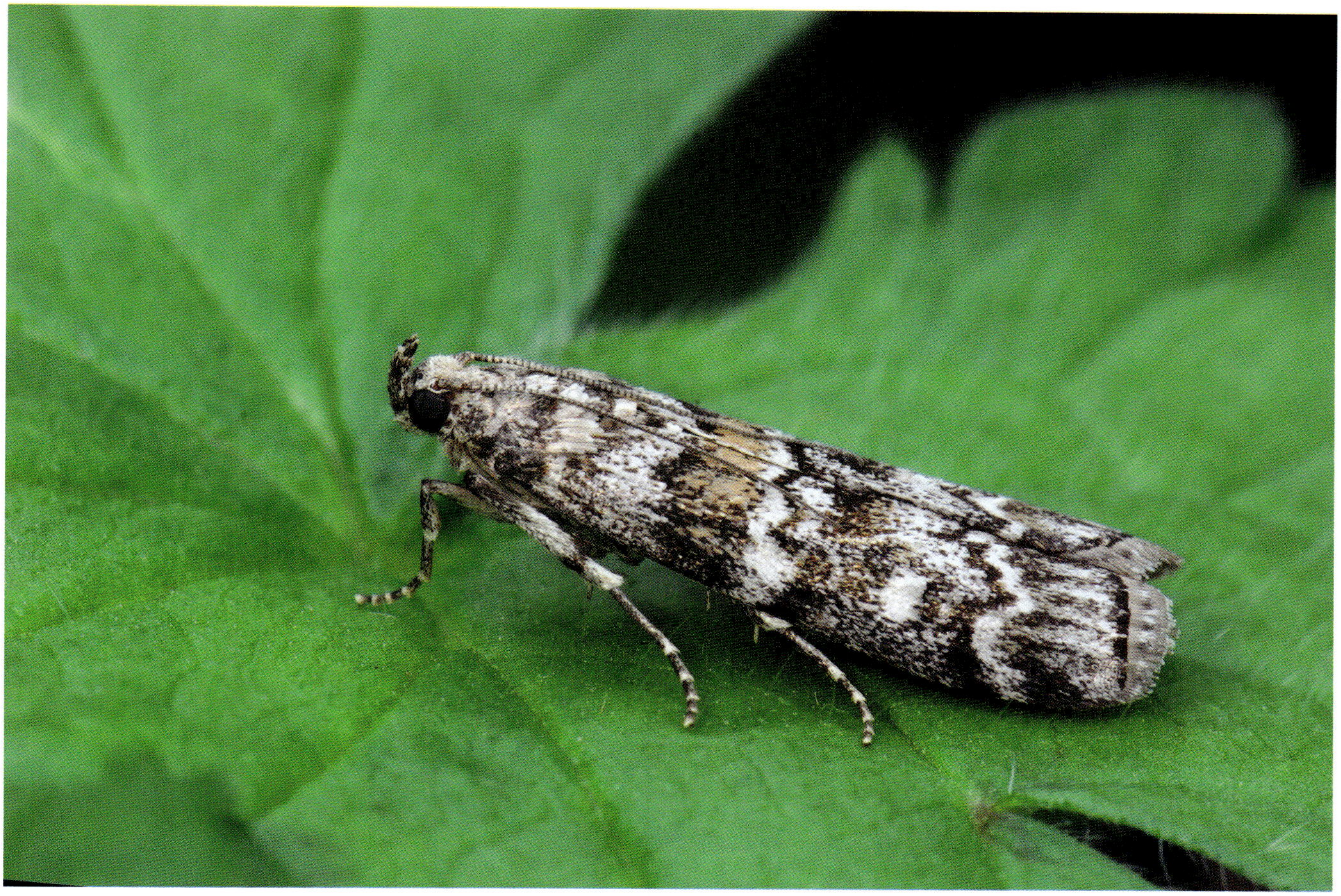

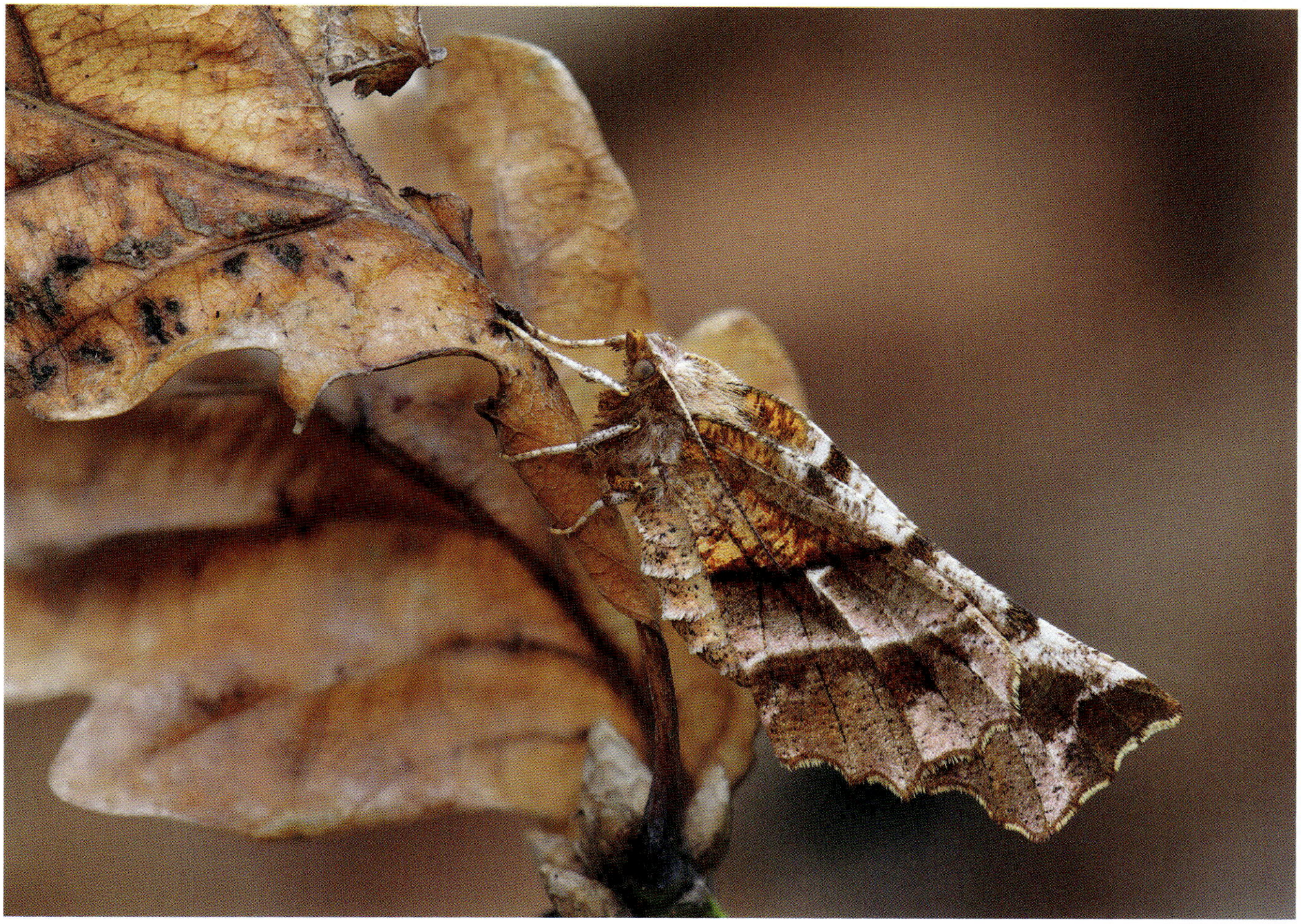

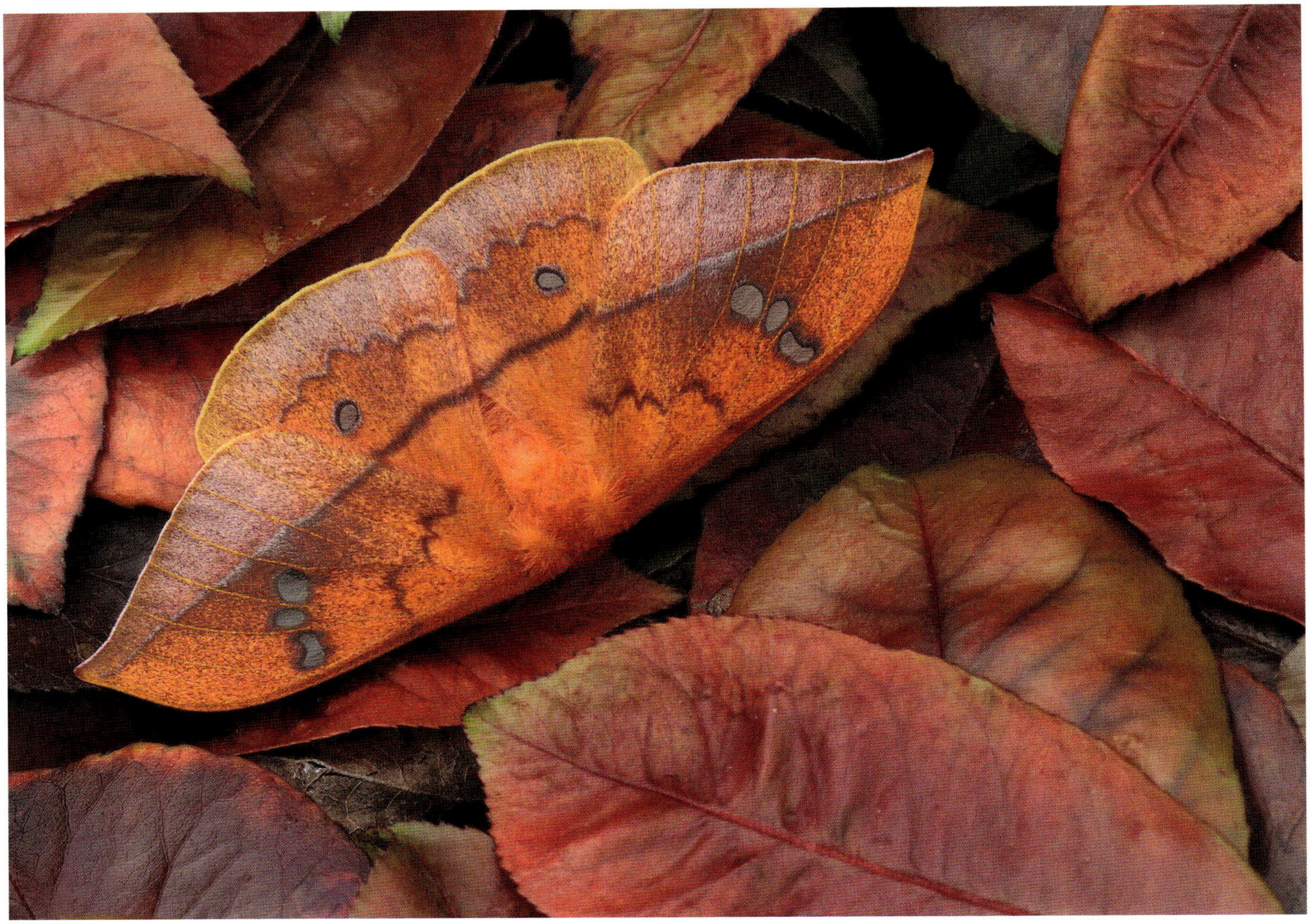

33.5 ~ **Scarlet Windowed Moth** *Cricula andrei* **(male)**
Many moths rely on cryptic camouflage to protect them from predators. Some assume the colouration and shape of leaves and seek protection among them.

↳ Kodak Pro SLR/n, 105mm micro Nikkor, 1/sec at f/11, ISO 160.

butterflies; both undergo a complete metamorphosis. Unlike most butterflies, the majority of moths pupate below ground among the moss and soil, often at the base of their foodplant, or among fissures in the bark. Some day-flying species spin hard, egg-like cocoons on the surface and are sometimes conspicuous in the vegetation. While butterflies in temperate climates are generally seasonal, moths can be found all year round. The majority, however, occur from spring until late autumn with only a small number flying during the winter months.

The colour and diversity of moths attract considerable interest among naturalists and photographers. They vary greatly in appearance and structure. The distribution of species is linked primarily to climate, habitat and the availability of the suitable foodplants, which they require in the larval phase of their development. Since the majority of moths fly at night, they rely much more than butterflies on concealment during the daytime. The vast majority use cryptic colouration and camouflage as their means of defence against predation. Many adults rest openly on rocks, branches and tree trunks, blending seamlessly with their backgrounds,

// FACING PAGE //

33.6 ~ **Merveille du Jour** *Dichonia aprilina*
A stunning moth when at rest blends beautifully with the lichens on the branches.

↳ Nikon D3X, 200mm micro Nikkor, 1/8sec at f/11, fill-in flash, ISO 200.

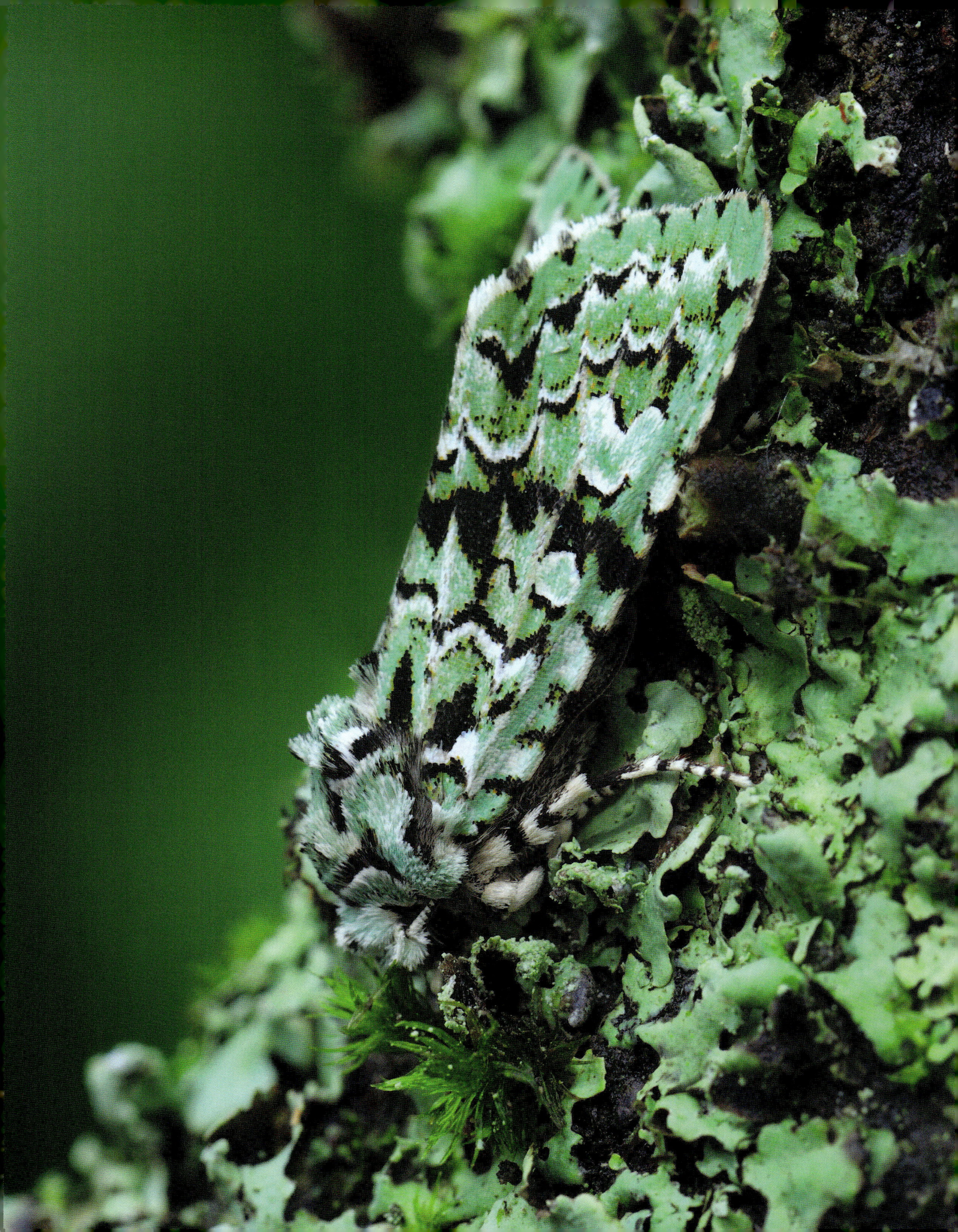

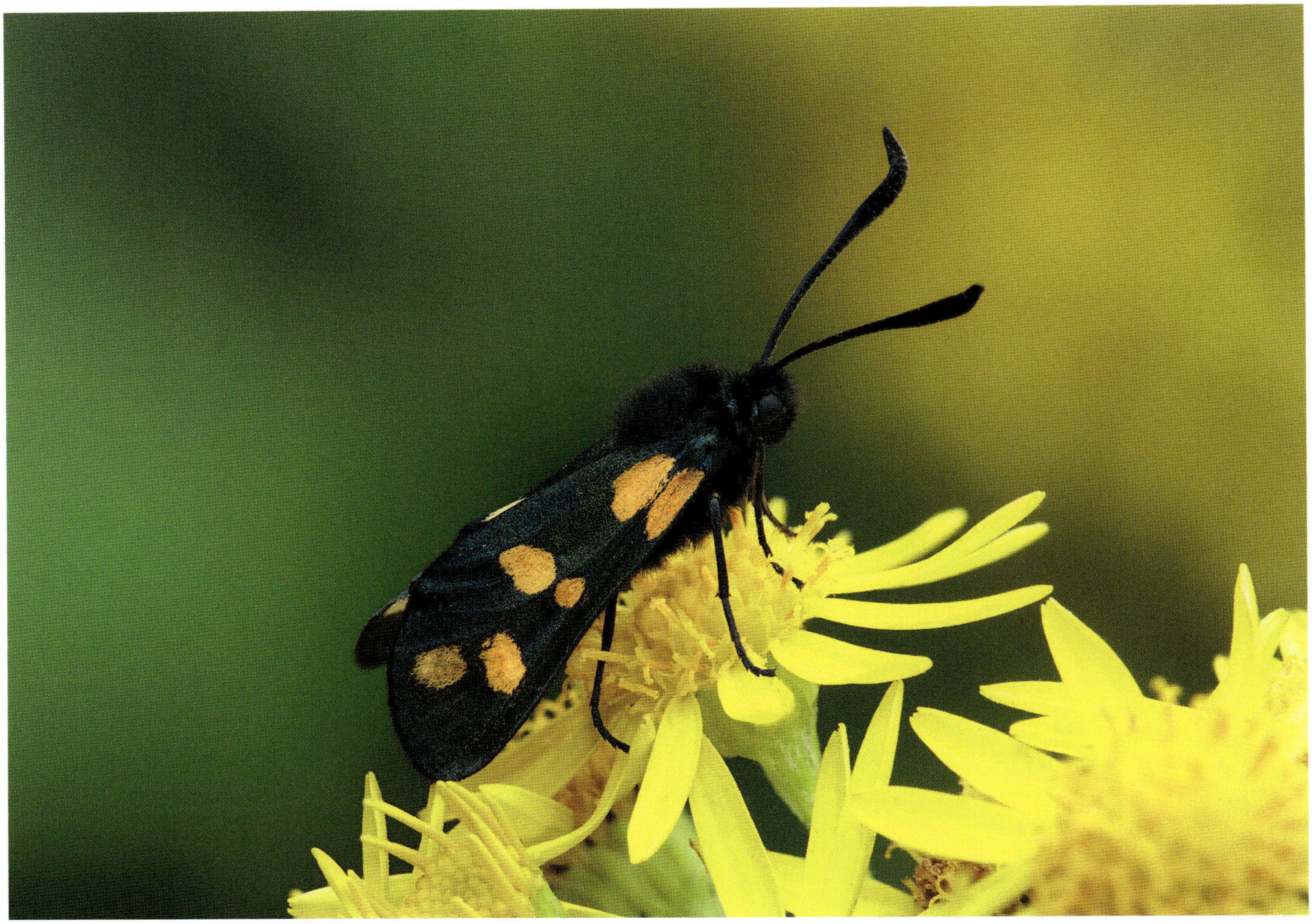

33.7 ~ **Six-spot Burnet** *Zygaena filipendulae* f. *flava*
A colourful day-flying species that inhabits flowery grasslands, roadside verges with large populations occurring in coastal sand dunes. It is one of the easiest moths to approach and photograph. The spots are normally red or rarely yellow as in this case. This is an aposematic species identified by its strong colouration which serves as a warning to potential predators that it is toxic.

→ Nikon D3X, 200mm micro Nikkor, 1/15sec at f/11, ISO 200.

making them difficult to detect by predators and even humans. No other insect group has evolved such elaborate strategies to avoid predation. Some moths resemble dead and withered leaves. Others have patterns and structures that give the appearance of bark, or broken twigs when at rest; all of these approaches are part of the strategy used by these denizens of the night to avoid detection. Many day-flying species rely on warning colouration as a protective measure. Strong, bright colours such as red, orange, yellow, white and black are easily recognised by a potential predator. A small number of species hibernate during the winter months and emerge

// FACING PAGE //

33.8 ~ **The Mullein** *Cucullia verbasci*
Many species resemble broken twigs and branches and blend beautifully with them when at rest.

→ Nikon D800, 200mm micro Nikkor, 1/25sec at f/11, ISO 200.

// OVERLEAF ~ LEFT //

33.9 ~ **Silver-ground Carpet** *Xanthorhoe montanata*
I disturbed this moth from vegetation and followed it until it settled again. Using a longer macro reduced my chances of hitting the surrounding vegetation and spooking it.

→ Nikon D800, 200mm micro Nikkor, 1/15sec at f/11, ISO 200.

// OVERLEAF ~ RIGHT //

33.10 ~ **Oleander Hawk-moth** *Daphnis nerii*
A stunning migrant species that occasionally turns up in the UK.

→ Nikon D810, 200mm micro Nikkor, 1/15sec at f/11, fill-in flash, ISO 100.

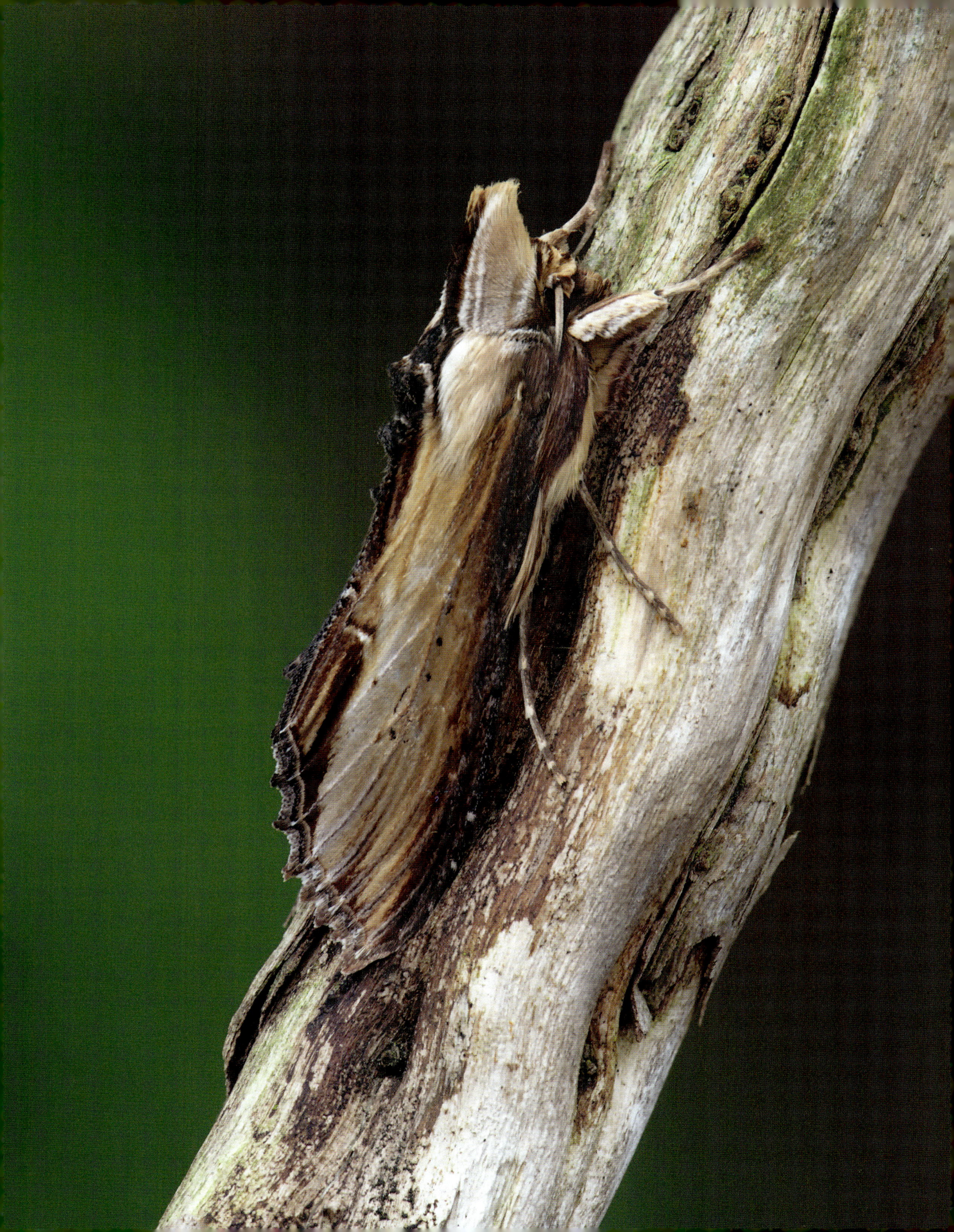

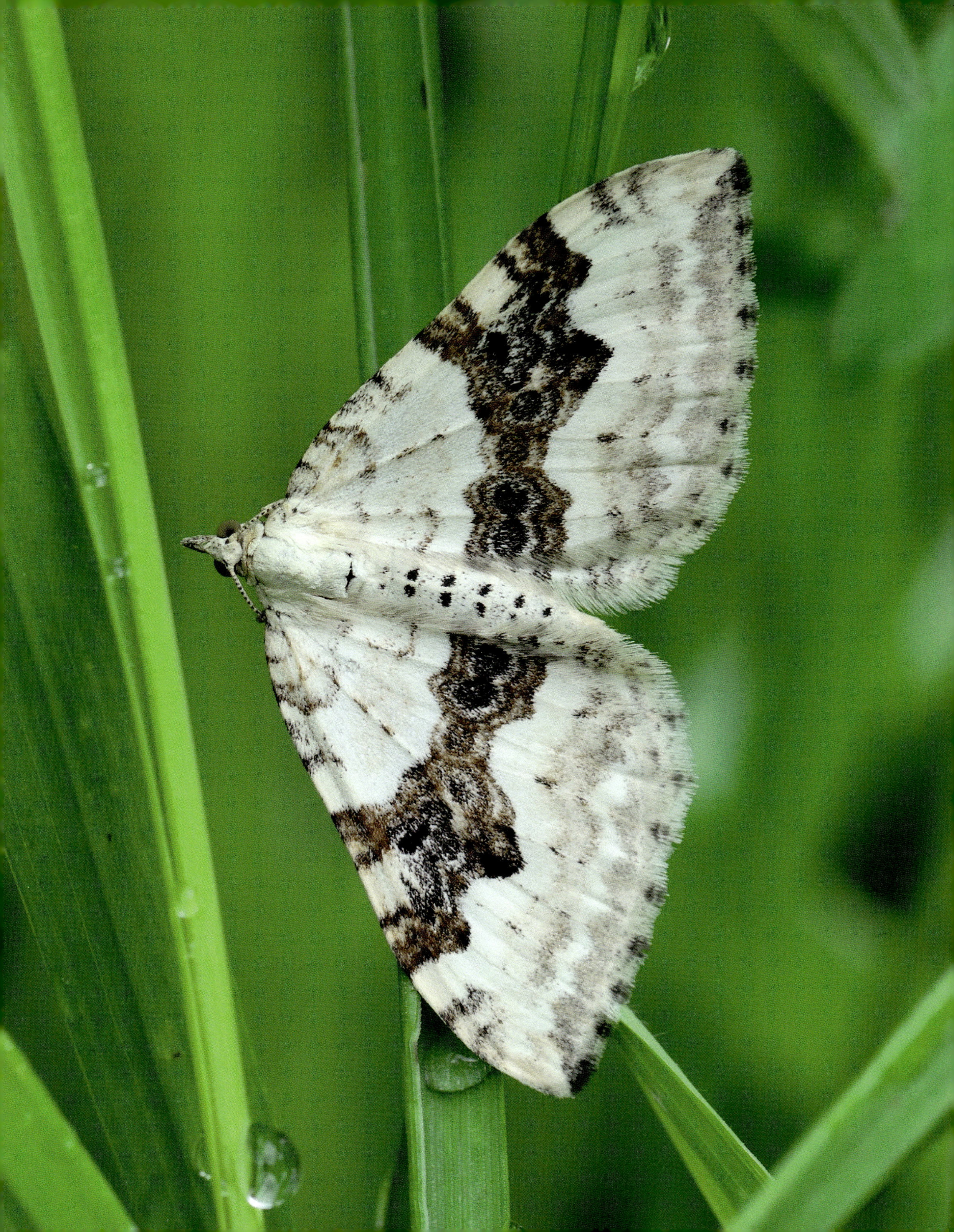

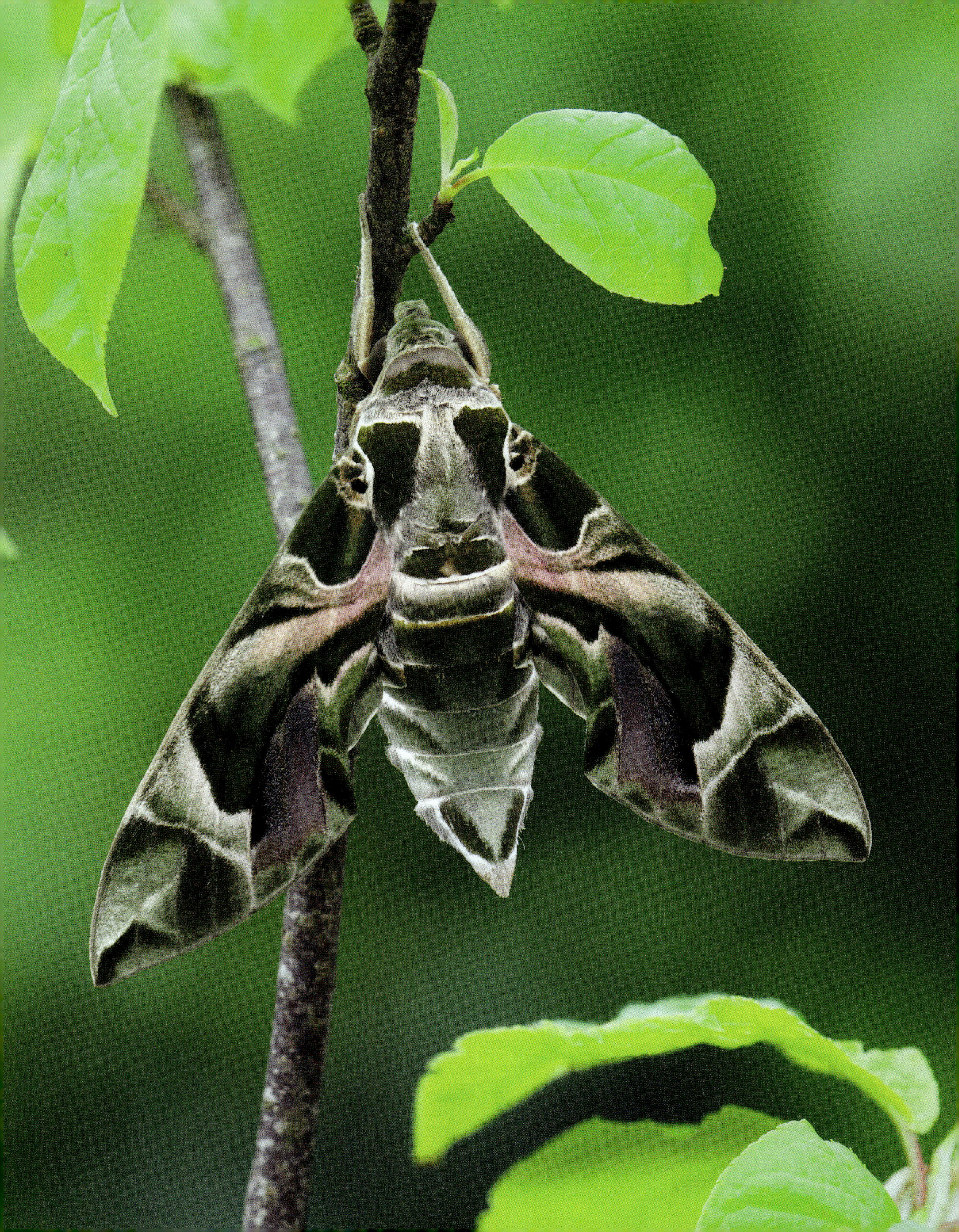

in early spring. In general, moths have a much longer flight period than butterflies with species being found in every month of the year.

Fieldcraft

Where to Find Moths

Moths can be found in almost every type of environment including your own garden. While the vast majority are nocturnal, a small number are day-flying. Those species that fly during the day can be treated in a similar manner to butterflies, although some are much more active and fast flyers, which makes them more challenging to photograph. Coastal habitats are among the best places to see and photograph day-flying species. These sites tend to be botanically rich with a wide diversity of flowers. Burnets are one of the most abundant species on coastal grasslands; their bright, vibrant colours make them conspicuous on flower heads and are an easy subject for the beginner to photograph.

Exploring the vegetation carefully often reveals resting adults, which, if disturbed, fly a short distance before settling again. Observing where they land will provide opportunities for photography if they are approached cautiously. Species which occur in woodland habitats are much harder to find and rely on their cryptic colouration and camouflage to avoid detection. But with a little knowledge and a bit of diligent searching, some can be located during the day. Many moths also rest on branches and tree trunks. These are always worth checking particularly on the shaded side, since many often settle in crevices and clefts in the bark, or at the junctions between the branches and the trunk.

Heathlands, bogs and marshy habitats are also excellent sites for moths. Old weathered lichen-covered fence posts, especially in upland regions are worth checking since the tree cover in these areas is usually scarce forcing moths to settle on whatever is available. Some prefer to rest on rocks, and in the crevices of dry stone walls where their colouration helps them to blend naturally with the surroundings. Anyone who has an interest in natural history knows that moths are attracted to artificial light at night, in particular, the UV part of the spectrum. We have all witnessed them flying up the windows at dusk attracted by the indoor lights. Leaving a strong porch or bathroom light on overnight, especially on a warm, humid evening will usually attract some species. This technique sometimes works best during the early and latter parts of the season, particularly in the country areas since there are little in the way of additional lighting to distract them. However, you have to rise early in the morning, as most moths will fly off before the sun forces them to seek cover.

Entomologists who study moths in their natural habitats use portable moth traps to attract species for scientific research. In ideal conditions, they can attract scores of adults and species. However, many get damaged and lose some of their scales when entering the trap, which becomes apparent when photographed in close-up. Some enthusiasts operate portable moth traps in their gardens throughout the year, and over a period of time accumulate quite a collection of photos of various species.

In the Field

Advances in digital technology have made the process of photographing moths reasonably straightforward. Most photographers can produce an acceptable image, but developing the skill for those that have the potential to be something beyond the average takes time and, more importantly, a creative eye. While set specimens still have a lot of scientific value, amassing a photographic collection of species offers a valid and important alternative providing they have location data embedded into the metadata. Photography also provides an insight into the behaviour of species, as well as showing emergence, wing expansion, feeding, mating and habitat preference – something that a preserved specimen can never do.

Many of the principles outlined in the butterflies' case study are also relevant to moths, but some are not. You will often find yourself working in shaded areas, which mean slower shutter speeds, and working on a tripod unless you intend to rack up your ISO, which I don't recommend. Many moths occur in woodland habitats. A significant number are cryptic and blend remarkably well with their surroundings. Their colour and wing patterns are extremely variable, which make them ideal subjects for photographic study. Many are skittish by nature, especially those that rest among the grasses and other ground foliage. Before you approach

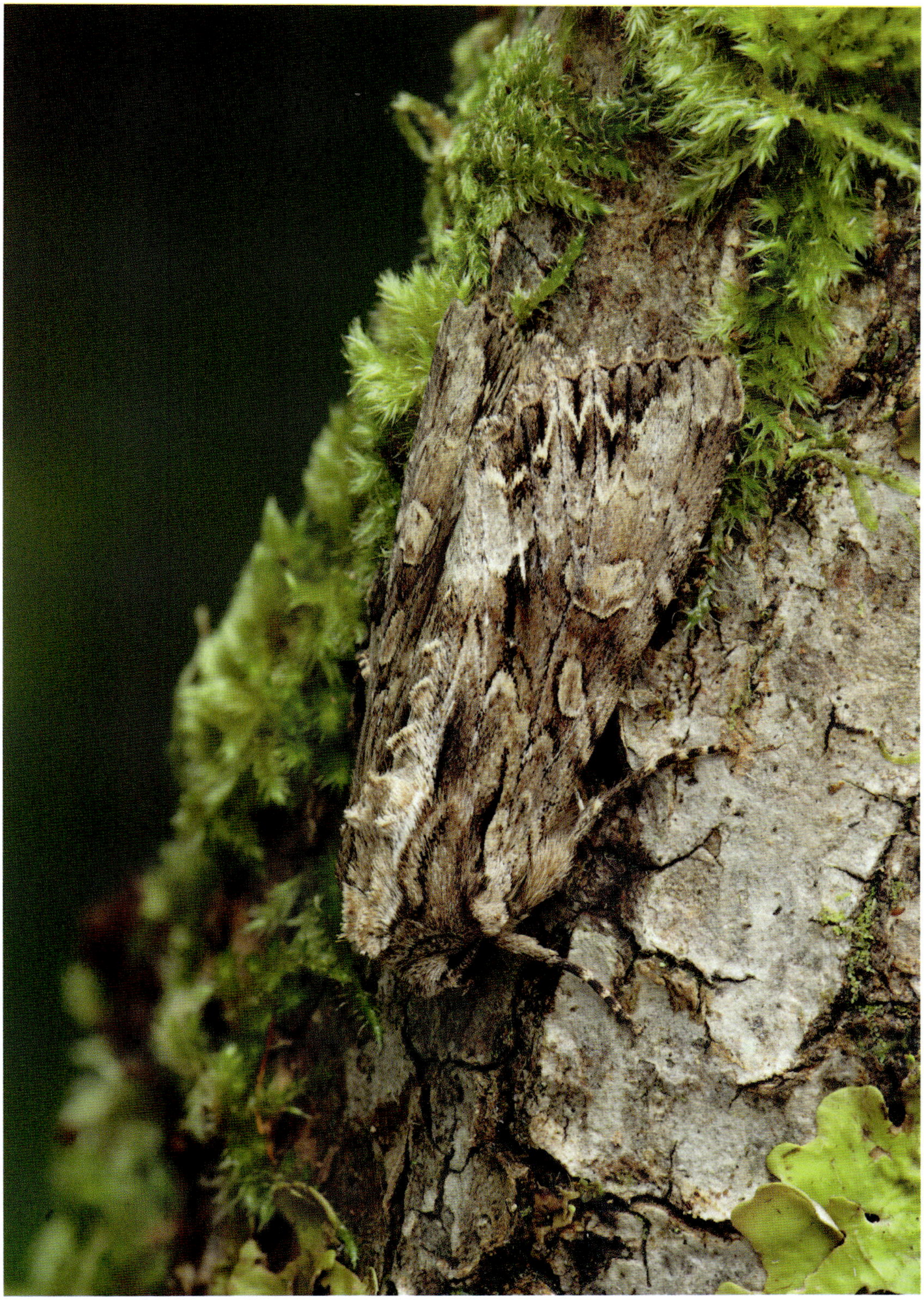

33.11 ~ Dark Arches
Apamea monoglypha
Having examined the bark of this tree for lichens I came across this moth by chance. It is a wonderful example of cryptic camouflage. I was careful not to touch the branch. Many species often rest upside down which helps to break up there colouration.

→ Nikon D810, 200mm micro Nikkor, 1/8sec at f/16, fill-in flash, ISO 100.

too closely, take a quick test shot of the vegetation first so you can make any corrections to exposure etc. You can then concentrate your efforts completely on the subject without the need to alter exposure settings.

Many larger moths do not have the capability of instant flight and require a warm-up period before they can fly if the temperature is low. It is always best to avoid touching the moth: unlike butterflies, they generally remain settled in the vegetation provided it is not disturbed too much. Species that rest flat against the trunk, or branch of a tree, pose few problems in terms of keeping the whole insect in focus. Others because of

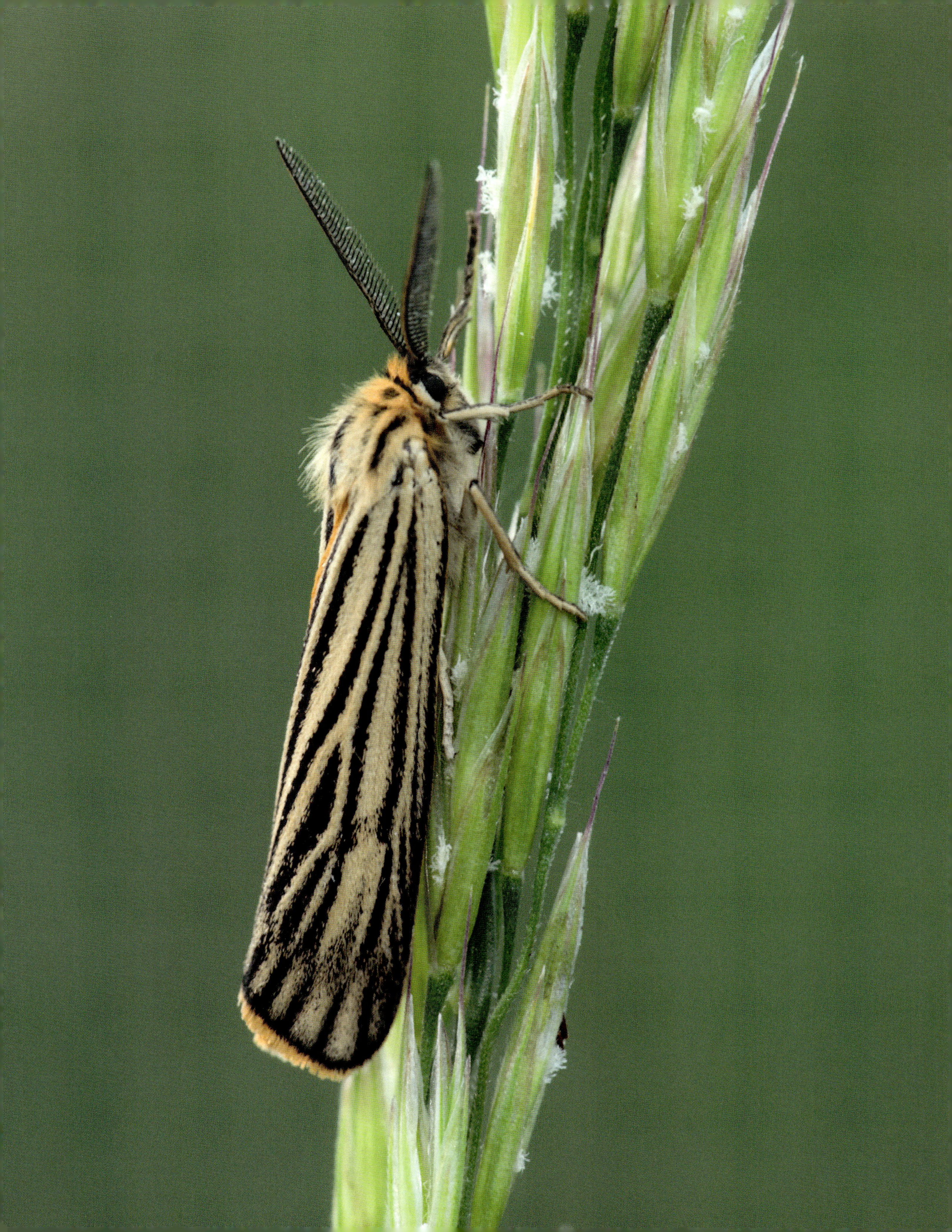

// FACING PAGE //

33.12 ~ Feathered Footman
Coscina striata
While running a workshop in France we came across these small day-flying moths. They are nervous by nature and best photographed with a long macro, or telephoto with ext. tubes.

↳ Nikon D810, 200mm micro Nikkor, 1/15 sec at f/11, fill-in flash, ISO 100.

// THIS PAGE ~ TOP //

33.13 ~ Buff Arches
Habrosyne pyritoides
Working in shade often requires slow shutter speeds and fill-in flash to boost colour and contrast.

↳ Nikon D810, 200mm micro Nikkor, 1/4sec at f/11, fill-in flash, ISO 100.

// THIS PAGE ~ BOTTOM //

33.14 ~ Peppered Moth
Biston betularia
Photographing in heavy shade often produces a colour cast. In this case I had to use manual flash as the main light source and dropped the shutter speed to allow the background to register.

↳ Nikon D800, 105mm micro Nikkor, 1/8sec at f/11, fill-in flash, ISO 200.

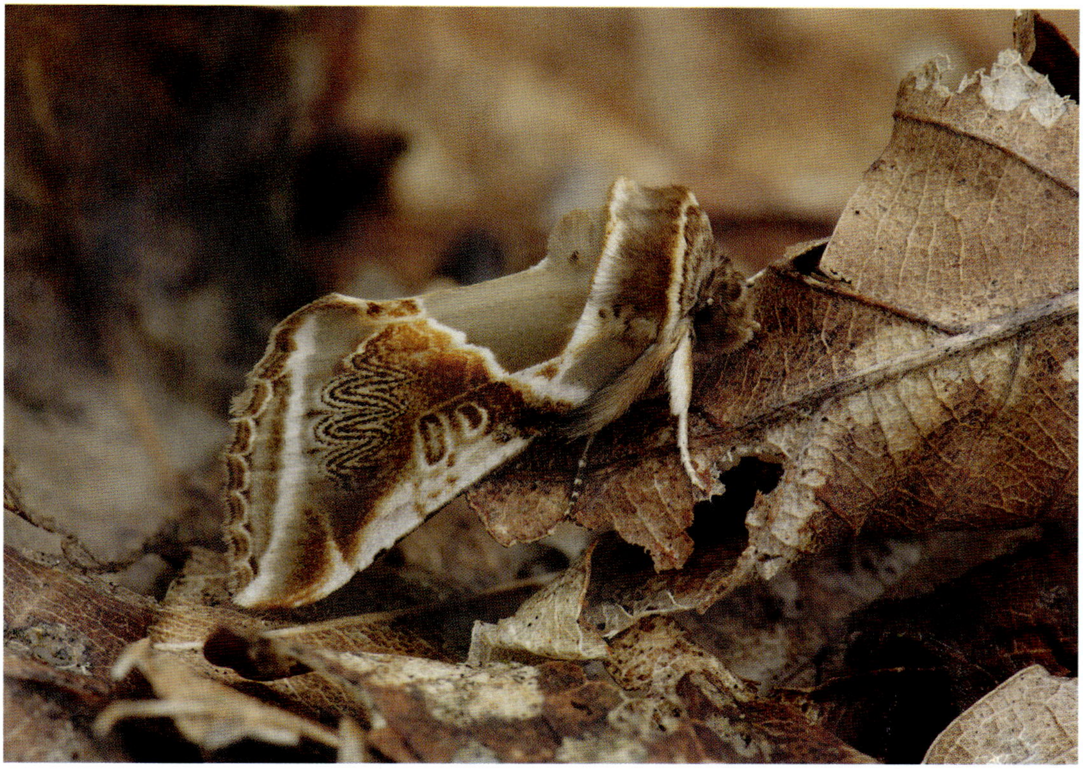

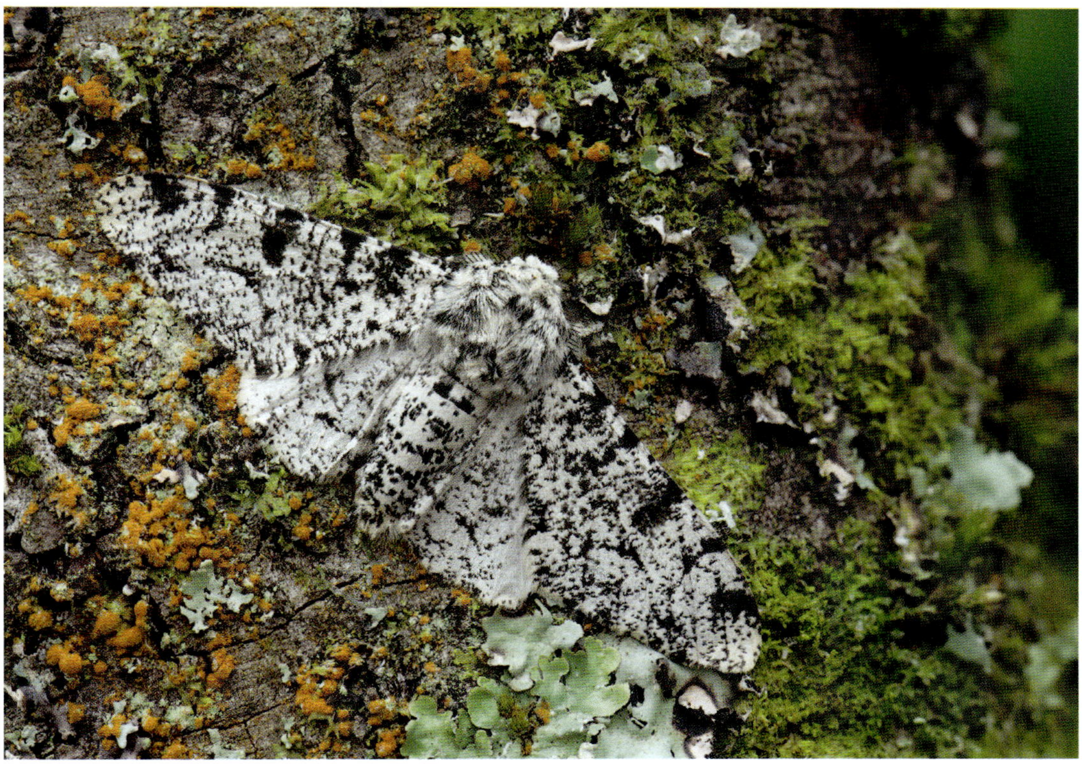

their resting posture require some thought regarding the composition to maximise the depth of field and retain acceptable sharpness throughout the subject. Where the difficulty can arise is keeping the whole insect in focus. Important features such as the eyes must be sharp, even at the expense of allowing the wing tips to soften – which is a more acceptable compromise. You need to look carefully at the species and its position and try to keep the camera back parallel to your chosen plane of focus. Photographing in the field invariably means being at the mercy of the elements. Swaying vegetation and branches with a resting moth can test your patience. If the wind is persistent with little or no lull, then it's a pointless exercise; you should pack up and try another day.

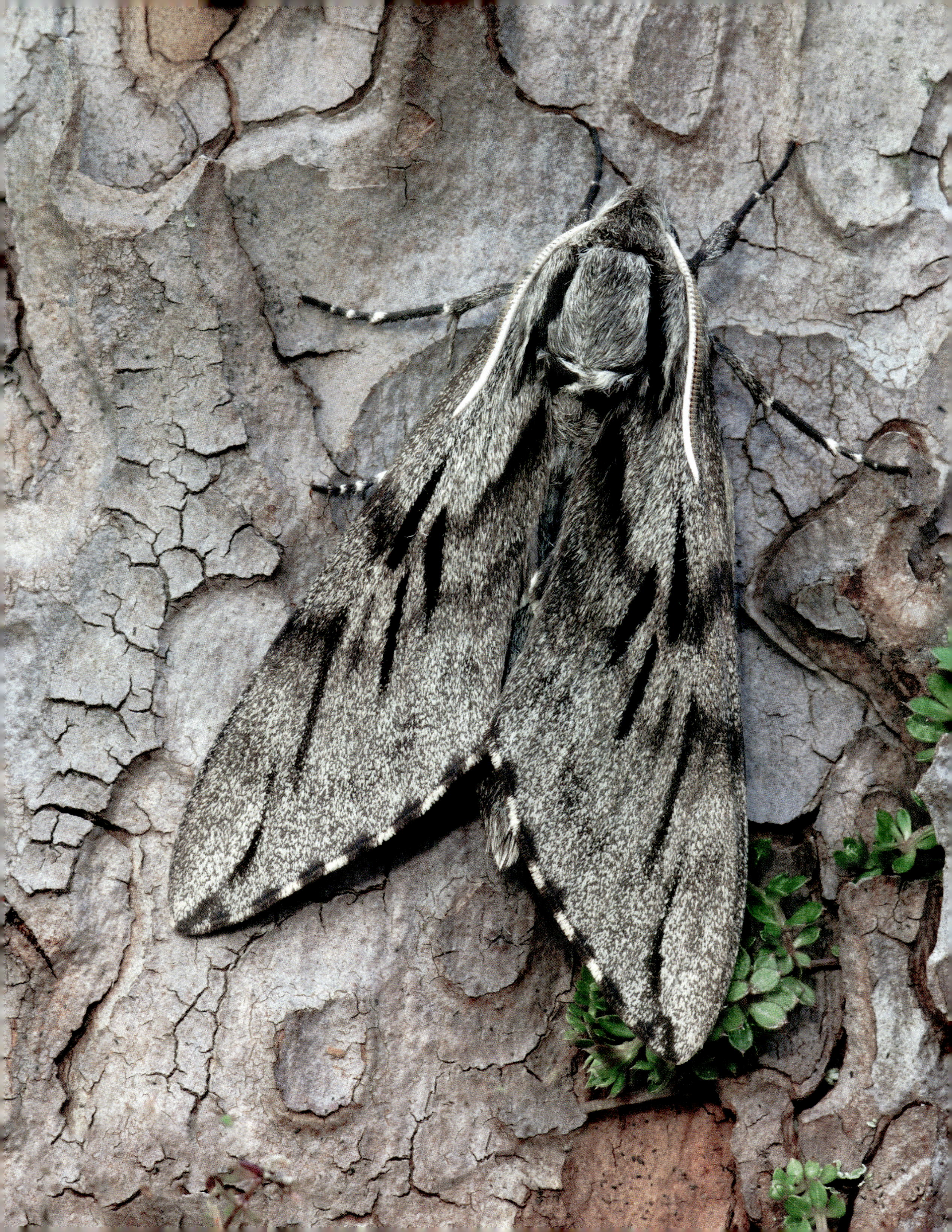

Photographic Hardware and Approach

The majority of moths are nocturnal and naturally they avoid sunshine, preferring to rest in the shade usually on the trunks and branches of trees or among the fallen leaves and foliage well out of sight from potential predators. Day-flying species are much more active in sunshine and can be a bit more challenging than butterflies. Colourful families such as the Burnets are a lot more approachable than many other day-flying species. In general, overcast days are best for moth photography, they are much more comfortable in these conditions, and there are fewer problems in terms of colour correction, contrast and exposure.

Photographing species that rest in woodland, often produces a greenish cast on the image, which you can reduce by switching your White Balance from auto to a fixed colour temperature. It is easier to make a global change when the images are transferred to the computer if necessary. I shoot most of the time in 'Aperture Priority' and use flash in some situations as it helps to reduce the colour cast a little. I sometimes use manual flash when the colour is severe or when the subjects are resting flat against the bark.

Backgrounds are also important, especially with moths, since they can significantly influence the meter's exposure readings. Moths resting against an unusually dark or light background will have a bearing on the exposure and adjustments to the camera's exposure meter must be made otherwise your photos will be over or underexposed. Due to the triangular shape of many moths when at rest they occupy less of the rectangular sensor frame than one might think. Off-centre placement of the subjects will show just how much the background takes up in the photograph. It is also important to analyse the subject in both formats and use a remote release to eliminate any vibration, which is hard to avoid if you are depressing the shutter button with your finger.

// FACING PAGE //

33.15 ~ **Pine Hawk-moth** *Sphinx pinastri*
Since the background was a similar colour to the resting adults I did not have to make any exposure adjustments.

→ Nikon D3X, 105mm micro Nikkor, 1/15 sec at f/11, fill-in flash, ISO 400.

You don't need very elaborate equipment to take successful photos of most moths. A short focal length macro is more than adequate, but not essential. Extension tubes in combination with short telephotos also produce excellent results. Moths which are at rest are unlikely to fly unless you disturb the branch or vegetation. While many of the geometrids, particularly carpet moths, are nervous by nature, the majority will tolerate a close approach with a tripod. It is also much easier to obtain environmental portraits showing them in their habitat settings. Flash is an important accessory and is useful as an additional light source when working in the shade.

Project Planning

Moths, unlike butterflies, can be found throughout the year, but the peak period is during late spring and summer when the greatest number of species are on the wing.

Finding Adults for Photographic Study

Photographing adult moths has always been a favourite pastime for many amateur entomologists. Much can be learnt about the species through photographic study. Adults can be found in the wild through some of the methods already described. If you are serious about photographing the adult stages of moths, then investing in a portable moth trap is the best method of obtaining specimens for photography. You will, of course, have to compromise sometimes on the condition of some adults, since as they enter the trap the delicate scales on the wings often get damaged. Setting up a moth trap on a regular basis in your garden is a worthwhile project and can provide a wide diversity of species to photograph throughout most of the year.

Although light trapping is one of the most popular methods for attracting moths, sweeping the ground vegetation is another useful technique for picking up species that are resting down among the foliage. You can easily purchase a sweep net, which is similar to a standard butterfly net but has a shorter, sturdier handle and a thicker frame. You simply sweep it through the ground vegetation and examine the contents. Many of the smaller micro moths are picked up in this way.

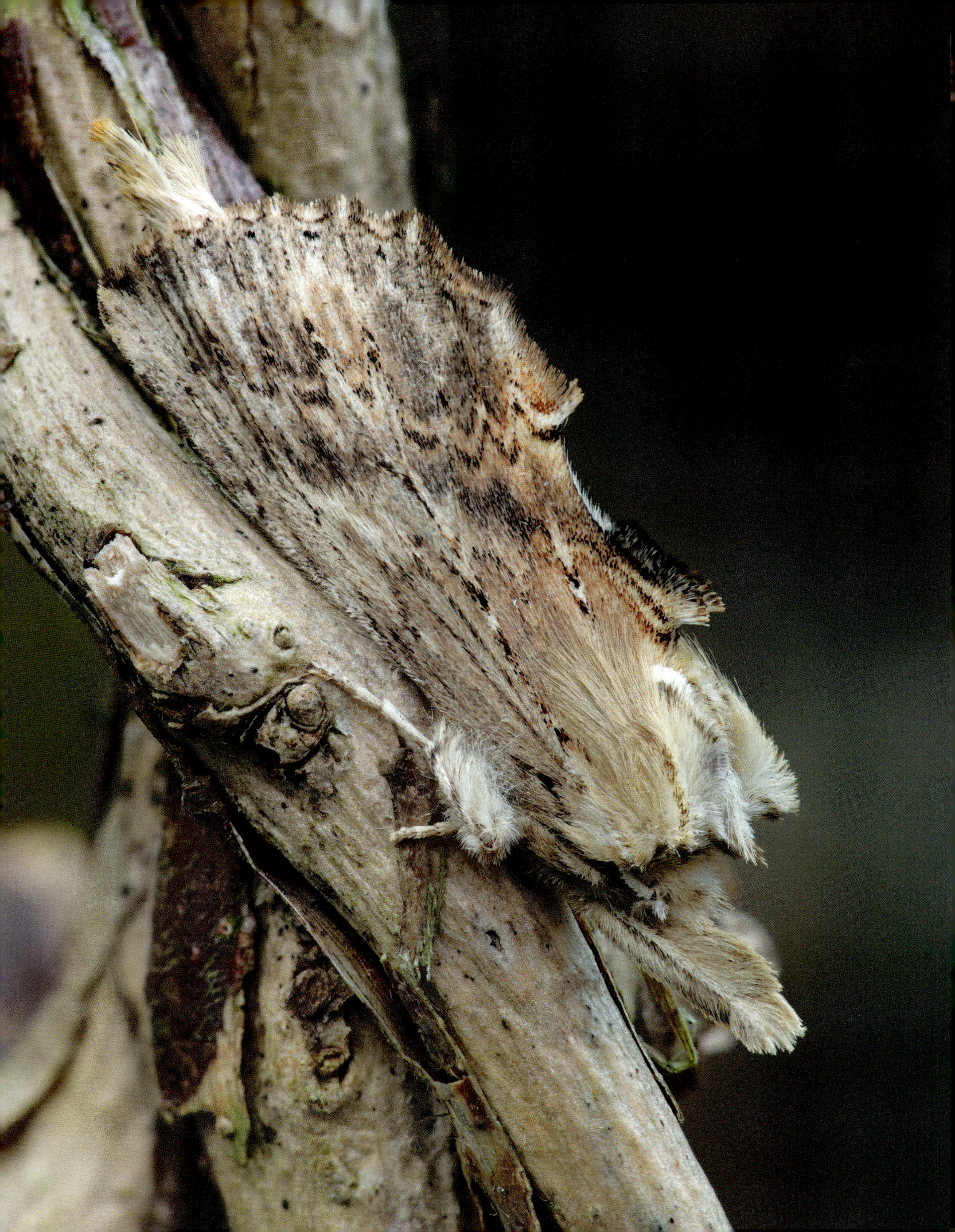

Rearing the larvae of moths is a traditional method of obtaining pristine adults for photography. The downside is that you often have to wait until the following year for the adults to emerge. See 'Life in the Foliage' (page 195) for the larval and pupal stages of butterflies and moths.

PHOTOGRAPHIC TIPS

- You can try to encourage moths into your garden by leaving a strong outside light on overnight. The ideal nights are those where the humidity levels and the temperature remains high. You need to get up early and examine the surrounding walls and trees before the sun forces them to seek shade. The most productive nights tend to be during the summer months.
- Check out suitable habitats in your area for day-flying species, particularly coastal locations, heathland and woodland rides and clearings.
- Examine the ground vegetation carefully and check branches, tree trunks and old fence posts for resting adults. Many moths are cryptic and easily overlooked.
- Confine your searches to overcast days; moths, with the exception of day-flying species, avoid bright sunlight.
- The vast majority of moths can be easily photographed *in situ*; there is no real need to remove them from their habitat. If you do, then return them to the same place. Do not remove any species that are protected by legislation; it is an offence to do so without the appropriate license.
- Always seek permission from the landowner or relevant authority before commencing any fieldwork or photography.
- Purchase a good book on moths, one that covers identification, distribution, biology and life history; this will provide the appropriate information, which will help you to identify and target individual species for photography.

RESOURCES

Below are some well-known publications and websites, which provide more in-depth knowledge on moths from different parts of the world.

FURTHER READING

Beadle, D. & Leckie, S. *Field Guide to Moths of Northeastern North America.* Peterson.

Clancy, S., Top-Jensen, M. & Fibiger, M. *Moths of Great Britain and Ireland.* Bugbook Publishing.

Leraut, P. *Moths of Europe.* NAP Editions.

Leverton, R. *Enjoying Moths.* Poyser Natural History.

Manley, C. *British Moths and Butterflies: A Photographic Guide.* Bloomsbury.

Powell, J. & Opler, P. *Moths of Western North America.* University of California Press.

Skinner, B. *Moths of the British Isles.* Apollo.

Sterling, P. & Parsons, M. *Field Guide to the Micro Moths of Great Britain & Ireland.* British Wildlife Publishing.

Thompson, R. & Nelson, B. *The Butterflies & Moths of Northern Ireland.* National Museums Northern Ireland.

Waring, P. & Townsend, M. *Field Guide to the Moths of Great Britain & Ireland.* British Wildlife Publishing.

Young, M. *The Natural History of Moths.* Poyser Natural History.

WEBSITES

Butterflies and Moths of North America: www.butterfliesandmoths.org

Butterflies & Moths of Northern Ireland: www.habitas.org.uk/moths

Butterfly Conservation Europe: www.bc-europe.eu

Butterfly Conservation UK: www.butterfly-conservation.org

Moths and Butterflies of Europe and North Africa: www.leps.it

UK Moths: www.ukmoths.org.uk

// FACING PAGE //

33.16 ~ Pale Prominent *Pterostoma palpina*
This moth was resting in very heavy shade. I switched to one of my custom White Balance settings for shade and used manual flash to eliminate a slight green colour shift and to darken the exposure in the background.

→ Nikon D2X, 200mm micro Nikkor, 1/8sec at f/11, fill-in flash, ISO 200.

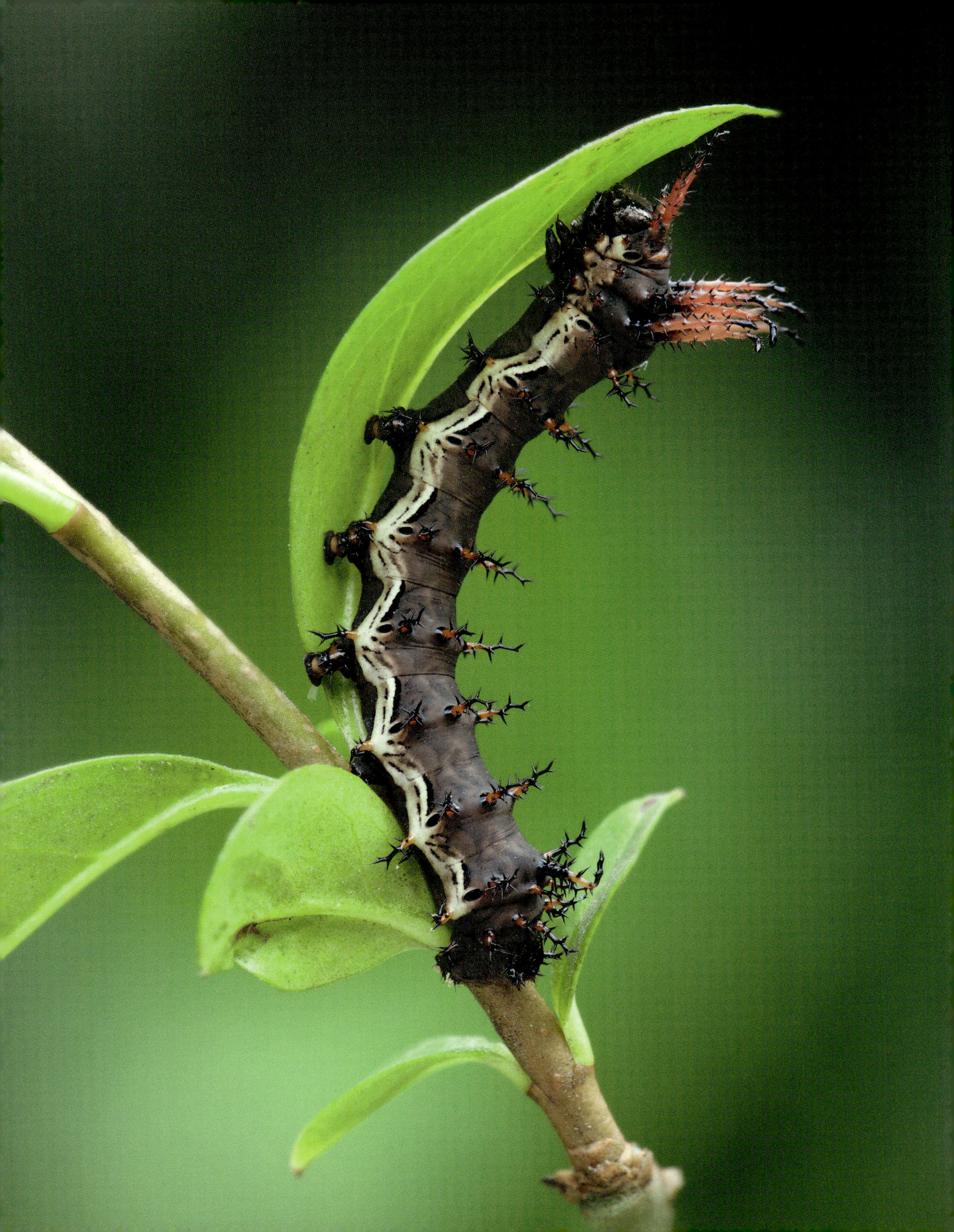

THIRTY FOUR

Life in the Foliage

The Larval Phase of Butterflies & Moths

Introduction

The life history of the adult stage of butterflies and moths has already been discussed in the previous case studies. The caterpillar or larval phase represents the most crucial stage in the development of these striking insects. The larvae are fascinating subjects in their own right, with extremely varied lifestyles that provide great photographic possibilities. Most people at some point have encountered caterpillars, be it as a child, walking in a wood or even in the garden. They are incredibly diverse creatures, not only in size but also colour and structure. They are the ultimate eating machine, with some being regarded as serious agricultural pests. There are over 20,000 species of caterpillar that have been described from around the world. Some of the largest and most colourful larvae belong to the giant silkmoths which are the largest and the most impressive group of moths in the world.

// FACING PAGE //

34.1 ~ *Citheronia laocoon* (larva)

→ Nikon D810, 200mm micro Nikkor, 1/8sec at f/11, ISO 200.

Biology and Life History

Once the egg hatches, the young larva has two functions in life, eating and surviving predation to adulthood. The large, formidable mandibles are designed to cut through foliage with the greatest of ease. Many species are polyphagous, (meaning they are capable of surviving on a wide variety of plants), however, others are monophagous and limited to a single foodplant.

The anatomical structure of a typical caterpillar or larva has three principal components. The head, which is essentially an armour-plated capsule, the thorax, consisting of three segments, has three pairs of true legs attached to it and the remaining part of the abdomen has ten segments with up to five pairs of prolegs depending on the species. The function of prolegs is simply to help the larva cling to the branches and leaves of the foodplant; these become redundant during the pupa stage. Despite having an elastic skin, which expands to accommodate food as the larva develops, it needs to shed it periodically to facilitate growth. To achieve this butterflies and moths go through a series of moults or instars (the latter being a term used to describe the stages between moults) until it reaches full size. These different phases

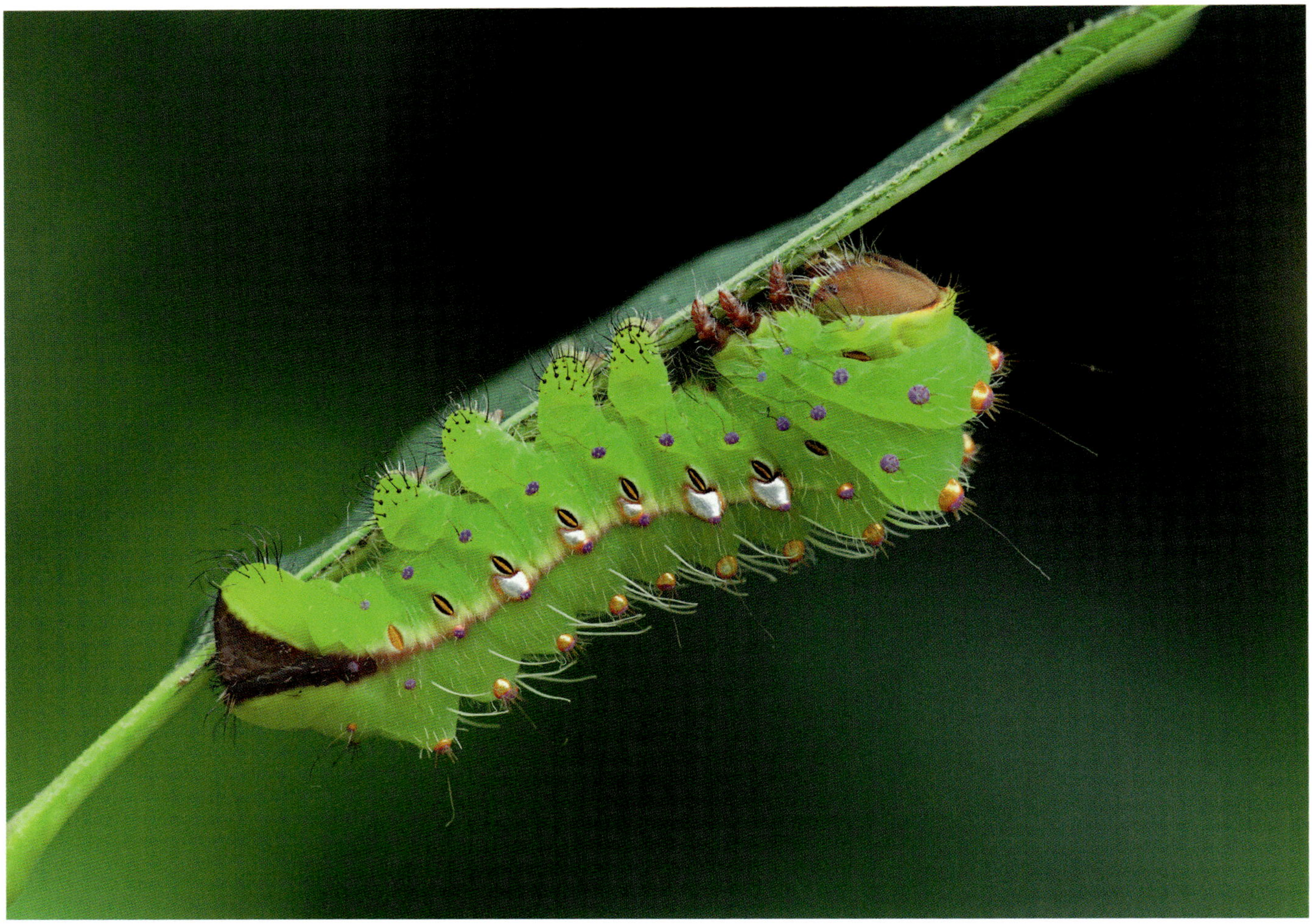

34.2 ~ **Tasar Silkmoth** *Antheraea mylitta* (larva)
One of the largest caterpillars found throughout India and Sri Lanka.
↘ Nikon D810, 200mm micro Nikkor, 1/15sec at f/11, ISO 200.

of larval development are worth photographing as they illustrate the progress of the caterpillar through to maturity.

The larval stage is the most precarious, for both butterflies and moths; mortality is high, and they are eagerly sought after by small birds who need an endless supply of food especially during the nesting season when demand is high. Although many lepidoptera are encountered as adults, the majority of species are more elusive in the larval phase. Their survival through to adulthood depends upon their ability to avoid detection and capture. The list of potential predators is considerable: birds, spiders, small mammals and parasitic wasps who tirelessly hunt them down to lay their eggs inside the young developing larva. Despite this relentless assault, many have evolved various strategies of their own to avoid detection. For example, some species rest openly on the leaves of their foodplant during the day; their bright, warning colouration and dense hairs send a clear message to a would-be predator that they contain toxins, which are distasteful if eaten. Others, when under attack, drop into the vegetation from a silken line, only crawling up again when the danger has passed. Feigning death, or emulating the foodplant where they blend seamlessly with the vegetation is another favourite stratagem. Many larvae hide during the day at the base of their foodplant and emerge under the cover of darkness to feed in relative safety. Whatever the strategy adopted, the vast majority of larvae rely to some extent on camouflage, which is the most effective method of avoiding detection.

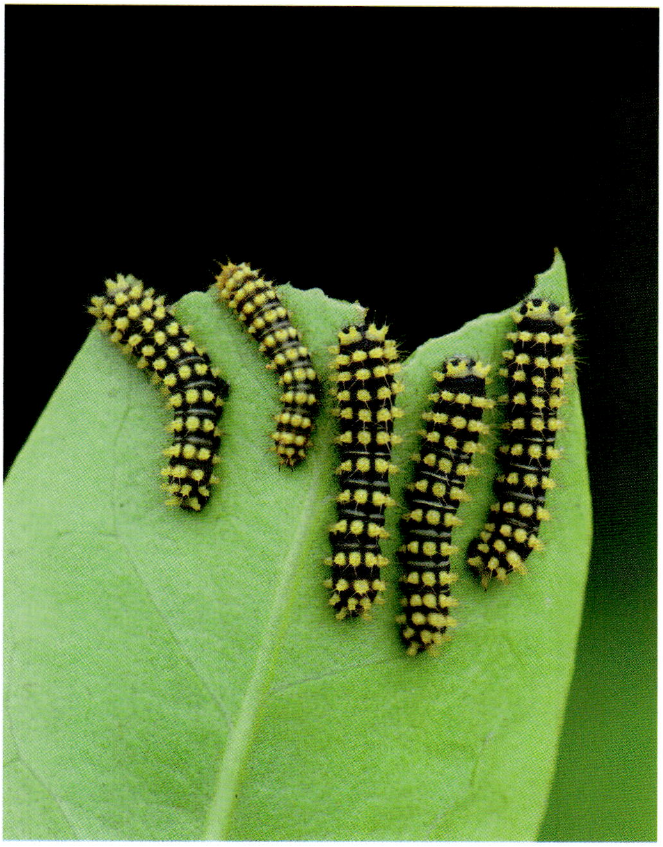

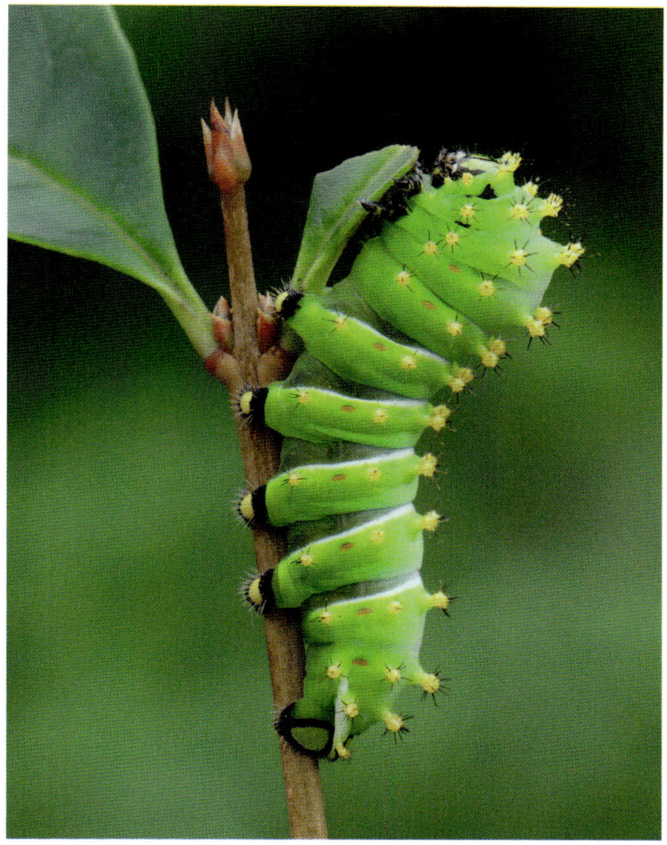

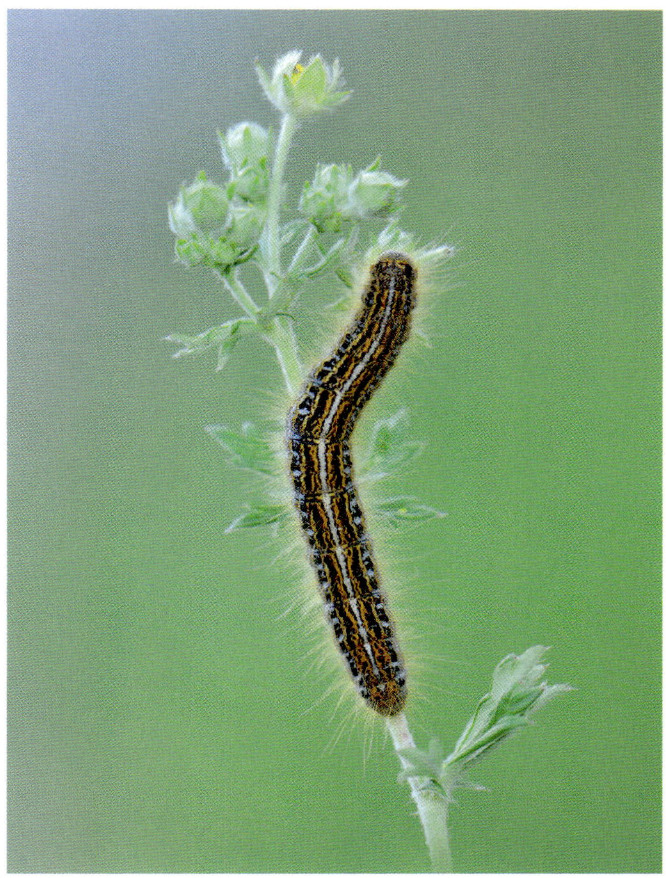

// TOP LEFT + RIGHT //

34.3 + 34.4 ~ **Forbes' Silkmoth** *Rothschildia lebeau forbesi* (larva)
It is always worth photographing the different stages of larval development. Both these images show how different they look when fully mature.

↳ Nikon D2X, 200mm micro Nikkor, 1/8sec at f/16, ISO 200.

// BOTTOM RIGHT //

34.5 ~ **Lackey Moth** *Malacosoma neustria*
The larvae of this species are gregarious, hairy and brightly coloured. They construct a communal silken tent on the food plant for protection from predators and temperature regulation. When fully grown they leave the tent and explore the ground vegetation and foliage for a suitable pupation site.

↳ Nikon D800, 200mm micro Nikkor, 1/15sec at f/8, ISO 200.

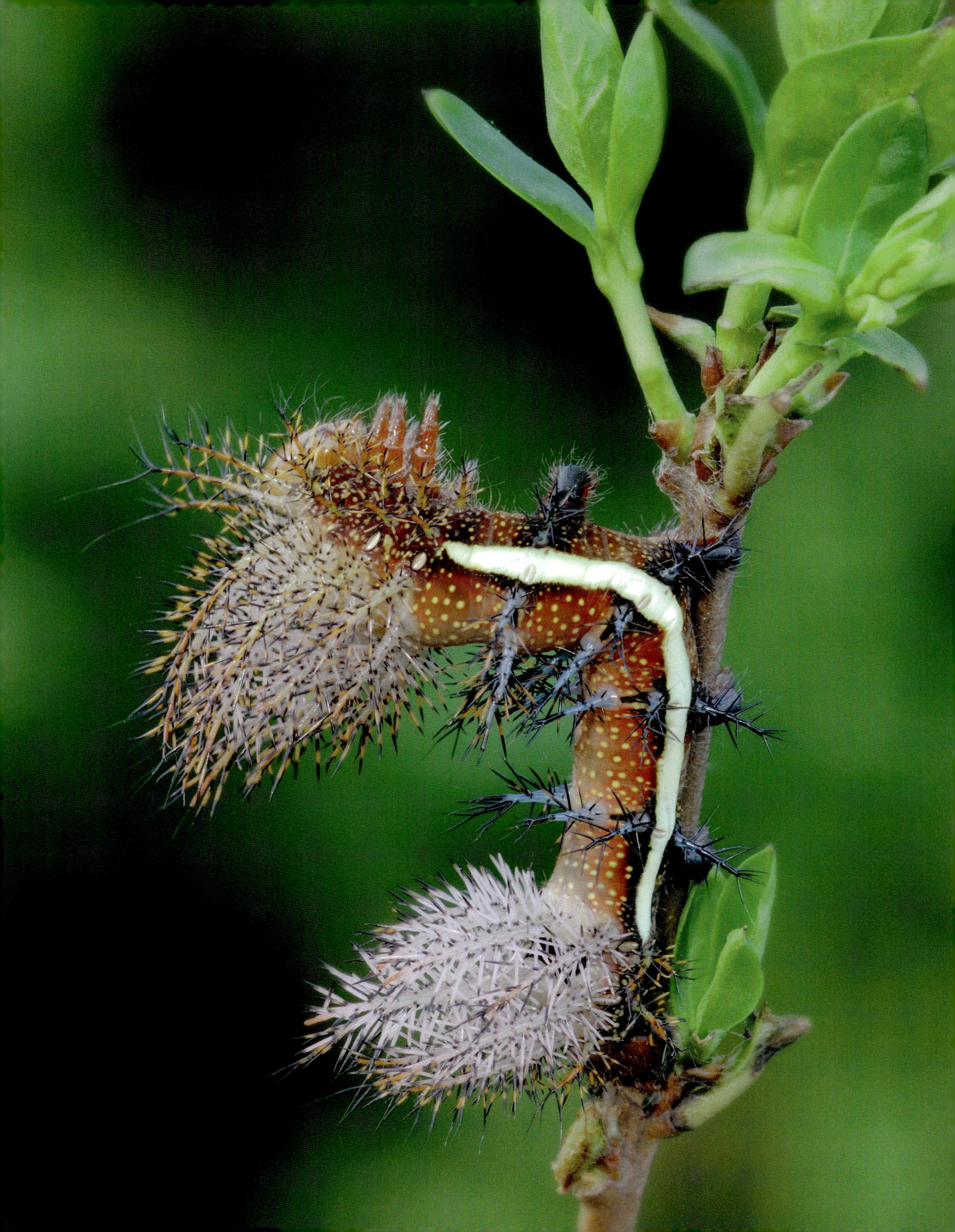

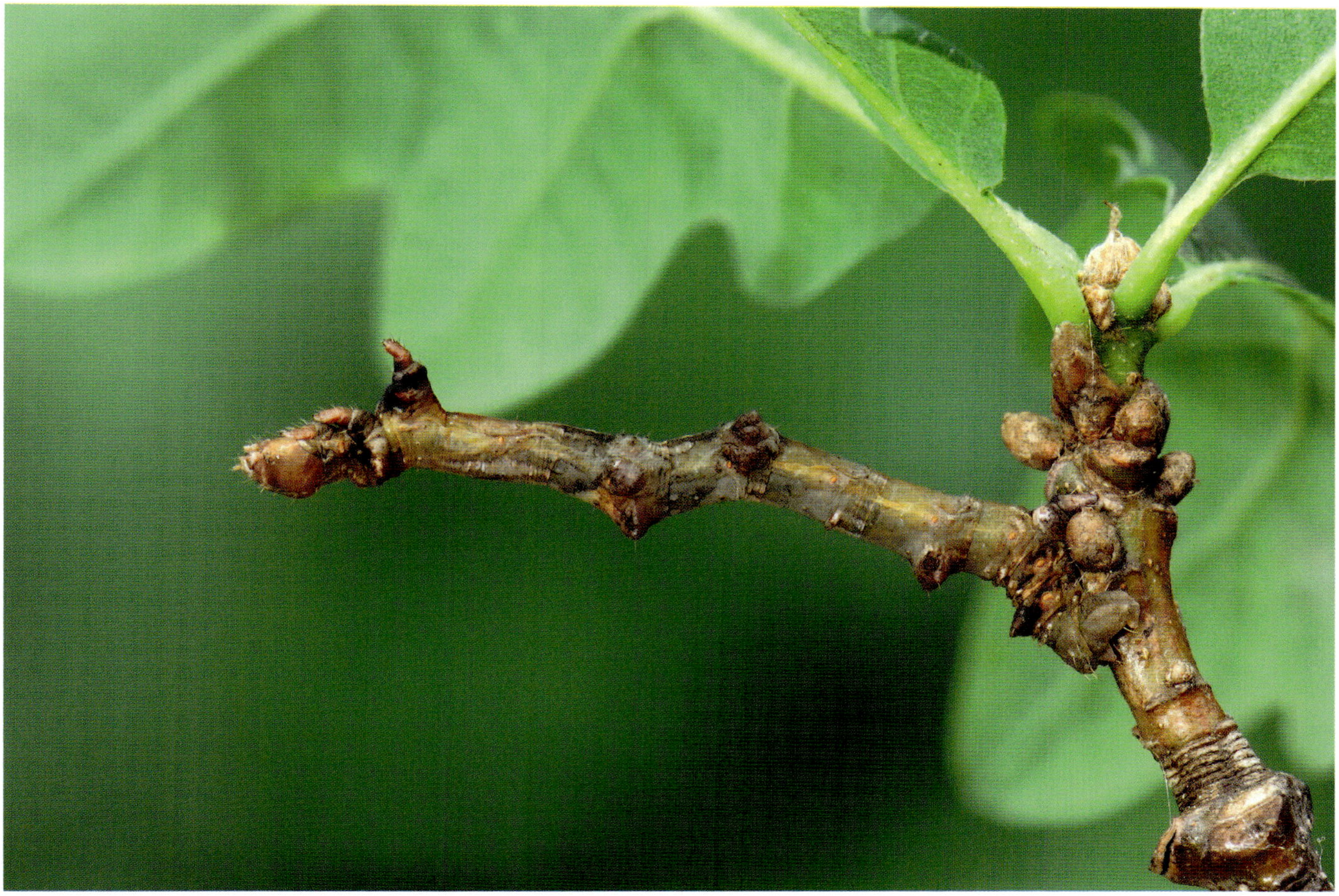

34.7 ~ **September Thorn** *Ennomos erosaria* (larva)
The survival of this caterpillar depends on its ability to remain motionless during the day. It's a wonderful example of natural mimicry.

↘ Nikon D2X, 200mm micro Nikkor, 1/8sec at f/11, fill-in flash, ISO 200.

// FACING PAGE //

34.6 ~ *Automeris larra*
A large impressive species with bright warning colouration and stinging hairs which are painful if handled.

↘ Nikon D2X, 200mm micro Nikkor, 1/15sec at F/11, ISO 200.

The Chrysalis or Pupal Stage

When the caterpillar reaches full size, it stops feeding and begins to wander in search of a suitable place in which to undergo the transformation from larva to pupa. It typically selects sheltered, inconspicuous places and escapes attention by camouflage, often assuming a colour similar to its background, which allows it to blend seamlessly with its surroundings. The larvae of butterflies pupate in different ways according to which family they belong to. They are diverse and colourful whereas moth pupae are more mundane. With the exception of a few common species, the pupae of many butterflies can be quite difficult to find in the wild since the larvae are very choosy where they pupate.

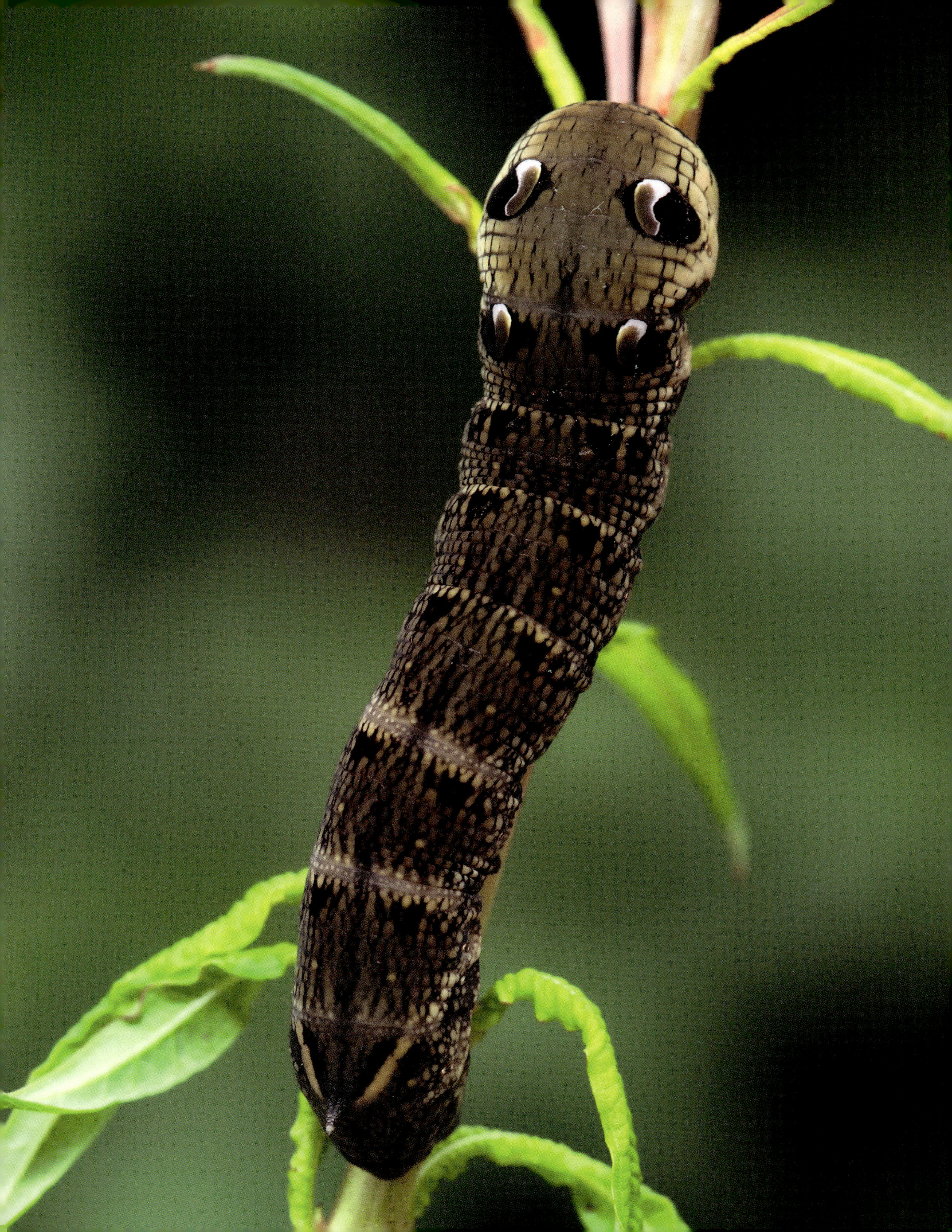

// FACING PAGE //

34.8 ~ Elephant Hawk-moth ***Deilephila elpenor*** (larva)
The fully grown larva. The following images show the transformation from larva to pupa and adult.

↘ Kodak Pro SLR/n, 200mm micro Nikkor, 1/15sec at f/8, ISO 160.

// TOP //

34.9 ~ Elephant Hawk-moth ***Deilephila elpenor*** (larva)
Notice how the larva has now shrunk in size taking on the shape of a pupa.

↘ Kodak Pro SLR/n, 200mm micro Nikkor, 1/8sec at f/11, ISO 160.

// MIDDLE //

34.10 ~ Elephant Hawk-moth ***Deilephila elpenor*** (pupa)
The pupa will now overwinter and emerge the follow year.

↘ Kodak Pro SLR/n, 200mm micro Nikkor, 1/8sec at f/11, ISO 160.

// BOTTOM //

34.11 ~ Elephant Hawk-moth ***Deilephila elpenor*** (adult)
↘ Kodak Pro SLR/n, 200mm micro Nikkor, 1/4sec at f/11, ISO 160.

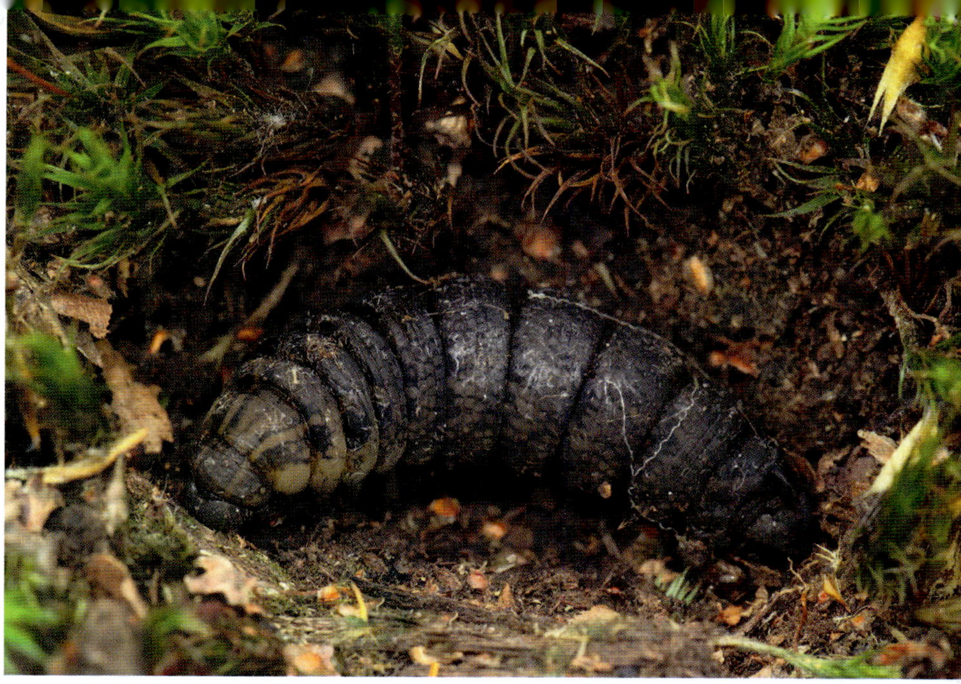

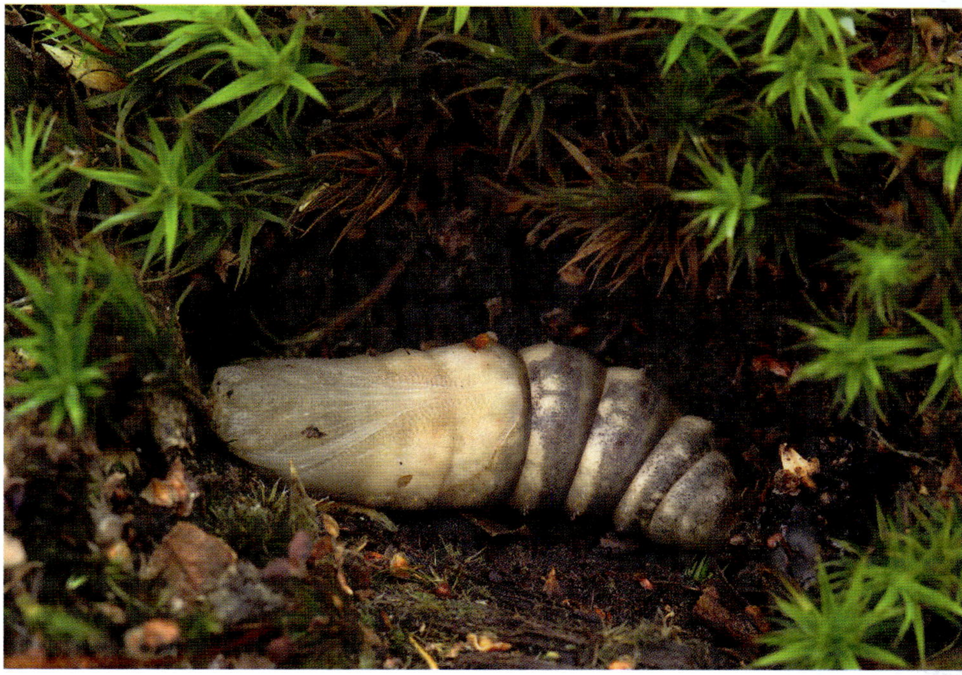

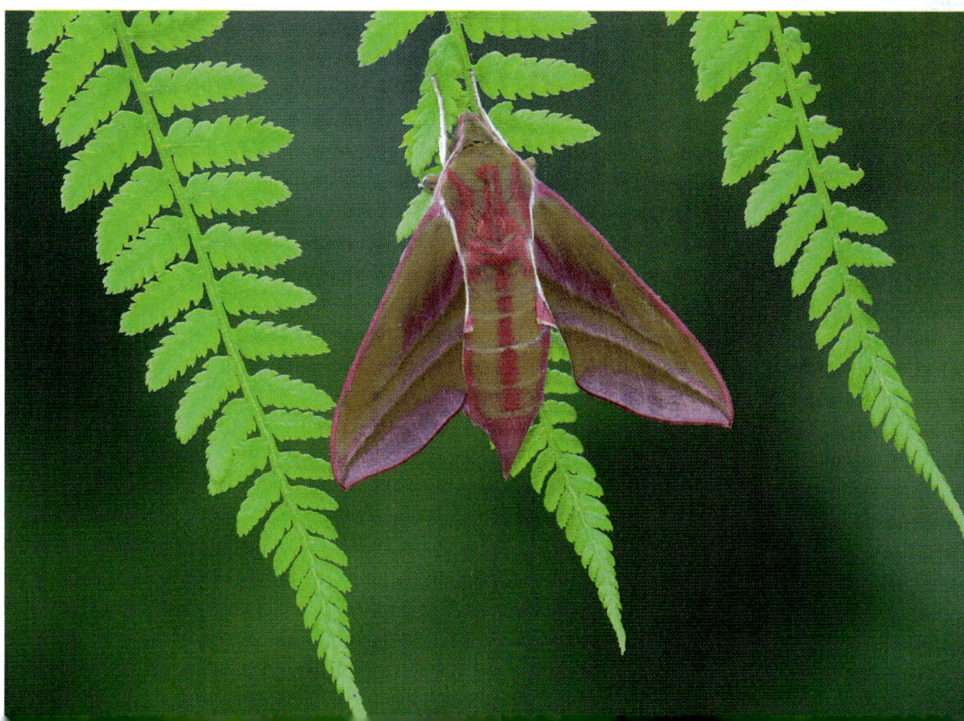

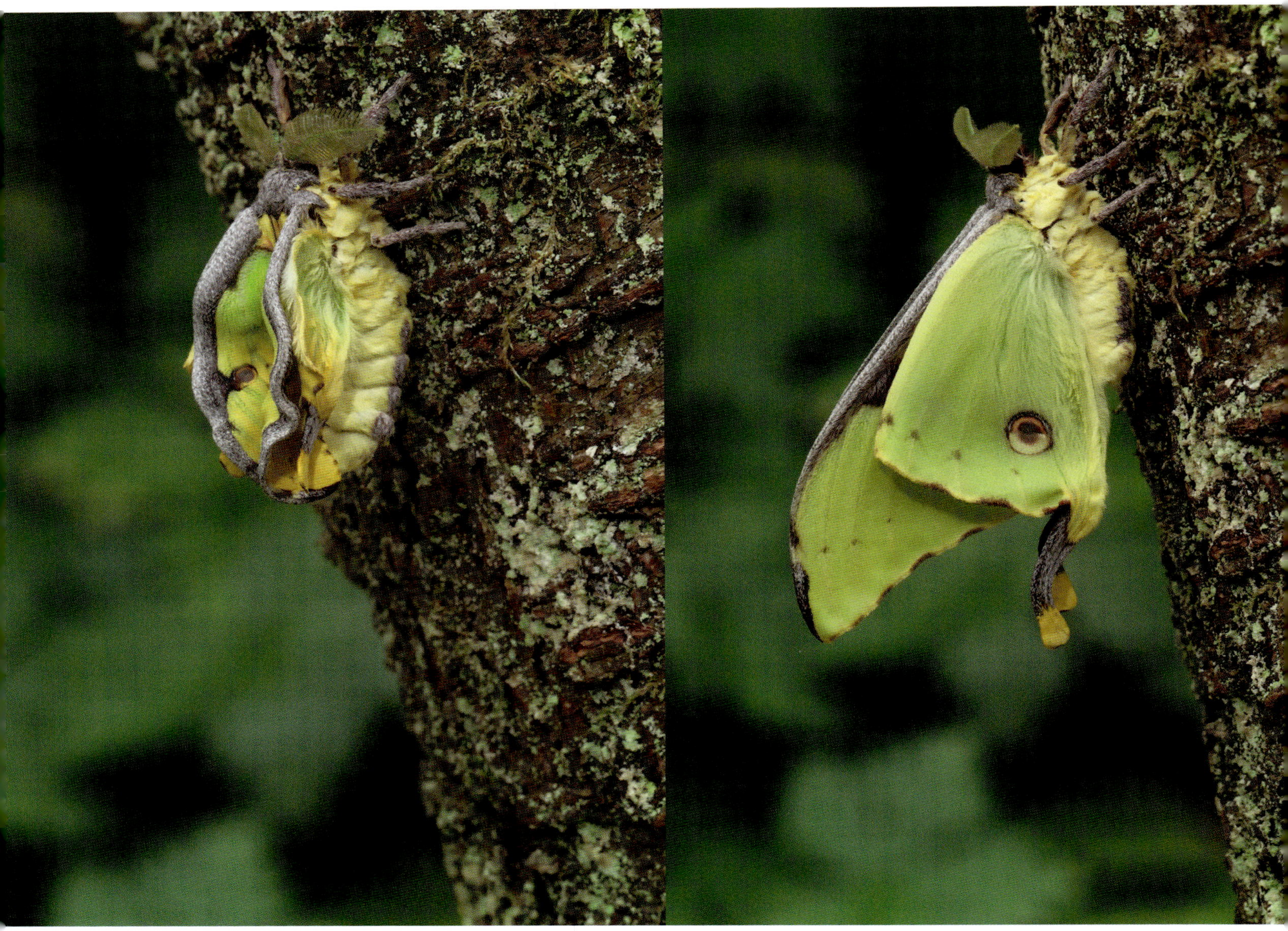

// FROM LEFT TO RIGHT //

34.12 ~ **African Moon Moth** *Argema mimosae* (male)
Emergence sequence showing the increase in size as the moth pumps fluid through its system to expand its wings and other structures.

34.13 ~ The wings are expanded first

34.14 ~ When wing expansion is completed the tails are then expanded

34.15 ~ The fully formed adult after expansion.

↪ Kodak Pro SLR/n, 200mm micro Nikkor, 1/15sec at f/11, fill-in flash, ISO 160.

The majority of larger moths pupate below the surface of the soil, or crevices in bark, or inside a flimsy cocoon among dead and living leaves. Moth pupae are not as attractive as those of butterflies and are mainly various shades of light or dark brown. Since there are so many more moths than butterflies, it is usually much easier to find the pupae and cocoons of some species, especially those that are pretty widespread and numerous.

The pupal stage is by far the most vulnerable for butterflies and moths, since they have no means of escape from a predator. However, survival to adulthood largely depends on the larva's choice of a pupation site.

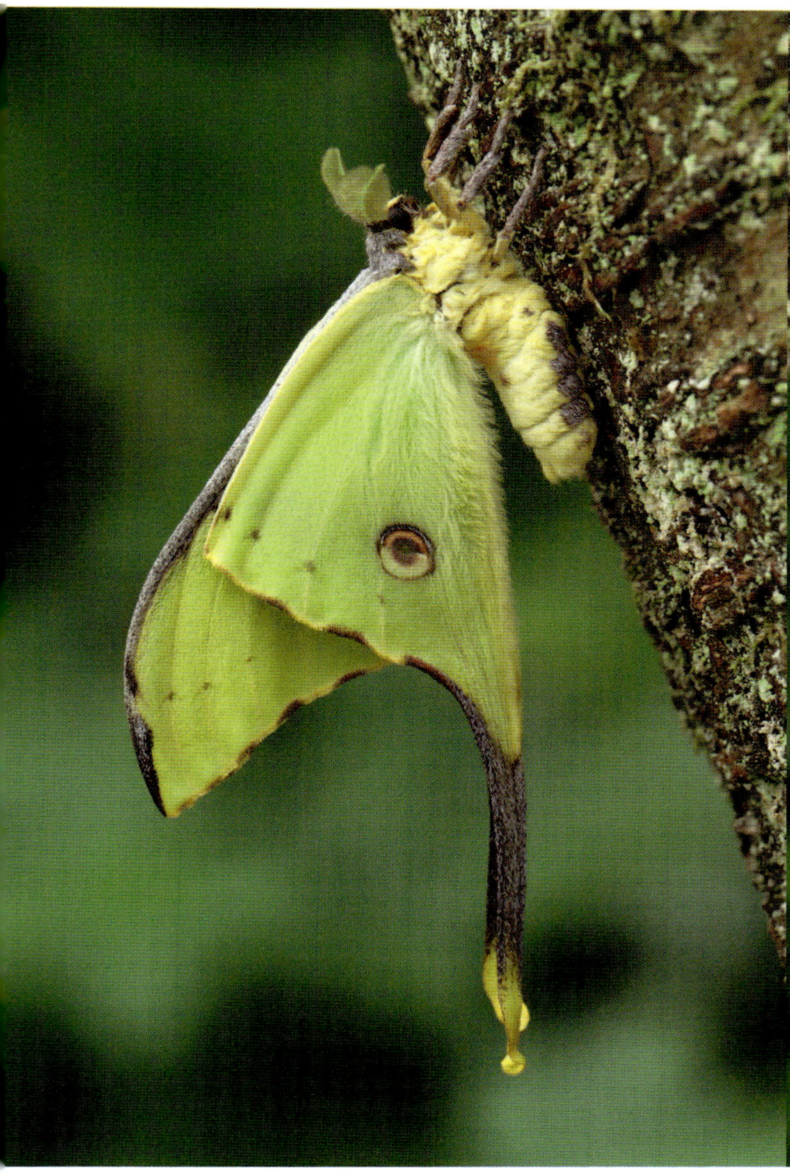

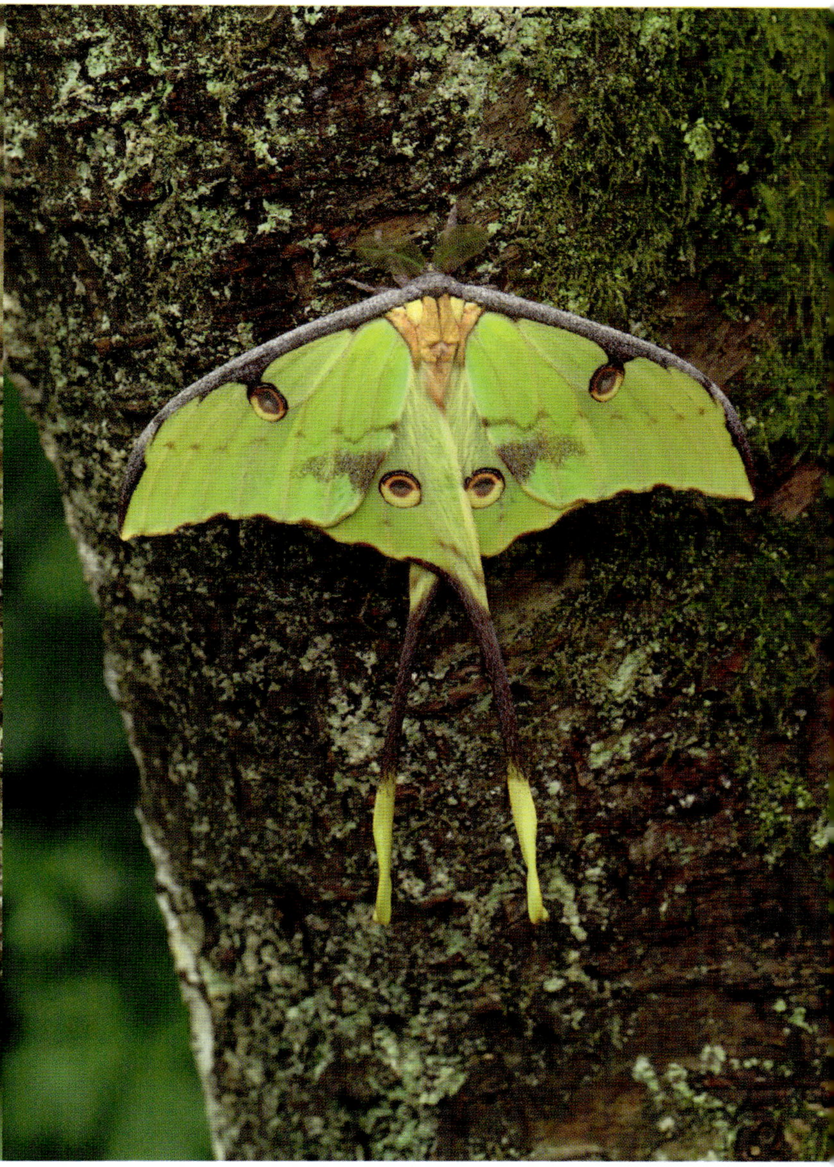

Passing the winter months as a pupa seems to be the choice of most lepidoptera. The transformation going on inside the pupa leading eventually to a winged insect is one of nature's amazing spectacles. It is much easier to predict emergence in butterflies, since the pupal case becomes transparent and you can see the adult clearly inside. Emergence in moths is much harder to ascertain. Some pale pupae darken considerably or become very soft to touch, which is often an indication that emergence is close.

The whole process of emergence is quite demanding. The adult butterfly or moth has to break open the pupal shell and if there is a cocoon present emit a special fluid, which softens it before it can force its way out. It then has to climb and find a secure branch, or similar structure, on which to facilitate the expansion of its wings which at this stage are compressed. Once suspended and secure the adult pumps haemolymph (the equivalent of blood) to expand them to their normal size. Any small glitch in this process is likely to leave it in a crippled state and therefore, unable to fly. The emergence stage is a fascinating process and well worth photographing the entire sequence.

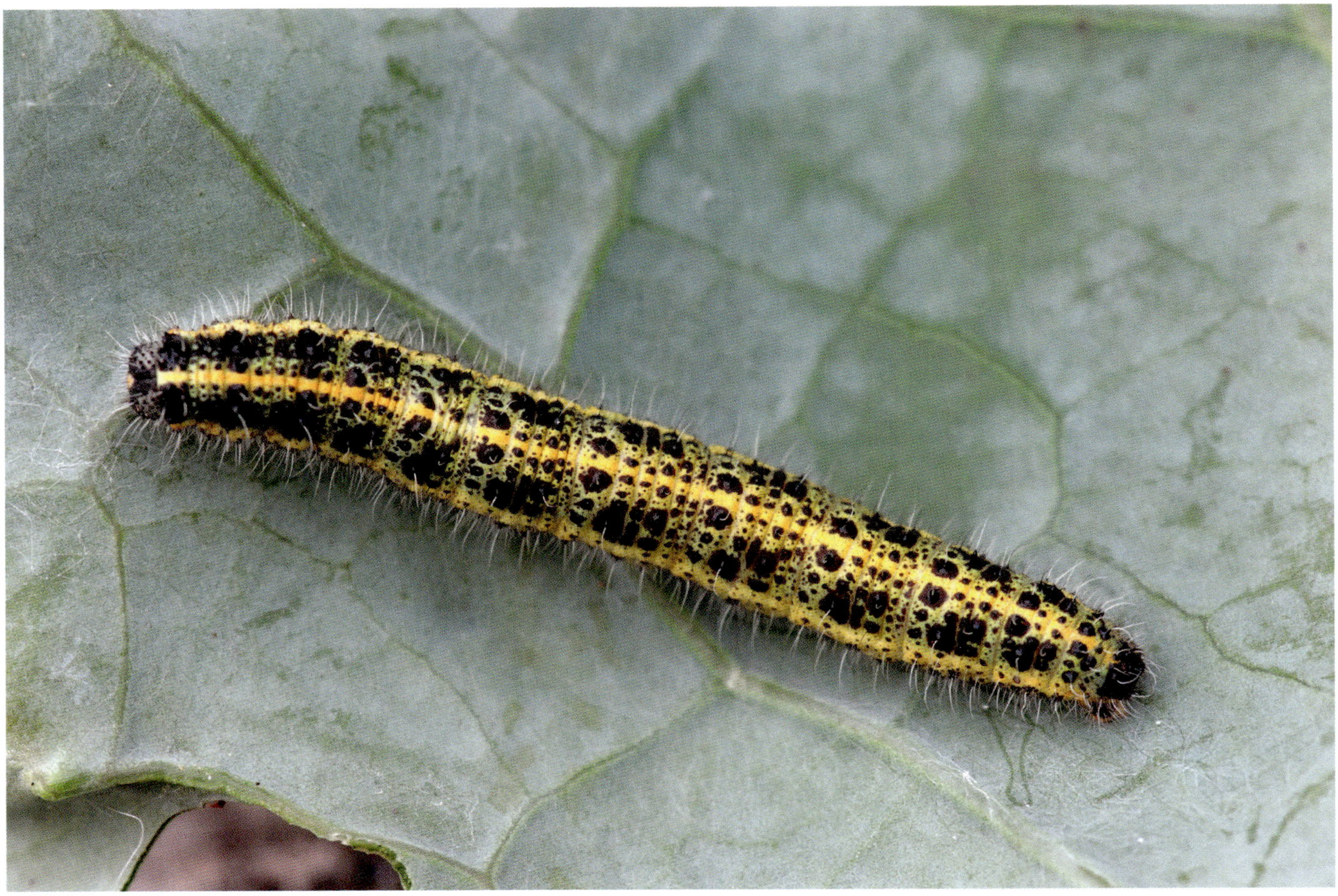

34.16 ~ **Large White Butterfly** *Pieris brassicae*
It's best to start with species which are easier to find.

→ Nikon D2X, 200mm micro Nikkor, 1/15sec at f/8, ISO 200.

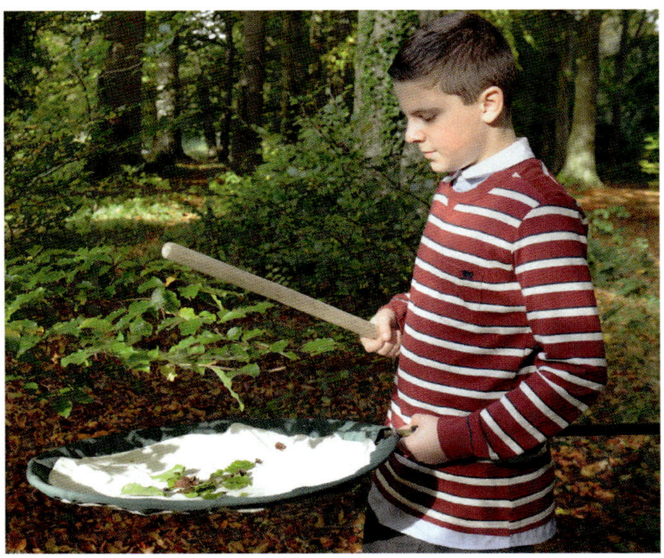

34.17 ~ **Beating tray**
Place under the branch and give a light but firm tap. Any creature on the branch will normally fall into the tray.

Fieldcraft

Searching for Larvae

Caterpillars or larvae come in many shapes and sizes. Among the most impressive are the hawk-moths and giant saturniids or silkmoths. Many have characteristic features such as stinging spines, irritating hairs, large eyespots or horn-like projections on the end of their abdomen. With a little knowledge and practice it is possible to locate some of the common species, for example the Large White Butterfly which feeds on cabbage or brussel-sprouts. Searching the appropriate foodplants in gardens and allotments is usually successful. As a photographer, it is important that you read up on the biology and habits of the species you would like to photograph. There are many excellent books, which will provide you with all of the relevant information, including the flight times of the adults and when to search for the larvae.

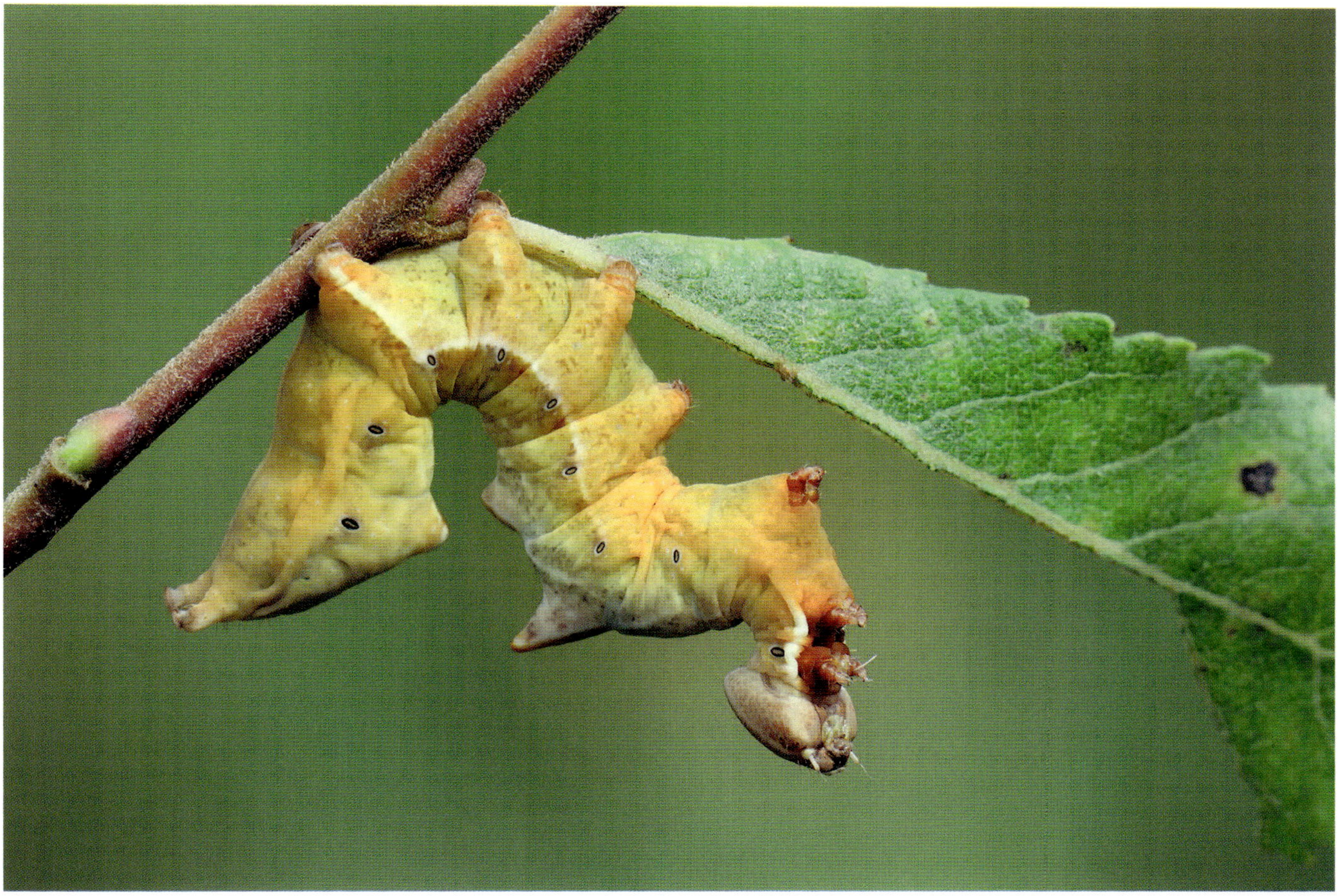

34.18 ~ **Pebble Prominent** *Notodonta ziczac*
I used a clip to hold back an intruding branch, which gave me a clear view and a diffused background.

↳ Nikon D810, 200mm micro Nikkor, 1/15sec at f/11, ISO 200.

Since butterflies and moths occur in a wide range of habitats, it's important to select the correct site to begin your search. There are many different techniques used for finding larvae. Some require specialist knowledge and are beyond the scope of this publication. However, many of the common species can be obtained by employing the methods outlined here. Searching small trees and shrubs in sheltered areas is a good place to start. Willow, along with birch and oak, are the most productive trees for caterpillars. You should begin your search by first of all examining the foodplant for signs of larval activity. Foodplants, which have larvae present, will have some visible signs; partially eaten leaves, stripped branches and frass (larval droppings), are all good indicators of occupancy. On close examination of the branches, you will often see larvae resting on the lower branches of the foodplant. Once you have found one chances are there are others, probably on other branches. Towards the end of summer is one of the most productive times.

The most popular method for finding larvae is by 'beating'. Entomologists use a specially constructed white canvas tray with a handle, which is placed below the branch which is then rapped sharply with a strong stick, this will usually dislodge any resting larvae. You can also use an upturned white umbrella or place a white sheet at the base of the shrub; both work equally as well.

Once you have rapped the branch, if you wait for a few moments before examining the contents any larvae that have lost their grip and fallen into the tray or onto the sheet will begin to move. Beating is best carried out on warm days when the foliage is dry. From a photographer's point of view, there are advantages and

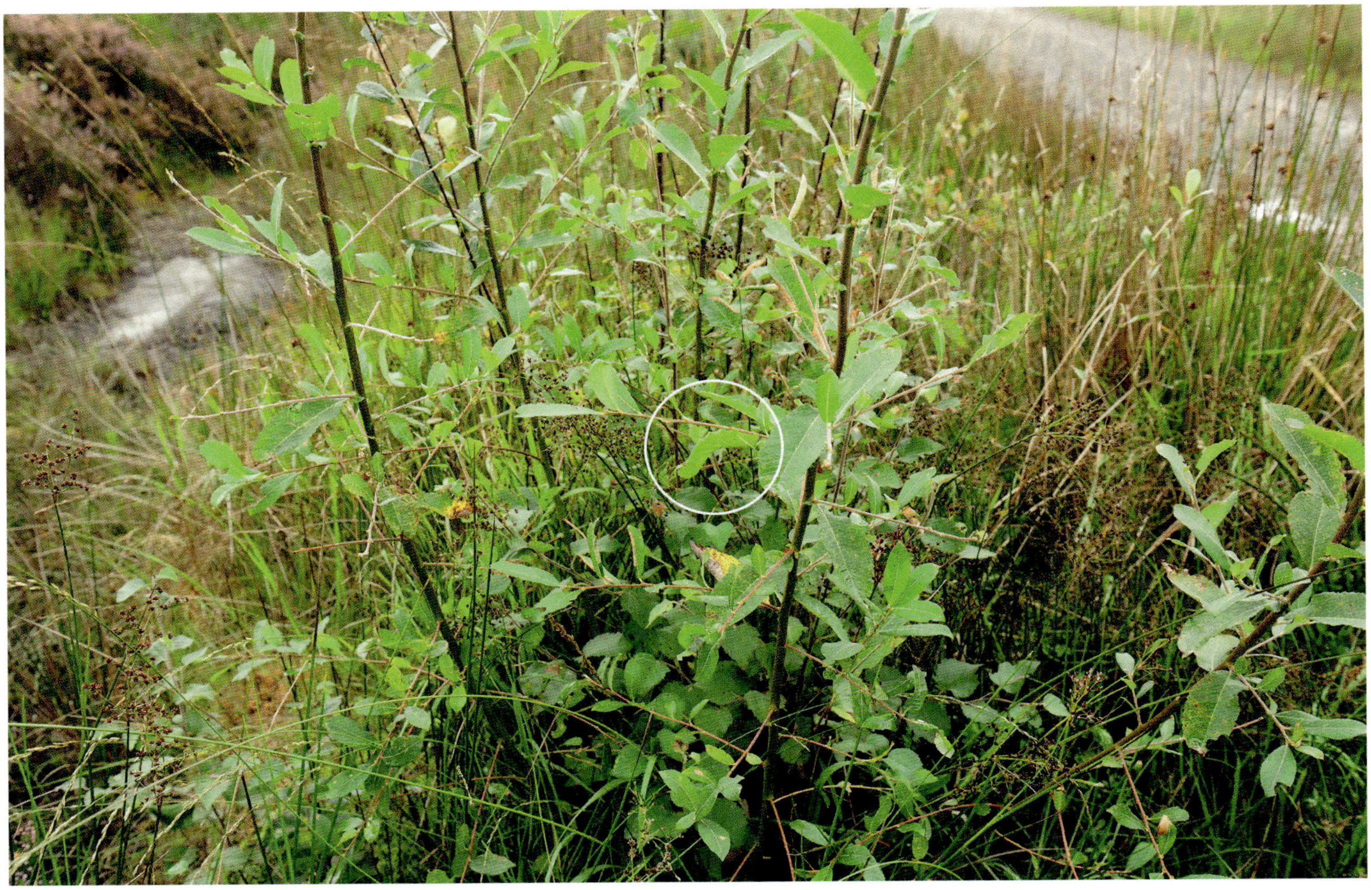

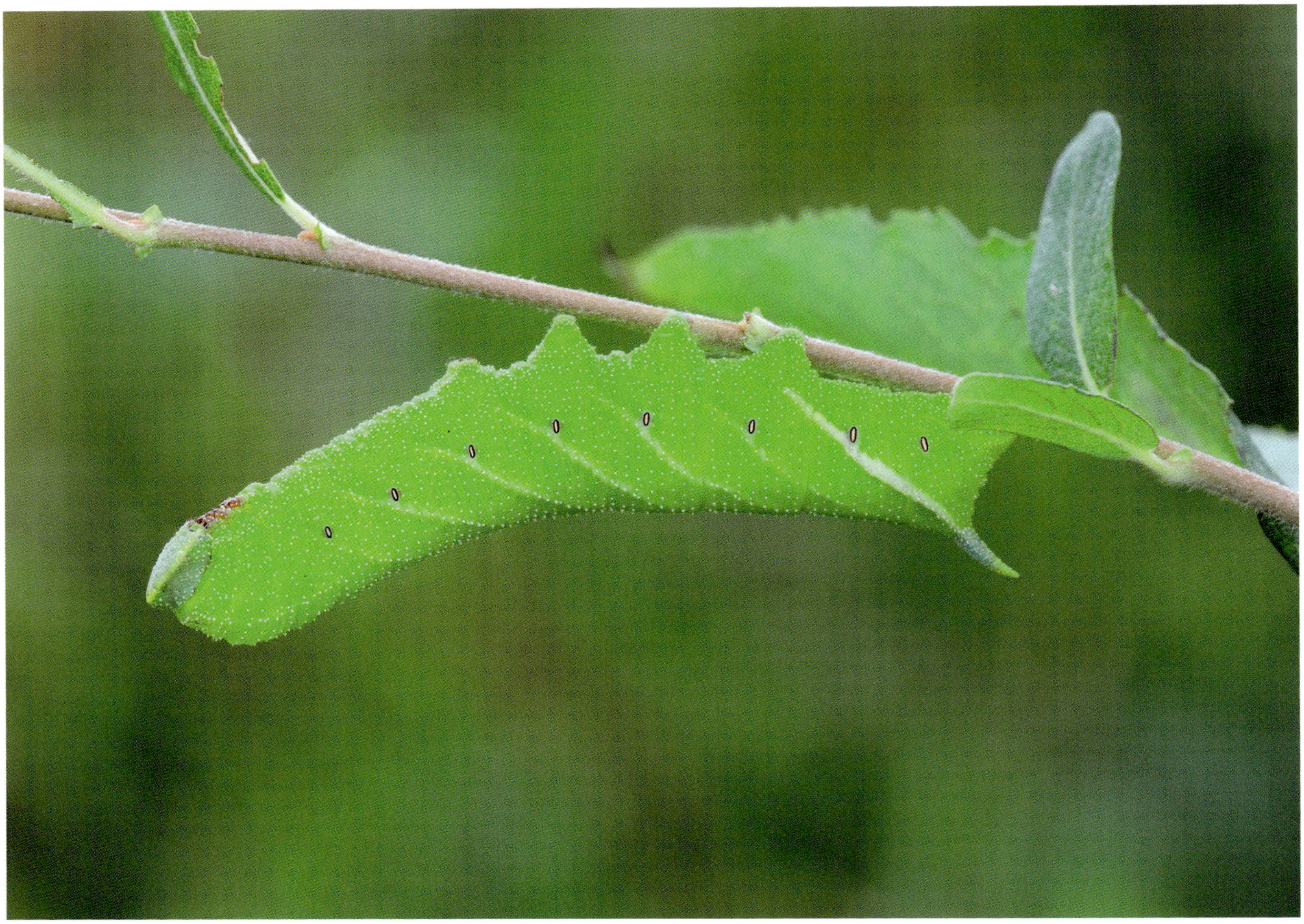

disadvantages to this method. You do find a lot more species, but you don't get to photograph them *in situ*. You have to resort to photographing them in controlled conditions, usually on cut foodplants, which you will have to replace on a daily basis.

In the Field

Caterpillars can pose more of a challenge in the field compared to the adults. They are more elusive and often rest in awkward positions, frequently twisting, or elevating parts of their abdomen, making it difficult to hold the entire larva in focus. Another problem is manoeuvring the camera and tripod into a suitable position without several branches obscuring your field of view. I carry clothes pegs and some larger crocodile clips, so I can carefully pull back those branches that are in direct line with the subject. Larvae typically remain still for a while in between feeding periods, providing that you don't accidently hit the branch they are resting on. Once disturbed, they get spooked and start to wander, which can be a frustrating experience. Some species tighten their grip and hold fast, but most head towards the base of the shrub for protection. You can spend a considerable amount of time trying to encourage them to settle again. I have often found the best strategy is to leave them alone; sometimes they settle quickly, and you can reposition your tripod and start again. If you search smaller trees and shrubs which are no more than five or six feet in height, then even if the larvae are resting high your tripod will still be able to reach them.

// FACING PAGE ~ TOP //

34.19 ~ Eyed Hawk-moth *Smerinthus ocellata* (larva)
The mature larva can be seen clearly on this small sallow bush. Background branches were a bit obtrusive in the background. I used a couple of clips to hold them out of view making the background more diffused. I was extremely careful not to touch the branch the larva was resting on.

↪ Nikon D3X, 24–70mm Nikkor, 1/60 sec at f/8, ISO 200.

// FACING PAGE ~ BOTTOM //

34.20 ~ Eyed Hawk-moth *Smerinthus ocellata* (larva)
Final image which has a much cleaner background.

↪ Nikon D3X, 200mm micro Nikkor, 1/8sec at f/11, ISO 200.

Photographic Hardware and Approach

Photographing caterpillars is not the most popular of macro subjects; they seem to receive less attention than most of the other insect groups. A short telephoto macro in the region of 105mm is ideal for larval photography, since you don't want to be too far away from the subject. My own approach is a rather simple one. I shoot the vast majority of larvae *in situ* where possible. Natural light is my preferred choice, even if I have to rack up the ISO a little.

It's worth taking a few minutes when you discover larvae to study their position and the background behind them. If there are branches which are likely to cause a problem, I carefully pull them back and secure with clothes pegs from the field of view. I handhold the camera first of all to establish my preferred shooting angle and position. I shoot a test shot analysing the composition, depth of field and the background, so I don't have to waste valuable time shifting the camera and tripod about increasing the risk of hitting the foliage. I also know how the image is likely to look when I take the actual shot and whether I need to make any adjustments. Larvae which are feeding require a fast shutter speed to arrest movement. The head and mandibles can move quite a bit while the remaining part of the abdomen can be quite still. Shutter speeds above 1/125sec will generally freeze any movement from the larva.

Wind is also an issue, which you may have to contend with, especially when photographing subjects on branches with leaves. Even on the calmest of days the foliage tends to catch the breeze. You have two options, shooting at a higher ISO, or using flash to arrest any movement. If there is sufficient background foliage I sometimes opt for flash, but where possible I prefer to shoot at a higher ISO.

Photographing in bright sunlight often creates unattractive highlights on foliage, which you want to avoid. To overcome this problem, I use a diffuser or flash to balance the shadows, or backlight the subject keeping the sun just out of the frame and slightly to the side. If adopting the latter technique, then you need to add fill-in flash to reduce the deep shadows in the foreground.

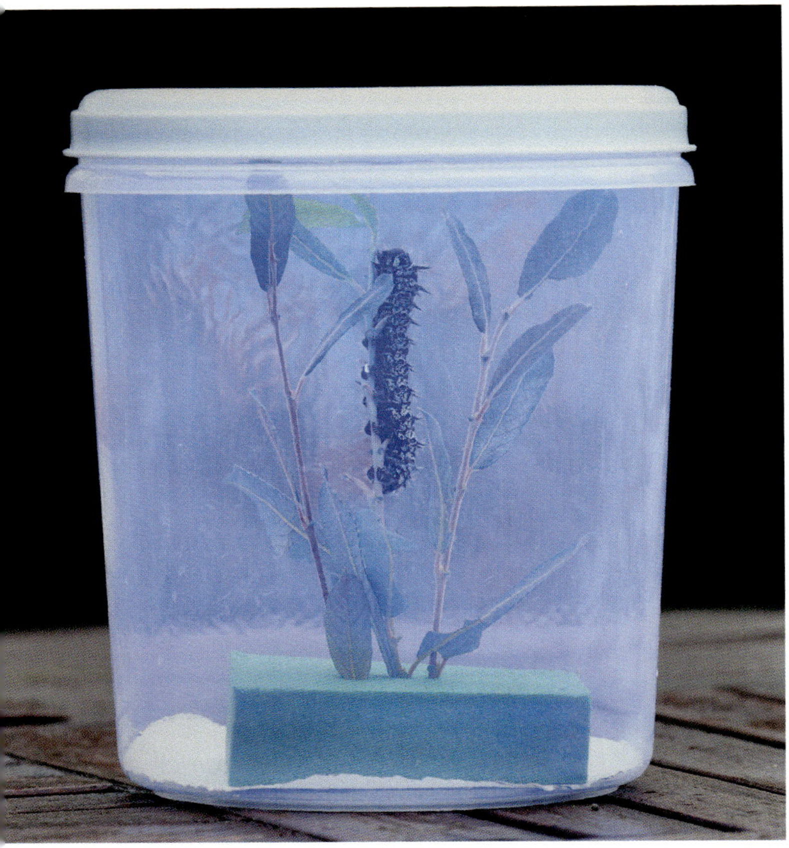

34.21 ~ **Larva being reared in large plastic tub**
When in their final instar it is best to split some of them up to prevent overcrowding.

Project Planning

Rearing Caterpillars for Photographic Study

Photographing the life history of moths has always been a popular pastime for many amateur entomologists and photographers. Much can be learned about these insects through photographic study. Rearing the larvae is often the best approach for obtaining adults for photography; you also get perfect specimens with no damage or wear. If you stick to a few basic principles and provide the correct foodplant, then it should be relatively straightforward. Hygiene is important, the containers need to be kept clean, don't overcrowd them and maintain the appropriate temperature and humidity and they should be okay. Start with a few easy species that are not too exact in their requirements. You also need easy access to the appropriate foodplant on a daily basis. Clear plastic boxes or Tupperware and even old margarine containers are fine. As the larvae get bigger, it may be necessary to spread them over several containers; you don't need to invest in expensive boxes or rearing cages. Whatever you use must be easily sterilised and washed out on a daily basis to prevent infection and disease. Line the bottom of the tub with a paper towel to absorb any excess moisture. You can also use oases foam blocks, just wet them lightly and then cover the block with cling film to prevent any moisture escaping and soaking the paper towel on the base of the container. Push the cut stems of the foodplant into the block. This method will delay the wilting in most cases for a couple of days. Once the cut stems show signs of drooping they must be replaced. When selecting foliage, pick those leaves which look fresh and free from pollution, viruses and other deformities. Check you're not introducing any potential predators such as spiders; this is especially important when the larvae are very small. Start with species which are considered easy. Each stage can then be photographed until the complete life cycle is attained.

When larvae reach their full size, they will require somewhere to pupate; this is a critical stage, and if you fail to act, then all of your efforts could be wasted. The larvae stop feeding and begin to wander about the base of the container. Their colour is also less vibrant, and the final droppings contain a lot more moisture often staining the paper towel. The larvae shrink in size but are still plump, but much firmer. Most butterflies pupate above the ground, and provision must be made for them. Depending on what species you are rearing, their preferred method can easily be found on the internet or from one of the field guides. The vast majority of macro moths pupate below ground level, but some spin protective cocoons around themselves above the ground attached to vegetation and leaf litter. You should remove each larva when ready to pupate into a small box of its own. Put a layer of peat, or soil that has been sterilised and place the larva on it with a piece of paper towel on top and leave for several days to transform. When this is complete, and the pupae have hardened, they can be transferred to an emerging cage or a container for overwintering. Fungal disease and dehydration are the two important factors to watch for. Overwintering pupae should be kept in a garden shed or similar place, which has good ventilation.

PHOTOGRAPHIC TIPS

- Look for small, isolated trees and shrubs and check for evidence of larval activity, e.g. partially eaten leaves, or in some cases stripped branches.
- Some species rest openly on the surface of leaves while others prefer the underside along the midrib; check both surfaces.
- When you find a caterpillar, try not to hit the twig or branch it's resting on. Check the other branches; chances are, there will be others, perhaps in a better position.
- Avoid touching caterpillars, especially if you have sensitive skin. Some species, particularly those with dense hair can produce an irritating rash.
- If you are collecting the larva to take back to the studio make sure you have access to the appropriate foodplant nearby.

Resources

FURTHER READING

Bartlett Wright, A. *Peterson First Guide to Caterpillars of North America*. Houghton Mifflin Co.

Manley, C. *British Moths: A Photographic Guide*. Bloomsbury.

Porter, J. *Colour Identification Guide to Caterpillars of the British Isles*. Viking.

Wagner, D. L. *Caterpillars of Eastern North America: A Guide to Identification*. Princeton University Press.

WEBSITES

Butterflies and Moths of North America: www.butterfliesandmoths.org

Caterpillar Hostplants Database: www.nhm.ac.uk/our-science/data/hostplants

Moths and Butterflies of Europe and North Africa: www.leps.it/indexjs.htm

The Lepidopterists' Society: www.lepsoc.org

United Kingdom Lepidopterists' Society: www.ukleps.org

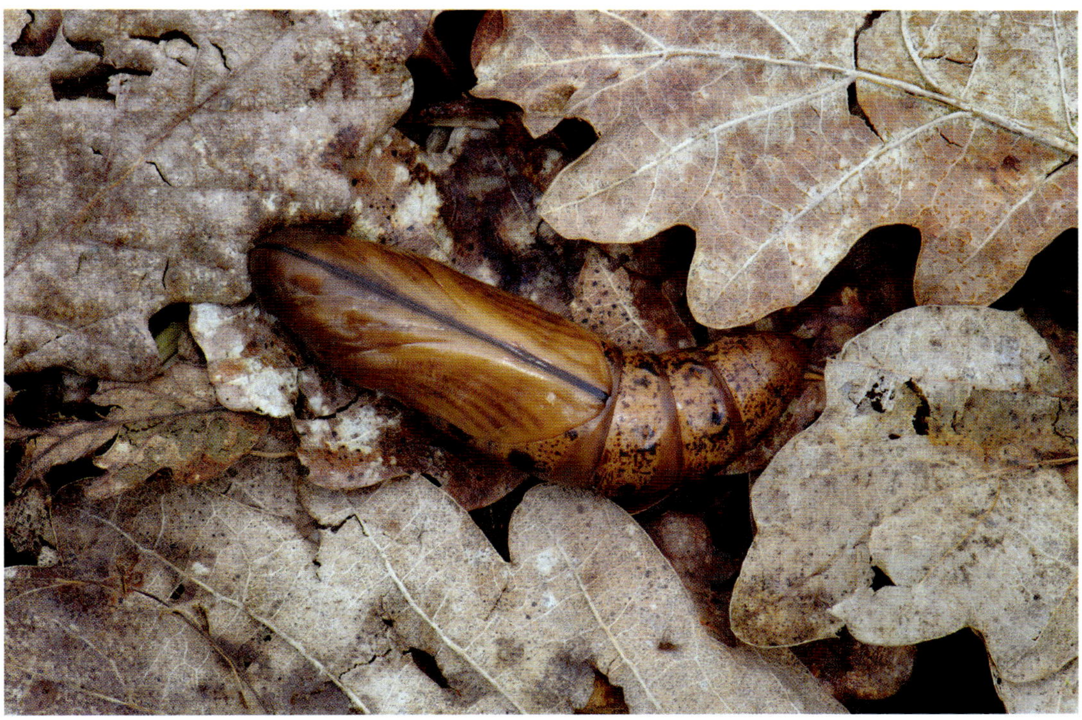

34.22 ~ **Oleander Hawkmoth** *Daphnis nerii* (pupa)
The pupae of many moths are some shade of brown and have a look of polished wood. Most moths pupate either among the leaf litter or below ground.

Nikon D800, 200mm micro Nikkor, 1/30sec at f/11, ISO 200.

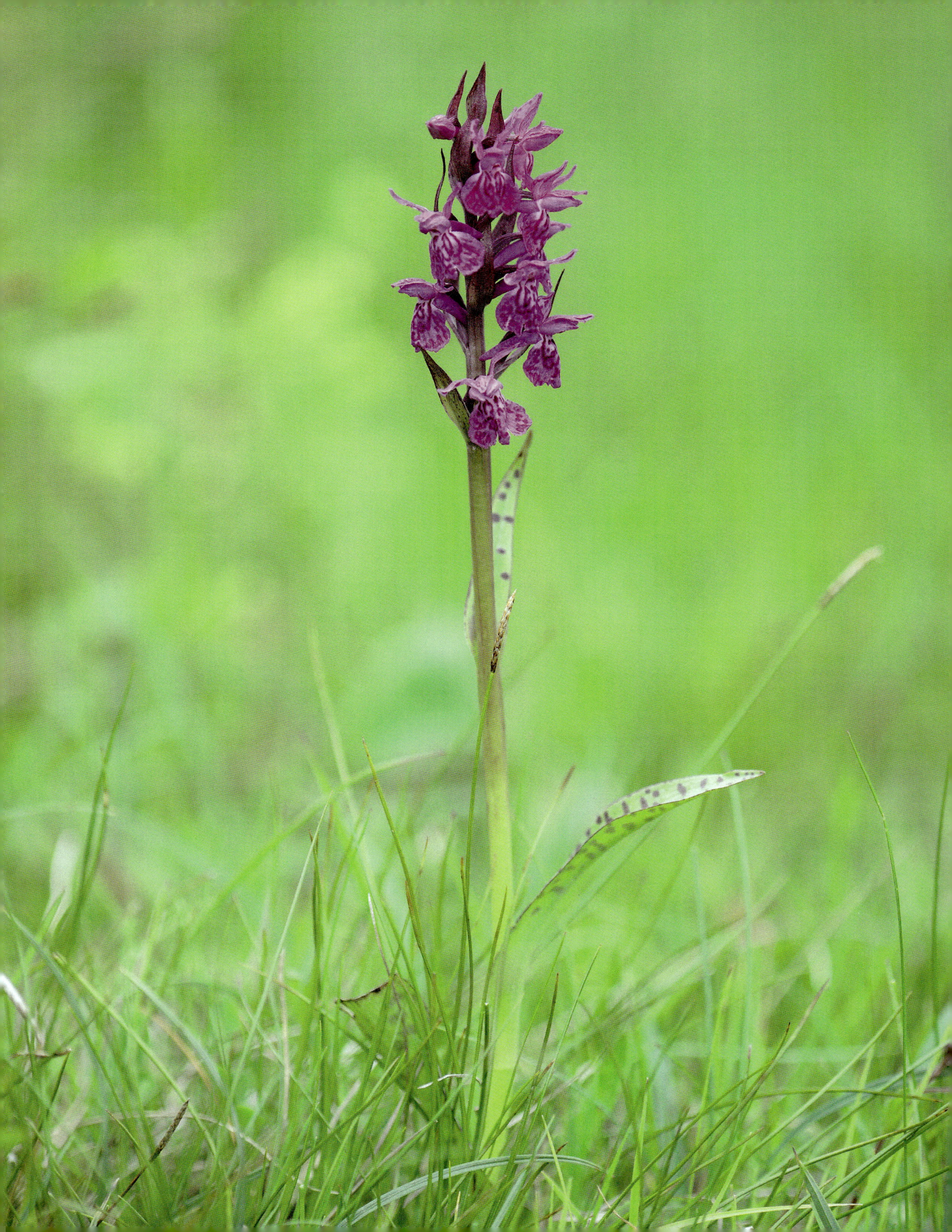

THIRTY FIVE

Nature's Floral Garden

Plants

Introduction

It probably comes as no surprise that flowers are by far the most popular subject among the macro fraternity. They are admired for their beauty, enticing scents and their delicate fragility. There is an inherent attractiveness about flowers; their extensive diversity of colour, shape and form make them unique and unlike any other organism. They occupy a varied range of habitats, from the driest deserts to the highest mountains, some even existing in the coldest regions of our planet. There are approximately 400,000 species of flowering plants in the world. Many are endemic to remote parts of the world while others may flower only once in a decade. Flowers symbolise love, life and immortality, yet their existence is ephemeral. Nevertheless, they are considered to be one of nature's most amazing gifts to the world.

I have often heard the remark that flower photography presents little in the way of a challenge when compared to other photographic subjects. Such a statement is, of course, simply untrue. Plants are one of the most challenging subjects in macro photography. Emphasising their beauty in a single photograph tests the ability and imagination of the most experienced photographers. Their lavish colours, intricate shapes, textures and elegant curves demand a creative eye and imagination to take it beyond a mere record depiction. Simplicity rather than complexity is often the best approach, although many grow in situations that make it extremely difficult to achieve clean, simple compositions. Virtually all of my plant photography is done in the wild, and in their natural settings. I prefer to capture them as they appear in nature.

// FACING PAGE //

35.1 ~ Alpine Marsh Orchid *Dactylorhiza alpestris*
I selected an aperture which gave me just enough depth of field to retain focus on the orchid but keep the background fairly well diffused.

↘ Nikon D800, 200mm micro Nikkor, 1/60sec at f/8, ISO 200.

Fieldcraft

Wild Flower Habitats

One of the benefits of living in a temperate climate is seasonal variation. Plants form the structure of all habitats. Our floral heritage is a significant factor in shaping the landscape and diversity of the habitats that we have today. After a winter devoid of colour, we re-emerge in spring with new-found enthusiasm, eager to re-immerse ourselves in the floral extravaganza that spring brings. Many plants have particular flowering times and seasons. Some species have an extended flowering period while others have only a short window. Whether you are photographing locally or further afield, it is important to have reliable information on flowering times especially if travelling abroad. Flowering periods can vary each year depending on the weather conditions and the severity of winter. As a flower photographer, it's important to understand a little about natural habitats and the flowers that occur on them.

Woodlands

Woodlands are one of the most important habitats, not only for flowers but many other forms of wildlife. Spring is the zenith in the floral calendar. Woods become revitalised with colour and vibrancy. Celandines, anemones, bluebells, wild garlic and early-flowering orchids, to name but a few, carpet the woodland landscape with a flush of colour and new growth. No other habitat from a photographer's perspective has the diversity of subject material throughout all of the seasons. Ancient woodlands are some of the richest in terms of botanical importance, and they also contain the greatest variety of species.

Grasslands

These charismatic habitats define not only the British countryside but also many other countries as well. Sadly, modernisation in farming practices has virtually eliminated most of the wildflower meadows in Britain, but in many countries where traditional farming practices are still carried out the floral display is amazing and a reminder to us all of what has been lost. Grasslands in general support some of the most colourful and alluring wildflowers. Orchids, gentians, cowslips, alpine primroses, clovers, globe flowers and many others pepper these incredible landscapes. I travel a lot in Europe and run some photographic workshops in the Mediterranean and the Alps. The flowers in the alpine regions are simply remarkable and a photographic paradise for any photographer interested in capturing their beauty and diversity.

Heaths and Bogs

Despite the floral richness and diversity of insect life in these unique sites, they are often regarded as wasteland and used for landfill or converted into conifer plantations by the Forestry Commission. The characteristic heathland habitat is one of heather and gorse, but many other attractive plants exist in these wetland havens. Some of the flowers from a photographic perspective include various species of heather, cowberry, sundews, bog bean, marsh orchids, bog asphodel, pitcher plants, various sphagnum mosses and many more. These underrated habitats have a lot to offer photographically.

Coastal Habitats

If you are lucky enough to live near the coast, you will be acquainted with cliffs, beaches, sand dune systems, machair grassland and rocky shorelines. Coastal grasslands, no matter where you live, come alive with an abundance of wildflowers in early summer. Lichen-covered rocks and the pink swards of wild thrift carpet many rocky headlands. Campions, sea holly, spring squill, viper's-bugloss and various orchids are to be found in these colourful coastal meadows.

In the Field

I have a particular passion for flowers, especially wild orchids. However, coming up with more creative ways to photograph plants in the wild is always a challenge. I do spend considerably more time in the field deliberating over how to portray them compared to insects and other subjects. There are a wide range of methods and techniques for flower photography, which merits a publication in its own right. The conventional approach is, of course, the standard portrait and close-ups of part of the plant, also a habitat shot of it *in situ* and vistas of flowers in the landscape or a woodland setting. To do justice to any plant, you need to be completely competent with your equipment and how to go about achieving the result you desire. My priority when visiting any site is to acquaint myself with the general area

// FACING PAGE //

35.2 ~ European Columbine *Aquilegia vulgaris*
This plant has a long, fine stem, which makes it quiver in the slightest of breezes. It used to be more widespread in the past along roadside verges in the Pyrenees. I used the stem stabiliser to secure it as there was a slight breeze.

↳ Nikon D800, 200mm micro Nikkor, 1/250sec at f/8, ISO 200.

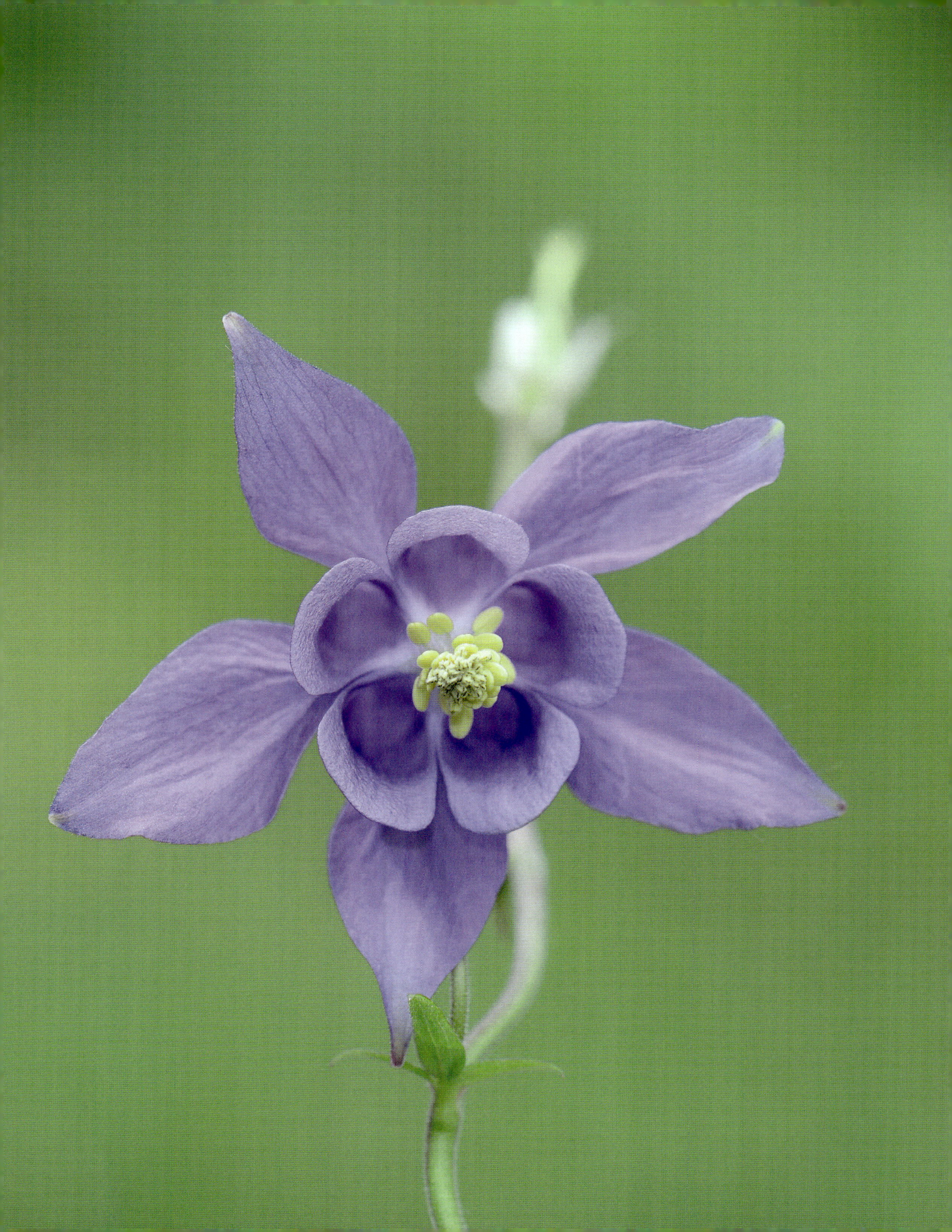

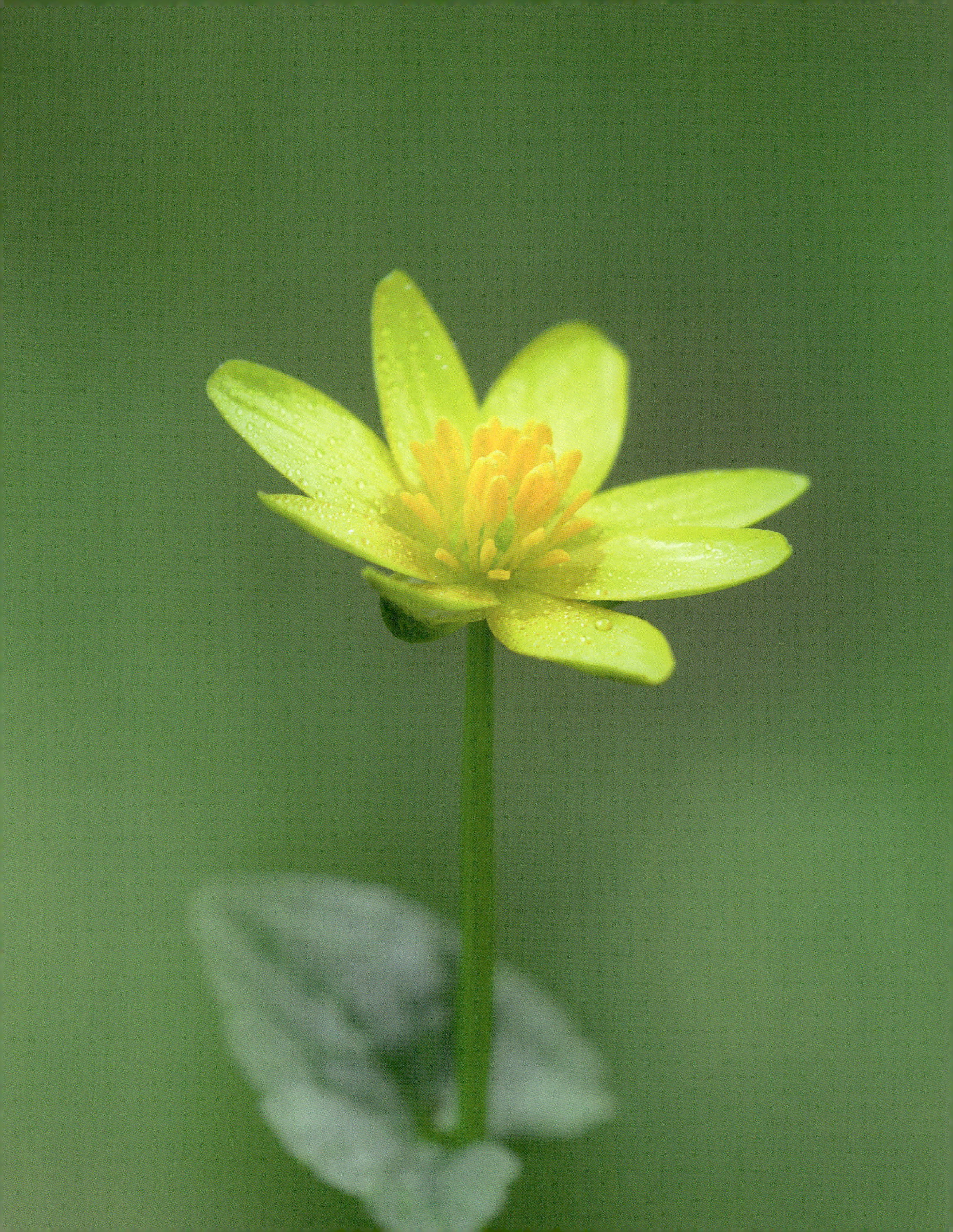

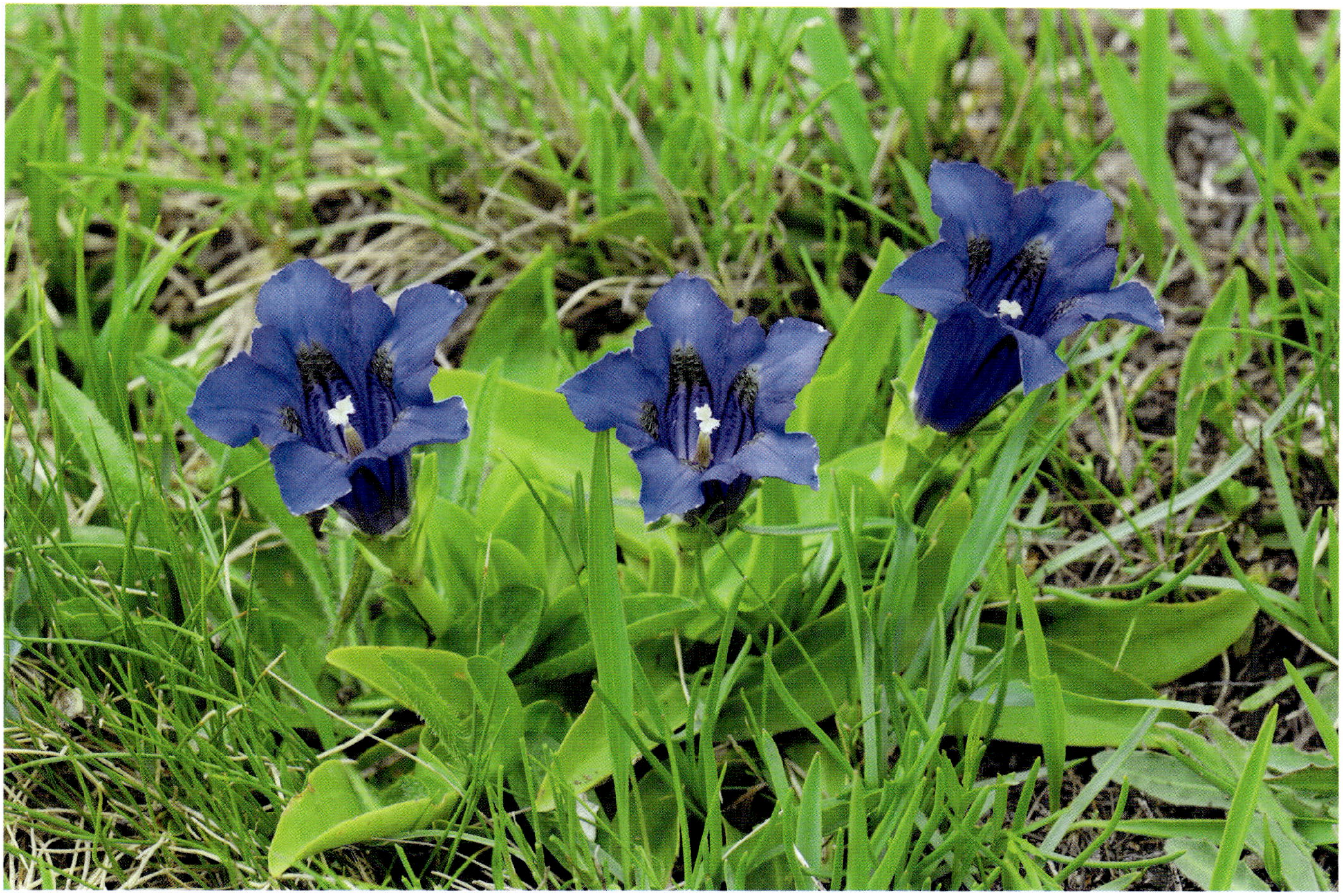

35.4 ~ **Trumpet Gentian** *Gentiana acaulis*
I normally like to spend a little time exploring a location before I reach for a camera. I usually have selected some subjects which have the most potential photographically. You want to try and avoid repetition as much as possible, since this wastes a lot of time.

↪ Nikon D800, 105mm micro Nikkor, 1/125sec at f/11, ISO 200.

// FACING PAGE //

35.3 ~ **Lesser Celandine** *Ranunculus ficaria*
I wanted to isolate this flower and used a wide aperture to diffuse the background. I shot through the foreground foliage to create the soft ethereal look.

↪ Nikon D800, 300mm Nikkor, + ext tube, 1/125sec at f/5.6, ISO 200.

and species present. I like to take some time wandering and exploring the floral diversity looking for those few plants that have the right colour, shape and form, but also growing in promising situations. Inexperienced photographers often make the mistake of photographing the first plant they see on their target list irrespective of its shape or position. Walking a few metres further on often produces a much better specimen with a more pleasing structure and background. It is easy to waste a lot of time photographing successive examples of the same species; what you inevitably come away with is photographic overkill. It makes more sense to set your bag down and explore the area first, identifying those that show the most promise.

Ideal Conditions

If you live in a temperate climate then you are going to experience a range of weather conditions, not all of them are conducive to good plant photography. Bright, calm, overcast days are the most productive. The cloud cover acts as a giant diffuser accentuating the finer intricacies such as texture and detail. Photographing flowers in sunlight brings its own challenges. Early and late evening light is more directional, and its softness can be used to your advantage, but the harsh lighting

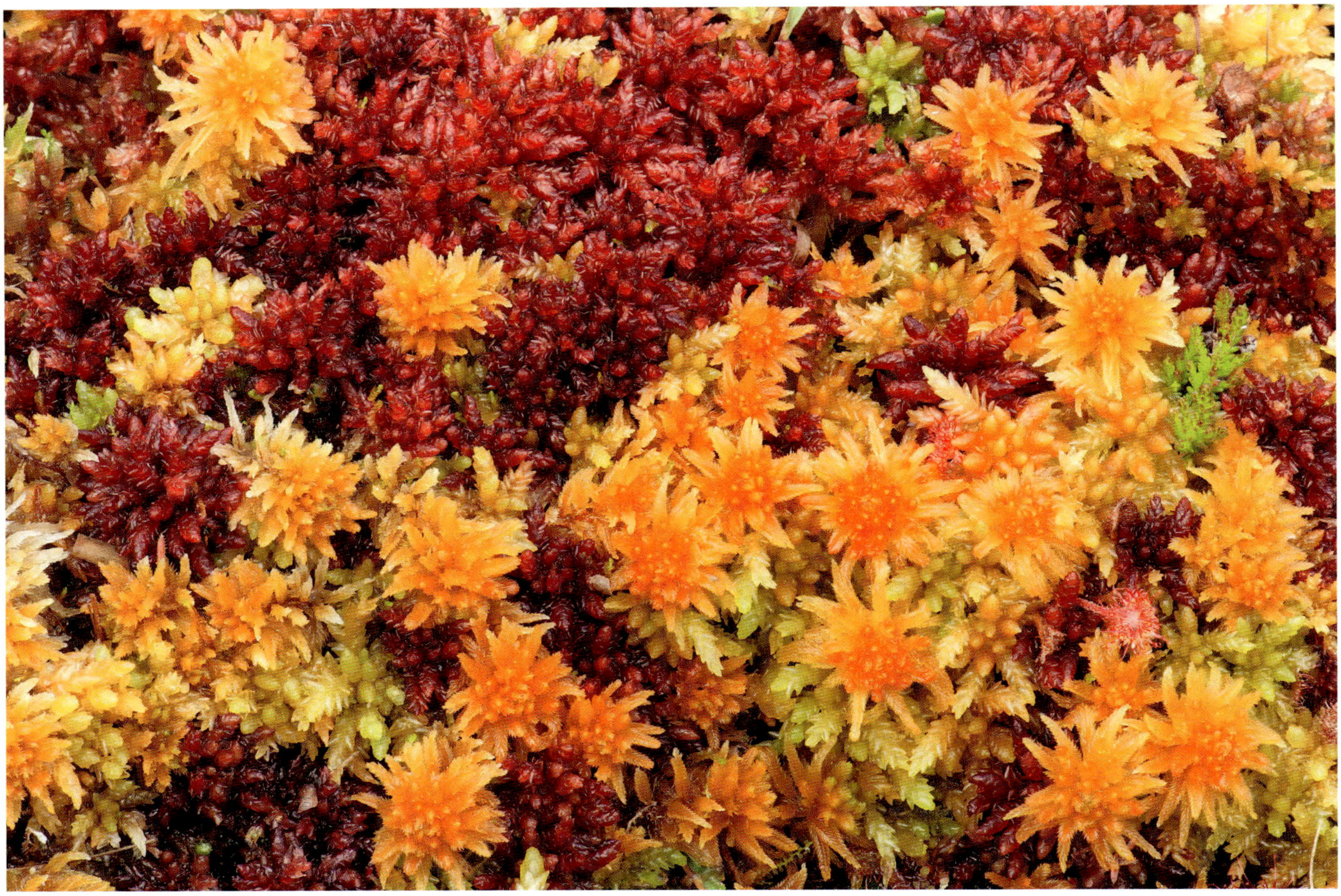

35.5 ~ *Sphagnum pulchrum* **and** *Sphagnum magellanicum*
Bogs and wetland habitats are great places for close-up photography. I focused in on the carpets of sphagnum isolating a small section which had a mixture of colour.

↘ Nikon D800, 105mm micro Nikkor, 1/30sec at f/16, ISO 200.

conditions during the middle of the day require diffusion especially when shooting pale-coloured specimens. Fill-in flash is a possibility in some cases and will help lighten the shadow areas. Reflectors can also bounce light back into the darker parts, but if the plant is not too large then placing a diffuser between the sun and the subject is the best option. Plants which have fine, hairy stems such as poppies, borage and pasque flowers often look well when backlit.

Photographic Approach

Plants are stationary, therefore you can slow down and take a more methodical approach and shoot on a tripod. I prefer natural light for all of my flower photography, but this is not always possible. There is no such thing as perfect light when photographing plants. Every situation will be different, and you will find yourself having to battle against the elements, harsh sunlight and heavily overcast conditions, or a combination of all of them; this is where experience pays off, being able to recognise the problem and how best to deal with it. There will be occasions when your expectations go beyond what is realistically possible, especially if you have travelled a long way only to be faced with really unfavourable conditions. I know this feeling only too well, having been there so many times. When shooting close-ups abroad, I frequently have to face many different types of weather conditions. I carry a lot of additional equipment with me to help deal with some of the challenges; otherwise, I would be confined to working at specific times of the day. Also, having incurred the cost of travel to a foreign destination, I want to ensure that I can maximise my time there and still obtain acceptable results irrespective of the weather conditions.

// TOP LEFT //

35.6 ~ *Anacamptis coriophora* subsp. *fragrans*
Before you commence any photography it pays to walk about and select the most suitable specimens; this will save a lot of time in the field.

→ Nikon D3, 200mm micro Nikkor, 1/250sec at f/8, ISO 200.

// TOP RIGHT //

35.7 ~ *Ophrys Lacaitae*
I had wanted to photograph this species for some time but it always eluded me. When I did finally get to see it the light was harsh. I used a diffuser to even out the contrast. In this case, it meant the difference in obtaining an acceptable result. It emphasises the point of always being prepared.

→ Nikon D3X, 200mm micro Nikkor, 1/30sec at f/11, ISO 200.

// BOTTOM //

35.6 ~ Borage *Borago officinalis*
I positioned the flash behind the subject to highlight the fine hairs on the stem and flower. I allowed the background to remain dark to make the plant stand out.

→ Nikon D810, 200mm micro Nikkor, 1/60sec at f/11, flash, ISO 200.

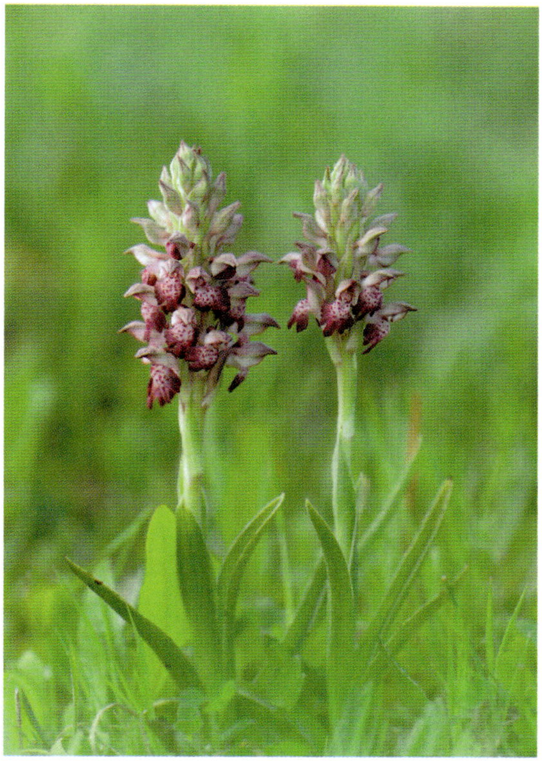

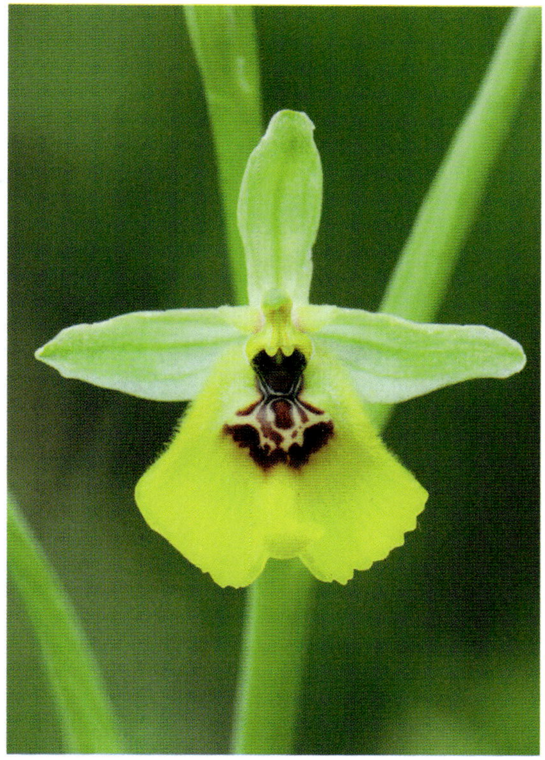

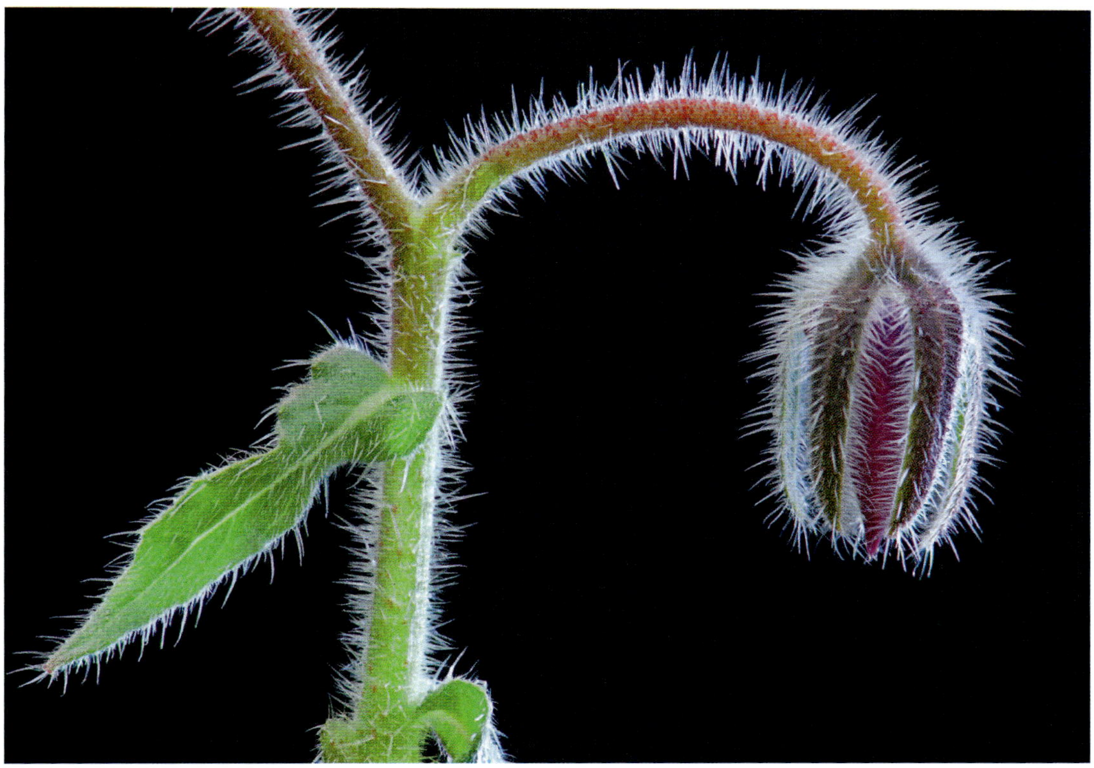

// OVERLEAF ~ LEFT //

35.7 ~ Early Purple Orchid *Orchis mascula*
What attracted me to this plant was the fact that it was growing in isolation within a grike among the limestone pavement in the Burren National Park in the west of Ireland. I was able to set the plant in context with its surroundings.

→ Kodak Pro SLR/n, 200mm micro Nikkor, 1/15sec at f/11, ISO 160.

// OVERLEAF ~ RIGHT //

35.8 ~ Martagon Lily *Lilium martagon*
A long lens in this situation helped to keep the background well diffused.

→ Nikon D810, 300mm Nikkor, + ext tube 1/250sec at f/8, ISO 200.

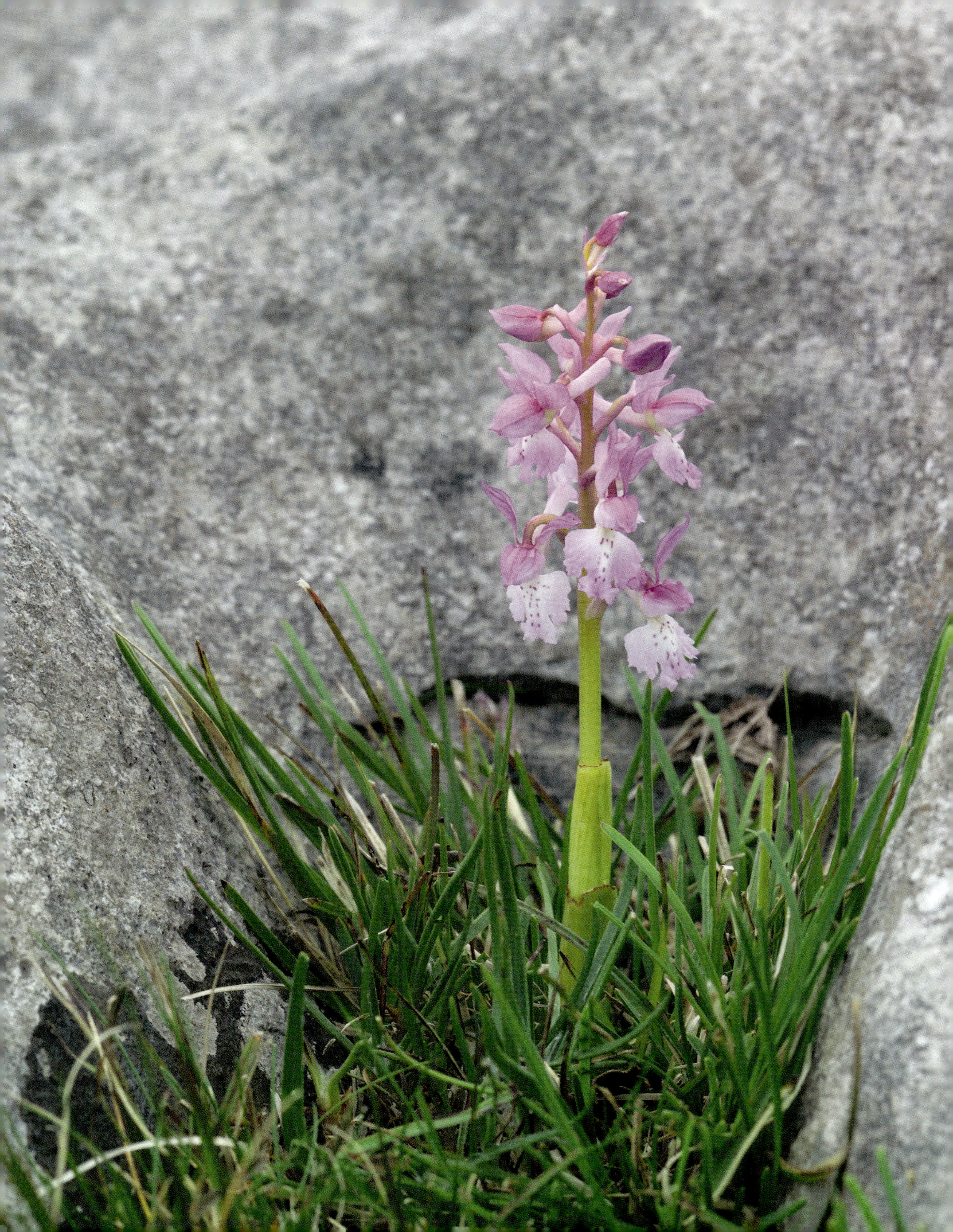

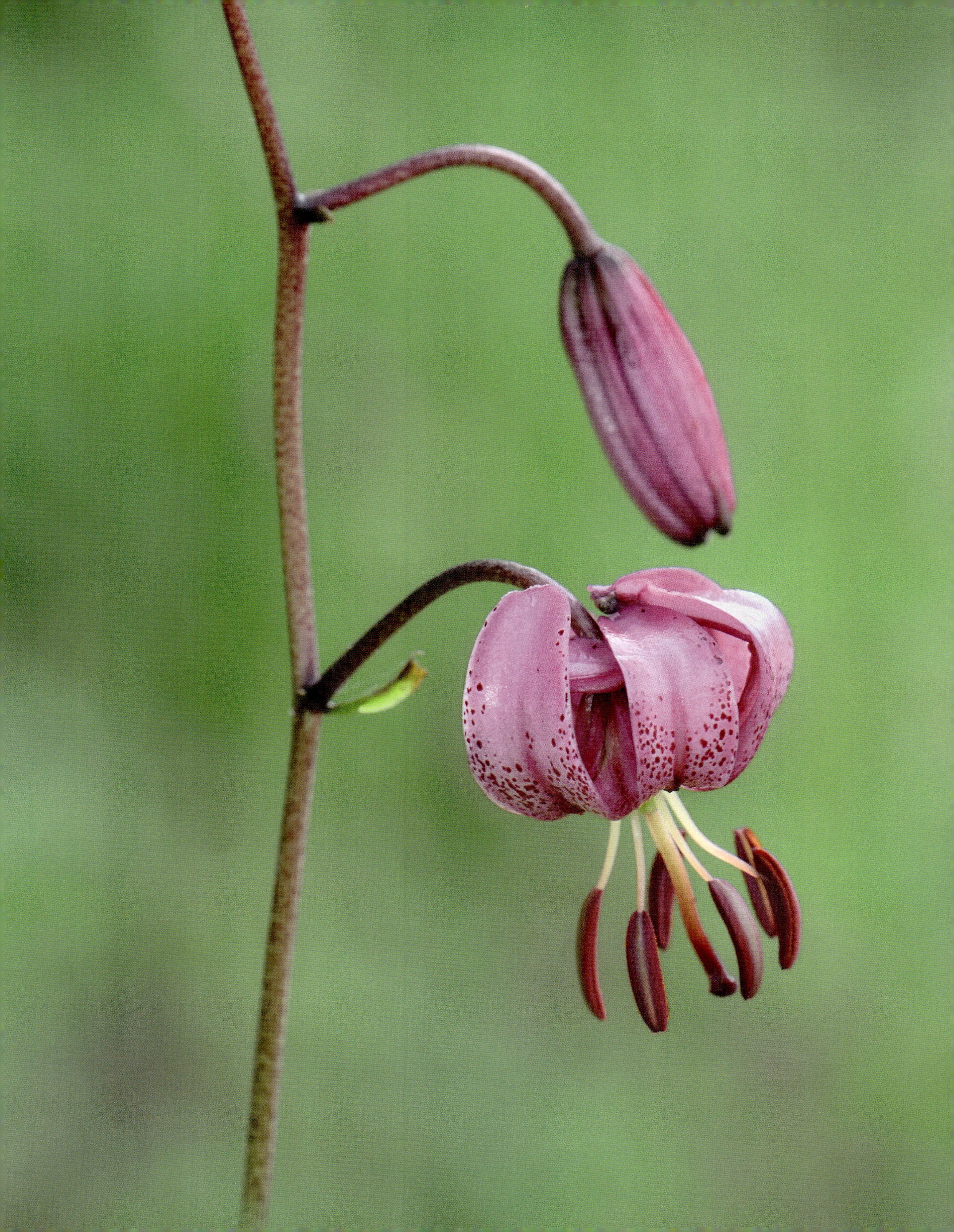

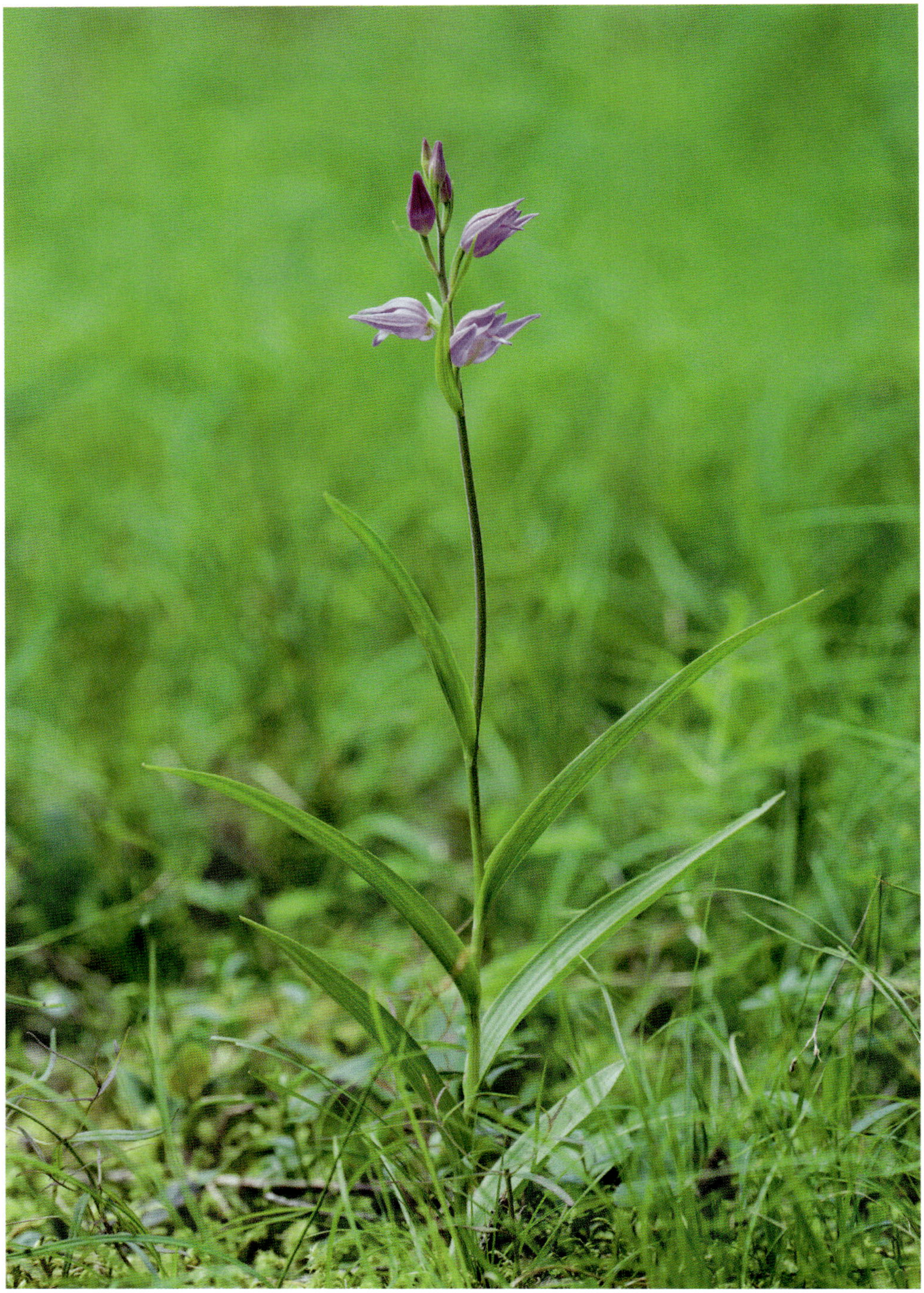

35.9 ~ **Red Helleborine**
Cephalanthera rubra
It pays to experiment with different lenses. I took the traditional portrait shot (left), but preferred the wide angle alternative (right), which conveys much more information about the orchid's habitat.

↘ Nikon D810, 200mm micro Nikkor, 1/125sec at f/8, ISO 200.

Selecting the Right Subject

I am a big fan of long lenses especially when shooting flowers. I prefer a low viewpoint employing shallow depth of field and shooting through the foreground vegetation keeping it well diffused. The narrow-angle of view and the increased working distance between the lens and subject make it a lot easier to frame and compose without the fear of damaging the plant or the adjacent flora. I have often seen the aftermath left by photographers with most of the surrounding vegetation left looking like a tsunami hit it. Working from a greater distance is a lot more comfortable for the photographer and reduces the visible disturbance.

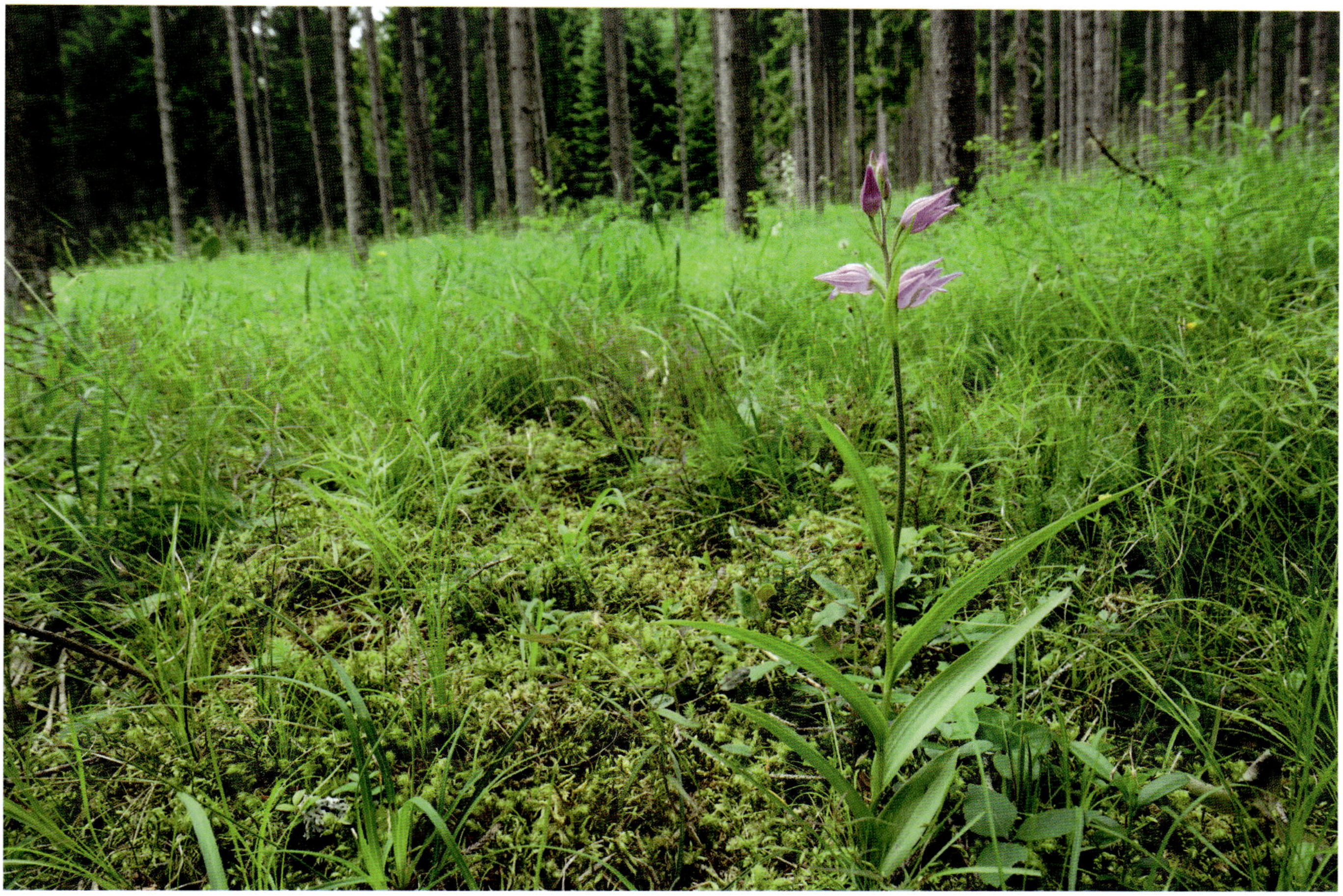

35.10 ~ **Red Helleborine** *Cephalanthera rubra*

↘ Nikon D810, 16-35mm Nikkor, 1/60sec at f/16, ISO 200.

It might initially seem irrational to talk about specimen selection when standing in a meadow overflowing with possibilities. Take your time and be choosy. Avoid plants which have blemishes, damaged flowers, or bent stems, or those which are past their floral peek. Try to select specimens which are typical of the species. Do not limit yourself to a single lens; many photographers habitually shoot close-ups with a single macro lens; experiment with various focal lengths and analyse the plant from different positions. Move in close and isolate component parts. A polarising filter is occasionally useful for removing reflections on foliage after rain and increasing saturation.

Colour accuracy is also important when photographing plants. Most DSLRs manage this pretty well. Many photographers prefer to use the auto White Balance setting and, in most situations, it produces a reasonably good result. Where colour is critical, some photographers shoot a frame using a Kodak grey card or equivalent; this is used as a reference when correcting any colour cast which can be eliminated in the RAW conversion software. However, natural light is constantly changing, therefore, if you need to make a global adjustment to your photographs, there could be some variation between images if you use an auto preset, since the light could change between shots. The background behind your subject is also important, and this should be looked at carefully. Sometimes a minor shift in the viewpoint is all that is required, or a longer focal length lens, for example, a 300mm with an extension tube to reduce the angle of view. Lowering the camera's viewpoint to increase the distance between the subject and its background can also help in some situations.

Occasionally the distance of the background in relation to the subject itself is not far enough away. You cannot obtain sufficient diffusion without shooting

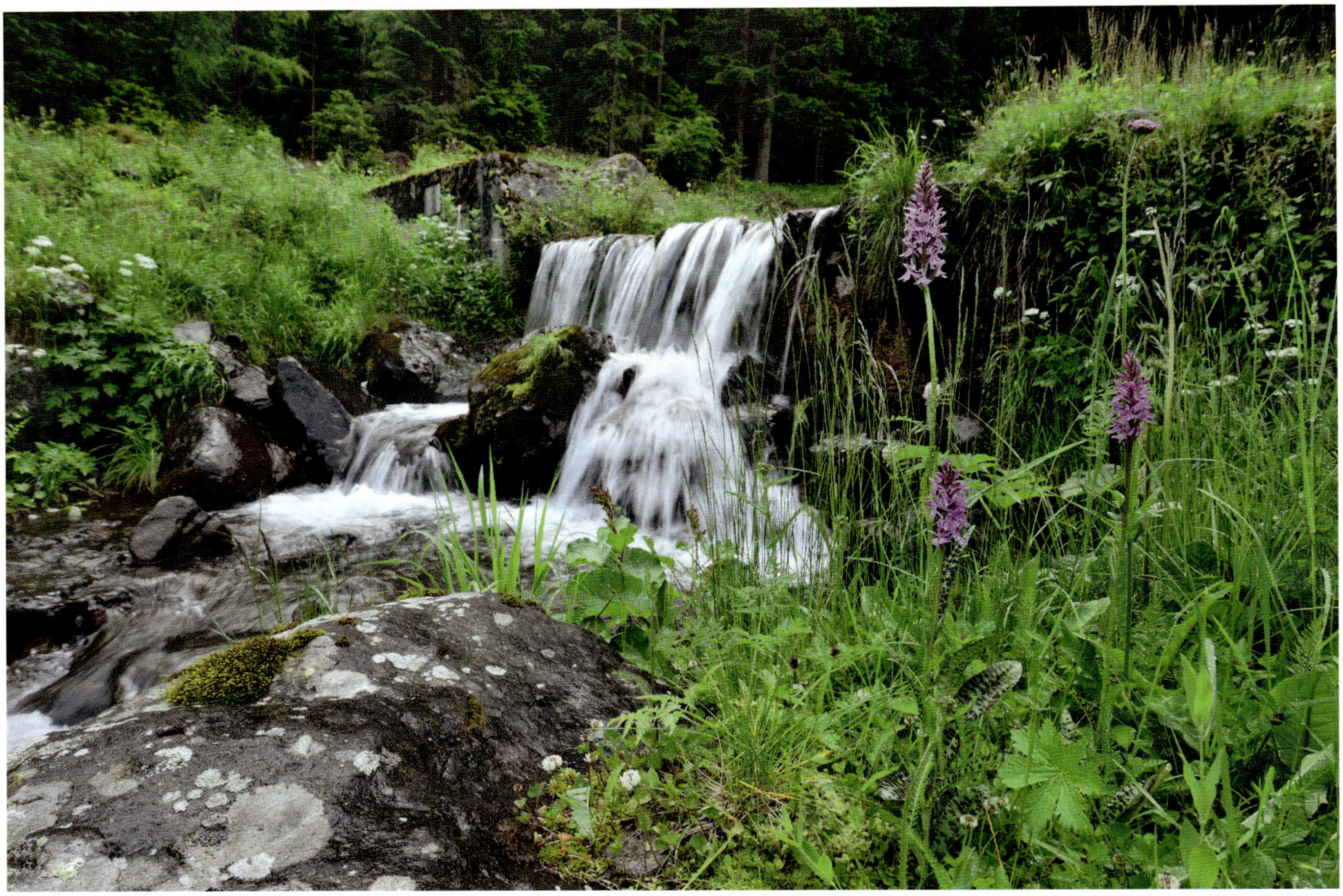

35.11 ~ **Alpine Marsh Orchid** *Dactylorhiza alpestris*
There are times when it is not possible to completely isolate a plant from its background. In this case I set it in context with its habitat which produced a better result.

↪ Nikon D810, 16–35mm Nikkor, 1/60sec at f/16, ISO 200.

virtually wide open, which you may not want to do. I describe this as the halfway house position where the background is not far enough away to blur and not close enough to retain acceptable focus. When the background is cluttered, it produces an obtrusive result. If you want to avoid this I suggest that you either reduce the magnification of the subject, therefore increasing your depth of field, or choose a smaller aperture, or use a wide angle lens which has a greater angle of view but will retain more detail in the background. Some photographers carry artificial backdrops which they can place behind the subject to emulate a diffused look, but this brings its own problems with lighting and potential reflections. With so much attention being given to the background it is easy to neglect the foreground, which is equally important. A messy foreground will detract from the photograph just as much as a cluttered background does. An adjustment to the viewpoint is usually sufficient to resolve most of the problems; if not, choose a long lens and shoot through the vegetation selecting a wide aperture and allow it to blur.

Selective Gardening

When photographing plants deciding what to include and exclude from the composition can often tip the balance either way. Your choice of position, background and f/number affect the look and also the background behind the subject. You can remove selectively, alter, or manipulate distracting bits of foliage in the background or foreground to produce a more pleasing result. It may be as little as a few blades of grass or a brightly coloured flower which can be a distraction if the background is

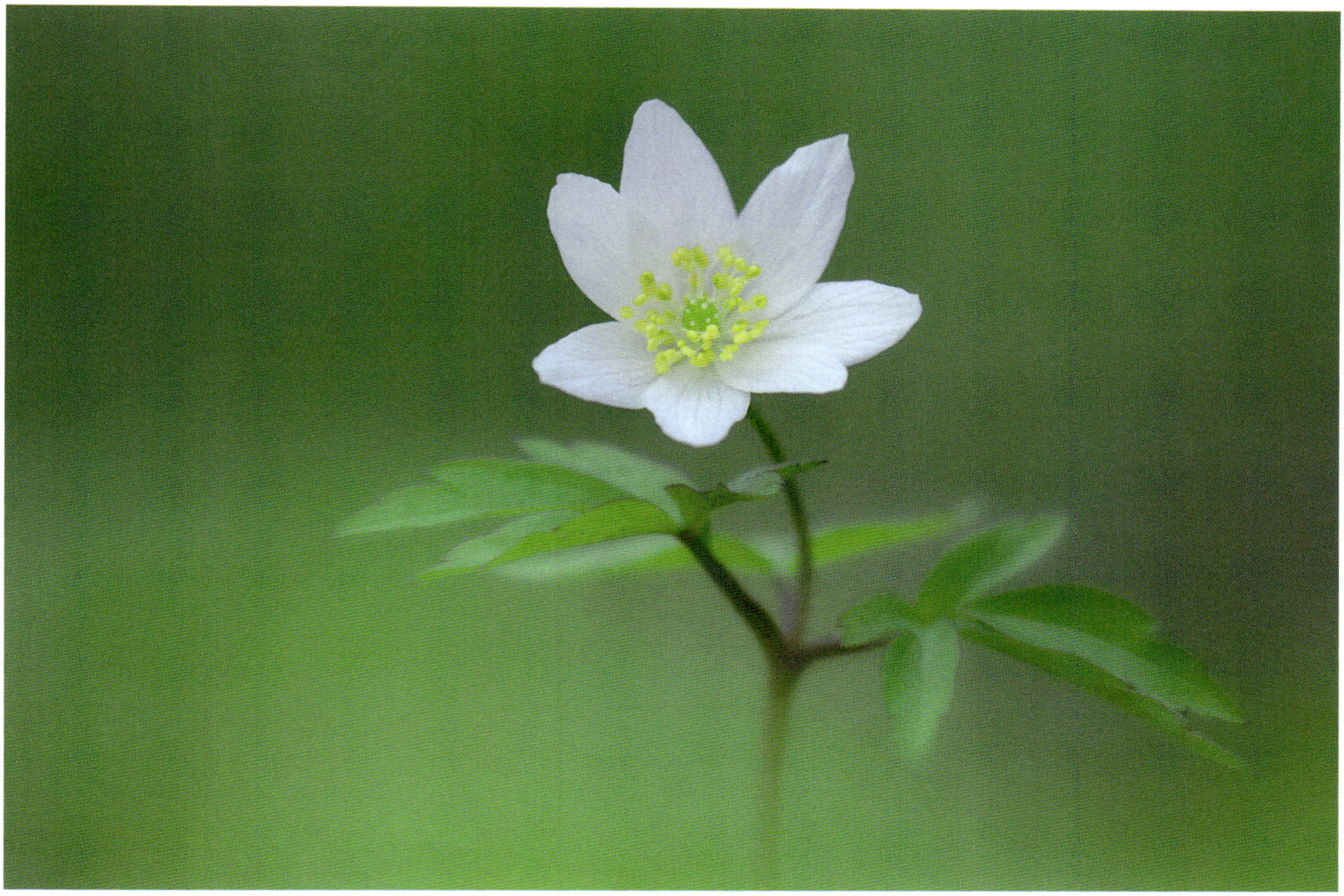

35.12 ~ **Wood Anemone** *Anemone nemorosa*
Anemones are the harbingers of spring. I never tire of photographing them. I do favour the impressionistic approach when the opportunity presents itself.

↪ Nikon D800, 300mm Nikkor, + ext tube, 1/60sec at f/5.6, ISO 100.

virtually a uniform colour. The purists would argue that you should not disturb or remove anything. However, I see no real harm in this providing that it's minor, and one is not uprooting plants or re-landscaping the site. Distracting foliage in the background can be dealt with by bunching it together and securing it with a clothes peg. You can remove it from the field of view and place a small twig or stone to keep it flat. Removing prominent blades of grass, twigs, small stones or leaves that are encroaching on your subject is fine. A brightly coloured flower or piece of foliage in the background can usually be bent out of the way, without plucking it! It is always a good idea before taking the shot to press the depth of field button and check for any obvious distractions, which can then be dealt with. Another option is to remove the offending object in Photoshop. However, an experienced natural history photographer can quickly tell if major reconstruction has been carried out on the image.

Photographing in Difficult Conditions

The weather is a significant factor, particularly with flowers. My worst experience was in Crete several years ago. The weather was so severe that for five of the seven days we could barely stand up at the sites let alone photograph due to the unseasonal severity of the winds. A light, intermittent wind is less of a problem since there are frequent let-ups in-between where you can take the shot. A stronger, more persistent breeze poses more of a problem keeping the subject in focus. In these conditions I look for subjects that are low to the ground and in sheltered positions. I also use a home-made

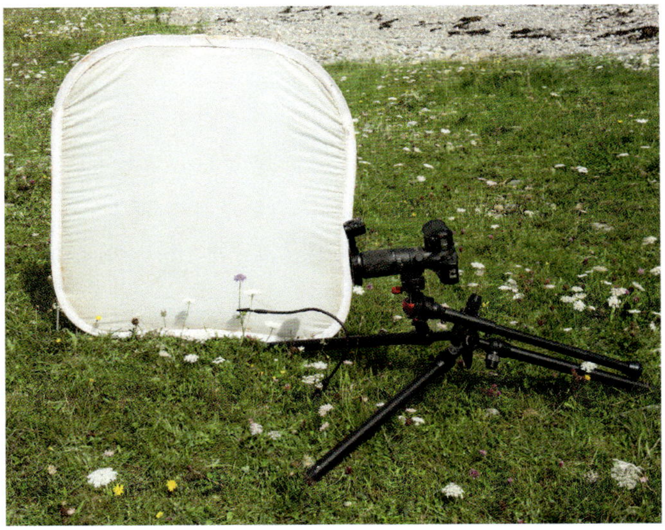

35.13 ~ **Wind shield**
I carry this home-made unit with me most of the time. It always proves extremely useful either diffusing sunlight, or reducing the wind blowing on a plant.

windshield, which also doubles as a large diffuser that I can erect quickly and is stable enough in a moderate breeze. It is secured into the ground with long aluminium rods. I also use my stem stabiliser for extra stability.

Light Diffusion Tent

Another accessory for plant photography is a translucent light tent. They come in various sizes and are relatively light and easily carried in the field. There are a number of different brands on the web, which are primarily used for photographing objects that require a white background for the internet. Not all light tents are suitable for the field.

The Lasolite cubelite is portable and easily erected. It can be used effectively on bright sunny days by scattering bright, harsh light, therefore, reducing contrast. The unit can be placed over small ground-dwelling plants, which can be photographed comfortably inside the light tent. The translucent material diffuses the sunlight producing a more balanced result. Taller plants require you to remove the back so you can photograph through the aperture to create a natural background, or you can keep it white. You can also place different backgrounds behind the subject, or use flash as the primary light source. The unit can help reduce movement in a light breeze, but there is little you can do when plagued with a persistent wind except pack up and return another day.

Conventional and Impressionistic Approaches

There are many varied approaches to flower photography. The traditional style favoured by botanists and naturalists focuses on the important features such as structure, colour accuracy and sharpness, also the biology and ecology of the plant. The different aspects are usually represented in a series of photographs depicting a full portrait followed by a close-up of the flowering spike and individual flowers. If possible, a wide angle shot of the plant in relation to its environment is also useful. Important as these aspects are in botanical illustration, it is not always necessary to stick to the rigours of convention. Adopting a creative or an impressionistic approach opens up fresh possibilities and is very much in vogue these days. Such an approach may involve isolating or magnifying part of the subject to create an abstract, or highlighting a small part of the plant with the lens wide open. In some ways, it seems a contradiction to the conventional images of plants that were deemed normal in the past. Isolating parts of the structure at higher magnifications also takes your images beyond the realms of normal vision. Utilising nature's natural elements like early morning dew or light rain provide atmosphere and a distinctive ambience to photographs.

Project Planning

Plants are so numerous and diverse that they lend themselves to many different applications and projects.

Themes and Collections

Photographing all of the wild orchids in your county, or better still the country is challenging but incredibly rewarding. Your photography can show particular aspects of the plant, including variations in flowers' colour and patterns, also any unusual aberrations. One such group within the orchid family is the genus 'Ophrys'. What makes them so interesting is the diversity of patterns

// FACING PAGE //

35.14 ~ **Orchid composite**
Composites are a great way of showing a range of similar species, or variations within a plant. In this case I have illustrated a range of orchids from the genus Ophrys.

OPHRYS SPECIES

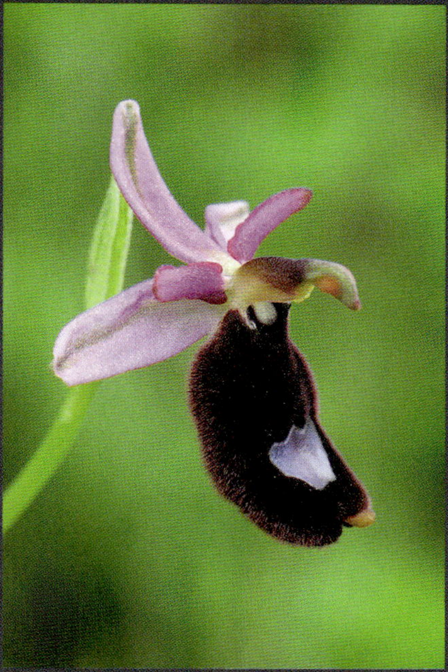
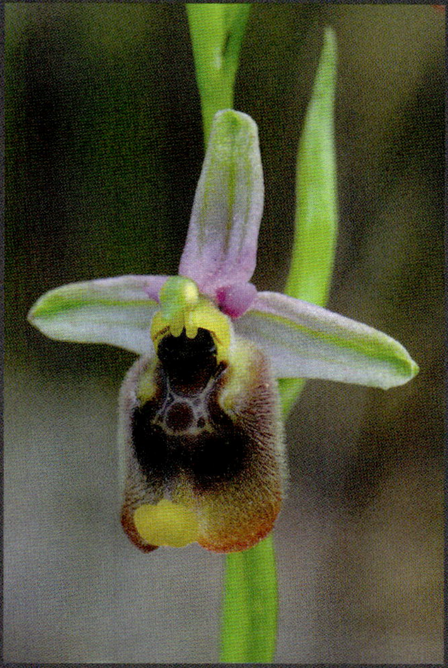
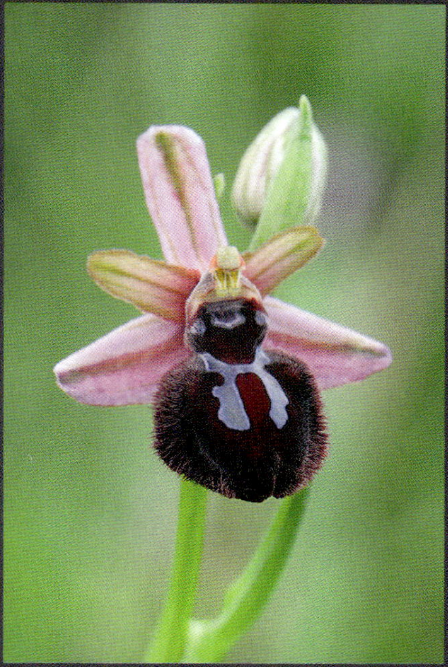
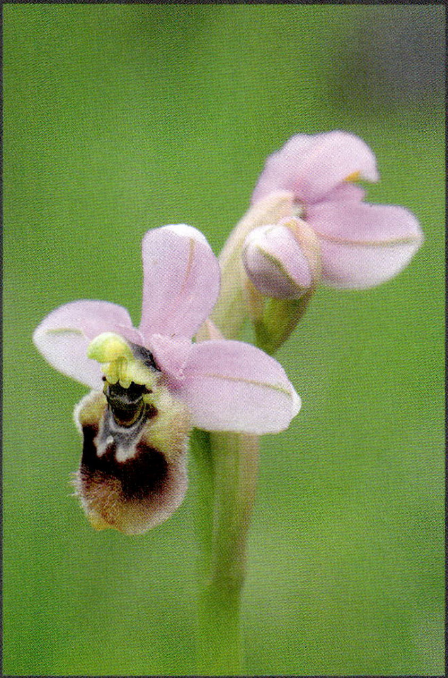
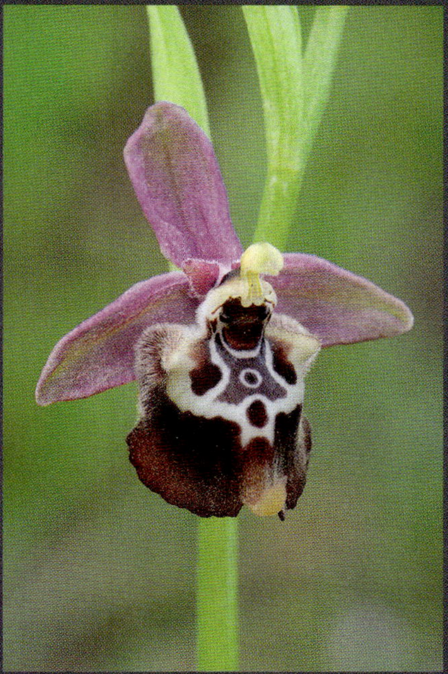
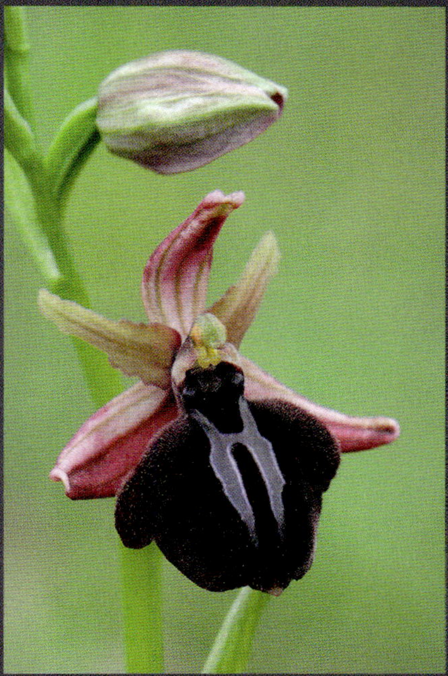

www.robertthompsonphotography.com

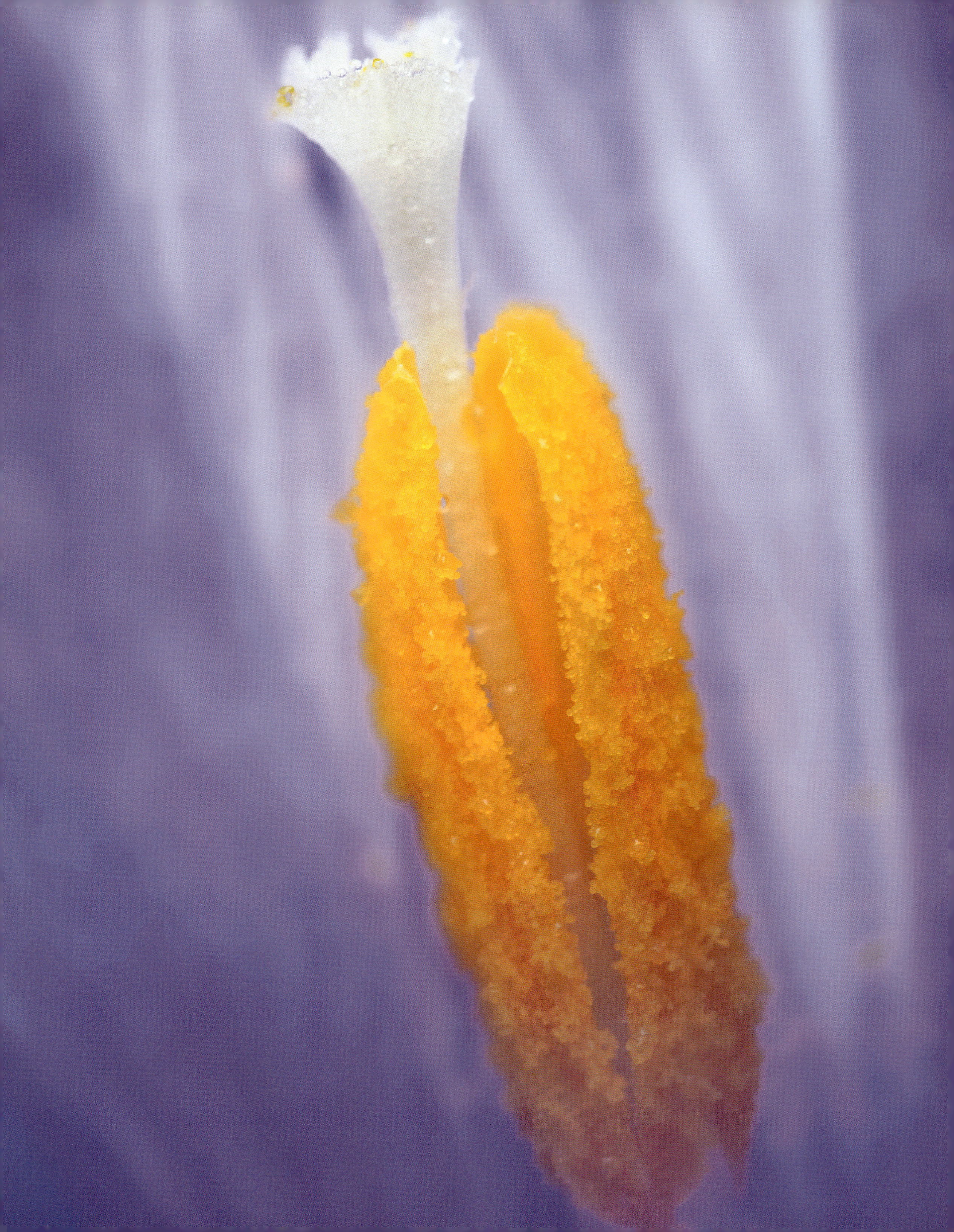

and colour on the individual flowers which have evolved to imitate insects in particular bees.

Composites

Compiling photographic composites of different species or aspects of their biology are popular approaches these days. Favourite subjects include families of flowers relative to their habitat. Foliage is another good example, especially the many varied shapes and textures of leaves. The bark patterns in trees such as birch have a diverse range of colours.

Abstracts

You could adopt an impressionistic approach to your photography by compiling a series of photographs that emphasises colour, shape and form, by isolating a particular aspect of the subject. Applying techniques such as selective focus, blur and creative lighting transcends the typical conventional approach.

PHOTOGRAPHIC TIPS

- Explore various types of habitats within your area including local nature reserves. These sites often have a good range of plants.
- Check the flowering times of plants you want to photograph to avoid disappointment and a futile journey.
- Check the weather forecast; it's pointless going out in conditions that are far from ideal.
- Refrain from photographing the first plant you see. Explore the surrounding area before making your decision.
- Examine your subject from different positions using different lenses. Keep your camera back parallel to the subject and work from a tripod, it makes it easier to evaluate your framing and compositional choice.
- Be mindful of the background behind the subject and how it might appear in the final image.
- Be aware of the surrounding vegetation when photographing; many other plants often get trampled in the process.
- Record some information about location and flowering period; this will be of use in the future if you want to return at some point.
- Experiment with flowers in your garden first using different lenses and setups.

RESOURCES

FURTHER READING

Angel, H. *How to Photograph Wild Flowers*. Stackpole Books.
Bishop, S. *Digital Flower Photography*. Photographers' Institute Press.
Bishop, S. *Photographing Flowers*. Photographers' Institute Press.
Davies, A. *Digital Plant Photography*. Bloomsbury.
Davies, H. *Photographing Flowers*. Focal Press.
Davies, P.H. *Photographing Flowers*. Collins & Brown Limited.

WEBSITES

Flora of Northern Ireland: www.habitas.org.uk/flora
Irish Wildflowers: www.irishwildflowers.ie
Wild Flowers of Britain and Europe: www.first-nature.com/flowers
Wild Flowers of the British Isles: www.ukwildflowers.com
Wild Flowers of the United States: www.uswildflowers.com

// FACING PAGE //

35.15 ~ Crocus species
Many flowers lend themselves to abstracts. In this case I have focused my attention on the stamens of the flower allowing the rest of the plant to blur.

Nikon D810, 200mm micro Nikkor, with Mamiya 80mmm reversed via a coupling ring. 1/60sec at f/8, ISO 100.

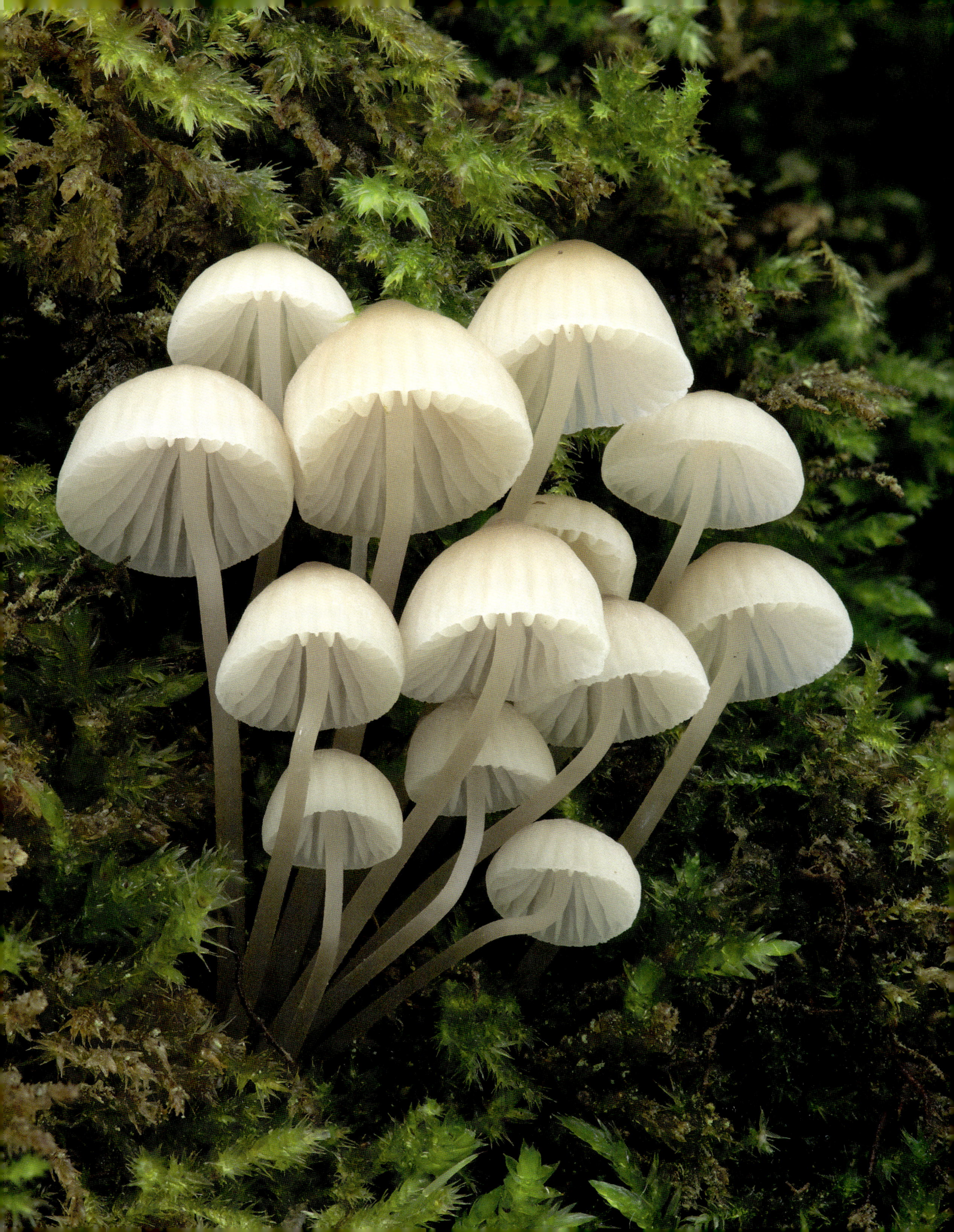

THIRTY SIX

The Kingdom of the Underworld

Fungi

Introduction

Fungi have always been associated with mystery and intrigue. Often described as the kingdom of the underworld, this idiosyncratic group of organisms has origins dating back at least 455 million years, and perhaps even longer. They are nature's undertakers, responsible for breaking down dead and organic material and recycling the nutrients through the bionetworks again. Many of the vascular plants rely on the mycorrhizae that infiltrate their root systems to nourish and supply them with essential nutrients.

There are approximately 99,000 species which have been described to date, with hundreds of new species being added each year. It's hard to estimate with any degree of accuracy the true numbers. They occupy virtually every type of habitat on the planet from the hottest deserts to the extreme conditions of Antarctica. There are many myths surrounding fungi; much of what is already known is the result of ongoing research, but many aspects of the life history and ecology of this bizarre kingdom are still a mystery. They play a significant role in everyday life, especially in the food and drink industry. More importantly, they have a vital role in medicine and are used in the form of antibiotics such as penicillin or cephalosporin to kill harmful bacteria which cause infections and disease.

It is fair to say that the majority of fungi are not that colourful and, therefore, difficult to get excited about. However, having said that, there are many which are; their bizarre shapes and structures make for real eye-catching photographs. Their popularity among photographers has increased significantly in recent times, probably due to the fact that more publications and online websites are now available to help with the identification of many of the common fungi. The fly agaric is perhaps the most widely known and one of the most photographed species. Others, such as yellow stagshorn, candlesnuff fungus, scarlet elf cup, sulphur tuft and various earth stars are equally colourful and photogenic. Many larger fungi have been ascribed vernacular names such as the panther cap, penny bun, death cap, destroying angel and the vibrant yellow brain fungus, but the majority of other lesser-known species have not. Some photographers specialise in fungi and travel to different parts of the world to see these weird

// FACING PAGE //

36.1 ~ Bonnet Mushroom *Mycena pseudocorticola*
I added fill-in flash to the undersides to help lighten the shadows.
→ Nikon D3, 105mm micro Nikkor, 1/4sec at f/16, fill-in flash, ISO 100.

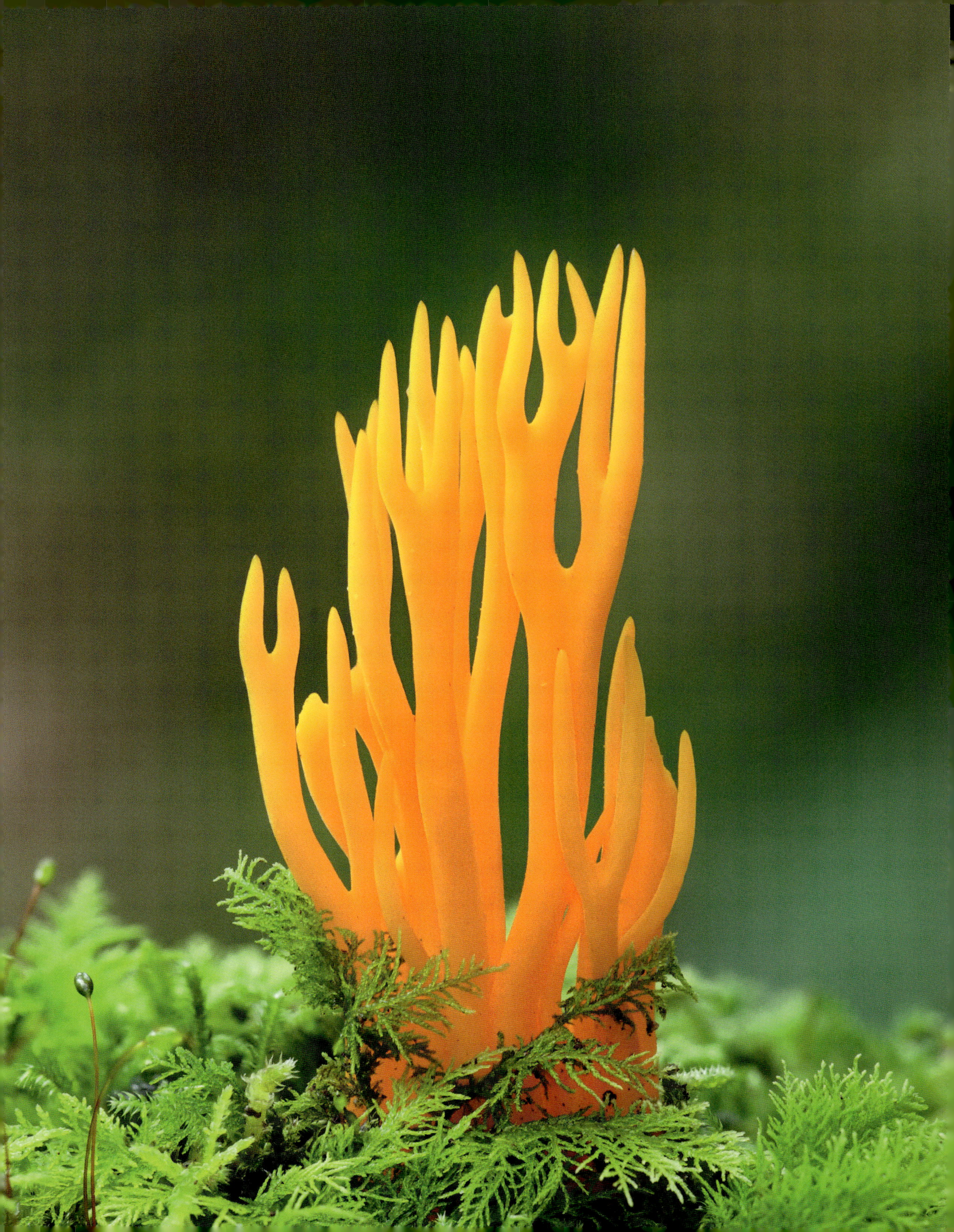

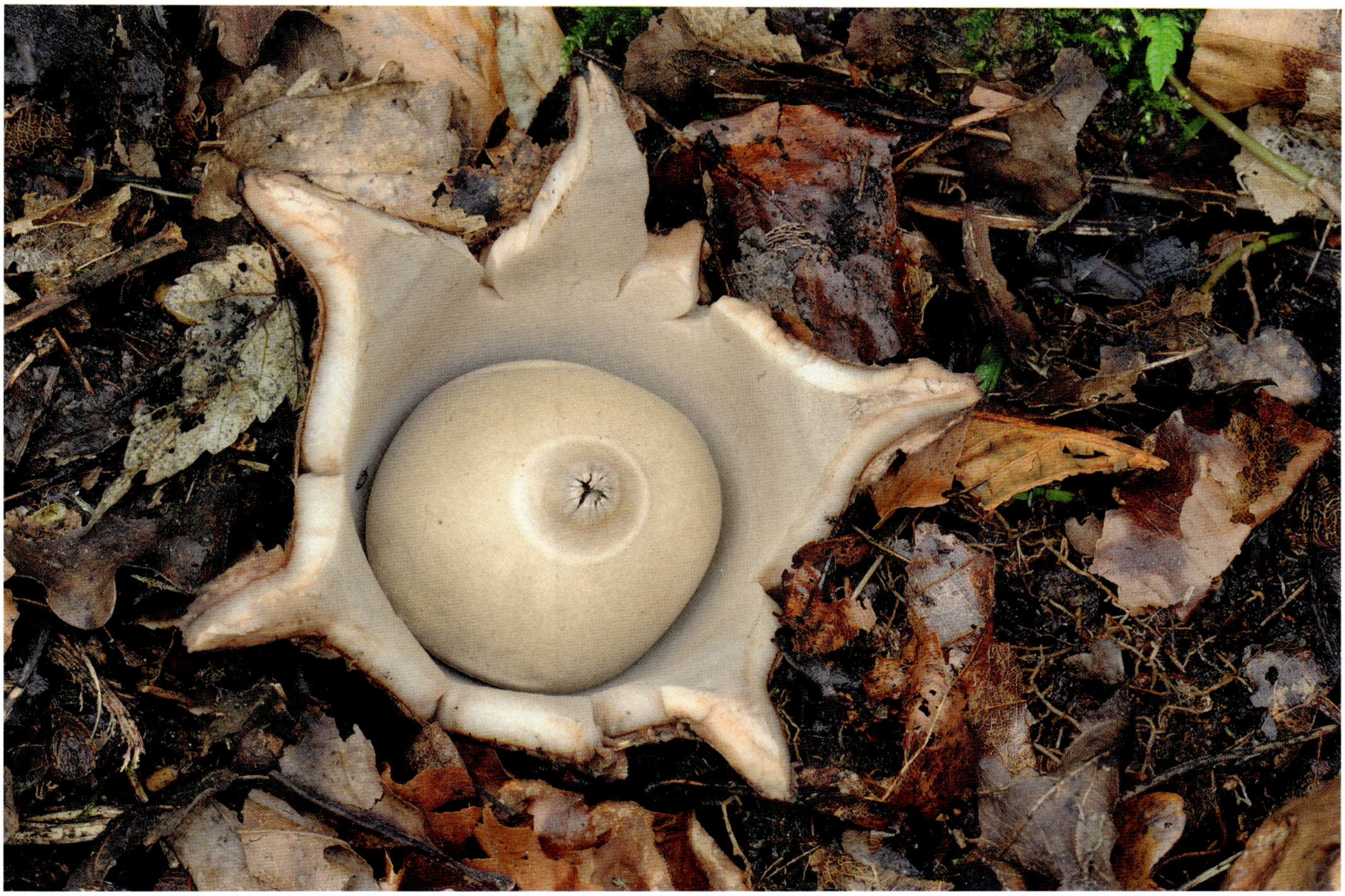

36.3 ~ **Collared Earthstar** *Geastrum triplex*
Earthstars are always a good find, especially when they are in reasonably good condition.
↳ Nikon D3X with 105mm Micro Nikkor, 1/8sec at f16, fill-in flash, tripod.

// FACING PAGE //

36.2 ~ **Yellow Stagshorn** *Calocera viscosa*
A common and widespread species found mainly on old decaying tree stumps. I used a long lens in this case to soften the background, making the species stand out.
↳ Nikon D2X, 300mm Nikkor, 1/2sec at f/11, fill-in flash, ISO 100.

and bizarre-looking organisms, some of which have rarely been photographed. All fungi, however, should be treated with extreme caution; many are highly poisonous, and a few are potentially fatal even if eaten in small quantities.

Biology and Life History

Most people assume that fungi are related to plants – scientifically they are not. Recent DNA research shows that fungi are more closely connected to animals than plants. Plants photosynthesise, but fungi do not since they lack the chlorophyll pigment. They also produce spores and not seeds as in plants. The mushroom or toadstool is known as the reproductive part, or fruiting body and is produced from a fine network of cobweb-like threads called mycelium, which exist in the soil. They obtain nourishment either as saprophytes feeding on the remains of plants or animals, or exist as parasites living off their hosts.

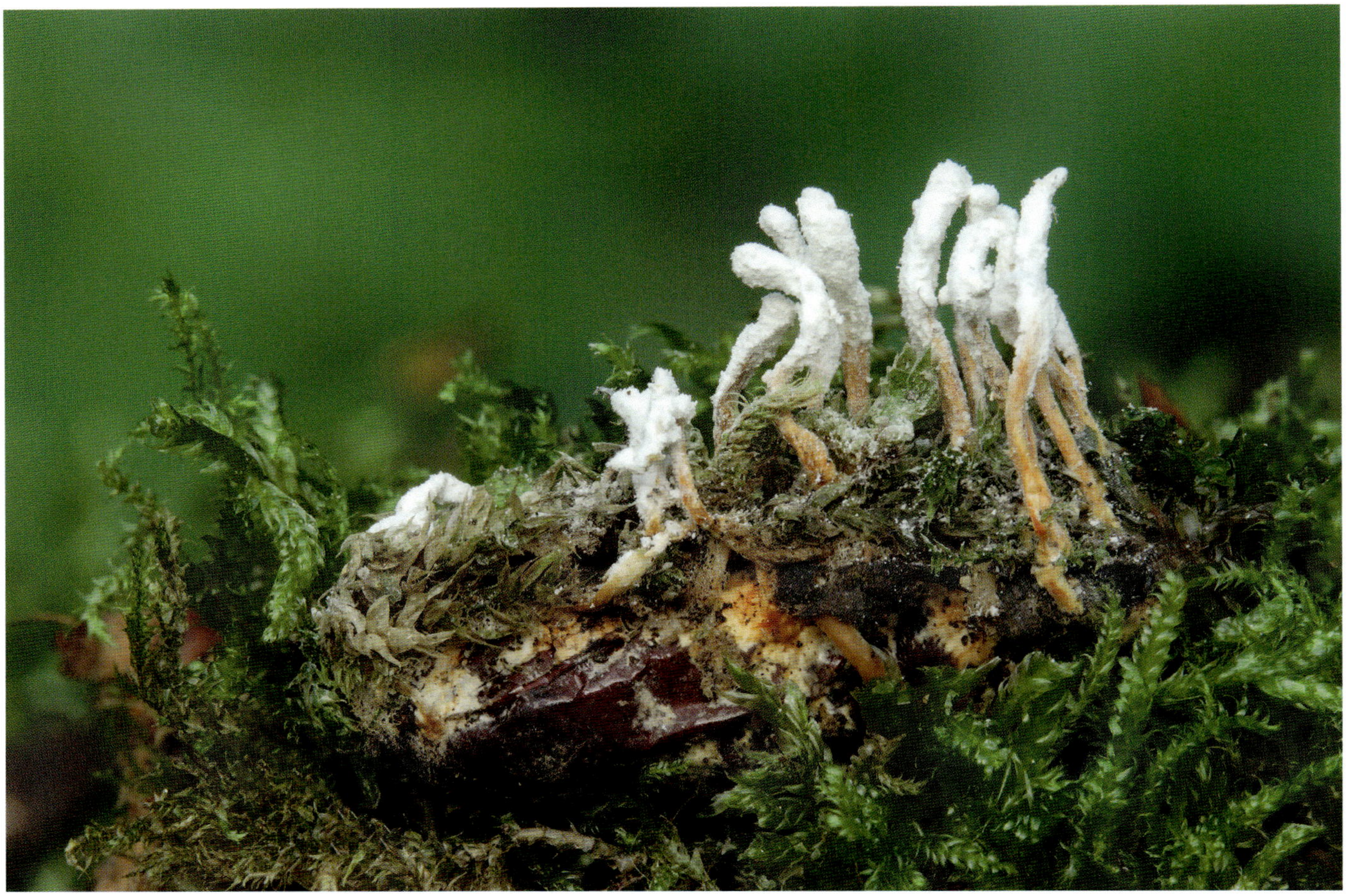

36.4 ~ *Isaria farinosa*
Some fungi are parasitic living off their host which in this case is the pupa of a moth.
↘ Nikon D810, 105mm micro Nikkor, 1/4sec at f/16, fill-in flash, ISO 200.

Searching for Fungi

My interest in fungi stems back to my early days as an aspiring macro photographer. Some of my natural history friends are real fungi enthusiasts. I picked up many useful tips and advice from spending time with them in the field. One of the most exciting aspects of fungi photography is the unpredictability of what you might find. Fortunately, the peak season is during the autumn months when most insects and flowers are virtually gone, and the woods and ground vegetation is a suffusion of yellows and browns.

Fungi occur in a wide range of habitats; woodland that contains mature populations of birch, beech and oak is generally the most productive. Conifer woodland generally has fewer species, but can still be pretty rewarding, especially mature pinewoods which are quite exceptional. Other habitats worth exploring are coastal sand dunes, roadside verges and unimproved grassland – the latter is often good for 'waxcaps', which appear in a variety of colours. Most fungi produce fruiting bodies from late summer until the onset of winter. A small number are to be found throughout the winter months and spring. However, September and October are the most productive months.

Many fungi have a close association with the habitats they occupy and in most cases with a particular host plant or tree. For example, the fly agaric is often found with mature birch and pine trees, which means you are more likely to find it where they occur. The fruiting bodies of many species have a relatively short lifespan and start to decay fairly quickly. It is, therefore, important to photograph them when they are at their best.

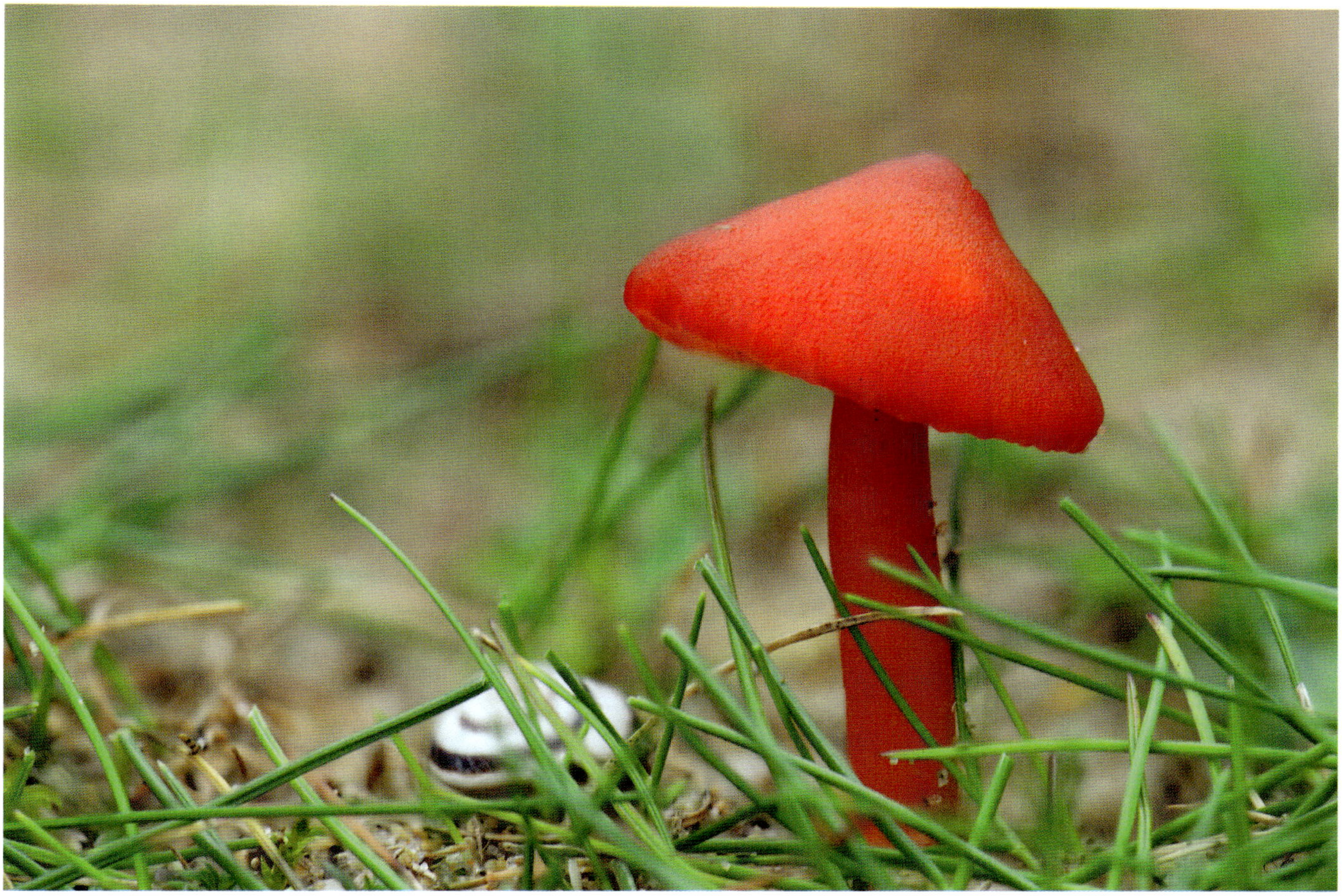

36.5 ~ **Scarlet Waxcap** *Hygrocybe coccinea*
An attractive species found on coastal grassland sites.

↘ Nikon D2X, 200mm micro Nikkor, 1/15 sec at f/8, fill-in flash, ISO 200.

Ideal Conditions

Unlike plants and other organisms, which appear year after year, fungi are much more unpredictable. Seasonal conditions play an important part in the reproductive behaviour of species, but there is no guarantee that they will appear in the same place each year. A warm summer followed by a mild, wet autumn produces the perfect conditions for fungi to flourish. The most productive time photographically is a few days after rain, especially if the temperature and humidity levels have been high. A sudden drop in temperature can stimulate a flush or emergence. Watching the weather conditions and visiting a local wood over several days will give you an indication when the peak of the emergence is. Fungi can appear remarkably quickly and it's important to try and photograph them when they are at their best.

Fieldcraft

In the Field

Finding pristine examples free from slug damage, even among common species, is always a challenge. It can be so frustrating when you find a rare or colourful specimen only to discover on closer examination that the slugs have beaten you to it. Despite their so-called lack of speed, they still manage to locate freshly emerged fruiting bodies with amazing rapidity. Many larger gill fungi are easily located close to the root structures radiating out from the trunk. Bracket fungi grow mainly on the trunk surface and on some branches. Fallen trunks which have been decaying for a while can also support a range of species. Smaller moss-covered branches are often a good source for various types of cup fungi. Photographers tend to focus on the large, well-known

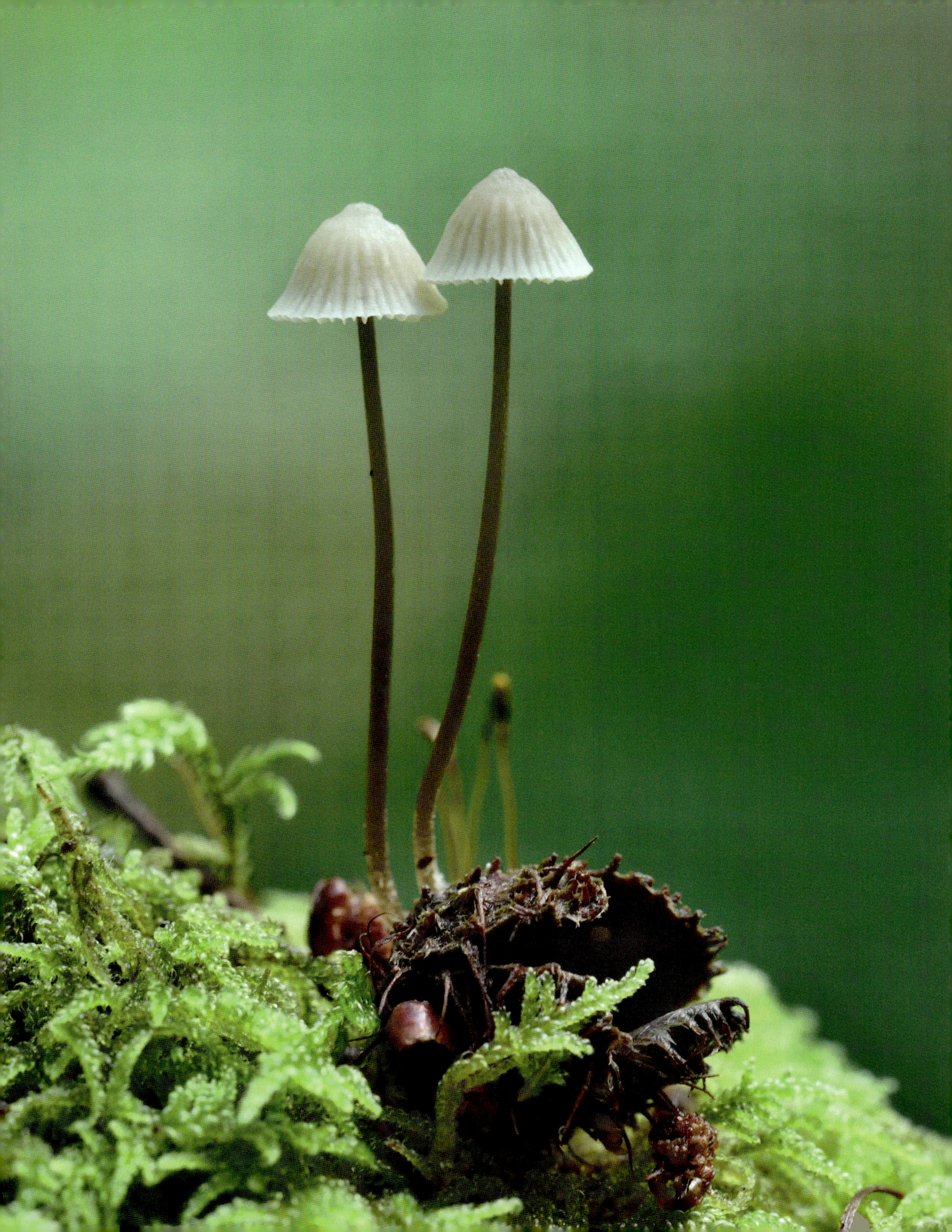

// FACING PAGE //

36.6 ~ Snapping Bonnet *Mycena vitalis*
These small fungi are always very delicate and easily damaged; this pair were growing out of a fallen beechmast pod. I had to exercise caution clearing any bits of unwanted debris from around them.

↘ Nikon D810, 105mm micro Nikkor, 1/4 sec at f/11, ISO 200.

// THIS PAGE ~ TOP //

36.7 ~ Eyelash Fungus *Scutellinia scutellata*
A colourful saprophytic species easily identified by the long dark hairs or eyelashes on the rim of the cup.

↘ Nikon D810, 200mm micro Nikkor, 1/2sec at f/16, fill-in flash, ISO 200.

// THIS PAGE ~ BOTTOM //

36.8 ~ Lemon Disco Fungus *Bisporella citrina*
A very common fungus found on old decaying wood which has lost its bark.

↘ Nikon D3X, 105mm micro Nikkor, 1/ sec at f/16, fill-in flash, ISO 200.

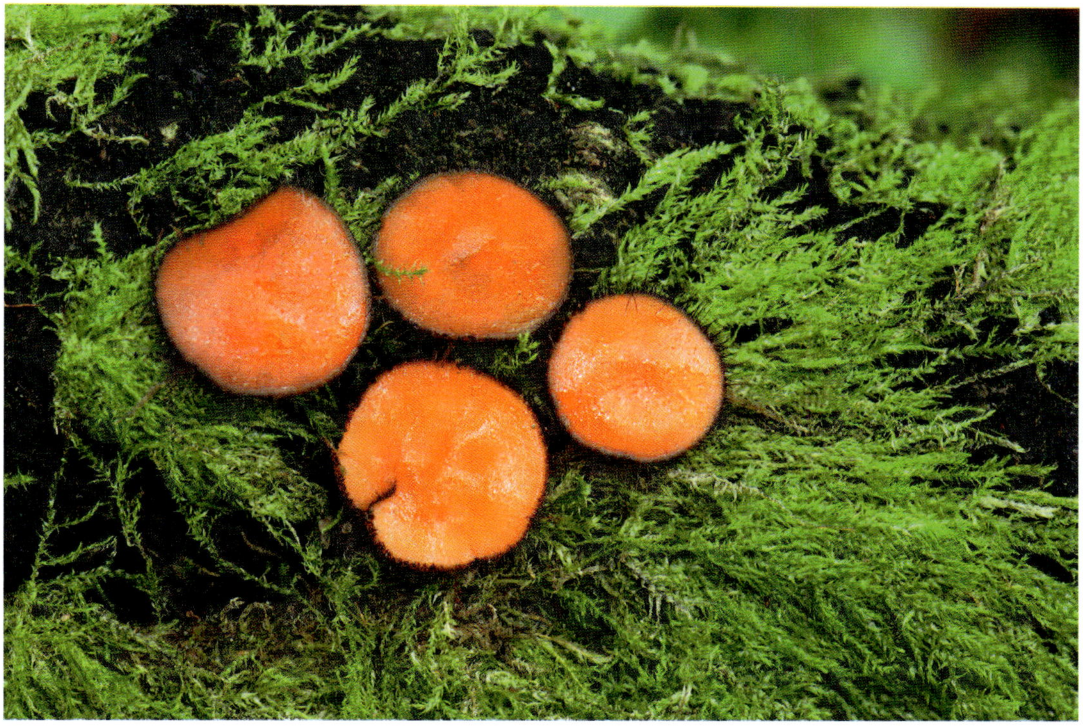

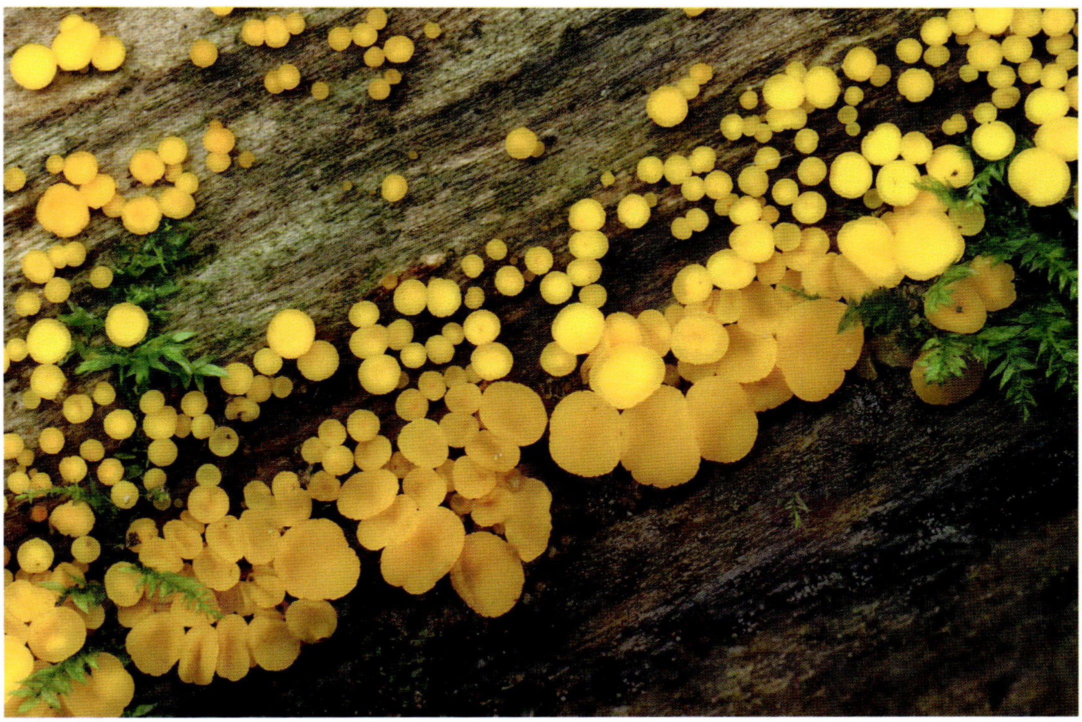

species, but many small fungi go relatively unnoticed. Don't neglect these; they often make great photographs. Superficially, many fungi look similar therefore visual identification is not always very reliable except in species which are very distinct. Taking a specimen for identification purposes does not harm the mycelium. Making a note of the habitat, the host tree, or plant and the date are extremely useful and will help with the identification process.

Many fungi like plants grow among the ground vegetation making them harder to isolate. Removing a few bits of obtrusive foliage will not do any harm, but don't overdo it. If you are not sure, then take shots before and after, that way you can choose which you prefer. Sometimes fungi have damaged areas in the top of the cap. You can try photographing it from a slightly different position, or place a couple of fallen leaves over the damaged area; this looks quite natural since many are often hidden under the fallen foliage.

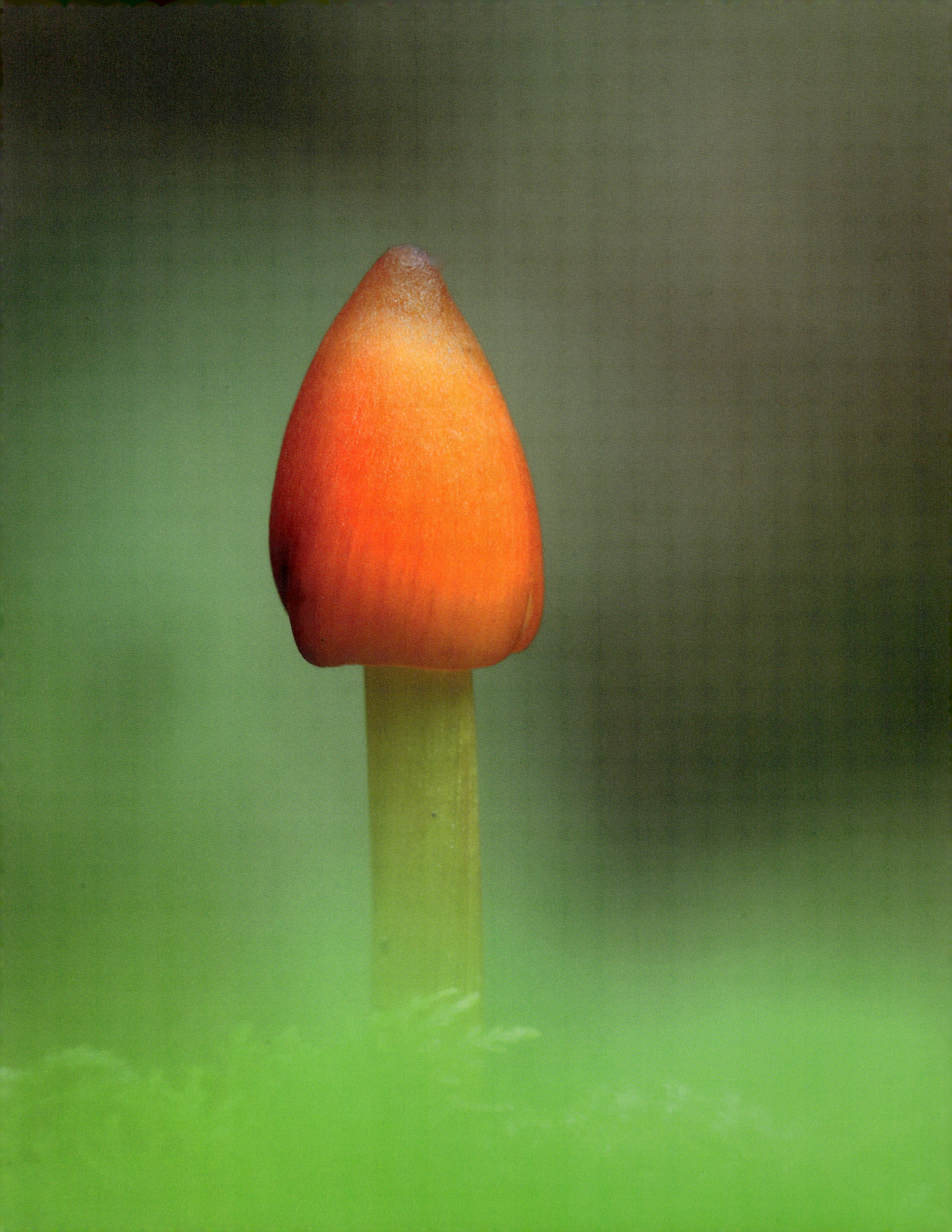

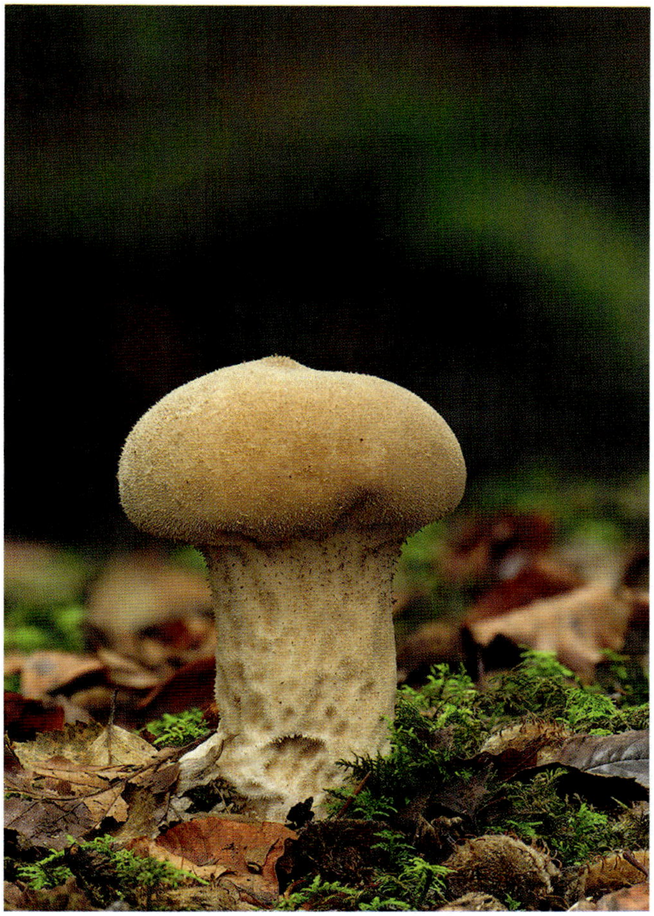

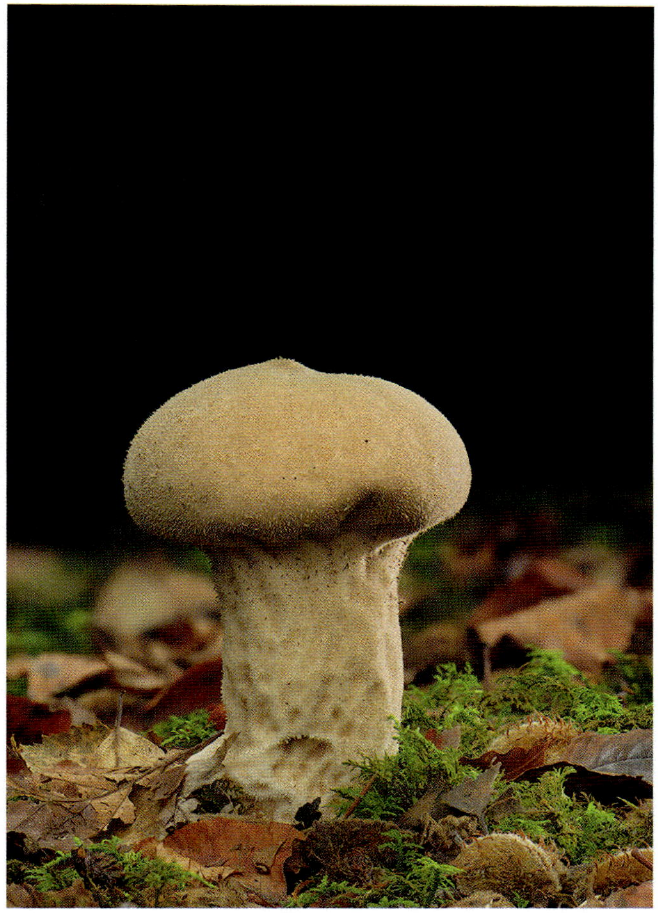

36.10 ~ **Pestle Puffball** *Calvatia excipuliformis*
In this example I wanted to reduce the distraction in the background visible on the left image. Using manual fill-in flash I was able to alter the amount of ambient light registering in the background.

// FACING PAGE //

36.9 ~ **Blacking Waxcap** *Hygrocybe conica*
I used a long lens here to shoot through the foreground vegetation to produce a soft impressionistic feel to the photograph.

↘ Nikon D3X, 300mm micro Nikkor, + ext tube, ISO 100 at at f/8, fill-in flash ISO 200.

Photographic Approach

I shoot the vast majority of fungi using natural light. I prefer this method whenever the conditions and the position of the subject allow me to do so. However, there are a few things to be aware of especially when in shady woodland interiors. If your White Balance is set to auto, you can sometimes experience a shift in colour as the overhead foliage in the canopy can influence the camera's sensor. As a rule, I change my White Balance to one of my custom settings, which I have set up specifically for shooting in dense woodland.

The general shape and structure of many fungi lend themselves to a vertical composition but don't be afraid to experiment with both formats. Many bracket fungi photograph well with wide angle lenses, placing them in context with their environment. I occasionally use flash as the primary light source when I want a

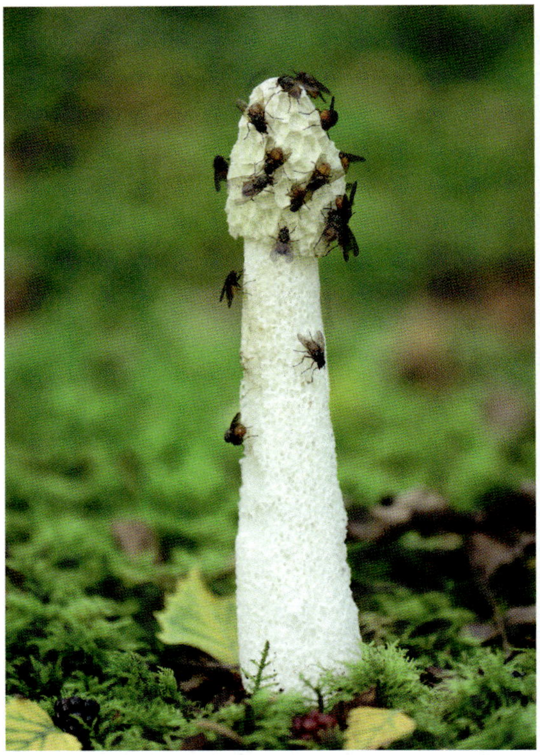

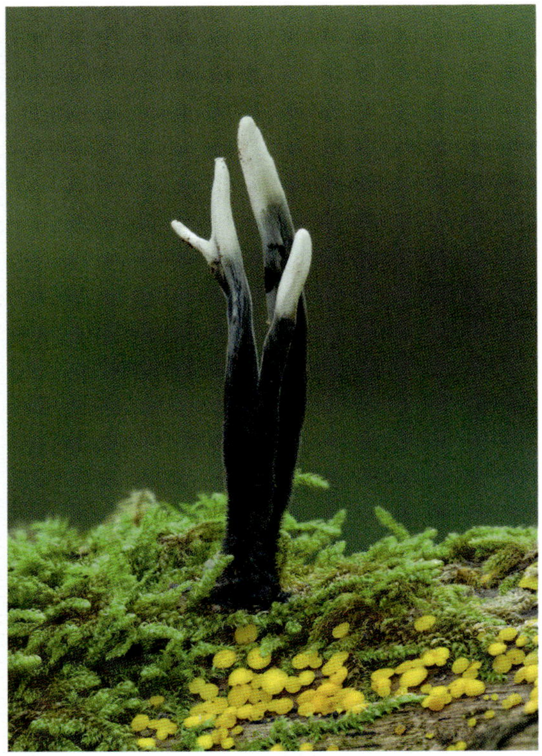

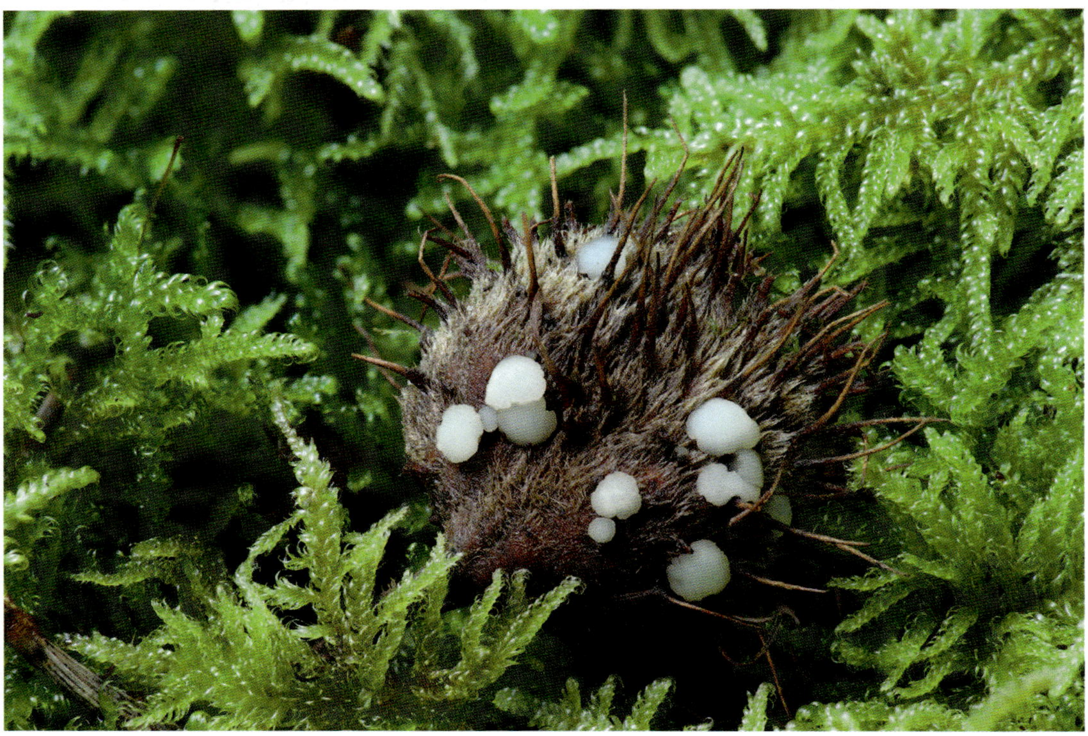

// THIS PAGE ~ TOP LEFT //

36.11 ~ Stinkhorn *Phallus impudicus* **var.** *impudicus*
A rather distinctive species not easily confused with any other. You can often smell these fungi before you can see them.

→ Nikon D810, 200mm micro Nikkor, 1/8sec at f/11, fill-in flash, ISO 200.

// THIS PAGE ~ TOP RIGHT //

36.12 ~ Candlesnuff Fungus *Xylaria hypoxylon*
A very common fungus found mainly throughout the late autumn and winter months. It is often seen growing in clusters on decaying wood. I used a custom WB setting and fill-in flash to help counteract the green cast which is often apparent when working in heavily shaded woodland.

→ Nikon D810, 200mm micro Nikkor, 1/2sec at f/11, fill-in flash, ISO 200.

// THIS PAGE ~ BOTTOM //

36.13 ~ *Hymenoscyphus fagineus*
A small pale disc-like species that grows on fallen beechmast seeds.

→ Nikon D810, 200mm micro Nikkor, 1sec at f/16, fill-in flash, ISO 200.

// FACING PAGE //

36.14 ~ Brown Birch Bolete *Leccinum scabrum*
This specimen was growing on the edge of a bank which gave me the height to use a wide angle lens, setting it in context with the stream and the distant woodland.

→ Nikon D3X, 24mm PC-E Nikkor, 1/8sec at f/16, ISO 200.

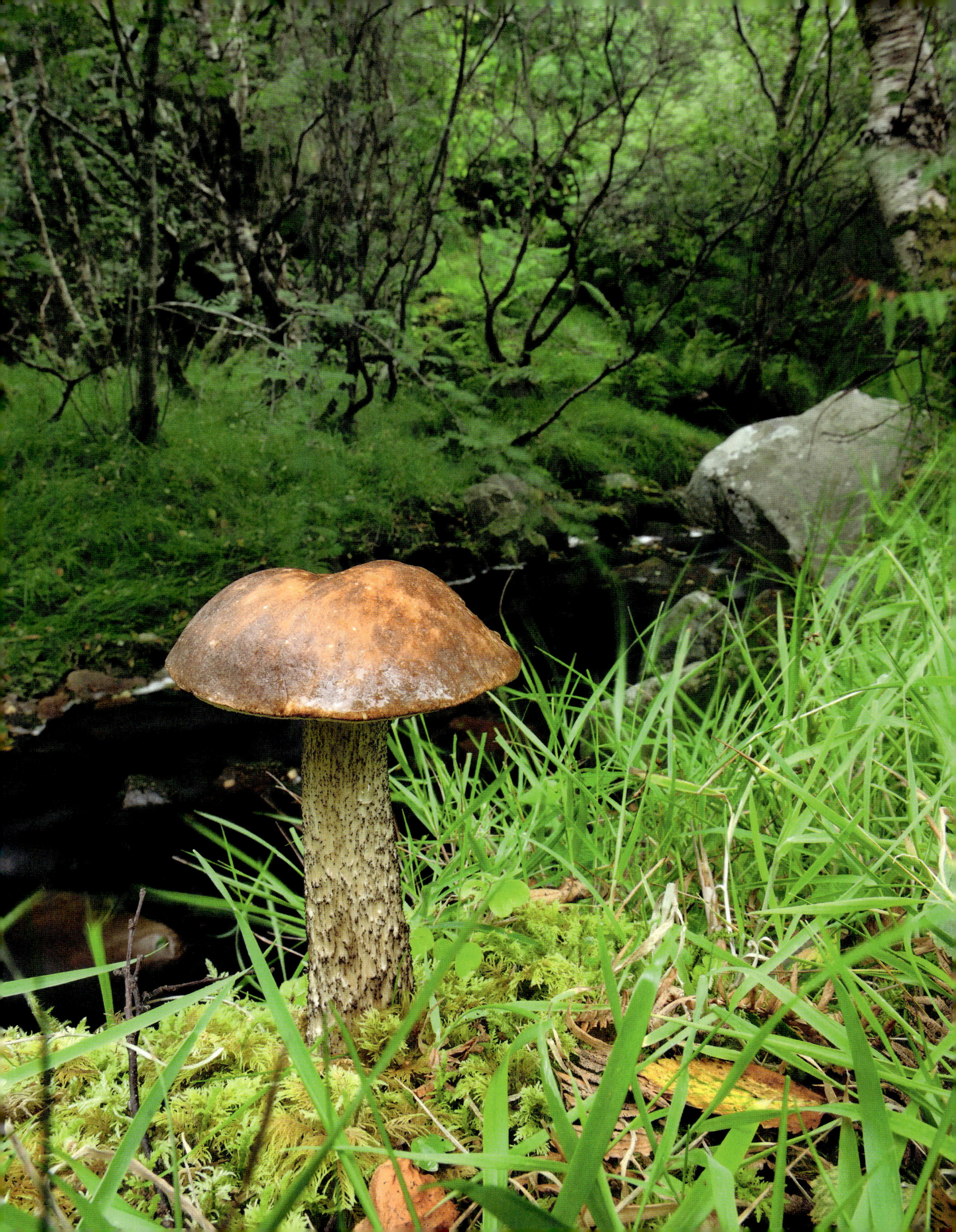

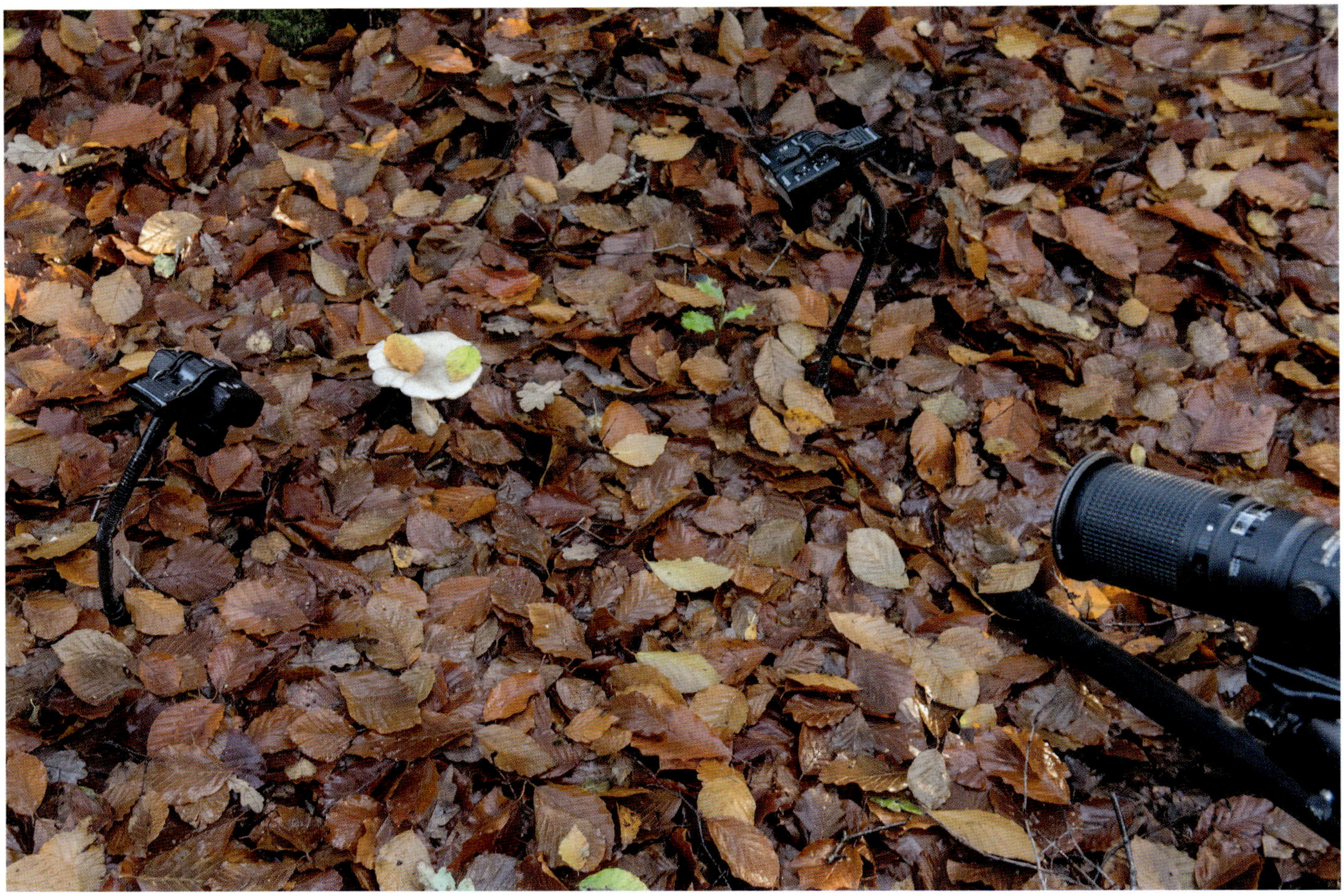

36.15 ~ Custom-designed flash spikes with flash units in place. They are controlled from the commander unit on the camera

particular lighting effect, or to darken an untidy background. Switching to manual and altering the ambient to flash ratio allows the background to appear darker and less obtrusive. I normally position the flash units 'off camera', on flexible spikes, which I designed (see page 88); this allows me to place them in any position I choose. Each unit can be programmed individually to create a particular effect.

The majority of my images of fungi are shot with a Nikon 200mm macro, but I will also use a 24mm–70mm or the 24mm PCE and occasionally a 15mm fisheye. These lenses are useful for placing subjects within the context of their environment. When space permits, the 200mm is a more comfortable lens to work with, and the rotating tripod collar allows a smooth transition from horizontal to the vertical format without the need to refocus or remove the camera from the tripod head. I also use a 300mm lens in combination with extension tubes when the background is a bit chaotic, and when I want to create a softer overall look to the image.

If you are serious about photographing fungi, then you really need to use a tripod. One that is capable of working at ground level since many of your subjects will only be a few inches above it. A beanbag or a ground spike with a platform is also useful when you need to position the camera body flat on the ground. Switching to Live View or using a right angle finder is an easier option when working at ground level. It's less awkward than lying on your chest and cranking your neck at right angles to look into the viewfinder. It is also worth keeping a small brush for cleaning dirt and bits of debris off the mushroom cap and stem, it saves time having to clone them out during post-production.

Exposure times, especially in shaded areas, frequently run well into seconds; even longer in some situations so working with a remote release is essential. Not all species grow in ideal locations, but it is important to record them as you find them rather than trying to contrive an artificial setting that will be obvious to anyone with knowledge on the subject. I don't use filters on a regular basis, but a polarising filter is useful when it has been raining and helps remove reflections and increases colour saturation.

Sunlight is another factor to consider as it can cause harsh shadows on the subject or a dappled appearance in the background. These conditions are best dealt with by using fill-in flash or a large diffuser, which produces a more balanced background. Sometimes using a longer lens and changing your viewpoint will also eliminate high contrast elements.

Project Planning

Fungi Development

Capturing the emergence sequence of a species, or photographing different aspects of its development make interesting case studies. Capturing spore release in puffball fungi is another popular approach.

Abstracts

The underside of many species have a complex network of gill arrangements in different configurations. These net-like structures often make for interesting abstracts, see page 274.

PHOTOGRAPHIC TIPS

- Visit local woodland sites in your area in late summer, especially a few days after rain. The warm wet conditions often encourage a fresh emergence.
- Many natural history societies have fungal forays during the early autumn. Most welcome newcomers and they often have some experienced fungi photographers. It is worth joining these field excursions; you can pick up a lot of hints and tips.
- Many fungi emerge quickly; it is wise to photograph them as you find them since they can be damaged or eaten virtually overnight.
- Don't overdo it with the gardening, it will be obvious to an experienced photographer.
- Avoid subjects that are in very bright contrasting positions.
- Shoot from a tripod and use a remote release.
- Pay attention to the background behind your subject.
- Explore the subject first from several angles before you set up your tripod.
- It's a good idea to keep a notebook of locations and dates so you can return in the future.
- Use Live View in situations where the light is inadequate to assist with framing and focusing.
- Use a polarising filter to help reduce reflections on caps after rain.

Resources

FURTHER READING

Bon, M. *The Mushrooms and Toadstools of Britain and North-western Europe*. Hodder & Stoughton.

Buczacki, S. *Collins Fungi Guide*. Collins.

Grünert, H. & Grünert, R. *Field Guide to Mushrooms of Britain and Europe*. Crowood Press.

Lockwood, T. F. *Treasures from the Kingdom of Fungi*. Privately published, Taylor F. Lockwood.

O'Reilly, P. *Fascinated by Fungi*. First Nature.

Phillips, R. *Mushrooms of Great Britain & Europe*. Pan Books Ltd.

Phillips, R. *Mushrooms of North America*. Little, Brown & Co.

WEBSITES

British Mycological Society: www.britmycolsoc.org.uk

European Mycological Association: www.euromould.org/index.htm

North American Mycological Association: www.namyco.org

Northern Ireland Fungus Group: www.nifg.org.uk/home.htm

Rogers Mushrooms: www.rogersmushroomsapp.com

Taylor Lockwood: www.fungiphoto.com/index.html

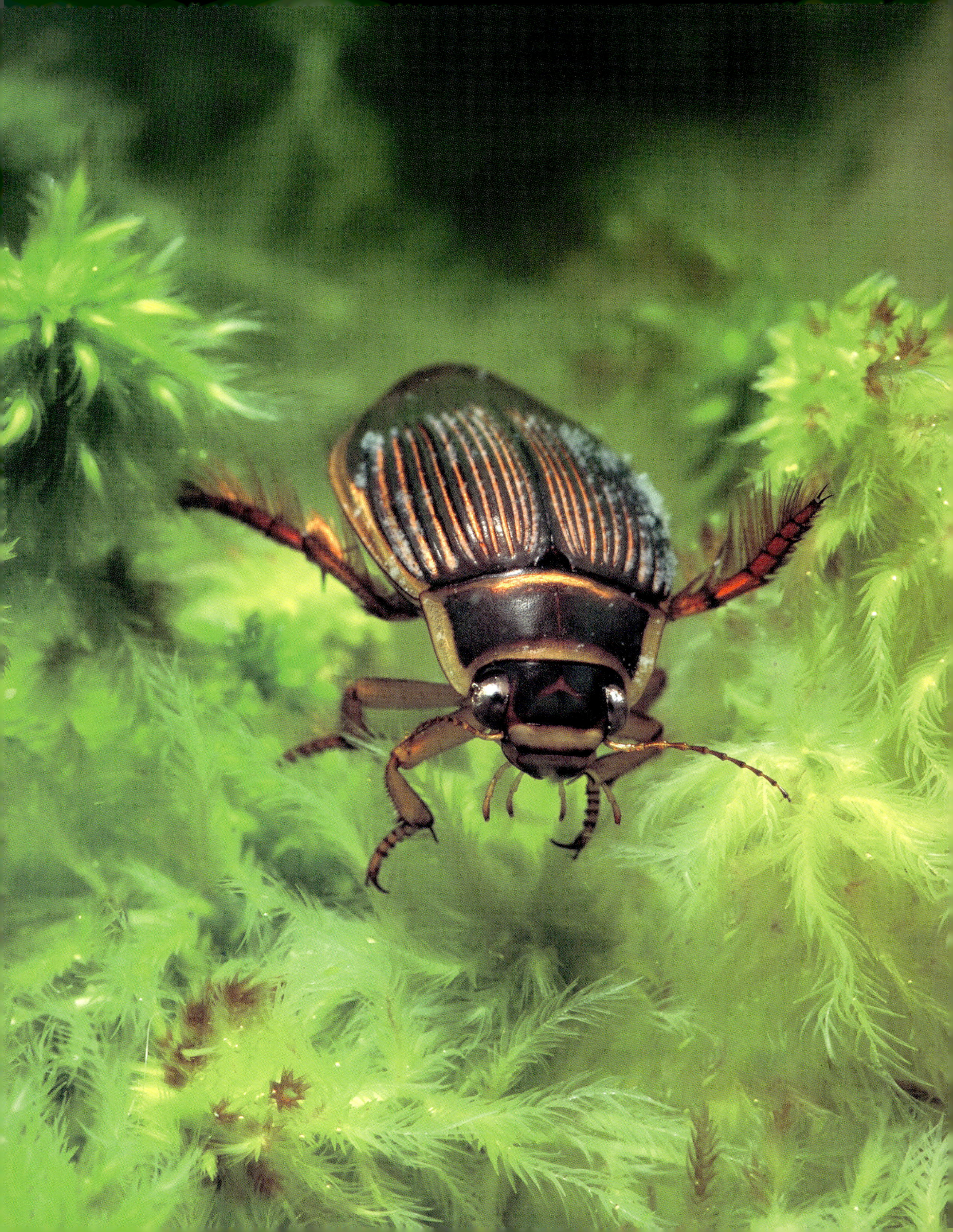

THIRTY SEVEN

Life in Freshwater

The Aquatic Environment

Introduction

Aquatic photography has always been seen as a minority interest among the macro fraternity when compared to flowers and insects. One of the primary reasons is the fact that it requires a lot more initial preparation than photographing terrestrial subjects. Aquariums need to be constructed, sets created and species introduced before the commencement of any photography. To produce an acceptable standard of images requires time and, most importantly, a rudimentary knowledge and understanding of the subject's habits and behaviour. Another equally important reason is their clandestine practices and in many cases their small size. Aquatic invertebrates are also less often seen since most of their time is spent below the surface in rivers and lakes. Despite their secretive nature, they are important indicators of the health and well-being of our freshwater ecosystems and of course essential to our own survival.

Proper preparation is essential if you want to obtain images that reflect their behaviour and charm. Although it may seem daunting at the beginning, it is a relatively straightforward process once you have everything in place. Researching suitable locations is the first priority. A quick search of your own area will reveal some freshwater habitats, and these are a good place to start. Even a quick sample of the site with a net will give you an indication of what creatures live there. It can be practised throughout the year, or at quieter periods when other subjects are long gone.

// FACING PAGE //

37.1 ~ Diving Beetle *Dytiscus semisulcatus*
↳ Nikon D3X, 105mm micro Nikkor, 1/60sec at f/11, flash, ISO 200.

Planning and Preparation

It is a good idea from the start not be over ambitious. It's better to confine yourself initially to relatively easy subjects until you become familiar with your setup. I have several aquarium tanks in different sizes to accommodate a range of subjects in freshwater and the marine environment. Standard aquarium tanks are not ideally suited for close-up photography and require some modifications. The glass is usually quite thick, which affects the clarity especially when photographing at higher magnifications, and especially when the subject is resting well back from the front glass. If you are using purchased tanks, then I would remove one of the glass sides and replace it with finer picture glass. An aquarium size of around 25cm x 20cm is fine for average sized

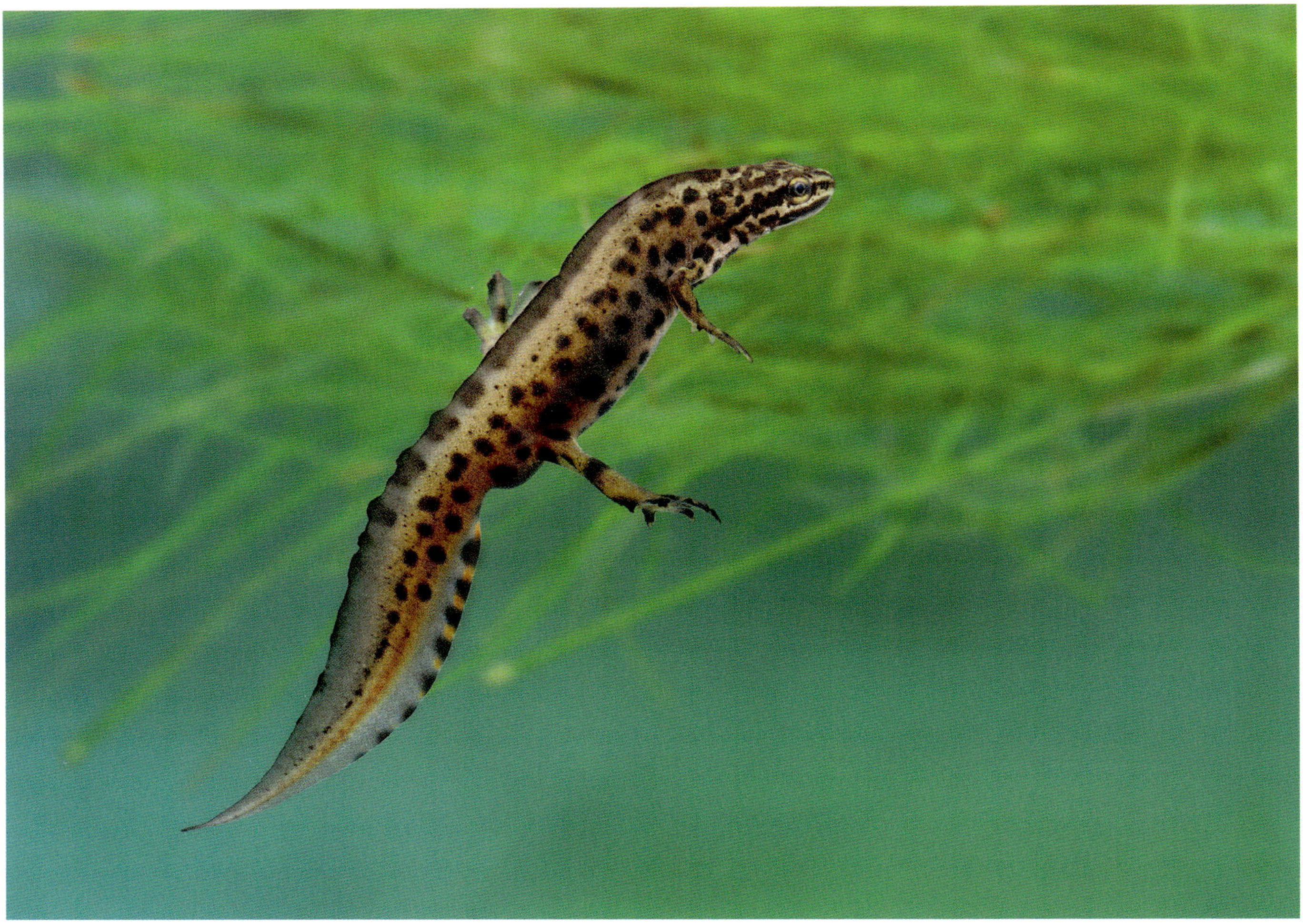

37.2 ~ **Smooth Newt** *Triturus vulgaris*
When working with aquatic subjects have everything set up in advance. Keep your sessions short as they are easily stressed. Early spring is a good time for newt photography. Males of many species take on bright colouring.

↳ Nikon D810, 105mm micro Nikkor, 1/60sec at f/11, flash, ISO 100.

subjects such as newts and small fish. Other creatures such as dragonfly and damselfly larvae work best in a smaller unit around 15cm x 10cm. I also have an aquarium tank constructed out of white Perspex for high key images (see 'The Outdoor Field Studio', page 113). I have a few micro aquariums for tiny creatures which are constructed from very fine optical glass.

I prefer to make my own aquarium tanks as I can control the size, height and depth. Any local hardware shop will cut glass to whatever dimensions you require. You also need to get a separate piece of glass cut, which will fit inside the tank and sit about 3cm above the maximum height of the tank; this will be useful for confining your subject to a particular area and keep it from

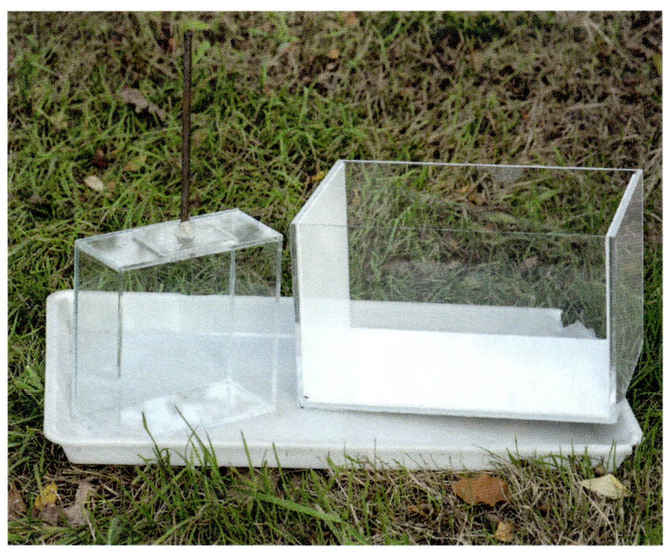

37.3 ~ **Glass aquarium tanks**
I have constructed a range of different sized tanks for photographing a range of subjects.

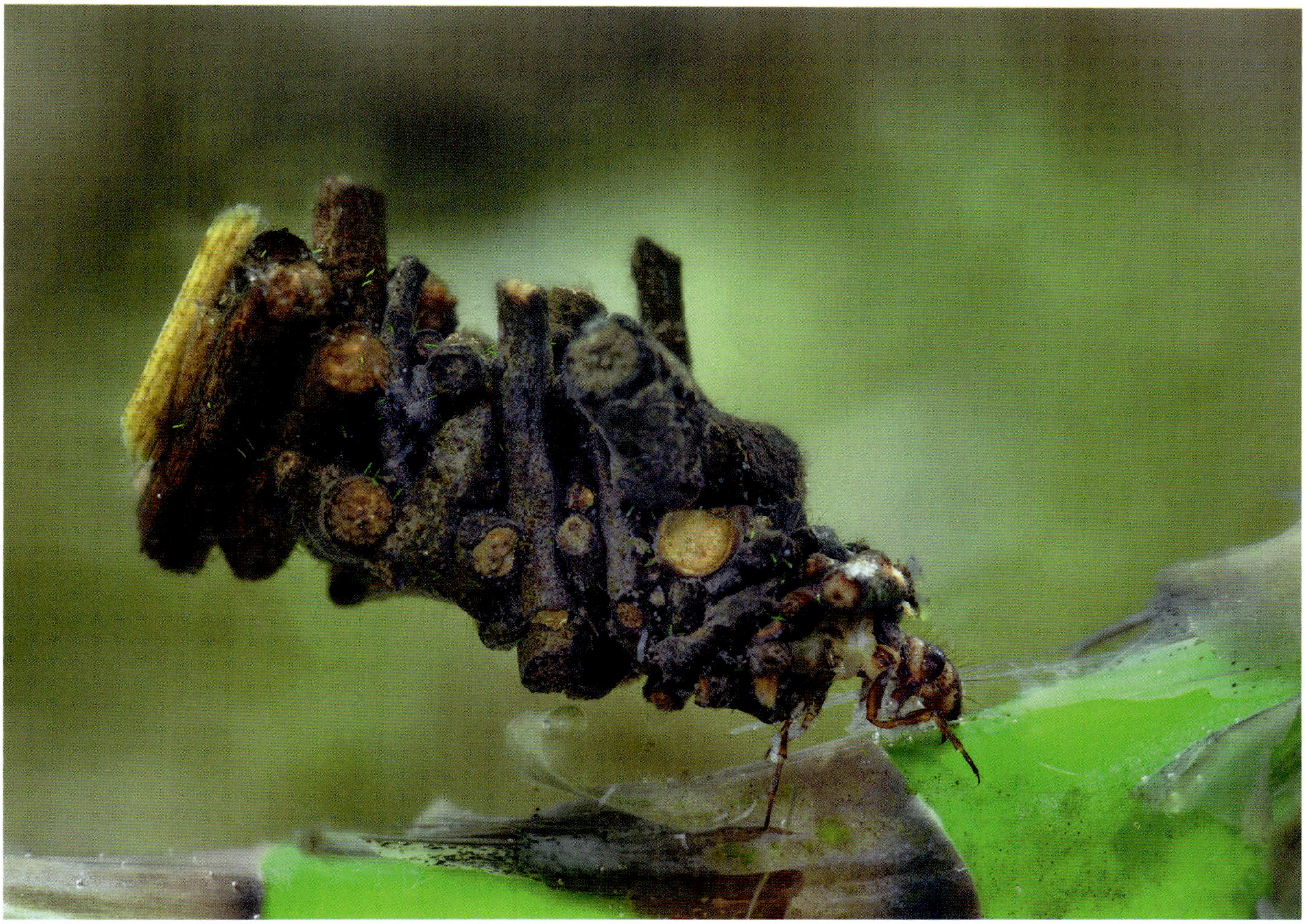

37.4 ~ **Caddisfly larva**
These small insects belong to the order Trichoptera which are related to moths. You can find them in lakes and rivers etc. They live inside protective cases and are excellent indicators for pollution. Their diversity makes them interesting subjects for photography.

↘ Nikon D810, 105mm micro Nikkor, 1/60sec at f/16, flash, ISO 100.

straying into your background props. You can make the back side longer, that way you avoid the junction lines at the sides of the aquarium. I have both designs so I can pick and choose depending on the size and behaviour of the subject. Clear silicone is ideal for cementing the various sides together. Micro aquariums can be constructed out of very fine glass which is secured between a u-shaped acrylic block about 2cm square. When photographing larger creatures such as fish I use a one-meter-long aquarium unit. I prefer to buy these and make the necessary modifications. They need to be constructed from 5mm glass on the base and sides. I replace the front side with strengthened 3mm glass since the aquarium needs to be fairly rugged when used at the water's edge.

Setting up Your Tank

It is wise to try and emulate the substrate and conditions as near as possible. Your subjects are more likely to behave naturally in an environment they are comfortable in. Keep all of your weeds and stones in a separate container; this will reduce air bubbles that normally occur when immersing dry stones and cut weeds into water. Choose the size of your props carefully. You don't want to have large stones that your subject can quickly disappear under, otherwise you will be continually disturbing the water trying to encourage it back into the frame. Keep your setup simple and try to arrange your props in a way that reduces the options your subject has to hide. It's important to wash all of your material thoroughly

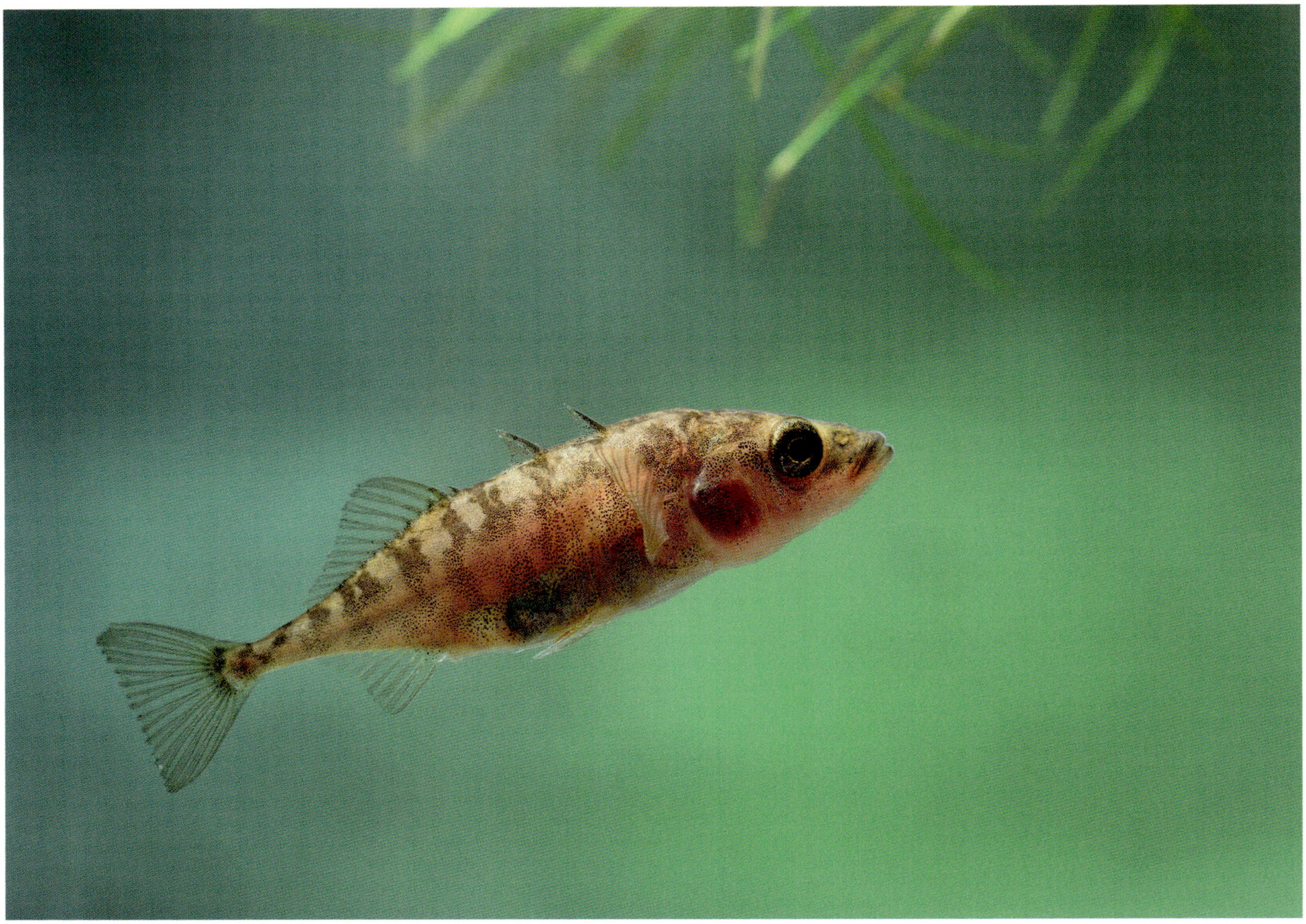

37.5 ~ **Three-spined Stickleback** *Gasterosteus aculeatus*
Keep fish separate and give them time to settle, you will obtain a more natural look to your images. Males of this species assume a red colouration during the breeding season.

↪ Nikon D810, 105mm micro Nikkor, 1/60sec at f/16, flash, ISO 100.

and carefully introduce the water into the tank slowly. You don't want to upset the props and create a plethora of particles floating about, which your flash will almost certainly pick up. Stones can also be used to anchor weeds in place or use heavy gauge foil or wire. Once the props are in place, you need to consider the background. Some photographers keep it black or blue, but I prefer to use greens and browns since they reflect the natural environment. Placing the background tight against the back glass can sometimes cause reflections. Putting it inside the tank eliminates the problem. I do vary it between subjects, otherwise all of your images will have a repetitive look to them. Keep your setup as authentic as possible. I know this is not always possible for a number of reasons but keep it in mind that a subject is more likely to be accommodating if you encourage it on to something that it may naturally rest on.

Filtration

The water that your subjects naturally occur in is not clear enough for photography, especially for small creatures. You can use mains water, but it should be boiled first and left to stand overnight. An alternative is rainwater which you can collect in a container, but you need to do this in advance. Use a filter to remove some of the particles and other micro debris from it otherwise when magnified they will create multiple distracting highlights when illuminated against a dark background. I also filter the water for a short while before starting the session.

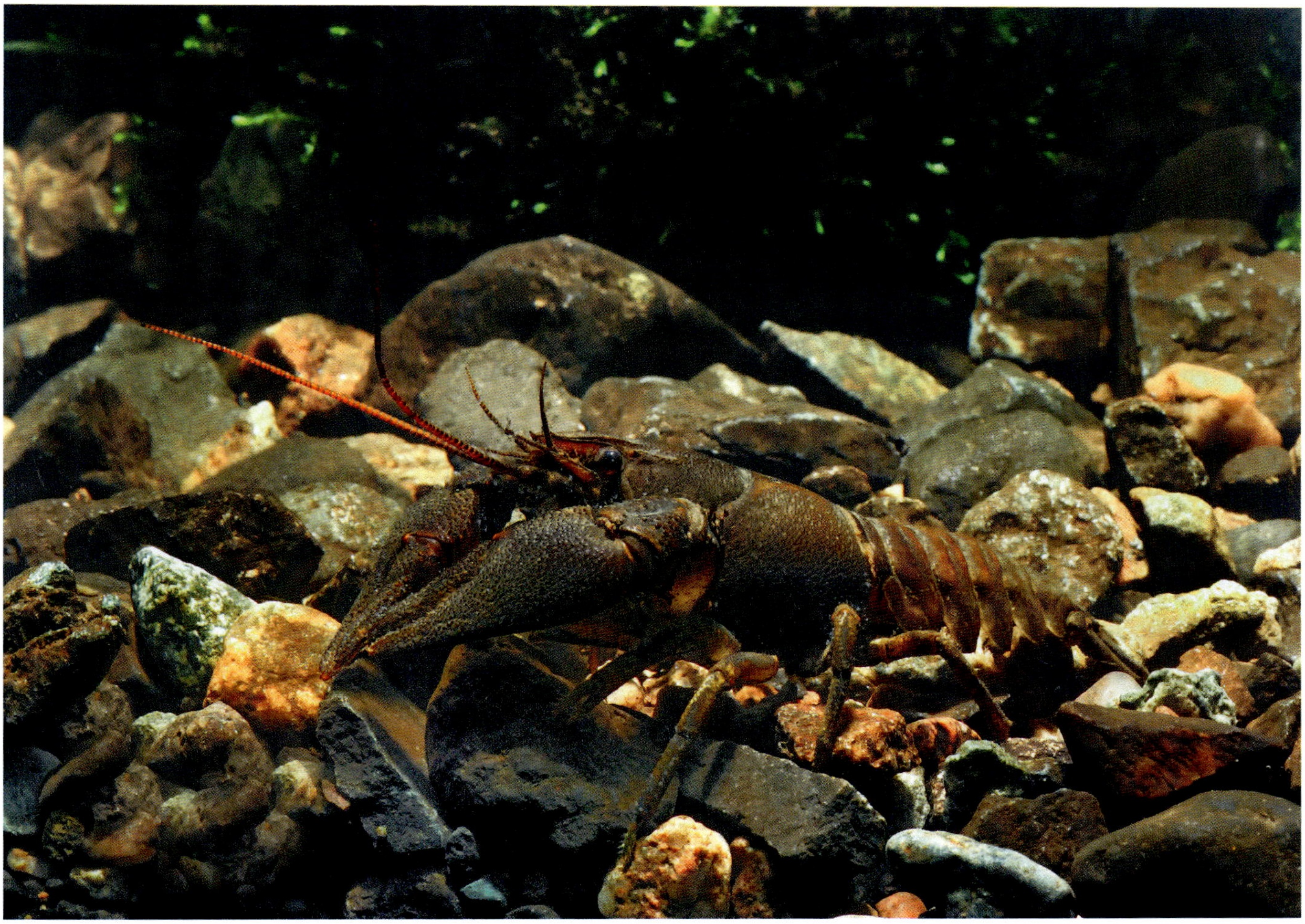

37.6 ~ **Freshwater Crayfish** *Austropotamobius pallipes*
Working *in situ* is always challenging. The tank was positioned near the edge of the stream and the substrate collected and placed on the bottom of the tank in a similar way.

↳ Nikon D2X, 105mm micro Nikkor, 1/60sec at f/16, flash, ISO 200.

Collecting Subjects

The best place to begin your search is your local river or pond. Use two separate containers, one for specimens and the other for any additional props that might be needed. A small, white plastic tray is necessary to examine the contents of your net. A general net is not that suitable for trawling the bottom of a river or the submerged bankside vegetation. Most of these are too weak, or the mesh size is too coarse. You can buy special nets in a range of mesh sizes from a local entomological store that are especially strengthened for this type of work. Sweeping the stones and immersed bankside vegetation at the edge of the river or pond will produce a good range of subject material, such as damselfly larvae, small fish, spiders, mayfly nymphs, snails and some beetles. Sampling for species in fast-flowing water requires a slightly different approach. Position the net into the flow when lifting stones and debris. Any organisms will get washed into your net which you can examine on your white acrylic tray. Examine specimens carefully and only keep a couple of those that are perfect. Don't keep all of your subjects in a single bucket, segregate any predators from the rest into other containers, otherwise they will eat or damage other species.

Many of the creatures if taken from ponds or slow-moving stretches of a stream or river will survive for quite a while if they are not overcrowded. Keep them cool, out of direct sunlight and segregate as many as possible. Inserting a small aeration pump into the container will increase the circulation of oxygen and keep your inhabitants more comfortable. Organisms collected from the fast flowing parts of rivers which are highly oxygenated are much more sensitive to temperature changes and reduced oxygen levels. They can die quickly if subjected to extreme variations in temperature and oxygen depletion.

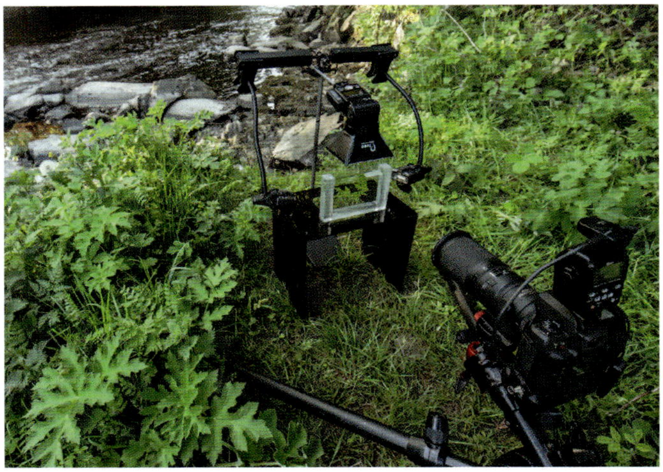

37.7 ~ **Mobile field studio**
My typical setup for photographing small aquatic invertebrates *in situ*. I use small micro aquarium tanks made up with a u-shaped acrylic block and optically fine glass.

Mobile Field Studio

Many of the suggestions outlined here apply equally in the marine chapter. I prefer to photograph most of the subjects at the collection site or in the boot of my jeep which acts as a mobile studio, that way I can quickly return subjects back when finished. Working with extremely sensitive creatures, for example fish, it's better to set up your aquarium at the river's edge or as close as possible. Photographing in a controlled environment can often be hit or miss, especially with fish. The problem with most fish is when you remove them from their natural environment they often exhibit signs of stress and behavioural changes. Dropped fins are one of the most visible signs, but setting up your aquarium at the water's edge has many advantages. You have instant access to the natural substrate and water, therefore, keeping environmental change to a minimum. The water will be at a similar temperature, which will reduce the initial stress on subjects. No matter how much preparation you do, one can never predict how the subject will react once introduced into the aquarium environment. From experience, fish can be extremely unpredictable. However, I have found that working with fish *in situ* and making use of the natural substrate to hand has produced better results. If working outdoors with fish, you need to be mindful of your movements in front of the glass, as they are easily spooked. Before commencing any photography, let them settle for a while in a holding bucket before transferring them into the aquarium. A nervous fish can not only wreck your setup in a few moments but can also leap out of your aquarium; I have had this happen on a couple of occasions with trout.

Electrofishing is a great way of getting a range of species and at the appropriate size. Don't select specimens that are too large as they can damage your carefully arranged setup. To get the fish to face the correct direction I had someone hold the irrigation pump on the surface in a particular direction, the fish will then orientate itself into the flow. This was the easiest way to control the subject's position within the tank.

Fieldcraft

Photographic Approach

Before commencing photography, it's a good idea to allow the aquarium to settle for a short while. Tiny air bubbles often appear on the inside of the glass. These can be removed with a small brush. I use flash for the majority of my photographs in the field, but occasionally I balance it with daylight depending on the conditions, the subject and the effect I want to achieve.

I light my tank with two small portable LED lights mounted on flexible goosenecks; this makes it easier to focus if the tank is setup in the dark interior of the jeep. I use a Nikon SB800 overhead with a diffuser. My SB-R200 flash units are positioned either side of the tank which illuminate the subject from the side. Experimenting with your lights will allow you to evaluate alternative lighting positions and their effects. Surface reflections on the front glass can be removed with a black card secured to the front of the lens with an old filter ring. A medium telephoto macro around 105mm is fine for most aquarium photography, but I also use a 200mm macro and 1.7X converter on the 105mm macro when I need magnifications above 1:1. I work from a tripod and shoot mainly in manual, but switch to autofocus if I'm tracking a moving fish. Before commencing any photography session, it's a good idea to let your subject settle for a while before you begin your session. Keep your subjects in the same environment as your tank to prevent significant temperature changes between the holding container and

// THIS PAGE ~ TOP //

37.8 ~ Brown Trout
Salmo trutta
These fish are always feisty and challenging. Don't select too large a fish and let it settle in a holding container before introducing it into the tank.

↘ Nikon D3X, 105mm micro Nikkor, 1/60sec at f/16, flash, ISO 100.

// THIS PAGE ~ BOTTOM //

37.9 ~ Perch
Perca fluviatilis
This species is difficult to photograph in controlled conditions. It tends to drop its fins, which looks unnatural. Working at the river's edge with the same substrate and water made a difference.

↘ Nikon D3X, 105mm micro Nikkor, 1/60sec at f/16, flash, ISO 100.

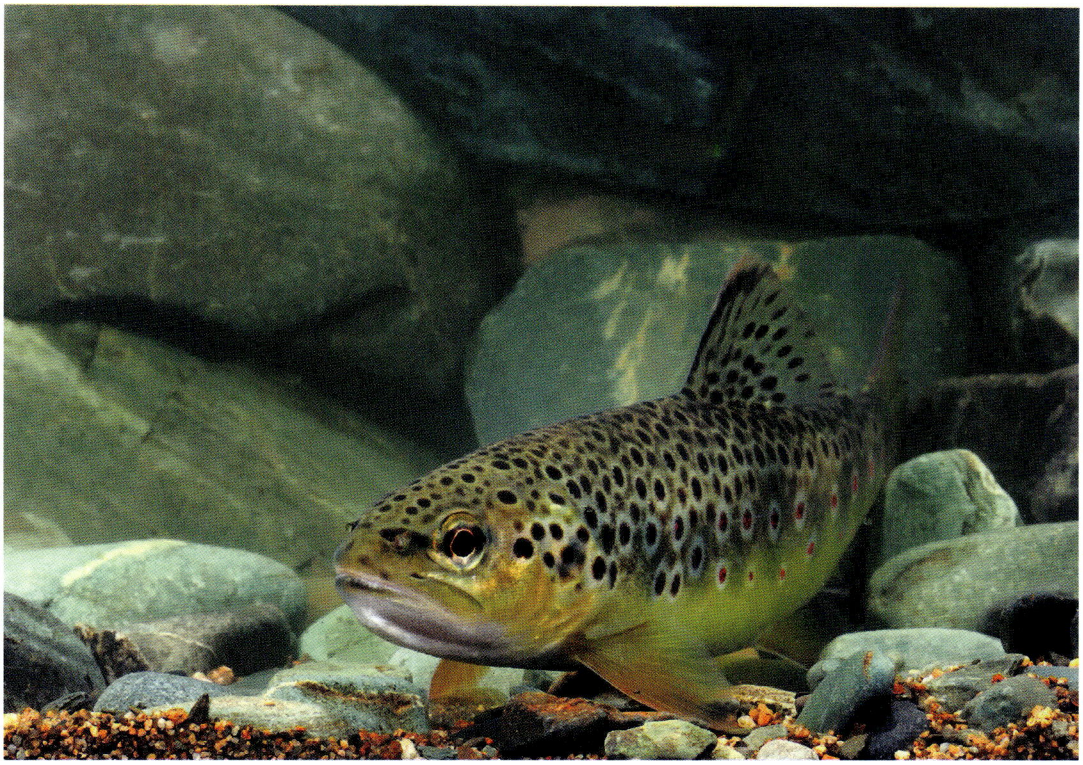

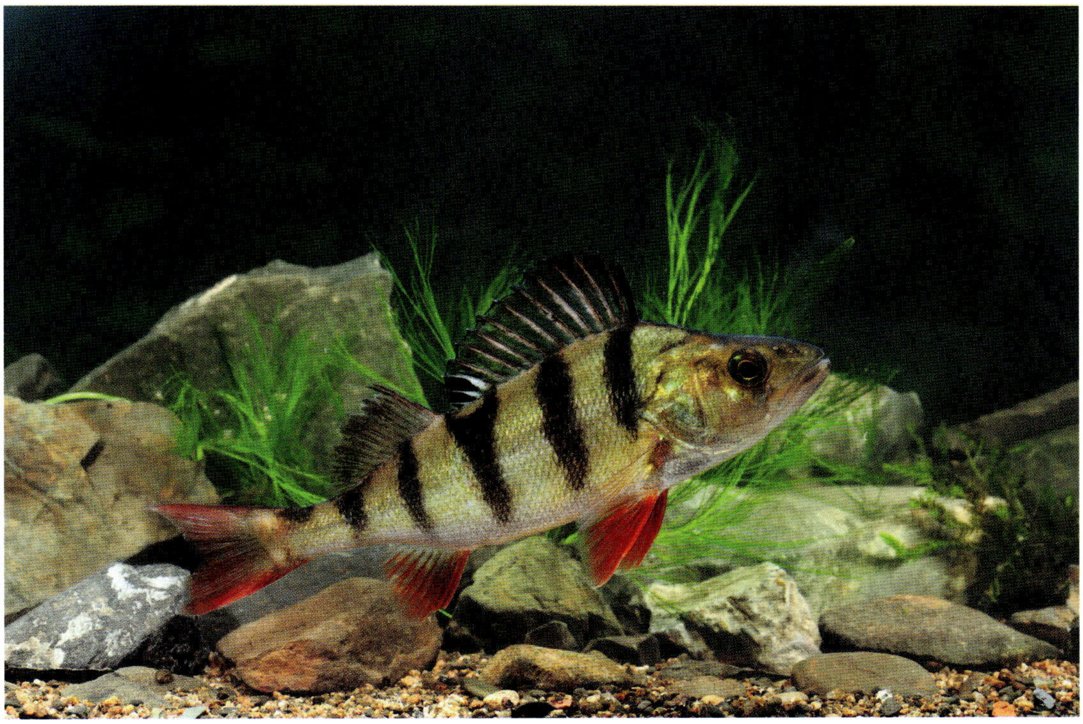

the aquarium. Remember also that the water temperature can heat up rapidly, I use ice cubes in smaller tanks to help keep the temperature from rising too quickly. Make sure your tank is longer than the largest subject you intend to photograph. Or, use one with a longer back to reduce the appearance of corners; this will give you some compositional latitude. Otherwise, you will be forced to try to keep the subject in the middle. It's also a good idea to restrict your subject to the front section of the tank using the glass insert; this makes it easier to keep track of where it is and keeps the disturbance to the background to a minimum. Remember, the subject's well-being should be paramount so keep your session short. Any creature that is under stress is less likely to behave naturally so don't overwork them. Sometimes a break for a while is the best approach.

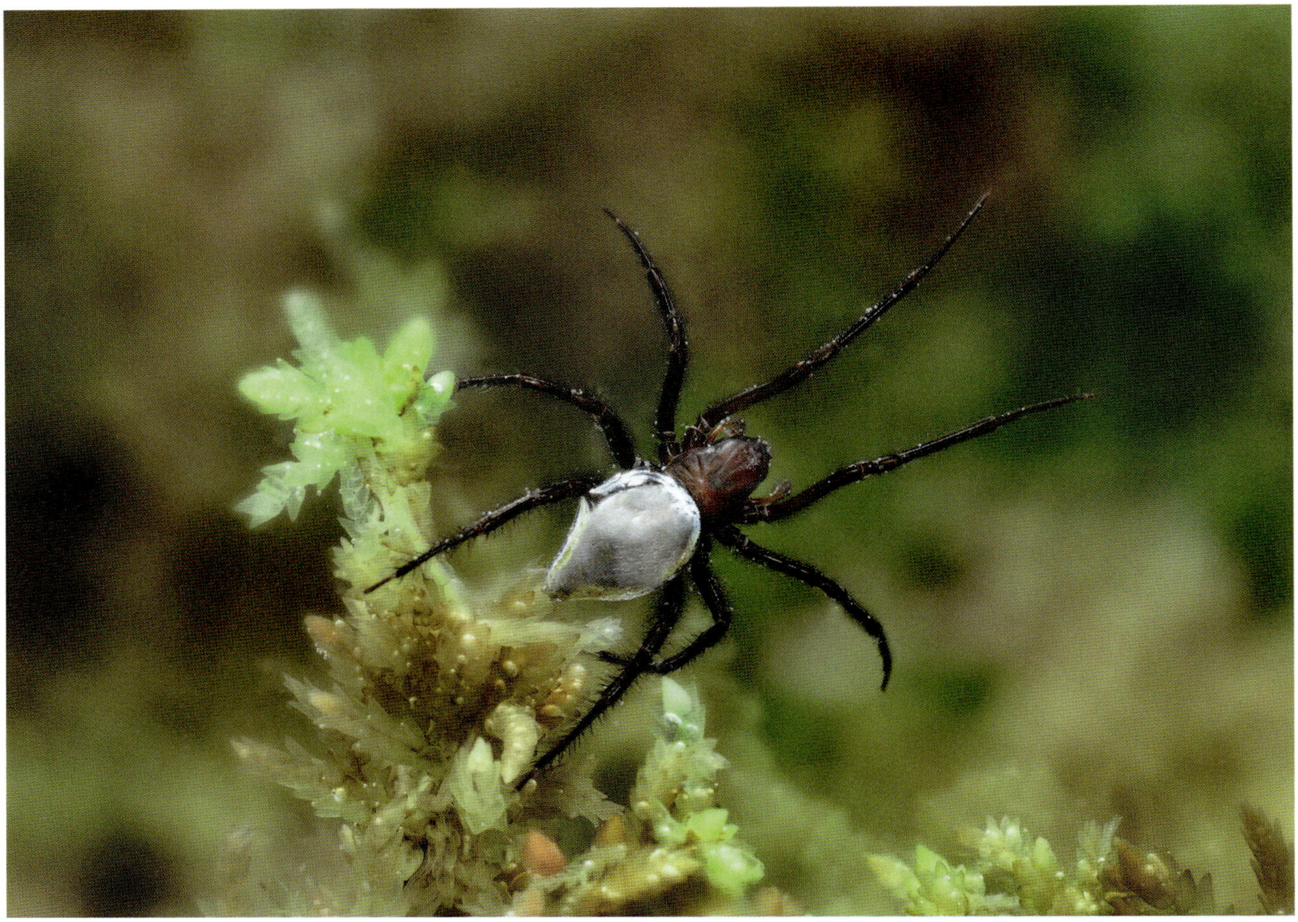

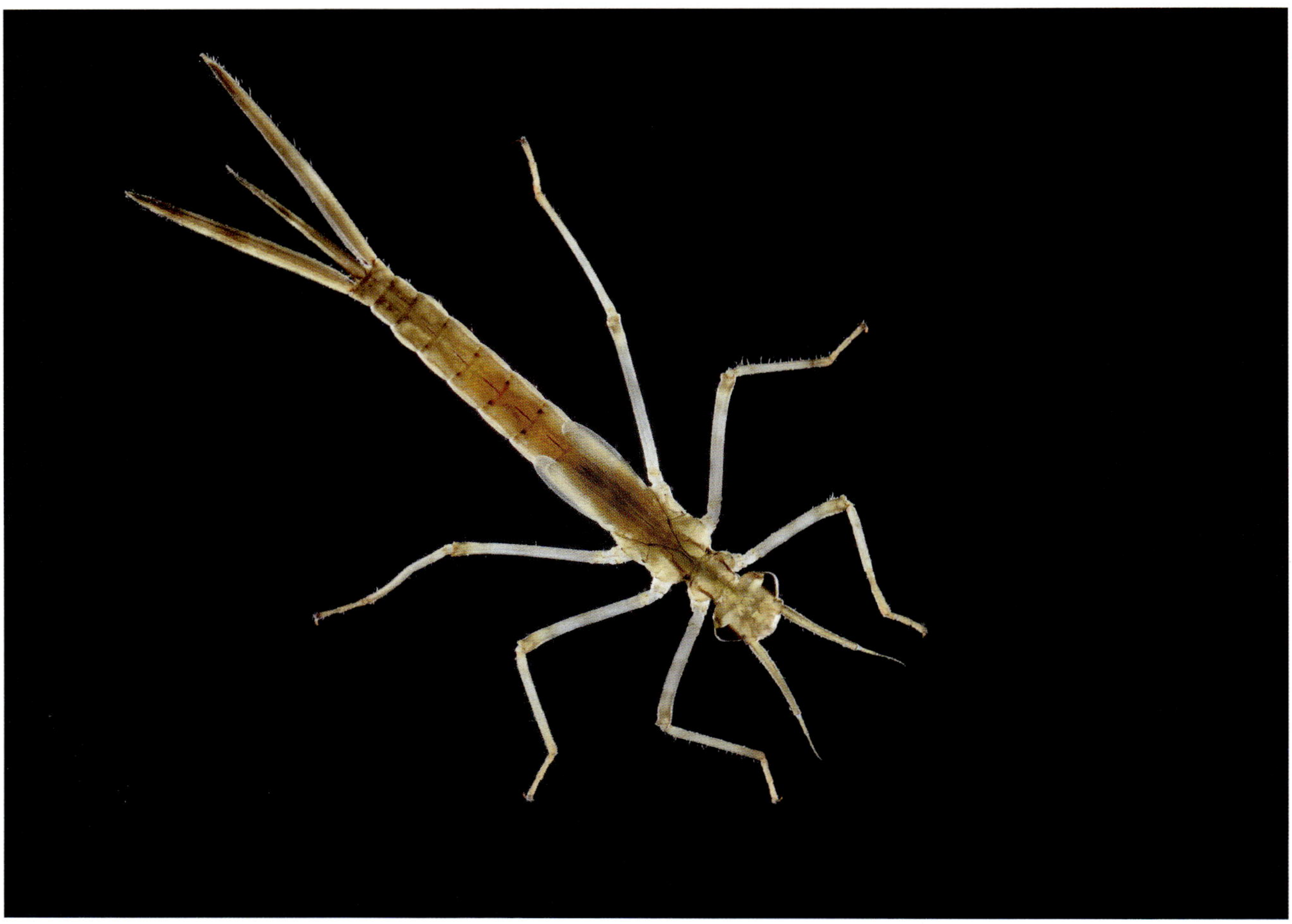

Dark-Field Illumination

Once you have obtained your photographs using conventional lighting techniques, you might want to consider an alternate way of illustrating your subjects. Dark-field Lighting is a technique that originates from the world of microscopy and is used for viewing transparent or translucent subjects. It is also a useful lighting technique in the macro world. Any subject that has reasonable translucency can be illuminated using this method. The technique is particularly well suited to many aquatic and marine organisms and is easily created by placing the organism in a glass petri dish with a small amount of water. A central hole is cut out of a small table or something similar and black velvet, or card is placed below the glass. The small flash units are angled up at approximately forty-five degrees, creating a rim-lit effect around the subject. You can use LEDs in place of flash, but if your subject is moving quite a lot, then the images are likely to be blurred. Flash is the best option when using this technique. See page 90 for setup.

Project Planning

Dragonfly Larvae

Dragonfly larvae vary considerably between families. I spent seven years rearing and photographing all of the species that occur in the British Isles.

// FACING PAGE ~ TOP //

37.10 ~ **Diving Bell Spider** *Argrpneta aquatic*
A common species and the only spider in the world to live entirely underwater. It has a velvet-grey body, which when submerged traps air around it giving it the appearance of mercury.

→ Nikon D810, 105mm micro Nikkor, 1/60sec at f/16, flash, ISO 100.

// FACING PAGE ~ BOTTOM //

37.11 ~ **Banded Demoiselle** *Calopteryx splendens*
Dragonfly larvae along with many other aquatic organisms lend themselves to this technique.

→ Nikon D810, 105mm micro Nikkor, 1/60sec at f/16, flash, ISO 100.

PHOTOGRAPHIC TIPS

- Keep your session relatively short to avoid undue stress on your subjects.
- Return them back to where they came from.
- Take only what you need and not more than you can cope with in any session.
- Set up your aquarium away from direct sunlight.
- Alternate your background and change your vegetation otherwise your photos will look similar.
- Separate your subjects from your props, otherwise some of them will disappear into the stones and weeds, etc.
- When working with fish and other larger subjects consider working at the water's edge rather than bringing them home.

Resources

FURTHER READING

Angel, H. & Wolseley, P. *The Family Water Naturalist*. Michael Joseph: London.

Benvie, N. *Outdoor Photography Masterclass*. Photographer's Institute Press.

Davies, P. H. *The Complete Guide to Close-Up & Macro Photography*. David & Charles.

Hamrsky, J. *Freshwater Life*. Self Published.

Shaw, J. *Closeups in Nature (The Photographer's Guide to Techniques in the Field)*. Amphoto.

Throp, J. H. & Rodgers, D.C. *Field Guide to Freshwater Invertebrates of North America*. Academic Press.

WEBSITES

Freshwater Biological Association: www.fba.org.uk
Freshwater Life: www.blurb.com/b/6306045-freshwater-life
Landcare Research: www.landcareresearch.co.nz

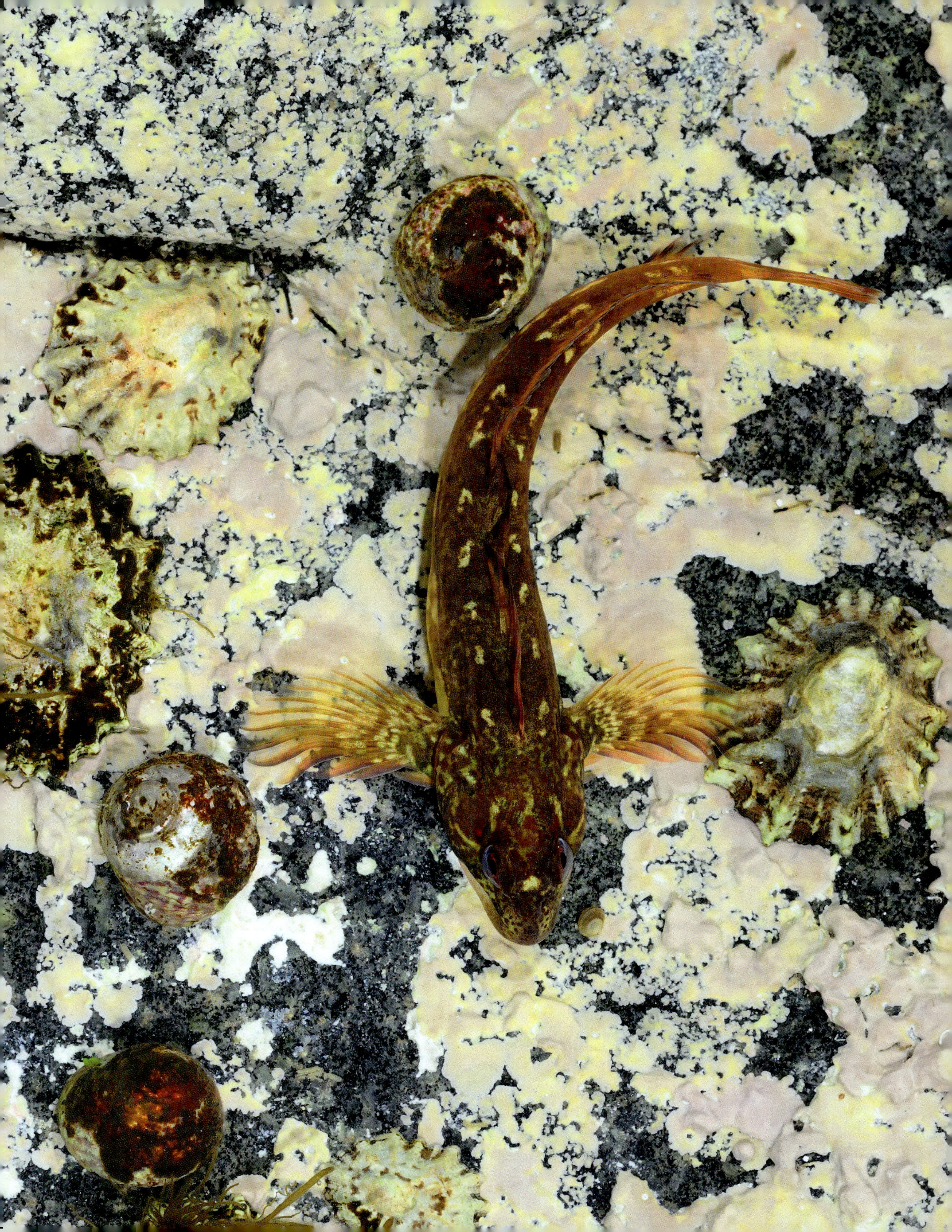

THIRTY EIGHT

Life on the Shoreline

Coastal Creatures & Rockpools

Introduction

Exploring the seashore, no matter where you live offers tremendous scope for any photographer interested in the world of close-up photography. Unlike a typical terrestrial habitat, the creatures that exist on the seashore are distinctly different than any land-based organism. Coastal habitats exist everywhere in the world from the Tropics to the Arctic. Despite its popularity as a mainstream photographic destination, the marine life on the seashore is one of the least photographed parts of this remarkable ecosystem. The diversity of habitats is amazing and they provide shelter for an astonishing number of organisms.

The interaction between the sea and the land defines the nature of the shoreline, which can be composed of rock, shingle, sand and mud; each has its charm and variety of organisms. Rocky habitats offer the most in terms of species diversity. Sheltered rocky areas tend to have a greater abundance of species than those which are more exposed. They also contain numerous micro-habitats in the shape of crevices, overhangs, gullies and boulders, offering a sanctuary for species during low tide. The type of rock and its hardness is also of importance. Soft rock erodes quickly and supports fewer species since they will constantly be on the move. Intertidal sandy habitats are more impoverished; creatures are exposed to predators and at low tide to the sun and wind. Species occupying this terrain usually bury themselves in the sand for protection and safety. Shingle beaches have less diversity, since the loose, rounded stones are mobile and unstable in rough weather, which prevents most organisms from using them. From a photographer's perspective, a rocky shoreline is far more productive even if it's more demanding photographically. The unpredictability of the weather and its ever-changing moods can make it a challenging environment to work in.

// FACING PAGE //

38.1 ~ Common Blenny *Lipophrys pholis*
One of the most commonly encountered fish on the seashore and in rock pools.

↪ Nikon D810, 105mm micro Nikkor, 1/60sec at f/16, flash, ISO 100.

Understanding Tides

Most places have two high and two low tides within a twenty-four-hour period. The area between high and low water level is called the intertidal or littoral zone. The regular way in which tides advance and recede

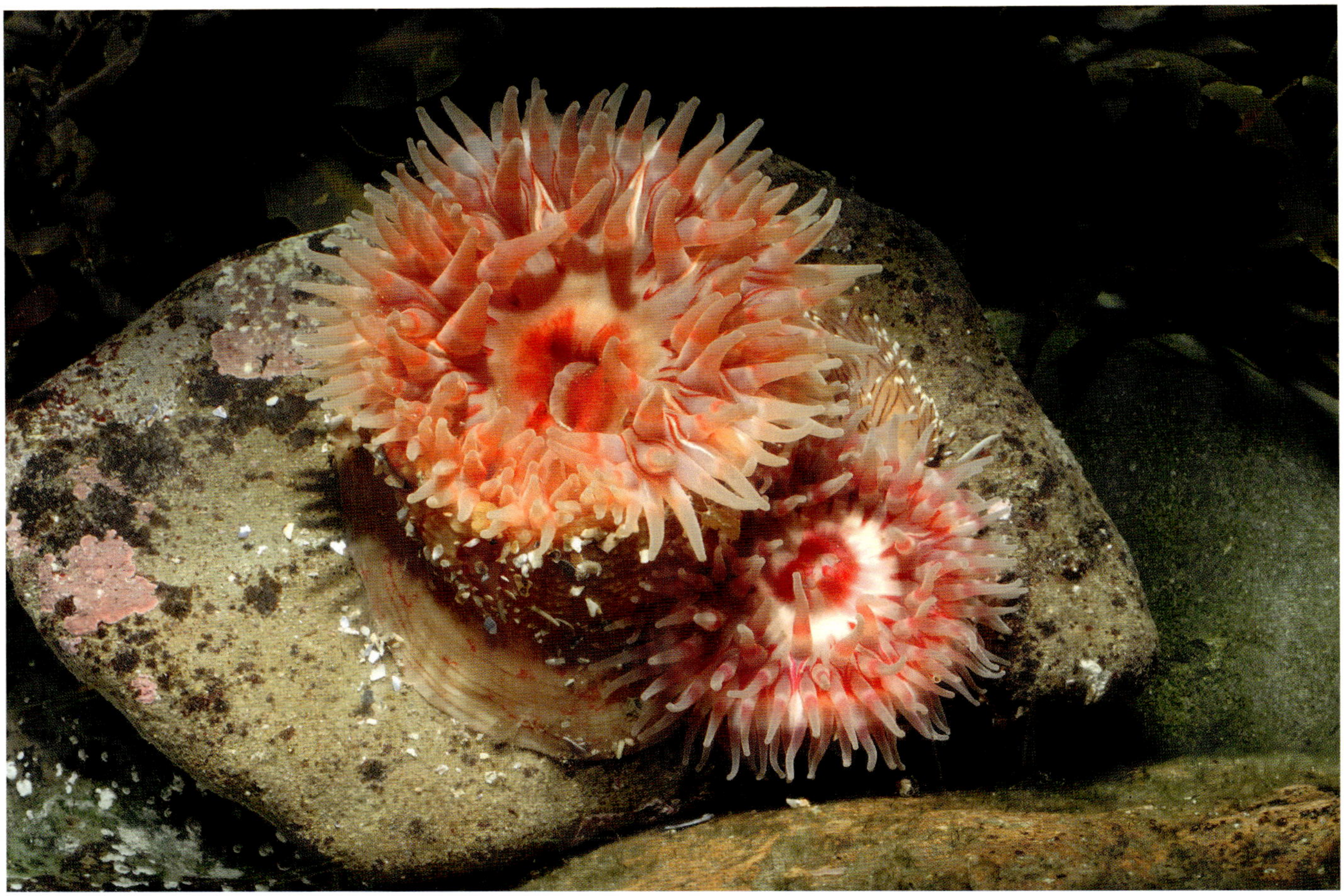

38.2 ~ **Dahlia Anenome** *Urtcina feline*
These are often found in rock pools. I raised the boulder until it was much closer to the surface which made it easier to photograph and it also reduced diffraction.

↳ Nikon D2X, 105mm micro Nikkor, 1/ sec at f/16, flash, ISO 200.

means that different parts of the shore are exposed at different times. Tides are heavily influenced by the relative position of the earth, the moon and the sun to each other, which changes on a daily basis. The most productive tides for photography are spring tides; they have the greatest variation between high and low water. Neap tides have the least variation between high and low water and are therefore less productive. Spring tides occur throughout all of the seasons and are not confined to spring, although some of the lowest tides occur during the spring and autumn equinoxes – confusing isn't it? During a large spring tide, more of the shore bottom is exposed, revealing many other animals and plants that would not normally be seen at any other time of the year. The whole tidal cycle has a controlling effect on the creatures that live on the shoreline. The animals and seaweeds which can withstand greater

// FACING PAGE ~ TOP //

38.3 ~ **Butterfish** *Pholis gunnellus*
Eel-like in appearance this species is commonly found among seaweed and under rocks. I photographed it in my mobile marine studio in the back of my jeep.

↳ Nikon D810, 105mm micro Nikkor, 1/60sec at f/16, flash, ISO 100.

// FACING PAGE ~ BOTTOM //

38.4 ~ **Common Sunstar** *Crossaster papposus*
Occasionally found in rock pools, I was fortunate to spot this large specimen in a fairly deep rock pool. I moved it along to the shallow end where it was easier to photograph.

↳ Nikon D2X, 105mm micro Nikkor, 1/60sec at f/16, flash, ISO 200.

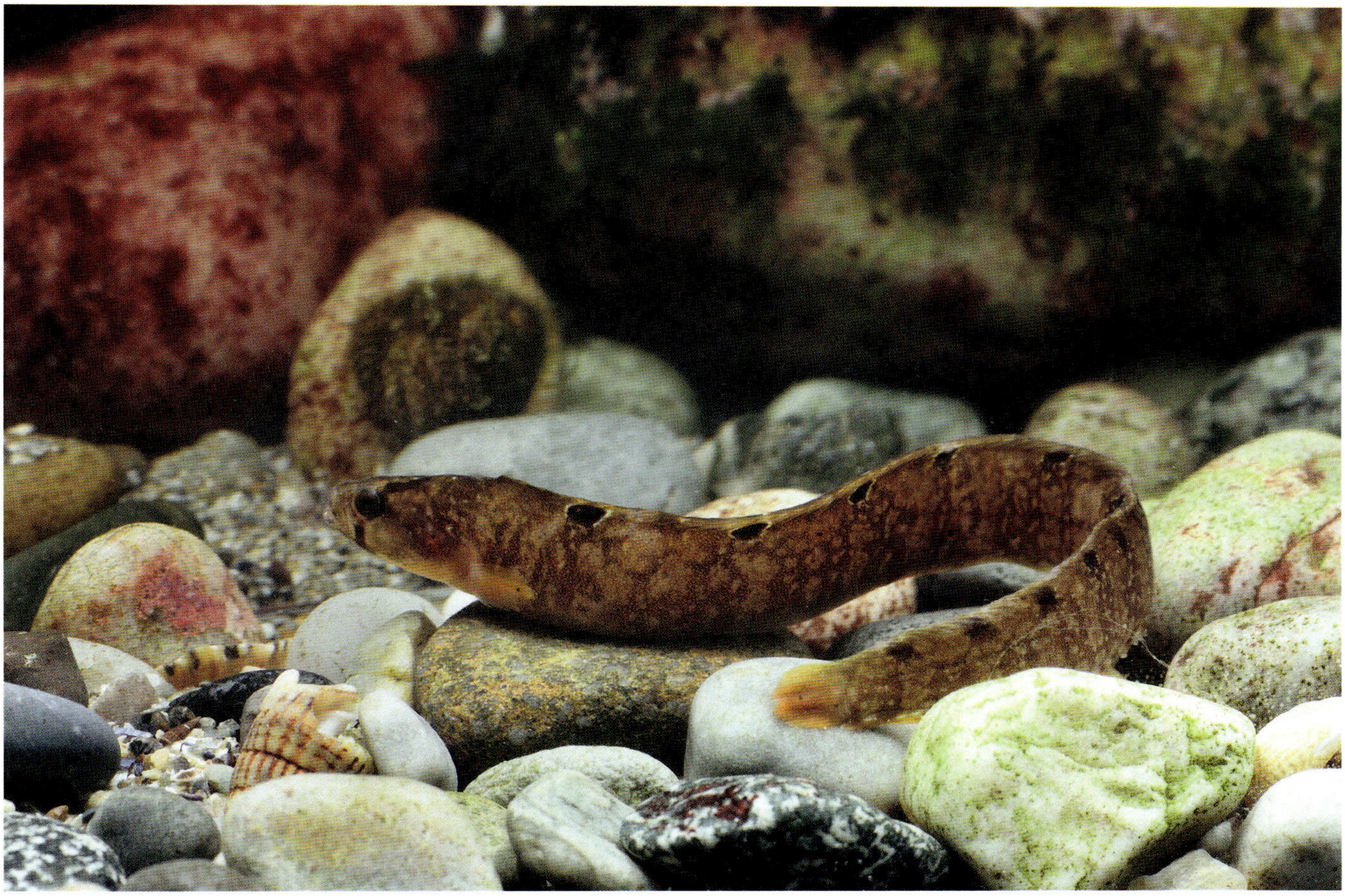

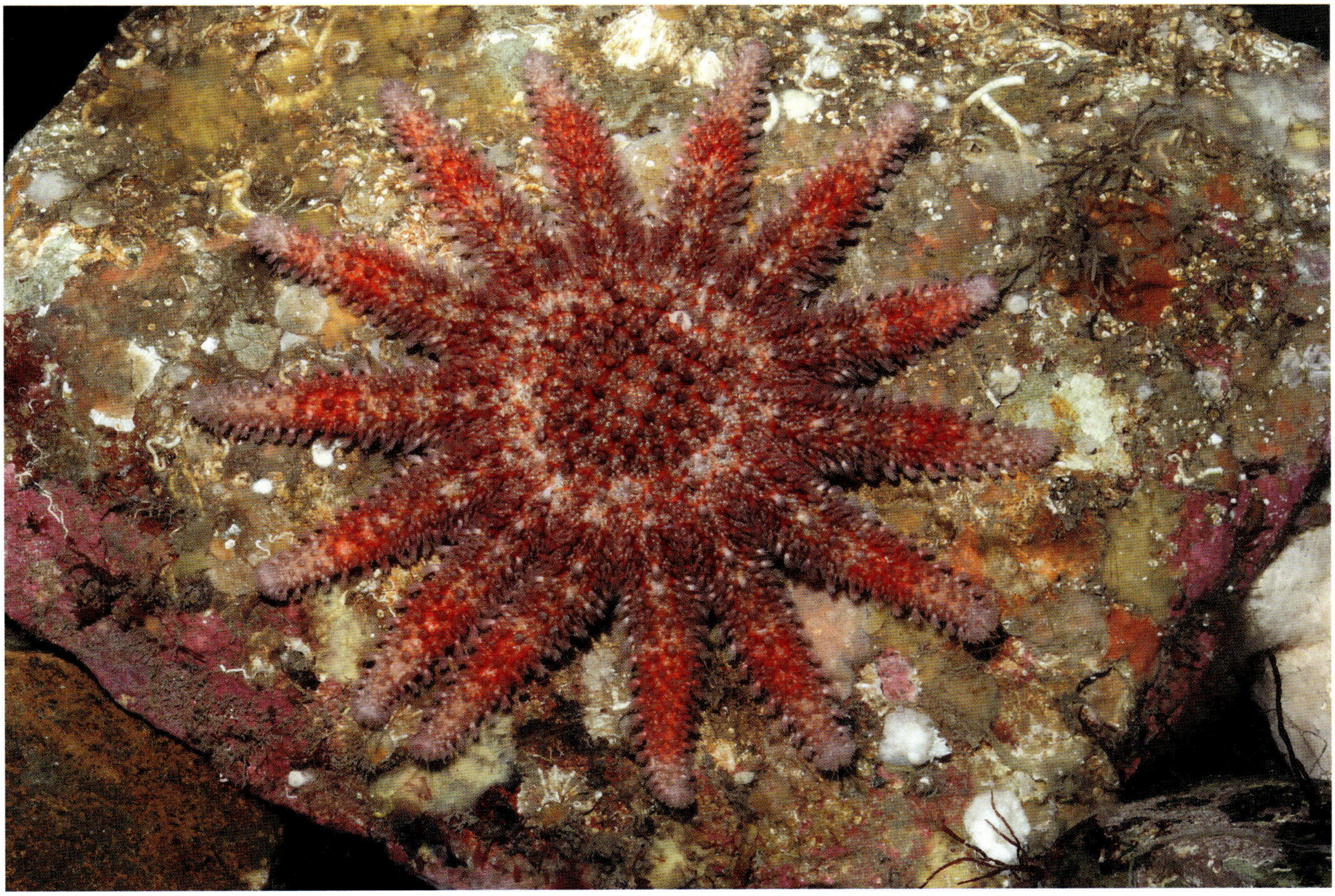

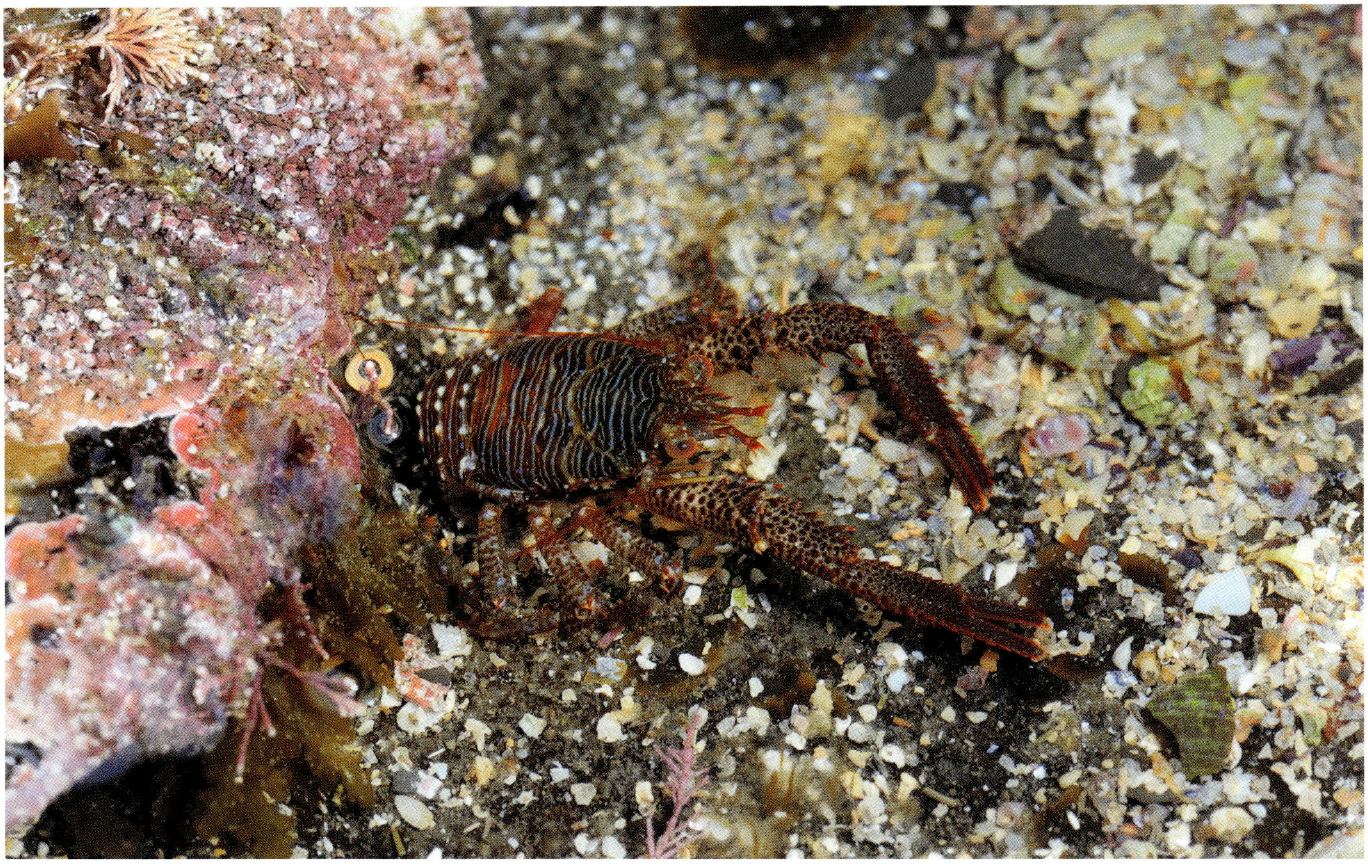

38.5 ~ Squat Lobster *Galathea squamifera*
These delightful creatures live under stones and rocks on the lower shore. Their colours are more radiant when in water.

↘ Nikon D2X, 105mm micro Nikkor, 1/60sec at f/11, flash, ISO 200.

exposure and drying out between tides are to be found in the upper regions of the beach, while those that cannot are restricted to the lower parts, usually hiding under boulders, stones and seaweeds to prevent drying out. These are the ideal places to look for subjects.

Preparation and Planning

The main inconvenience of working on the seashore is the changing cycle of the tides, which can often mean very early starts or working late into the evening at particular times of the year. Planning and researching an area in advance is essential for this type of photography; you don't just turn up and leave everything to chance. Checking the tide times for low water in your area is a must, or you run the risk of a wasted journey. You also need to be there well before low water and work your way down the shoreline with the receding tide. The most interesting and productive part is the area at the low water line. The seashore is not a static environment, but one in a constant state of flux.

The shore is a challenging environment to work in, the weather is not always sympathetic, your equipment is exposed to more hazards than normal; drop a lens or a flash unit here, and it is likely to be a write-off! Perhaps these are some of the reasons, along with a limited knowledge of the marine environment, that makes it less popular among macro photographers. Proper clothing is also essential. You need to be comfortable when working in a changeable environment. I tend to wear sandals or wellingtons depending on the weather and time of year. Another useful item is light knee pads. These are handy and protect your knees from imprints from stones and other sharp material. Be careful where you set your gear, working down at the lower end of the shore often means there are few places to put your bag. I usually carry a bit of polyethene and put my bag on it. When the tide is on the turn don't forget about it, you

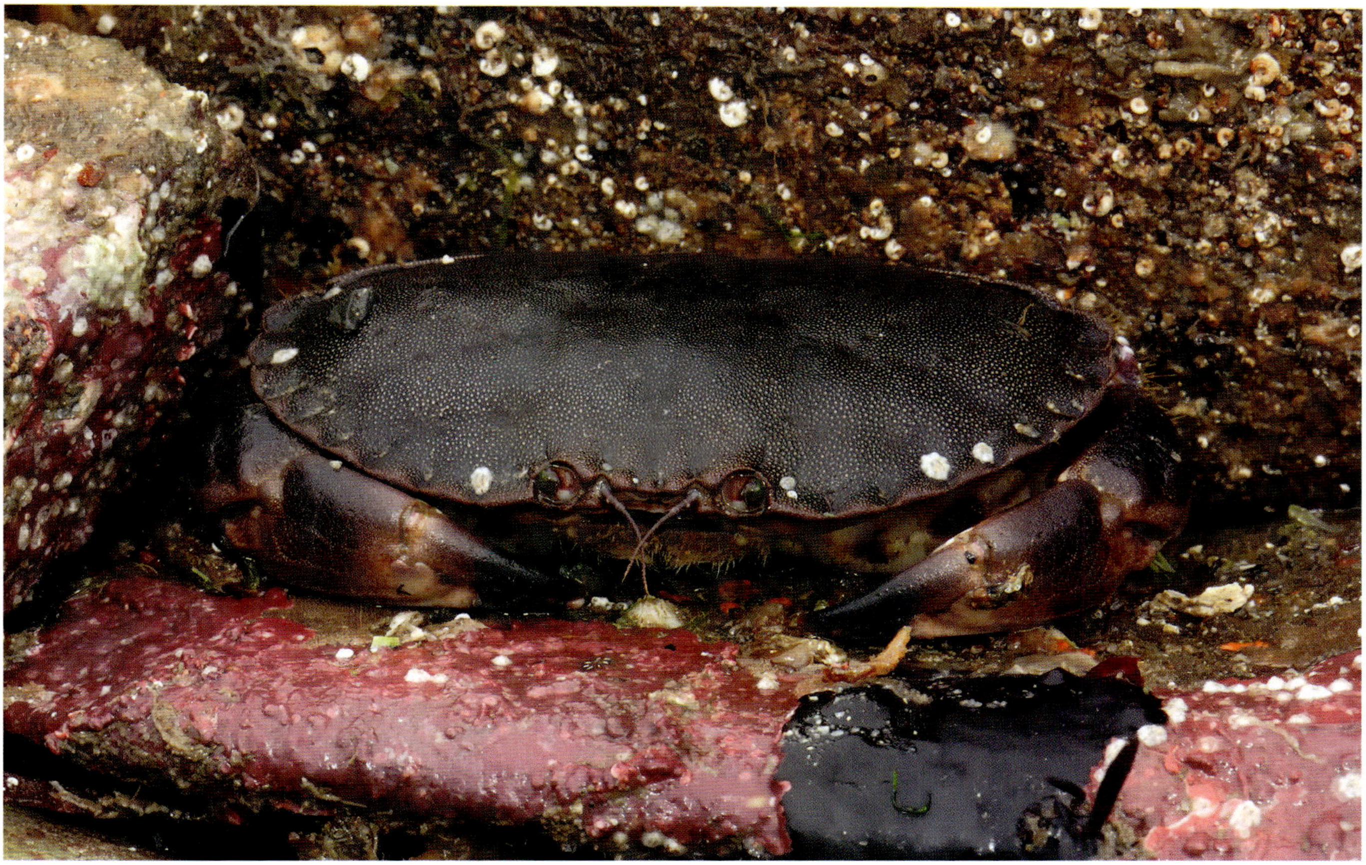

38.6 ~ Edible Crab *Cancer pagurus*
Searching carefully among the boulders and seaweeds turns up a wide variety of creatures. The black-tipped tooth pincers and the pie-crust edging to the shell separate it from other crabs.

↝ Nikon D2X, 105mm micro Nikkor, 1/30sec at f/11, flash, ISO 200.

don't want to see it floating towards you on an incoming wave! I also carry some disposable gloves which come in handy when looking among the boulders and stones.

Fieldcraft

In the Field

I would not claim to be a dedicated practitioner of sea-shore photography. I enjoy the contrast between it and photographing inland. Although the shore may seem chaotic with plants and animals dispersed in what seems a haphazard manner, there is a structure which is commonly referred to as 'zonation', where the rise and fall of the tide creates a number of distinct zones. In a rocky shoreline, the area at the top of the shore is known as the splash zone, which has limited contact with the sea other than perhaps occasional salt spray. Here the rocks are occupied mainly by various species

// OVERLEAF ~ LEFT (TOP) //

38.7 ~ Broad-clawed Porcelain Crab *Porcellana platycheles*
A small pretty crab with broad front claws. You often find it on the underside of rocks. Like so many marine creatures, their colour and beauty are better revealed when photographed under water.

↝ Nikon D810, 105mm micro Nikkor, 1/60sec at f/16, flash, ISO 100.

// OVERLEAF ~ LEFT (BOTTOM) //

38.8 ~ Purple Sea Urchin *Paracentrotus lividus*
A scarce species found mainly in the west of Ireland and also in rockpools. I found quite a few at low tide among the stones. I used a polariser to lift some of the reflections of the rock.

↝ Nikon D3, 105mm micro Nikkor, 1/60sec at f/11, polariser filter, ISO 200.

// OVERLEAF ~ RIGHT (TOP) //

38.9 ~ Common Starfish *Asterias rubens*
Widespread and frequently found among gravel and rock especially where mussels and barnacles occur.

↝ Nikon D3, 105mm micro Nikkor, 1/60 sec at f/11, ISO 200.

// OVERLEAF ~ RIGHT (BOTTOM) //

38.10 ~ Common Blenny *Lipophrys pholis*
One of the most common fish in rockpools in a range of colours. Photographed in the mobile studio.

↝ Nikon D810, 105mm micro Nikkor, 1/60sec at f/11, flash, ISO 100.

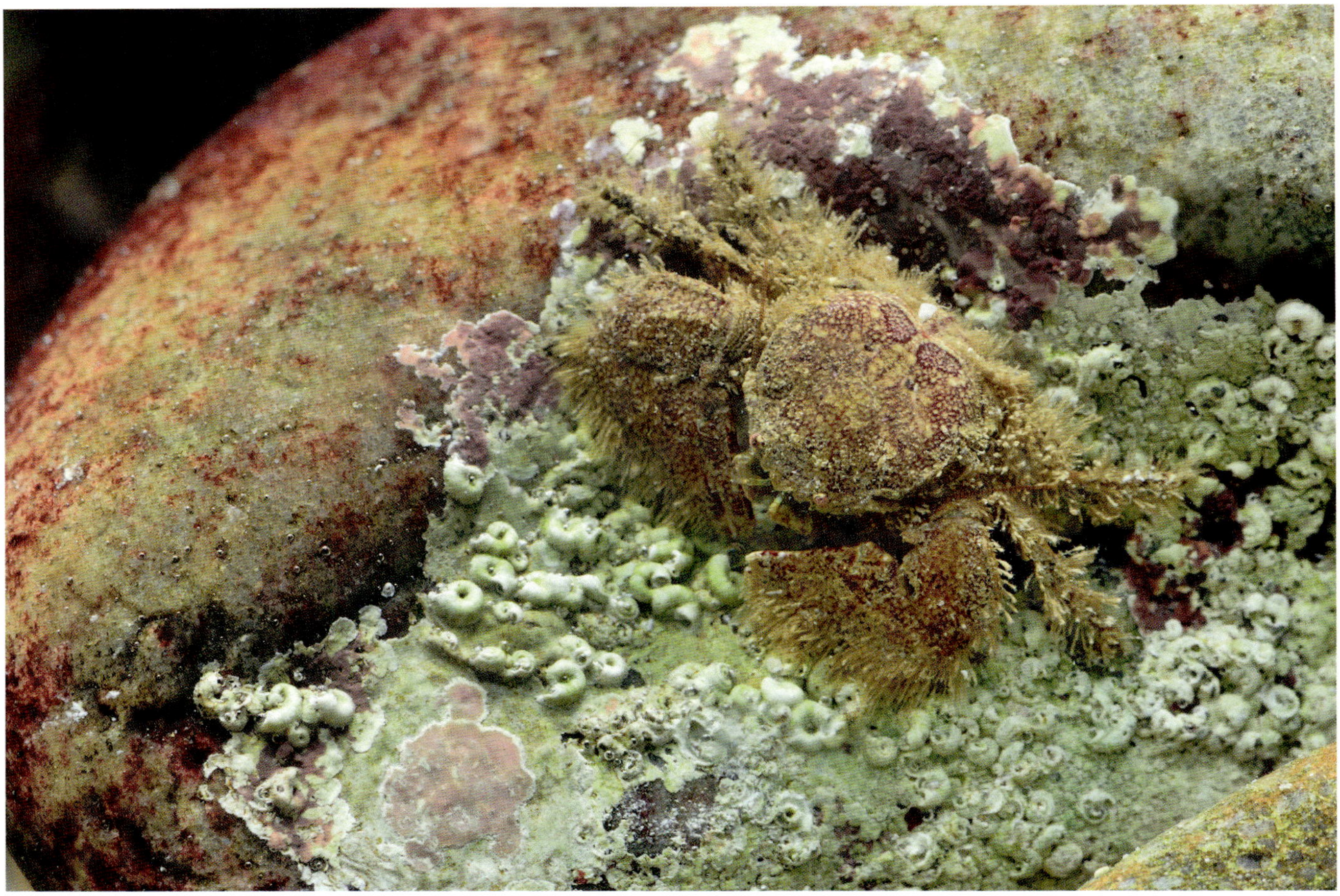

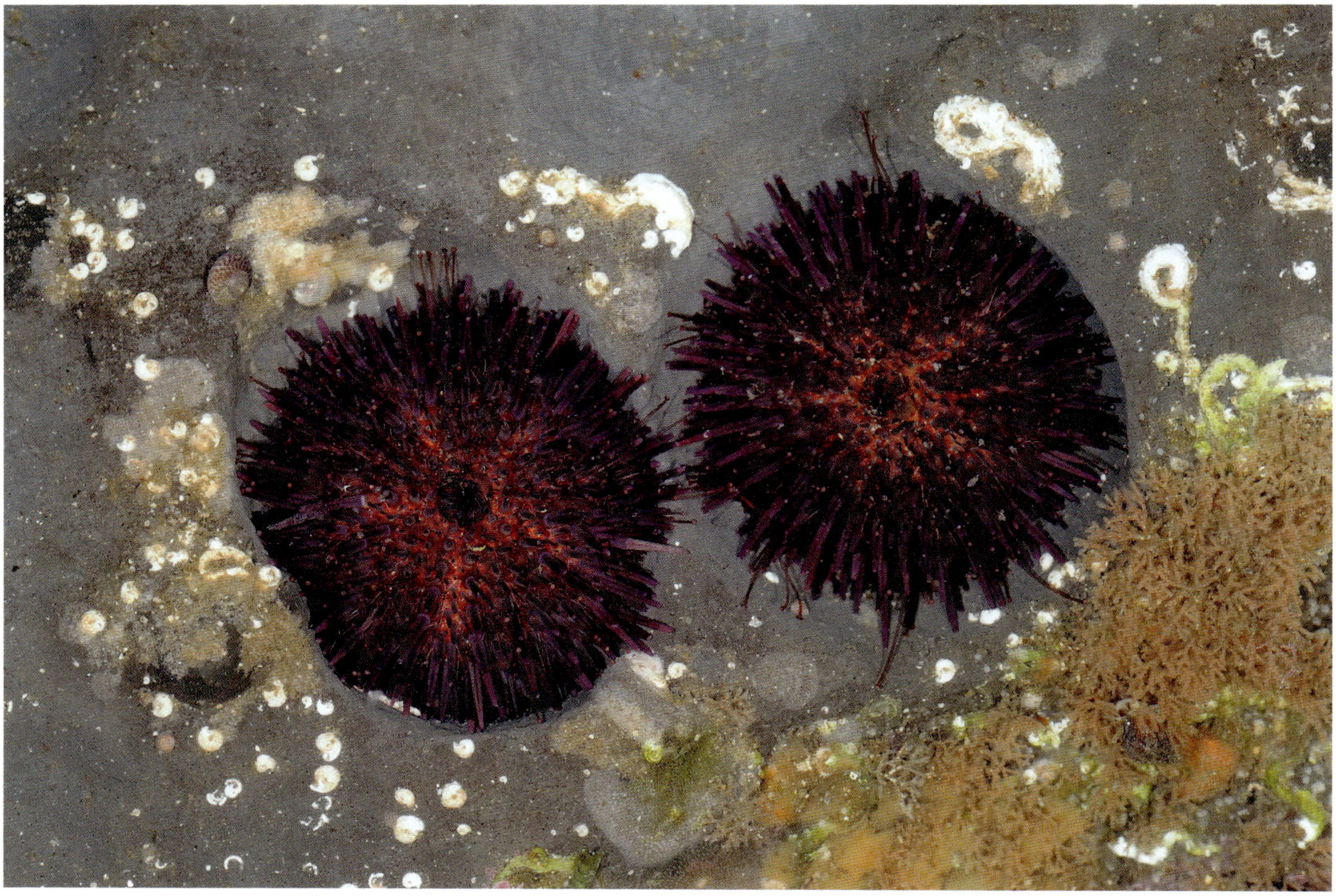

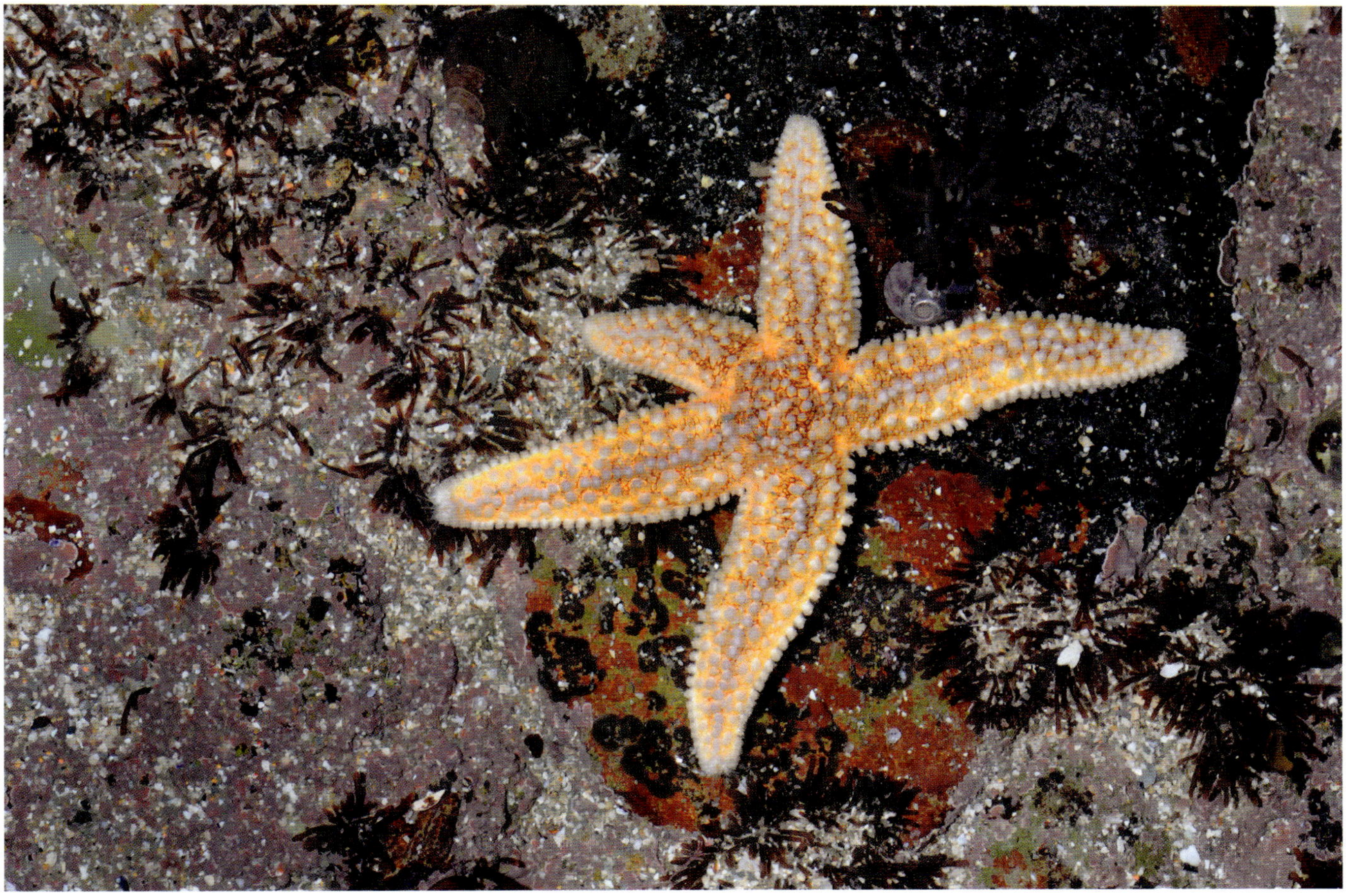

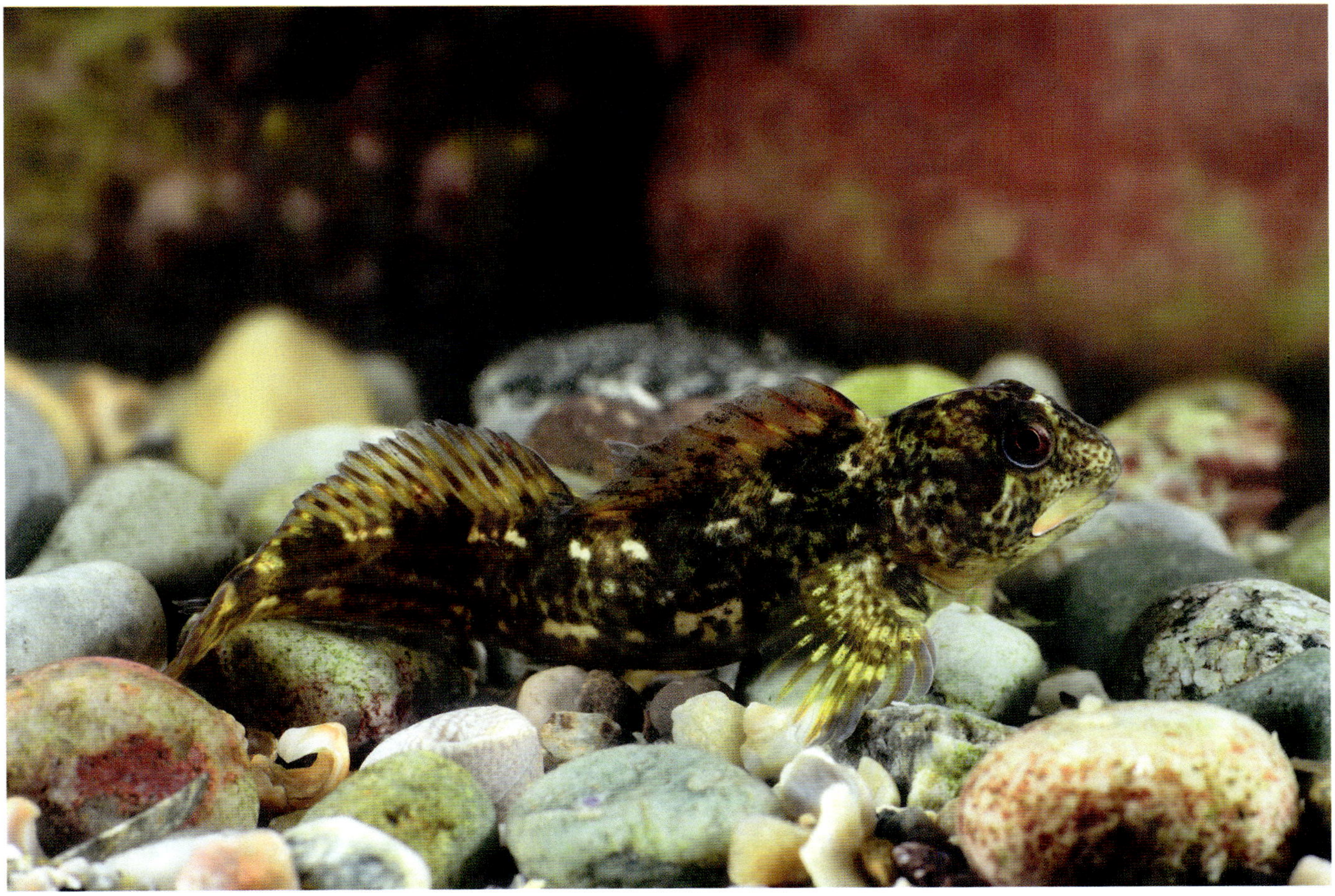

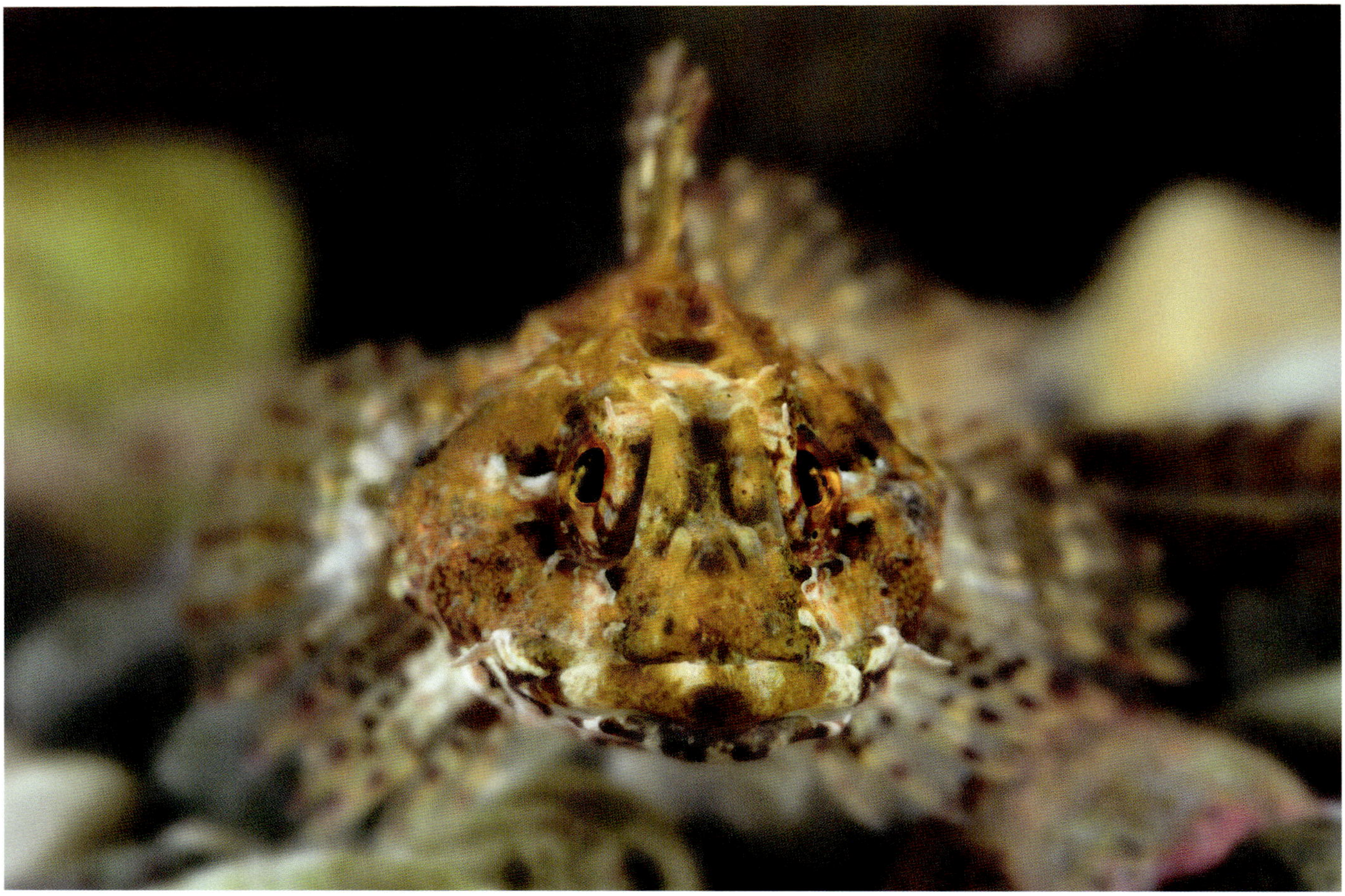

38.11 ~ Long-spined Sea Scorpion *Taurulus bubalis*
A mean-looking creature capable of changing its colouration to match its habitat. I have photographed it many times in rockpools but wanted a head-on shot, which I set up in my mobile studio. I kept the depth of field shallow to focus on the head.

↳ Nikon D810, 105mm micro Nikkor, 1/60 sec at f/11, flash, ISO 100.

of lichens and salt-tolerant flowers, such as thrift, which often carpet the lichen-covered rocks. The upper shore is the zone above the mean high water mark and is only covered during high spring tides. Conditions here are often extreme with only a limited number of creatures able to survive the long periods of exposure. Seaweeds such as channelled and spiral wrack predominate here, along with animals with protective shells such as periwinkles, limpets and barnacles, etc.

The middle shore or zone lies between mean high water and mean low water. This area is subjected on a daily basis to spring and neap tides. Here limpets, top shells, anemones, dog whelk, crabs including porcelain and common shore crabs and many other species are to be found.

The lower shore or zone below mean low water is usually the most productive area, but is only accessible during spring tides. It contains the greatest species diversity but is only exposed for a short time. The plants and creatures in this zone are virtually marine and, therefore, cannot tolerate persistent exposure to the air. Photographically this is the richest area with a wide diversity of subject material available. Clingfish, snakelocks anemones, brittle stars, urchins, common starfish, sea squirts, snake pipefish, velvet swimming crabs, various sponges and painted topshells are typical of the creatures you are likely to encounter.

Rockpools

Coastal rockpools are a feature of rocky shores and have something special that appeals to people of all ages. They are fascinating environments and are the ocean's portholes, or mini aquariums, allowing us a glimpse into a microcosmic world of exquisite beauty. These natural aquariums exist in all manner of shapes, sizes and

38.12 ~ **Sea Slug**
Coryphella lineata
Marine gastropod molluscs or Nudibranchs are extremely beautiful creatures, much more colourful and diverse than their land-based cousins. Although most species are restricted to the lower shore there are a number that can be found at low tide in rockpools.

→ Nikon D2X, 105mm micro Nikkor, 1/60sec at f/11, flash, ISO 200.

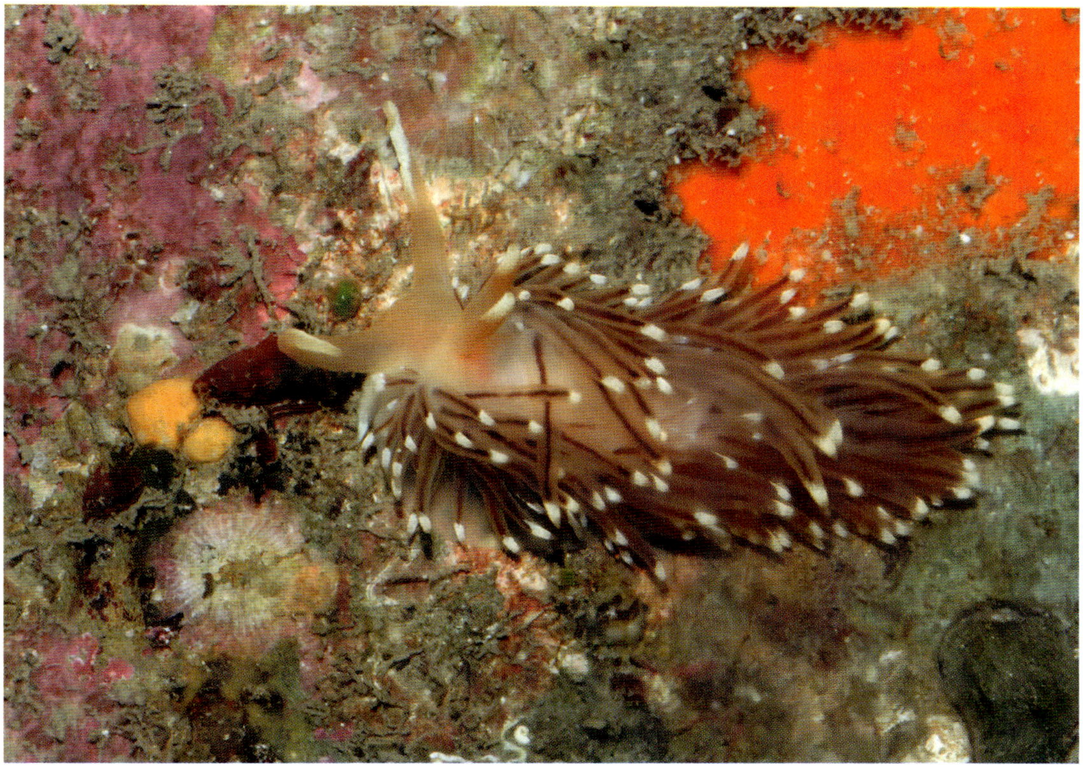

depths. Those pools that are close to the high water line are largely unsuitable – many suffer large fluctuations in temperature and usually contain little in the way of interesting subject material. Also, pools at the end of the shoreline (although rich with marine life) are generally cluttered with seaweeds and too deep to be useful photographically. It is often the small, shallow pools, which lie in the middle, or near the lower shoreline that are the most interesting photographically.

Photographic Approach

The best rockpools for photography are those which are several centimetres deep. They are more evenly illuminated with available light. Diffraction and illumination are a problem when you work in deeper pools. I tend to target those which have light coloured encrusting alga on the bottom rather than those which are covered in seaweed or bare rock. A lighter background will naturally reflect more light upwards. It is also a good idea to examine the pool with your camera for surface reflections; they will be much more prevalent in one direction than another. Naturally, you want to select the position that gives you the best view of your subjects. On overcast days, you can get a lot of surface reflection from overhead clouds. A polarising filter will overcome this to a point but at the expense of losing two stops of light, which will affect your exposure or force you to increase your ISO. Many photographers and books recommend it, but I rarely use one myself. A large matte black board or black umbrella will reduce the surface reflection and any generated by the camera. I also shoot with flash which solves the problem. A bright sunny day provides the ideal conditions, and small shallow pools are usually very evenly illuminated and clear from visible reflections.

The wind is another major annoyance and creates ripples on the surface. A simple frame, which floats on the surface secured with a gooseneck usually, resolves the issue. I don't as a rule use natural light as the primary light source and prefer flash to arrest any movement. If your flash units are attached to the lens, you are likely to create flare on the surface of the water. I use my own custom-designed gooseneck brackets that attach to the legs of my tripod. I can manipulate these into any position to overcome surface reflections. If you are photographing in rockpools, some experimenting is required to ascertain the ideal position, which is about 45 degrees to the surface. I prefer to use a medium telephoto macro for rockpool photography. There are occasions where having too great a working distance can work against you. Check for floating weed or other debris; they can cause shadows when magnified.

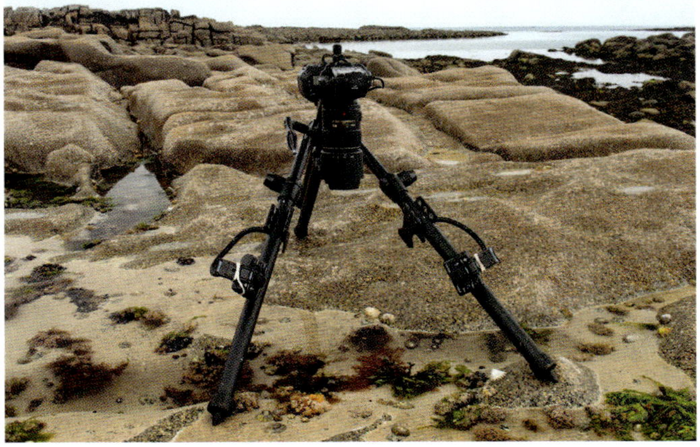

38.13 ~ **Flexible custom flash units**
Flash units are clamped to the tripod legs which makes it easier to adjust the angle and position.

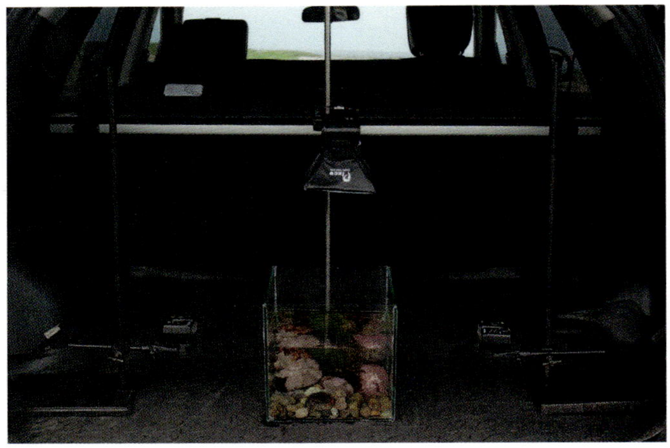

38.14 ~ **Mobile studio**
One of my medium-sized tanks positioned in the boot of my jeep, which is close to the shore. I can operate between the rock pools and my tank when required. The tank is lit with a diffused overhead flash and two smaller units placed at the side when required.

The Mobile Studio

One of the limitations of rockpool photography is the restriction on your compositional approach. Normally you have to shoot mostly from above, which means all of your images are taken from the same viewpoint. It is much harder to portray your subject in profile unless you place your camera and lens into a protective housing of some sort. Also shooting obliquely can create issues with the contrast, lighting and diffraction since the density of the water will not be even throughout the subject. It can also cause a reduction in image quality.

The best option for profile photographs is a tank. It does not have to be large, but sufficient to accommodate a reasonably sized subject. Unlike freshwater photography, where the creatures have a greater tolerance of the variations in temperature and water quality, marine species are much more sensitive to changes and can become stressed quite quickly. You can overcome some of the problems by having a mobile studio. I carry a series of tanks with me when photographing at the seashore, which are of different sizes and shapes. The boot in my jeep is black and serves as a mobile studio. The advantage is I can park it close to the shore, collect suitable substrate from a rockpool or the beach and create the ideal habitat within the tank. I can also use the same water and try to emulate the current conditions as close as possible. Subjects can be collected from a rockpool and transferred into a small bucket, which is placed in the water and then transported several metres to the jeep and the bucket placed into the tank. Your subject is more likely to behave in a natural way if the disturbance is kept to a minimum. I find this method works extremely well for the majority of subjects. My flash guns are attached to laboratory clamps which I can position exactly where I want them. When the session is complete, I return the subjects to where they were found. I also use a small tank rigged up to a laboratory stand and clamp. I can position this beside a rockpool and attach my flash guns to it giving me the option of using a range of lighting techniques from high key to dark-field (see page 113).

Ethical Responsibilities

Rockpools are extremely fragile environments, even when exercising due care delicate organisms are still easily damaged. Keep disturbance in the pool to a minimum. When turning over stones on the shore always replace them in the same position. Many organisms attached to the underside of the rock would become stressed, or even die if left exposed for any length of time. The majority of your subjects naturally look their best when in water, but not every subject that you may find among the stones belongs in, or inhabits, a rockpool. It is a good idea to start with some of the common occupants such as anemones, starfish and crabs, etc.; this also provides the opportunity to experiment and polish your techniques. We can all at times get enthusiastic and carried away, but be mindful of your time with subjects as they can become stressed if being handled for long periods. Always keep in mind as nature photographers, we have a duty of care, and the welfare of the subject comes first. Animals showing signs of stress will always be apparent to those who understand their biology and ecology.

Project Planning

The seashore has such a rich and diverse fauna that there are many projects you could undertake.

Photographically documenting the various zones and the creatures that inhabit them is one approach worth exploring.

Many creatures such as anemones have different colour forms. It is useful to show the variations that can exist within a single species.

Nudibranchs or Sea Slugs are a highly photogenic group of marine molluscs. Some species occur in rockpools and the lower shore under stones. Many are extremely attractive and worth photographing.

PHOTOGRAPHIC TIPS

- Check local tide and weather forecast before you set out.
- Arrive in good time and follow the tide down as it recedes.
- Be mindful where you set your bag.
- Carry a diffuser with you and also a pair of knee pads.
- Select rockpools that are reasonably shallow.
- Handle creatures with care and wet your hands first.
- Always replace overturned boulders exactly as you found them.
- Return your subjects back to where you found them after photography.
- Wear appropriate clothing; it can get very cold when photographing for several hours.
- Make sure someone knows where you are.
- Carry a mobile phone with you.
- Be careful when handling some creatures such as large crabs which can give you an unpleasant nip.
- Don't leave creatures in a bucket for any length of time. The water heats up, and the oxygen levels will drop.
- Watch where you put your feet when exploring.
- Don't try to prise creatures off rocks as this can kill them.
- Take your rubbish away with you when you leave.

Resources

FURTHER READING

Angel, H. *Photographing Nature: Seashore*. Fountain Press Ltd.

Duane Sept, J. *Beachcomber's Guide to Seashore Life in the Pacific Northwest*. Harbour.

Kricher, J. & Peterson, T. *Peterson First Guide to Seashores*. Houghton Mifflin Harcourt.

Meinkoth, N. *National Audubon Society Field Guide to North American Seashore Creatures*. Knopf; Chanticleer Press.

Oakley, J. *Seashore Safaris*. Graffeg.

Plass, M. *RSPB Handbook of the Seashore*. A&C Black Publishers Ltd.

Sterry, P. & Cleave, A. *British Coastal Wildlife*. Collins.

Wildlife Trust. *Concise Seashore Wildlife Guide* (Wildlife Trust). Bloomsbury.

WEBSITES

BBC Seashore: www.bbc.co.uk/nature/habitats/Tide_pool

Encyclopedia of Marine Life of Britain and Ireland: www.habitas.org.uk/marinelife

The Seashore: www.theseashore.org.uk

Wildlife Trust: www.wildlifetrusts.org/bsoup

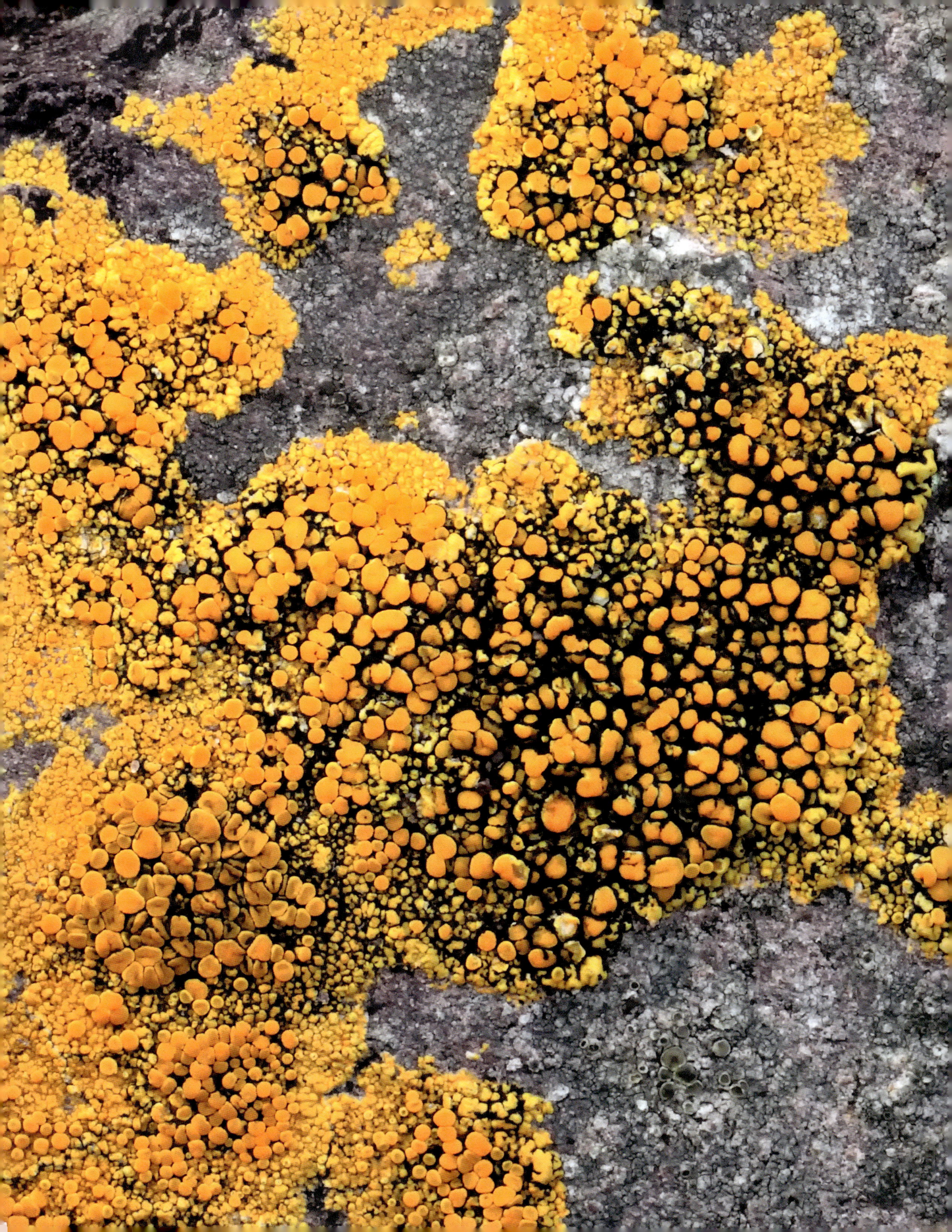

THIRTY NINE

Patterns on Bark & Stone

Lichens

Introduction

Lichens are a fascinating group of organisms that mostly go unnoticed by the majority of people. From a photographer's perspective, they are colourful, diverse and more attractive as close-up subjects now than in the past. They are an important part of the natural world, and their role in everyday life is not appreciated or understood. There are approximately 20,000 species that have been described worldwide. They occupy some of the most inhospitable habitats on the planet, and can survive the intense cold in high, altitude regions, while in contrast endure extreme heat in many of the hottest climates. They are often referred to as the pioneers of the botanical kingdom, being one of the first species to inhabit some of the most extreme regions of the world where little else grows.

Unlike most other plants, lichens can withstand very extended periods of desiccation, entering a state of suspended animation and not resuming growth until rehydration occurs again. Many species are extremely sensitive to atmospheric pollution and are excellent indicators of the air quality where they grow, which is why towns and local industrial areas have an impoverished lichen flora. They are also one of the slowest-growing organisms in the world, with some species managing only a millimetre or two in a single year. Lichens obtain minerals through the absorption of rainwater and moisture from the atmosphere. Many have extremely long life spans with some communities being reputed to be at least 9000 years old.

These particular plants have many applications in the natural world, including medicines, perfumes and dyes for colouring wool and other fabrics. They are also an important food source for many animals including reindeer and caribou during the winter months; snails, slugs and many other insects, including the larvae of some moths, depend on lichens. The larger eye-catching species form patchworks of colour on rocks and decorate the trunks and branches of trees and gravestones. The vibrant orange and yellow Xanthoria and Caloplaca species add rich, vibrant colour along rocky coastal shorelines. They also contribute to the aesthetics and the ambience of the environments which they inhabit.

// FACING PAGE //

39.1 ~ *Caloplaca marina*
Photographing lichens can test even the best photographers. Getting pin sharpness to the edge of the frame means careful positioning of your tripod and camera.

↘ Nikon D3, 105mm micro Nikkor, 1/8sec at f/16, ISO 200.

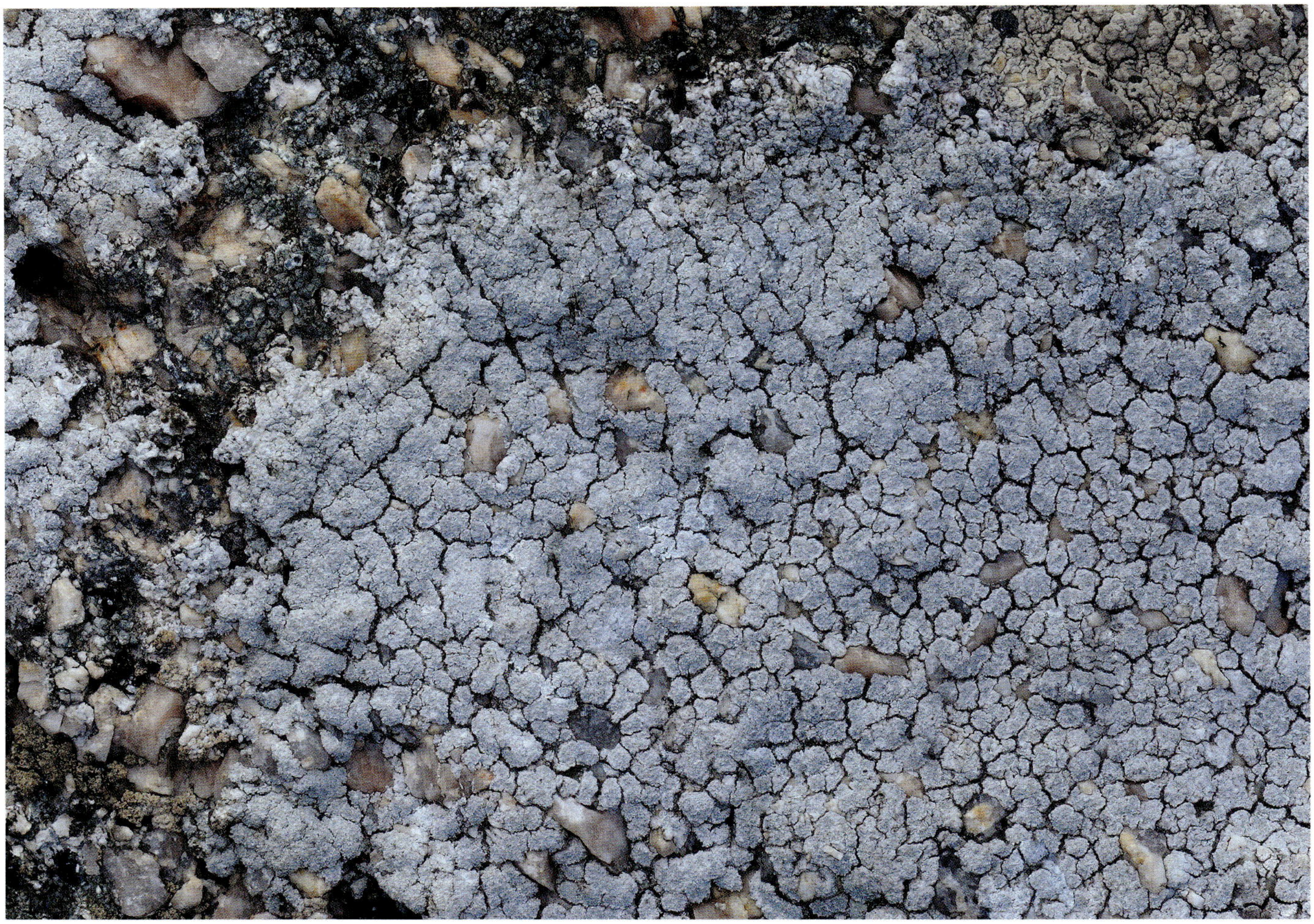

39.2 ~ *Pertusaria amara*
Colour can often vary between species. This is a particularly nice colour form which I photographed on a remote island in the Atlantic. I used a diffuser to even out the contrast.

↘ Nikon D3X, 105mm micro Nikkor, 1/15sec at f/16, ISO 200.

Biology and Life History

Lichens have an interesting life history, which is the result of a successful partnership between a fungus, an alga, or a cyanobacterium, or sometimes both, existing together in a congruous symbiotic relationship. The fungus provides the structure (or the thallus as it is known), and the alga, or cyanobacterium, through photosynthesis provides the essential nutrients. It's a highly productive partnership that stems back millions of years.

Lichens range in size and colour from small, inconspicuous dots on branches to large, colourful patches that decorate many types of hard surface from the bark of trees to rocks and gravestones. They come in a variety of shapes, sizes and are divided into four growth types: crustose, foliose, squamulose and fruticose. Crustose lichens are crust-like in appearance, forming coloured mosaic-like structures on rocks and similar surfaces. They are attached or integrated into the substrate on which they grow and cannot be removed without breaking it. Squamulose lichens are scale-like in appearance with flat lobes and similar to crustose lichens in size and stature. Foliose lichens are leaf-like and spread horizontally across the surface of the substrate and are attached by tiny threadlike structures. The upper and lower surfaces of the lichen are clearly different in texture. Fruticose lichens grow either vertically or pendent, often shrubby in appearance and attached only at the base.

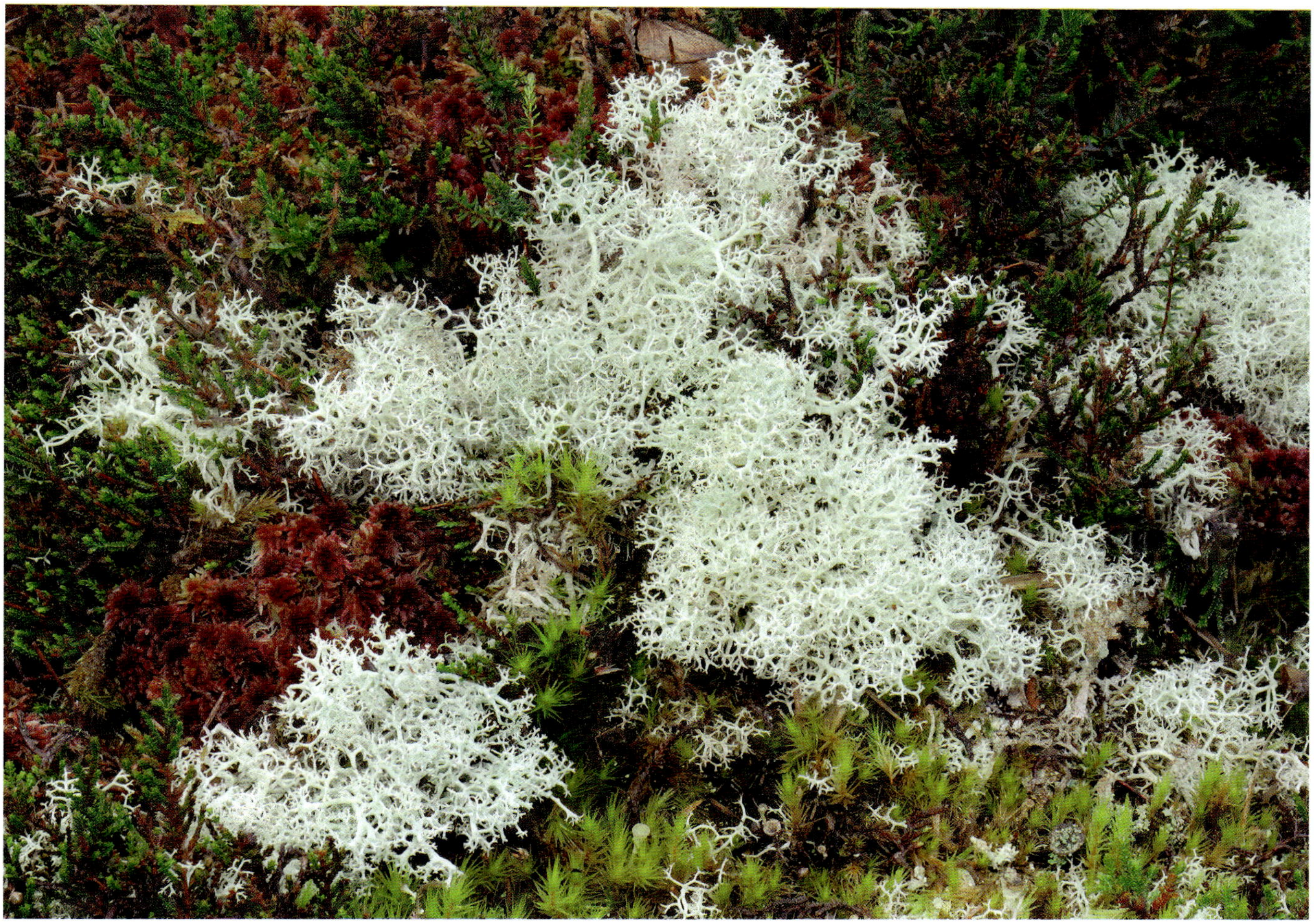

39.3 ~ **Reindeer Lichen** *Cladonia portentosa*
A common, fruticose species of bogs and heathery habitats. Although called reindeer lichen, it is not the same species commonly found in the Arctic tundra that the herds of wild reindeer feed on.

↘ Nikon D3X, 105mm micro Nikkor, 1/8sec at f/16, ISO 100.

Searching for Lichens

From a photographer's viewpoint, lichens are at their best during the late autumn and winter months when the trees are devoid of leaves and the moisture level in the air is higher. Many species have a real colourful vibrancy to them, particularly after rain, which is a good time photographically for some species. One of the best places to start your search is the rocks that occur along the seashore. Bogs and wetland habitats also have some colourful species. The rocks and boulders in upland regions are also worth exploring. The lichen communities in these locations have much less exposure to pollution or habitat change.

Ancient woodland also contains a good range of species, but a little more diligent searching of the trunks and branches of trees is required to find some of the most unusual types. Some lichens form patterns and mosaics on certain trees such as holly and hazel, and these should be examined, especially the older specimens. Weathered fence posts in upland regions, especially those which have been there for a long time are also worth a look. Heaths and bogs are excellent locations for Cladonia species, which resemble red-headed matches and deer's antlers. Old churchyards are good habitats for crustose species – these are lichens that spread and embed themselves into the rock and cannot be removed from the surface. Many thrive on the various types of gravestones and monuments, forming patterns. The most productive are those which are well weathered and have been neglected for many

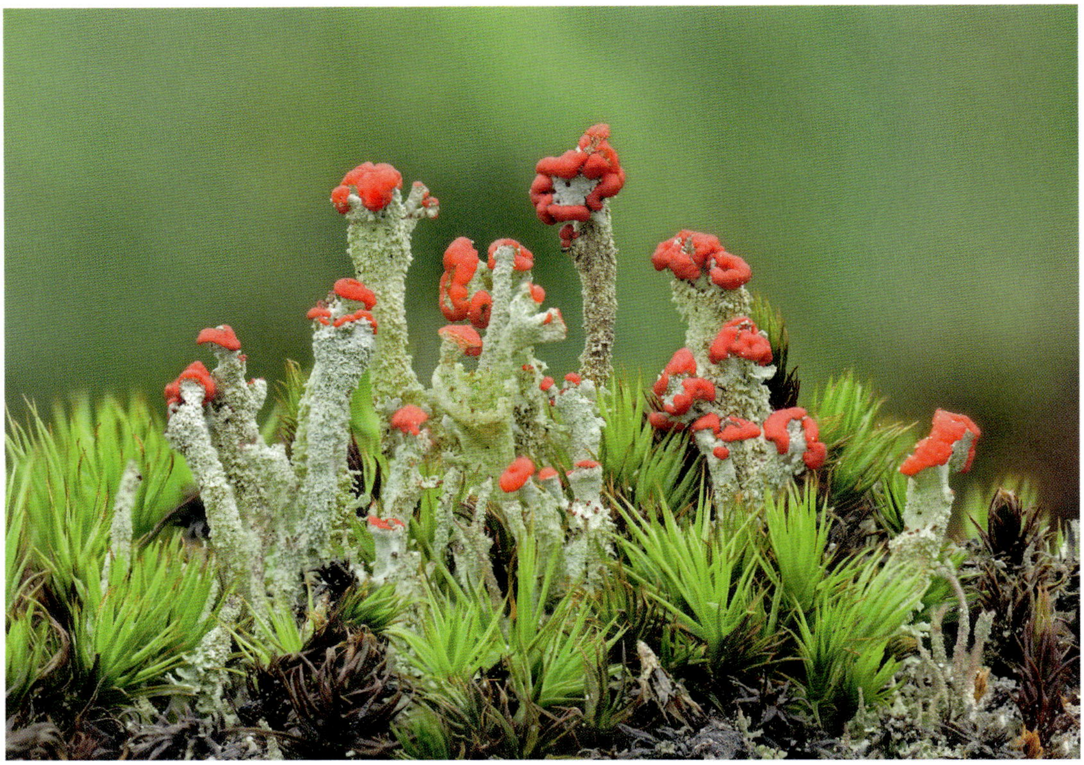

// THIS PAGE ~ TOP //

39.4 ~ Cup lichen *Cladonia coccifera* One of my favourite groups and particularly photogenic.

↘ Nikon D810, 200mm micro Nikkor, 1/8sec at f/16, ISO 200.

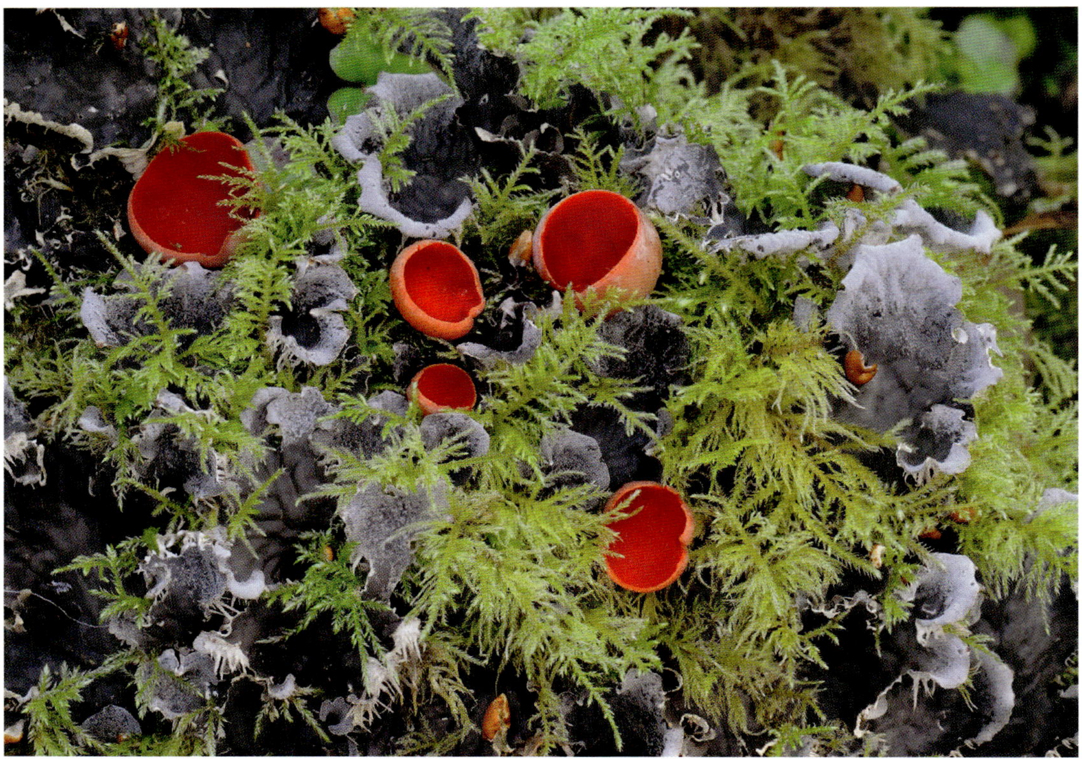

// THIS PAGE ~ BOTTOM //

39.5 ~ ***Peltigera membranacea*** **and Scarlet Elf Cup** ***Sarcoscypha coccinea*** What attracted me to this lichen was the fact that it was growing alongside an attractive cup fungus which appears in the spring. I used a diffuser to even out the exposure in the background.

↘ Nikon D2X, 105mm micro Nikkor, 1/15sec at f/16, ISO 200.

years. Old metal railings around graves often support species, especially if they are in a state of decay. If you plan a photographic trip to a churchyard, pick a day with no rain as many of the species that inhabit rocks are better photographed when they are dry. This also applies to upland mountainous areas as well.

Fieldcraft

In the Field

Believe it or not photographing lichens can be a frustrating business; I often find the most interesting specimens grow in extremely awkward places. My

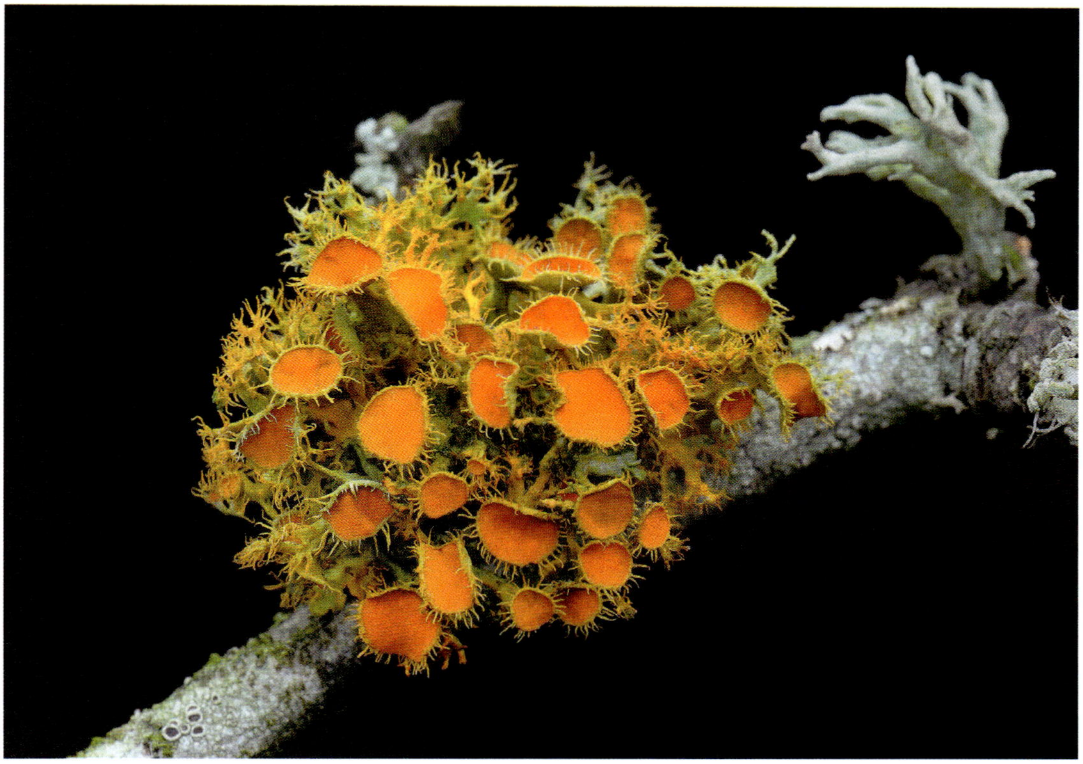

39.6 ~ Golden-eye Lichen
Teloschistes chrysophthalmus
With a size of a one-pence piece, this species is the holy grail among lichens. It was rediscovered in Ireland in 2008 and recently in the UK as well. I made a round trip of 500 miles in a day just to see and photograph this remarkable species.

↘ Nikon D2X, 105mm micro Nikkor, 1/60 sec at f/16, flash, ISO 200.

interest in this group was purely casual, up until ten years ago when my involvement in a high profile photographic contract, along with some of Britain's leading lichen experts, changed my opinion. Having to photograph subjects from half a centimetre upwards in the field in all sorts of conditions was indeed challenging. I ended up devising all manner of devices that would make the process easier, especially when dealing with smaller species. There were times I had to climb steps to reach specimens on branches or lie flat on my chest in bogs.

Lichens are rich in detail and a great test of your focusing skills and technique. Although a subject may at first glance seem sharp, once magnified any flaw in focusing or if vibration is present during exposure will be apparent. I shoot most lichens with natural light and when faced with direct sunlight I use a diffuser clipped to my tripod leg via a clamp, which is usually adequate for photographing species that commonly occur on rocks. I prefer the 105mm macro as it gives me a comfortable working distance. Also, the tripod is relatively close to the subject making it easier to clamp the diffuser (when required) onto the tripod leg. I can position it to soften the light and reduce the shadows. Making sure the tripod is secure before shooting is a critical factor as the terrain is not always that stable. Since all macros are corrected for flatness of field they will deliver edge-to-edge sharpness, which makes them ideally suited for this type of photography. However, if you don't own a macro you can still take excellent close-ups of lichens using a short telephoto lens around 100mm combined with extension tubes. The curvature of the glass in non-macros make it difficult to retain sharpness right to the edge of the frame. You are better reducing the magnification of the image to take this into consideration and then crop.

I have had my large Benbo tripod in every conceivable position and some of the most challenging environments just to get the shot. I learned a lot about these organisms during my prolonged commission to photographically document the lichen flora of Ireland. It also convinced me that the combination of a natural history specialist working in partnership with his/her photographic equivalent produced a far more successful outcome as they each brought their own level of expertise to the project. This was a very successful formula, and I have worked on many similar commissions since.

To be perfectly honest the majority of photographers do not set out specifically to photograph lichens, but encounter some of the richly coloured species by chance and can't resist the opportunity to photograph them especially if there is little else about. Identification is the biggest problem and the lack of appropriate publications to assist with this process was a major drawback.

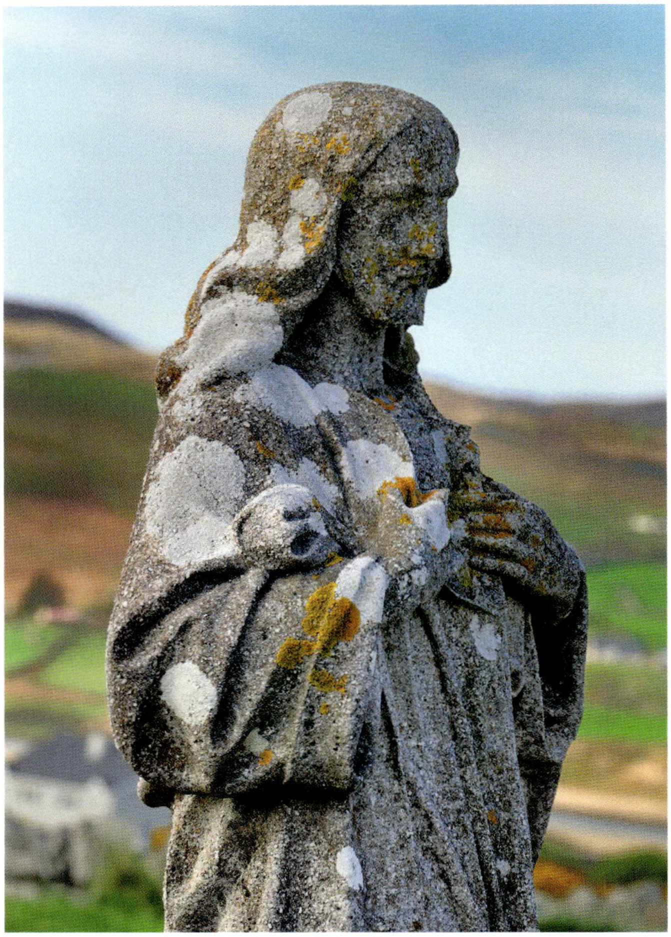
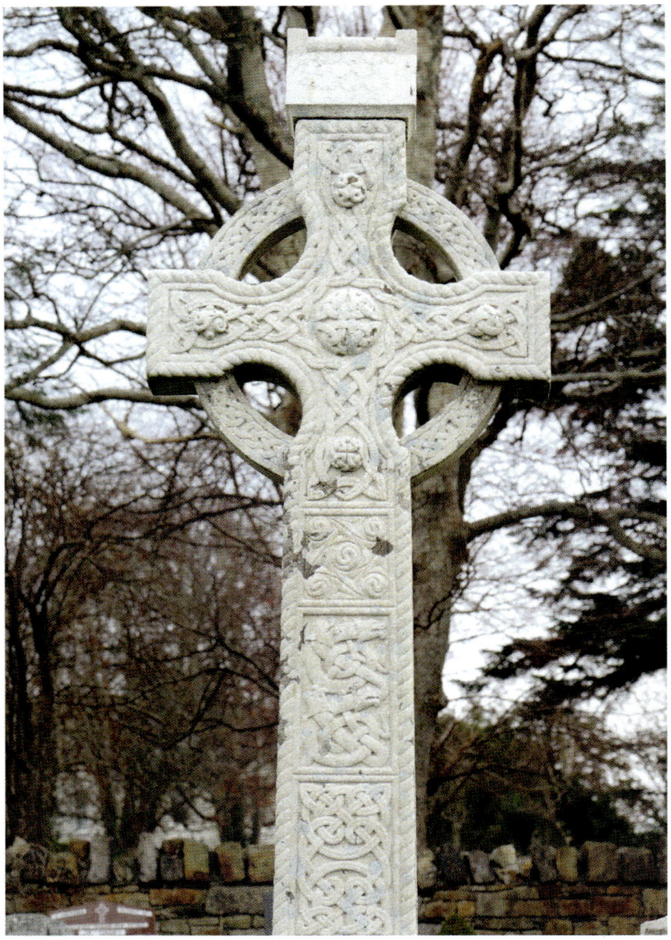
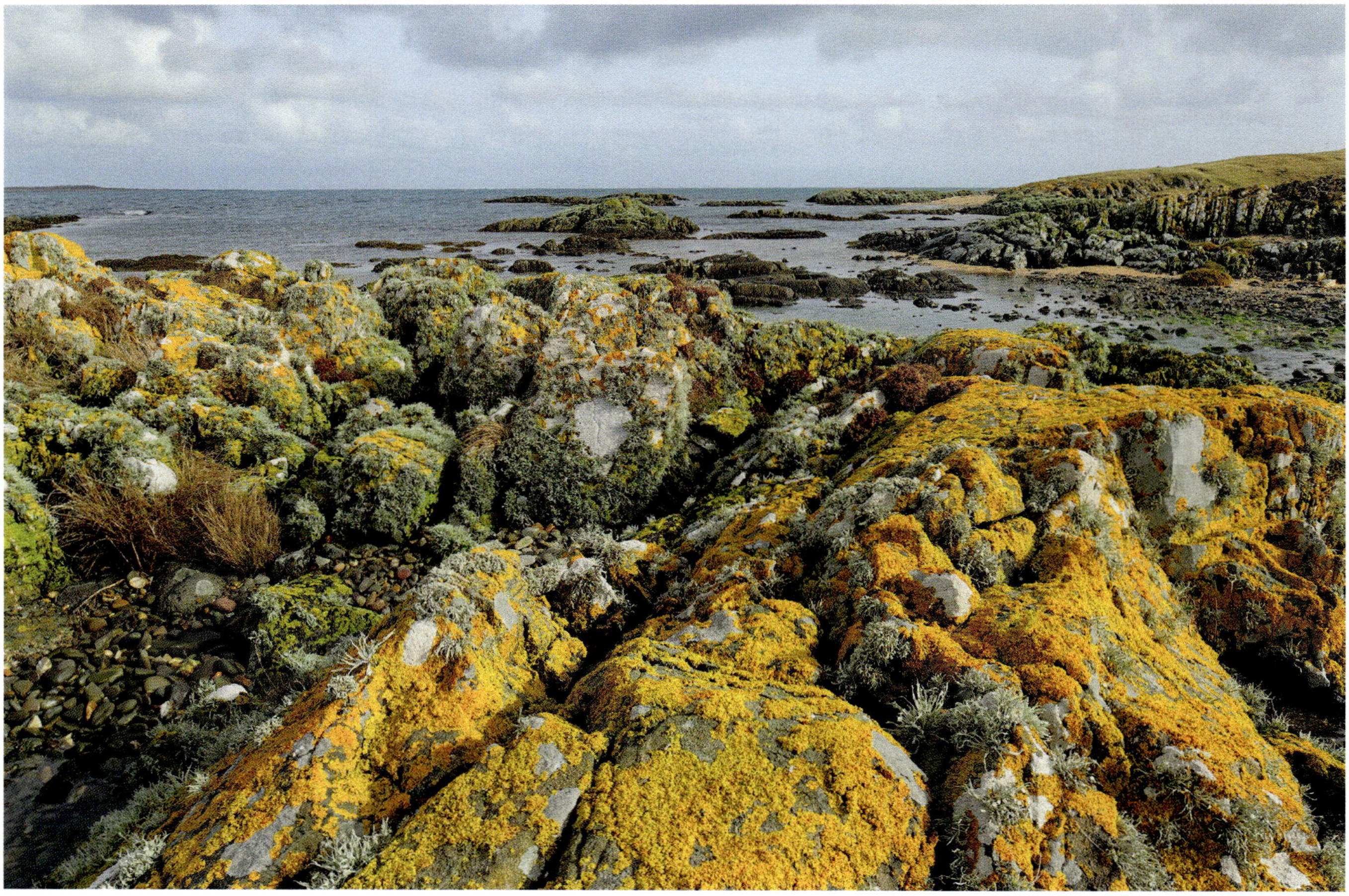

However, times have changed, and there are some publications and websites now, which are devoted to the study of lichens and include photography to assist in the identification of many commonly encountered species. Unfortunately, only a small number of lichens have established common names.

Project Planning

Photographically Documenting Lichens by Habitat

Many lichens are restricted to particular habitat types. For example, old churchyards have a wide diversity of species. Many grow on weathered gravestones and tombstones. Building a photographic reference collection from a particular site or from various habitats is an interesting project. It also serves as an excellent reference library of species which you can refer back to when necessary.

// FACING PAGE ~ TOP LEFT //

39.7 ~ **Graveyard statue**
Old abandoned graveyards are often great sites for lichens, especially those which have fallen into neglect for many years. The autumn and winter months are good times to explore them when there is little else about.

↳ Nikon D3X, 200mm micro Nikkor, 1/40sec at f/16, ISO 100.

// FACING PAGE ~ TOP RIGHT //

39.8 ~ *Ochrolechia parella* & associated species
Old neglected graveyards are often ideal locations to look for lichens. This old celtic cross was completely covered in several species.

↳ Nikon D3, 105mm micro Nikkor, 1/60sec at f/8, ISO 200.

// FACING PAGE ~ BOTTOM //

39.9 ~ *Xanthoria aureola Ramalina siliquosa* & associated species
Lichens make great environmental portraits especially Xanthoria species when they pepper the surfaces of rocks on the coast. I used the 24mm shift lens to allow me to hold both the foreground and background in sharp focus.

↳ Nikon D3X, 24mm PC-E Nikkor, 1/30sec at f/11, ISO 200.

PHOTOGRAPHIC TIPS

- Lichens on rocks are best photographed in dry weather; the fine detail in the thallus is more easily seen.
- If you want to record the finest detail and choose the point of focus, then use a tripod and remote release.
- Make sure you position the camera body up parallel to the plane of focus to ensure the maximum depth of field for your chosen aperture.
- Live View is helpful in establishing the degree of sharpness in the overall image.
- Photographing dark specimens on light-coloured rock will require adjustments to the camera's suggested exposure reading.

RESOURCES

FURTHER READING

Brodo, I. M., Sharnoff, S. D. & Sharnoff, S. *Lichens of North America.* Yale University Press.

Dobson, F. *Lichens: An Illustrated Guide to the British and Irish Species.* Richmond Publishing Co Ltd.

Dobson, F. *Lichens: Guide to Common Churchyard Lichens.* Field Studies Council.

Jahns, H. *Guide des fougères, mousses et lichens d'Europe.* Delachaux et Niestlé.

Sharnoff, S. *A Field Guide to California Lichens.* ASIN: B00OL3ONCS.

WEBSITES

Irish Lichens: www.irishlichens.ie
LichenIreland: www.habitas.org.uk/lichenireland
Lichens of Australia: www.anbg.gov.au/abrs/lichenlist/introduction.html
Lichens of Ireland Project: www.lichens.ie
Lichens of northwest North America: www.waysofenlichenment.net
Lichens of Sweden: www.stridvall.se/la/galleries.php#lichens
Mike Sutcliff's UK Lichens: www.britishlichens.co.uk
Scottish & British Lichens: www.lichens.lastdragon.org
Stephen Sharnoff Lichens website: www.sharnoffphotos.com/index.html

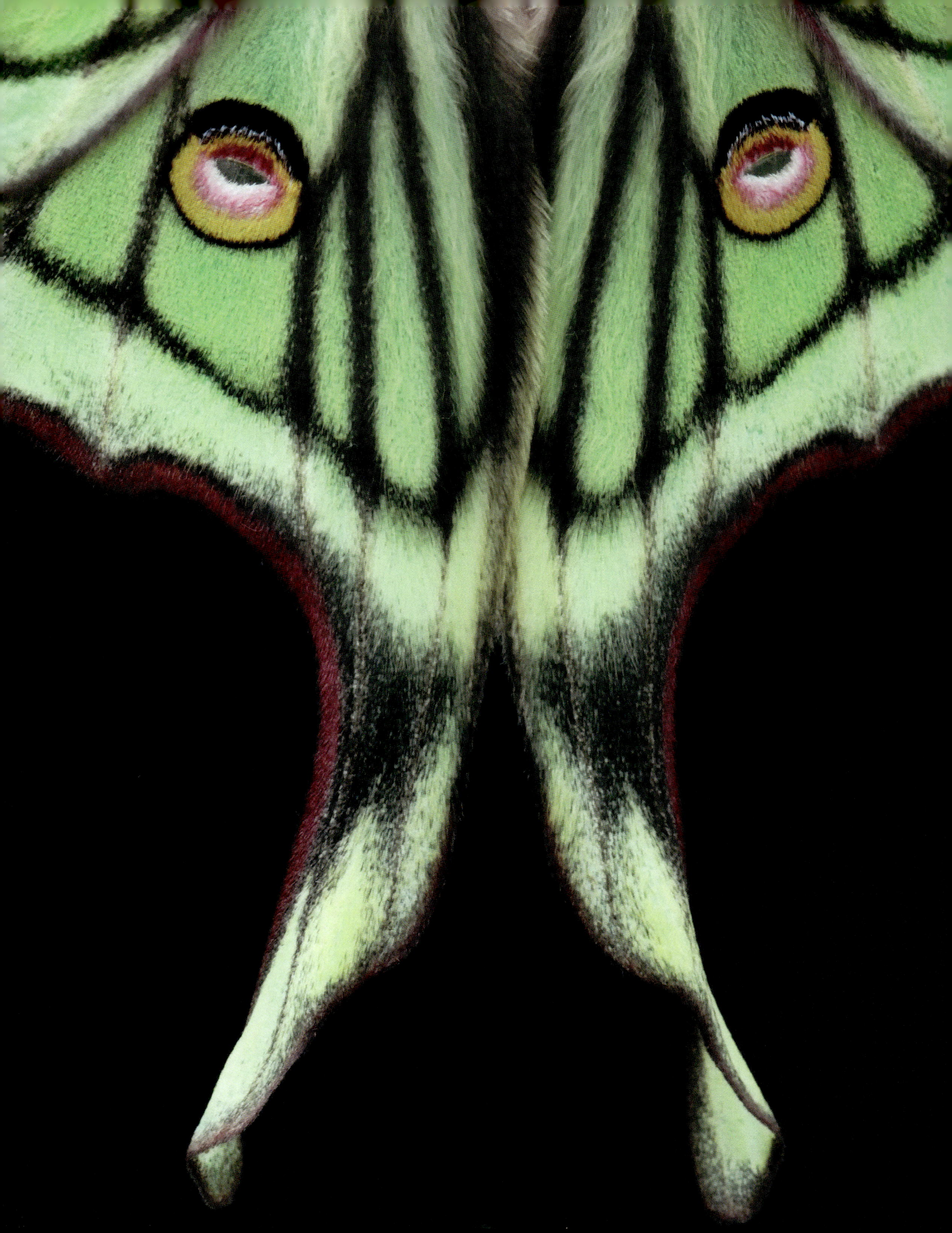

FORTY

Nature's Grand Designs

Patterns & Abstracts

Introduction

I am always amazed just how diverse and complex the natural world is. The more I see and engage with it, the more I realise how insignificant my knowledge and understanding of its complexity is. The world below our feet is equally mesmerising, the abstract possibilities here are simply endless. Many photographers, however, see only the 'big picture' and in doing so miss the beauty and diversity that it has to offer. Nature's grand designs are all around us; there are endless possibilities to explore with a camera.

// FACING PAGE //

40.1 ~ Spanish Moon Moth *Graellsia isabellae*
Identifying those subjects that make for interesting abstracts comes with practice. It can be obvious in some subjects but subtle in others. The eyespots in this moth are what attracted my attention. I used flash to kill the background giving it a ghost-like appearance.

→ Nikon D2X, 200mm micro Nikkor, 1/60sec at f/11, flash, ISO 100.

Discovering Patterns

Patterns exist everywhere in nature; they may be obvious in some subjects but subtle in others. The key to recognising patterns is becoming familiar with repetition and uniformity within a subject. It could be petals in a flower, feathers, veining in leaves or the gills in fungi. Being technically competent with your camera is only one aspect of the process, observation and the ability to look beyond the familiar and to recognise colour, shape and form require an experienced eye. Getting into the routine of not only seeing the subject in its entireness but looking for and recognising repetition within it comes with practice. Patterns become apparent when shapes, colours and lines repeat within a scene. However, we tend out of habit to focus on the subject, often unaware of the textures and shapes which in their own right make for interesting photographic studies. Inherent patterns are initially the most apparent, for example, the colour and structure of bark, spider's webs, pebbles on a beach and the arrangement of feathers on a bird, etc. Other subjects which display patterns and equally worth exploring are, lichens, fungi, mosses and flowers; the wing structures of insects have attractive colours, textures and shapes; all are capable of providing endless opportunities.

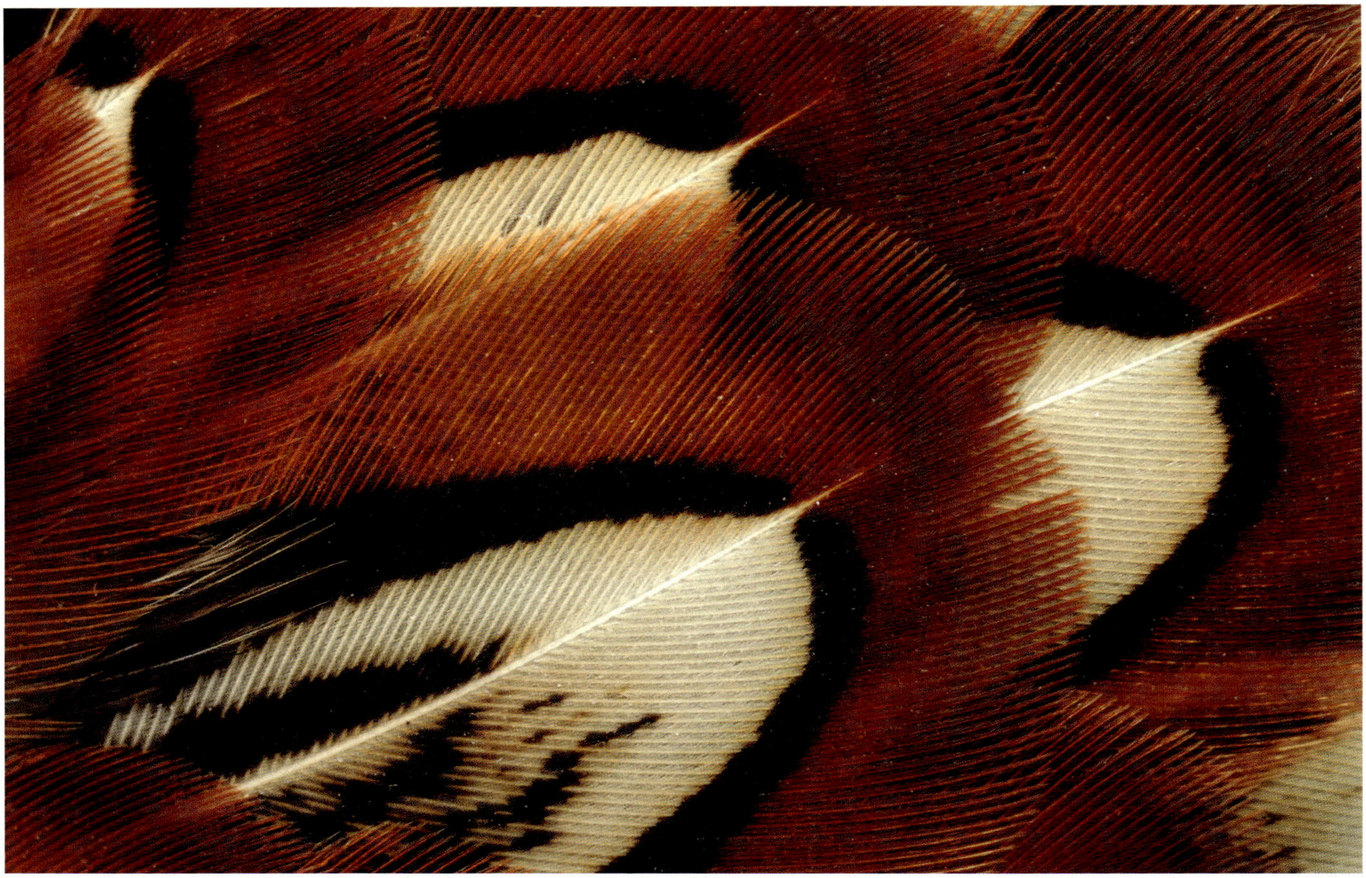

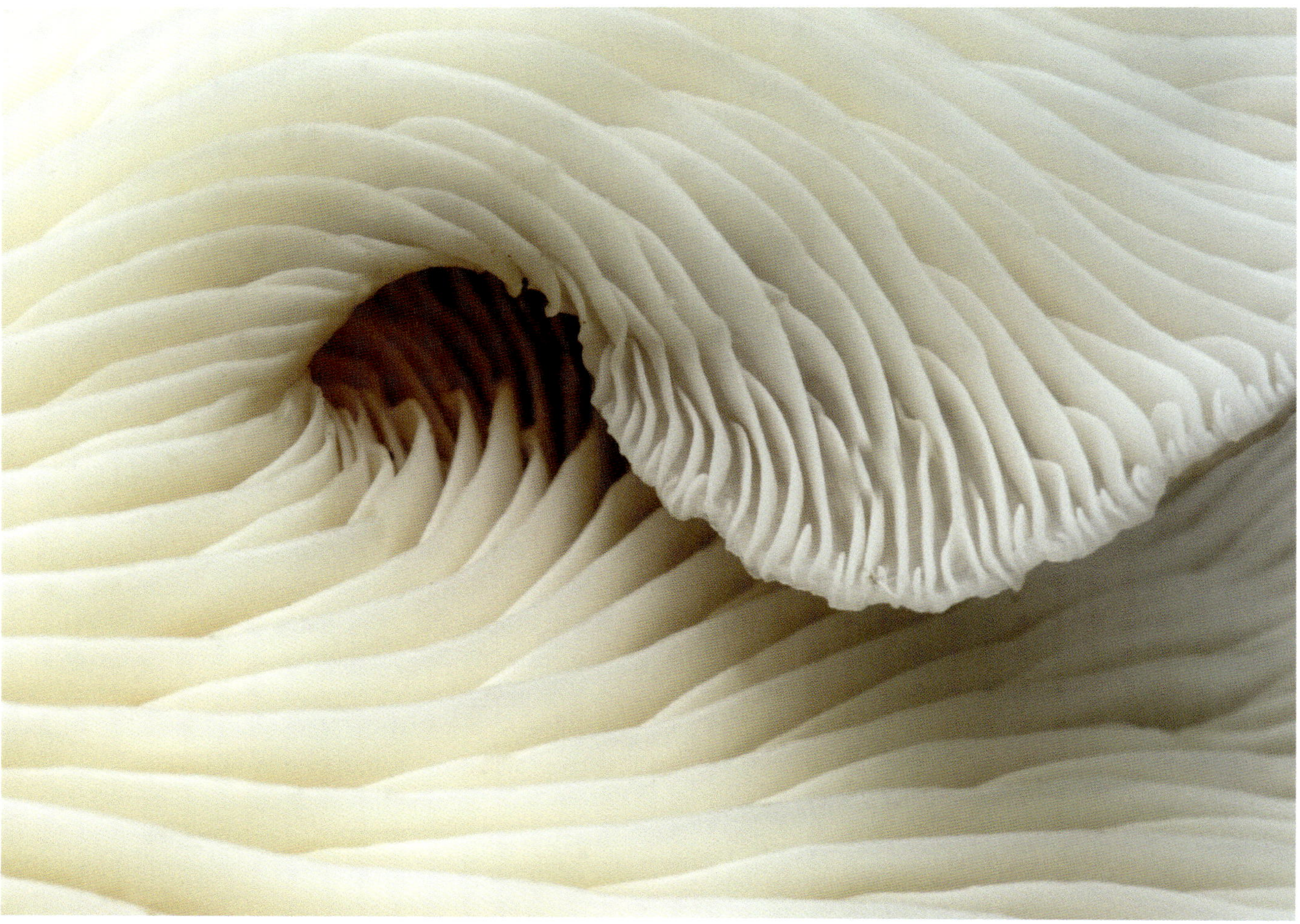

Abstracts

Abstract macro photography is about the exploration of the components that make up the structure of a subject and, when viewed in close-up, often conceals its identity, but not necessarily in every case. It is also about breaking the rules, focusing one's attention on a particular component, or multiple parts including colour and texture in an attempt to inhibit recognition. Some key elements are fundamental to creating interesting abstracts. Shape defines the visual structure in an image; it is one of the main parts and must be pleasing to the eye. It can also make or break the overall balance of a photograph depending on how it's placed within the frame. Colour is also a key element; especially those that complement each other and is important in holding the viewer's attention. Lines, if present, will often define the artistic element to the overall composition. Diagonal lines are generally more visually pleasing to the eye; whenever possible seek these out, it may mean rotating the camera between formats to achieve this. Repetitive lines may form a pattern and, therefore, indicate predictability within the photograph.

The most successful abstract compositions are usually simple in design but have a strong visual quality that may baffle or intrigue the viewer. Describing what defines an abstract is a difficult question to answer. There are many opinions on the subject and no universal consensus that I have come across. The success of abstracts, in my opinion, is largely down to presenting the familiar in an unfamiliar way. An interpretation may focus on a small section of a subject, which highlights its shape, colour or texture, but light, lens selection, perspective and a discerning eye will determine the look of the final photograph.

Fieldcraft

In the Field

When you become familiar with patterns, you begin to see them everywhere; this is particularly the case when working in close-up. Pictures that depict strong graphic content are generally more appealing than cluttered images that convey little to the viewer other than confusion. The rules of composition also apply equally in close-up and careful attention to natural focal points are just as important, but not essential if it reduces the impact of the photograph. Reducing an image to its essential components is a useful discipline that often helps to focus the mind directly on the subject. You don't have to look very far for potential subjects that photograph well as abstracts. Plants are one of the best examples when it comes to colour, shape and form. The unfurling fronds of ferns, the many variations in bark, especially birch and pine, are popular subjects. Close-ups of foliage, especially fallen leaves with autumnal colours, create patterns on the ground. Frost, dew, rain droplets on the underside of leaves with prominent veining add additional interest to the composition. Leaves can also be brought back home and positioned on a lightbox in various patterns and backlit to emphasise the texture and veining. The wings of insects, in particular the scales and patterns on butterflies and moths, are another popular subject among photographers.

The coast is also an excellent place to find patterns and abstracts. Barnacles, limpets and whelks attach themselves to rocks often forming attractive patterns. Seaweeds, sponges and patterns in the sand are also excellent subjects. Shingle beaches provide pebbles in all shapes, sizes and colours which provide many abstract opportunities among the stones; you can even arrange your own compositions. Developing an eye for abstracts requires patience. Look for subjects that have good colour and symmetry. Work at higher magnifications and eliminate peripheral information that may weaken the impact.

// FACING PAGE ~ TOP //

40.2 ~ Pheasant *Phasianus colchicus*
Feathers often have repetition among the patterns. I found this dead pheasant on the roadside and selected an area that was not damaged.

↳ Nikon D3X, 200mm micro Nikkor, 1/15sec at f/11, flash, ISO 100.

// FACING PAGE ~ BOTTOM //

40.3 ~ Oyster Mushroom *Pleurotus ostreatus*
Don't neglect the underside of some fungi, the gills make interesting abstracts.

↳ Nikon D2X, 200mm micro Nikkor, 1/8sec at f/11, ISO 200.

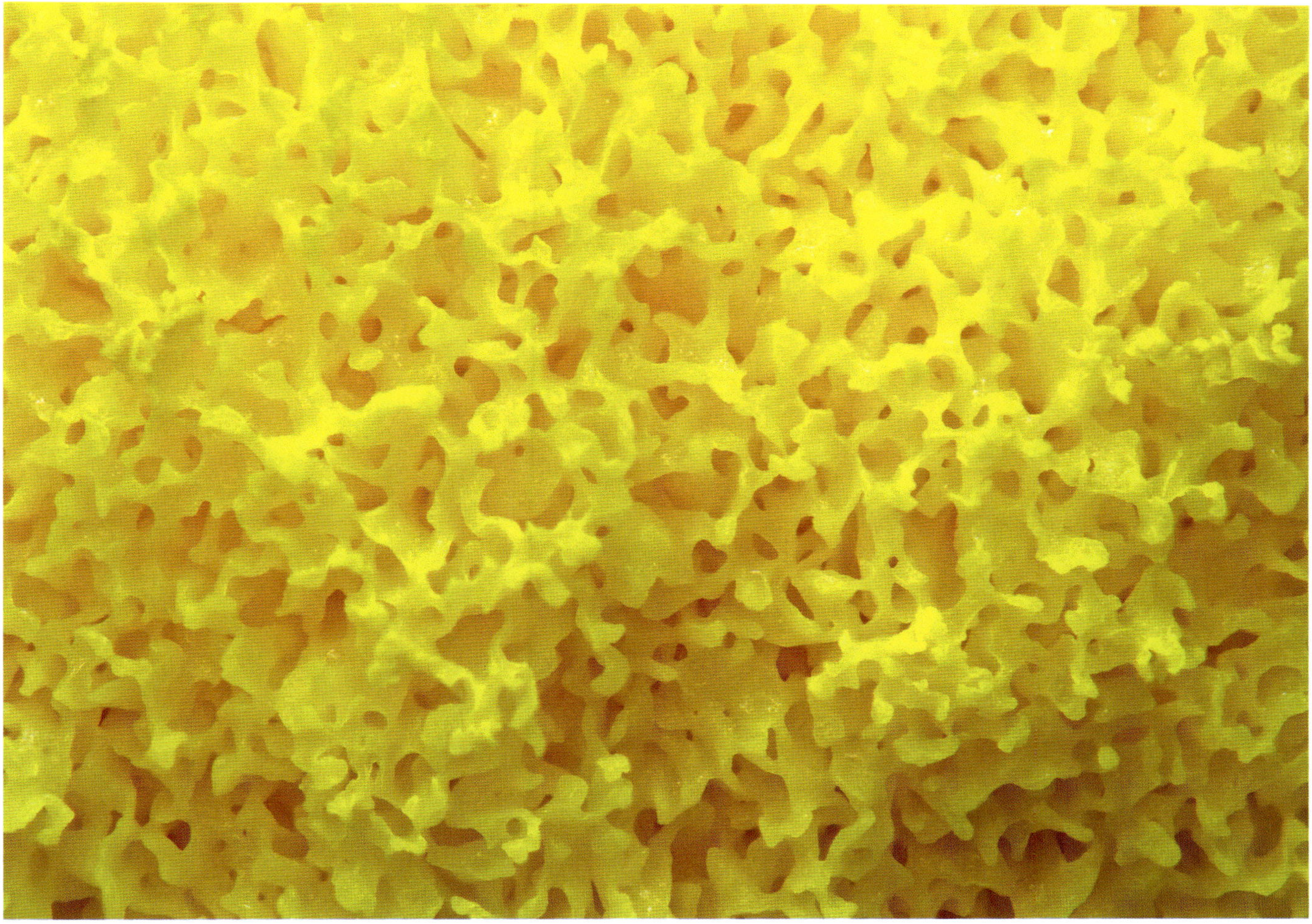

40.5 ~ **Slime Mould** *Fuligo septica*
Originally classified as fungi, slime moulds are now thought to belong in the kingdom of Protoctista. Many are quite colourful and have fascinating structures.

↪ Nikon D810, 105mm micro Nikkor, + 2X converter, 1/4sec at f/16, fill-in flash, ISO 200.

// FACING PAGE //

40.4 ~ **Silkmoth eyespots**
In this example I have compiled a range of wing abstracts of the eyespots on the wings of different silkmoths. Composites are an excellent way of showing diversity in a group.

Photographic Approach

You don't need an elaborate setup or equipment to capture patterns and abstracts; a macro lens is an advantage, especially when you need to increase the magnification to isolate a part of the subject, but it's not a necessity. Any lens between 60mm and 100mm combined with extension tubes will be okay. You also need a tripod capable of operating at ground level along with a remote release, which should be adequate in the majority of situations.

Although there is an abundance of subject material, it takes time and practice to get proficient at identifying those which have potential. While technical ability is important, technique is perhaps of less significance in this particular case since the secret of creative abstracts lies with the ability of the photographer to see and visualise those subjects that are likely to work. Operating at higher magnifications requires moving in close to your subject and cropping out everything else that is not relevant. Keep your configuration simple and try not to over-complicate the arrangement. Remember less is more. Also, depth of field becomes shallower as magnification increases. Resist shooting every subject at f/16. Many of the best abstracts are photographed with minimal depth

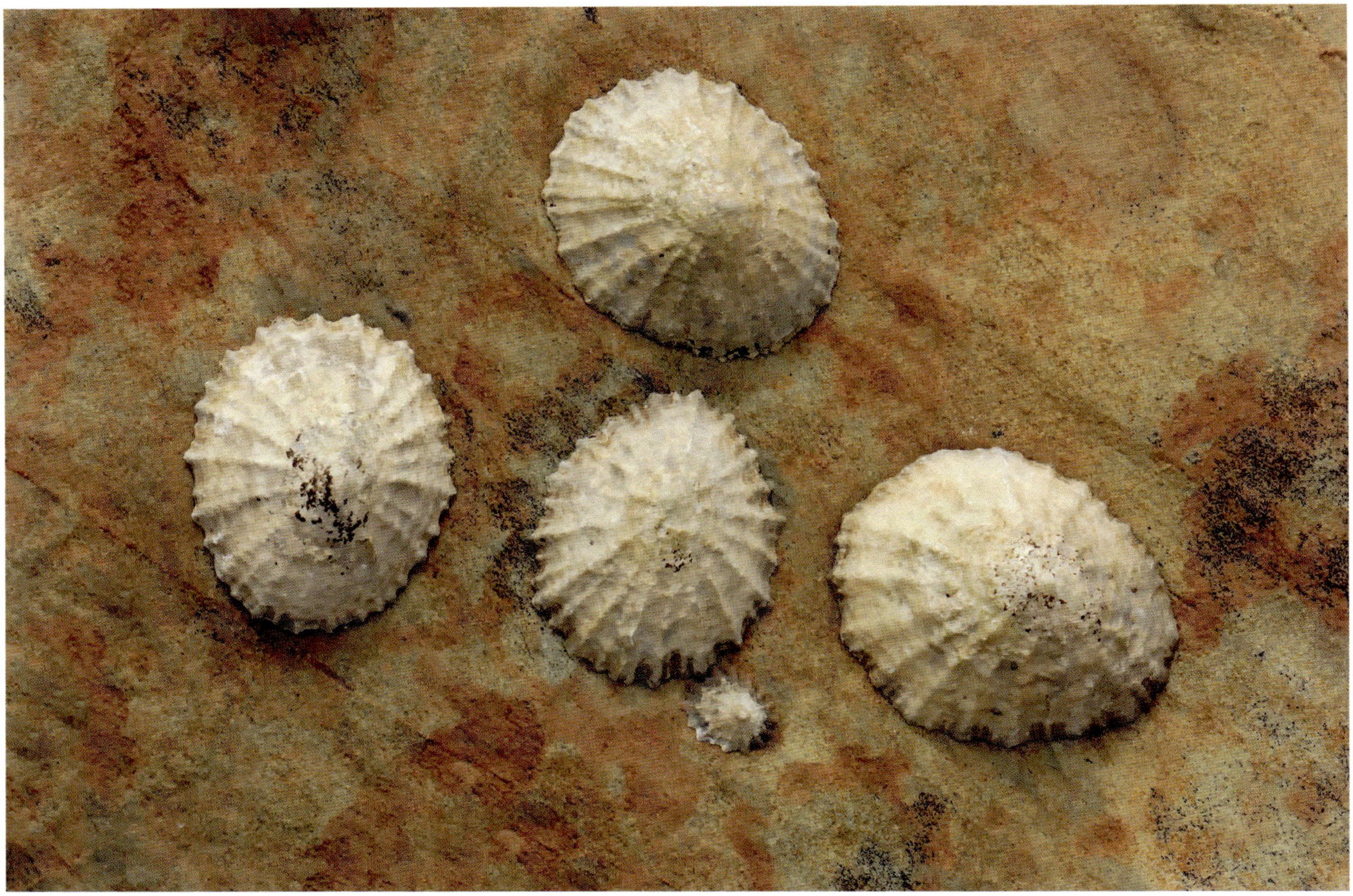

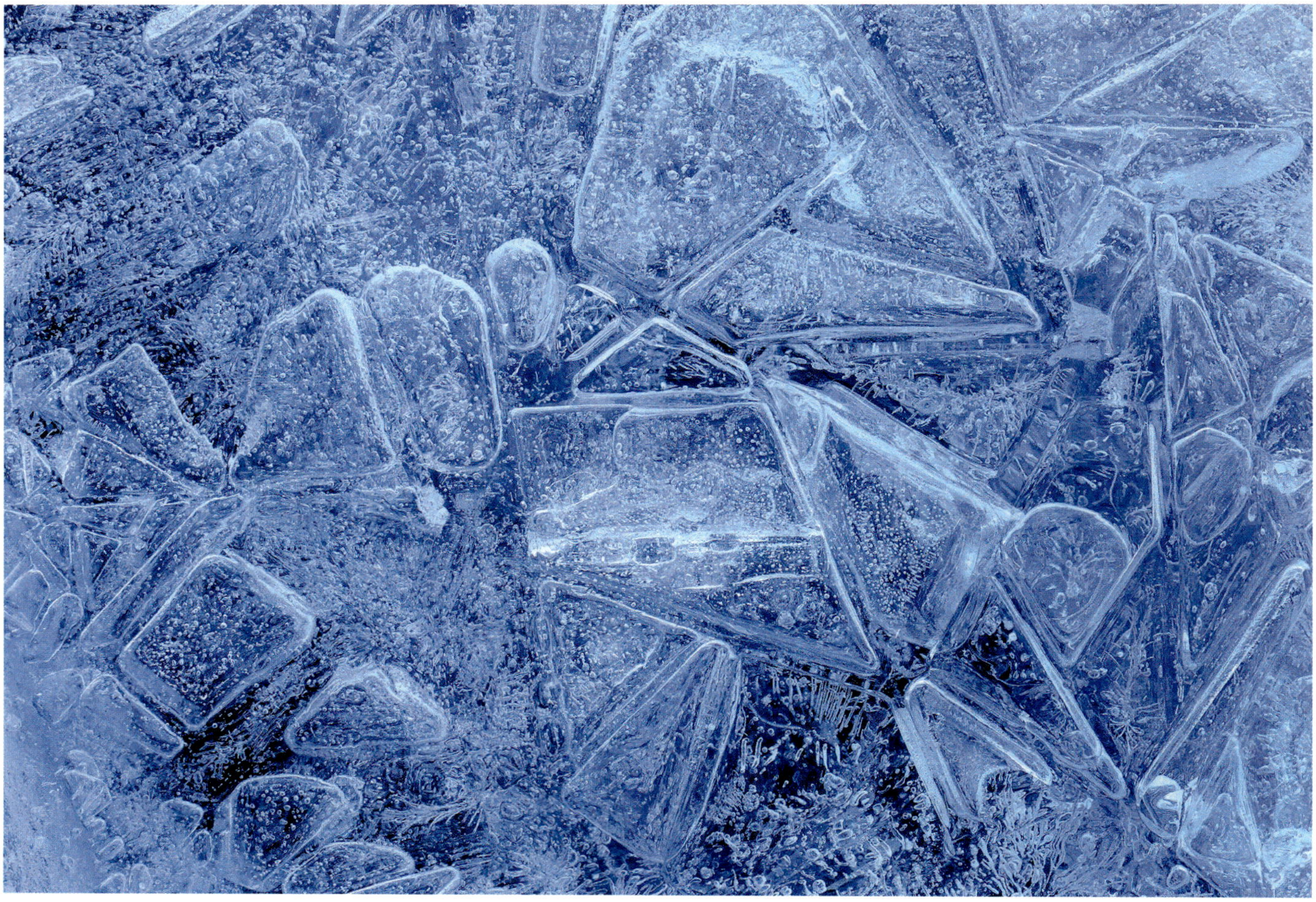

of field. Take time to explore the subject from different viewpoints. Keep your framing tight and exclude backgrounds and any other encroaching parts that are not relevant. Try using Live View for focusing and framing; it helps you to gauge how the final image is likely to turn out.

Photographing Through the Winter

I always find the winter months to be an ideal time to experiment with patterns and abstracts. There are fewer distractions from other subjects to monopolise your time. Frost can transform ordinary things into intriguing designs. Freezing temperatures and peripheral frost on vegetation creates great opportunities for shooting natural patterns. Foliage will be encrusted with tiny ice crystals, bracken fronds, dead grasses, numerous seed heads and spider's webs are all excellent subjects to begin with. Puddles, ponds, and lakes are transformed when covered with ice. Focusing in close reveals a wealth of shapes and patterns within the ice. Trapped air bubbles along with leaves and feathers that are entombed in ice make great subjects. Overcast lighting is ideal for shooting frost and ice. Areas with lots of shade often provide dark backgrounds, allowing the intricate detail in the tiny frozen ice crystals to stand out. Be mindful that bright subjects such as frost and snow can fool the camera's metering system, resulting in underexposure which renders your subject grey rather than white. You will need to pay particular attention to the histogram and make the necessary adjustments to ensure the subject is rendered correctly. It is also prudent to select a cooler colour temperature; you want to replicate the conditions and preserve the cool look in your images. If you are shooting in RAW, then you can easily make the corrections during processing. A polarising filter is a useful accessory when you need to reduce the reflections, it also has a blue cast, which is not a disadvantage in these situations.

Getting out during the winter months also prevents you from going off the boil and entering periodic hibernation as many photographers often do during this time. Inactivity does affect your skill level so, if you want to stay on top of your game, you need to keep your hand in at this time of the year.

PHOTOGRAPHIC TIPS

- Keep your compositions simple and clutter-free.
- Vary your approach and avoid including the background where possible.
- Crop tightly and eliminate any redundant parts.
- Analyse your subject at different f/ numbers and evaluate the overall appearance of the image.
- Shoot from a tripod, it will make the process of evaluation and framing much easier.
- Take a range of photographs from different viewpoints.
- Use a polarising filter when you need to remove reflections.
- Carry a diffuser to reduce contrast and shadows when shooting in bright light.

// FACING PAGE ~ TOP //

40.6 ~ Common European Limpet *Patella vulgate*
The seashore is often a good location for patterns. Limpets and barnacles make good subjects to experiment with.

Nikon D2X, 200mm micro Nikkor, 1/15sec at f/11, ISO 200.

// FACING PAGE ~ BOTTOM //

40.7 ~ Frozen ice crystals
Winter is a good time to explore frozen streams for patterns in the ice or trapped leaves.

Nikon D2X, 105mm micro Nikkor, 1/8sec at f/16, ISO 200.

Resources

FURTHER READING

Braasch, G. *Photographing the Patterns of Nature*. Amphoto Books.
Wilson, A. *Photographing Pattern and Design in Nature*. A&C Black Publishers Ltd.

WEBSITES

Art in Nature Photography:
www.artinnaturephotography.com/gallery/abstracts

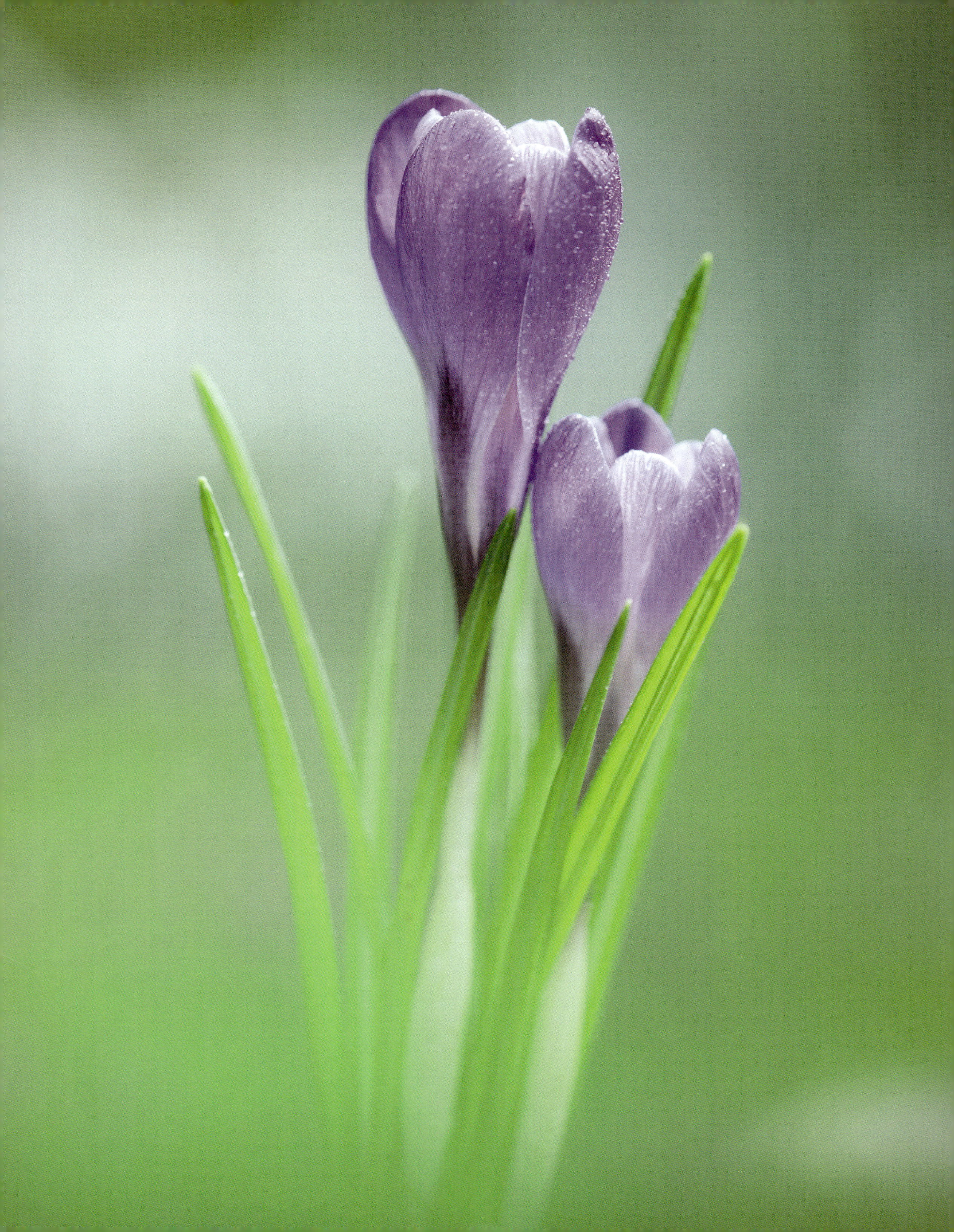

FORTY ONE

Nature on Your Doorstep

Macro in the Garden

Background Information

Over the past several years garden photography has grown in popularity with many competitions initiated specifically for images taken both in formal and ordinary gardens. The International Garden Photographer of the Year is one example which receives thousands of entries and continues to flourish each year.

The pressure on the countryside has never been greater than it is today. We live in a landscape dominated by concrete and expanding urbanisation, where natural habitats and their occupants are frequently squeezed to the limit. Much of the wildlife either has to adapt or face extinction, which makes gardens an extremely important refuge. Gardens don't act in isolation, but link up to form an extraordinary mosaic of different habitats. They serve as corridors connecting major habitats and allowing species to move about between the various locations. If you are considering developing your garden to encourage wildlife and further your photography, some organisations offer advice and support to those who want to encourage wildlife and biodiversity in general. Not everyone has instant access to the countryside, and a well-planned garden can provide a variety of different plants and creatures that are conveniently placed right on your doorstep. With a little bit of thought, you can have a garden that provides not only pleasure but endless hours of photography. You also have the advantage of not being disturbed and can choose your own time when the weather conditions are ideal to practise your art.

// FACING PAGE //

41.1 ~ Crocus species
Photographers coming new to macro photography often underestimate the potential of their own garden. There is a wealth of subject material to explore. It is also a good place to experiment with your equipment and techniques.

↝ Nikon D810, 200mm micro Nikkor, 1/250sec at f/5.6, ISO 100.

Encouraging Subjects into Your Garden

Most people underestimate the importance of the average garden. You may be surprised to learn that even the smallest of urban patches has a range of minibeasts engaged in all sorts of activities right under your nose. A friend of mine lived in a small townhouse in the heart of the city with a very small garden but still managed to record over two hundred species of moth

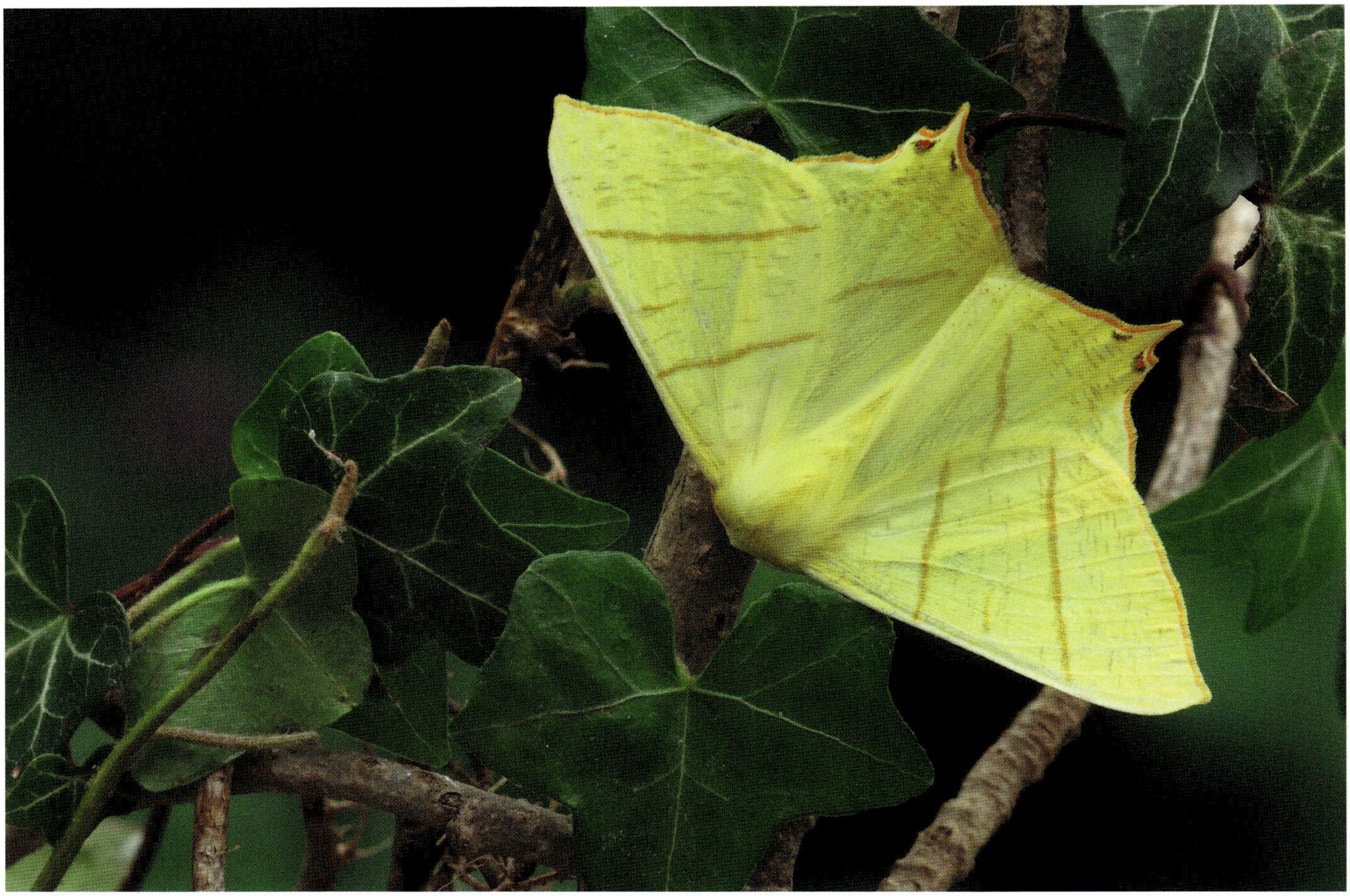

41.2 ~ **Swallow-tailed Moth** *Qurapteryax sambucaria*
I have mature ivy at the bottom of my garden which is the foodplant for this attractive moth. Every year there are always adults to be found among the ivy.

↘ Nikon D2X, 200mm micro Nikkor, 1/8sec at f/16, ISO 200.

over a three-year period. Your garden can also act as a large outdoor studio, providing you with a rich source of subject material available at your convenience.

Flowers are the heart of any garden along with trees and shrubs; they are a food source for numerous insects and provide shelter for many different creatures. They have an important role when it comes to insects. Buddleia, lavender, ice plant, michaelmas daisy, red valerian, aster and scabious are just some of the nectar plants that butterflies and other insects find attractive. Night-scented flowers such as jasmine, honeysuckle, evening primrose, sweet rocket and the tobacco plant are among the most effective for attracting moths at dark. A garden that includes many of these plants will have a rich source of species. Some dedicated enthusiasts/photographers run a moth trap throughout most of the year and can easily record well over a hundred species just from their garden. Bees, hoverflies, lacewings and ladybirds are frequent visitors to my own garden. Banded and garden snails are also abundant in a variety of colours. Every year I also get adult swallow-tailed moths in early summer as the old wall at the bottom of my garden has mature ivy growing along the top which is the foodplant for the larva of this attractive species.

We all tend to keep extremely tidy gardens these days, but it's a good idea to leave an area and let nature take its course. Avoid using any pesticides or artificial fertilisers and leave a small shady area in the corner covered with leaf litter, dead wood, and moss-covered logs to encourage beetles, woodlice, and fungi. It will also provide hibernation sites for other creatures.

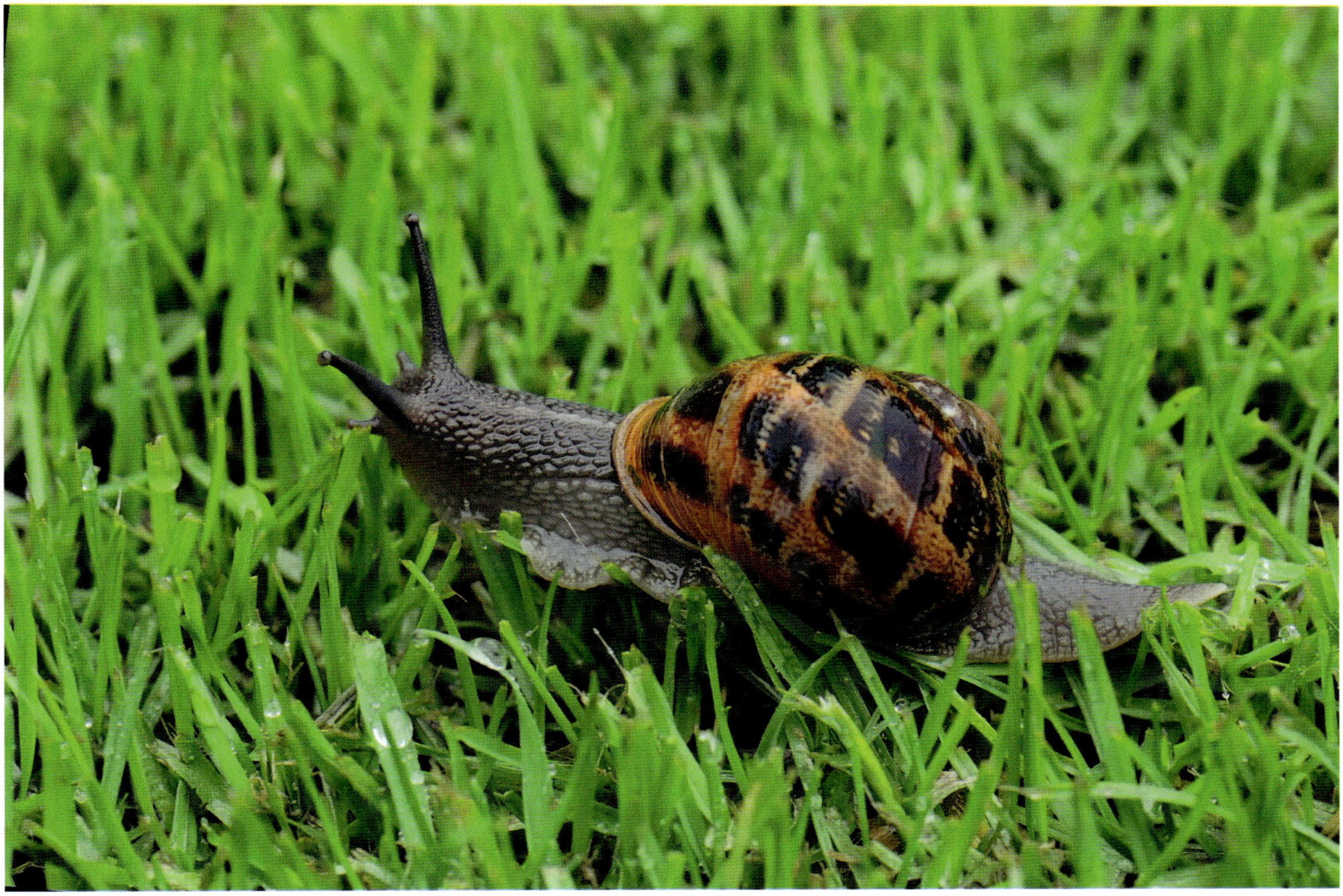

41.3 ~ **Garden Snail** *Helix aspersa*
Virtually every garden has a population of molluscs. I get a wide variety of banded and garden snails. They are frequently active early in the morning. I photographed this specimen slipping across the lawn while the dew was still fresh on the grass.

↳ Nikon D3, 105mm micro Nikkor, 1/15sec at f/16, ISO 200.

Leaving some of this year's perennials uncut over the winter will provide shelter for hibernating insects, which like to rest in the hollow stems. Stones piled up in a shady corner that is sheltered will provide possible hibernating sites for amphibians and reptiles.

If your garden is large enough, then creating a garden pond opens up many other possibilities. Amphibians, especially frogs, newts, and the larvae of dragonflies and damselflies are just some of the aquatic insects that will quickly colonise it. You will be able to get emergence sequences of dragonflies and damselflies in spring if you examine the vegetation early in the morning. Great diving beetles, mayfly nymphs, pond skaters and water boatmen are just some of the other aquatic species that are likely to make their home there too.

Fieldcraft

Photographic Approach

For any photographer coming fresh to close-up photography, the back garden is the best place to begin. Being on hand means you can witness any interesting behaviour or activity and be in a position to act quickly when necessary. It is also an ideal location to practise your photographic techniques. Your garden can become your outside studio, and you can grow and arrange suitable props to facilitate your photography.

For example, growing flowers in containers has some advantages, in that they are portable and you can position them precisely where you want them. Placing them on a table at a more comfortable height makes it easier to organise and position things. You can also

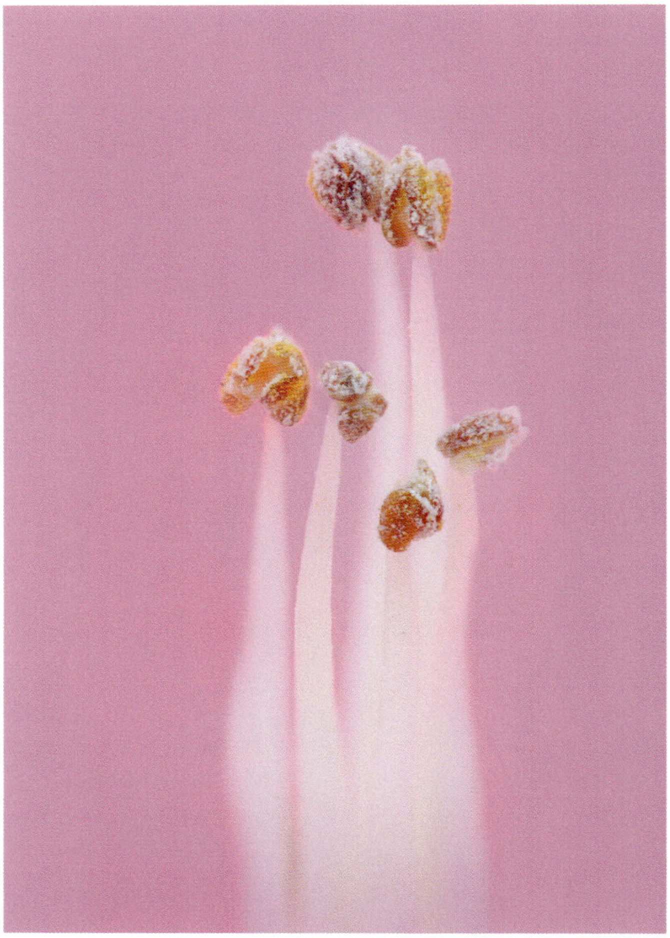
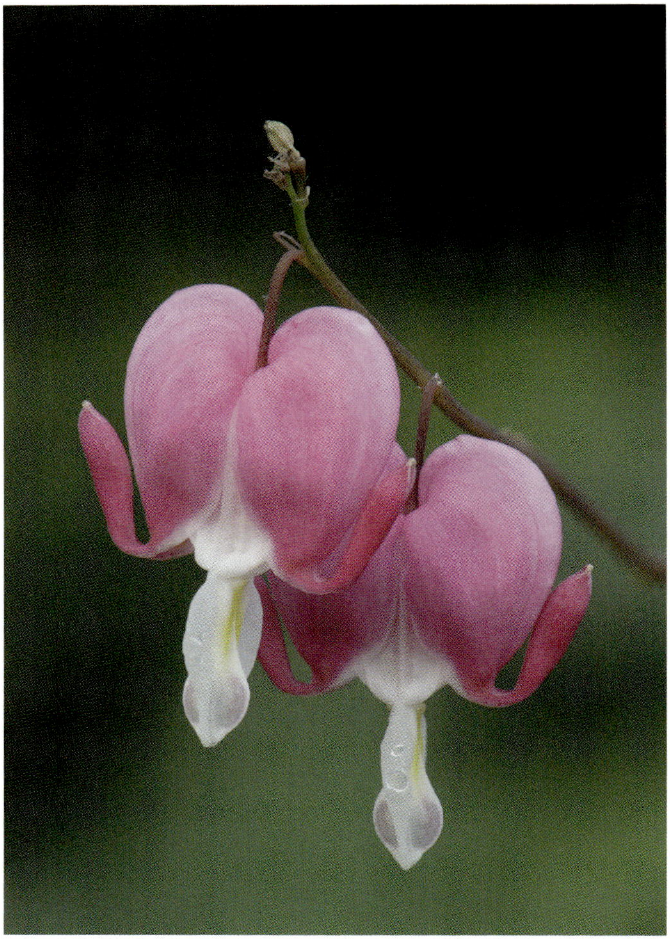
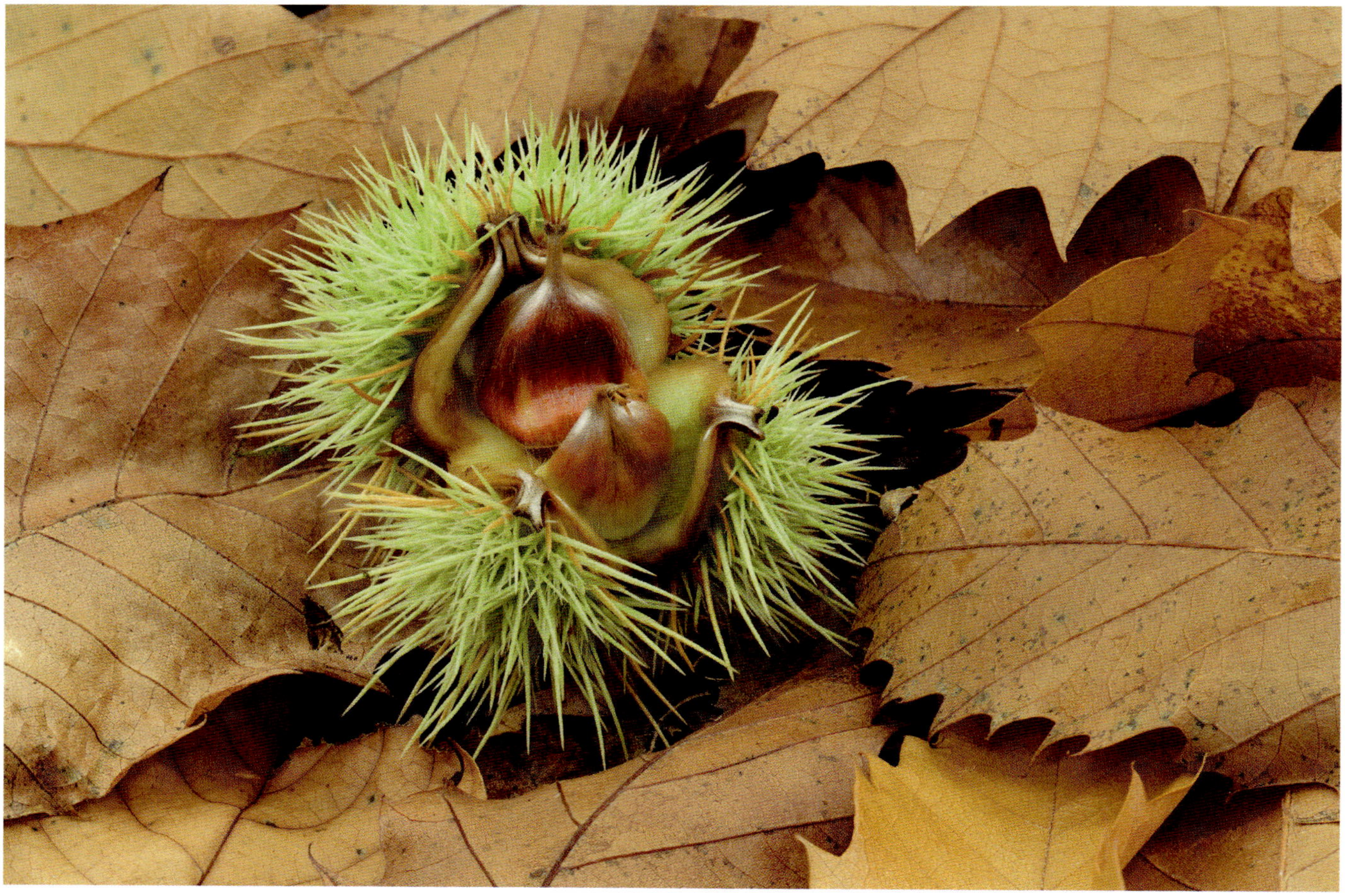

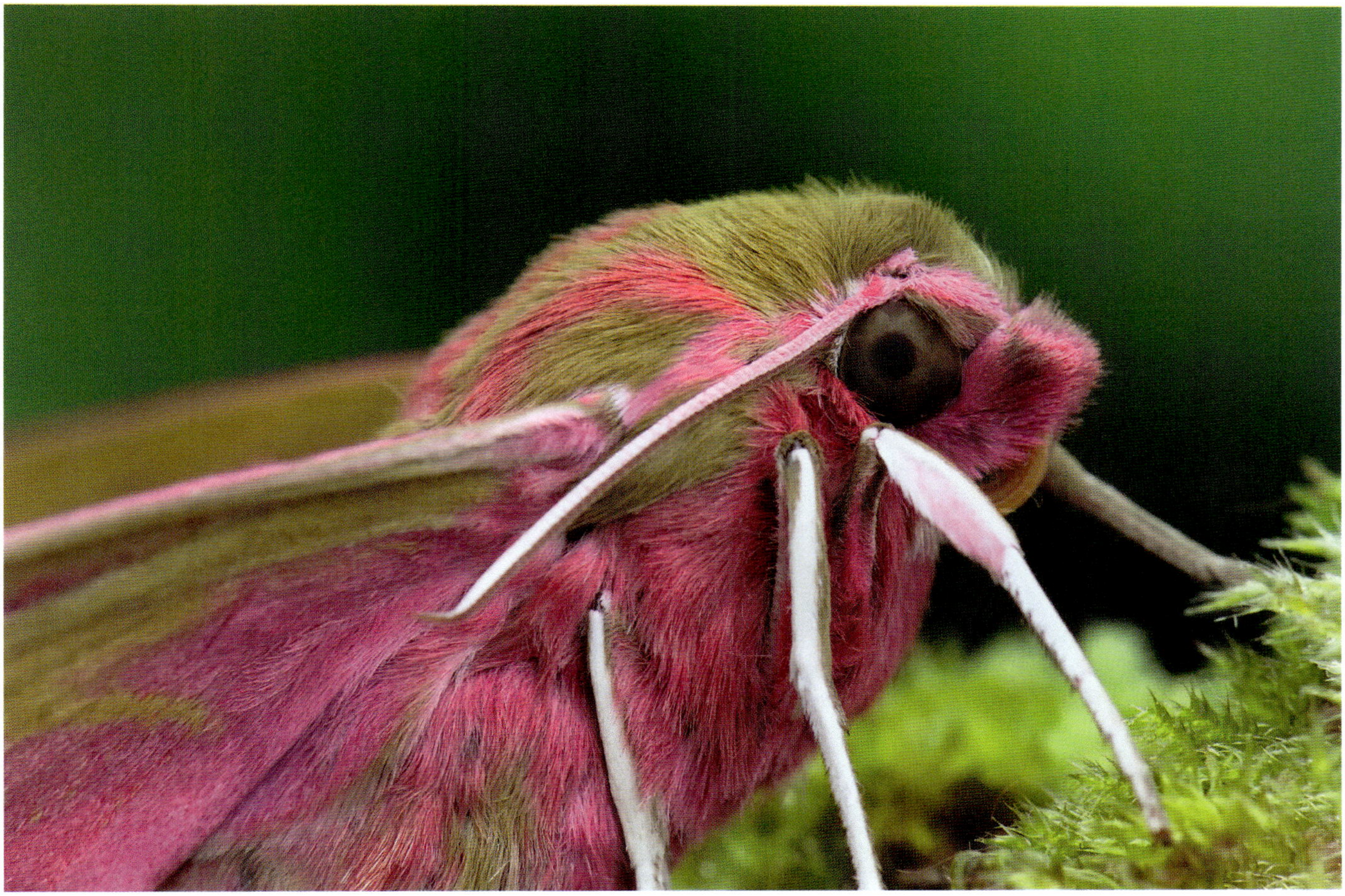

41.7 ~ Elephant Hawk-moth *Deilephila elpenor*
A common and attractive hawk-moth that frequents my garden, on some occasions, to feed on the honeysuckle. I have also found the larvae on my garden fuchsia.

↳ Nikon D3X with 105mm micro Nikkor lens and 1.7X converter,1/8sec at f16, ISO 200.

// FACING PAGE ~ TOP LEFT //

41.4 ~ Stamens of the Camellia Flower
I have photographed the Camellia flowers in my garden many times, however, in this case I focused in on the stamens. Reproduction is around 2.5 times life-size.

↳ Nikon D810, 200mm micro Nikkor, with Mamiya 80mmm reversed via a coupling ring. 1/15sec at f16, ISO 200.

// FACING PAGE ~ TOP RIGHT //

41.5 ~ Bleeding Hearts *Dicentra spectabilis*
One of my favorite garden plants. These photogenic flowers move at the slightest of breezes. I photographed them early in the morning when still in shade. The heavily overcast conditions allowed me to render the detail in the pale parts of the flowers.

↳ Nikon D3X, 200mm micro Nikkor, 1/15sec at f/11, ISO 200.

// FACING PAGE ~ BOTTOM //

41.6 ~ Sweet Chestnut *Castanea sativa*
The green spiky seed cases that protect the reddish-brown fruits are always worth exploring in parks and gardens during the autumn months. A custom WB was used here to deal with the slightly green cast from the overhead canopy.

↳ Nikon D810, 105mm micro Nikkor, 1/8sec at f/16, ISO 200.

arrange your lighting and any other additional props which give you more control of the final photo. You can also create sets where you can introduce your subject and achieve images that would be more challenging to accomplish away from home. A good example would be high-speed flash shots of insects visiting flowers. Banded and garden snails are extremely common in my garden and are active early in the morning especially after rain. I have also found the larvae of the elephant hawk-moth (see page 200) on a few occasions feeding on my garden fuchsia along with several others. It is also worth getting up very early in the morning when dew is still on foliage. You can often find visitors that have settled on the vegetation overnight. Once the temperature rises, they are quickly on their way. Early morning is also a good time to obtain atmospheric shots with dew before the sun or the rising heat burns it off.

Project Planning

Moth Trapping

One of the most popular photography projects in gardens is moth trapping. If it is carried out on a regular basis throughout the year, you can photographically document the number of species that visit your garden throughout the seasons. Not all of your specimens will be good enough to photograph; you can select the best ones and release the others.

Insects

You may be surprised throughout the summer months just how many insects visit flowers in your garden. You can build a photographic portfolio of the creatures that live there or pass through during the seasons. Also, recording insects, in particular butterflies and moths, is a worthwhile project. Many organisations such as Butterfly Conservation collect data on species that frequent gardens. The information is added to the national database which periodically produces reports on the state of the country's butterflies and moths.

Formal Gardens

If you have limited space or no garden, then visiting public gardens is a good alternative. Many have a broad range of flowers and mature plants laid out in a formal design and all within an easy reach. Some offer year-round access, but it's always worth checking on opening times and any restrictions they may have about photography. Some gardens do not allow the use of a tripod which is critical for any serious macro work. Also, check the closing times as you may be able to avail of evening light if they stay open late enough. The National Trust has numerous properties throughout the UK. Many have formal gardens, but some have restrictions on tripods so check before you go. Also, most operate a relatively strict code of practice which often means no straying from the designated paths.

PHOTOGRAPHIC TIPS

- Keep compositions simple and make sure your background compliments the subject.
- Photograph in natural light and use diffusers and reflectors to help overcome difficult lighting situations.
- Don't overcrowd flowers in pots; you want sufficient space around them to compose properly.
- Examine your subject carefully looking at its colour, texture and structure and select a viewpoint that complements it.
- Observation is the key; look closely at what plants are being frequented the most by insects.
- When planting flowers out in your garden be mindful of the background behind them and where they will be in relation to the sun.
- Choose the best specimens for photography.
- Before you start photographing in earnest, take some test shots first to establish the lighting, exposure and check out the background.
- Be careful when handling sensitive creatures. I prefer to photograph subjects where they are. If you must move a creature, then return it back to where it was.

Resources

FURTHER READING

Adams, I. *The Art of Garden Photography*. Timber Press.
Angel, H. *How to Photograph Flowers*. Stackpole Books.
Detrick, A. L. *Macro Photography for Gardeners and Nature Lovers*. Timber Press.
Nichols, C. *The Art of Flower and Garden Photography*. Argentum.

WEBSITES

Royal Horticulture Society Wisley: www.rhs.org.uk
Cambridge University Botanic Gardens: www.botanic.cam.ac.uk/Botanic/Home.aspx

// FACING PAGE ~ TOP //

41.8 ~ Canary-shouldered Thorn *Ennomos alniaria*
A very attractive species that frequents my garden in late summer each year. It takes its name from the canary-yellow thorax.

Nikon D3X, 200mm micro Nikkor, 1/8sec at f/11, ISO 200.

// FACING PAGE ~ BOTTOM //

41.9 ~ Borage *Borago officinalis*
An annual herb native to the Mediterranean and also known as the starflower. A very photogenic plant found in many gardens.

Nikon D810, 200mm micro Nikkor, 1/60sec at f/8, ISO 100.

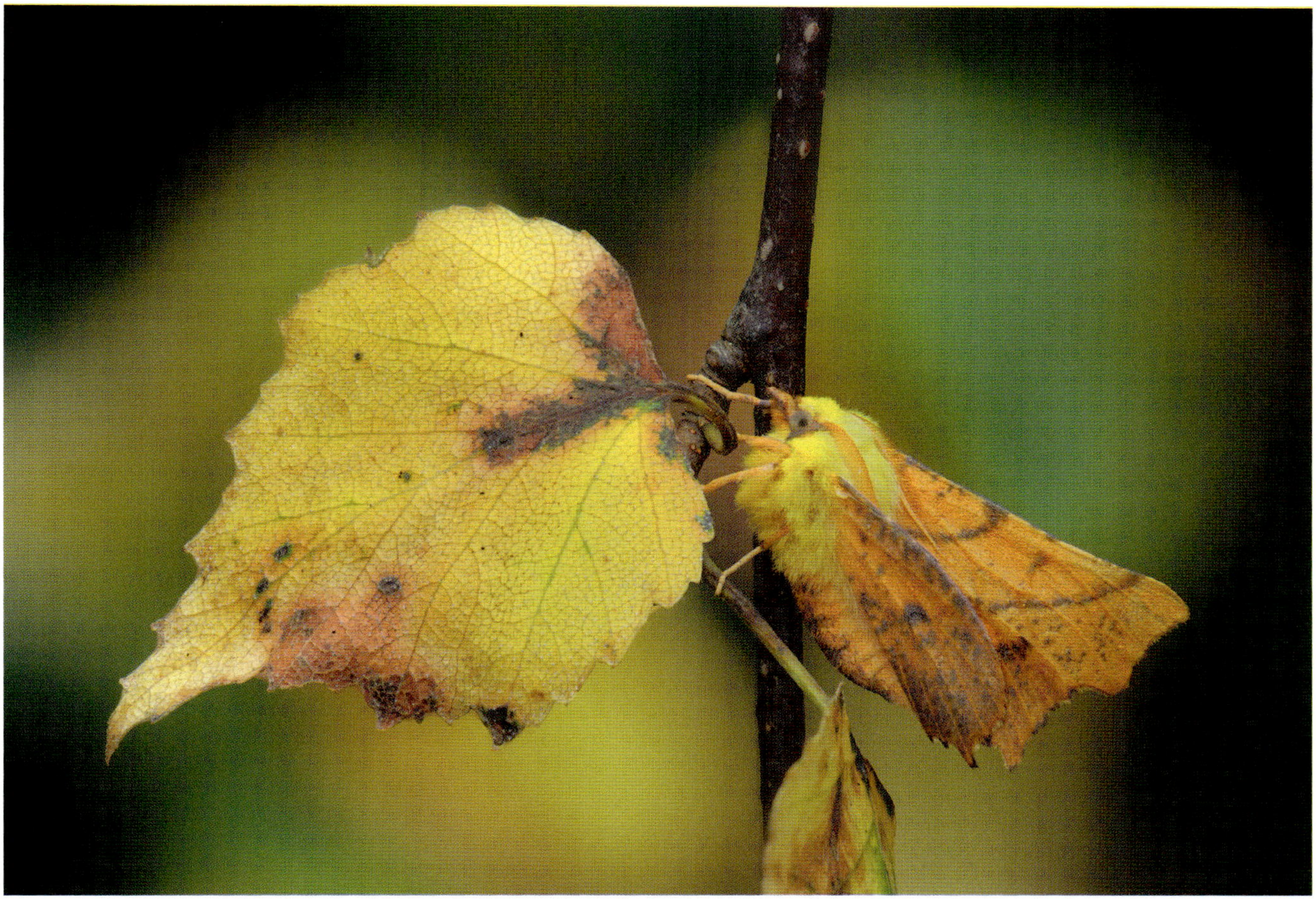

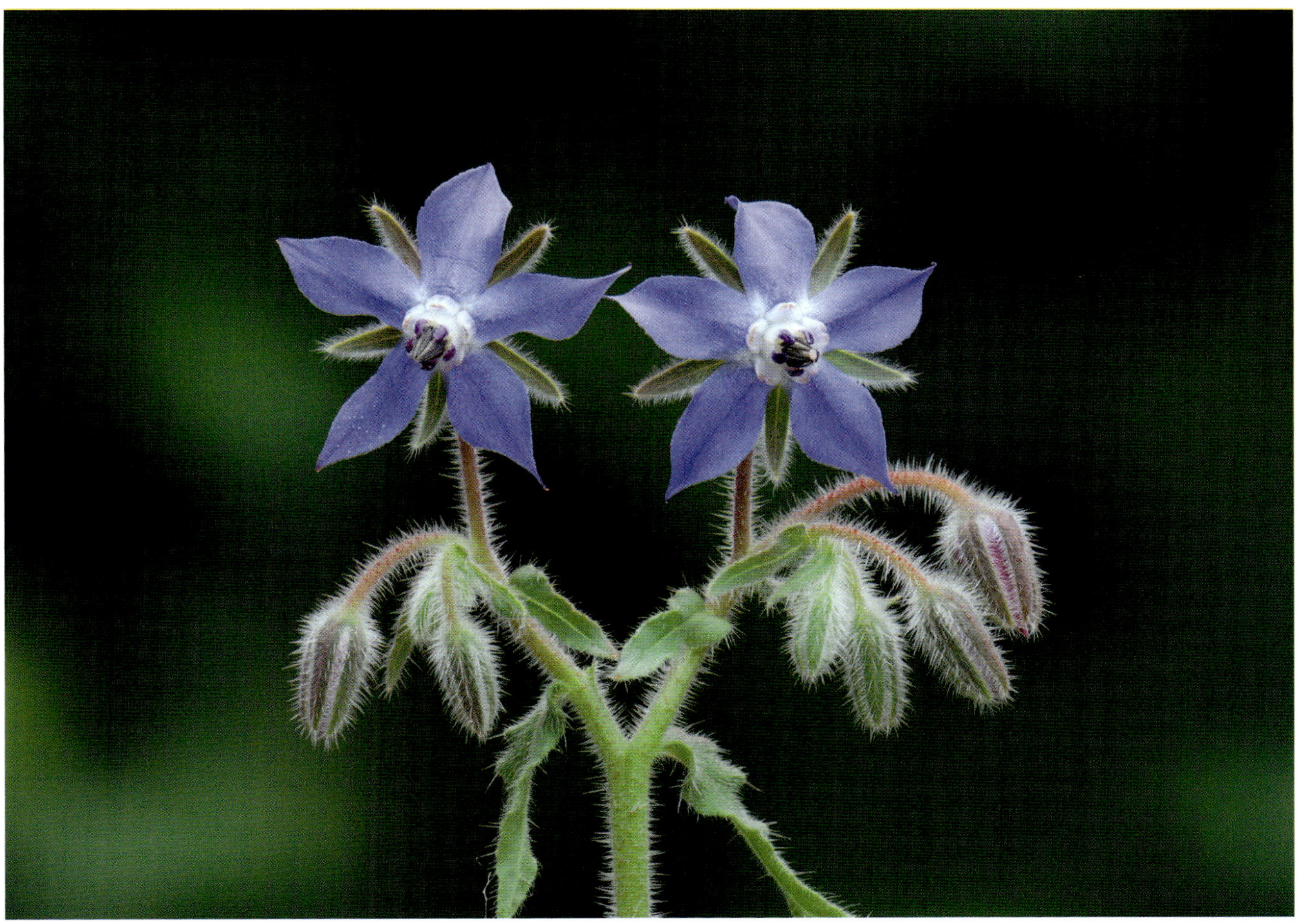

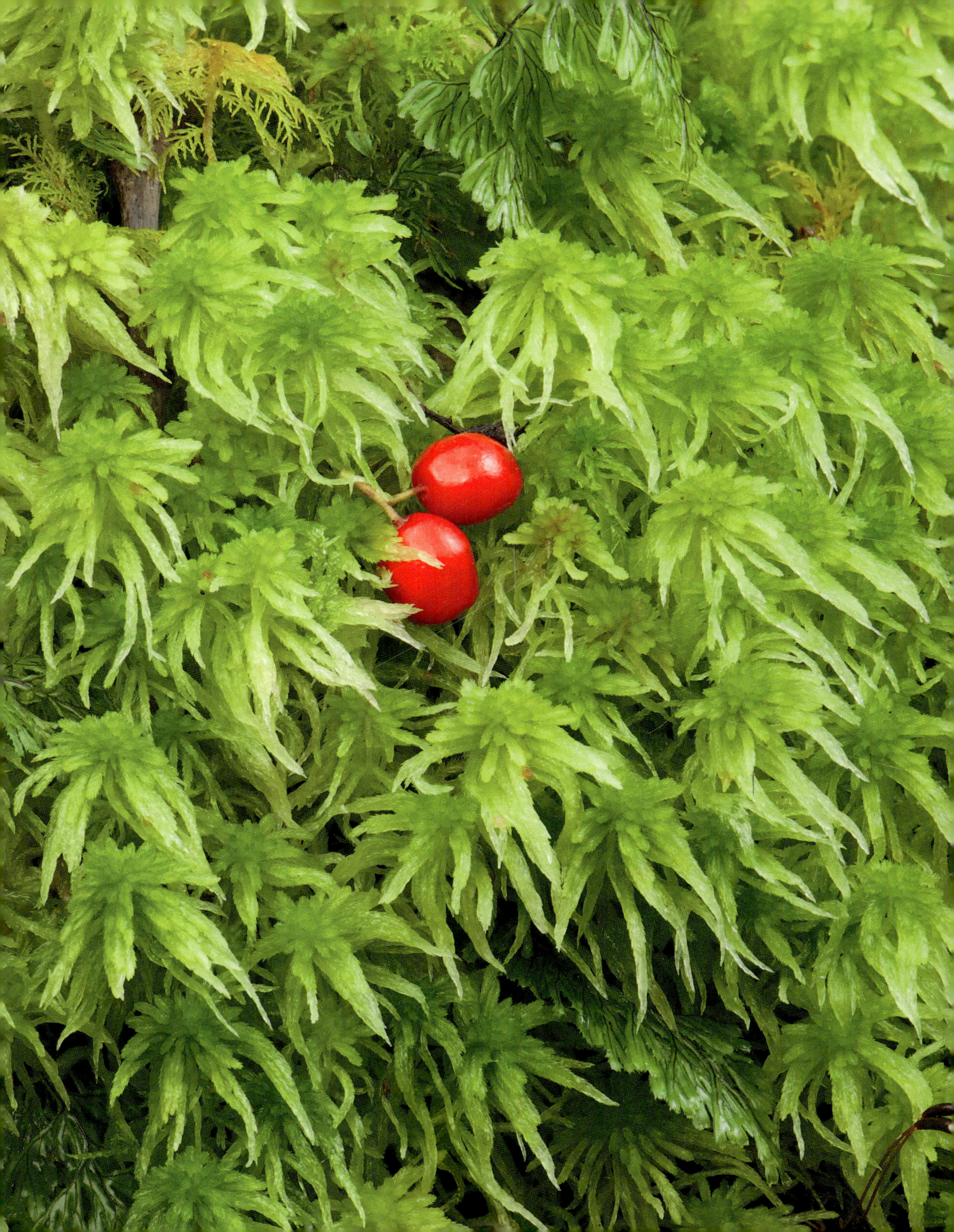

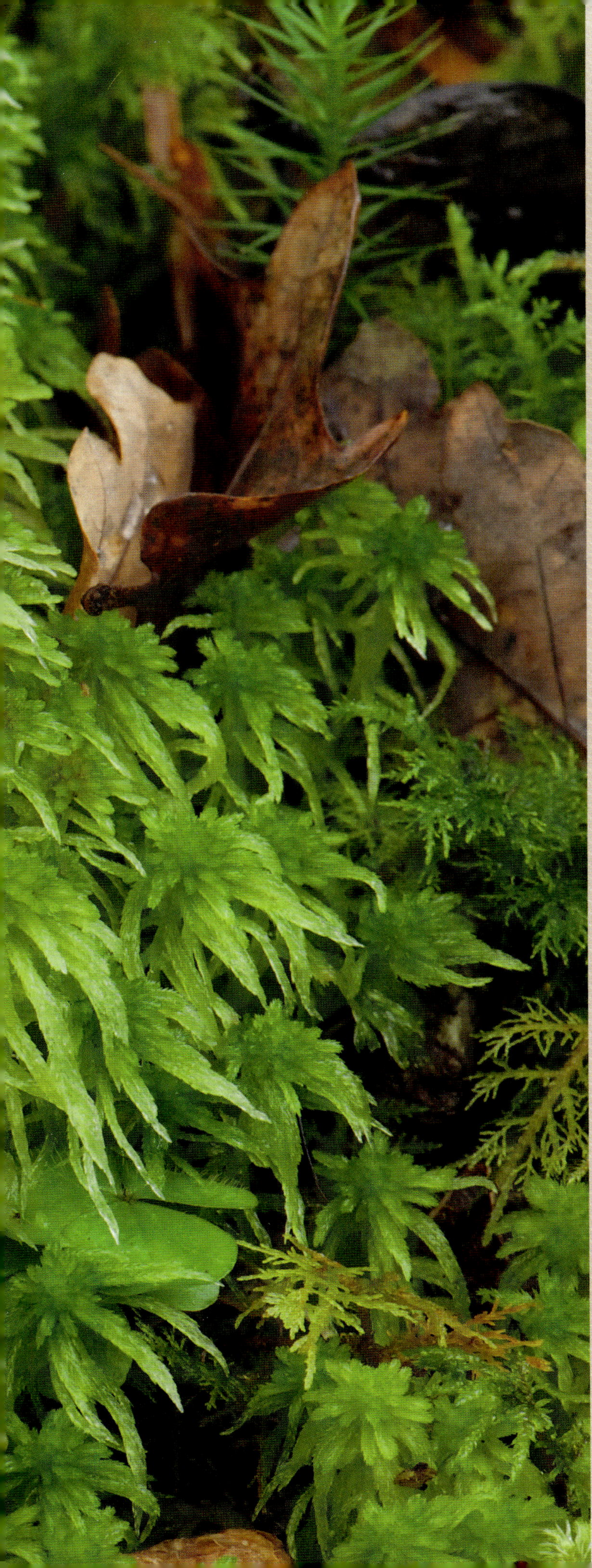

Part Four

Digital Workflow & Presentation

Sphagnum quinquefarium

FORTY TWO

Digital Workflow & Presentation

CAPTURING images is only one part of the photographic procedure. The digital darkroom is the next step where you will download, edit and process your images. The methods for digital post-processing, workflow and archiving your work are major subjects in their own right. There are many books which have been written specifically on these topics. Discussing them in any great detail is beyond the scope of this publication. However, the workflow outlined in this section is a reduced version taken from my own editing procedure. I do not claim to be an authority on the subject nor am I suggesting that you adopt my approach. It is merely a guide to assist you in developing your own workflow, one that suits the kind of photography you do. There are many good publications on the subject; see Additional Resources (page 304).

Developing a workflow procedure is about having an efficient system of work from capture to delivery involving a series of interrelated processes. It's important to have a structured workflow so your digital files can move quickly and proficiently through the post-processing stage. There is no single correct workflow; what suits one photographer may not necessarily work for another. You need to give some thought to developing a simple workflow that suits you. Plan it out on paper first; try to envisage some of the problems that might occur and most importantly is the data at the end of the process safe and secure. Run a test setup for a couple of weeks so you can identify any issues or shortcomings in your workflow structure before beginning in earnest. Working systematically will improve not only your speed but also help to standardise your methodology, improve your efficiency and bring continuity to your work. You want to avoid switching between different software applications; this will make it harder to establish an organised approach to your work.

Computer and Monitor Calibration

The most important part of your digital workflow process it your computer and monitor. I'm not going to get into the deliberations of Mac versus PC; it's a personal choice, but I have used Macs for many years, and they suit my purpose. While any modern computer with a reasonable processing speed would be adequate, I would advise adding additional RAM (Random Access Memory). You can never have enough memory especially since digital files are getting larger and image manipulation is more complex. Investing in a high-quality flat screen monitor is also important; buy the best you can afford and one that you can calibrate. If you are not using an iMac which has a built in monitor then a decent one is likely to cost you more than your desktop, so don't cut corners on it. You will also need a good calibration device. The X-Rite i1 Display Pro 2 or the Spyder Pro are excellent units. Colour management is important, and it's better to get things right from the beginning so your images will appear correctly on-screen and on other people's screens as well.

Image Editing Software

There are many image editing software programs about these days; one could devote a whole section to the pros and cons of each. It is fair to say that Photoshop and Lightroom are the most popular and widely used editing platforms. Most software programs offer free trials, and it's worth taking a little time to see what works best for you. Resist the temptation to jump from one program to another. It's better to become familiar with a few and learn them thoroughly; this will speed up your workflow. I have used the same software programs since my conversion to digital and have resisted the temptation of moving around. It's important to get your images right in camera or as close as possible; this saves a lot of valuable time trying to correct and resolve issues in the editing software.

Adobe Photoshop has been the flagship for many years. It is essentially a pixel based image editing program which is primarily designed to work with single images rather than multiple groups. Unlike most other software programs, it allows you to combine, manipulate, blend and stitch images together. It is not, however, a RAW file editor and therefore needs to be used in combination with other programs such as Adobe Camera Raw or Adobe Lightroom. I use Photoshop for certain tasks, but I am not slavishly addicted to it. I can't afford to spend endless time processing a single image. I want to replicate what I see in nature as accurately as I can not drastically alter it. If you are using Photoshop, then you have to process your images in a RAW converter such as Adobe Camera Raw, Lightroom, or an equivalent and then import them into Photoshop for any final tweaking. Photoshop by nature is an expensive program and widely used in the publishing and graphics industries.

Adobe Lightroom, on the other hand, is an image management program designed specifically for photographers, with an impressive set of features and a rather slick interface which aims to allow you to work through your images in a more efficient and practical manner. It is, in many ways, a complete workflow system, ideally suited for working with multiple images. You can import your RAW files directly into the program, sort, edit and apply a broad range of adjustments and changes in addition to organising your collections, even creating slide shows and galleries on the web. It is also much less expensive than Photoshop and easier to learn. Lightroom is an excellent program that works well for general adjustments to photographs but not at a more detailed level or where you need to do more extensive retouching or produce composite images. One of its big advantages is its non-destructive editing feature; any changes you make to any individual file are totally reversible.

Directory Structure

There are many different approaches as to how to organise your images. Everyone has their own method, but it is important to have some systematic structure otherwise, you will create problems for yourself at a later date. I have always preferred a directory-based library rather than having a catalogue-based photo management structure which is favoured by many photographers who use Lightroom and similar programs. There is nothing wrong with this method but it relies heavily on key wording and if you caption incorrectly you may not find all of your images, especially if you have thousands in your catalogue. Think carefully about how you want to manage your photos and whatever approach you adopt stick with it. You don't want to be making frequent changes to it especially if it contains thousands of images.

A simplified version of my own structure is illustrated. It has a main directory called Master Photo Library from this are a series of sub-directories and libraries entitled, RAW, TIFF, JPEG, Print, Agency and Processing. There are further sub directories off these which form the core of my image database. All of my images from a shoot go into my RAW in-folder which is organised by year, e.g. 2016. Every shoot is given a subdirectory and labelled with a location or a species name and the date, e.g. Clare Glen 24th April 2016. The subdirectory contains all of the RAW files from that shoot. It will remain there until I get around to editing and captioning it. When I have edited this folder all of the kept RAW files go into the RAW library into the the relevant directories, e.g. butterflies. The RAW library and the TIFF library are cloned and identical in their directory structure. That way I can see an image in the TIFF butterflies' directory and can then

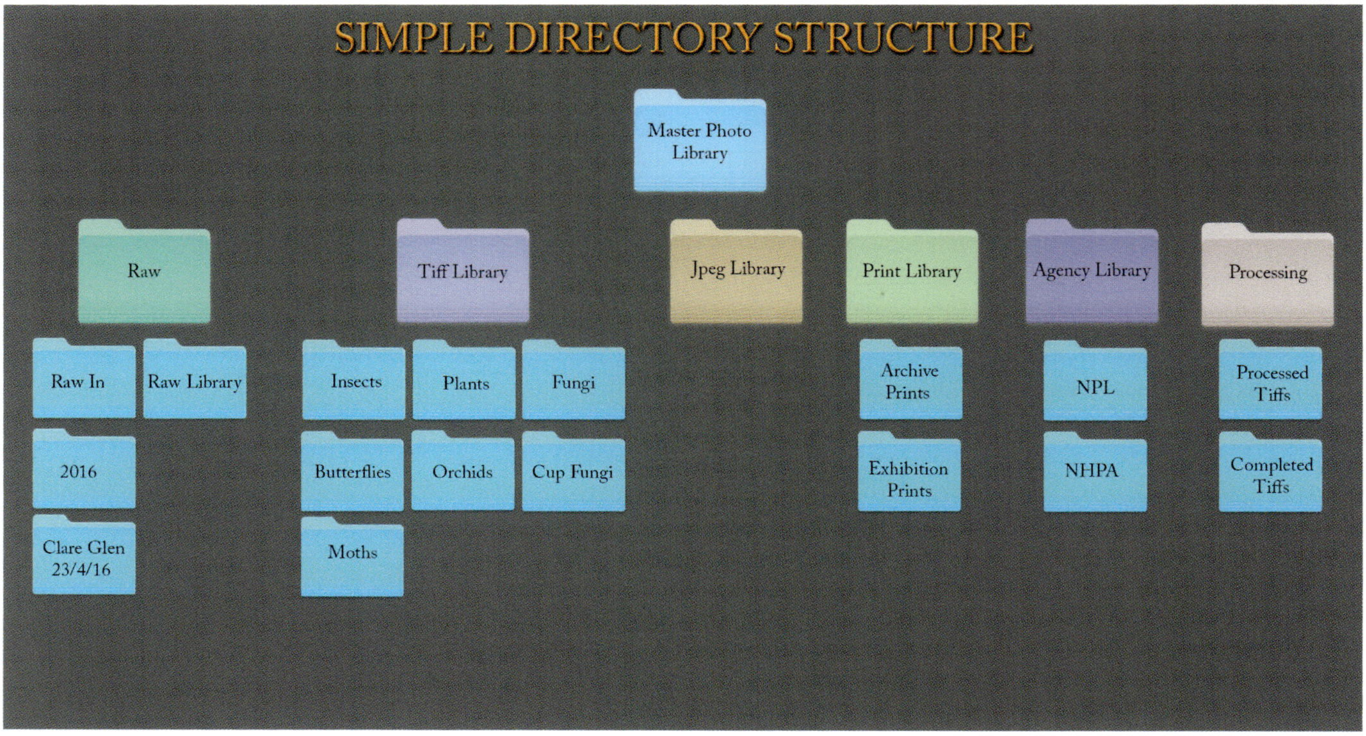

42.1 ~ Simple photographic folder structure for managing your images

go to the equivalent RAW butterflies' directory and find the original NEF file there. All have the same numbers. It's a simple approach but works very well. You can see from the illustration that the TIFF library has many sub folders for various orders. For example, the Insect folder has many sub folders for different families, e.g. butterflies, moths and so on. The same is repeated for plants, fungi and other major groups; this is all replicated in the RAW library as well to maintain continuity.

Downloading and Importing Your Files

For file importing I use Nikon Transfer, I prefer to use my camera manufacturer's software. You can alter some of the settings before importing including the renumbering of the RAW files which I need to do to ensure they have six digits. I also have a metadata preset constructed in Nikon Transfer, which inserts my personal information and copyright details into each file. I can also specify where I want the files to be imported, which is into the RAW in-folder. Many photographers now use Lightroom as their primary editing software. The web is full of information on virtually every aspect of it so there is little point in repeating it here. It does an excellent job and offers additional import options, such as copying your files and importing them directly into your catalogue or converting to DNG if you wish. You can also rank your images, but I see absolutely no point in this at all. I keep only those images that I consider good enough to print and publish; the rest hit the trash can. Irrespective of the software or method you use, having a systematic workflow and sticking to it is the important factor here.

Editing Your Images

Once the files are downloaded to the appropriate directory, they are opened up automatically in Nikon's View NX-i software, which I use for preliminary editing only. Metadata entered in the RAW file on third party software does not transfer with the original RAW file unless entered in Nikon's original software. NX-i displays all of the images initially as thumbnails along

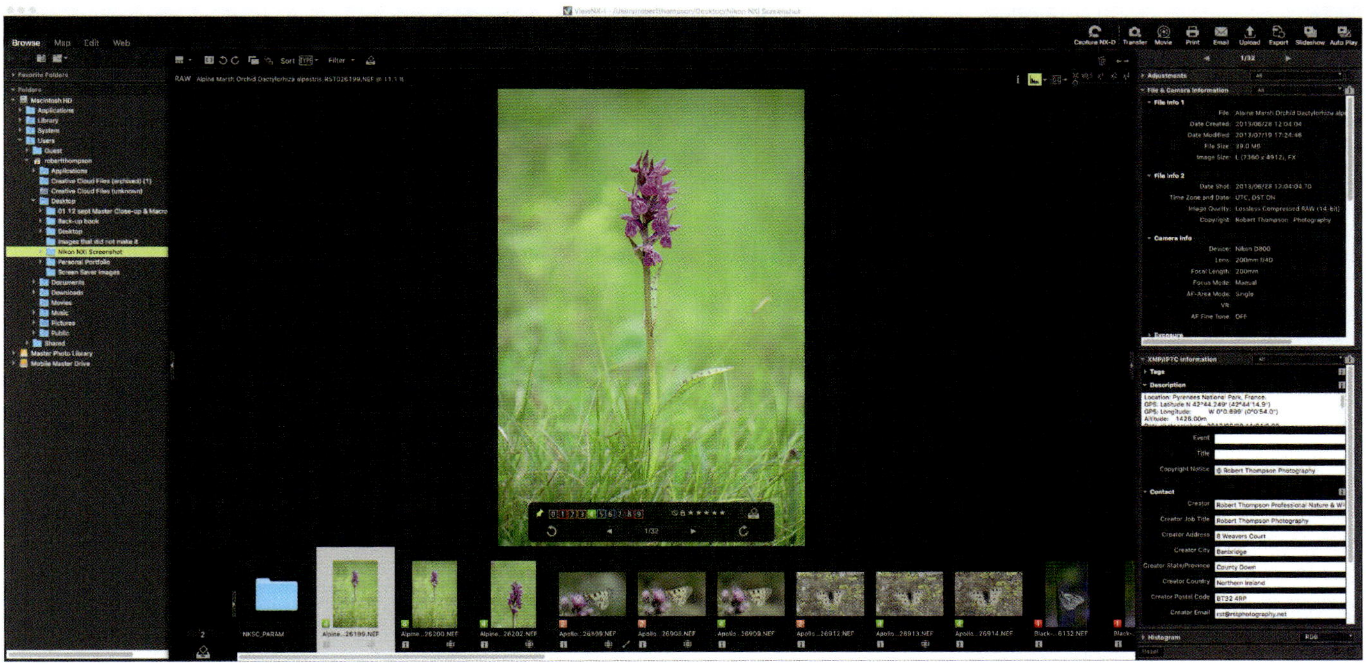

42.2 ~ Nikon's View NX-i which I use for initial viewing, captioning and preliminary editing. The program is available from Nikon's website and is free

with the metadata. Selecting any image automatically enlarges it for critical checking. From the filter menu, I assign a colour code to each image. Green are my keepers, amber require a more detailed look, and red are automatic deletes. My panoramic images are blue; I shoot a blank at the start and the end of the sequence to identify the group of shots. My preliminary edit is very much a visual scan removing all of the non-starters that I consider to be below par; these are assigned to a red button and can be deleted with a single action.

In the second edit, I look carefully at those that are left, enlarging each image to 100% and individually checking and comparing the sharpness and the histogram readings between similar images for tone and brightness etc. They are assigned a green or amber filter. When the second edit is complete, I will delete the amber images. I do tend to edit critically, keeping only what I think I can realistically use. I don't see the point of retaining images which are unlikely ever to see the light of a screen; this habit is a hangover from the days of film when photographers routinely kept slides that were not up to the mark. There was always that fear that the best image would get lost or damaged. Storing thousands of digital files clogging up hard drives is not best practice.

Metadata Captioning Keywording

The remaining green coded images need naming and information entered into the IPTC data fields. The IPTC Photo Metadata is the most widely used standard to describe and disseminate information about photographs and is universally accepted among photographic agencies, libraries museums etc. All major software has the IPTC's descriptive fields incorporated into it. Each image in addition to the default metadata includes my own information such as: location (details of where the image was shot); GPS co-ordinates, including altitude other relevant facts relating to the image; camera used; © copyright details; email and website address etc. This can be applied to all images from one location in a single action. The additional information entered into the RAW file can be viewed with any third party software. It is also carried through on conversions to other file formats. Since the majority of my work will be archived in the National Museum, it's critical that the information added to the RAW file is visible on any piece of third-party software. Last of all the vernacular and scientific names of each species where relevant are added, and they also double as the file name. I also add

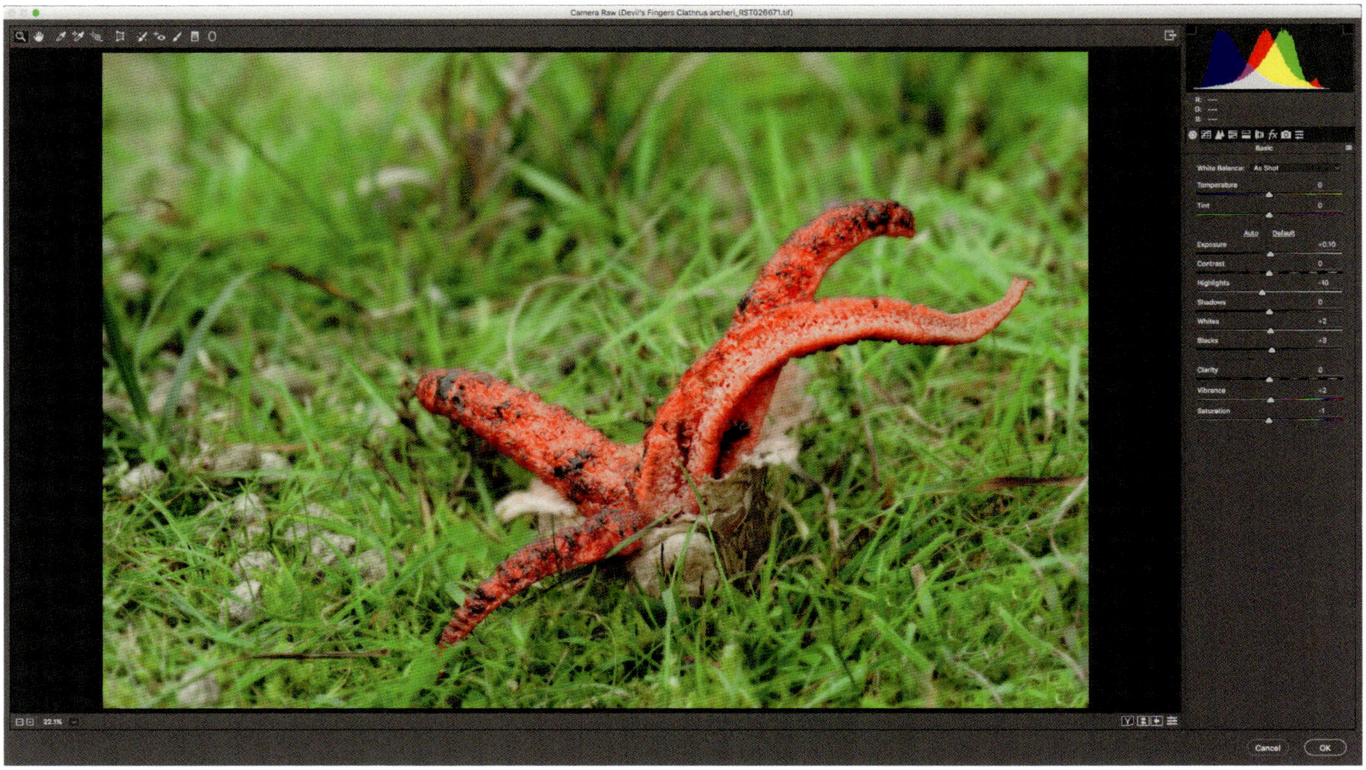

42.3 ~ **Devil's Fingers** *Clathrus archeri*
Adobe Camera Raw interface. I now use Adobe's Raw file editor since Capture NX was withdrawn.

a few basic keywords. As a rule, I don't store any of my photographic libraries on the computer's hard drives; not that they could accommodate the libraries anyway.

Processing RAW Files

If you shoot RAW, your photographs will need a certain amount of post-processing and conversion to a suitable format for printing, publishing on the web or social media sites. To convert them into a readable format they will need processing in software that can read your camera's RAW file format. The amount of processing they require depends on many factors, such as the complexity of the image, metadata input, and the final result you are aiming to achieve. I use Adobe Camera Raw for processing my RAW files and conversions to different formats. I make use of some of Lightroom's features but still prefer Photoshop for any additional tasks. Like many Nikon photographers, I used Capture NX until it was no longer supported by Nikon. Its replacement Capture NX-D is a significant step backwards in my opinion.

Once the editing process has been completed the files which are retained will be processed and any adjustments carried out. The selected files are then converted into TIFFs and sent to the processed TIFFs folder; any final tweaking is completed from that folder in Photoshop. The files are then sent to the completed TIFF folder awaiting transfer to the appropriate folders in the TIFF library. I also convert these files into JPEGs for the web or client light boxes using a Photoshop action script. All of my JPEGs are a standard size of 900 pixels on the linear; this is an acceptable size for emailing and for client viewing. Each image has copyright text embedded into the picture and are copied into the JPEG library. If a client wants a large number of images, I produce an interactive web gallery in Lightroom; see online web galleries (page 297).

The 16-bit TIFF files are copied first of all to the relevant agency folders and then to the TIFF library and to the relevant subfolders. The RAW files which have been processed are sent to the RAW file library folder which is essentially a digital negative library. All of the RAW files are stored in the same way in a duplicated directory structure. It's essentially running two cloned directories, one for the RAW files or digital

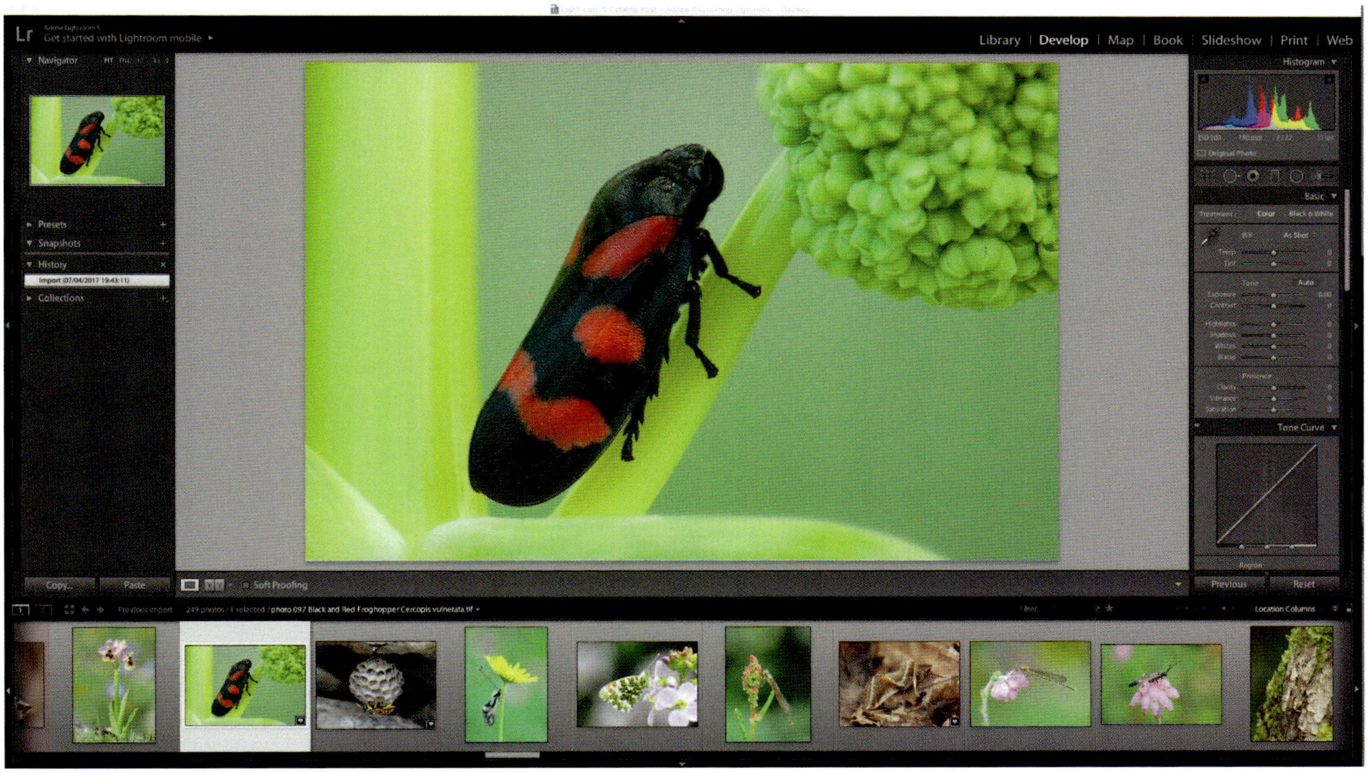

42.4 ~ The develop module in Adobe Lightroom
Many photographers now use Lightroom as their standard Raw file converter.
All of the edits and tweaks you carry out are non-destructive.

negatives and the other for converted TIFF files. The RAW file library will naturally contain more images because the TIFF library will not have every RAW file converted; only those which I consider are likely to be used. There is no point in converting every RAW file; you can always retrieve any one of them at a later date and convert it when necessary.

If you are shooting JPEGs, there is less flexibility when it comes to post-processing. It is important to ensure that all of your settings are correct. Since all of the information is processed in-camera make sure they have been exposed correctly and all of the parameters have been followed. Your options for making major corrections are more restricted.

Backup and Exporting Your Finished Files

Losing data is a profoundly painful experience for any photographer. It's a position none of us wants even to experience. However, it does happen and those who have experienced it know only too well the heartache and pain associated with it. Years of work and photographs can be lost in the blink of an eye. It is essential from the start to have a good backup strategy for peace of mind. As I said earlier, I do not store any of my photographic library on any of my Macs. I have three sets of external drives. I also have a Raid 1 configuration where my photographs are spread across two drives in a mirror configuration. Should one drive fail I only replace that drive, but I still have a copy of my images on the other. Once the new drive is fitted you begin the rebuilding process. One thing to bear in mind is Raid 1 should not be treated as a backup, it is not. It allows you to keep on working should you experience hard drive failure but you still need to have additional backups. I also have two other backups of my libraries. One of these is the primary backup and is kept on-site, the other is kept off-site and is backed up once a week. You could opt for cloud storage as an option for off-site backup, however, I am not prepared to send my entire library to the cloud, but that's me! Whatever you decide make sure your backup strategy is safe and robust.

FORTY THREE

Contact Displays & Panels

THERE are many situations when you may need to show a group of images collectively. For example, it might be for a client who wants to choose from a collection of photographs for publication or when you want to illustrate a community of organisms from a particular habitat or variations within a species or for identification purposes. Contact sheets can be used in a variety of ways, but especially when you want to illustrate photographs collectively. During the days of analogue capture, contact sheets were standard procedure for viewing multiple images. They were usually a positive print of the rolls of film used in a shoot. The images could be analysed and the best selected for enlargement. With the advent of digital, there seemed less need for them. However, with so many different digital platforms these days they have, along with interactive web galleries, become popular again. Many of my own clients like this approach and most importantly it adds a professional look to your images. Digital contact sheets and web galleries are still used frequently by wedding and fashion photographers for quick previews for their clients. Some examples of contact or composite panels have been used in this book.

Some current software programs allow you to create contact sheets/panels relatively quickly. Photoshop, Bridge and Lightroom have the facility to produce them to you own particular specifications. Many photographers use Lightroom as their default software for editing and managing their workflow. It is a relatively straightforward process in Lightroom to construct contact sheets quickly and in whatever format you require. There are a series of default templates which you can use or simply create your own. You can also change the background colour along with other features to whatever suits your needs. The easiest way to produce a digital contact sheet in Lightroom is by creating a new directory and inserting your selected images. Navigate to Lightroom's print module and select all of the images. Insert them into one of the preformed templates in the browser. In the Lightroom panel set the pixel size, I tend to stick at around 900pixels; this gives a reasonable size image for viewing or placing. You can then customise the template and include file names and watermarks etc. if you wish. When completed, save as a PDF or another format and export to your desktop.

Online Contact Panels

Another very useful feature for presenting your work to a potential client or uploading new images to your website is the web gallery module in Lightroom. You can generate an interactive online gallery similar to the contact sheet in Lightroom. Copy your images into a new directory. Open up Lightroom and go to the web module and import your pictures. You can save your customised configuration as a template in the collections panel and use the same default custom template or use the many others available. Once you are satisfied, you can export it to your drive or desktop and activate by clicking on the index file within the directory.

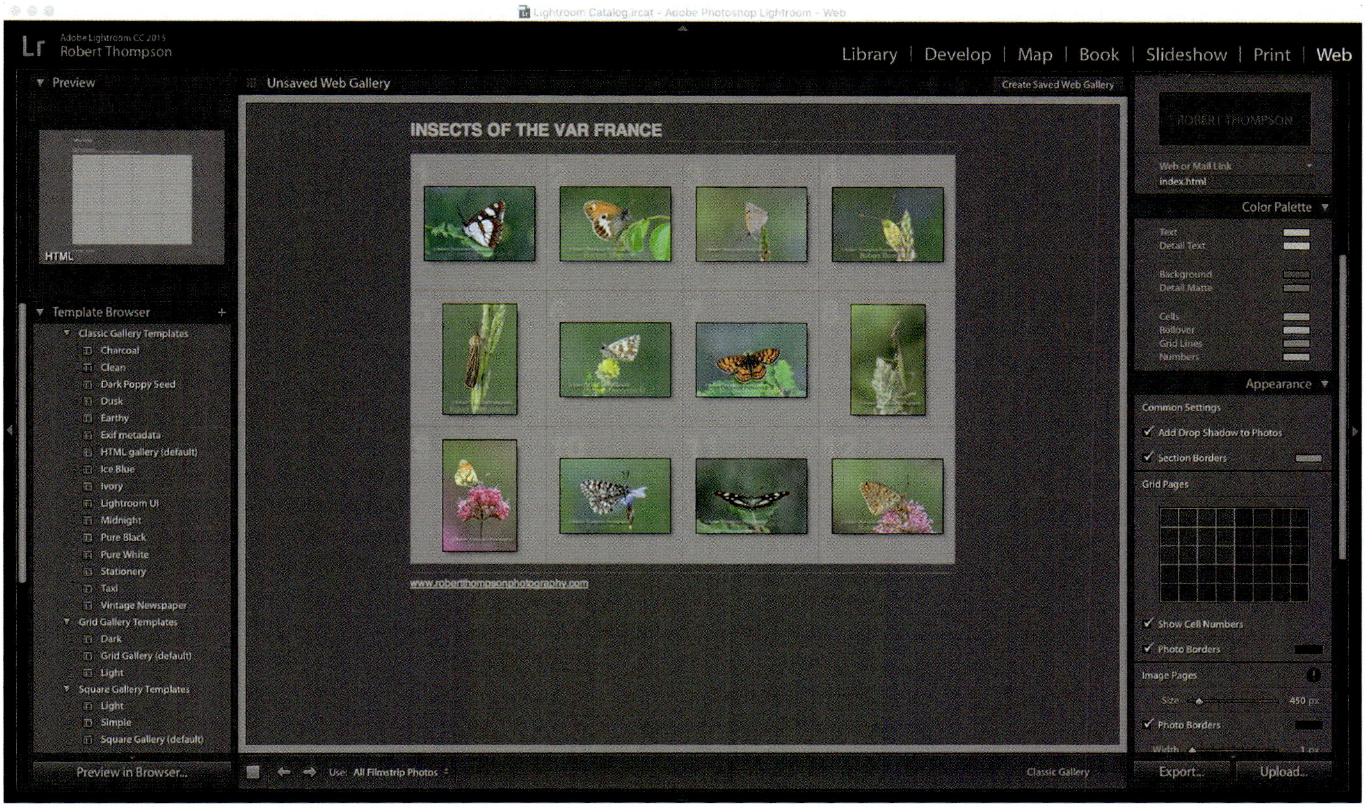

43.1 ~ Online gallery contact panels are a great way to assemble a group of images to upload to the web or to send to a client. They are easy to construct and can be tailored to your requirements. You can click on an individual image to see a larger view

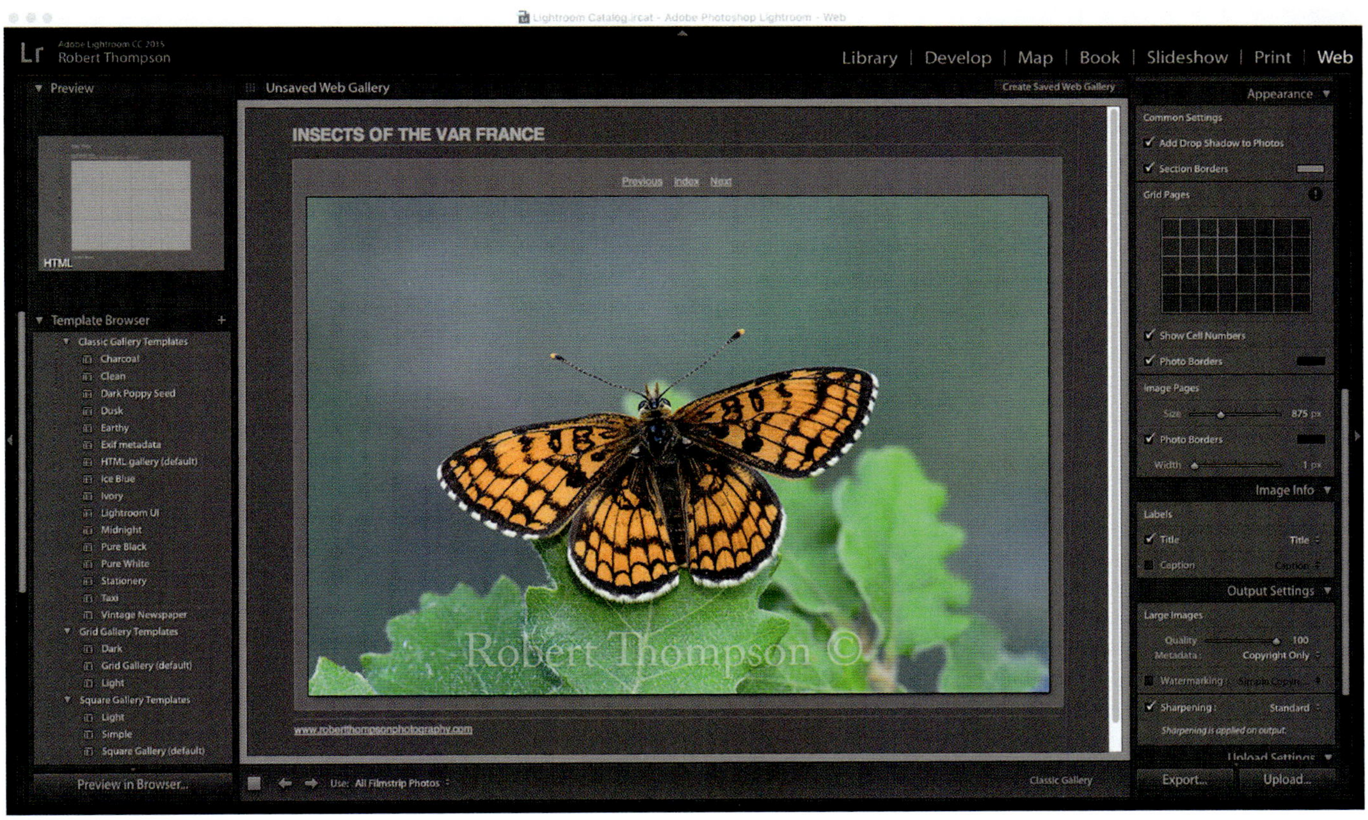

43.2 ~ Expanded view of the species when the thumbnail is clicked on

Creating Customised Panels

There are occasions when you might want to create an entire customised panel showing a single image or a collection illustrating a particular theme or diversity of a subject. You have complete control of the text fonts and colour etc. Photoshop is better suited to this approach since it will involve layers. Once the panel has been constructed, you can save it as a template for future use. These are various methods which can help you promote yourself and your work. Don't underestimate the importance of design and presentation; it's often a key factor in tipping the balance in your favour!

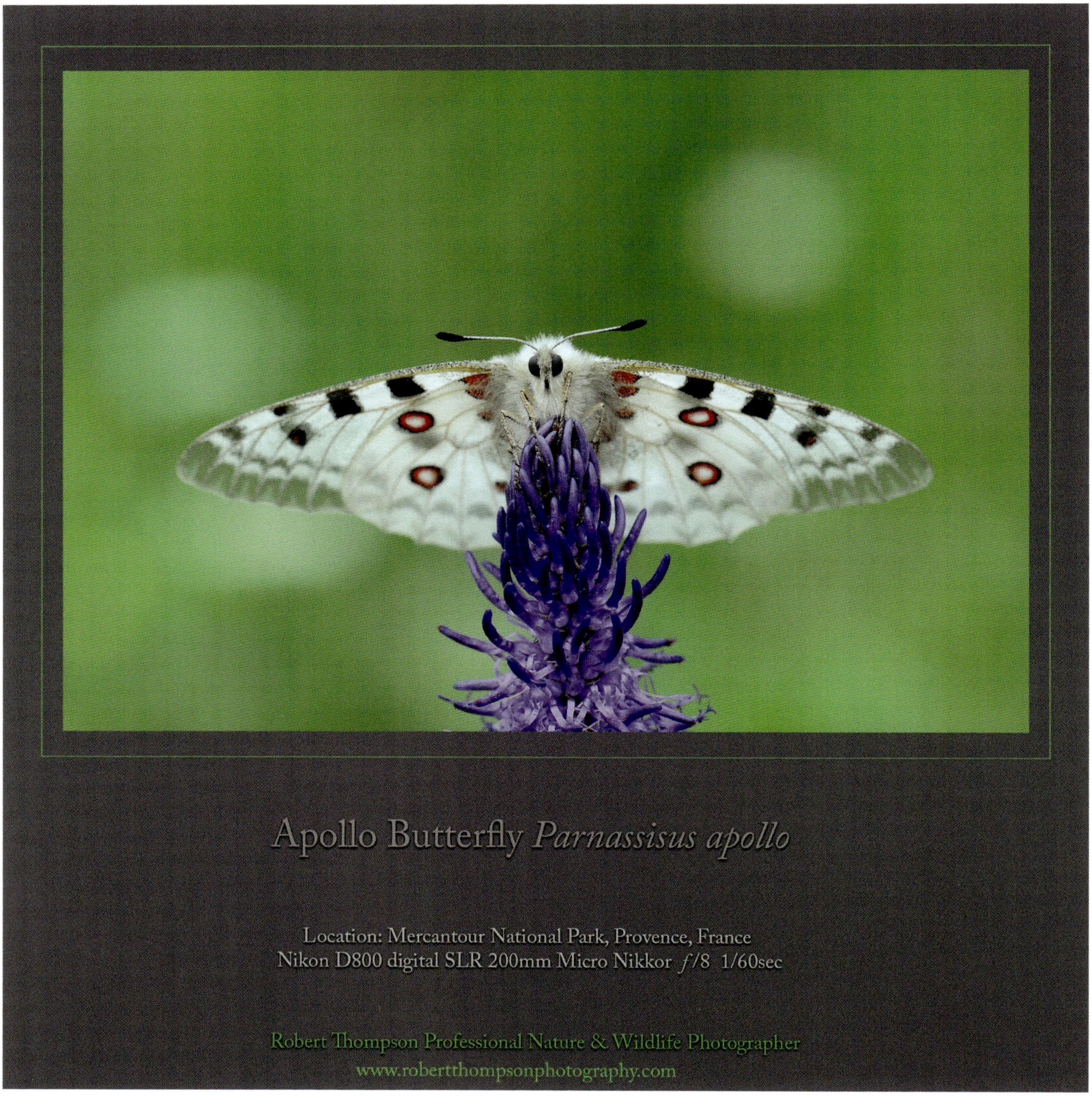

43.3 ~ A single customised panel. You can save as a template and change the image and text when required

FORTY FOUR

Presenting & Publishing Your Photographs

THERE are many ways these days to showcase your work from the world wide web to social media. Twenty years ago no one could have envisaged the scale and power of the internet and the changes that digital technology would bring. However, the well-known cliché of a picture paints a thousand words still holds true today. We live in a visual world, and the vast majority of information that is communicated to our brains is visual. Pictures have the power to deliver meaningful stories and form part of everyone's lives in many different ways. In the pre-digital era, every household had a photo box or something similar of prints, charting the lives of their families throughout the decades. The computer now dominates each home and has taken over the role of storing the family's life history.

It is also a fact that we print far less than we did in the past and completely rely on mobile phones and the computer's hard drive to be the guardians of our valuable photographs. If you consider the number of images you take in a year, realistically how many of these do you actually print, probably very few. Just look at the collection of pictures that you have accumulated since the digital revolution and you will see that only a small number ever make it to print. Most images remain abandoned on your computer's hard drive. I have always felt as a photographer that you need to set yourself goals, have a purpose for your photography; it's a great incentive and motivator when you have a purpose. Sharing your images with other fellow photographers on the web and through social media is an important platform these days, but ask yourself where will that material be twenty years from now? Perhaps buried in the archives of the web somewhere. The exception being those few who own a print gallery in a busy town or tourist area.

Many would say photographs have a natural affinity with paper; its where their origins lie. Printing provides you with a physical entity which is there for a lifetime; it can be passed on, and it's not dependent on any electronic device. It will always be there irrespective of whatever changes come along in the future. I offer a print service online and have an Epson large format printer. I do get a reasonable number of requests for prints throughout the year, but it's not a game changer. Most photographers offer a print service on their websites and if the truth be told very few make any substantial income from online printing requests. I certainly don't know any nature photographer who could survive on print sales alone. Although the web is an essential platform for showcasing your photography you should also be thinking beyond that and having some long-term plan for your work and the best way to ensure its future is to print.

Having been involved for much of my photographic career in high profile photographic contracts and monitoring programmes for government and NGOs documenting the country's flora and fauna, I felt that it would be a great pity if much of this work in later years would eventually lie in the archives of the National Museum without ever seeing the light of day. Much of the imagery was often of rare and threatened species, and I felt it would be worth having something

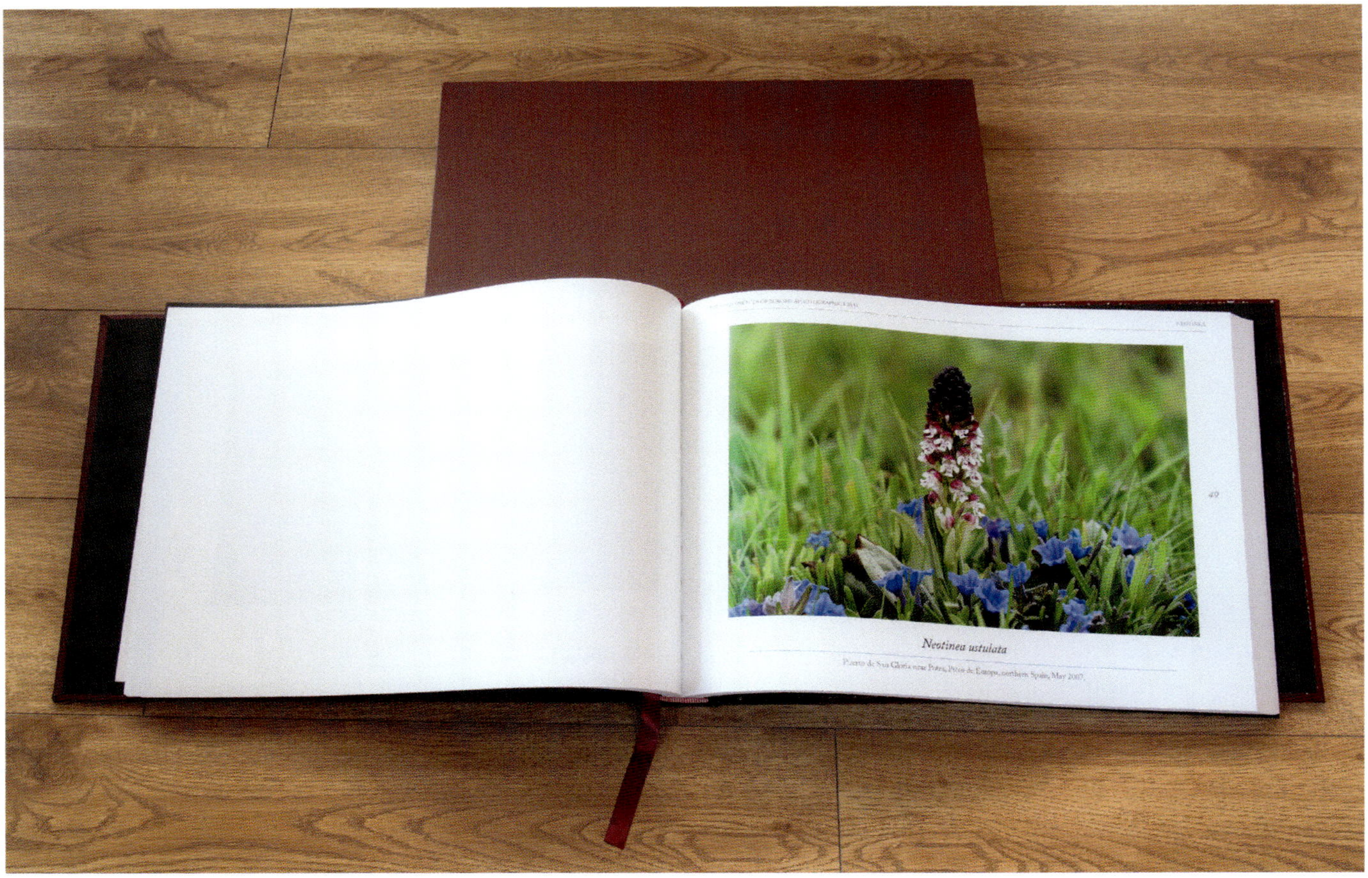

44.1 ~ An example of the portfolio on the Wild Orchids of Europe. The A3+ prints are hand bound and the whole book in protected in a large slip case. It's a great way to preserve your most valuable images for decades to come irrespective what changes take place in the future

in print, which is much more accessible in the years to come. It would also have a value in that the information attached to the image would provide an important marker many years on for future monitoring projects. It would also be there for my family to have and enjoy should I unexpectedly have an early exit. I made the conscious decision some years ago that I would produce a series of portfolios documenting some of my most important work. Each portfolio would contain approximately one hundred A3+ images, these would be hand stitched and bound by a bookbinder and protected in a large slipcase. These are no light-weight books, but they have a valuable role in the future. I have worked on these over the past five years and have now produced six on various topics.

Photographic Portfolios

Designing and creating a portfolio of your work is a significant achievement as a developing photographer. Not many photographers actually produce a portfolio of their best work, for a number of reasons; sometimes it's due to time or lack of confidence or simply experience. A portfolio acts like a calling card: it defines your capabilities as a photographer and is often what potential clients use to evaluate your ability.

Portfolios are an ideal way to showcase your work, but it's not just a case of selecting twenty-four of your best images and displaying them in a bound book, presentation case or online. A portfolio is more than images, it's a whole visual experience which requires careful thought not only about the imagery but also design and presentation. Design is a critical factor in photography as is presentation and it's often undervalued. I have designed many of my own books over the years and have always spent time carefully looking at various options before making up my mind. A friend of mine who was an excellent photographer and an accomplished graphic designer once told me that a good design could make an average photograph look good and a great one look outstanding. I have always remembered that comment.

Your portfolio should follow a theme, have continuity and the images should work together. Be selective in your choice of content and don't include images that are closely related or variations of the same thing. Your selection should be strong, inspiring and the type to linger in people's minds. Another common mistake is putting all of your best photographs at the beginning of your portfolio which becomes evident as the viewer turns the pages. Mixing formats is also to be avoided if possible; it breaks the continuity of the presentation. Diversity is important but keep to the central theme.

Once you have made your selection, organising them into a cohesive layout is the next stage. The opening image needs to be strong, eye-catching, its job is to entice the viewer to explore further. Avoid putting your weakest images at the back; your last image should be a jaw-dropper. Leave the viewer or editor with a parting memory. The final question is whether to print or produce an electronic version. There are benefits of both, but prints are often seen as the last part of the photographic process. Prints are organic; you can feel and touch them but, most importantly, you will always have them. A web-based portfolio while extremely convenient and versatile can only be viewed on an electronic device, which is not always convenient.

Other Ways of Publishing Your Work

One of the biggest growing industries in photography at the moment is self- or vanity publishing as it's sometimes called. It is not a new approach by any means, but one that has taken off post-digital. Every photographer at some point wants their name in print. It has indeed become harder to publish books, and the reality is that very few photographers become authors; the rejection rate is high. Many of the smaller photographic publishing houses are gone or have been absorbed by larger conglomerates. It's even becoming more challenging for existing authors to get additional books published. Self-publishing is now more popular than ever. E-book publications are very much in vogue at present; this trend is likely to expand even more in the future as hard copy declines even more. The potential audience is the world wide web; the cost is insignificant compared to the production of a printed copy.

Print on Demand

Blurb is one of the leaders in self-publishing and provides a print-on-demand service. It offers the inexperienced photographer a series of pre-designed templates through its BookSmart software. The software is compatible with Mac and PC. It is also compatible with Adobe's InDesign and now Lightroom, for those who are experienced in graphic design and want much more control over the format and appearance of finished publication. It also has a colour management profile so you can get the best out of the software and the printing process. They also provide a range of book sizes, paper types and cover selections. There is also an option for you to sell your publication through their site. The downside to self-publishing is cost. Producing a book through any of the major self-publishing companies makes the individual cost of your book very expensive. Nevertheless, if you want to publish a book of your own work, then this is a route to consider. There are many other self-publishing companies online and which are also worth exploring.

The Self-financing Route

Self-financing your own publication is a challenging and risky business. It is a well-known fact that most sell less than half of their print run. You really have to do your research carefully and have a product that's different from what's already out there backed up with inspiring photography. Opting for self-publishing means the photographer has to incur all of the costs including design, editing, proofreading, printing

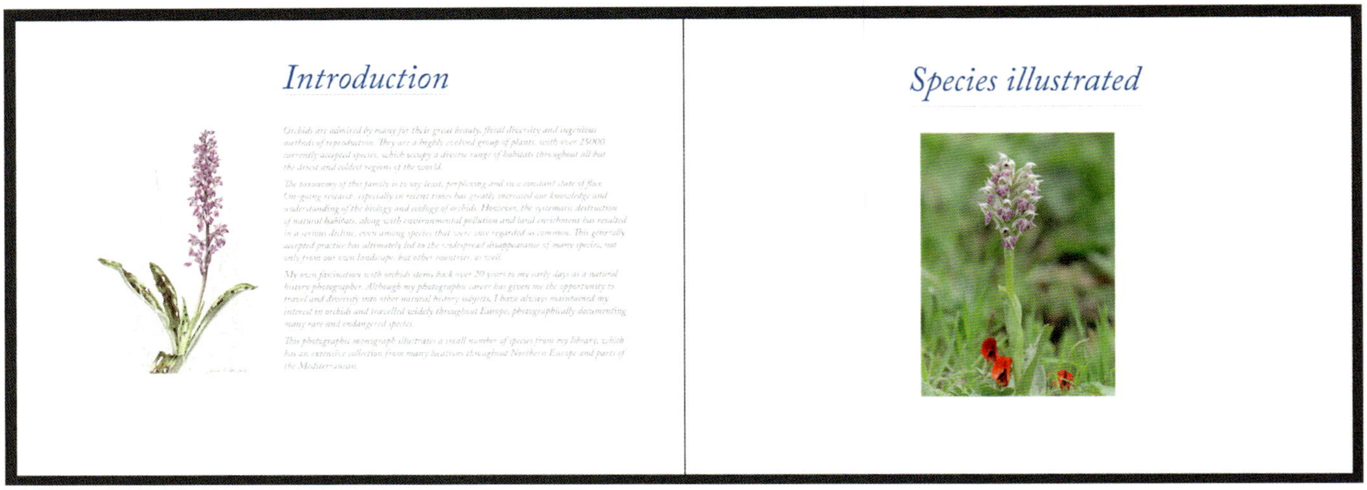

44.2 ~ Many companies now offer online book printing. Once you have installed the software you can lay out your images and have them print and bind your publication

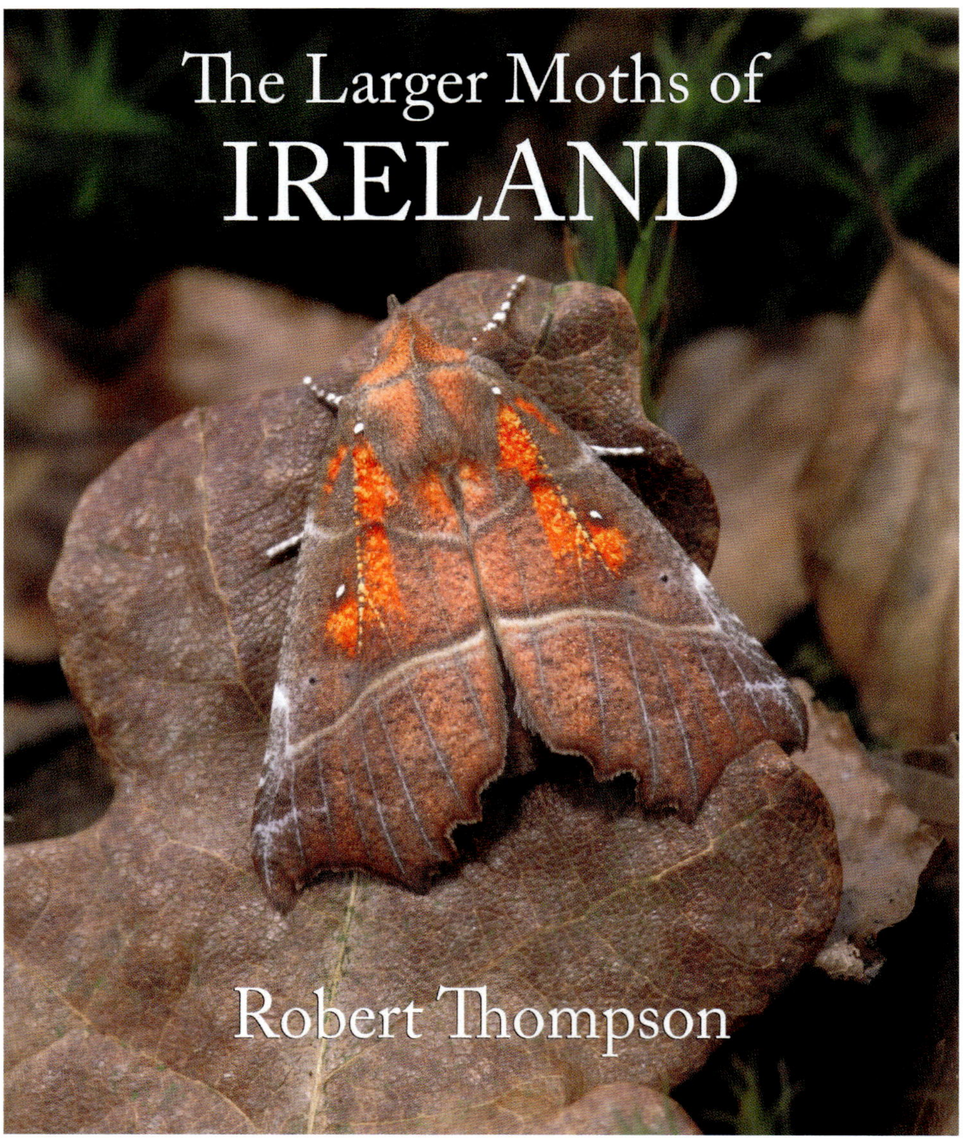

44.3 ~ Producing PDF publications is a relatively cheap and easy way to get your work out there. You can create a template and produce your images in Photoshop as single pages and then combine them using Adobe Acrobat.

and binding. You have also got to consider storage of your books, postage, packing and delivery, which may involve sending your publication to other countries. The number of pages affects not only the production costs of your book, but also postage as well. The one aspect that you as a self-publisher can't bring to the table is marketing and distribution. Most large publishing companies have outlets in many countries and have access to bookshops, clubs and other online outlets. The advantage of self-publishing is of course that you retain all of the profits, which if contracted through a publisher could be as low as 10% and often less. Nevertheless, I do know some photographers who have taken this route and have been mostly successful, although they have told me it involves a considerable amount of time and expenditure to achieve it.

E-PUBLISHING

Electronic publishing has become hugely popular among photographers for a variety of reasons. It's a cheaper, more economical way to produce a book with little overhead costs, higher profit margin and no middlemen. If you are thinking of publishing a book, then exploring this route first might be a better option. It will allow you to gauge the interest of photographers in your topic and whether there is merit in producing a hard copy. You need to give some serious thought to your target audience. Is the circle of interest in the topic broad enough to warrant the time and effort? Are there already publications on the subject? Have you something to say that's different? These are questions you should ask yourself before you consider starting down the route of publishing.

If you are inexperienced in using specialist software there are many programs available which make it relatively easy to do your own design using a selection of pre-formed templates. It becomes a simple task of dragging and dropping your images into place. Photoshop and Lightroom both allow you to create books from single page layouts into PDF books using Adobe Acrobat to combine pages together. It is a very simple but effective approach and involves only time and a little practice. Although the production of an e-book may seem relatively straightforward, there still is a lot of work; writing is the easy part. Marketing and selling your publication is the most demanding and challenging part. Advertising your book on a blog or through social media is one way, since they will do a lot of advertising for you. I have produced a couple of e-books in-between my other publications, and they have worked out extremely well. My target audience was my own country since they were particularly relevant to Ireland. I produced a limited number of printed copies along with an e-book copy.

Many companies such as Blurb allow you to convert your hardback publication into an electronic PDF copy which can be downloaded onto tablets and computers. It is also a relatively simple procedure to set it up for sale through your website. Digital book publishing is the future, and it's a great platform to launch your first book.

PDF (Portable Document Format) is another popular way you can show your work. Images can be designed out in Photoshop as single pages and then combined into a PDF for sharing on the web. You can add pages of text along with images and a front and back cover. No matter what you decide there are many avenues for you to get your work out there for other fellow photographers to see.

Additional Resources

BIBLIOGRAPHY

Angel, H. *Macro Through a Nikon Lens*. Chris Weston Publishing Ltd.
Bebbington, J. *Insect Photography Art and Techniques*. Crowood.
Benvie, N. *The Field Studio.* E-book. Privately published.
Bishop, S. *Colour Light & Composition: A Photographer's Guide.* Photographers Institute Press.
Cremona, J. *Extreme Close-Up Photography and Focus Stacking.* Crowood.
Davies, A. *Close-Up and Macro Photography.* Focal Press.
Davies, A. *Digital Plant Photography.* Bloomsbury.
Davies, P. H. & Bolt, C. *Wide-Angle Macro: The Essential Guide.* E-book, privately published.
Davies, P. H. *Close-Up Photography Q&A.* pixiq.
Davies, P. H. *Small Things Big.* David & Charles.
Krogh, P. *The Dam Book: Digital Asset Management for Photographers.* O'Reilly Media.
Shaw, J. *Closeups in Nature*. Amphoto Books.
Thompson, R. *Close-Up & Macro Photography: A Photographer's Guide.* David & Charles.
Thompson, R. *Close-Up on Insects: A Photographer's Guide.* GMC.

ONLINE

www.alexhyde.photoshelter.com
www.claybolt.photoshelter.com/index
www.guyedwardes.com
www.heatherangel.co.uk
www.johnshawphoto.com
www.meetyourneighbours.net
www.naturephotographers.net
www.niallbenvie.com
www.paulharcourtdavies.com
www.stephendalton.co.uk
www.suebishop.co.uk

MACRO EQUIPMENT SUPPLIERS

www.kirkphoto.com
www.reallyrightstuff.com
www.speedgraphic.co.uk
www.wildlifewatchingsupplies.co.uk

SOFTWARE

www.heliconsoft.com
www.google.com/nikcollection
www.on1.com
www.zerenesystems.com

FORUMS

http://www.bythom.com
www.dpreview.com
www.learnmacro.com
www.naturephotographers.net

PHOTOGRAPHIC ORGANISATIONS

American Photography Association: www.americanphotographyassociation.org
North American Nature Photography Association: www.nanpa.org
Royal Photographic Society: www.rps.org

Index